One Hundred Havens

One Hundred Havens

THE SETTLEMENT OF THE MARLBOROUGH SOUNDS

HELEN BEAGLEHOLE

MASSEY UNIVERSITY PRESS

Contents

Introduction

MY INTRODUCTION TO THE MARLBOROUGH SOUNDS was in 1977 when I arrived in our first, and small, yacht from Mana. The yacht sailed at about 2½ knots and it had been a long and stormy crossing. Our small daughter and I huddled on the cramped cockpit floor, soaked with spray and being sick into the same bucket. Now and again, my husband Tim leaned over the tiller to empty the bucket overboard. Our boys, a little older, were sick, then slept below.

At last we reached the sheltered waters behind Perano Head, and then Tory Channel itself. The sun came out, we shrugged off our sodden coats — and the wash from the inter-island ferry drenched us as it smacked against the side.

That trip began an exploration of the Sounds — by boat, by bike and by foot — that lasted almost 40 years, with the two of us, with our children and with our children's children.

Writing this history of settlement in the Sounds has taken me further into this unique environment. I knew something about Captain Cook, his visits and his relationships with the people he met, but little about other early explorers, visitors and surveyors. I was aware Sounds Māori had been tragically affected by the Waipounamu, and earlier, purchases but I knew nothing of their subsequent lives and situations.

In 1977 we were surrounded by farmland over which scrub was steadily encroaching; in other places, the play of light and shade of the bush was being obliterated by the relentless march of rows of pines. But of the story behind that bush and the creation of that landscape, I knew nothing. Researching — and writing — this book has therefore been a fascinating and moving journey.

There are many strands to the history of the Sounds. To ensure that they do not become too confused and to give each strand its due, my account is organised thematically. It is further focused on four broad time periods: from first human settlement to the time of Bellingshausen's visit in 1820; from 1820 to 1856, by which time the land was no longer in Māori hands; from 1856 to 1920 when the first exodus of settlers was underway; and from 1920 to about 1980, when the major options still underlying economic development of the Sounds come into focus. The final chapter brings the story to the present day, exploring what the Sounds now offer to permanent residents, and to Māori in particular as they look to develop ways to sustain and nourish their people.

The story is of two people and two fates. Māori, of East Polynesian origin, first settled in Titirangi in Pelorus Sound about 1300. When Cook arrived in Tōtaranui (Queen Charlotte Sound) in 1770, Māori were living as nomadic hunter-gatherers in a pattern of living well attuned to their environment. Today, archaeological maps and exploration attest to the multiplicity of scattered, often transitory, habitation sites all over the Sounds. But it was only when archaeologist Reg Nichol pointed out to me the pā sites on hills and headlands, the canoe haul-out places on beaches and the kūmara pits that I began to appreciate fully the extent to which Māori had once peopled the Sounds.

By 1856, however, the Crown had 'bought' all the Sounds land from Māori, setting aside modest reserves for them to live on. But the reserves were too small to be formed into economic farming units, and the land too poor. And even some of that was subsequently taken for scenic and roading reserves. Māori patterns of settlement and the Māori way of life were set for obliteration.

The early years of Pākehā settlement typify early colonial life in the New Zealand backblocks: a story of new settlers — mostly not well off and lacking the necessary skills — struggling to establish and maintain livelihoods in the face of limited resources and obstacles that ranged from the merely difficult to the nearly impossible. Axe, fire, herds of cattle and flocks of sheep slowly transformed the landscape. A government keen on 'closer settlement' funded carefully benched tracks through a rugged landscape of deeply indented bays and steep, high hills; roads would follow. Some settlers graduated from subsistence farming to more profitable enterprise.

Local papers, always keen to report success stories, heralded the opportunities for settlement and for exploiting the Sounds' other natural resources — the forests, fish, minerals. The direct benefits settlers reaped from those activities were largely fleeting, but lasting indirect benefits included improved shipping and communications.

That second wave of settlers, with their old-world institutions and patterns of existence, had worked with an expanding farm frontier, but after 1920 that frontier contracted and reducing opportunities saw Pākehā leaving the Sounds. However, from the late 1960s, forestry and mussel-farming began to offer new opportunities. Meanwhile a third wave of settlers, long-term intermittent, often inter-generational visitors in the form of boaties and bach owners, had been growing from the 1920s. Their increasingly vocal protests against some of the new commercial developments and their implications for conservation introduced a new view not previously articulated in the Sounds.

Māori were trapped in a different reality. Their participation in the colonial world as traders, whalers, gardeners and landowners fell away from the 1860s onwards. They no longer controlled the land, and lack of capital, contested land titles and systemic and widespread discrimination constantly created barriers to economic opportunities. Well into the twentieth century, Māori survived on mahinga kai (what smaller amounts remained), subsistence farming and a little cash from seasonal work on European farms. In the midst of poverty, illness and epidemics, they got their children to one of two schools available to them. In the 1950s, families began a steady move from the Sounds and surrounding hinterland into the regional centres.

Māori had lived in a rich ecosystem in which they saw themselves in a practical and spiritual relationship with their physical world, and over which they exercised a custodial role, managing the environment for subsequent generations (kaitiakitanga). The arrival of Pākehā and the loss of their land changed all that. With an increasing inability to 'express their cultural values in practice' and transmit them to successive generations, iwi faced a loss of 'material, cultural and spiritual sustenance'.[1]

It is a story that historian Rachel Buchanan suggests all New Zealanders must encounter so that they can 'step up now and take the time to learn, know and feel the history of the places they call home'.[2]

The final chapter provides an overview of the past 30–40 years. From a Pākehā perspective, earlier trends can be seen working themselves through. From a Māori perspective — and the story, having begun with Māori, aptly ends with them — Treaty of Waitangi settlements are enabling cultural renewal and exciting new futures for many Sounds iwi.

IN NARRATING THE EUROPEAN STORY I had access to a plethora of official reports, parliamentary records and media reports. The redoubtable and 'patriotic' *Marlborough Express* and *Pelorus Guardian* in particular provided a sometimes embarrassing amount of rich detail, almost all of it relentlessly positive. In this already extensively documented world, local histories and family memoirs, letters and diaries, and conversations with those who lived or are still living in the Sounds provided further detail and insights.

By contrast, what is publicly accessible on Māori lives from the 1860s to the 1930s is largely official documents and reports written from a European perspective.

Equally, local newspaper reporting tends to throw more light on European responses to an event than on the event itself.

I am very conscious that I am a Wellington writer and have almost no contact with Māori in the Sounds. My account is therefore, inevitably, a Pākehā account; it cannot be otherwise. However, to have left out the Māori history would have invalidated my account, so, wisely or unwisely, and hoping that my Pākehā sensibilities do not intrude more than is inevitable, I pressed on.

In that mission I am indebted to Hilary Mitchell and John Mitchell for their invaluable, detailed three-volume *Te Tau Ihu o Te Waka*. I have drawn considerably also on the Treaty of Waitangi's nuanced 2008 report *Te Tau Ihu o te Waka a Maui: Report on Northern South Island Claims*. Through that report I have been able to access the extraordinary work, dedication and courage of those who brought their stories to the tribunal. That largely unseen and unsung work, and the tribunal's considered assessment of the material, have allowed me to gain some understanding of Māori history in the Sounds.

All perspectives have enriched my understandings; I hope my readers will be able to say the same.

Finally, I remain particularly indebted and grateful to Rangitāne kaumātua Richard Bradley for his account of growing up in the Sounds in the 1960s, for his narrative of land, legend and belonging, and of the past and presentness of history.

A word about place names

One of the things that struck me as I researched this book was the almost total loss of Māori place names in the Sounds as new European arrivals took over the land. I don't imagine the new settlers gave any thought to this, but for Māori that process must have intensified the loss of land and deracination from the world they knew. They no longer owned the land; they saw the names that had long carried their history unilaterally replaced in a further annihilation of culture, even of identity. To quote contemporary historian Danny Keenan, names were part of a link to living 'ancient landscapes'; their loss, part of that existential loss that Māori faced when their land was alienated, was one that 'cut the essence of Māori society'.[3]

Today, a new naming system is evolving to rectify that loss. In this book, apart from place names in the captions, I have attempted to highlight the issue in a small way by using, at first mention in the first and last chapters, a hybrid Māori–European name (where both forms exist). For second and subsequent references I have defaulted to the Māori name, unless referring specifically to names bestowed by European explorers. In the chapters between, I default to the name most commonly used today. I include below a reference guide to these usages.

Anaho — Cannibal Cove
Kākāpō — Guards Bay
Kura Te Au — Tory Channel
Meretoto — Ship Cove
Motungarara — Tītī Island
Ngāwhatu Kai-ponu — The Brothers
Puna-rua-whiti — Endeavour Inlet
Rangitoto Ki Te Tonga — D'Urville Island
Raukawa Moana — Cook Strait
Takapourewa — Stephens Island
Te Akaroa — West Entry Point
Te Anamāhanga — Port Gore
Te Hoiere — Pelorus Sound
Te Tau Ihu — top of the South Island
Te Koro-o-Kupe — Cloudy Bay
Te Pākekā — Maud Island
Te Taonui a Kupe — Cape Jackson
Te Waipounamu — South Island
Te Whanganui — Port Underwood
Tōtaranui — Queen Charlotte Sound

Maps of the Marlborough Sounds

Marlborough Sounds

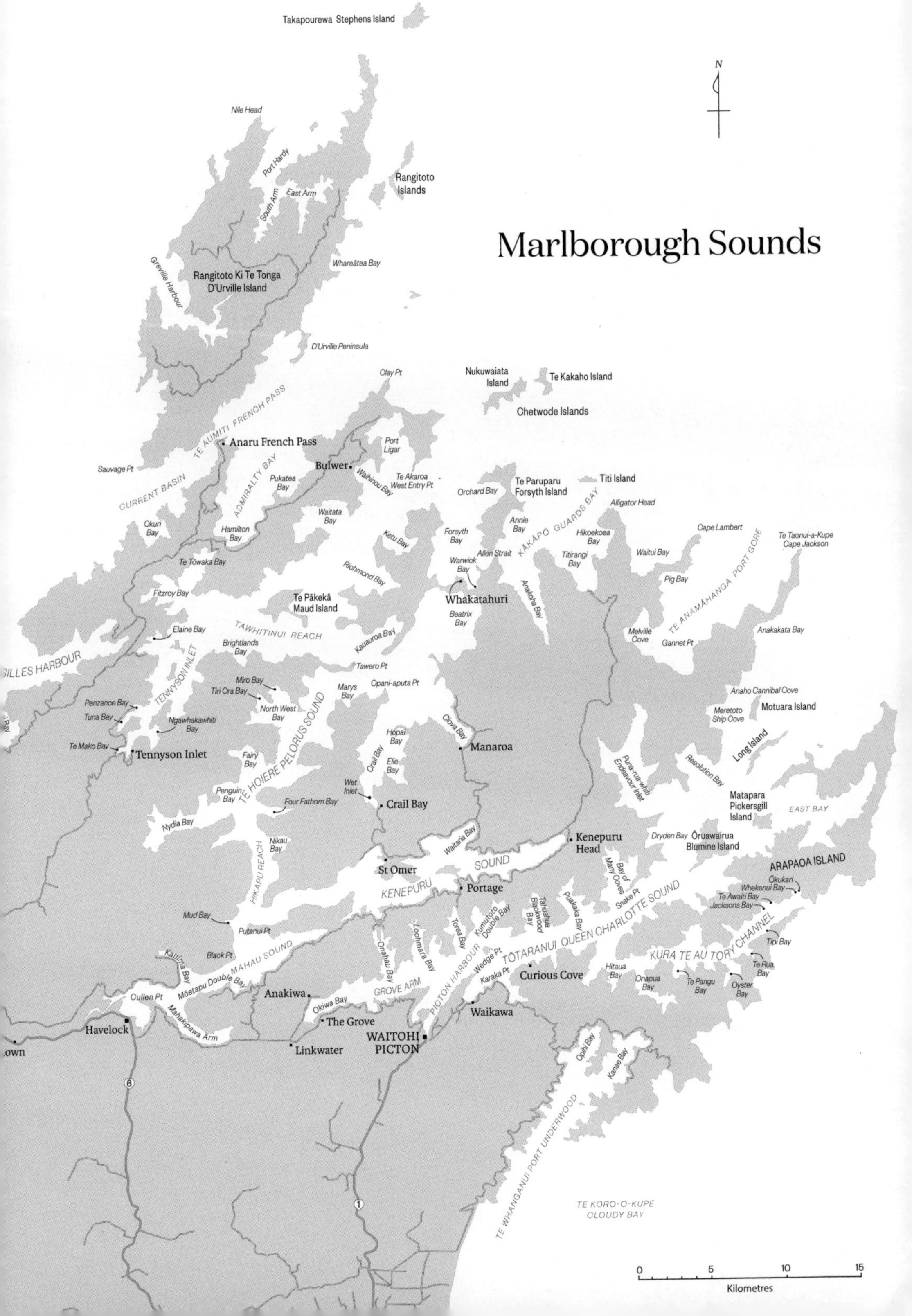

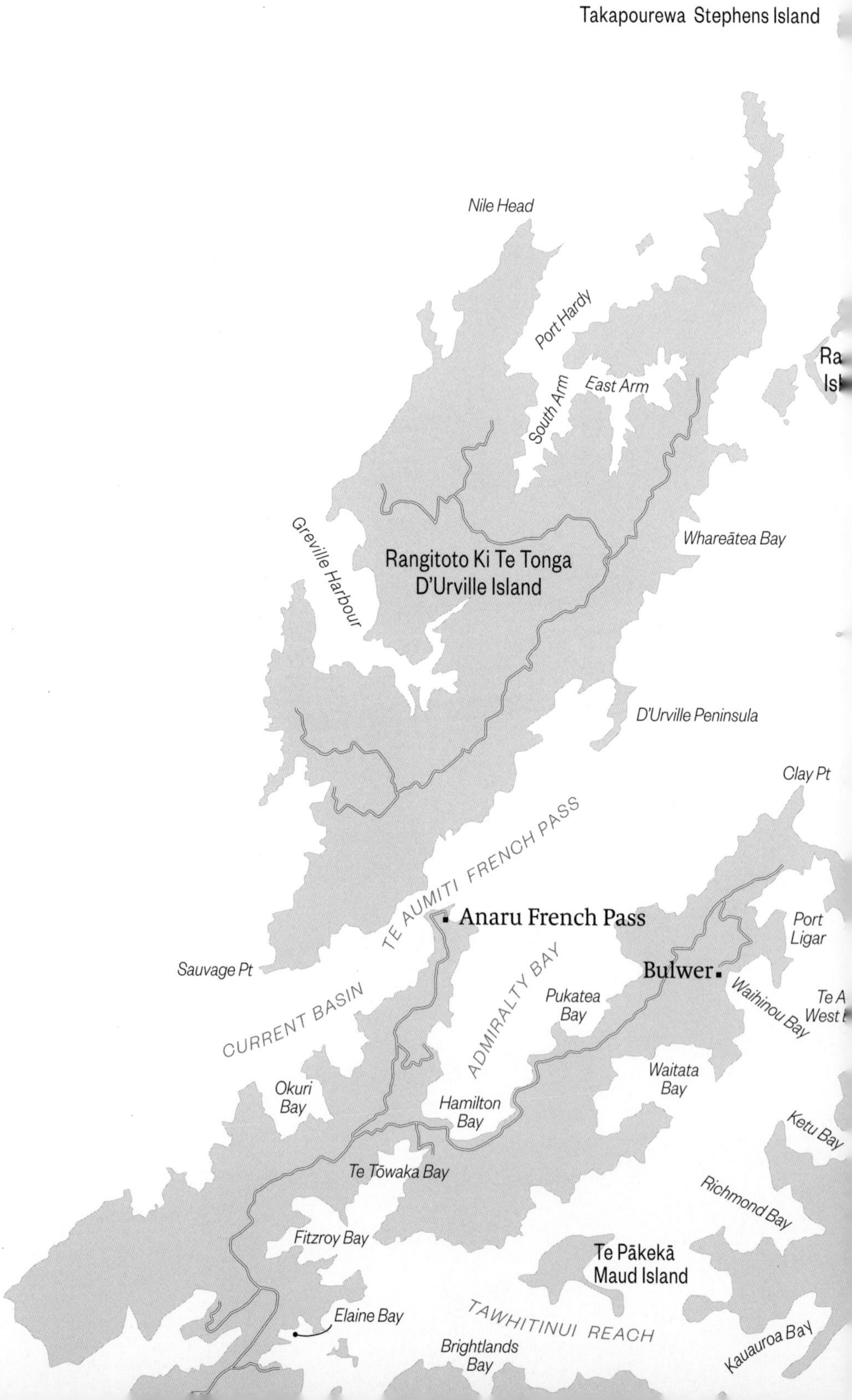
Takapourewa Stephens Island
Nile Head
Port Hardy
South Arm
East Arm
Greville Harbour
Rangitoto Ki Te Tonga
D'Urville Island
Whareātea Bay
D'Urville Peninsula
Clay Pt
TE AUMITI FRENCH PASS
Anaru French Pass
Port Ligar
Sauvage Pt
Bulwer
CURRENT BASIN
ADMIRALTY BAY
Pukatea Bay
Waihinou Bay
Waitata Bay
Okuri Bay
Hamilton Bay
Ketu Bay
Te Tōwaka Bay
Richmond Bay
Fitzroy Bay
Te Pākekā
Maud Island
Elaine Bay
TAWHITINUI REACH
Brightlands Bay
Kauauroa Bay

Marlborough Sounds (detail)

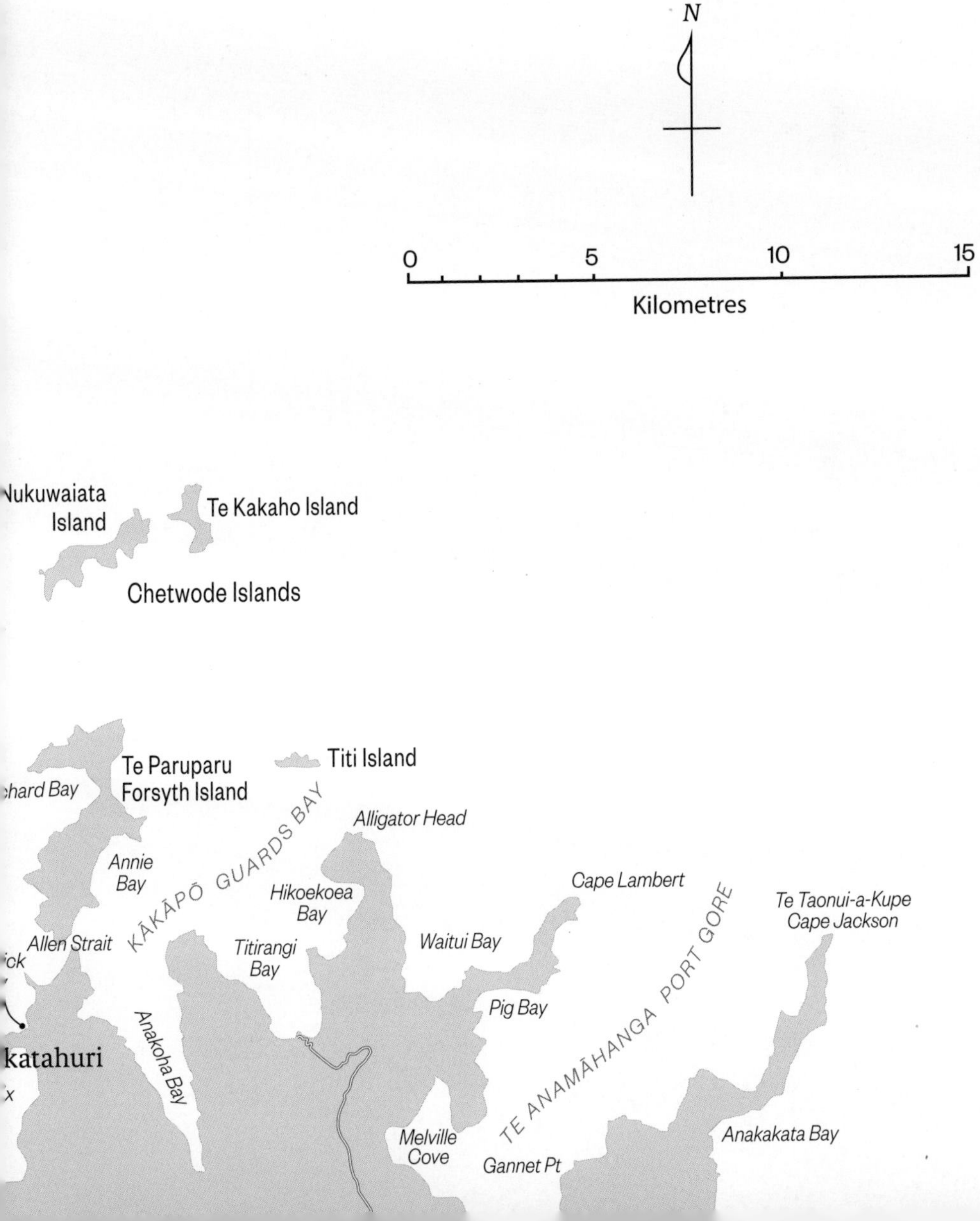

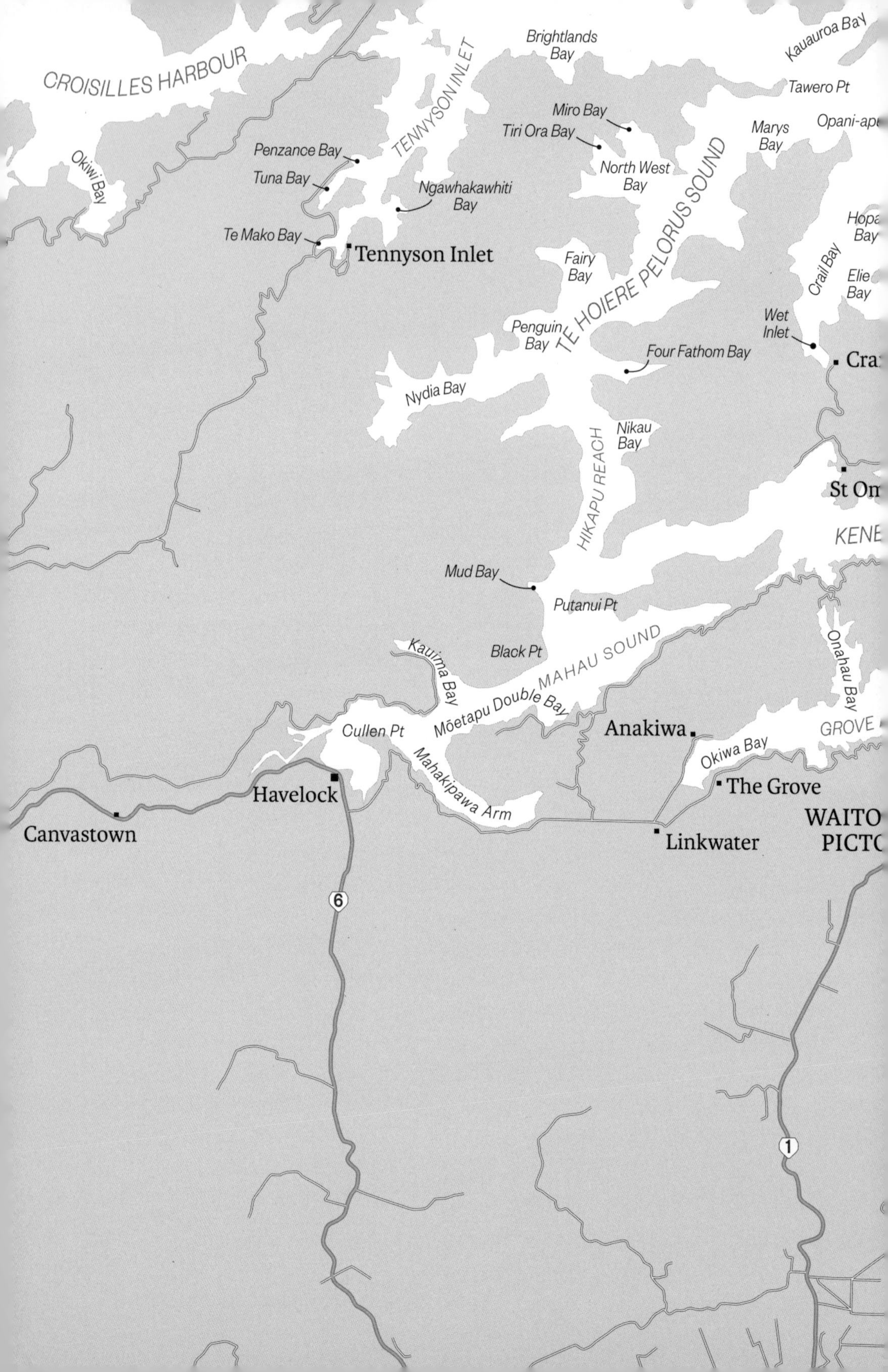
CROISILLES HARBOUR
Okiwi Bay
TENNYSON INLET
Penzance Bay
Tuna Bay
Ngawhakawhiti Bay
Te Mako Bay
Tennyson Inlet
Brightlands Bay
Miro Bay
Tiri Ora Bay
North West Bay
Kauauroa Bay
Tawero Pt
Marys Bay
TE HOIERE PELORUS SOUND
Fairy Bay
Penguin Bay
Four Fathom Bay
Nydia Bay
Crail Bay
Wet Inlet
Nikau Bay
HIKAPU REACH
Mud Bay
Putanui Pt
Black Pt
Kauima Bay
MAHAU SOUND
Mōetapu
Double Bay
Cullen Pt
Mahakipawa Arm
Anakiwa
Okiwa Bay
The Grove
Onahau Bay
Havelock
Canvastown
Linkwater
6
1

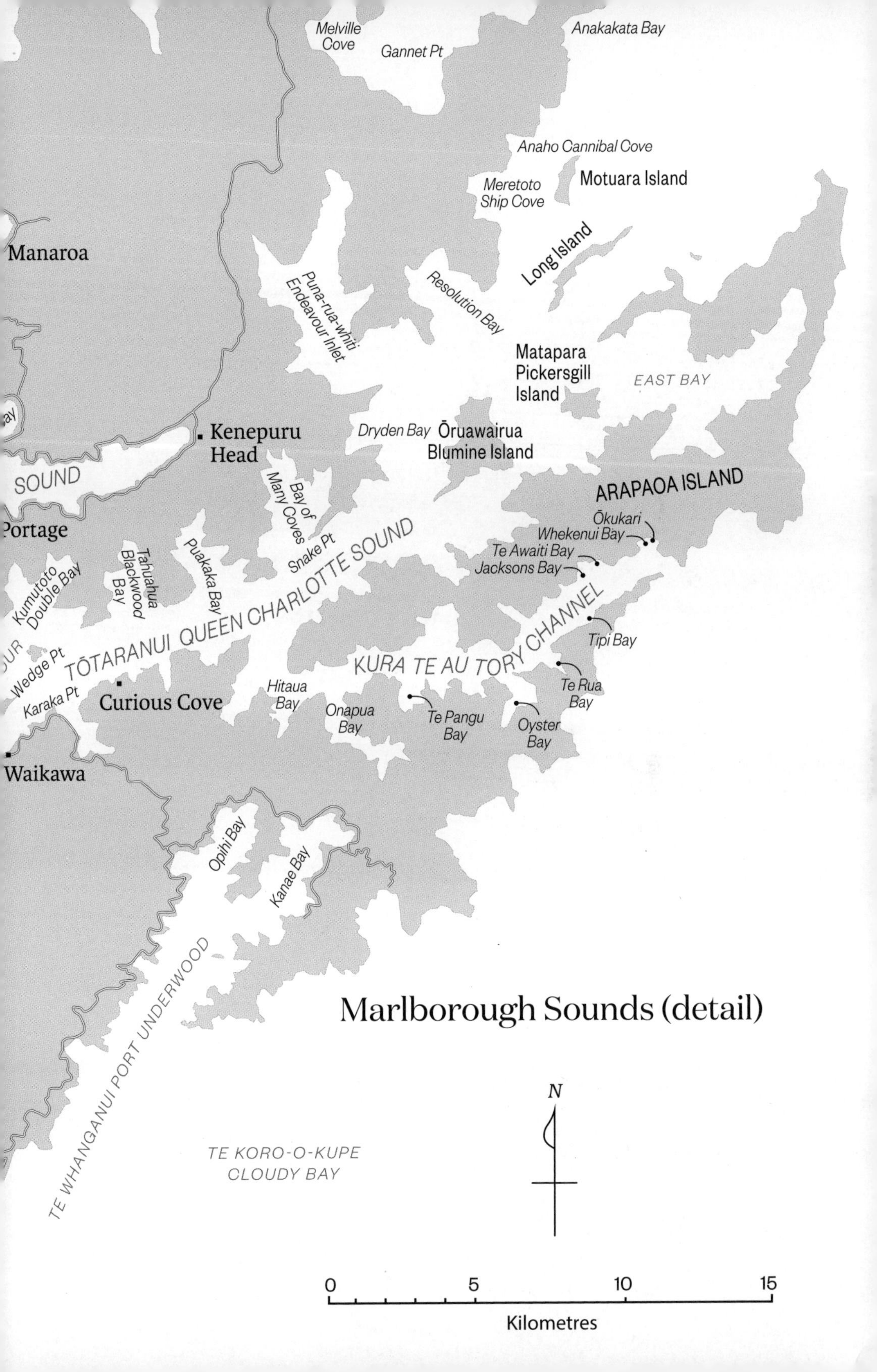

Marlborough Sounds (detail)

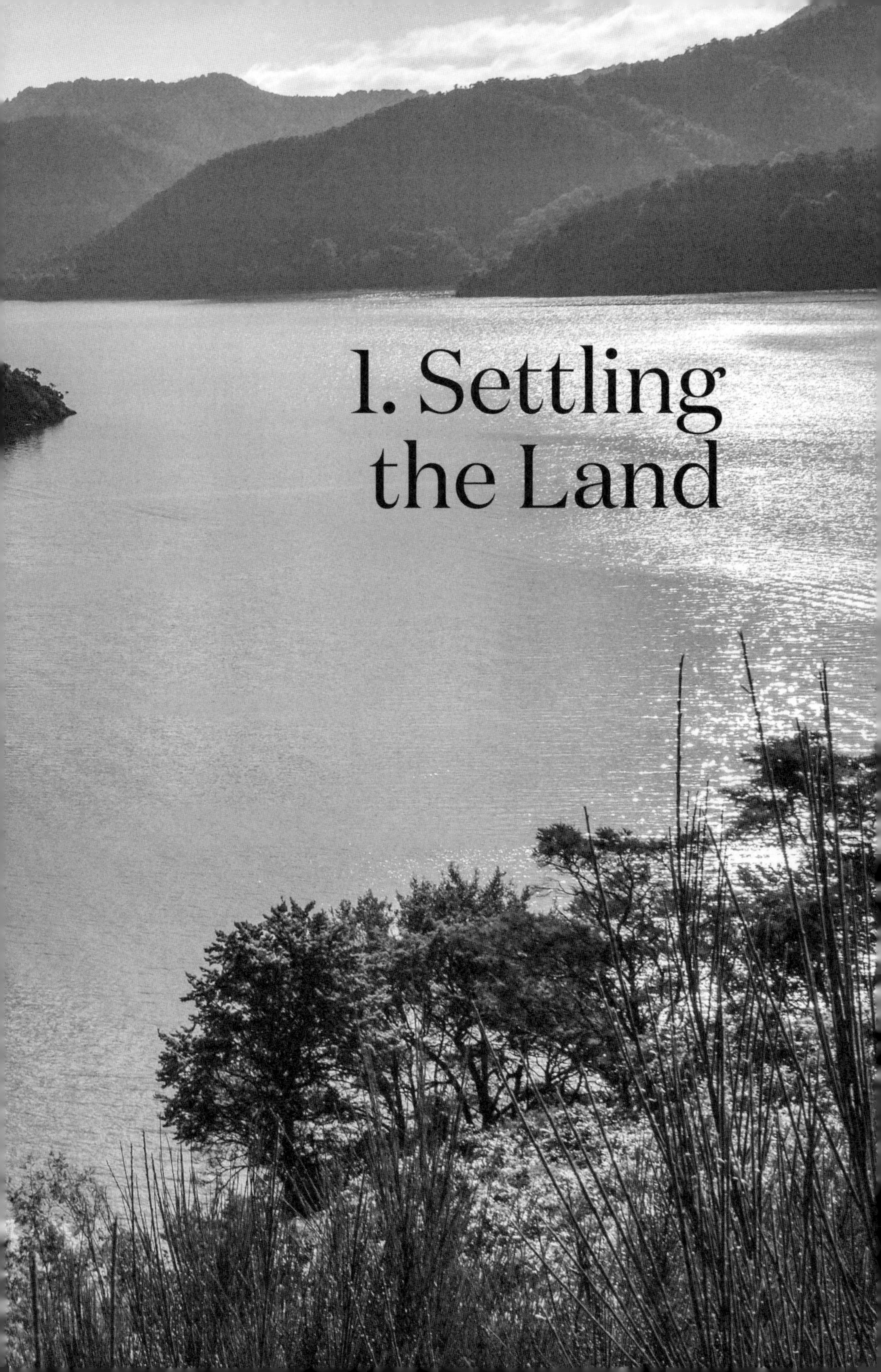

1. Settling the Land

> At times, with the sea barely touched by wind, the islands in the Sounds appear to be floating. At other times, katabatic winds sweep down the valleys . . . and solid sheets of rain reduce the world to a grey mass of water.

Planes flying into Marlborough across Raukawa Moana Cook Strait pass over the steep eastern cliffs of Arapaoa Island. Formed, like others in the Sounds, by heavy coastal swells beating on exposed rock, they delineate the south-east side of Kura Te Au Tory Channel.[1] The narrow, rocky entrance of the channel, which appears suddenly, almost improbably, from this coastline, was long feared by ships' masters for the force of its tides and, in southerly blows, the violence of the sea at its entrance. Kura Te Au winds west towards the many bays that typify Tōtaranui Queen Charlotte Sound. Behind those bays, precipitous, tortured land on the western side snakes out towards Raukawa Moana Cook Strait, separating that sound from the great reaches of Te Hoiere Pelorus Sound. The dramatic peaks that dominate the skyline behind Tennyson Inlet lie to the far west.

Massive geological forces shaped these ranges and waterways. As the Australian and Pacific tectonic plates collided, land was uplifted, faulted into blocks and tilted towards the newly forming Raukawa Moana. This tilting and the consequent river erosion along faults aligned Tōtaranui and Te Hoiere to the north-east, towards the strait; Kenepuru Sound was dragged to the east-north-east, along the major alpine and

Looking down into Kura Te Au Tory Channel, Arapaoa Island and to Tōtaranui Queen Charlotte Sound. WHITES AVIATION, ALEXANDER TURNBULL LIBRARY, WA-47659-F

ABOVE Looking across Forysth Bay, just through Allen Strait (Guards Pass), in the outer Te Hoiere Pelorus Sound, 2007. HELEN BEAGLEHOLE

BELOW Yacht at anchor, Tawa Bay, Endeavour Inlet, Tōtaranui Queen Charlotte Sound, February 2011. Summer in the Sounds does not necessarily bring good weather. HELEN BEAGLEHOLE

other nearby faults that run parallel throughout Marlborough. Such tilting, too, may have altered the course of Te Hoiere. Today it flows out past Havelock; it may formerly have flowed south-east, through the Kaituna Valley, as a tributary of the Wairau River.

After several million years of tectonic upheaval came the numerous glacial cycles of the Pleistocene era; the last one peaked about 20,000 years ago. At that point an estimated 30 per cent of the earth's surface is thought to have been covered with ice, and permafrost, which stretched from the edge of the ice some hundreds of kilometres into, for instance, North America and Eurasia. Sea levels fell dramatically around the globe, only to rise again as the ice sheets melted and the sea flooded in. During that time, Aotearoa New Zealand's two islands were connected by a land bridge so that much of what is Raukawa Moana today was dry land. As the sea began to rise at the end of that glacial period, and as the land in the area began to tilt downwards, the ancient rivers running through the Marlborough valleys were progressively drowned, forming the Sounds we see today.

Today the dull green of exotic pine forest in parts of Tōtaranui seems to absorb the light. Clear-felling can denude whole flanks of hills; dead trunks on the skyline indicate attempts to control wilding pines. Elsewhere, high rugged country, now increasingly covered with the native bush that earlier European settlers strove so hard to burn off, rises from the sea's edge. Large areas of easily cultivatable land are rare in Te Hoiere and almost non-existent in Tōtaranui.

At times, with the sea barely touched by wind, the islands in the Sounds appear to be floating. At other times, katabatic winds sweep down the valleys, even in the almost land-locked Kenepuru and Mahau sounds, and solid sheets of rain reduce the world to a grey mass of water. Williwaws — 'whirlwinds that come walking out of every bay and all over the place' — appear from nowhere, making 'clouds of water spray, and white foam dance high into the air'.[2] On a good day, a clear sea drops from the deeply indented coastline to translucent depths; in poor weather the water moves restlessly against a grey, forbidding shore.

MĀORI CREATION MYTHS EMBODY cataclysmic forces. In one version associated with the Sounds area, Ranginui, the sky father, and Papatūānuku, the earth mother, lay in a close embrace. From them came their children, the gods. Longing for light and air, they forced their parents apart, creating the world and its diurnal and seasonal cycles. Later, as the great chief Aoraki and his brothers were visiting their father Ranginui's second wife, and exploring the southern oceans of Papatūānuku, they incurred the wrath of Tāwhirimātea, god of weather, who whipped up such storms that the waka in which they travelled, its crew and its cargo were all turned to stone. This was the origin of Te Waka o Aoraki (the canoe of Aoraki) or the South Island. Following a different tradition, the South Island is also known as Te Waka a Māui. The intricate traceries of the great carved prow of the canoe formed Te Tau Ihu o Te Waka a Māui — the top of the South Island: Farewell Spit, Golden Bay, Tasman Bay and the bays and islands of the Marlborough Sounds and Cloudy Bay.[3]

Many place names in the Sounds are linked to that legendary traveller Kupe. Differing versions of the stories of his shaping of the Sounds are common to all local hapū. Kura Te Au is said to have been named from the red blood of the wheke (octopus) that Kupe fought and killed and that still stains the waters of the channel. Te Umu Wheke, the octopus oven, now Umuwheke Bay on the western side of Arapaoa (formerly Arapawa) Island, was where Kupe's adversary was cooked. Near Picton, the spring Te Mimi o Kupe (place of urinating) or Wedge Point was formed before Kupe's party left the Sounds. He left his companions Kokomohua and Amerikiwhati, tiny islets just south-west of Cape Koamaru, to guard his resources in Tōtaranui. Te Koro-o-Kupe Cloudy Bay is held to derive from the dredge or scoop with which Kupe harvested oysters.[4]

The long reef off Te Taonui a Kupe (now Cape Jackson) was Kupe's fishing net, and his footprints are visible in the rocks at Te Anamāhanga Port Gore. Other myths associate Kupe with nearby Rangitoto Ki Te Tonga D'Urville Island and Takapourewa Stephens Island. Early Europeans were told about the islets to the north of Arapaoa Island called Ngāwhatu Kai-ponu The Brothers. They were the eyeballs of Whekenui, the giant octopus killed by Kupe. This was a place of such extreme tapu that until the 1820s Māori crossing Raukawa Moana for the first time covered their eyes with kawakawa leaves to ensure that they saw only the paddles of their waka and the sea. The eyes in the great canoe prows were also covered, the leaves being removed only when the islets were left far behind.[5]

Twentieth-century ethnographers attributed a particular importance to the myths and legends, arguing that they were conceptualised as 'detailed oral maps', providing an understanding of geography, of how to move around the country, exploit its resources and facilitate settlement. The Kupe stories in particular were seen as naming the coast for future generations of travellers. '[C]omplete with survey posts and warning beacons of the most dangerous passages', their intricate detail enabled people to voyage across the vast Pacific and arrive at precise points.[6]

The legends of Ngahue, explorer contemporary of Kupe and the atua (god) of pounamu (greenstone), and Poutini, the taniwha who assisted him, played a similar role in helping iwi (tribes) locate such resources as the deposits of metamorphosed or 'baked' argillite on Rangitoto Ki Te Tonga, which early Māori used extensively, and the outcrops of pounamu in the outer part of Te Hoiere.[7]

There is no single strong oral version of these myths, however. Some scholars have more recently become sceptical about some interpretations and the existence of oral maps, yet the stories, in their varied forms, have continued to be passed down.[8]

First peoples

Māori, descended from people of East Polynesian origin, first settled in New Zealand in substantial numbers over a thousand years ago. There was a large settlement in Te Hoiere, at Titirangi Bay, around AD 1300 to 1320,[9] but 'differing traditional narratives . . . different perspectives . . . and competing interests'[10] mean that today there is no single, generally accepted account of the area's occupation and settlement.

However, in the seventeenth century, Rangitāne, Ngāti Apa and Ngāti Kuia, descendants from *Kurahaupō*, one of the seven great waka said to have come from the homeland of Hawaiki, slowly migrated from the Mahia Peninsula to Te Tau Ihu, the top of the South Island. ('Kurahaupō waka' now serves as a kind of shorthand for a complex genealogical history that includes 'original peoples' — Ngāti Wairangi, Ngāti Tara and Ngāti Tūmatakōkiri — encountered when the waka first arrived in Te Tau Ihu.)[11]

The Waitangi Tribunal report (Wai 785) on Te Tau Ihu posits that Ngāti Māmoe, Ngāti Tara and Ngāti Tūmatakōkiri were established in Te Tau Ihu in the seventeenth century. In the mid-to-late 1600s some Rangitāne and Ngāi Tahu, bound by close whakapapa links, crossed to the Sounds from the North Island. Late that century, Rangitāne settled in Te Whanganui Port Underwood and fought with Ngāti Māmoe; in Te Hoiere, Ngāti Kurī (a Ngāi Tahu hapū or subtribe) battled with Ngāti Tara. Intermittent fighting followed as Rangitāne and Ngāti Kurī attempted to move into the Wairau area.[12]

Towards the end of the eighteenth century intertribal conflict was constant, and during the first two decades of the nineteenth century other northern iwi groupings became dominant. The situation was fluid and territorial dominance was not fixed.

‘Regions could be shared along with whakapapa’ because boundary adjustments, marriage over a number of generations and successive migrations saw different descent lines intertwined. Thus people could live together in some places, while ‘settlements belonging to one group could be found interspersed within a general locality dominated by another’.[13]

As a major staging point for travel across Raukawa Moana, the Sounds were closely linked to, and traded with, a wider world. The early discovery of the Nelson mineral belt and the extensive mining of argillite on Rangitoto Ki Te Tonga placed Tōtaranui in particular on an important trade route for pounamu from the West Coast and obsidian (volcanic glass) from the North Island.[14] A block of argillite found on Hippa Island (at the southern tip of Motuara Island), for instance, and the small stone carved faces found at Titirangi Bay, indicate an extensive and effective network in which Sounds iwi played a part.[15]

Around the fourteenth to sixteenth centuries, the local iwi used argillite from Rangitoto Ki Te Tonga and on the mainland to make adze heads. Evidence of adze-head manufacture at a number of sites suggests a thriving industry.[16] Flaking the hard stone produced sophisticated artefacts and ornaments. But by the end of that period, and once Māori across the country had learned to cut and polish pounamu, a burgeoning creativity overlay many aspects of their lives, with the production of highly fashioned and beautifully styled ornaments and weapons. The use of pounamu to make carving tools also led to the creation of elegantly carved wooden combs, weapons, carvings and house fronts.[17] A quadrangular adze-head was developed, often associated with pā walls and ditches that were a feature of Māori habitation in the Sounds.

The 200–400 people living in the Sounds in the late eighteenth century[18] appear to have continued their nomadic hunter-gatherer pattern of moving between the hundreds of small, transitory habitations on the mainland,[19] propelled by conflicts with neighbouring communities, seasonal opportunities to forage, and access to fortified pā offering protection.[20] In winter they repaired their weapons and boats and made clothes. Over the summer they moved ‘up and down in different parties . . . sometimes laying in the Canoes and sometimes on shore, as there is a number of huts in every Cove’.[21] Far from haphazard, these stopping places were part of ‘a carefully, perhaps ritually, regulated seasonal round of fishing and food-gathering activities’ in which, during the summer, Māori were able to provide against winter shortages.[22]

Basic, prefabricated temporary shelters were erected with practised aplomb in the small camping places during food-hunting expeditions. Māori carried the framework with them. Lieutenant James Cook observed: 'The moment the Canoes landed men leaped out and at once took possession of a spot of ground, by tearing up the pla[n]ts etc or sticking up some part of the framing of the hut.' The women 'were not idle, some were takeing care of the Canoes, some securing the Provisions, and the few utensils they are possessed of, and others went to gather dry sticks to make a fire to dress their victuals'.[23]

Some sites were substantial, most were small;[24] many were so thickly clustered that to map them is to almost delineate the coastline itself — the map on page 28 gives a sense of an extraordinarily habited landscape. The sites were not limited to sheltered bays offering apparently good food resources and opportunities to garden. Their diet was wide-ranging, with middens found containing shells of mussel, pipi, cockle, whelk or mud-snail shells, as well as remains of fish, berries, dogs, seals and birds.[25] Even an incomplete list of the fish caught by Māori living throughout Te Tau Ihu reveals a rich variety: crayfish, mullet, elephant fish, sole, tarakihi, moki, blue cod, salmon, gurnard, skate, mackerel, parrotfish, leatherjacket and butterfish.

Birds were another source of protein. Kākāpō, mokai, kākāriki, robins and tits, kiwi (highly valued for their feathers for weaving cloaks), kākā (easy prey and particularly prized for their tender, well-flavoured meat),[26] rail, shags and penguins were all fair game. Kurī or dogs were bred and killed for meat,[27] and, in all probability, Māori made short work of the breeding pigs, hens and goats that Cook and his men liberated, though hens may have survived briefly in the bush behind Meretoto Ship Cove.[28]

Particularly after the cooler conditions of the Little Ice Age (1303–1860) precluded kūmara cultivation in the South Island, fern and fernroot became an important (and apparently pleasant) food source.[29] Fern and fish were both dried to last over winter and were carried on the seasonal migrations. New dating techniques mean that earlier conclusions reached in terms of dating gardening activity can no longer be assumed to be correct, but it seems that, like their counterparts in northern coastal and warmer inland regions, and coastal parts of the South Island, Māori in the Sounds gardened from the time their Polynesian forebears arrived.

Some garden sites, like that in Titirangi Bay, one of the most complex and important, were sufficiently large to challenge some assumptions about seasonal movements.[30] To date, archaeology has uncovered nine distinct garden sites in the bay. The Cattleyards Flat site, with its middens, terracing and earth walls, was '[p]robably the most impressive garden site in the South Island'.[31] Using sometimes quite substantial stones, Māori developed single stone heaps, stone lines, double

Current, pending and inactive NZAA sites, June 2020.

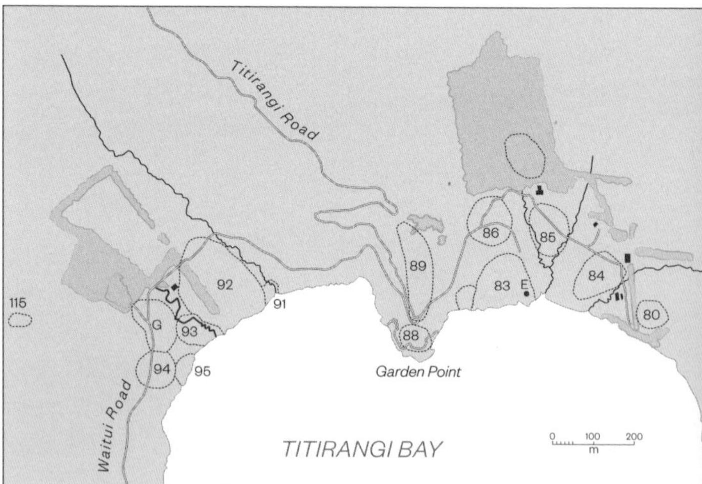

KEY

80	Garden	91	Midden
83	Occupation material	92	Cattle Yard Flat
84	Garden	93G	Garden — extends under pa
85	Garden	94	Garden
86	Garden	95	Garden
88	Pit complex	115	Terrace and pit site
89	Terrace and pit site	E	Excavation site

ABOVE The archaeological record of the Sounds covers some 600 to 700 years of habitation. Although only a small number of sites would have been in use at any one time, the range and extent of visitation of favoured spots is striking. As a Rangitāne kaumātua said, 'My people covered the ground like ants.' ARCHSITE, NEW ZEALAND ARCHAEOLOGY ASSOCIATION

RIGHT Titirangi Bay archaeological map, showing the extent and number of garden sites. AFTER MICHAEL M. TROTTER, MAP 7, *TITIRANGI ARCHEOLOGICAL SURVEY: AN INTERIM REPORT* (CHRISTCHURCH: CANTERBURY MUSEUM, 1977)

stone lines, and double stone lines with what appear to be paving stones between them, perhaps to hold soil. As elsewhere in the surrounding area, pebbles were added to the soil to warm and aerate the ground.[32]

At Brightlands Bay in Te Hoiere a low stone wall may indicate early Māori agriculture,[33] as do the gentle slopes and lie of the land at the largest of five villages on the north-west side of Te Pākekā Maud Island.[34] In Tōtaranui the number of garden sites in East Bay on Arapaoa Island indicates extensive cultivation.[35]

The gardens grew kūmara. Although the cooler, wetter weather from the end of the fourteenth century made kūmara cultivation more difficult in the Sounds and farther south, mounds built with organic matter at the core provided an excellent nursery and growing environment and encouraged the plants to develop roots.[36] Pits were dug for kūmara storage, although there has been some fanciful speculation about other uses. Little fireplaces, quite distinct from the stone-lined hearths used in house floors, may also have been built to keep crops warm during cold spells.[37]

Fire was a useful tool in cultivation. Ernst Dieffenbach, naturalist on the New Zealand Company vessel *Tory* in 1839, recorded kūmara growing in the bays around Te Awaiti, with bush on the hillsides burned to improve soil fertility before planting. In 1845 Samuel Stephens, surveying for the company, noted that in Tōtaranui, possibly thousands of acres had been cleared by burning,[38] though this may have been to encourage bracken growth.

Although archaeological evidence indicates that both Māori men and women were taller than their European counterparts,[39] and Cook and his men commented on their healthy appearance, life for Māori, in the Sounds as elsewhere, could be short, hard and sometimes hungry. Evidence of the abrasive diet of gritty shellfish and fernroot that gradually prevailed after 1500 suggests that agricultural produce was too unreliable to be a main source of sustenance. Poor diet resulted in bone deterioration and occasional malnutrition; people died early. Yet there is no doubting the admiration with which Cook's men viewed the Māori they met. 'When a New Zealander stands forth,' wrote American John Ledyard, with Cook on his third voyage, 'the subsequent idea is . . . there stands a man.'

COOK'S MEN ALSO ADMIRED the psychological strength that Māori brought to the turbulent times in which they lived. During the periods Cook and his men spent in the Sounds, violent and often intergenerational tribal warfare was still a constant.

A south-east ridge on Motuara Island looking towards Long Island, Tōtaranui Queen Charlotte Sound. The steep drop-off to the sea illustrates the challenge marauding parties would have faced when attacking. COLLECTION OF HAWKE'S BAY MUSEUMS TRUST, RUAWHARO TĀ-Ū-RANGI, 15751, GIFTED BY JASPER HERRICK

Even as Māori constructed their temporary shelters, they were careful to place their weapons within easy reach.[40] James King, second officer on Cook's final voyage, was alive to the psychological pressures of the constant warfare. An account of 'their surprizes by night & other adventures' gave King 'a terrible picture of their mode of living, keeping constant guard and sleeping with their arms in their hands'.[41]

Cook, too, described Māori living 'under perpetual apprehinsions of being received some injury or a nother from some other'. They would attack at night and, if finding their enemy unguarded, could kill 'every soul that falls in their way' and eat or mutilate the dead. Because seemingly minor slights like brief hunting incursions into others' tribal areas could cause such incidents, war 'keeps them continually upon their guard'.[42] Fear of cannibalism, Banks suggested, meant that warriors, even when looking to pick a fight, often travelled with '[w]omen and young children in arms as if they were afraid to leave them behind'.[43] Such constant harassment must have occasioned considerable tension, yet Ledyard gives testimony of the 'native courage of Maori, their great personal prowess, their ineversible [sic] intrepidity, and determined fixed perspective'.[44]

This pattern of warfare brought 'massive disruptions' among Sounds Māori,[45] who resorted to their pā or fortified villages when circumstances warranted. The large numbers Cook saw on Hippa Island on his first visit were villagers from Anahou, Little Waikawa and Anakakata, expecting a retaliatory raid from northern and eastern tribes beyond the Sounds. They dispersed during Cook's three-week stay. On his second voyage three years later the pā was abandoned and the vegetable garden where Cook had planted English vegetables was overgrown. By the 1777 voyage the houses and palisades had been rebuilt and were in good order, though the pā was unoccupied.[46]

In 1839 James Coutts Crawford, who would become the region's provincial geologist, recorded that the 100 or so people living at Anahou had been dreading an attack by Ngāti Raukawa, who were themselves fighting Ngāti Awa, the parent tribe of the Anahou people. Those at Anahou had set up watch stations and had fortified the pā, though they were reportedly reluctant to retreat because they would have lost their vegetable gardens.[47] However, pā had other than defensive purposes. One of Cook's men considered a pā near Amerikiwhati Island as a defended 'separate . . . place of retreat and a magazine for securing . . . dried fish, fern root, and other provisions'.[48]

Pā built with extraordinary ingenuity, skill and effort supported the many kāinga (villages), urupā (burial grounds) and tauranga waka (canoe landing places) dotted around the coastline. They help reinforce that understanding of the Sounds as a well-inhabited region. A pā employed geography to maximise the tribe's hold on it. Te Akaroa

J. W. Barnicoat's sketch of Ngākuta Bay, Tōtaranui Queen Charlotte Sound, March 1843, shows the relationship of village with pā. Here, the pā is on the forested foreland, with the village and its raised food store on the shore. HOCKEN COLLECTIONS UARE TAOKA O HĀKENA, UNIVERSITY OF OTAGO, 94/244 A & B

West Entry Point, the high, narrow headland opening the eastern entrance to Port Ligar, has multiple terraces, pits and a defensive ditch. At Cannon Point, a pā that is open to north-west Raukawa Moana weather looks across to Te Akaroa and the land rises steeply above the sea on both sides to offer good natural defences.[49] At the entrance to the sound, in Kākāpō Guards Bay, there are two pā sites, one in Titirangi Bay, the other on the promontory of Dan's Nose, where, despite challenging geography, the carefully designed village and the high terraces are invisible from the sea.[50]

When Cook and others visited the pā on Hippa Island, Joseph Banks thought that sides of the island were so steep that fortifications were almost redundant. On the highest point was a 'town', and when William Bayly, astronomer on the second voyage (1772–75), visited he estimated there were 32 or 33 houses on a reasonably level area about 90 metres long and 9 metres wide.[51] Posts driven into the ground formed a palisade. Long vines were interwoven between these posts and the gaps filled 'with small brushwood'. An additional defence was the small entrance door to the interior of the pā, which allowed only one person at a time to crawl in.[52] The island also had middens and a pit.

There were at least six other fortified villages in the vicinity of Meretoto, each with strong defences that capitalised on their geography. At one, 'evidently a rock lying off Blumine or Pickersgill Island', the cliffs and rocks formed excellent natural defences. They were so steep, said Banks, 'that it was almost in danger of our necks that we climbed up'.[53] There, too, was evidence of Māori's extraordinary ability to create 'living space out of every habitable metre'. Along with one 'fighting stage' there were 80–90 houses.[54]

Within such fortifications most structures were small, low, squat rectangular huts. Heavily, and effectively, thatched with bark covered with long grass or flax, they looked rounded; their single low door necessitated entering on hands and knees; one of the two fires was just inside the door (the smoke may have helped to repel the tiresome sandflies); low sleeping places were covered with dry grass and rushes. The small interior spaces made for warmth,[55] but William Anderson, the naturalist on Cook's second voyage, described them as 'poorly ventilated, smoky and too low to allow their inhabitants to stand upright'.[56] Lean-to style constructions, perhaps used for cooking or manufacture, and solidly built storage huts were sometimes added, as well as larger buildings 'exactly', William Anderson thought, in the style of an English country barn and apparently for a 'principal' person.[57]

Surprisingly, given the constant warfare, none of these pā had a permanent water supply. But deceitful attacks, where the hosts were slaughtered by those coming in apparent friendship, appear to have been favoured over laying siege, so residents did not fear being imprisoned for long periods without supplies. Moreover, as the water in containers at Amerikiwhati pā demonstrated, a fair amount of water could be stored if needed.[58]

AS LIEUTENANT JAMES COOK SAILED into Tōtaranui, which he would call Queen Charlotte Sound, on 15 January 1770, he passed the pā on Hippa Island, the islet off Motuara Island. The people there then 'set up a loud shout and every man brandished his weapons which none of them were without'.[59] He anchored at Meretoto — Ship Cove to him. On all three of his voyages he would come here for the same reasons as Māori: in search of sheltered anchorage, abundant fresh water and open ground for gardens. Cook also sought a campsite offering space for his carpenters and sailmakers, and the long sloping beach would allow him to careen his ship.

When the *Endeavour* was at anchor, canoes full of well-armed Māori from Hippa Island 'rowed round and round the ship defying and threatening us as usual and at last hove some stones aboard which we all expected to be a prelude of some behaviour

Meretoto Ship Cove has sheltering hills, deep water close inshore, freshwater streams and flat land where Cook could careen his ship and set up his observatory. It was a haven to which Cook returned on subsequent voyages. V. C. BROWNE & SON, 13361

which would oblige us to fire upon them'. An old man indicating he wanted to come aboard defused the situation. The English encouraged him and, although some of his companions tried to hold him back, he was 'receivd in as freindly a manner as we possibly could and had many presents given to him, which he returned to the canoes who immediately joind in a war dance — whether to shew their freindship or enmity it is impossible to say, we have so often seen them do it upon both those occasions'.[60]

The Māori left and Cook's crew set about fishing, pulling up 300 pounds (136 kilograms) with a few hauls of the seine — more than they could possibly use, something they often did. They also shot some shags and 'some few other wild fowl which to people in our situation was fresh food not to be dispised'.[61] Banks, a few days later, recorded that the shags, which 'we roast or stew', were 'not bad provisions, so between shags and fish this is the place of greatest plenty of any we have seen'.[62]

The following morning when Cook's crew began careening the ship and making good the storm damage suffered on the voyage, Māori arrived with fish, and although the English thought it stank, Cook had it taken on board to encourage trade. He appears to have overreacted to a somewhat aggressive-seeming trader and fired some small shot,[63] but the locals remained willing to talk and to answer questions.

In spite of two further shooting incidents, which both Cook and Banks deplored though there is no record of the officers involved being disciplined, there were constant interchanges between Māori and Europeans — trading, visiting and seeking information, with Tupaia, the Tahitian navigator who had accompanied Cook, interpreting. Most of the English accounts compiled during all three voyages reported Māori as remarkably fearless and friendly (a word repeatedly used).[64] Even after the fraught initial contact, the Māori at Hippa Island pā, wrote Cook, 'shew'd not the least dislike of our coming but on the contrary shew'd us all over the place'.[65] Banks, too, recorded 'all possible demonstrations of friendship, if the numberless hugs and kisses we got from both sexes old and young in return for our ribbands and beads may be accounted such: they also sold and gave us a good many fish with which we went home well pleased with our new acquaintance.'[66]

There were, of course, strains on this reciprocal relationship: the exasperation caused by petty pilfering, the discord over Cook's requests for further provisions and, of considerably more moment, the massacre at Grass Cove on the second voyage, when the 'hasty, foolish behaviour'[67] of master's mate Jack Rowe, 'who evidently thought you should take a high hand with "Indians"',[68] ended in his and all the crew members of one of Captain Tobias Furneaux's cutters being killed and eaten.

However, Cook, visiting the beach on his third voyage in February 1777, acted with forbearance and restraint, writing that killing anyone 'cou'd answer no purpose at all'[69] and, wanting to reassure those involved,[70] made it clear he sought neither revenge nor punishment. His crew, however, saw things differently; Cook's officers felt that Māori had become contemptuous of them — indeed, historian Anne Salmond argues that Māori regard of the visitors was in fact lowered, as Cook's failure to avenge the killings would have upset their concepts of spiritual balance and harmonious societal relationships.[71]

On the first visit, however, Cook's men over the few days following their making landfall, worked on the ship, collected water and cut wood. The main aim of the first voyage had been to observe the transit of Venus on Tahiti, but the Admiralty had also ordered Cook to look for, explore and chart the great land mass that contemporary geographers imagined lay at the bottom of the world, and his scientists were to explore and record the flora, fauna and peoples they encountered. Finally, he was to take possession of that country in the name of the king.[72] And so, shortly after arriving in Meretoto, Cook set off for the head of his newly named Queen Charlotte Sound.

Headwinds slowed progress, but on 22 January he climbed to a high point (Cooks Lookout) on the southern ridge of Kaitapeha Bay, on Arapaoa Island. Although the view was partly blocked by densely wooded higher hills, the swirling waters of Kura Te Au beyond suggested a link to the sea. Given the existence of what Cook soon confirmed was the strait that bears his name, and his own coastings down the North Island, he realised that any elusive southern continent was most unlikely.

He sailed south to Ruakaka Bay but no further. None of his detailed and beautiful charts of Queen Charlotte Sound and Cook Strait show Kura Te Au.[73] On his second voyage, however, on 5 November 1774, Cook took the ship's boat up Kura Te Au to where they could see that it opened out into the sea, but the tide, which they had battled all the way up, prevented their clearing the entrance.[74] The channel thus effectively remained unknown to Europeans until whaler John (Jacky) Guard entered it in 1826/27.

A few days later Cook took men across to survey the big (now) East Bay of Arapaoa Island. There, on an unnamed hill between Onehunga Bay and Ōnauku Bay, the further sight of Cook Strait dispelled any lingering doubts that it might be a huge bay. Wanting a lasting monument, he built a small cairn from loose stones and buried musket balls, shot and anything else they had with them that would last. He also left a cairn at the top of the hill overlooking Ship Cove, one in the cove itself and one on Motuara

Island. On Motuara Island, too, without consulting Māori, he hoisted the Union Jack and 'dignified this Inlet with the name of Queen Charlotte's Sound and took formal possession of it and the adjacent lands in the name of and for the use of his Majesty'.[75] The names of these 'adjacent lands' Richard Pickersgill, with Cook on his first and second voyages, discovered a few days later were Te Ika a Māui (North Island), Arapaoa and Te Waipounamu (South Island).

ON 6 FEBRUARY 1770, HAVING been delayed by a typical summer blow, Cook sailed from Meretoto. He and his men carried accounts of the inhabitants of the Marlborough Sounds and their world that would be eagerly received at home. They reported on the freshness and newness of the plants, and wrote fulsomely on the beauty of the birdsong, little knowing that the Norwegian rat (*Rattus norvegicus*) they had taken with them would go on to devastate the country's fauna.

But what might this land offer Britain? As Cook and his men had left the 'miserably barren' land at Cape Jackson and moved deeper into the sound,[76] they had found country that was steep, with deep valleys and little room for cultivation. They were amazed by the dense, impenetrable but majestic vegetation. From a commercial perspective, the trees, Cook thought, would be excellent for everything but masts, for which they were too hard and heavy. John Reinhold Forster, botanist on the second voyage, was similarly impressed by the New Zealand flax (*Phormium tenax*) that he saw growing in the Sounds. A perennial, it grew everywhere, could be cut back and needed no special care, and its hemp was 'excessively strong, soft, glossy, and white'. He predicted it would be immensely useful in Europe. Fabian Gottlieb von Bellingshausen, in 1820, gathered seeds to plant in the Crimea.[77] Banks, the first to make this mistake, considered the soil's quality was

> best indicated by the luxuriant growth of its products, for the hills (except a few towards the sea which are covered with smaller bushes) are one continued forest of lofty trees which flourish with a vigour almost superior to any thing imagination can conceive, and afford an august prospect to those who are delighted with the grand and beautiful works of nature.[78]

Cook's visits had little immediate impact on Māori settlement in the Sounds. Most of the livestock he established got eaten or died, and his gardens lay untended. For the next half-century Māori probably continued to live in much the way that Cook had observed. Apart from the odd whaler or sealer, no other European visitors came.

By 1820, the year Bellingshausen and his Russian polar expedition arrived in Meretoto on 9 June, Rangitāne had become 'associated with Tōtaranui, the Wairau, Cloudy Bay and possibly as far south to the Clarence River'.[79] They shared the Kaituna River Valley with Ngāti Kuia, the dominant tribe throughout Te Hoiere as far as Rangitoto and adjacent mainland areas. Ngāti Apa, relative newcomers to the area, had interests from Nelson west. Critically, the Sounds and surrounding districts were relatively stable.

Bellingshausen, who could make comparisons because he carried with him accounts of Cook's three voyages, noted a growing appetite among Māori for European clothing. Sleeves had been added to outer garments; Māori may have acquired seamen's sweaters from a whaler or sealer, and the barter with his own crew in which Māori so enthusiastically engaged was frequently in Russian greatcoats, shirts, handkerchiefs and jackets.[80]

From some 200 metres off the beach, Bellingshausen and his men spotted 'long rows of baskets' full of potatoes. These had been recently dug from a headland that is probably between Anaho (which Cook named Cannibal Cove after his crew found human bones there in the remains of a meal) and Little Waikawa Bay.[81] Such cultivation, it is now known, appears to have contributed to a change in local Māori diet and possibly their way of life — although fernroot was still extensively used as a food, regular seasonal potato-growing had become part of the subsistence cycle. In Tōtaranui the observant Russians noticed '[c]ultivation of the headland; a stone-edged stream; a village with a single, ditchless palisade: all pointed to a relatively settled way of life, based upon trade and agriculture, ferns and fishing — and not on warfare.'[82]

Bellingshausen judged the population to be only about a third of Cook's estimate. Had Cook overestimated the numbers or were they affected by seasonal migrations or moves away in time of local disturbances? Whatever the reasons, the small number and meagre defences of Māori in Tōtaranui and Te Hoiere left them highly vulnerable to attacks by those equipped with European muskets. By 1828, many in Kura Te Au, Tōtaranui and Te Hoiere would be dead, captured, hiding in remote places in the Wairau or living in a vassal-like state in and around Te Whanganui and the Lower Wairau. Nor would it be long before a second wave of settlers struck more fundamentally at the world Māori had built in the Sounds.

2. New Arrivals

> 'We are yet a people, a living people, and have the right to speak when our land is being sold without our consent, and no payment is received by us . . . we will not give it up.'

From 1820, the relative stability between the various iwi groupings in the Sounds was dramatically upset by a series of heke (migrations) spanning some 20 years. These were initiated by Te Rauparaha, a Ngāti Toa leader and master tactician from Kāwhia.

After decades of tribal warfare in the North Island over control of land and resources, Ngāti Toa began to eye the South Island as fertile new territory. They joined forces with a large party from the neighbouring Taranaki district, comprising Ngāti Tama, Ngāti Koata, Ngāti Mutunga and Te Ātiawa, to look for somewhere else to settle well away from 'a seemingly endless and hopeless situation in the north'.[1]

In 1827 Te Rauparaha led various allied northern iwi, including Te Ātiawa, Ngāti Toa and Ngāti Rārua, on a major raid into Tory Channel. The Rangitāne pā at Ōkukari on Arapaoa Island was destroyed as the invaders swept into Port Underwood before pushing further south. Two years later a further taua (expeditionary force) again crossed Cook Strait.[2]

Once in the Sounds, the taua split. Led by Te Ātiawa, one force sailed down Queen Charlotte Sound; Te Rauparaha took his allied iwi across the top of the South Island, traversed Pelorus Sound, then moved south in a series of attacks against Ngāi Tahu.[3]

Most of the invaders had muskets, against which the Sounds iwi were as good as unarmed.[4] As they traversed Queen Charlotte Sound, Te Ātiawa destroyed Ngāti Apa and Rangitāne pā; in massacres at Karaka Point, Waitohu, East Bay and Endeavour Inlet people were enslaved, killed, eaten or driven back into the interior. In Pelorus Sound, Te Rauparaha and some 340 allied warriors destroyed Ngāti Kuia villages and people at Alligator Head, Titirangi, Forsyth Island, Whakatahuri and, within the sound, the settlements at Crail Bay, Hikapu, Moetapu (in Mahau Sound) and Māhakipawa.[5]

In 1830 young whaler James Heberley was 'very frightened' when he saw 'a great many dead bodies' in the bush:

> I told an Irishman . . . he laughed at me and told me there were plenty more in the next bay. So I went and had a look. I suppose there were about fifty or sixty on the ground, besides heads and arms and joints. Some of the joints were cooked. There was what looked like a young child stuck upon a stick before a fire that had been lighted. It looked as if the natives had had their fill and had left the rest.[6]

Years later, Eruera Wirihana Pakau-wera recalled the devastating speed and destruction of 'the Ngāti Toa invasion' in Pelorus Sound. Ngāti Kuia at Hikaupu were warned only

> a very short time before the fleet was seen approaching, coming on at a very great pace. Ngati Toa landed and dashed into the village, and commenced slaughtering right and left. The unfortunate inmates had nothing but their native arms to defend themselves with, and were so panic-stricken that they became easy prey for the invaders. My informant was a child of about eight or ten at the time, and was led away by his father, who managed to make good their escape to the forest. 'What are those lights and the smoke we see at the village?' asked the child. His father replied, 'That is Ngati Toa burning our ancestors and our houses!' . . . It was a massacre pure and simple.[7]

Scattered bands of Kurahaupō, their leaders dead, survived by withdrawing into the Wairau Valley and the headwaters of its river, or existed in an insecure vassal-like state in coastal areas. Explorer, agent and politician Edward Jerningham Wakefield, exploring Pelorus Sound in 1839 and seeing a party of Rangitāne living at Anakoha, noted the raids' demoralising and corrosive effects. The party, collecting flax from river swamps for a tribute to Te Rauparaha, were terrified, both of further mistreatment from members of the victorious iwi and of being caught up in reprisals from Rangitāne who had escaped into the hills.[8]

THE RAIDS USHERED IN A new power balance. Te Ātiawa now dominated most of Queen Charlotte Sound and, along with Ngāti Toa, Tory Channel and Arapaoa Island. Ngāti Koata held land on D'Urville Island and in the outer Pelorus Sound, and shared land with Ngāti Tama in the Croisilles Harbour area. Ngāti Toa occupied the inner Pelorus and Kaituna. Ngāti Rārua and Ngāti Toa predominated in Port Underwood and into the Wairau.[9]

Of the original Kurahaupō iwi, Ngāti Apa lived at Port Gore alongside the victors. Ngāti Kuia remained alongside the Ngāti Koata, who had settled on D'Urville Island and in Pelorus Sound. As noted above, isolated pockets of Ngāti Kuia also continued to live as refugees in the depths of the bush in the Sounds and their environs, while scattered groups of Rangitāne and Ngāti Kuia remained in Māhakipawa, the Pelorus Valley and the Sounds.[10]

The impact of those 1820s raids reverberated beyond the immediate fallout. The ambiguous relationship of defeated and victorious iwi, the absence of any agreement on how they might share districts or assets, and fluid understandings of conquest and the transference of mana whenua (territorial rights) to the new arrivals would take decades to be resolved.[11]

On a deeper level, the losses also meant that the oral history of the 50–100 years before Pākehā arrived had been lost, and the 'memory bank of traditional history' had been 'savagely reduced'.[12]

The changes in occupation would take on a new importance as Europeans sought and achieved title to the land. British people were settling in Tory Channel, bringing with them a new form of settlement and various accoutrements of European civilisation — such as a cash economy, land ownership, widespread land clearances and Christianity. Māori enthusiastically embraced many aspects of that economy, yet over time, the impact left Māori in the Sounds, and across New Zealand, dispossessed of their land, their language and their 'knowledge of tikanga, waiata, karakia'.[13] Those losses continue to reverberate today.

Whaling in Tory Channel

In 1826 or 1827 ex-convict and experienced whaler and sealer Captain John (Jacky) Guard and his men found themselves being driven south through Cook Strait towards the steep and unforgiving cliffs of Arapaoa Island. At almost the last minute the entrance to Tory Channel became visible and the tide carried their vessel through into the sheltered anchorage and bush-clad hills of Te Awaiti on Arapaoa Island.[14] They were probably the first Europeans to have made that entrance.

From about the early 1800s, whaling and sealing ships had been dropping men off in bays and on offshore islands in the Sounds, and 'significant' numbers of vessels were in the area taking in flax.[15] The long history of ships using the Sounds as shelter from storms and as a base for repairs and restocking had begun, and contact with local Māori was largely peaceful. Guard's arrival, however, signalled something different. He immediately — albeit briefly — imposed European place names on the bay. Wickett did not last long, and Fairhaven was soon supplanted by Te Awaiti or, as the whalers had it, Tarwhite, a pronunciation that continued into the 1970s.

More significantly, Guard realised the potential for hunting right whales. In early May the females came up the South Island's east coast, stopping to calve in the sheltered harbours of Otago, Akaroa and Cloudy Bay. Guard, demonstrating the initiative, energy and determination that typified many settler endeavours, decided to exploit the fact that the whales' migratory route allowed them to be caught close to shore. In 1827 he set up what was possibly New Zealand's first shore-based whaling station and got to work.[16]

Initially, the seasonal venture was miserable and unprofitable. Te Rauparaha's taua harassed and frightened the whalers, local Māori had neither potatoes nor provisions to trade, and Guard and his men existed on wild turnip tops and whale flesh. With inadequate numbers of whalers, and with no equipment for extracting or storing the oil, Guard's men extracted only the bone from their occasional kills and sold this to passing ships.[17]

However, their fortunes changed rapidly. In New Zealand's northern waters, ship-based ventures had long hunted sperm whales for their oil, an excellent lubricant. The odourless spermaceti, the light liquid wax inside a sperm whale's head, was particularly valued. In 1823 the English slashed their duties on colonial oil so its export to England became more profitable. However, sperm whale numbers had declined. By 1830, when the Greenland right whale oil fishery was also collapsing due to overfishing,

View of Kura Te Au Tory Channel, pencil sketch by Charles Heaphy, 14 October 1839. Jacksons Bay is in the foreground, with White Rocks, Te Awaiti and Ōkukari in the background. The whalers' lookout was on the right headland. The ships anchored off are *Honduras* and *Tory* (right).
ALEXANDER TURNBULL LIBRARY, C-025-006

New Zealand whalers were discovering the value of the right whale. It was relatively large and peaceful, it did not sink when harpooned, and its baleen made excellent corsets for women, and whips for the dandies of the burgeoning rich and middle classes.[18]

New Zealand's high-quality right whale oil was competitive and valuable. From at least the late 1820s, Port Underwood and the northern end of Tory Channel had 'sizeable mixed-race communities of people attached to the whaling establishments'.[19] In 1830 these dispatched 522 tuns of oil (a tun is just over 950 litres) to Sydney and upwards of 30 tonnes of bone. Sydney merchants were paying high prices and looking for ways to facilitate their New Zealand trade.[20] It was cheaper to establish shore

stations than supply and provision seagoing ventures, so stations were set up on Kāpiti Island, along the South Island east coast from Kaikōura to Moeraki, and west around the coast at Preservation Inlet.[21]

The number of stations in Tory Channel grew. In early 1830 James Hayter (Jimmy) Jackson, James 'Worser' Heberley — both surnames still strongly associated with the district — and Joseph Toms came to Te Awaiti. In 1832 John Agar (Jacky) Love, Richard (Dicky) Barrett and William Keenan arrived with Te Ātiawa from Kāpiti. In the mid-1830s Guard left for his shore station in Kākāpō Bay, Port Underwood, and sold the Te Awaiti station to Barrett and Love. Joseph Toms operated his own station in the same bay.

Jimmy Jackson, the first of three generations of whaling Jacksons, had by then established his own station at Onepapata (later named Jacksons Bay).[22] By 1839 some 40 people lived at the whaling stations and in the adjoining (mainly Māori)

James Worser Heberley and Maata Te Naihi (Te Ātiawa). ALEXANDER TURNBULL LIBRARY, PACOLL-5800-12

communities at Ōkukari and Whekenui.[23] Fifteen to twenty boats hunted whales more or less exclusively from Tory Channel and out into Cook Strait. Other whalers, wary of the channel's tide and narrow, rocky entrance, preferred the safer Cloudy Bay.[24]

When Jerningham Wakefield arrived at Te Awaiti in the summer of 1839, as part of the New Zealand Company party on the *Tory*, he noted that some whalers procured potatoes and pigs from local Māori, both for themselves and for trading, but others were 'either cultivating a patch of ground which the natives have tacitly allowed them to take possession of, or depending entirely on their native connexions for fish and potatoes'.[25]

Over a decade after the station had been established, Māori were still providing, not entirely altruistically, forms of assistance. They were interested in forming alliances with Pākehā as a way of securing a source of barter for arms and clothes and because, as one Te Atiāwa chief, Te Wharepouri, commented, 'I should be able to keep these White men under my hand and regulate their trade myself.'[26]

The whalers also established other sorts of relationships with Māori. William Keenan, involved with Taranaki Māori from the early 1820s, had come south with factions of Te Ātiawa, Ngāti Mutunga, Ngāti Tama and other iwi, along with Barrett and his trading partner Jacky Love, when they left Taranaki in 1832 for the Kāpiti coast and the Sounds. Keenan's wife was Hikimapu Takune (aka Katarina, Catherine, Ikimapu or Ike Mapu). Jackson, before he married Englishwoman Eliza Roil, had a Māori common-law wife; Heberley was similarly bound to Maata Te Naihi (aka Te Wai, Mata Heberley or Martha) of Te Ātiawa descent.

Several whalers' wives were high-born. Dicky Barrett married Wakaiwa Rāwinia, sister of the war leader Te Wharepōuri and niece of Ātiawa chief Te Puni.[27] Jacky Love married Rāwinia's close relative, Mereruru Te Hikanui, also of Te Ātiawa and 'related to all the influential chiefs living at Port Nicholson [Wellington]'.[28] Joseph Toms married Te Ua Torikirikiri, the only daughter of Ngāti Toa chief Nohorua, Te Rauparaha's oldest half-brother.[29]

Such relationships gained the European husbands access to the tribal chiefs of Ngāti Toa and Te Ātiawa under whose agreement the whalers at Kura Te Au and elsewhere in the Cook Strait region used the land. Māori, however, saw themselves as granting access and use, not ownership. They saw such transactions as 'a transfer of particular rights which remained subject to Māori rights to the land'.[30] In the late 1820s these relationships also provided protection to the whalers during Te Rauparaha's raids. But this did not extend to skirmishes in 1833, when two Ngāi Tahu raiding parties burned the whalers' homes and wrecked their processing plant.[31]

Power balances were, however, not stable, and while the whalers' relations with Māori remained relatively amicable, they were at times 'unwilling victims' in the open hostilities between previous allies in the 1820 raid, Ngāti Toa and Te Ātiawa. In 1838 Māori on the island of Moioio were repeatedly robbing Joseph Toms of a considerable amount of his property. Such behaviour appears to have ended, in this instance, when HMS *Pelorus*, under Lieutenant Phillip Chetwode, put in to Te Awaiti. *Pelorus* was visiting coastal whaling stations on a routine survey (an indication of how the whaling was already enmeshed in the British colonial commercial world). Representing a concrete and significant European presence and indication of European power, the ship contributed to Māori fears of retaliation and the stolen property was recovered.[32]

WHALING WAS A BRUTAL BUSINESS. Because the whalers mistakenly believed that lactating females produced more oil than bulls, calves were harpooned without compunction to ensnare the mothers. Dieffenbach saw a 24-foot (7.3-metre) calf being dragged back to shore, its mother tightly secured by a rope but still alive. 'Gasping in the agonies of death, the tortured animal, when close to our ship [the *Tory*], threw up jets of blood, which dyed the sea all around.' Then the calf, threshing with its tail, broke 'a boat right in the middle, and threw the crew into the water'.[33]

Appalling injuries to crew were also common. On one occasion a whale caught Jackson with its tail, broke many bones and left him unable to continue whaling.[34] Care was always needed against Cook Strait's sudden squalls or gales, which could swamp any boat that failed to reef in time, leaving men drowning as other boats were swept helplessly past. Because the lives and livelihoods of everyone on the station depended on instant compliance with orders, Guard, Toms and Jackson imposed a discipline as brutal as the job and ruled with their fists.[35]

The clinker-built whaleboats, commanded always by European headsmen (or helmsmen) who worked the steering oar and whose word was law, needed six or seven men at the oars, including the harpooner. Until a land-based system of lookouts was established, crews scanned Cook Strait waters for whales. All boats, each with a little flag to celebrate a success, helped to tow catches ashore.[36] But these could be from miles offshore and, with tide or wind against them, could take hours. In bad weather the whalers might have to put in at whatever inhospitable cove offered shelter, haul their boat to safety, using oars as skids, and then huddle overnight until the weather cleared.[37]

The work of dismantling the vast carcasses was carried out skilfully and pragmatically. 'In the water huge sunken carcases of whales, on shore, great skulls, vertebrae, shoulder blades, and ribs met the eye, while the soil was impregnated with the smell of oil, and the air was loaded with the stench of decayed whale.'[38] With all possible speed, flensers climbed over the carcass, cut off strips of blubber, chopped them into blocks and threw them into the trypots. As the oil rose to the surface it was skimmed off and put into casks. Scrag, the remains of the previous renderings, was used to fuel further fires.[39] 'Over everything, like a great odiferous blanket, there was the smell of oil; the very sands of the beach were soaked with oil. Scraps of whale flesh and the remains of carcasses' added to the stink that 'pervaded every corner of the station'.[40]

European crews, working as indentured labourers for the season, were paid by the whale or by the oil collected and might net about £35 for a good season (about $4000 today). A bad season meant no pay, 'and the only wages consist[ed] in a share of the produce'. And the Sydney-sourced clothing and bedding, tobacco and spirits were vastly overpriced and ensured that the employees were never out of debt. Headsmen got about 10 shillings a tun of oil. The best paid, Wakefield reported, were the artisans, coopers and carpenters, who earned ten shillings a day. They made the oil barrels used for storing and shipping the oil, maintained the whaleboats and had the clout to insist on hard cash.[41]

Māori may have fared better. Some had gained whaling experience on British and Tasmanian ships, indicating their early involvement in the new economy. At Te Awaiti their reputation as capable, skilled and sober oarsmen, willing to put in sustained hard work, made them preferable to a European crew.[42] Thus, even as the whaling industry was bringing 'immediate, massive and lasting change to . . . Māori tribes . . . in the whaling districts', Māori participated in 'this new way of life with vigour and enthusiasm'.[43]

The power Māori wielded as skilled boat-handlers allowed them to dictate their terms. Many spoke English and knew the going European rates of pay; they could command the going rate or highly sought-after muskets, ammunition and powder. They also demanded rents or fees for most services and goods they supplied to the whaling ships, sometimes expecting ships' masters to pay dues to take wood and water, or to occupy land. Whalers in the Sounds resented this practice, though it does not appear to have led to the friction it occasioned in other places.[44] When disputes arose over whose harpoon had hit a whale first, and who therefore owned it, Māori had no qualms about staking their claim.[45]

Quite how many Māori were living in Kura Te Au when the *Tory* glided up the channel in September 1839 is not clear. Dieffenbach estimated that there were about 40 Ngāti Awa in the pā on the tiny steep-sided island of Moioio and another 150 in the bays of Whekenui and Ōkukari.[46] Those aboard the *Tory*, however, focused their attention on the two whaling stations at Te Awaiti, then operating under Joseph Toms and Dicky Barrett.[47] The township boasted about 20 homes, whose construction reflected social distinctions. Barrett's whare was 'a very superior edifice, built of sawn timber, floored and lined inside, and sheltered in front by an ample veranda'. The young Arthur Elmslie, 'from a prosperous middle-class London family', had built himself a cottage away from the beach on a terrace on the northern hill.[48] By contrast, the walls of the whalers' houses were 'generally constructed of wattled supplejack, called kareao, filled in with clay; the roof thatched with reeds; and a large unsightly chimney at one of the ends, constructed of either the same materials as the walls, or of stones heaped together by rude masonry'.[49] Dieffenbach judged some of the houses 'not inferior to those of the villages in many parts of Europe'[50] — though European peasantry lived hard.

Whaling station life, many observers agreed, was tough. Whether recorded in the thunderous biblical cadences of Methodist missionary Rev. John H. Bumby,[51] or in others' somewhat more objective language, it was clear some considered the European whalers volatile, lawless, drunk and pugnacious.[52] However, both Edward Jerningham Wakefield and Ernst Dieffenbach differed, noting their willingness to provide assistance when needed, and their manliness, courage and hospitality.[53]

Dieffenbach found Māori 'easy to deal with, confident, and hospitable'. Their sobriety and their reliability have already been noted.[54] The Māori women of Te Awaiti and their children also received high praise from both Wakefield and Dieffenbach. Expressing British virtues, Wakefield thought the 25 children 'strikingly comely, and many of them quite fair, with light hair and rosy cheeks; active and hardy as the goats with which the settlement also swarmed'. The women, dressed in 'loose gowns of printed calico' and with their hair 'always clean and well-combed', were 'remarkable for their cleanliness and the order which they preserved in their companion's house'. They 'seemed proud of belonging to a White man, and had often, we were informed, protected their men from aggression or robbery'.[55]

'These women,' Dieffenbach observed, 'do all the domestic labour, and excel their European husbands in sobriety and quiet disposition.'[56] The children's survival at a time when so many Māori were dying of introduced disease was

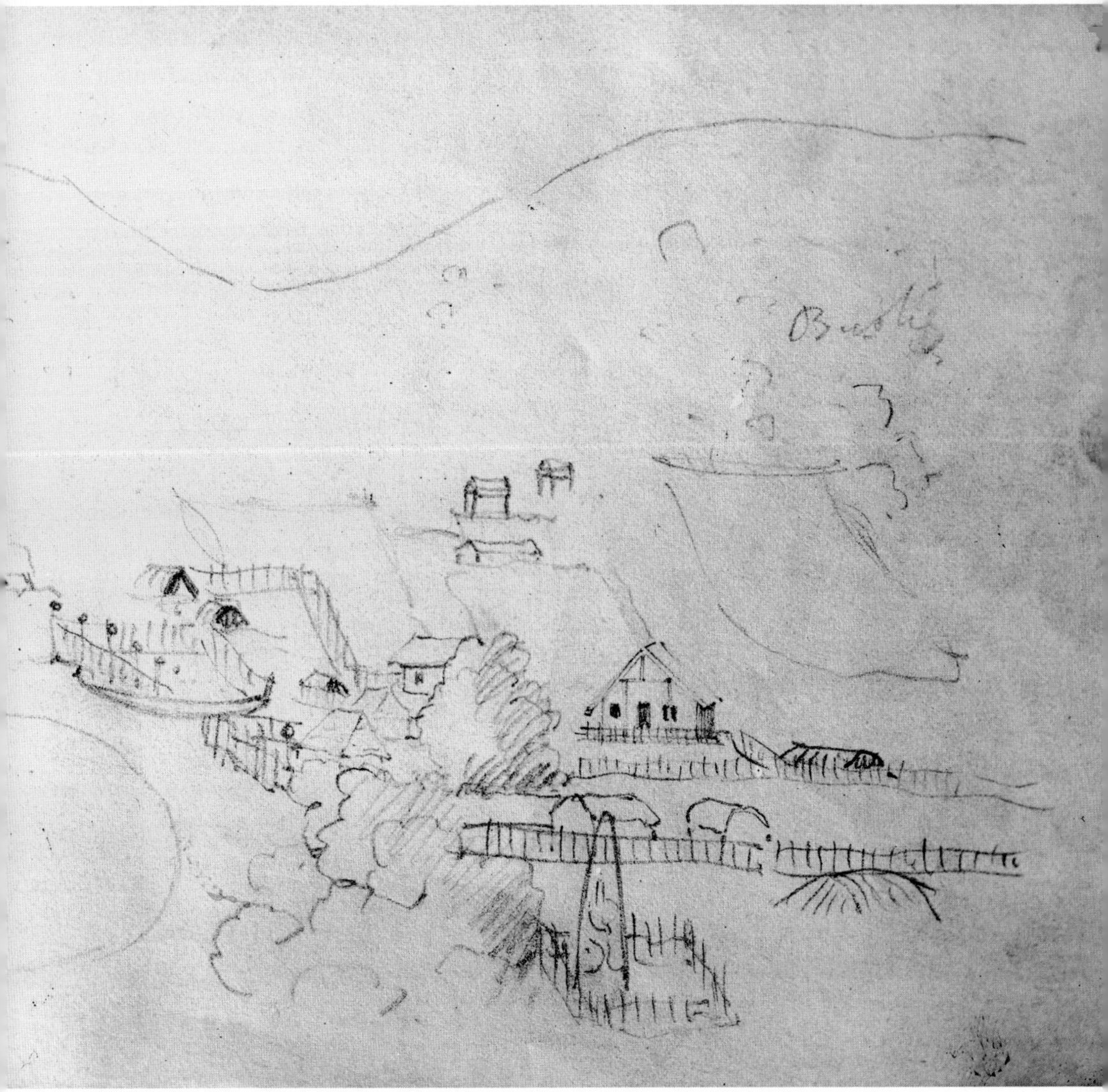

J. W. Barnicoat sketch of the pā at Ōkukari, 1843. Ernst Dieffenbach reported that some 150 Ngāti Awa lived at the Whekenui and Ōkukari settlements, where they had carefully cultivated, well-fenced gardens in which they grew taro and potatoes. They had a lot of pigs and seemed 'well off'. They did not appear to drink and comprised 'very friendly communities'. Augustus Adolphus Alexander Hood claimed that he had set up a whaling station in Ōkukari in 1853, though whether it actually operated there is still a matter of conjecture. BETT LOAN COLLECTION, NELSON PROVINCIAL MUSEUM, 314892

possibly because of better housing than most would have enjoyed, as well as good diet and strong genes. But how those women interpreted their changing world, to what extent they maintained Māori custom or habit or felt its loss — even the extent to which they could communicate with their European husbands — is lost to history. Perhaps the 'vibrant mixed-race community' provided support.[57] (By the same token, what did Eliza Roil, who arrived in 1843 as Jackson's wife, and Maria Toms, the other English woman on the station, feel on arrival at a place so many worlds away from the gossipy English village?)

MEANWHILE, ECONOMIC AND SOCIAL CHANGES were affecting the Tory Channel whaling community. As early as 1841 the *New Zealand Gazette and Wellington Spectator* reported that whaling was no longer profitable to individuals nor a significant export for the country. In 1847 not one whale was caught from Port Underwood; for almost two decades, newspapers would have little to say about whaling. Whalers had to look to other income sources.

Settlement within the Sounds was also increasingly taking on a European face. On 1 October 1831 Elizabeth (Betty) Guard, reputed to be the first European woman to settle in the South Island, had married Jacky Guard (probably in 1830) and given birth to a son, the first European child to be born there. Her daughter Louisa was born in 1833.[58] A decade or so later, as European immigration and settlement increased and as other whalers started to marry Englishwomen, Te Awaiti's mixed-race whaling community began to change. It is not known what happened to Jimmy Jackson's Māori common-law wife, with whom he had a number of children, but on 19 February 1843 he married seamstress Eliza Roil, who had arrived in the new New Zealand Company settlement of Nelson with her family as an assisted immigrant on the *Bolton* in March 1842.[59]

The Treaty of Waitangi had been signed at Port Underwood on 17 June 1840, a nascent agriculture was becoming established, missionaries had brought European traditions and new faces to the Māori world, explorers were assessing the Sounds for settlement potential. Māori would find their initially valued participation in that European world becoming steadily more constrained.

Farming, felling, trading

Coastal whaling was seasonal, meaning that additional ways of earning an income were essential even before the market downturn. In 1844 the whalers kept goats, sheep, rabbits and pigs on the outer islands of the Sound, suggesting that they were farming for food and for supplementary income;[60] Jacky Love organised his men into tree-felling gangs. One season the gangs prepared 100,000 staves for casks for the Sydney market.[61]

By 1849, working towards at least a measure of self-sufficiency, Jackson had an orchard, and 4 acres (1.6 ha) fenced and growing wheat, potatoes and vegetables; with later clearances he had over 50 acres (20 ha) and ran 24 cattle, 30 goats and 15 pigs.[62] Presumably to grind flour, he built a watermill, probably in Jacksons Bay; it was possibly New Zealand's first water-powered flourmill.[63] By 1855 he was running a store in the small settlement of Waitohi (now Picton). He maintained the farm on Arapaoa Island and returned there in 1857, buying more land and continuing as farmer and part-time whaler.[64]

The increasing influx of European immigrants provided opportunities for local men with local knowledge of difficult waters to supplement their incomes. Arthur Elmslie, who had 'a considerable reputation as a boatman and navigator', was involved with piloting and shipping around the Sounds.[65] Jimmy Jackson began trading. By 1842 his *Nelson Packet* regularly carried passengers as well as freight.[66]

These men had considerable experience and expertise as boatmen and navigators, having built up their knowledge of local conditions and navigational hazards. Tory Channel was charted in 1842, and the wider Sounds area first surveyed in 1854. But even when charts did exist and were to hand, the long history of wrecks and notices of new rocks or shoals shows the extent to which they were works in progress. There was no substitute for local knowledge.

Across New Zealand, the first decade or more from the 1840s appeared to confirm Māori expectations of small, scattered European settlements near the coast that provided markets for their produce — potatoes, pigs and flax. In turn the settlers provided sought-after goods such as nails, tools, equipment and cloth and new technologies. They did not seriously interfere with the use of Māori waterways or the seasonal exploitation of mahinga kai (cultivation or food-gathering).[67]

In the sheltered inner reaches of Queen Charlotte Sound, settler need saw Māori expanding their customary gardens to exploit new economic possibilities.[68] We don't know what that meant in terms of their nomadic lifestyle, but Europeans viewed it positively. As early as 1832 Captain William Steine, a Tasmanian who navigated Queen Charlotte Sound down into what became Picton Harbour, reported that 200 Māori at Waitohi had acquired hoes from Te Awaiti and were growing potatoes.[69] In 1845 New Zealand Company surveyor Samuel Stephens wrote admiringly of potatoes, pumpkin, cabbage, melons, Indian corn and kūmara flourishing in the 50–60 acres (20–24 ha) of native gardens there,[70] and pumpkins were growing in Grove Arm, probably at Momorangi.[71]

At Te Awaiti in 1839 Dieffenbach reported that Māori burning and planting had created a micro-climate for potato-growing.[72] They managed their crop to be assured of a harvest before Christmas.[73] It was from Māori, too, that some whalers bought pigs and potatoes for profitable trading with the whaling ships moving around the coast.[74] At Arthur Elmslie's summer home at Cannibal Cove, just north of Ship Cove, 80–100 Māori were growing a profusion of 'potatoes, kumara, cabbages, swede, turnips, many other vegetables and a number of fruit trees', as well as a field of wheat grown from seed given by Jacky Love.[75]

When the *Tory* arrived, they were rapidly able to amass 500 basketfuls of potatoes and a stock of pigs sufficient for her company for six weeks.[76] The scale and skill of Māori food production was not inconsiderable. The canoes moving from Admiralty Bay to Cloudy Bay laden with potatoes and pigs for barter shortly after the *Tory* arrived in Ship Cove indicate that the extensive trading and communication channels that Cook had observed were still in place.[77]

Māori also part-owned several locally built trading ships. Toms' *Three Brothers*, one of the first vessels to be built at Te Awaiti, was registered in 1845 in the names of Rawiri Puaha, Solomon Matakapi and Joseph Henia. Henia was one of two masters; the other, a European named George Hempleman, handled the Kāpiti Coast–Cloudy Bay trade. *Eleanor*, a 33-foot schooner, was jointly owned by Thomas Hempleman and three Māori whose names were recorded as Amion, Hopi Te Oio and Amicapi. The *Elizabeth Warren*, a 39-foot schooner built in 1848, was registered in 1851 with Hohepa Ngapaki as master. Māori were also recorded as owning vessels that resembled large whaleboats.[78] From at least 1854 two small traders were taking a weekly supply of wheat and potatoes to Nelson from the large native settlement of Māhakipawa in Pelorus Sound.

By the 1840s, with cash supplanting the traditional barter, Māori had a wider range of food choices themselves. They rapidly took up flour, pork and tea, and increasingly adopted European clothing; tobacco use was widespread by 1839. Yet, Māori did not always find it easy to adapt to this new economy. In 1843 John Wallis Barnicoat, in a survey of Queen Charlotte Sound, painted a grim picture. Māori were existing on the fish and potatoes Europeans rejected; dirt, disease and ulcerous sores were commonplace.[79] By the late 1850s, alcohol, which both Cook and Bellinghausen had earlier noted that Māori did not like, had become a problem.[80] Moreover, as Europeans became self-sufficient, Māori skills and produce were no longer so much in demand. By the mid-1850s, partly because valuable cultivation lands in Motueka were lost to land grants and also because goldmining had arrived in western Te Tau Ihu, Māori trading interests were in decline.[81]

Spreading the word of God

At the end of the eighteenth century Methodists and Anglicans had formed societies of voluntary members to preach the word of God in foreign parts.[82] Missionaries, largely ignorant of the world they were coming to and fuelled by a desire to introduce Christianity and 'civilisation' to curb Native 'impulsive "savagery"' and 'propensity to excess and violence'[83] arrived in the Sounds in 1839, under the auspices of the Church Missionary Society, founded in 1799. This would herald a considerable evangelical effort. In May 1839 Methodists Rev. Bumby and John Hobbs travelled to Port Underwood with some 20 young Methodist-educated Māori from the north. In a practice adopted by a number of missions, they left some behind as teachers at Port Underwood, at Te Awaiti and at the native villages at 'Wangenui' and 'Okokurri' and Moioio, all close to Te Awaiti.[84]

A year earlier, the Anglican Church Missionary Society's Rev. Octavius Hadfield (who, like others in the field, did not seem to welcome competition)[85] built a school at Ōkukari — soon some 80 adults were attending, and further schools were established. At Anaho, Wirimu, a native teacher trained in the Bay of Islands by the Anglicans, was preaching, and teaching reading and writing.[86] In 1841, when the Māori population in Cloudy Bay, Queen Charlotte Sound and Tory Channel was about 1200, Hadfield reported that Māori were very interested in getting a minister and becoming Christian; by 1843 there were estimated daily congregations of 300 to 400 that on Sundays swelled to up to 800.[87] The Ōkukari people were firm believers.[88]

Enormous physical effort went into missionary work. Anglican Charles Lucas

ABOVE Octavius Hadfield, the first priest to be ordained in New Zealand, had accepted a posting to the Kāpiti area, where he worked with Te Ātiawa and paid occasional visits to those in Tōtaranui. An early visitor to Waikanae, where he was based, described the young missionary as 'a tall, straight, slender, active, sinewy, sunburnt, smiling Pākehā . . . an agreeable intellectual cheerful young Gentleman well up in the Māori Language, Habits and Manners'. ALEXANDER TURNBULL LIBRARY, 1/4-006801F

RIGHT Father Antoine Marie Garin was parish priest in Nelson for nearly 40 years, and had seven years in Northland prior that. His accounts of his time among Māori in Te Tau Ihu suggest something of a suspicious authoritarian, too credulous about stories of vice. ALEXANDER TURNBULL LIBRARY, 1/4-016333-F

Reay's 'itinerant evangelism' took him from Nelson, where he was based, to Kura Te Au, Arapaoa Island and Queen Charlotte Sound during 1843, 1844 and 1845. Samuel Ironside, who was the son of a Sheffield minister, had established a Methodist mission at Ngākuta Bay in Port Underwood in 1840. He used the steep Māori track between Hitaua Bay in Tory Channel and Port Underwood — a track settlers were still using decades later. Māori crewed a whaleboat to carry him to the western shores of Arapaoa Island, where there were many Māori villages, to Pelorus Sound and beyond.

Roman Catholic priest Father Antoine Garin arrived in 1850. His parish boundaries would be reduced in the 1860s, but for 14 years he travelled by foot, horse and boat to minister to the 200–300 Catholics over a parish that covered Buller (including the Sounds' tortuous country), Nelson and the northern parts of Westland.[89]

Māori may have been attracted to a new god as their world order changed. Many may also have found religion a useful way of accessing European goods and engaging with the outside world.[90] Settlers' reports depicted a new world imbued with European values. At Anakiwa in 1853 Archdeacon John Salisbury, touring his Wellington diocese, found an 'orderly' village of about 100 'very quiet, sober and diligent' Māori, whose well-built chapel was decorated with 'consummate taste'.[91] Māori were participating as preachers, teachers and catechists; Anaho residents were practising 'writing assiduously, writing on all occasions and on all substances . . . with a good, firm, decided hand'.[92] New Zealand missionaries were quick to interpret that urge to literacy as a strong belief and desire to read 'in *their own tongue, the wonderful word of God*'.[93] Bumby, for instance, considered the missionaries' 'errand of mercy to the Sounds' had resulted in fervent belief, and that Māori had turned their old, out-of-date muskets 'into church bells', and their swords into ploughshares.[94] In Queen Charlotte Sound and Tory Channel, Ironside found Māori anxious for 'spiritual truth and the meaning of God's word'.[95]

Food was eagerly traded for copies of the Bible. This almost insatiable desire for Christian publications was replicated throughout New Zealand; by the early 1840s a 'cautious estimate' considered that about half of the Māori adult population was able to read and write a little in their own language.[96]

Samuel Ironside's Methodist mission in particular developed a considerable framework to support the new faith. A vigorous and energetic man, within three years of arriving he had established schools at Cloudy Bay, Te Awaiti (in 1841, 116 adults and 14 children were reported as attending) and in Queen Charlotte Sound, possibly in East Bay,[97] and 'at least' 16 chapels where 'more than 30 Local Preachers and

Leaders' preached to large congregations.[98] By then, too, the mission reached across to Punekerua in Pelorus Sound and to D'Urville Island.[99]

Methodist Māori also evinced their faith in building. By 1842 a staggering nine Methodist churches were scattered through Queen Charlotte Sound and Tory Channel; there was also one in Pelorus Sound and another on D'Urville Island. Ironside, unsurprisingly, was pressing for assistance in dealing with his flock.[100] The buildings were by no means insubstantial. Generally, the smallest were 20 by 25 feet (6 by 7.6 metres), the largest 40 by 50 feet (12 by 15 metres).[101] The effort and manpower that went into chapel building may have been testament to the strength of Māori belief, and it certainly demonstrated their skill in using new tools and techniques.

Ironside recorded in his diary:

> From 100 to 150 [Māori] gave all their time and labour to the work for months. Large and lofty pines grew in the hills behind, and a good many of these were felled . . . and crosscut into the required length. They were hauled out by main force with the aid of blocks and tackle lent by the whaling ships. The sawpits were constructed, each trunk was cut down into three or four slabs. These were adzed to a perfect smoothness. They were set up for the walls.[102]

IRONSIDE'S ABILITY TO ATTRACT MĀORI helpers and servants who worked willingly with or for him suggests their considerable regard for him.[103] His mission was marked by his Wellington superiors.[104]

This situation did not last. By 1842 the New Zealand Company, needing land for the English settlers it had brought to New Zealand, started investigating the Wairau Plains. Local Rangitāne, Ngāti Toa and Ngāti Rārua opposed this. In December 1842 whaler Richard Cook raped and then murdered Ngāti Toa chieftainess Rangiawa Kuika, a close relative of Te Rauparaha's nephew Te Rangihaeata and married to the locally respected and liked trader James Wynen. Cook also killed her son. The court, citing lack of evidence, failed to convict the whaler. Ironside later remembered that Te Rangihaeata had told him that the court's failure to punish Cook had led to his actions in what is now known as the Wairau Affray.[105]

The Wairau survey, undertaken to provide the new settlers' land, began, despite deputations led by Te Rauparaha and several iwi to ask that the Wairau not be included in the survey. Matters escalated. On 17 June 1843 Arthur Wakefield's impetuous

Punekerua Wesleyan Mission Chapel, Te Hoiere Pelorus Sound, 15 March 1843. The substantial nature of the building well represents the effort and skill that Māori put in to constructing their churches. J. W. BARNICOAT, HOCKEN COLLECTIONS, UARE TAOKA O HĀKENA, UNIVERSITY OF OTAGO, 94/247

attempt to arrest Te Rauparaha and Te Rangihaeata after their party had disrupted the Wairau survey left four Māori and 22 Europeans dead.[106] Attitudes of settlers in Port Nicholson and Nelson towards Māori hardened, a tapu was placed on the Wairau because of the numbers of dead, and Ngāti Toa and members of Te Ātiawa and Ngāti Rārua left Marlborough for the safety of their Kāpiti/Horowhenua settlements. Many did not return.[107]

With his congregation melting away, Ironside had little option but to leave himself. In 1843 he was appointed to the Wellington ministry. A lay preacher, William Jenkins, was appointed to the Sounds, but after six years he left for Motueka. The Methodist Māori mission in the Sounds collapsed.

Some of the issues that surfaced at the 1905 Methodist Conference suggest systemic problems within the church's approach to its Māori missions — its Māori parishioners had been neglected because there was inadequate funding and the church had failed to appreciate 'that the Maori methods of working were different to those of the Europeans, and allowance should be made on that head'.[108] Methodist minister T. J. Hammond asserted that Māori 'had been handed over to the Church of England'.[109]

These issues probably contributed to the failure of the other mainstream denominations in the region. By 1860 there were only 16 baptised Roman Catholic Māori in Queen Charlotte Sound.[110] Father Garin, who claimed that the Catholic Church's late arrival in the area left no room for him to work with Māori, seems never to have been a sympathetic figure — indeed, his writings suggest a censorious man.[111] Although in 1868 Wellington's Bishop Viard identified Hauhauism (a set of militant religious beliefs that arose in the 1860s) as a cause for the low numbers, a more perceptive analysis came from Archbishop Redwood, who was appointed bishop after Viard's death: priests tended to focus on European settlers instead of Māori.[112] The Anglicans, while involved in educational effort at the Māori settlement at Okoha at the top of Pelorus Sound towards the end of the nineteenth century, largely directed their energies towards the European settlers.

The overall impact of the missionaries on Māori society in the Sounds was, however, considerable. The building of churches may have been one factor in Māori becoming less nomadic, so that they became more vulnerable if crops failed or spoilt and could not be sold. Even more fundamentally, native teachers with no traditional authority or status may have eroded the authority, prestige and mana of traditional chiefs.[113] This could have worked to undermine social structures, leaving Māori open to unscrupulous aggression and without clear leadership to help them deal with it.[114]

Scoping new territory

In 1832, Tasmanian captain William Steine claimed to have travelled some 40 nautical miles (80 kilometres) around Queen Charlotte Sound, naming Queen Charlotte Sound and Tory Channel Queen Adelaide River and William the Fourth River respectively. His description, the first European one recorded, of where Picton now stands spoke of 'a beautiful bay surrounded with magnificent timber interspersed with extensive tracts of the richest soil'.[115]

In 1839 the New Zealand Company party on the *Tory* spent 13 days in Queen Charlotte Sound assessing the potential of the sound for the settlements the Wakefields wanted for the new immigrants they were bringing to New Zealand. They were not convinced. The 'historical associations' might be rich, the primeval majesty of the impenetrable forest that ran down to the water's edge impressive, the birds harmonious,[116] the harbour at Waitohi magnificent, but they had no idea who they should approach to buy the land. Nor, they thought, did Queen Charlotte Sound offer land suitable for a town centre, or the 201 acres (81 ha) of land with which the company was planning to meet its obligations to supply its planned rural allotments for farming.[117]

Four years later, in 1843, John Wallis Barnicoat, contracted to the New Zealand Company to survey part of the Wairau Plains, waxed eloquent after exploring the inner part of Queen Charlotte Sound. It was a land of 'surpassing beauty and fertility' and 'of the most inviting character': the sound, he wrote at the time, had 'arable potential' — land, timber and streams in each bay and a huge area available for settlement, particularly in Grove Arm.[118] Two years later he had not substantially altered his conclusion. The connection of the Waitohi Valley, despite the mudflats that some considered hindered the development of Port Cooper (later Lyttelton), with the Wairau Valley still led him to consider that 'the probable site of the important settlement that *must* one day be formed somewhere on these shores [Queen Charlotte Sound]'. 'Mocapahwah' (Māhakipawa) contained 3000–4000 acres (1214–1618 ha) of 'gently sloping land, the greater part magnificently timbered, and the whole well watered and of the finest possible description. The native who accompanied us . . . assured us that it had never been visited by white people before.'[119]

Then, two years after Barnicoat, in early March 1845, the New Zealand Company sent surveyors William Fox, Samuel Stephens and others on a further expedition to

Queen Charlotte Sound. They were specifically tasked with looking at where a port, and the town to service it, might be sited.

Stephens's lively account of the journey appeared in the *Nelson Examiner*. He recorded adventures — of sailing through the treacherous waters of French Pass, which very few English gentlemen had done; of the gales; of 'the romantic little pā called Tetarangi' (Titirangi), usually occupied by Te Rauparaha's men; the 'small clearings on slopes of wooded hills'; the signs of pigs and the 'elephantine fleas' in Melville Cove where weather again detained them. In Ship Cove, Stephens was thrilled to be in 'the favourite resort of the famed navigator Captain Cook', and to stand where the 'celebrated voyager' had been and indulge romantic fantasies. His conclusion: in Queen Charlotte Sound there was land ready be tamed and developed.

The low but rocky and precipitous hills at the entrance to the sound were 'covered with grass, fern, and low bush, well suited to the grazing of cattle and sheep'. Although, beyond Ship Cove, the land became 'undulating, abrupt, and often precipitous', it was 'capable of cultivation on a limited scale, there being many very charming sites for small individual settlements'. At the confluence of Queen Charlotte Sound and Tory Channel the scenery increased in 'beauty and grandeur at every turn of its passage'. After a side trip to Te Awaiti, where they replenished their supplies with oysters, milk and butter, the surveyors retraced their steps to explore the western arm of the sound and, they hoped, enter the Wairau district.

Of the possible town sites they investigated — the Wairau River mouth and various places in Cloudy Bay and Queen Charlotte Sound — Stephens firmly recommended Waitohi. The northern entrance to the sound, he wrote, was open to all-weather navigation and the sound itself 'was one of the finest harbours in the world'.[120] Waitohi itself 'affords good anchorage for vessels within a very short distance of the shore, where boats may discharge their cargoes at any state of tide'. The prolific gardens and bush around the pā suggested good soil.

Waitohi, too, gave easy access to the Wairau Plains, with opportunities for growing corn or running big flocks of sheep or cattle. The favoured town site was flat and high enough to be easily drained and had room for 200–300 sections; a river and other streams with good flows provided a town supply of water; and there was plenty of timber for building. A potential further port and town site at Milton Bay (now Waikawa Bay) was inferior to Waitohi only because its waters shoaled more gradually and it was further from the plains. Shakespeare Bay could be another harbour.[121]

THE EXISTENCE OF PELORUS SOUND came later to European consciousness. Jacky Guard, who had taken refuge during a gale in what he described as a river between Queen Charlotte Sound and Admiralty Bay, must have been one of the first to enter. Again, it was the New Zealand Company's search to identify suitable land for settlement that lay behind the early European incursions into the sound. Lieutenant Phillip Chetwode, temporary captain of HMS *Pelorus*, which was assessing the suitability of the area for the company's settlements in 1838, took Guard with him as pilot. Coming up from the south, they sighted the sound on 1 September. Over the next 10 days they worked up it for 35–43 nautical miles, surveying Crail Bay and making their innermost anchorage about a mile past what is now Black Point, where the water shoaled suddenly. They had come to the tidal mudflats, which for so long would bedevil Havelock as a port. Like Cook, Chetwode was impressed with the value of the heavy timber, with 'some spars as large as a line of battleships lower mast'.[122]

The following year the *Tory* was not long at Te Awaiti before trader Jimmy Jackson was urging the merits of Pelorus Sound as a site for the company's settlement. In another extraordinary adventure in testing country, a small boat set off, manned by Māori, with Guard and John Wynen as pilots, and carrying William Wakefield and his nephew Edward Jerningham Wakefield, Wynen's wife Rangiawa Kuika, and Hōhepa Tamaihengia (aka Hengia), a young Māori chief. The two Māori, both related to Te Rauparaha, provided Wakefield senior with the authority he needed to enter the sound.[123] They were also people through whom the English could negotiate. Jackson, worried that Guard and Wynen would exclude him from any deal, followed shortly after.

They made good speed, rounding into the sound two days after leaving Te Awaiti. They covered the same ground as the *Pelorus*, to about a mile from where that ship had reached, then pressed on, tacking and dragging a pinnace, into the Pelorus River. When the river was no longer navigable by boat they used a canoe, then proceeded on foot. They passed a large pā, whose 'solitary and decaying relics told the whole history of *Rauperaha*'s devastating raid'. They then retraced their steps, 'after setting fire in pure mischief to the fern. The blaze spread far and wide, and its glare was perceptible all night from our camp.'[124]

Jerningham Wakefield was impressed by Pelorus Sound. He wrote,

> For forty miles we continued to advance along this magnificent arm of the sea, which only differed from Queen Charlotte's Sound in the grander

> scale on which are the mountains, the woods, and the spacious bays and harbours branching out in every direction . . . The scene forms a labyrinth on an immense scale, in which you may lose your way among tortuous paths of water two or three miles broad, and between hedges composed of mountains from 2000 to 3000 feet in height, clothed to the summit with the most luxuriant and majestic timber.

Seamanship was critical. 'Even our pilot guided himself in some of the most intricate passes by watching the set of the tide.'[125] But Pelorus Sound, was not, William Wakefield determined, where he wanted settlements. He did, however, decide to purchase it as a bad-weather refuge and as a way into the open country behind.[126]

Fifteen years later HMS *Pandora*, under Captain Byron Drury, would carefully chart the Sounds and Port Underwood as part of a marine survey of New Zealand begun in 1848 by HMS *Acheron*.

In his 'Sailing Directions [for] Pelorus Estuary (Cook's Straits)', which appeared in the *Government Gazette* in November 1854 and was reprinted in the *Nelson Examiner* the following January, Drury gave a detailed assessment of the area and its suitability for settlement. Apart from the identified flat land at the anchorage where Havelock now lies, and some 200–300 acres (81–121 ha) of cultivable land at an old Māori settlement at 'Kopai' (Hopai) in the outer sound, he saw 'few acres in any one spot that could be brought under cultivation'.[127] Might Pelorus Sound serve as a port? Some 30 mostly land-locked bays did offer anchorages, safe depths, an abundance of fish and shelter: 'The gusts in bad weather are very furious,' Drury wrote. But:

> I cannot believe that the Pelorus offers a better means of shipment of the produce of the Wairau plains than Port Underwood. The swamps are barriers to road making, and even if this were overcome, the difficulties of navigating the Pelorus to the anchorage are considerable.

Also problematic for shipping were the mudflats at the mouth of the Pelorus River, which made getting close to shore difficult in any tide, and — because of the considerable tidal ranges — re-anchoring was essential with every tide.[128]

Drury's sailing directions contained no mention of any existing European settlement. In 1849 sawyer and farmer William Harvey and his wife Augusta, a dressmaker, with their four small children, had set sail from Nelson for Pelorus Sound.

They put into Port Ligar and Waitata Bay, searching for good land, before they finally settled at the head of Clova Bay, where they would not have been visible to the ship as she sailed down the main sound.[129] The Harveys were the first to settle in an area where, despite Drury's and Wakefield's opinions, European settlement would focus. By the time Drury visited there were indications of the transformation this would bring. The wild cattle seen by the Wakefields as they came into Pelorus, the domestic animals that Stephens noted in the outer part of Queen Charlotte Sound and the huge wild pigs that Drury's expedition came across would all in time destroy the bush. Jerningham Wakefield's careless fire was the first of many that would be deliberately lit to create farmland from impenetrable vegetation. All too often these would get out of control and denude even the land most unsuited to farming.

Extensive lists of the local flora and fauna drawn up by the *Pandora*'s surgeon, Dr John Jolliffe, and appended to Drury's sailing directions, indicate something of the new world into which the Harveys had settled. He named some 17 different types of birds (some of which had a number of varieties) and 13 different types of trees; and noted 90 kinds of ferns and clubmosses, six of which had not been found elsewhere. The tree ferns, he wrote, were 'particularly large and beautiful'. He identified 15 species of fish, and four types of shellfish, plus lizards and a few insects.

Jolliffe provided more than just names. He noted the cormorants' nesting habits, the abundant quail, the exceedingly tame robins and the equally tame (or stupid) pigeons, the variety of seabirds found in the outer Pelorus, the ease with which weka could be caught, and the sight of jellyfish floating in the water, 'showing beautiful golden and silver colours, as the sun's rays were reflected from their various surfaces and fringes'.[130]

Buying the South Island

When, on 16 September 1839, the *Tory* left for Wellington and Whanganui, with Heberley and Barrett on board as interpreters and pilots, the Wakefields were intending to purchase and gain formal title to much land across the top of the South Island (Te Tau Ihu) for the New Zealand Company.

What did English notions of land ownership mean in this new land? In the first decades of European occupation some Māori had allowed early settlers to use land for settlement or mission stations. As settlement proceeded, further land was bartered and traded. But in the minds of Māori, they were not ceding ownership of this land. They were allowing it to be used by others.[131]

The signing of the Treaty of Waitangi in 1840 accorded the British 'sovereignty' over New Zealand. In June 1841, with New Zealand a colony in its own right, Governor Robert FitzRoy established the Old Land Claims Ordinance to investigate land transactions made before the Treaty. Article Two of the Treaty of Waitangi guaranteed Māori 'the full, exclusive and undisturbed possession of their lands and estates' and banned future private individual land purchases from Māori — not to protect Māori but to confine land sales to government-employed Native Land Purchase Commission men, who proceeded to buy up as much land as possible, using often dubious methods.[132]

Until its demise in 1850, the New Zealand Company developed an interesting relationship with government. Although by law only the government could purchase land from Māori, in the South Island the New Zealand Company was permitted to administer all government-purchased land and, acting as an agent for colonisation, could sell this land at 'stipulated minimum prices'. That money, when received, was to be used to reimburse the government for what it had paid to Māori.[133] Through this and other such agreements with the government, the company became 'essentially an agent of Government in disposing of waste land for the purposes of emigration and settlement'. That being the case, its claims to purchase were not open to the provisions of the 1841 Land Claims Ordinance, which decreed that a title of ownership could be invalidated unless the Crown confirmed the sale to have been genuine and fair.[134]

In Te Tau Ihu, as in the rest of the country, very few advanced their claims for review under the new ordinances, as most claims were disallowed. Jackson, claiming land at Te Awaiti to establish the legitimacy of his occupation, was one of four claimants in Queen Charlotte Sound. He stated that he had given 'blankets, pipes, tobacco and other things, including calico and prints amounting to £32 or £33', and that the sale had been witnessed by many Māori and William Keenan.[135] He pointed out that he had lived in New Zealand for seven years and in Jacksons Bay for two and that over this time he had built a house, he had land partly under cultivation and a fully operational whaling station, all of which had cost him considerable money and time.[136] He did not have the necessary documentation, but his claim was finally investigated in 1869 and he was awarded 150 acres (60 ha).[137]

Meanwhile, events laying the basis for European title to the land and for 'colonial' settlement in the Sounds moved ahead. Between 16 and 25 October 1839 the New Zealand Company signed what has come to be known as the Kapiti Deed. This gave it ownership of a vast area of land on the north and south sides of Cook Strait, all of Te Tau Ihu, as far south as Kaikōura, including Queen Charlotte Sound and across to Cape Farewell, in exchange for 'a quantity of merchandize, value not stated'. (Today the details are readily available. Three purchases totalling over 20 million acres of land were made for goods — arms, clothing and utensils, plus reserves to be allocated (though the company's previously stated intention to set these aside was not mentioned) — valued at less than £9000.) Te Rauparaha, who had more or less dictated the deed's terms over the preceding days, signed it on 25 October 1839. The deed was then taken to Kāpiti, where 10 Ngāti Toa, including Te Rangihaeata, signed. Te Whetu represented Rangitāne interests. The company then took the deed to Tōtaranui for agreement with Te Ātiawa, who signed on 8 November 1839.[138]

Focused on getting as much land as possible before the British annexation, the New Zealand Company had negotiated primarily with Te Rauparaha and other Ngāti Toa rangatira, nominating them the holders of primary rights. Company agents were well aware that this did not reflect the complexities of rights within the district. The legal implications, the concept of land ownership, the size of the proposed settlements and reserves were foreign to Māori and misleadingly translated. The goods the company gave as purchase payment might, traditionally, have been construed as tuku or gifts, which, once accepted, 'would have enhanced the mana of the recipients over the land in question'. What Māori expected was that 'both groups would utilize the land and its resources together'.[139] Before long Te Rauparaha, Te Rangihaeata and others would repudiate the deed.[140]

BY 1844 THE NEW ZEALAND COMPANY — and its Nelson settlement in particular — had run into severe financial problems. It remained desperate to maintain British capital investment in the Nelson settlement, and determined to lay out a new town of about 1000 quarter-acre sections that would serve as a shipping port for the Wairau district, where many of the company's first English Nelson landowners had moved. The 1845 Fox expedition had recommended Waitohi as the best site. Then in 1847 the company, rescued from its precarious financial situation by a £236,000 loan from the British government, acted under enabling English legislation as the

Crown's agent for colonisation and became the New Zealand government's agent for the continued colonisation of central New Zealand.

The company then benefited from the government's 1847 'purchase' of the Wairau district as ransom for the release of Te Rauparaha who, following the Wairau incident, had been imprisoned for 18 months without charge or trial. The government granted the New Zealand Company the land in late 1848. Governor George Grey also promised a road to make a valued connection between the Wairau and Picton; in 1849 surveyors Ward and Goulter laid out a line for it,[141] on Māori land even though the deed did not include Queen Charlotte or Pelorus sounds, which would be covered in later purchases.[142]

However, the land that Ngāti Toa 'sold' in the enforced Wairau Purchase did not include land at Waitohi or in the adjacent Queen Charlotte Sound district where Te Ātiawa, not Ngāti Toa, held mana whenua (authority over the land). Further negotiations were thus needed to secure land for the port and town. Confident of a good outcome, colonists began these discussions at the end of 1848. It was a long-drawn-out process, and from today's standpoint it is not obvious why Māori agreed.[143] The Waitohi deed of sale was finally signed on 4 March 1850 by four chiefs — Ropoama Te One (who had been heavily involved in the whole sale process), Hēmi Potaka, Witikau and Te Retimana — and 18 others.[144]

Māori preference was to remain in Waitohi and have the port developed at Waikawa[145] because they were concerned that the land at Waikawa was poor, but the final agreement was that the company would pay £300 and Māori at Waitohi would resettle at Waikawa. One hundred pounds was for the land at Waitohi; £200 was to compensate Māori for the work of having to re-establish their cultivations. The company also agreed to build a chapel at Waitohi, a building finally finished in 1860.[146]

Francis Dillon Bell, the company's resident agent in Nelson, considered that the agreement created a model for subsequent settlements. He had little time for Governor Grey's belief that Māori needed larger areas in which they could continue their traditional lifestyles — running pigs, gathering fernroot, catching eels, fish and birds — or Grey's reservations about the extent to which Māori could be pushed immediately into a model of European agriculture.[147] The Waitohi agreement, Bell said, would encourage Māori to 'abandon their filthy pahs and their cultivations in commonality, for the advantages of individual property'.[148]

Shortly after the purchase, Māori vacated Waitohi (where a larger amount of land was taken than the vendors had agreed to)[149] and moved to Waikawa, which had been formally designated a reserve[150] (an act that would make it subject to Treaty

The Love brothers, possibly seated in Kura Te Au Tory Channel looking out to the southern hills. Their family were leaders in the Te Ātiawa Tōtaranui Queen Charlotte Sound community, and would subsequently occupy prominent positions within Te Ātiawa iwi and the Pākehā world. PICTON HERITAGE AND WHALING MUSEUM, COURTESY PICTON HISTORICAL SOCIETY

considerations). Former whaler John MacDonald, his Māori wife and three children remained the sole inhabitants of Waitohi until about 1854. Vacant sections were marked out by survey pegs and advertised in Nelson, the provincial capital. Absentee Nelson businessmen and entrepreneurs began buying from the New Zealand Company, speculating on land-hungry immigrants' need for land and the apparent potential for milling the heavily bushed Waitohi. The long arms of the sound were hailed, not for the last time, as an immediate transport system on which boats could ply efficiently, cheaply and relatively safely.[151]

In 1856 a post office was established at the tiny settlement of Waitohi. On 4 October 1859 Marlborough Province was established, with Waitohi, under its new official name, Picton, as its capital. But its future as a centre or springboard for settler development in Queen Charlotte Sound was ended by a massive earthquake in January 1855. This deepened the Ōpawa River and made it navigable for sea-going vessels, whereupon the focus of settlement moved to Blenheim, which replaced Picton as provincial capital in 1865. The provincial government then refused to spend the £4000 appropriated for the Picton–Wairau Road — the road Goulter and Ward had surveyed in 1849 would finally begin to progress 10 years later.[152] The South Island main trunk railway line did not arrive until 1945. The long saga of ensuring adequate infrastructure and communications vital for settlement between Picton and the outside world was underway.

BY EARLY MARCH 1850, MĀORI had been coerced into selling 117,248 acres (47,450 ha) of the adjacent Wairau district for a 'very trifling'[153] sum.[154] They had seen thousands more acres at Waitohi bought for a mere £100, their good-quality cultivated lands there exchanged for the poorer soils of Waikawa. They received no compensation or replacement for their Waitohi homes, or for the cost of moving to Waikawa.[155] Further European actions would soon give rise to more fundamental concerns.

The Waitohi Purchase was one of the government's final acts on behalf of the New Zealand Company. Four months later, on 4 July 1850, and with its financial position continuing to deteriorate, the company surrendered its charter. Government officials took over responsibility for extinguishing native title not caught up in previous purchases. Many company agents became public servants and, when representative government was created in 1853, a number became elected politicians.

In order to reconcile the conflicting assumptions of Pākehā law and Māori concepts of land tenure, the New Zealand government worked on the understanding that Māori owned the whole country and that those rights had to be extinguished or alienated. Alienation was largely achieved by government purchase.[156] That purchase complete, the land could be offered to new settlers. Between 1850 and 1856, in a series of transactions known as the Waipounamu Purchases, and in subsequent deals with individual iwi up to 1860, vast tracts between Wairau and north-west Nelson districts, as well as the reserves set aside for Ngāti Toa in the 1847 Wairau Purchase, were alienated from native title. In the Sounds, government agents made their first purchases from Ngāti Toa, assuming, as the New Zealand Company had, that that tribe had superior rights over the resident iwi over land taken in the 1820s.[157]

Governor Grey considered land purchases a way of 'consolidat[ing] military conquest'.[158] In 1853 he appointed Donald McLean as Chief Land Purchase Commissioner. A few months later, in one of his final acts as governor, Grey negotiated the broad terms under which the government was to buy all Māori land in the South Island that it had not already bought. Reserves, which the governor was to designate, were to be set aside for Māori cultivation and subsistence. Following these instructions, and to help overcome Ngāti Toa chiefs' understandable reluctance to sign away all their property rights in Te Waipounamu, McLean agreed that 15 would receive £50 to buy land of similar value elsewhere in the colony, and a further 26 would each get a 200-acre grant of Crown land at a location to be decided by government. However, these conditions were not included in the Deed of Purchase,[159] and no provision was made for them in later settlements.[160]

The terms, for what amounted to about 8 million acres or one-fifth of the South Island, were shockingly final. For £5000, Māori were to recognise

> the final transfer or sale of all our lands on the said Islands . . . with its trees, lakes, waters, stones, and all and everything residing on the said land . . . and all and everything either under or above the said land, and all and everything connected to the said land to Victoria, the Queen of England, for ever and ever.[161]

On 10 August 1853 some 73 men and women signed the deed of Kemp's Purchase. Te Ātiawa, Ngāti Koata, Ngāti Rārua, Ngāi Tahu and Rangitāne were all cited as participating in the deal.[162]

Today there are many questions: around who actually participated; around Māori understanding of the terms of the agreement; around Ngāti Toa's right to make deals with regard to the land areas involved; and around Grey's, and then McLean's, assumption that Ngāti Toa were legitimate vendors.[163] They had paid Ngāti Toa chiefs £2000. The other £3000 was to be distributed to the cited participants in six annual instalments of £500 each (though it was two years before McLean concluded transactions with some iwi.)[164]

Local iwi were concerned that the Ngāti Toa absentee vendors who had received that initial instalment but never actually lived in the district sold had effectively extinguished the rights of local iwi to their lands and cultivations. Resident chiefs were even more insulted when they learned that in December 1854, McLean, to help finalise the South Island settlement, had paid Ngāti Toa a further £2000 of the purchase price and Te Ātiawa £700.[165]

Widespread alarm and anger were aroused when government surveyors moved to set aside the reserves in each district before any payment had been made. Residents resisted the surveying parties until they and the Crown agents came to negotiate directly, and denied that many places had been sold. Some Ngāti Kuia in Te Hoiere Pelorus Sound spoke forcibly, claiming:

> We are yet a people, a living people, and have the right to speak when our land is being sold without our consent, and no payment is received by us . . . and now we positively say that unless the Government pay it to our hands a fair share of payment, we will not give it up, neither will we allow it to be surveyed.[166]

In Tory Channel, Te Ātiawa chief Ngawheua, or Whitikau, said he would not part with any of his land. Other chiefs were willing to sell, but conditional on a fair price and a right to choose the reserves.[167]

McLean had £300 left out of the original £5000 with which to settle with the residents of about 8 million acres (3.2 million ha).[168] He hoped to achieve this at an average sum of about a farthing an acre.[169]

He went beyond that limit. In 1853 Te Ātiawa, Ngāti Toa, Ngāti Rārua, Rangitāne and Ngāi Tahu were paid £5200 for all their claims in the South Island. In 1854 North Island Te Ātiawa were paid £200 for the Wairau and Queen Charlotte blocks; Taranaki Te Ātiawa extinguished their claims in the South Island for £500; Te Ātiawa of Queen

Charlotte Sound got £200 for their block; Te Ātiawa of Waikanae received £100 for the Port Gore and Queen Charlotte block; Te Ātiawa of Queen Charlotte Sound got £200 for Te Awaiti; Te Ātiawa of Arapawa received £500 for all claims in the South Island. All Ngāti Rārua and Ngāti Tama claims for much of the South Island were settled in 1856 for £600. The same year, Ngāti Kuia and Rangitāne were paid £100 for their blocks in Kaituna, the valley running roughly south-east from today's Havelock.[170]

Not all land sales were completed under duress. Ngāti Kuia, for instance, had sold in order to gain the Queen's protection, and believing that she would sponsor education and trade. Agents had frequently promised help with roads (providing vital access to Pākehā markets and employment opportunities), hospitals and education. Ngāti Kuia, having seen that in Nelson European settlement attracted wealth, believed their wealth, mana and well-being would be enhanced.[171] However, where necessary, McLean did not shy from using 'elements of coercion', leaving the chiefs with the choice of accepting the money on offer or receiving nothing for their land which had been 'purchased' by the government, regardless of their response.[172]

Most agreements included the offer of reserves. In the Sounds, the 1850 Waitohi Purchase, and two sets of agreements with Te Ātiawa in 1854 and in 1856, saw 18,767 acres (7600 ha) being reserved in Queen Charlotte Sound, Tory Channel, on Arapaoa Island and in Port Gore.[173] The inadequacy of these reserves and their inability to support Māori in either continuing their traditional way of life or becoming equals in the new European venture did not begin to be resolved until the Waitangi Tribunal report on Te Tau Ihu in 2008, almost 150 years later.

3. New Agriculture

> 'Timber might last for some time and gold might be a good thing, but the real bone and sinew of all places was the cultivation of the land.'

In the middle of the nineteenth century the government needed the land settled and productive. Settlers, who had an overwhelming practical imperative to carve out a living from the land, were willing to assist. Unsurprisingly, then, in 1857 the Nelson Provincial Council, anxious to benefit from its newly acquired right to spend revenue from land sales,[1] opened the Pelorus district for purchase.

The Nelson Examiner and New Zealand Chronicle lost no time in boosting the initiative. The 'two single hills or saddles' between long 'necks of land' meant, it argued, that a straightforward boat trip could be made from Nelson to Port Underwood, via Croisilles Harbour, Pelorus Sound and Queen Charlotte Sound, involving only 5–6 miles (8–10 kilometres) of land travel. Travellers could then move on to the Wairau district without needing to enter the dangerous Cook Strait waters.

However, noted the paper, while the peninsulas were mostly steep and covered with 'timber or scrubby bushes', most of the 'innumerable' bays had at least some good flat land at their head, and in the Waitohi, Pelorus, Kaituna and Rai valleys up to several thousand acres were available. With thousands more acres of 'rich' land reported to have been sold already, the paper was sure more such valleys would be found. Any notion that the area should remain as Crown land was, the paper considered, to ignore its true potential. It was cattle country, and the long arms of land and sea meant that only short fences would be needed to separate runs. Here 'small agricultural settlers' with 'a few milking cows or working bullocks, brought in every day, and not suffered to grow wild, might be advantageously kept by each cultivator of the soil'.

There was timber for firewood and fencing, the sea provided 'ready-made roads that cost nothing to keep in repair', and if the government and the Nelson Provincial Council constructed the road between the Wairau and Awatere districts and Picton there would be ready access to what would certainly be a thriving town market there. Farmers in Queen Charlotte Sound and Tory Channel would not need roads at all, while those in Pelorus had only the short distance over the hill, or they could go round by 'small vessels' into the northern entrance of Queen Charlotte Sound. Cheap freight, too, was on its way, with a steamer about to ply the route between Picton and Nelson.

The area was not suited, the paper opined, to large pastoral run-holders, with its 'rugged hills' and thick forests. With small holdings offered and the anticipated infrastructure in place, including a road through Waitohi Valley, the paper was confident the district would become a favourite resort for small farmers, while the beauty of the bays and the picturesque scenery could also make the place a kind of summer retreat for many families from other parts of the province.[2]

A 'hundred havens'

Other publications painted an even greater future for the area. The 1862 *New Zealand Handbook, or, Guide to the 'Britain of the South'* noted that the steepness of land in Queen Charlotte Sound precluded much ploughing, but the 'hundred havens' the sound offered could grow corn and fruit 'in luxuriant abundance', and fish and timber would sustain 'flourishing little communities (fishers, sawyers, ship-wrights, small farmers, health-recruiting visitors etc.)'. And the sound was so conveniently positioned between Nelson and Wellington. Meanwhile, 'dominating the noble waters of Queen Charlotte's Sound, there may some day be found a great metropolis of the Pacific in which New Zealand may find her London, her Portsmouth, and her Pembroke combined'.[3]

These seductive narratives paid scant regard to the area's geographical and physical realities, its isolation, or the difficulties of instituting efficient sea transport, let alone track or road construction.[4] Early promotional literature also peddled throughout the colony a notion of majestic trees and luxuriant growth as clear evidence of rich and fertile soil.[5] Such narratives held significant sway until well into the next century. They were imbued, too, with the widely held beliefs that country life was superior to that of the towns, breeding comely, capable girls and skilled, wiry and tough boys;[6] that farmers were the backbone of the economy; and that a vigorous rural district contributed to the country's well-being.

Biblically phrased injunctions infused and reinforced such beliefs.[7] The colony's 'primeval carpet', an official 1879 report noted, was to be replaced by a 'bright landscape' and '"the earth and the abundance thereof" [was] being turned to its legitimate use — the blessing of the many'.[8] The Fox government's economic and development policies in 1869–70 reflected these beliefs and subsequent Liberal governments also subscribed to them.

Personal ambitions and aspirations contributed to the dream too. Many Pākehā settlers arrived wanting life not as a 'tenant-grubber' but as a 'landlord' whose small capital would make him independent, farming his own estate and seeing, within a few years, his family 'married, settled and provided for',[9] security against want assured and family succession achieved.[10] The unflinching optimism of media and official accounts reinforced established myths of the wealth that could be realised through working the land.[11] Few doubted their ability to wrest a living from the land, whatever its suitability.

'The forest is behind me and the sea in front,' wrote Sarah Harris soon after arriving in New Plymouth.[12] Settlers in much of New Zealand arrived to an extraordinary landscape where a tangled undergrowth dominated by majestic podocarps formed a dense, dark, threatening barrier. Successful farming meant transforming that landscape. Slashing and cutting could do only so much.[13] Fire, that essential tool, created a temporary fertility that masked the true nature of the country. Greenhorn farmers would buy up land, not realising that south-facing slopes were too often sunless and that even the perennial native grass *Danthonia* (now more commonly known as *Rytidosperma*) was threatened by bidi-bidi, bracken, mānuka, the ever-constant potential for second-growth bush,[14] and an expanding range of imported weeds.

The Sounds reflected that wider world. Even when title to land was achieved, enormous effort was needed to make and maintain a farm on what was mostly steep, infertile land. Success was modest, and for many unattainable.

THE OLD LAND CLAIMS ORDINANCE 1840–41 impacted little on the Sounds. As noted in the previous chapter, only four settlers made any claim to have their settlement in Queen Charlotte Sound reviewed, and there were no European settlers in Pelorus Sound until 1849. (There is no record of retributive action against any in the Sounds who failed to claim.) By the late 1850s, with provincial governments elsewhere beginning to offer land for sale, and wanting a fair share of prospective immigrants, the Nelson superintendent placed what appears to be the first notice for land sales in the Sounds: two sections in Deep Bay (Tory Channel), seven in Ōtānerau Bay (on Arapaoa Island), two on Blumine Island as well as sections in Wharehunga, 'Kaitepea', Whatamonga Bay, Kahikatea Bay and 'Kahikatea East' (all in Queen Charlotte Sound). All were advertised for auction.[15] A couple of months later, at 'the town of Bulwer' (Outer Pelorus), where steep hills loom over a narrow foreshore, the enterprising settler could buy land for a similar sum.[16] In 1861 Courtney Kenny, who already owned the Lochmara Run and would become a prominent politician, applied for and got the estimated 10,000 acres (4046 ha) of Kenny Isle, the large block of land west of Piripāua Neck (now known as Pohuenui).[17]

But 7000 acres (2833 ha) of the Kenny Isle land was soon on the market again, along with its goodwill (however that might have been built up by then). The soil, the advertisement claimed, was 'extremely good in general, parts covered by grass, fern, flax'. The remainder 'had extremely close scrub, and everything could be easily burned off'. The holding's small bays had excellent anchorages, there was sufficient flat land for homestead sites, and steamers continually passed within a few miles.[18]

Many advertisements of land for sale at the end of the 1850s and into the 1860s boosted such a narrative. When, in 1863, the 5097 acres (2063 ha) of the Blencathara Run, 6 miles (9 kilometres) from the 'fine port of Picton', was up for sale or lease, its accessible water frontages on both Queen Charlotte and Pelorus sounds and good facilities for shipping stock were stressed.[19] Facilities and accessibility were constant themes. At Tahuahua or Blackwood Bay — only 7 miles (11 kilometres) from Picton, 'the future capital of New Zealand' — 80 acres (32 ha) of bush and scrub mixed with artificial grasses were 'well adapted for a small dairy farm' and an excellent weatherboard house had 3 acres of cleared land around it, suited for a market garden or orchard.[20]

In Endeavour Inlet, itself 'rich in the recollections of Captain Cook', 103 acres (42 ha) of formerly native cultivation were now half bush, half cleared. In Kenepuru a number of small lots of 50–70 acres (20–30 ha) were advertised, along with their ‘excellent’ soil, water frontages, timber, level ground and existing cleared land. Ten thousand acres with pre-emptive rights to 80 acres (these gave occupants the right to purchase specified public land at nominal prices provided they improved it) of the Kenepuru Run was also on offer. This run straddled the southern end of the peninsula between Pelorus and Queen Charlotte sounds, 7 miles (17 kilometres) from Picton and 12 miles (19 kilometres) from Havelock. Its promoted advantages included water frontages, facilities for shipping and landing stock and, in this case, existing clearing, grassing and track work.[21] Resales and, presumably, disillusionment, began early.

By 1864, about 400 people occupied or owned sometimes multiple sections or large holdings (or both) in or around Picton, Blenheim, the Wairau Valley and south towards the Clarence River. By contrast, in Queen Charlotte Sound and Pelorus Sound, 28 people occupied or owned land (see Appendix 1a). The freight that the *Elizabeth* delivered to Havelock in 1868 is indicative of the tiny population and the subsistence nature of their enterprises — 40 sacks of flour, 20 sacks of chaff, four bags of sugar, two boxes of tea, four boxes of soap, two cases of jam and two cases of kerosene.[22]

The 1881 Census, 20 years later, provides another snapshot of settlement. The Sounds’ population had risen to 540. In Queen Charlotte Sound, most were involved with milling and mining; in the various bays of the still sparsely populated Pelorus Sound, milling at Black Point and Nydia Bay accounted for congregations of population; the rest were largely farming 10–20 acres (4–8 ha) in clusters in the bigger bays in Kenepuru Sound and in Crail and Clova bays in the Outer Pelorus. A couple of big stations in the east of the Outer Pelorus also accounted for small groups of people (see Appendix 1b).

Yet, if the freight on the 36-tonne ketch *Argus* Pelorus-bound from Nelson in 1879 is any indication, optimism was in the air. She was carrying 20,000 feet of timber, 4500 bricks, 20,000 feet of shingles, eight kegs of nails, one bale of paper-hangings, two bales of scrim, eight packages of doors, 14 packages of sashes, five sacks of lime, 12 packages of mouldings, 11 kegs of paint and 47 packages of sundries, as well as a large cargo of building material for the Ketu Bay people.

Getting to that stage had not been straightforward. Regularising and identifying title to unoccupied land was not a simple process. In 1872 the Department of Lands and Survey, sometimes helped by locals (who would have doubtless appreciated the additional income),[23] began a second survey based on the Torrens system. This allowed titles of unoccupied land that the government was releasing onto the market to be registered prior to purchase or settlement. It also required those whose holdings had been acquired through provincial council sales to have their land resurveyed so as to gain title. By the mid-1880s a backlog of settlers' applications to have land resurveyed and titles registered was testing departmental manpower.[24]

The 'old, inaccurate' provincial surveys had created problems, and in the mid-1880s old boundaries had to be reconciled with new.[25] The promised Crown grants of land were held up and the settlers were complaining. But the department could not grant titles because the descriptions of the land were inadequate. While sorting this out was 'tedious and troublesome work' and 'a serious drag on progress',[26] the department, wanting to ensure it got full value for what was falling to the auctioneer's hammer, was not prepared to open land for settlement without at least a preliminary topographical survey.[27]

The Sounds' 'tortuous' wet country (a much-used description) did little to facilitate progress. Bad weather could hold the work up for days, and much time was lost in chopping down trees and in the sheer slog of 'opening up lines through fallen tree-tops and entangled undergrowth encumbering the ground'.[28] The 'hilly bush country' demanded that 'every corner [be] pegged'[29] and surveyors battled in high, steep country bushed to the water's edge and heavily tidal beaches.[30]

Even into the 1890s the Marlborough Land Board, when processing applications for land, had not required topographical surveys and had 'little or no information as to the nature of the country, the quality of the land, best fencing-boundaries etc.'. The board was working in the dark and settlers were being offered land to which there was no access, or access only by 'paper' roads, or which had no water over the summer. To make matters worse, for a period around 1890 the Lands and Survey Department employed one solitary officer in the district.[31]

Surveying for road-lines was also fraught. By the early 1880s, roads were considered essential if productivity was to follow settlement.[32] Yet the 'hilly bush district' in the Sounds necessitated 'much research' to find 'the lowest saddles and the best possible grades and location of road-lines'.[33] The department would frequently return to this plaint.

Land lease schemes

By 1883, with the government proclaiming a focus on settlement rather than revenue,[34] various land-holding schemes were operating. The Land Act 1877 had

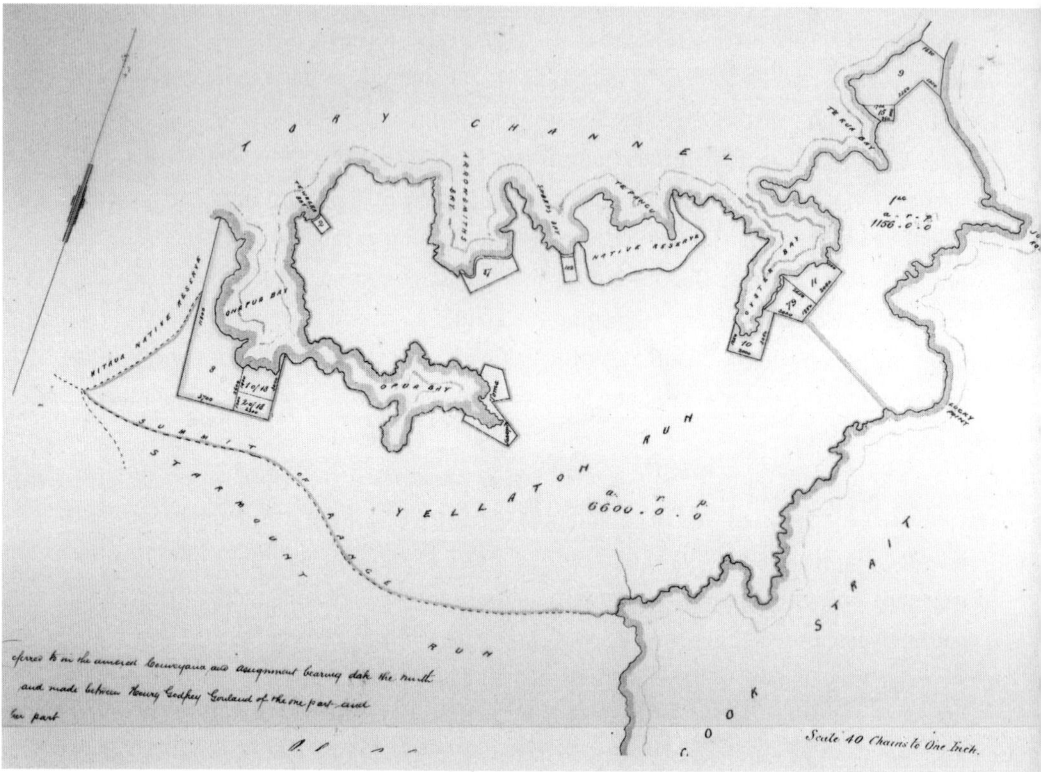

The Yellaton Run, Kura Te Au Tory Channel. This substantial block of land running from Onapua Bay to Te Rua Bay was first auctioned off in small blocks in the early 1890s. PICTON HERITAGE AND WHALING MUSEUM, COURTESY PICTON HISTORICAL SOCIETY

provided for deferred payments, intended to promote not large individual holdings but land 'as a boon and encouragement to families' who had 'the labour and the will to cultivate' and the skill to make the land profitable.[35] Those participating in the scheme paid a deposit of one tenth of the value of a block of pastoral land up to 320 acres (130 ha). The rest of the price was to be paid over 10 years, as long as the leaseholder lived on the land and improved it. Married women and women who owned up to 640 acres (260 ha) could also participate. The intention was to cap how much land any one person could buy from the Crown. The scheme was popular, and the Lands and Survey claimed it had had a transformative effect in parts of the country. Without it, the land 'would still have presented, unbroken, the monotonous sombre hues of fern, brown tussock or bush'.[36]

The Land Act 1882 introduced perpetual leases: an initial term of 30 years could be extended for another 20. (With male life expectancy then about 50 years, the term perpetual was not inapt.) Land was offered at a maximum annual rent of 5 per cent of its value. A residence had to be built, and improvements made. Three years later, under the Liberal John Ballance, the Land Act 1885 provided for small grazing runs. These allowed sheep farming on a small scale on an area that a family, rather than an imported workforce, could manage. Runs were up to 5000 acres (2023 ha), rent was about 2.5 per cent of the land's value, and, 'as the land was often rough bush country worth only about five shillings an acre', it was envisaged that the resulting low rents would enable farmers to spend on improvements and stock.[37] With such favourable terms, the government argued in 1890, no one should experience problems with compliance.[38]

The redoubtable *Marlborough Express* regularly ran notices of settlers' applications for land, and the results of the ensuing auctions for what were not insignificant farms. In March 1887 Henry Baxter and William Davenport applied for licences for 730 and 250 acres (295 ha and 101 ha) respectively of the Yellaton Run in Tory Channel, and Isaac Landall applied for 1150 acres in Oyster Bay. In May 1887 G. Maxted got the 730-acre lease for £3 annual rent; Davenport secured the licence he wanted for 10 years at £1 1s per annum. In the same auction J. Heberley got tenure for a further 10 years of the Oyster Bay land that Landall had wanted, for 1d (1 penny) an acre. A 10-year lease of 550 acres (223 ha) at Māhakipawa at 1d per acre went to John Duncan. D. Love, like Heberley doubtless wanting a further income stream to supplement the decidedly unprofitable whaling at that time, secured 400 acres in Anatoi (Anatohia?) Bay. All tenants were to have the boundaries surveyed at their own expense.[39]

In 1888 another 1700 acres (688 ha) in Pelorus Sound were gazetted for auction as small grazing units under amended terms that the government envisaged as particularly suited to the Sounds.[40] That year, too, 21-year leases at 3d an acre annually went to W. H. Keenan for 1350 acres in Onapua Bay, Tory Channel; J. P. Salisbury for 400 acres (162 ha) in Queen Charlotte Sound; and Mrs John Mills for 830 acres (336 ha) in Tawhitinui Reach, Pelorus Sound. The Land Board also announced its intention to auction a 10-year lease of 13,500 acres (546 ha) for a pastoral run in Onapua Bay at 1d an acre per year. At an auction a few months later the Harris brothers at Ketu Bay secured the lease of 3160 acres (1279 ha) of land as part of the Kenny Isle (Pohuenui) run, paying 1d an acre.[41]

Settlers' 'land hunger' put pressure on government to open further land for settlement.[42] The government's slow response meant that growing or felling seasons were lost (no small matter to settlers) and potential buyers discouraged.[43] When land was notified for auction, the settlers frequently had things to say about the boundaries and the varying cost of land in different parts of the district. Small runs in Pelorus Sound, for instance, often reached top-of-the-range prices but for useless land. Elsewhere, complained one newspaper correspondent, one person 'has the run of a whole island for 25 years with peppercorn rental . . . the rest of us pay 3d, or deducting the useless land, 6d an acre'. On one shore of the sound, and in the Nelson district too, land could be obtained at 17s 6d per 100 acres (40 ha), while in the Marlborough land district it went for 25s.[44]

The Marlborough Land Board was balancing a lot of complicating factors. It wanted settlement but sawmilling was depressed and some of the Sounds' best settlers were having to leave the district to earn a livelihood. The board was not averse to giving newcomers advice to keep them on. If they were not meeting the deferred payments scheme's residence requirements after four years (some struggled with inaccessible land or land without a water source), they could, the board advised, put up a temporary shack on their property and sleep in it. They only had to do this a few times to prevent the land being taken back.[45]

As an overall percentage of land in the Sounds, what was taken up in the first stages of settlement was small. In 1874, as settlement in Canterbury boomed with over 334,000 acres (135,165 ha) taken up, in Marlborough only 6343 acres (2567 ha) of land had been leased.[46] In Pelorus Sound in 1880 there was perhaps one settler every 25 kilometres.[47] In 1883 official records put the total number of holdings in the Sounds as 62.[48] Increases were slow. Bush clearance would peak only between 1910 and 1920.[49]

However, the appointment of John McKenzie as minister of lands in the new

Looking down into Kaiuma Bay, Te Hoiere Pelorus Sound. By 1962, when this was taken, milling had removed most of the timber, but the challenges of the steepness of the land and the paucity of flats to farming are clear. MARLBOROUGH HISTORICAL SOCIETY

Liberal government in 1891 was hailed across the country as opening 'the gates of opportunity for the ordinary people of New Zealand'.[50] By the mid-1890s Pākehā families whose names became prominent fixtures in the settler landscape had reached Pelorus Sound and adjacent areas — the King-Turners, for instance, and the Archers, Mills, Fells, Macefields, Godsiffs and Neaves. The Bowdens, Turners and William Baldick arrived in Queen Charlotte Sound (see Appendix 1c for details on where these people settled).

McKenzie's childhood memories of dispossession and despair during the Scottish Highlands evictions of thousands of crofters from their small farms marked him indelibly. He wanted land to be distributed in a more equitable way and believed that the state should break up monopolistic land practices that discouraged settlement. He also wanted to provide easier capital to encourage individual initiative.[51] A strong subscriber to ruralism, McKenzie saw land as the key to successful colonisation. 'Timber might last for some time and gold might be a good thing, but the real bone and sinew of all places was the cultivation of the land.'[52]

If land was to be fully cultivated, leases had to take such improvements into account, not be subjected to public auction at the end of a tenure.[53] McKenzie's 1892 Land Act enabled farmers to buy land outright, though certificates of title were awarded only after improvements were made. Settlers could also apply for 25-year leases to occupy land, with a right to purchase after 10. And finally, the earlier lease 'in perpetuity' for 50 years was replaced by a 999-year term for less than 640 acres (259 ha) of first-class or 2000 acres (809 ha) of second-class land.[54] These leases were drawn up to enable people with no capital to take up land, and the practice continued until well into the twentieth century.[55]

By 1894 the small grazing runs scheme, under more flexible legislation, appears to have encouraged settlement in the Sounds. The government was by then bearing a lot of the survey costs, rents were comparatively low, and tenure was almost always a perpetual lease. Switching to such a lease was straightforward and lessees did not have to comply with residence clauses — they could live a few miles away.

That year 36 small grazing runs had been established in the Sounds over about 22,706 aces.[56] Government land was becoming regularly available for settlement, primarily in Pelorus, the 'working sound' as it was later known, and sometimes in Queen Charlotte Sound.[57] By 1906, claimed Lands and Survey, all land within Sounds county with water frontage, apart from reserves, was occupied under some form of Crown tenure. Most people had held their lease for at least 10 years, had complied with lease conditions or made improvements beyond what was required, and the value of their land had increased by 50 per cent over the previous three years. Anyone who wanted to sell could do so advantageously.[58]

Dream meets reality

In 1893, politicians had stressed the soil's 'undeniably rich character', land that was 'much better . . . than people have been led to believe'. '[S]kill, capital and energy [would] make comfortable homes in these bays.'[59] From 1897, in the Sounds and elsewhere, the government was parcelling out what was often a reoffering of second-class land. For over 10 years it had been known that the land in the Sounds was rugged mountainous country that was hard and expensive to clear.[60] Lands and Survey itself was well acquainted with such facts and the expenses involved.[61] Towards the end of the first decade of the twentieth century, when the refrain of the costs and time of providing road access in such isolated difficult country was fully established, the department continued to report high survey costs where 'the surrounding freeholds were small and sometimes intricate',[62] often landlocked, and thus 'useless' to anyone who did not own the frontage.[63]

Did prospective settlers know this? Did they look at and understand maps? Did they have any idea of the distances and transport difficulties they would face? We do not know. We do know that the demand for land continued and by 1911 was greatly exceeding supply. The uptake of what was known to be poor land in the neighbouring Pelorus Valley did begin to slow in 1913, and in the Sounds that year only some 1300 acres (526 ha) of small holdings were applied for, as opposed to the 22,000 (8903 ha) in 1894.[64] But the impact of even that settlement was not insignificant. In the 30 years between the late 1880s and the early 1900s, two-thirds of the native bush in the Sounds had been cleared.[65] By 1916, Bishop William Sadlier reported to a friend, 220 families were scattered over 1058 miles (1700 km) of coastline in 225 named bays[66] and the available land was, by and large, all spoken for.

TODAY, WHEN INTRODUCED MAMMALS HAVE modified even the densest bush, it is difficult to imagine the daunting barrier it must have presented to the new settlers. In 1849 William Harvey and his wife Augusta arrived at Clova Bay with their four small children.[67] Did they have any expectations beyond survival as they pushed past the whitened driftwood and the untidy barrier of grasses and flax that edged the beach, into the next barrier of ngaio, kawakawa, native fuchsia, coprosma, akeake? Were they at all familiar with the mānuka, tauhinu (*Ozothamnus leptophyllus*) that so readily sprang up on cleared land, the tutu (*Coriaria*) that killed horses and stock, the stinging nettle (*Urtica ferox*) that all too often colonised bare ground on which they might have pitched their calico tent?

Bigger trees such as hīnau, kohekohe, tawa, tītoki, pigeonwood and kaikōmako formed yet another layer. In the gullies, ferns and tree ferns proliferated. Above a tangled undergrowth were supplejack, rātā and bush lawyer. Majestic podocarps — kahikatea, rimu, mataī, and tōtara up to three metres across and tens of metres high — dominated the bush. Beech, kāmahi and the occasional southern rātā grew on the steeper land. The Harveys were in untouched bush where gleams of sunlight occasionally broke the shade;[68] bird calls and the sea worrying at the shore were all that broke the silence.

The steady, rhythmic thud of an axe would soon be heard. William was a sawyer by trade; he and his new wife had lived in the north, where William had worked in the kauri timber trade. His skill and knowledge would be vital to the success of their settlement.

Their experience of clearing the land would be typical. It could take a week to cut down perhaps four trees. The enormous effort of underscrubbing, clearing and grubbing out the massive roots was all done by hand, and dragged on day after day while the sandflies ate the new settlers alive.[69] At some point the Harveys used a jack to help lift the roots, then horses to drag them out of the ground.[70] Only later was gelignite used to unearth the roots. The logs were probably left to rot and grass was grown between them. Later, fires that burned on a scale and with a ferocity and speed beyond any English settlers' experience[71] were lit and land was cleared 'at an expense little beyond the price of a box of matches'.[72]

From the early 1860s, in the Sounds as in many other parts of New Zealand, millers began steadily encroaching on the bush, establishing that important symbiotic relationship between millers and farmers. As they logged the best trees in the bush in advance of settlement, they lit fires to burn what was left. In their aftermath, farmers cleared stumps and logs, burned, and sowed seed in the still-warm ash to provide good grass on which, for a time, sheep or cattle would do well. For settlers, often fulfilling lease conditions on land clearance, the fires were a boon.

The dreams of good land and bright futures touted by the early advertisements

Taken from Te Tara-o-Te-Marama Mount Freeth, above Picton. Two women and a girl seated among stumps of fallen trees look down on the freezing works in Shakespeare Bay and across to Waikawa. Today, where we see charred stumps, detritus and debris, settlers saw progress. PICTON HERITAGE AND WHALING MUSEUM, COURTESY PICTON HISTORICAL SOCIETY

were not easily abandoned. In 1880 one settler in Pelorus Sound bought into this idyll: beautiful bays of 10–200 acres 'famous' for their pasture, where a family might keep a cow, aspire to a comfortable homestead, and where the water was full of fish and the hills had enough beech to supply all New Zealand's railways. 'Doubtless there are many fishermen in the old world who would think they had entered Paradise if located in one of them,' opined the *Nelson Evening Mail*.[73] Fourteen years later the *Pelorus Guardian*, ever upbeat, described the felling in the bays and hills as a 'pleasing prospect'.[74]

Whatever the prospect, the reality was invariably harsher. Farmers were trying to make a living from steep, densely bushed land whose value was only as permanent forest providing scenic climatic and erosion control. The soils in most of the Sounds are inherently low in nutrients. The higher and wetter the country, the fewer the nutrients, while high runoff (in places up to 2540 millimetres a year) from steep, denuded slopes further leaches fertility. With the forest gone the land eroded easily; in the inner Sounds, particularly on south-facing slopes that got little or no winter sun, frost froze the already poor soil, making the ground hard for weeks. A century later, scientists would say that only 10 per cent of little-eroded pasture was 'reasonably good'; the rest was poor or deteriorating — good only for sheep farming and the odd 'cattle product' for export.[75]

The higher reaches of many holdings simply did not warrant the effort needed to clear or maintain them. Native shrubs regrew persistently, broom and gorse invaded. Clean musters became increasingly difficult: cattle and sheep got lost and went wild. A tourist in Queen Charlotte Sound in 1882 was one of a handful to recognise the struggle involved in making a living for those in the small bays of the sound. Few settlers, he recorded, seemed to have cleared land apart from a 'few yards in front of the houses'. One resident kept bees. In 1892 the Golden Point settlement (where Māori had earlier established a peach orchard) was 'looking dreary and deserted'.[76]

The sea, too, was an enemy. 'We have had another very high tide with a very rough sea and heavy wind that blew salt spray all over the garden,' Edward Hope reported to his mother from Deep Bay in 1884. 'I fear [it] has seriously injured our trees (peaches, apples, pears, raspberries, gooseberries etc) in fact the sea gravel was driven right through my paling fence.'[77] Storms pushed tides to record heights, swept heavy timber into the sea and created slips and mud that damaged fencing, homes, tracks and, later, phone lines.[78]

PESTS, CREATING NATIONWIDE PROBLEMS, ADDED to the relentless work of keeping farms as paying propositions. Scabies, caused by a mite that creates terrible itchiness, as well as loss of wool, appetite and lamb weight, attacked the sheep. Rabbits were not then a problem, but by 1910 the Sounds were a 'veritable hotbed' of ferrets, stoats and weasels that, quite apart from their destruction of native birds, attacked settlers' poultry and caused considerable anxiety about loss of a food and income source.[79] Possums, liberated by acclimatisation societies from 1870 to 1921 to help build a homegrown fur trade and 'absolutely protected' in some counties, including the Sounds,[80] stripped domestic gardens and were later found to carry tuberculosis that infected dairy herds. Into the 1940s, 'wild pigs used to come down from the bush and kill the lambs and skin them . . . you'd go into the paddock and just find the legs and bones still in the skin but all the meat would be gone.'[81] Deer, released into areas of the Sounds for hunting in the 1890s, grazed and badly damaged paddocks. Even the more expensive higher-than-normal fences were little deterrent.[82]

In 1894 porina or grass grub, which attacks most grasses, appears to have made its first appearance. Newspaper reports were generally limited to initial outbreaks but a severe attack could result in the complete destruction of the grass on a farm. Similarly, scale beetles, then tortoise beetles, left trees looking 'like a lot of bare yacht masts'. One early attempt at farm forestry at Kaiuma was destroyed.[83]

Imported weeds arrived to flourish. In 1910 foxglove, which smothers grass, was noticed in Marlborough and rapidly became a significant pest.[84] A year later the Californian thistle arrived. It spread easily and its thistles cut the mouths of stock, allowing entry to the virus scabby mouth. Settlers called it the 'worst weed' they had yet met. Large areas of land became 'covered more or less with briar, blackberry and [some] patches of broom, gorse and St. John's Wort'. This last, poisonous to stock, spread rapidly and was 'difficult and expensive to keep in check when once established'.[85]

Briar and blackberry, spread by birds even into virgin bush, affected grazing and ensnared sheep,[86] and dairy farmers had to waste time looking for cows that hid themselves and their calves in the flourishing big clumps. Bidi-bidi was prevalent, downgrading fleece value.[87] By 1910 barberry, very difficult to eradicate and springing up all over the district, was pronounced 'the biggest curse that New Zealand had yet seen in the form of noxious weeds'.[88]

Not all of the Sounds were equally affected, but where the weeds did establish themselves the measures of the Noxious Weeds Act 1900 seemed ineffective. The

Sounds Farmers' Union had no luck with spurring the government into action to eradicate or prevent infestations,[89] and settlers did not possess the necessary capital. As the twentieth century moved into its second decade, some farmers regularly and illegally allowed their cattle to stray onto adjourning reserves to forage for feed, spreading the seeds further.[90]

THE FIRES THAT HELPED BREAK in the land carried their own threat. A wind change could fan smouldering embers into flames; simple carelessness could ignite burns that destroyed homes, buildings, fences, grass, stock and the Sounds timber that, exported for railway sleepers, buildings and pavements, underpinned much of the country's development.[91] Against such fires settlers were largely helpless. With their clothes soaked in water and their heads wrapped in wet sacking against the intense heat, families or small groups of settlers might form bucket brigades or nail wet sacking onto buildings to save them and their contents, but only rain or a wind change could bring the fires under control.[92]

A daughter of Isaac Landall at Oyster Bay died in a scrub fire[93] — not the only such tragedy. Droughts saw fires spreading from people's careless burning-off, and deer hunters burnt bracken to flush out their game.[94] In Kenepuru, settlers lost homes and fencing to fires that raged round the Sounds in 1898; fires devastated the landscape in Pelorus and Kenepuru sounds in 1904 when gale-force winds carried live sparks that started further huge blazes.[95]

In the terrible summer of 1908, when fires burned across the entire country, great palls of smoke hung over the Sounds. Eli Bay to Beatrix Bay was ablaze with 'roaring mountains of fire': 'hundreds of sheep', grazing and some outbuildings were destroyed and homes were saved only after bucket brigades waged terrible battles.[96] The supply of milk dropped to a few cans; the Paradise Bay dairy company had to close temporarily. Homes and valuables were lost. For small farmers on poor land, and with little or no compensation available, the loss of grazing and fencing was compounded by the horror of burned stock and the choking, acrid smoke. Decades would pass before legislation and education greatly restricted such outbreaks.[97]

FARMERS WERE WORKING WITH SOILS, plants and weather patterns that were very different from those in their home countries. In 1888 the establishment

Isaac Landall, Dieffenbach farm, undated. PICTON HERITAGE AND WHALING MUSEUM, COURTESY PICTON HISTORICAL SOCIETY

of Lincoln Agricultural College and then the Department of Agriculture in 1892 signalled a growing understanding of the economic importance of farming across the country, and the need for better science to help farmers. A handful of the department's agricultural advisers made occasional visits to the Sounds from about 1902. They, and the Farmers' Union via its growing number of local groups, gave leadership, information and opportunities to share experiences that helped engender an environment in which struggling farmers could see a way forward and believe that their efforts were not in vain.[98]

From the end of the nineteenth century the nation's papers carried increasing numbers of practical articles on noxious weeds, animal husbandry, good dairying practice, the depth and extent of ploughing, the best time to burn, the advisability of sowing gorse on poor land for sheep fodder, the best grasses to use (and so on), adding to farmers' store of knowledge.

At the end of the 1890s Isaac Newton Harvey, son of William and Augusta Harvey, was farming the family land around Manaroa in Clova Bay, where his parents had first settled almost 50 years before. Following earlier correspondence on the matter in *The Press*, he put pen to paper in the *Marlborough Express* to detail his method of dealing with scrub and weeds. Burn the fern, he advised, any time from Christmas to March. Mow any fern not burned off with fern scythes. Sow grass as new fern comes through, fence to keep pigs in so that their rooting among the fern would prepare the land for ploughing (and the pigs for market), then crowd on sheep until the young fern is cropped off.

Harvey recognised that more fern would sprout in October but, he wrote, its growth would be weakened and after the above cycle had been repeated over two seasons there would be few weeds and little scrub left. Mānuka and possibly young gorse (largely confined to the inner Sounds) might also be tackled by close cropping, though young mānuka might have to be pulled out until the seed in the ground was exhausted.[99]

Ploughing and harrowing twice in a season was important. Of the specialised ploughs available, Isaac preferred Duncan's double-furrow plough that 'can go anywhere a horse can, and is easily managed'. Where old timber prevented ploughing, he ingeniously shackled condemned cable chains together, crossing and recrossing them to form a square harrow connected to a stout cross-bar. A pair of 'powerful horses' dragged this through the fern, killing it temporarily.[100]

Such treatment, and the resulting sheep dung, much improved the land, he claimed. Grass sowing was the next step and he offered advice on the various grasses available. Cheap cocksfoot, used with large quantities of fog, a cheap ryegrass containing large portions of white clover, the poas, plantain, red-headed bend grass (*Agrostis*), and as much as could be afforded at seven pence a pound of the hard native fescue (*Festuca duriuscula*), lots of good Dutch clover 'which, loving good strong land, yet has a curious affinity for some poor birch country', was very good for hills covered in fern and mānuka scrub.

Isaac Harvey described the native *Danthonia*, which grows near bush and scrub, as 'the most valuable of all for much poor or medium fern country'. (Hopes that it would help destroy tauhinu would soon be dashed.)[101] He advised that grass seed be sown in March, the area grassed stocked lightly during the winter until the fern showed up again, then any bare patches resown in spring.[102]

THE ABILITY TO INVEST IN farming equipment was obviously critical to success. Yet '[f]encing, ditching, track-making, the buildings, the animals themselves'[103] were so costly that it may have bred a certain conservatism. Many farmers continued burning almost annually, hoping the grass would grow again. It was not a recipe for success. Land reverted to fern,[104] and too often the grasses sown were unsuited to the poor soils, giving ferns an even greater chance.[105]

As early as 1898 it was officially recognised that the key to success on poor forest land was larger holdings.[106] The Harveys had shrewdly consolidated earlier, buying up little farms lost to the bracken that sprang up so quickly after land was cleared. By 1882 they owned all the free and leasehold land from Okoha to Manaroa. Their holdings were not contiguous, but could provide the additional grazing needed to make the total viable.[107] Others similarly benefitted from such moves. Robert Woodgate, then Thomas Buxton, farmed the 1170-acre Ravenscliff Run that ran north from Endeavour Inlet to Cape Jackson. In 1866 the Turner Brothers (soon to be involved in the various mining operations in the area) had acquired the provincial government lease for the run. By 1875 it was stocked with one sheep to the acre (90 of them fat halfbred Leicesters, a breed that would come to be well regarded), horses and pigs. A 'substantial' six-room house, a men's cottage, a boatshed and stockyard had been built and 150 acres (61 ha) of the run had been largely cleared and sown with 'English' grass. The store for the Ravenscliff Goldfield (proclaimed in 1872; see Chapter 4) was also sited on the run and arguably added to its value.[108]

In 1899, when any flock over 2000 was considered large, the Harris brothers at Pohuenui were running over 6000 sheep; in 1900, they bought Port Ligar to complement their Kenny Isle farm, as well as the steep (though cleared) land at Bulwer,[109] and continued clearing, fencing and sowing grass.[110] At Anakoha, where Francis Digby Neave had amalgamated local farms between Anakoha and Port Gore, his son Digby managed 9000 acres (3642 ha) or so, carrying 2–3 sheep to the acre (not unusual after those flushes of fertility that accompanied the early burning). Within two years he spent over £8000, brought in managers, felled the bush and developed station buildings. However, in 1912 the farm was beginning to revert to scrub and was sold. Its new owner, Ebenezer Hay, reduced sheep numbers, introduced cattle, improved the cattle yards and built a new wharf. Gangs of Russians and Finns, as well as locals, were brought in to build the tracks so critical to farm management and to battle with foxglove — until they realised that trying to destroy it made it come back even more strongly.[111]

Small farms, however, continued to characterise Sounds settlement. In 1901, in the sheltered and relatively fertile Kenepuru, 'farm after farm' had sea frontages and were nestled among the trees, with only the 100 acres (40 ha) of government-designated scenic reserve remaining unoccupied. But with only about 200 bales of wool exported from the area that year it is hard to see these farms as economic units.[112]

SETTLERS ALSO TRIED HORTICULTURE AND cropping. From the early 1880s, the Sounds' 'early producing', mild climate allowed some in Kenepuru and Queen Charlotte sounds to move from subsistence farming to productive cropping and orcharding. It began on a tiny scale,[113] but in 1881, 50 tonnes of potatoes went direct to the Sydney markets, possibly the first such shipment.

As more land was devoted to cropping,[114] the variety increased. In the early twentieth century farmers put in cocksfoot (for the back-breaking return of only 3d a pound),[115] oats (to feed the horses), turnips, choumollier (a type of kale), mangles (a type of sugar beet, also called mangolds), and produced silage.[116] For a couple of decades in the 1900s early strawberries did well in the sheltered bays of the inner Queen Charlotte Sound.[117]

From the early 1890s farmers grew a rich variety of fruit — 'probably a dozen varieties of apples, six of plums, several pears, quinces, medlars, apricots, peaches, nectarines, cherries, grapes and walnuts' in 'sheltered nooks'. Citrus could be grown on headlands where wind movement prevented frost. Figs, Kentish cherries, boysenberries and raspberries produced prolifically.[118] By 1915, wherever orcharding in the Grove Arm had 'found a foothold on the coastal flats, autumn tints are now the distinguishing features of the Marlborough Sounds. The bright red and yellow tones of cherry, peach and walnut groves relieve the long stretches of placid blue water, curving round green and brown hillsides.'[119]

Horticulture may have returned a small profit, though this was always constrained by the steep hills, and thus cropping always played a relatively minor role in the economy of the Sounds. In 1916 the *Marlborough Express* reported that farmers in Kenepuru owned nine stationary engines for cutting chaff and wood and about nine chaff-cutters and several binders, and were growing several hundred acres of rape and turnip; wartime prices meant good financial returns.[120] Orchards apparently thrived in Kenepuru and the inner Queen Charlotte and Pelorus sounds, but it is unclear how much fruit was actually marketed.[121] Farmers were still seeking seasonal contract work to supplement income, suggesting that revenue was limited.

CATTLE, AS WE HAVE SEEN, were introduced to the Sounds early on; by 1865 cattle thefts were not unknown. In the early 1890s the Archers, on their valuable and relatively extensive flat land at the head of World's End, Tennyson Inlet, were fattening cattle before driving them out over the rough, steep cattle track into the Rai Valley and on to Blenheim — said to be a full day's journey[122] — and at least one paper envisaged a rosy future for fat cattle farming.[123] Yet sheep remained the mainstay of Sounds farming, despite the discovery that cattle played a minor role in suppressing mānuka.

Wild pigs were shot, both for their meat and to keep their numbers down. Domestic pigs, particularly after the Marlborough Bacon Company's factory was established in 1914, provided another source of income.[124]

By the turn of the century most Sounds homesteads had one or two house cows, and by 1891 Liberal party politician Charles Mills ran a 'large butter business'.[125] Developing any kind of dairy industry was a formidable undertaking. Butter shipped from the outer Sounds could be ruined in the three or four days it took to reach Havelock; what happened to the business of one producer who tramped from Manaroa to Māhakipawa and over densely bushed hills to Endeavour Inlet to drum up a market for his butter is unknown.[126]

ABOVE A scene on a farm near Dieffenbach Point, Tōtaranui Queen Charlotte Sound, around the turn of the nineteenth century. MARLBOROUGH HISTORICAL SOCIETY, 012482

BELOW Havelock Dairy Factory with horse and carts delivering cream and milk. PICTON HERITAGE AND WHALING MUSEUM, COURTESY PICTON HISTORICAL SOCIETY

However, in 1893 a Mr Bond, a new and energetic Pelorus settler, imported a Jersey bull so he could 'launch out into the dairying industry'.[127] Five years later the government began offering cheap credit to establish dairy cooperatives.[128] Could the Sounds compete in this environment? Most potential suppliers had tiny herds of five or six cows — Peter Archer, who ran 20 milking cows in Tuna Bay in 1905, was an exception — and most hand-milked until after World War II.[129]

Optimism was in the air. Creameries, predicted one government official, would be dotted all over the district; Wairau and the Sounds 'have the natural resources that would make . . . for complete success'. Others were expecting success like that in Taranaki. Despite there being only one milking machine in the district,[130] the Havelock Co-operative Dairy Factory opened in 1901.[131] In November 1905, as the dairy industry and cooperatives boomed all over the country,[132] the 'commodious and well equipped' Sounds Co-operative Dairy Company opened in Paradise Bay where several families farmed. Columns of local reporting were devoted to the VIPs in attendance, the promises and praise for the refrigerator, butter worker and churner (supplied by Topliss Brothers, Christchurch), boiler and steam engines (Luke and Sons, Wellington, and Chambers and Son, Auckland, respectively) and the Rose turbine tester.[133] By 1910 the Linkwater Co-operative Cheese Dairy Company, near the Grove wharf, was also operating.

With the small dairy farmers maintaining their promised yield, a bright future could well have seemed assured. In 1907 the Sounds Co-op factory was delighting its 23 suppliers with payouts and its directors with how it was meeting its contract obligations. Butter was reaching the Wellington market, and the anticipated completion of the phone line would soon create that vital facility for 'rapid communication with the outside world'.[134] In 1909 the big Wellington creamery Hill and Barton introduced a new fast, shallow-draught, Picton-built steam launch as another link in their extensive cream collection operation in Queen Charlotte Sound.[135] Production increased and the number of cooperatives grew.[136] In the year ended 30 April 1911 two Sounds butter factories produced 7 tonnes of butter.

The factories worked to increase the rate of cream collections, both to stop the spoilage as the cream stood awaiting pick-up and to lure farmers away from competitors. The Sounds Co-operative Dairy Company's launch collected the cream every second day, but as supply increased, daily collections were envisaged.[137] The Linkwater factory picked up cream from specified spots three times weekly, with suppliers paying three shillings a trip.[138] In 1911 the new manager offered more competitive rates and was prepared to send his Wells' Whakatahuri-built launch, *Whareatea*, to any part of the Sounds. He covered Pelorus and Kenepuru sounds on alternate days.[139]

Outside competition arrived when the Marlborough Dairy Factory opened in 1914. Its central position in the district allowed it to capitalise on the Blenheim–Wellington shipping that came up the Ōpawa River, and on the nearby Picton–Blenheim railway line. It could make collections in its new motor van, picking up milk and cream from Havelock and the Sounds to the lower Wairau and Blenheim. Its up-to-date Topliss churn could make 570 kilograms of butter in one operation; its buttermilk and cream pumps, ice-making plant, retail sales to Wellington and export plans dwarfed anything Paradise Bay could offer.[140]

Meanwhile, the Sounds Co-op struggled to make high-grade butter with cream of varying quality. It continued to operate at least until 1924, but Pelorus Sound farmers increasingly sent cream to the Marlborough factory via the Havelock mail launch.

Harry Williams' recollections put the whole venture into perspective. Paradise Bay was a small butter factory that later became tourist accommodation.[141] In about 1917 Harcourt Williams, Harry's father, recognised the limited future of dairying in the area and sold his cows and pigs (which ate the skimmed milk) and increased his sheep flock.[142]

He was well behind the trend. Between 1884 and 1890, with much of the land still unopened for settlement, sheep numbers increased from 47,000 to 61,000. This number more than doubled over the next decade[143] and new crossbreeds were in demand. Individual flock sizes varied considerably,[144] but by 1905 Sounds farmers saw sheep as the way to make money,[145] and sheep numbers continued to rise rapidly.[146] By 1915, sheep were being shipped to Wanganui and substantial numbers were being sent to the Picton Freezing Works.[147]

Exaggeration about the feed the land produced, the fertility of even high ground and its carrying capacity accompanied such developments. Pelorus farmers, ran one claim, could run three to seven sheep per acre all year round — and then had difficulty disposing of them in winter because they were 'so grossly fat'.[148] The extraordinarily high lambing rates, even on the rigorous slopes of Tory Channel's steep southern side, demonstrated, claimed another, the advantages of not overstocking and of good fencing and, more generally, the Sounds' valuable grazing country where good fencing allowed large numbers.[149] Farmers on this land, one newspaper reported, could lamb early — with ewes in good condition, bad weather was not the scourge it was thought to be.[150] Today, we know that it was only the early flushes of grass after burning that permitted such stocking rates, and that over time even good country ran only about two sheep to the acre.[151]

The external environment favoured sheep farming. An attempt in 1871 to start a tinned meat factory in Pelorus Sound proved abortive,[152] but the first frozen meat export to England in 1882 proved 'a turning point in New Zealand's economic history, and for sheep farming'.[153] While the frozen meat trade was not consistently profitable until the mid-1890s, the 'marvellous' trade had commentators anticipating that the country's farmers could expect solid profit from 'every sheep fattened on the matchless grass of this fine country'.[154] The meat trade burgeoned — 2.3 million carcasses in 1895 had risen 5.8 million in 1910 — creating a 'profitable outlet for . . . surplus sheep' that before might previously have fetched only a small sum for tallow. The typically small Sounds farm was becoming viable.

THE FROZEN MEAT TRADE SPAWNED freezing works all over New Zealand, and the Sounds were no exception. In 1891 the experienced Nelson Brothers[155] established the Wairau Freezing Company at Spring Creek, some 23 kilometres from Picton. Carcasses were taken to Picton, frozen, then shipped. Sounds farmers, envisaging 'a brilliant future', promised their support.[156] That year, too, punts (that 'economical and reliable mode of transport'), which could carry up to 300 sheep each, were used to send sheep to the works. Towed by a steamship, the punt reached Havelock within a few hours; handling was minimal and the sheep arrived at the works in good condition.[157] It cost only 1d a head, a rather better rate than the 3d for wethers and 2½d for ewes that it cost to get a mob to Wellington.[158]

A Picton-based frozen meat industry took off after the Nelson Brothers brought the Dunedin-based *Prince of Wales* to Picton as a freezer ship. The following year the Tyser Line, already a big carrier of agricultural and other cargo to London,[159] began the first direct Picton–London frozen-meat shipments.[160] The Nelson Brothers, with difficulties in sourcing adequate supplies, sold out in 1899 to the Christchurch Meat Company (which became the New Zealand Refrigerating Company Ltd in 1916). That company bought 300 acres (120 ha) of land in Shakespeare Bay for a modern meatworks and for holding paddocks. Killing began on 21 January 1900.[161] East Indiaman *Edwin Fox* was used as a freezer ship until 1905, when the plant's own freezing facilities became operational.

Prince of Wales, the first ship to act as a freezer unit for the thriving Picton freezing works.
PICTON HERITAGE AND WHALING MUSEUM, COURTESY PICTON HISTORICAL SOCIETY

Further competition eventuated. Stock driven south to Kaikōura and Canterbury could bring in high prices;[162] other stock went to the Wanganui saleyards.[163] In 1902 the Picton works was putting through about 30 per cent of the total exported. By 1912, almost 94,000 sheep were killed annually at the works.[164] At last farmers in the Sounds had a viable outlet for their sheep.

The trade put welcome cash into the economy. Some farmers spent on better grasses and on the long-wools and crossbreeds (good for meat and for wool) that New Zealand farmers were demanding.[165] David Godsiff worked with the stud Lincoln sheep breed that his father, Henry, had bought in about 1879.[166] In 1892 a new consignment of crossbreed sheep with a good freezing carcass and a 'good payable fleece' typified the new breeds flooding onto the market.[167] Six years later further breeds well suited to the local environment became available, including the Halfbred (a Merino crossed with a Romney or an English Leicester). It was bred especially for New Zealand conditions, had a very good constitution and did extremely well on Sounds wetlands, producing a good fat leg of mutton.[168]

Such benefits did not escape the *Pelorus Guardian*. Mr and Mrs D. Wells in Four Fathom Bay, who had begun by having to pay the government £2 per acre for milling rights to valueless timber, were running 1000 Lincoln and Halfbred sheep by 1894.[169] By the end of the first decade of the twentieth century, Sounds breeding ewes were said to be in demand, and the quality of the mutton and lamb and the thriving freezing industry attracted attention.[170]

The frozen meat trade brought other economic spinoffs. Early in 1903 the Peranos (whose name would soon become more associated with whaling than transport) built a new steam launch, *Waitohi*, the biggest in the Sounds, to take sheep to the Shakespeare Bay works.[171] By 1910 the Anchor Company's new ships, *Alexander* and *Waimea*, were taking consignments also. The Union Steamship Company's older *Monowai* carried them on deck in large pens all forward of the bridge. A pungent smell of sheep pervaded the ship, and the decks were so filthy that the animals kept losing their footing. Similarly, not all passengers appreciated the little Sounds trader, *Manaroa*, carrying sheep in her hold.[172]

IN 1901 THE GOVERNMENT IMPORTED a small number of Angora goats as breeding stock. The country's papers lost no time in enthusing about the animal. Its close cropping kept weeds under control and killed undergrowth, and it provided rich milk, good leather and welcome manure. The goats made good pets as well as good game for sportsmen.[173] In 1906, having already established an experimental breeding farm at Bickerstaffe in the Kaipara district, the government set up a second station on Motuara Island.

It was not an entirely straightforward operation. The light timber on the western slopes was cleared easily, but mānuka elsewhere had trunks over a foot thick. Harvey Turner, appointed caretaker of the Angora goats' 'sanctuary' and of Ship Cove, was primarily responsible for keeping the island free of tauhinu. The department built him a comfortable cottage, the fences and yards were 'an object lesson in sustainability' and a pure-bred angora buck was crossed with local nannies that Robert Ewing, owner of a grazing run in Resolution Bay, caught from the many running wild on Cape Jackson.[174]

Within a year there were 200 goats on Motuara and plans were afoot to increase the area to accommodate more. Demand exceeded supply, and as goats were liberated around Picton and Blenheim (as well as elsewhere in the country) there was speculation on a possible meat market.[175] But in 1908, having spent an estimated £283 on 'improvements',[176] government decided that Motuara Island was too inaccessible and too free of the blackberry and briar needed as goat fodder to function properly as an experimental station.[177] Two years later fat lambs were on the island and the goats had been transferred to Bickerstaffe. In 1913 the eastern side of Motuara Island was declared a scenic reserve, and by 1915 it was a sanctuary for native birds that elsewhere were shot as game.[178] Any hopes for new livelihoods were extinguished.

HOWEVER, AS EARLY AS THE 1890s, some settlers were doing well enough to indulge in some discretionary expenditure. Thomas Mills, sawmiller, dairy farmer, then sheep farmer, had a 12-room residence at Hopai Bay on his several-thousand-acre estate.[179] The walks and flower gardens at the 'superb residence' at Mary's Bay (part of the Homewood Run) demonstrated the owner's taste and energy.[180] Within a few years of his arrival, William Macefield would be running 3000 sheep over Manaroa's 2000 acres (809 ha). He and his mother lived in a homestead 'built in the old English style', and he was soon able to take time off for jaunts in his recreational Una boat.[181] In the early twentieth century David Godsiff's stallion and breeding mares gave his sons a dozen or so mounts to choose from.[182]

These places must have been havens for homesick new settlers in the raw, burned land, but they are unreliable as indicators of any wider prosperity. Better ones are the

McNabb's garden at Glenlee, Crail Bay, Te Hoiere Pelorus Sound. This would later become one of the well-known Sounds accommodation houses. To visitors, the sheltered English-style garden, with its little fence, must have seemed a welcome shelter against the wilderness around them.
MARLBOROUGH HISTORICAL SOCIETY, 0000.200.2

30 new 'oil-launches' that Sounds residents owned in 1904.[183] These were taking hold all over the country, and Pākehā ownership in the Sounds grew rapidly. In 1906, too, mutton and wool buyers were noticing the improved quality of Sounds sheep, and the desirable *Danthonia* was becoming established in the hills and valleys. 'Sounds settlers, after many years of vicissitudes, may now be considered comfortable, with the prospect of their land continuing to rise in value', the Department of Lands and Survey reported that year. It also noted, ominously or presciently, that the rise was 'not altogether from [the land's] productive power, but from the desire of retired people and caterers for the tourists to become possessed of land in this exceptionally beautiful district'.[184]

In 1908 the department continued the good-news story: healthy prices for wool, cattle, sheep and produce were encouraging farmers to get another 7000 acres (2833 ha) of bush land under cultivation; thousands more acres would have been broken in had bushmen been available; and farmers' improvements to their land were almost twice the level required by legislation.[185]

Some of this new farming community, then, were establishing a solid existence. The dwellings did not measure up to those of Nelson's upper crust, but the holdings, as the following advertisement suggests, were substantial. In 1911 a block of 930 acres (376 ha) — 200 acres freehold, the rest leased in perpetuity at an annual rent of £13 2s 2d — that formed 'one of finest and best situated properties in Pelorus Sound' was up for sale. Fifty acres (20 ha) were under plough, 800 (324 ha) in grass, the rest was bushed. The property ran 800 breeding ewes, 700 hoggets, six horses and some cattle. There was a seven-room house, a sheep dip, a woolshed, outbuildings, implements; a post office and phone were handy, two Wellington–Picton steamers called weekly so the 3–4 tonnes of chaff per acre could be shipped direct to Wellington, and a creamery was 'within reach'. Pelorus Sound tourist traffic was rapidly increasing — 'a golden harvest could be induced to roll in for eight months of the year . . .' The asking price was £6500.[186]

Today, we might be interested in why such an attractive proposition was being sold. In 1916 the vice-president of the Marlborough Farmers' Union was blithely optimistic: in 'the early days' anyone setting out for the Sounds 'was put down as an born idiot' but a 'good future' was in the offing, particularly if people listened to the advice of the Department of Agriculture's visiting experts.[187]

But however healthy the sheep and the wool prices might have been, many Sounds farmers struggled, their situation largely invisible amid the promotional

ABOVE The substantial-looking Mulcock house, at Bulwer, outer Pelorus Sound, was already built when Edward Mulcock bought it in 1903. By then, the 15 people living in the bay were served by a post office where mail arrived, its timing dependent on the tide, on alternate days via casual steamers plying to and from Havelock. PICTON HERITAGE AND WHALING MUSEUM, COURTESY PICTON HISTORICAL SOCIETY

BELOW Homewood, Te Hoiere Pelorus Sound, undated. The cluster of buildings and the boats in the bay suggest something of an established existence. Almost all of the hills were subsequently cleared. PICTON HERITAGE AND WHALING MUSEUM, COURTESY PICTON HISTORICAL SOCIETY

partisanship of the local papers. They were small farmers, initially operating a 'peasant economy' on what were little more than subsistence farms, attempting to sell tiny amounts of produce from their homes, often on 'a near barter basis'.[188] Men needing to establish their own farms sought paid work on the bigger runs, tried to find other contract work, diversified where they could.

Yet lack of capital to effect improvements or improve their stocking rates too often held families back.[189] And whatever was done, the basic problems remained — poor land with a low carrying capacity, largely unsuited to cattle, and overrun with the mānuka, tauhinu, fern and bracken that by 1908 was still growing over a 'great deal' of the Sounds, and which today will still rapidly regenerate on open country.[190]

In 1909 the homes in Tory Channel's Hitaua Bay and Te Weka had well-cultivated gardens.[191] Launches and big steamers passed close in, and a phone line to Te Awaiti ensured that 'it is never really lonely'. But that was not everyone's experience. Queen Charlotte Sound in particular was a 'hard country from which to make a living'.[192] Long-running advertisements of land for sale with no takers suggest unprofitable, unwanted holdings. The bays towards the outer north-west of the main sound are south-facing and lose the sun early in winter. In 1910 there was still no phone line and the little steamers such as Captain Henry Fisk's mailboat *Torea*, long employed on the Wellington–Blenheim–Sounds run, had become rusted relics on Waitohi Beach. Captain Bowden's *Gannet*, delivering mail and taking out produce, came only once a week; those without a launch had to summon help by lighting a fire. '[T]he fern and scrub and bare hillsides give a sterner aspect to the landscape; the shadows are more sombre . . . The settler learns that his bread must be wrested from these hills.'[193]

The small Blackwood Bay (Tahuahua) settlement had the vital minimum number of children needed to retain its aided school, but the Almyers, who from 1899 had cleared and laboriously established pasture, were finding much of their 292 acres (118 ha) of poor beech land unusable and incapable of sustaining two families. Ruakaka Bay had only two homes and an abandoned cherry orchard. The earlier busyness that antimony mining (see Chapter 4) had brought to the inner Endeavour Inlet was gone, reduced to a post office, one bungalow, an accommodation house and a few further homes at the head of the inlet. The old wharf had been reduced to three or four piles on which a rough jetty had been fashioned.[194]

Reality was hard. 'North and south winds tear straight up and down the inlet and it's too far from Picton,' wrote a *Marlborough Express* reporter.[195] Moreover, with the gold rush finished, Picton's 'magnificence' was itself in decline. Its present inhabitants '[were turning] their eyes to the misty pages of the future and look[ing] for the grandeur that is to arrive with the completion of the Main Trunk Line, the establishment of a Naval Base, and other entrancing but mistily outlined dreams of a great day to come'.[196]

Māori, land alienation and the reserves

In the 1840s, whaling, farming and trading had allowed Māori to begin to create a niche for themselves in the new Pākehā economy. From the 1860s, despite the limited reserve land available to them, some Māori established orchards.[197] They also ran cattle and pigs and grew potatoes and a range of other crops. But by the early 1870s, as the new settlers established their own farms, the market for Māori produce and animals declined and Māori, like the Europeans, were finding cropping uneconomic on its own. By the mid-1880s, Sounds Māori had increased the area sown in grass and significantly increased their sheep numbers so the majority of Māori-owned sheep in the Marlborough/Nelson district were in the Sounds, with the largest flock on Arapaoa Island. This, however, was not on Māori reserve land.[198]

That qualification is important. Tracts of land had been put aside in the Sounds as occupation reserves for Māori when the New Zealand Company and then the government made their purchases. These were not like endowment or trust reserves or the tenths reserves created in other parts of Te Tau Ihu. Rather, Grey, in relation to the Waitohi Purchase, stipulated that there be 'sufficient land for Maori to run their future operations'. In the Waipounamu Purchases 1853–56 in the Sounds, 'certain places' were to be reserved for groups to live. In some places iwi agreed to the blocks to be established, but in Queen Charlotte Sound, as elsewhere, politics, poor process and misperceptions of the extent to which the iwi valued the land underlay the allocations of the occupation reserves.[199]

Simply put, the reserves they had been given were too small for Māori to farm successfully. Moreover, while the Europeans had purchased what was judged to be good land with the best access, Māori reserves were too often on inaccessible, steep, bush-covered land whose fertility was dubious.[200] And without capital, they were unable to effect improvements.

In time, poverty saw much reserve land alienated through sales to private individuals, or acquired by government for scenic or road reserves. A survey of some

Queen Charlotte Sound occupation reserves. Of the almost 19,000 acres, 3050 acres were at Waikawa, 8192 acres were in other parts of Queen Charlotte Sound, and 5957 acres were on Arapawa (Arapaoa) Island and on the shores of Tory Channel. The final 1568 acres were at Port Gore. Not included here are the reserves subsequently set aside for the 'landless' natives.
TREATY OF WAITANGI TRIBUNAL, *TE TAU IHU O TE WAKA A MAUI: REPORT ON NORTHERN SOUTH ISLAND CLAIMS*, VO. 2 (WELLINGTON: LEGISLATION DIRECT, 2008)

of the reserves on the eastern side of Queen Charlotte Sound shows that, despite Māori farming abilities, the nature of the reserves prevented much economic participation in the new Pākehā society.

Initially, Māori may not have been entirely dissatisfied with the reserve land. They had had some say in where the reserves were sited, but those early preferences were dictated by a range of considerations, including historical associations and access to bush or to the sea where they could fish, or where the land nearby remained unoccupied and available for Māori traditional use. So the economic limitations of what they had chosen may not have been apparent.[201] Some recipients of reserve land made good through milling or farming, or by leasing the land.[202] But those without capital who wanted to farm for a living were in for a difficult time.

In Queen Charlotte Sound and Tory Channel, including Arapaoa Island and Port Gore, a total of 18,767 acres (7595 ha) had been set aside in nine occupation reserves.[203] Only five were bigger than 1000 acres (404 ha). Two were 200–300 acres (81–121 ha). Only the smallest, at Whatamongo, had flat land.[204] There were also reserves at Pelorus and Kaituna.

The Waikawa reserve was over 2500 acres (1012 ha) and had been intended to compensate the 'ousted Waitohi residents'. It was initially given communally but this changed in 1889 when the Native Land Court divided up the reserve and its village area; further partitions would occur from 1904.[205] The intention of the court in enacting the Native Lands Act 1865 was to convert land from being communally owned to individually owned, ensuring that no parcel of land had more than 10 named owners, making it easier for Pākehā to transact purchases.

In a community of 89 people, the apportionment averaged out at only about 30 acres (12 ha) per person, of which only 3 acres were at sea level and only two were cultivable. As we have seen, reserve land was of 'indifferent character, chiefly steep hillsides, with small patches, suitable for Native cultivation, scattered here and there on the shores of the Sound'.[206] Additionally, the move from Waitohi cost Māori some of the best farming land in the Sounds. The exchange of land also removed them from what would become a centre of European commercial activity.

In the two Port Gore reserves, created for Ngāti Hinetuhi and Ngāti Apa, the land rose from small flats on the coast to steep, high hills; again, Māori were settled far from other employment opportunities.[207] In the inner Pelorus, the Kaiowahine and Rangiawea reserves (200 and 100 acres respectively) and the 68 acres at Oruapuputa provided 6–8 acres per person.[208]

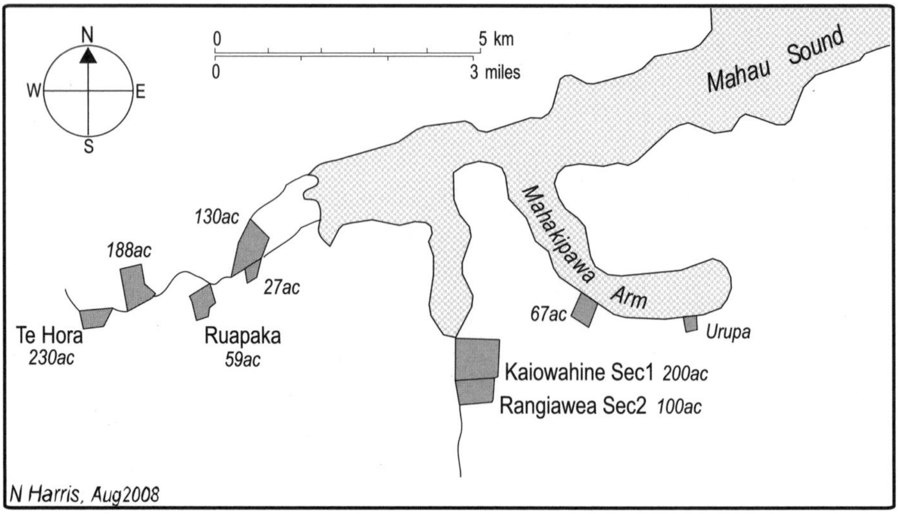

Pelorus occupation reserves close to Havelock. Our story concerns particularly the Kaiowahine and Rangiawea reserves (200 and 100 acres respectively) and the 68 acres at Oruapuputa allocated to Ngāti Kuia and Rangitāne. Ngāti Kuia were also allocated several town sections, one of which may have been one of the sections near the Kaituna River mouth. Now significantly modified by reclamation, this area was particularly important in the iwi's history. TREATY OF WAITANGI TRIBUNAL, *TE TAU IHU O TE WAKA A MAUI: REPORT ON NORTHERN SOUTH ISLAND CLAIMS*, VO. 2 (WELLINGTON: LEGISLATION DIRECT, 2008)

THE SETTING ASIDE OF THE 'landless natives' reserves' is a longer story. The inadequacy of the Māori reserves set aside as an economic basis in the 1840s and 1850s had, by the late 1880s, become a matter of concern to some in the government as well as to Māori. Of particular note was the situation of Rangitāne and Ngāti Kuia living in Pelorus Sound and Wairau, who simply did not have enough land on which to support themselves. 'Landless natives' reserves' were eventually established for these largely Kurahaupō people. (Sounds Māori were not the only ones affected. In the Buller area, Rangitāne in particular were hard-hit, and 'landless' tribes in the Croisilles Harbour area and on the West Coast also needed assistance.)[209]

In 1884 Teone Hiporaiti of Ngāti Kuia and 20 others, showing an unflagging resilience in the face of an unfamiliar and unresponsive European bureaucracy, petitioned the government. They were in a dire situation. In 1856 Ngāti Kuia had signed a sale document, understanding its terms and, taking Nelson as an example of the benefits signing could confer, expecting that Pākehā settlement would bring wealth and mana to the district. Government agents, too, had promised roads (attractive because of access to markets and employment opportunities), schools and hospitals. Some Ngāti Kuia had been promised opportunities to repurchase land, and there had been promises of Crown grants to two chiefs.[210] The tribe sought to gain the Queen's protection. Their petition set out in dignified terms the position to which they had been reduced. The very small portion of land reserved for them had reduced them to 'a suffering people. We pray for an extra portion of the land to be given us, that we and our descendants might be enabled to live.'[211]

In 1887 Alexander Mackay, then a Native Land Court judge whom government tasked with investigating the situation, found that an estimated 245 Kurahaupō people in Pelorus and the Wairau — 57 Rangitāne, 74 Ngāti Kuia, 48 Ngāti Rarua, 22 Ngāti Toa and Ngāti Koata from the Pelorus and Wairau areas, 33 he described as 'half-castes' belonging to the Ngāti Kuia, Rangitāne and other tribes (these included Ngāti Rārua, Ngāti Toa, Ngāti Koata and Ngāti Tama, as well as those he referred to as 'Ngatiawa' and 'Ngatihinetu'), and 13 Ngāi Tahu (11 living in the Pelorus and two on D'Urville Island)[212] — had been allocated land that amounted to 6–8 acres per person and, had they not repurchased Crown land to supplement this amount, they would have been very badly off.

Mackay also pointed out that Māori needed more land now than they had at the time of the initial allocation; moreover, European occupancy and the fact that the new settlers could cut off or 'interfere with' Māori food supplies further reduced their ability to earn a living.

In 1888, with Mackay's report in front of it, the government had to do something for these landless people. But it found that remedying the problem was problematic.[213] Liberal perceptions had it that Māori were not turning land 'to good account or endeavouring to make something out of it for themselves and for family';[214] Lands and Survey practice, therefore, was to provide more land for Pākehā than for Māori use. Individual European families had strong, binding relationships with Māori they knew, but a *Pelorus Guardian* editorial in 1894 presumably struck a chord with its readers:

> Māories still own nearly twelve million acres of land and the young [European] men who have been born and bred in that locality are also landless . . . whilst justice is done to the Natives, a very great injustice is done to those who would make sterling settlers.[215]

No thought seems to have been given to the government buying back private land, although in the early twentieth century it did move to break up some large estates in southern Marlborough.[216] Meanwhile, by 1896 the number of Māori affected had grown to 681, at which point the government determined that anyone born after that date was not eligible.[217]

In the Pelorus area in 1891, four years after Mackay's report, a committee of Māori was formed, comprising, as Rangitāne kaumātua Richard Bradley describes it, 'the original half-caste George MacDonald, son of that early Picton settler Hemi Whiro (headman for Ngāti Kuia), and Meihana [Martin] Mason — the headmen of these families'.[218] The other committee members were officials, including Crown ranger Joshua Rutland. They set off from Havelock in the sawmilling company Brownlee and Co.'s tug SS *Pelorus* to begin identifying available land on which the people could settle. The *Pelorus* went first to Okoha at the head of Anakoha Bay and Cockle Cove in inner Port Gore, where land rose 'to great prominence'. They then rounded Cape Jackson to look at land in Endeavour Inlet.[219]

The choices were limited. Bradley comments:

> Quite often, [the Māori committee] would say, we like that area over there because they knew they had an old kāinga there and it was a headland or because they still had an affinity for the land. And the ranger would say, 'Oh no, we need that for a scenic reserve.'[220]

Kipa Hemi Whiro and his wife, Haromi Kikiroa or Kiharoa. Kipa Whiro and his sister Ina Key fought to retain rights to harvest tītī from Te Kakaho and Nukuwaiata (the Chetwode Islands) and Motungarara Tītī Island. Kipa and his brother Te Pou were the first trustees of the mutton bird islands after an agreement was reached with the government in 1910, allowing Ngāti Kuia families with a permit to harvest tītī. In 1933 a second agreement nominated Wiremu Waaka and Te Mutini Meihana as trustees. In 1964, harvesting tītī was prohibited. PICTON HERITAGE AND WHALING MUSEUM, COURTESY PICTON HISTORICAL SOCIETY

It is not clear exactly how much any preferences expressed on this trip influenced the eventual government allocations, but in 1894 the process of settling the 6328 acres (2561 ha) of reserves in the Sounds began. In Queen Charlotte Sound, land was chosen at two sites in Endeavour Inlet — in Big Bay and Edgecombe Bay, near the western entrance to the inlet. The nine children of Kura Huruata and Alymer Kenny were allocated 360 acres at the head of the Bay of Many Coves adjacent to the existing Ruakaka Reserve. At Okoha, in the Outer Pelorus, 50 Ngāti Kuia selected 1924 acres where they, and some families from Rangitāne, Ngāti Koata and Ngāi Tahu settled. At Port Gore, two blocks totalling 518 acres were established either side of the existing Otaki reserve and accommodated 18 owners, all members of Rangitāne. In Kenepuru 1138 acres were allocated mostly among Ngāti Kuia.[221]

Along with another 28 Rangitāne who settled in Big Bay (Endeavour Inlet), Peter Hohua MacDonald, a man of considerable note and stature,[222] and his wife established themselves at Punaruawhiti in the innermost part of Big Bay, where, Richard Bradley noted, 'the sun goes from the land at about three o'clock'. 'It wasn't a thriving agricultural centre,' Bradley notes with some irony.

> There were no boats going from Endeavour Inlet to Picton. The perception, carried on to the present day, was that the land didn't have to be good quality, because the natives could live off the land. But the value of the land was in the timber, so the farming consisted of cutting out native timber because that was what was valuable, and running a few cows for milk to sell. But of course, the difficulty of getting it from Endeavour Inlet in a dinghy all the way to Picton meant that cutting timber didn't work, so our old people were basically subsistence farming.[223]

The MacDonald cows got ill or died from eating the ubiquitous tutu.[224] Landslips were common after trees were felled. 'Of course, when you cut the timber down, the land became unstable and started sliding away into the sea,' says Bradley. In 1910 one huge slip and then another left the home engulfed by a foot of mud and sludge.[225] Half the farming area had gone. They had no resources or building materials. 'It was just too much for them to cope with so they moved to Picton.'[226]

In 1896 a reserve was identified in Tennyson Inlet and allocated to 175 Sounds Māori, but Marlborough's Commissioner of Land halted the proposed reserve, saying, 'It would be a stupendous folly to allot this land to Landless Natives.' No reason was recorded. A few other sites were considered in the Wairau but nothing eventuated. Then in 1921, without consultation or negotiation, those who had been promised allocations were paid a few pounds per promised acre and that was that. In 1923 the 6000-acre block in Tennyson Inlet was declared a scenic reserve.[227]

The final years of the century saw 308 people still unplaced. In 1899, 10,000 acres (4047 ha) at the remote Port Adventure on Rakiura Stewart Island was approved in principle. The land was allocated in 1905, but once again the reserve came to nothing and those involved were neither compensated nor given land elsewhere.[228]

The South Island Landless Natives Act 1906 provided for new blocks to be formally reserved and individual titles granted. The prospective owners, however, had to agitate before titles were finally issued during 1910 and 1911. Other matters remained unresolved, including eligibility for land allocation. In 1917 a judicial inquiry recommended that an additional 135 people be added to the 'landless' list, and monetary compensation be given if land was not available.[229]

In the landless natives' reserves, each adult was allocated 40 acres and each child 20, though land held elsewhere would be deducted from these totals.[230] Three acres were allowed for a homestead section and the rest was included in communal land. It is unclear how the amount was determined. Interesting comparisons can be drawn with other land allocations: the 30 acres per person allocated at the time of the occupation reserves; the 50 acres per man, woman and child legislated for under the Native Land Act 1873; Alexander Mackay's 1881 comment that 100 acres per Pākehā farmers was barely viable;[231] or the 25 acres of first-class land per head, 50 of second-class or 100 acres of third-class defined as sufficient under the Native Land Purchase and Acquisition Act 1893.[232] The experience of one European farmer in the 1930s who was struggling on 2000 acres of better Sounds land provides another perspective.[233]

Regardless of quantity, the quality was poor. Descriptions of the allocated land today note the steep, hilly or rugged and often southern-facing slopes, the marginal amount of flat land in some, the flood-prone nature of others, and remoteness and inaccessibility. The remote Okoha reserve, for instance, was a long way from where the owners usually lived in Havelock and Canvastown. Already poor, Māori had no capital to sink into the work required. When the land was partitioned among four families in 1914, those families bore 'enormous' survey costs. The result was often absentee ownership.[234] At Port Gore, on land as poor as that at Okoha and possibly more isolated, some were reduced to subsistence farming.

The Native Land Act 1909 replaced the specificity about what Māori should be given as reserve land with broad generalisations about sustainability — land allocated had to be adequate to ensure that Māori had sufficient total interests in Māori land to maintain themselves.[235] Though it purported to be aimed at protecting Māori rights, under this legislation much undeveloped Māori land was sold and huge chunks of the reserves sold or acquired by the Crown.[236]

IMPOVERISHMENT AND MARGINALISATION deriving from the progressive alienation of reserve land had been occurring over decades. In 1862 and 1865, part of where Te Ātiawa were living in the Waikawa reserve was leased; from 1889 the land was divided and awarded to individual Māori owners. Small amounts of land were then sold in the 'buying surge' of 1909–10,[237] though those sales had nothing like the impact of those that took place from 1963.[238] In Tory Channel some land was leased early on, and private purchasing from 1910 to 1920 saw significant parts of the two mainland reserves alienated. The land in Port Gore was largely lost in sales from 1912 to 1929.[239] In Pelorus Sound, Oruapuputa survived in Māori ownership until 1971, but most of the rural land in the district purchased by Māori was sold by 1915.[240]

Elsewhere, the loss of land was facilitated by the way individualised titles were determined under the Native Land Court. Individuals' new legal rights were poorly defined and recorded, and the government's failure to actively protect Māori ownership further fragmented the holdings. Te Ātiawa, for instance, whose reserves until 1899 had been 'communal in nature', found that '[c]ommunal interests were no longer represented. It was easy for sales to take place . . . there were no longer any rights for iwi.'[241] 'What is most upsetting to us,' Anthony Keenan submitted in the Waitangi Tribunal hearing, 'is how quickly the land went from us. We lost all this land by 1910.'[242]

As Native Land Court rules of succession made the titles increasingly crowded, owners had little option but to sell and to adopt a European lifestyle — but without an adequate economic basis to help ensure success.[243]

MĀORI RESERVES WERE FURTHER ERODED when, under the Land Act 1892, the government took, without compensation, 20-metre-wide coastal reserves along lakes, coasts and waterways, ostensibly for future road construction. Despite protest by Native Land Court judge Alexander Mackay, hundreds of acres were taken in the eastern and western Marlborough Sounds (including on D'Urville Island and the smaller islands). This effectively removed the only flat land Māori had for housing, cultivation and boatsheds, while the permitted public access over the riparian strip lowered the land's monetary value. Very little of this land was ever used for roads, yet none was ever returned.[244] Nor were roading reserves compulsorily imposed on European-owned coastal lands in the Sounds. Today, some residents still hold 'Blue Water titles to Mean High Water Springs' and can prevent public access to the beaches that front their properties.

The Scenery Preservation Acts 1903 and 1906 enabled identified land to be taken for scenic reserves (and compensation given). This added significantly to the land losses for Te Ātiawa. While today we might applaud the 18,000-plus acres (7284 ha) of scenic reserves in the Sounds, they were created by at best questionable procedures and in the face of Māori opposition. In Tory Channel, for instance, the 515-acre (208 ha) scenic reserve at Ngaruru was created in the early 1920s over long, eloquent and reasoned protest that embodied the sense of loss as land and livelihood were taken:

> We would respectfully point out to you, sir, that practically all the native land of any value to us has now been taken for scenic or other purposes . . . We would point out that no matter what monetary value you gave us in exchange, you cannot adequately reimburse us for the loss that we will suffer.[245]

Today, 88 acres (36 ha) remain in Māori ownership.

As Pākehā rapidly took up land adjacent to Māori reserves, new issues arose, such as fencing. On the one hand, Māori wanted to allow their pigs, whose breeding and running were critical to their livelihood, to wander. But this invited trouble with their European neighbours. And how also, without fences, would they prevent settler cattle trespassing on their land on which they already struggled to earn a living? In 1861, with significant hostility growing, Alexander Mackay had the following put into the local newspaper:

> Whereas certain persons have, at various times, annoyed the Natives residing at Queen Charlotte and Pelorus Sounds, by burning houses, stealing fruit, and permitting their cattle to trespass on the Native Reserves, and cultivations there situated . . . I hereby inform such persons that all complaints made by the Natives will most strictly be attended

> to, and investigated, and all persons so offending and trespassing will be prosecuted with the utmost rigour of the law.[246]

Another proclamation warned Europeans about hunting pigs on native reserves in Bottles and Daveys bays, Queen Charlotte Sound.[247] As early as 1874 government was being advised by Mackay of the dire situation:

> . . . as the settlement of the country progresses the natives are necessarily restricted to narrower and narrower limits, until they no longer possess the freedom adapted to their mode of life. The settlers hunt down, for pastime or other purposes, the birds which constituted their food, or, for purposes of improvement, drain the swamps and watercourses from which they obtained their supplies of fish; their ordinary subsistence failing them, and lacking the energy or ability to supplement their means of livelihood by labour, they lead a life of misery and semi-starvation.[248]

As Pākehā pressure for land grew, there are countless instances of government-appointed administrators overriding the interests, wishes, occupation and even ownership of the Māori 'owners' of the occupation reserves.[249] Economic opportunities were increasingly being denied them. Their earlier hunting and gathering was restricted. Like Pākehā, they were having to abandon their mixed cropping and livestock as uneconomic. Their former flourishing provision of market goods was now restricted to growing only enough for their own needs. At the same time, European settlement was increasingly limiting the stock they could run; lack of capital and the difficulties of dealing with poor land meant that Māori struggled with what they were left with.

While state aid was not comprehensive in any sphere, the government did little to foster Māori economic development.[250] In 1863 there was Alexander Mackay's implement scheme providing farming tools; nine years later Māori learned that they were to pay half the cost of whatever carts and implements they bought — not a condition attached to European purchase;[251] the landless natives scheme provided poorly in comparison with the sort of assistance that small-scale Pākehā farmers received under, for example, the Lands for Settlement Act (1892) and the Government Advances to Settlers Act (1894).

In stark contrast to the new settlers, Māori 'were expected to make their own way in the new economic world they were confronted with'.[252] The chairman of Arapaoa Māori Council in 1910 asked pointedly, 'Why does Govt not advance money to the Maori, yet it lends it so readily to the Pakeha?'[253]

Prior to European settlement, Māori had been living in a landscape replete with natural resources. These made up a rich, flourishing ecosystem of birds, fish and plants.[254] They had accepted tiny, isolated, unfarmable reserves of poor-quality land with significant misgivings, because that was the only option on offer.[255] By the end of the 1920s, Māori in the Sounds, along with rural Māori communities elsewhere,[256] were subsisting chiefly on what they could grow, whatever irregular or seasonal employment they could find and, for those who still had holdings, minimal land rents. Many were experiencing considerable economic and social difficulties.[257]

Yet some communities continued to cling to the poor reserve land on which they had been settled. The reserves, as Bradley said, might have those old 'affinities' with the past. They gave access to kaimoana, hunting, forest products, and to the highly valued fishing grounds whose importance increased as further land was lost. Today, the descendants of those people do suggest one positive outcome. The tiny areas of land that, for instance, Ngāti Kuia had, provided a base for whānau to visit and access the area's natural resources.[258]

The loss of land and, with it, tino rangatiratanga (sovereignty), created a profound and lasting cultural loss. 'Land and sovereignty,' writes historian Danny Keenan,

> were the same thing; you can't have one without the other. Te tino rangatiratanga was anchored by whakapapa into ancient landscapes 'posited as living beings, enhanced by founding tūpuna, enshrining ongoing cultural expressions of mana'. The loss of land was an existential loss that cut to the essence of Māori society.[259]

4. Whales, Minerals and Fish

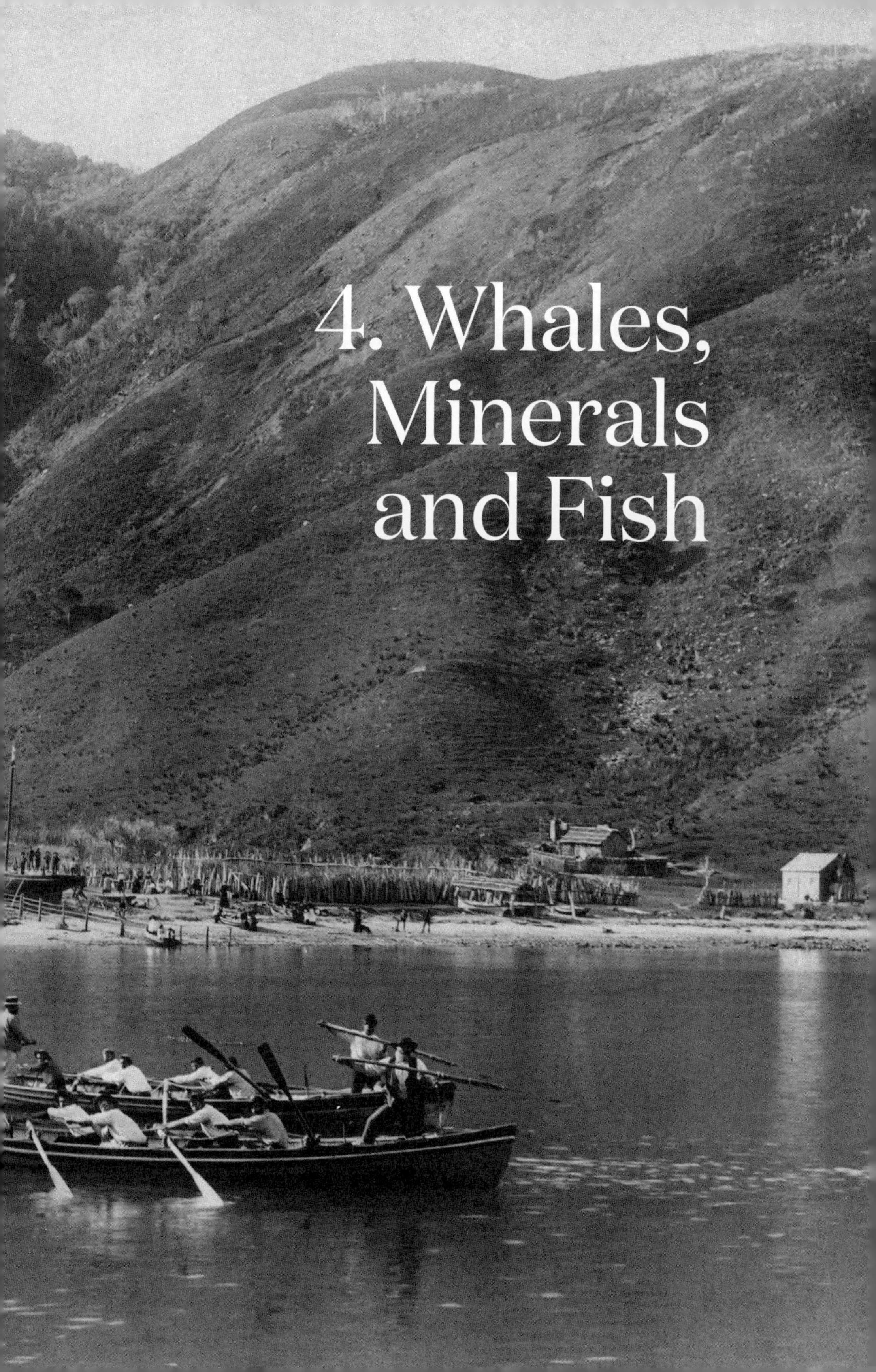

> The northern Marlborough waters would 'teem with purse seine boats'; thousands would be employed using 'high-class machinery'; and 'girls' could make good wages.

From the 1860s and into the twentieth century, provinces made every effort to attract settlers, and the media by and large promulgated the call. At a stage when a lighthouse and a jetty were envisaged as a way of consolidating and encouraging settlement,[1] the *Marlborough Express* over the decades created pictures of the Sounds as a place of great natural wealth and potential profit. Here, ventures other than farming would do well. With local fish for a Wellington market whose tastes ran beyond the tinned variety, fish-curing looked set to thrive. Artificially created oyster beds would cater for the nineteenth century's insatiable demand for this shellfish, and the reintroduction of salmon promised a substantial industry. In the second decade of the twentieth century even whaling was picking up again. Over the years, too, a tiny boat-building industry, using local timbers, turned out the distinctive, elegant Sounds boats, launches and dinghies that settlers used for moving round their world.

Wealth might also derive from the heavily bushed hills that came down to the sea. In 1864 gold was discovered in the Sounds' hinterland and prospectors were drawn into the area. When, in 1872, the vast Queen Charlotte Sound Goldfield was proclaimed after exciting discoveries in Port Gore, newspaper columns were devoted to prospects of rich finds. Substantial lodes of antimony were discovered, and rewarding overseas markets were rapidly envisaged. Even as the elements of the pristine landscape so constantly evoked were being destroyed, the Sounds' romantic settings, their backdrops of dark hills against 'translucent water' on which the shadows of nīkau, beech and 'punga' (probably mamaku, *Cyathea medullaris*) played,[2] were constantly lauded and increasingly available to a growing tourist market.

In 1886 the *Marlborough Express* looked to a rosy future. Picton's fish-curing business it pronounced solidly established; its fish-curing works, flourmill and malthouse would create strong employment and turn out high-quality produce. The snug little town would be thronged with people. There were, the paper concluded, multiple resources and opportunities for all; the industries were examples of how capital and talent could be deployed in directing appropriate investments and developing natural resources.[3]

How did this play out? Brief histories of these ventures provide an opportunity to assess how, and to what extent, the boat-building, whaling, fishing, aquaculture, milling and mining ventures, as well as the embryonic tourism industry addressed in the next chapter, contributed to the settlement of the Sounds.

GIVEN THE SOUNDS' HIGH HEADLANDS and deeply indented bays, boats were essential for day-to-day living. Māori in the Sounds had long built small, workaday craft as well as imposing waka, and they were quick to adapt European-style dinghies and, later, other powered craft for themselves and their families.

Many European settlers, too, were adept at building their own small rowboats, picking out the right timbers for knees, sternposts and planks.[4] Others might buy in from other parts of New Zealand. Nevertheless, a small boat-building industry was long present in the Sounds. From 1869, William Pire Henry Keenan was already making craft in Hitaua Bay.[5] A Mr Nixon in Onapua Bay apparently, in 1896, built a smart, fast little cruising yacht that was finished in Wellington. Rather better known was Benjamin McCauley at Bulwer, who built six boats, among them the *Dove*, *Ofar* and, in 1908, the *Ark*.[6]

There were also commercial ship-building yards. The first, operational in 1873 in the Grove Arm, where Queen Charlotte Sound runs south-west beyond Picton, launched five vessels of 40–60 tonnes.[7] In 1907 Ernest Richard Lane, who came from a

The jetty at Waihinau Bay, near the settlement of Bulwer, Te Hoiere Pelorus Sound. The boat, taken out of the water for careening or repairs, probably belonged to the Irisman Patrick McCauley (also known as Patsy, and not to be confused with Mr McCauley, the employer at the fish plant in Bulwer). After labouring, gold-digging, piloting and working at a sawmill at Crail Bay, McCauley moved to Bulwer in the 1870s, where he farmed, delivered mail and built boats.
ALEXANDER TURNBULL LIBRARY, 1/2-010313-G

boat-building family, set up a yard in Picton and capitalised on the demand for sizeable commercial 'oil-launches'.[8] Lorna Orchard's father, Robert William Wells (known as Claude), whose 'natural talent' allowed him to 'take a pencil and a length of timber and draw a pattern for a curved shape without any guide', built a number of boats and in 1911 set up the only commercial boat yard in Pelorus Sound, at Whakatahuri, where the family also farmed. His elegant and distinctive boats included the *Tanekaha*, made of double-skinned kahikatea. Used as a commercial fishing boat, she was noted for her power, speed and service.[9] Many of his craft, like those of Lane and McCauley, lasted for decades. But these small ventures provided little employment and their overall contribution to the Sounds' boat fleet was small.

'Whaling on modern lines'

On 22 August 1868 James Keenan and party caught the seventh whale that season. One of the largest they had taken that year and worth £300, it was the best catch for a long time. Almost 20 years on, in 1886, he and his party harpooned what was said to be one of the biggest whales then seen in the Sound; in August 1887 a Māori crew from Te Awaiti captured an 85-foot (25.9-metre) whale worth £400. Large parties, sumptuously catered, celebrated such successes with dancing till dawn. Keenan's kill rate increased as he upgraded his equipment, and passengers in the little steamers running up and down the Sound might enjoy the frisson of a chase.[10]

These were highlights but overall, the dramatic decline of right whales that had begun at the end of the 1840s continued. A capture in 1884 was possibly the first in years. By 1907 the average catch had for years been only three whales a month.[11] High prices were paid for whalebone but numbers continued to decline.[12] In 1910 only two or three right whales were taken from Tory Channel over the entire season.[13] No press report of 'unfortunate' years or of the catch of the largest whale in the season, or of 'shy' whales causing poor seasons[14] or of old hands' comments on coastal steamers scaring the whales away could hide the fact that both whale numbers and whale size had been declining for years.

The impact on the Te Awaiti station was marked. Some 'modern' homes, reported one visitor in 1910, had been built among the early bare, functional structures, but the place, he reckoned, functioned primarily as a post and telegraph station where settlers from nearby bays collected their mail, brought in by the little local steamer *Gannet*, then as a sheep station; a whaling station was the least of its purposes.[15]

Industry-wide changes were afoot. Whatever the experience of the Tory Channel whaling industry, in 1909 Lake Falconer Ayson, the Marine Department's chief inspector of fisheries, reported sightings that, after 30 years of little harassment, indicated that whale numbers were on the increase. He argued for 'whaling on modern lines — i.e. from whale factories', which would create important employment opportunities. With whale numbers growing, he reported, anyone interested in whaling with 'properly equipped' shore-based factories should be encouraged. Canada, America and Norway were already extracting not only oil but 'other more valuable products' from the carcasses.[16] New Zealand, he considered, should do the same.

Two years later, in 1911, Joe and Charlie Perano, sons of the erstwhile Picton herring canner Agostino Perano,[17] built a 'spartan' factory in Yellerton Bay, now Te Rua Bay and, presciently, began taking the previously largely ignored humpback whales.[18] A humpback gave less than half the oil of a right whale but there were more of them. In 1912, with their catch doubling from six the previous year to 12, the Peranos moved to Tipi Bay, closer to Cook Strait and the whaling grounds.[19] The Jacksons, Keenans, Nortons and, over the 1915–16 season, the Bergs continued to provide competition,[20] but within a year or two Joe and Charlie Perano were the only Cook Strait whalers.

Meanwhile they were shrewdly investing in soundly based and practical innovations.[21] Their steamer, the 65-foot (20-metre) *Waitohi*, was built in 1903 initially for trading and to take sheep to the Picton freezing works. Now, as the largest steam launch in Sounds, she served as mother ship and tug, pulling the fuel-hungry chasers around Cook Strait.[22] Their new motorised cruisers, each costing £400, were in sharp contrast to the open rowboats still used by the Loves, Jacksons, Nortons and Keenans. In 1912 the Peranos imported the first explosive harpoon-gun to be used in Cook Strait. Fired by a cannon, a barbed harpoon hooked into the whale, and the harpoon's head exploded to kill it. A hit now meant a catch.[23]

By 1916 further investment in their whaling fleet and increases in catch size suggested that things were looking up.[24] The following year the six Perano motorised launches, one of which, Charlie Perano's Picton-built *Cachelot*, could do 29 knots, were whaling from Tory Channel. Two years later the tug *Tuatea* replaced *Waitohi* as the mother ship. Catch and employee numbers grew correspondingly, and 1917 was the most successful season on record. The 200 tonnes of oil from the 57 whales

The Tipi Bay whaling station, Kura Te Au Tory Channel, in 1918, where the installation of steam-driven mincers and digesters had improved oil extraction. The men are standing in a whale's mouth, an adventure also offered to tourists. ALEXANDER TURNBULL LIBRARY, PACOLL-8880

caught was valued at £3800 (almost $500,000 today). By 1919 the Tipi Bay factory employed 16 men: six as whalers, 10 onshore.[25]

The Peranos' focus on sea craft and consequent low investment in the land-based side of their operation meant tough conditions. Stationed high up on one of two sites on the ridge separating Tory Channel from Cook Strait, their lookouts had only their oilskins, gumboots and wide-brimmed felts to protect them against the spray from the waves crashing against the cliffs below and the 'hissing, whining wind'. Smoke from fires, sometimes lit by Joe's wife, Pattie, who watched for whales from the 120-metre hill overlooking Cook Strait, formed prearranged signals to indicate the whales' location and direction of movement.[26]

Work at the Tipi Bay factory involved 12-hour days of hard physical and, from today's perspective, unsavoury labour with improvised tools — ordinary knives were used, so the men flensing and cutting up the blubber became covered with oil.[27] Once the blubber had been boiled down, they didn't waste time burning the carcasses (which was mandated) but towed anything left out to sea and abandoned it to the waiting sharks and raucous gulls.

The men's accommodation was sparse, with the choice of rowing across each day from Te Awaiti or living in tents and a big marquee on site. A bach a little closer to Tory Channel provided further shelter and was something of a social centre, though, not unusually, there was no running water.

The impact of whaling on settlement appears to have been marginal. Whaling provided seasonal employment, particularly for Waikawa Māori, but the sums the crews were paid two decades on suggests that the money would have done little to alleviate the situation of people struggling with poverty or leave them with much to contribute to the local economy.[28] Nor, although in the 1880s Te Awaiti station was something of a tourist destination, can whaling have done much to attract new settlers.

Like rural children elsewhere, whalers' children (mostly Māori) worked at the station, doing adult jobs. They caught fish, smoked them then sold them to a Picton merchant. They shot wild goats on Arapaoa Island, they foraged for semi-wild berries and the wild cape gooseberries that were particularly golden after a burn-off — such expeditions were necessary to supplement household rations.

Canned fish, wet fish and shellfish

In 1865 hundreds of tonnes of herrings stranded on Picton's beach. They putrefied and stank, but the papers were quick to note the commercial quantities and pointed to a potentially profitable industry.[29] People paid vast sums for imported tinned fish,[30] and Picton was ideally placed as a port. In 1873 John Heberley set up Picton's first curing factory and by 1881 his quality 'Picton bloaters' were shipped all over the colony. In the off-season he diversified into a range of other smoked fish.[31]

Competition arrived that year, when Oscar Alfred Norgrove and his brother Horace, Picton entrepreneurs of some standing,[32] emerged from a raft of unsuccessful ventures in partnership with the Whiting brothers. Trading initially as Whiting Bros., they developed a substantial fish-curing business that offered permanent and casual employment.

By 1886 Horace Norgrove, profiting, as had Heberley, from 'the great luminous shoals of herrings that still congregated so conveniently off muddy banks close to the town',[33] seems to have bought out his erstwhile partners. Overcoming the 'trials and vicissitudes' that attended colonial enterprises, Norgrove developed a Picton business whose importance to the town can be seen in the constant and lengthy reporting of the latest developments. On one day alone, several newspaper columns went into extolling his works, worth £4000, that, along with his house, stood on a foreshore reclaimed at the owner's expense. Norgrove had three or four fishing boats built; his nets, imported but tanned in the colony, were worth £100 each; he employed six permanent staff and as many casually. Over the April–September season his six smokehouses could turn out 10,000 cases of fish, each case containing 24 dozen herrings of a quality that took honours in various colonial exhibitions.[34]

Norgrove kept abreast of the times, applying under the Fisheries Encouragement Act 1885 for an available bonus on canned and cured fish exported from the colony — by 1887 his 'far-famed Picton bloater' had reached Sydney.[35] During a temporary hiatus the business appeared to suffer in 1888, Norgrove displayed his usual ingenuity and enterprise by offering to take passengers on the 'Shortest, Best and Cheapest route to Mahakipawa Goldfield' ('Gold! Gold! Gold!' his advertisement proclaimed),[36] and, later, by providing a Sounds passenger service. In 1893 his fish business, once again in good heart and now trading as the Union Preserving Company, continued to send fish around the country and to Australia.

John Heberley's not inconsiderable business lasted until about 1888. By then

Agostino Perano and his sons were in on the act, sending fish, smoked or in brine, to Thompson and Co. in Dunedin, as well as fresh and smoked fish to the Wellington, Picton and Christchurch markets. By 1896 the Perano cured herring business was locally acclaimed.[37]

Within a few more years, however, the herring boom had ended. The Perano sons moved into whaling and trading. Norgrove, as master first of the SS *Phoenix* and then the SS *Elsie*, ran the postal service in Queen Charlotte Sound. He retired in 1904, sold the *Elsie* to Eugenio Charles Perano, and died in Wellington in 1928.

Fish-canning ventures were not limited to Picton. In 1871, pre-dating Heberley's venture, Charles Finnie, a very early settler, reportedly had ambitious plans for competitively priced fish canned in Pelorus Sound. Commentators lauded the idea. Today it seems an extraordinarily audacious venture. His factory would lie among heavily bushed ranges in an almost unpopulated world. Where would he get his materials from, how would they be got in, and the finished product out? Where were his workers and fishermen? Such obvious questions did not deter newspapers from anticipating success. In either event, neither Finnie nor his venture got further mention in local papers until 1880, when his children and a friend were drowned in a boating accident.[38]

In 1885, responding to Sir Julius Vogel's 'Great Public Works' scheme to promote the colony's industries, Joshua Rutland, Crown Lands ranger in Picton, listed sites he thought would be ideal for fishing stations in the Sounds.[39] Over the next 10 years applications were granted for factories in Endeavour Inlet, Ship Cove and Resolution Bay. Nothing eventuated, possibly because applicants were required to furnish £250 necessary capital.[40]

Smith and Coventry's 'fishing establishment' at Bulwer had been running for about a year[41] when, in 1887, a bailiff seized everything to cover debts — the wash boilers, scales, barometer, oars, rope, troughs, fish nets of all sizes, tinning plant, tinned fish, barrels, lead press, machines, soldering irons and so on. Three years on, John Smith, 'Fishcurer at Bulwer', applied for bankruptcy.[42] The problem, according to local MP and member of the New Zealand Legislative Council Charles Houghton Mills, was that the large plant had 'cost hundreds of pounds [and] got the owners into chancery' primarily because the proprietors could not easily communicate with the outside world.[43] Such problems must have undercut so many fledgling Sounds ventures and hopes of constructing livelihoods.

WHILE SOUNDS SETTLERS HAD ALWAYS caught fish as a necessary supplement to their diet, the first sign of a commercial wet-fish industry in Queen Charlotte Sound emerged only in 1884, when a Mr Jones introduced fresh kahawai, crayfish and oysters to Blenheim. Four years later John Heberley (of the herring business) was catching fish mostly outside Tory Channel and sending them twice weekly to Picton and Blenheim, and to the more distant Dunedin market. Other men fishing in Tory Channel were supplying the Picton market, while 'foreigners' were said to be planning a fishing business in Kenepuru.[44] By the end of the 1890s the growing Sounds fresh-fish industry was selling Tory Channel hāpuku in Wellington (for 6d per pound).

The Wellington market was close to Picton, and by then a regular ferry service was operating, so the idea of developing a fresh-fish market in the capital cannot have seemed too daunting. In the distant outer reaches of Pelorus Sound, meanwhile, more ambitious plans were spawned. By 1896 (in a venture that lasted into the first decade of the twentieth century) a Mr McCauley, 'the largest employer in Bulwer' and with 'Home' experience in the industry, employed a 'large' workforce at his fishing station.[45] The men were often away fishing for days at a time.

In 1902 the Hikuraki Fisheries and Electrical Power Co., already running successful fishing operations in the far south, planned a fish-freezing plant in the 'capitally sheltered' waters of Beatrix Bay and its permanent and profitable fishing ground, which had not previously been exploited because of the difficulties in landing fish in Wellington in good condition. Their new steamer was fitted with a freezer and a well, to ensure fish would arrive fresh to market at lower prices.[46] Speeches, demonstrations of the equipment and even a ball marked the plant's opening, although by now it was in Forsyth, not Beatrix, Bay.

The firm changed owners and name when in 1905 F. J. Sullivan, 'Fish, Oyster, Rabbit Salesman and General Commission Agent' from Dunedin (the colony's entrepreneurs had a remarkable capacity for reinvention), took over. At the now Pelorus Refrigerating and Fishing Company all initially appeared well.[47] Sullivan had the works connected by phone, and, because it was a seasonal operation, locals could supply the firm during the winter when the cows had dried off and were well paid for their efforts. (There is one report — the only one to mention Māori — of them catching 1½ tons of blue cod.)[48] The fish were promptly cleaned, packed and frozen before being dispatched to Wellington, or Sydney, where blue cod was in demand.

For a time it all seemed to work, with the firm making good money. However, the firm ceased to operate about 1910, a subsequent attempt to recommission it failed,[49] and in 1915 the Marine Department revoked its licence to use and occupy the foreshore and land below low-water mark at Forsyth Bay as a site for a wharf.[50]

In 1910, 38 licensed fishermen in the Sounds (about 20 of these from Pelorus Sound)[51] were reported, as they would be in successive years, as catching a wide variety of fish mostly for the Wellington market.[52] A snapshot in 1917 and 1920 of the Picton industry shows only line and net-fishing rowboats were in use, no 'oil-launches' (motorised small craft), though in 1920 one steam-trawler was in use.[53] Similarly, in Pelorus Sound until the 1930s men used time-consuming methods tailored to particular fish and locations. They set nets over the winter to catch mostly flounder but otherwise used hand-seining. From Maud Island out towards the sea they line-fished with wind buoys, mostly going after groper; and the time-consuming hand-lining was used for blue-cod fishing all over the Sounds, as well as for snapper, conger eels, barracouta and groper off Tawero Point. These fishermen were facing competition for that crucial Wellington market from bigger, more powerful boats that accessed not only Cook Strait but also the rich Cape Palliser fishing grounds from where the catch was got efficiently to market.[54]

In 1921 fishermen all over the country were finding that the increases in catches were failing to offset the costs of petrol and gear, administration and travel times. More and more, they tended to go out only when conditions assured payable catches.[55] The Pelorus fishermen in particular, working part-time from small boats with little gear, struggled to earn enough to gain a toehold in the increasingly efficient commercial scene. They fished only in the winter when the cows had dried off, and when it was cold enough to get the fish to market in good condition.[56] Their small open boats had a limited range, and weather might prevent their getting out at all — and certainly not into the productive Cook Strait waters.

Nor was market access easy. Both Pelorus and French Pass fishermen had to transfer their catches to the relatively regular and frequent steamers or scows that sailed past the top of Pelorus Sound on the Nelson–Wellington run, yet even at the best of times these transfers were dangerous. The collecting ships, too, might be delayed by bad weather or by missing the French Pass tide; or the weather might be too bad to attempt a transfer: catches were then simply tipped overboard.

Such irregular and unreliable supply did nothing to foster the local industry's development, and even if fishermen did get their fish to market and ensure a fair price,[57] they were not in a position to make sure they got paid. Yet, in the Sounds' tight economic environment, even tiny amounts made vital contributions to family finances and to keeping the settlers on the land.

Wharves in what was known as Whebby's Corner, Māhakipawa Arm, Te Hoiere Pelorus Sound. Alexander Brown's wharf (built 1876) is on the left, Dive and Gaby's (built 1864) on the right. William Fortesque, on the wharf dressed in an apron, was, in 1881, the first baker at Cullensville, a now abandoned town at the head of Māhakipawa Valley. He reportedly lived to the age of 106.
MARLBOROUGH HISTORICAL SOCIETY, 1768

AT THE END OF THE nineteenth century the world was eating oysters. Londoners consumed some 50,000 tonnes annually;[58] in the US and Canada the annual take was much higher. In New Zealand, oyster bars, saloons and shops advertised their wares, and the *Marlborough Express* ran tips on what to look for when buying oysters, recipes for how to prepare them, and an advertisement for a 'boy who can open oysters with a reference'. At the turn of the century, oysters were linked to outbreaks of typhoid, mostly overseas but with the occasional outbreak in New Zealand, and by 1906 they were recognised as a potential source of acute gastrointestinal illness. Yet New Zealanders continued to eat oysters enthusiastically. The Sounds rock oysters, from Queen Charlotte Sound and Tory Channel, had a high reputation.[59]

The resource was, as usual, over-exploited. From 1874, legislation, orders in council and regulations had imposed closed seasons, limits or outright bans to prevent oysters being exterminated and 'one of the most important industries in this colony' being destroyed.[60] In 1889 the natural beds in Tory Channel closed for some months, not for the last time, and the government was considering how to best ensure that the country's oyster beds were farmed sustainably.[61]

One approach was to create artificial oyster beds. In 1894 the New Zealand Company laid down thousands of oysters from Auckland and Sydney in Pāuatahanui Inlet, on the west coast north of Wellington. In 1895, with the Tory Channel beds again closed, Henry Baxter and William Davenport were granted licences to form oyster beds at the entrance to Eire Bay, Tory Channel.[62] A year later government leases were handed out to Alexander Maule of Havelock for 48 acres in Mud Bay, Hikapu Reach; Peter Ewing got four acres in Hitaua Bay, Tory Channel; and in 1896 Percy Neave leased 16.5 acres in Mahau Sound.[63]

The *Pelorus Guardian*, that indefatigable advocate, considered that 'Pelorus Sound oysters will ultimately 'acquire a name for delicacy of flavour which cannot be rivalled in the Colony'.[64] However, Percy Neave's initiative does not appear to have got off the ground and the other ventures failed. All had been initiated by settlers of small means who put countless hours of work and resources into developing walls and conditions in which oysters, they hoped, would flourish. They were thwarted by landslides and slips creating sedimentation, seaweed that grew too quickly in the warm sheltered bays, and inexperience. The oysters, lacking essential stonewalls, cairns and enclosures, did badly.[65]

Nationally, closed seasons continued to be imposed, and recommendations and reports on creating artificial beds proliferated. During 1915 and 1916, and as part of another 'entirely experimental' government initiative to revive depleted beds, rocks with oysters attached to them were planted at various sites around the country. Against local advice,[66] this was done in Tory Channel, Queen Charlotte Sound and Pelorus Sound.[67] The Marine Department, firmly backed by fishing industry interests,[68] also made a couple of attempts to plant Foveaux Strait oysters off White Bluff and the Awatere River mouth.[69] The importance of cooler waters for oyster reproduction would not be recognised for another couple of decades. By 1920 all efforts had met with almost blanket failure.[70] In 1935 interest was revived in Queen Charlotte Sound and Tory Channel but the beds' poor quality offered no certainty of supply, and by 1946 the industry was effectively finished.[71]

Oysters were not the only aquaculture venture in the Sounds. In 1916 government advisors were claiming that quinnat salmon would spawn a further 'important industry'.[72] Having been introduced in 1901, the fish had returned to breed in the rivers of the South Island's east coast, and in 1917 the Department of Fisheries built a small hatchery in the upper reaches of Marlborough's Wairau River. The *Marlborough Express* waxed eloquent on a venture of 'possibilities of a magnitude that, safe to say, is quite unsuspected by the average person'.[73]

The fish, one enthusiastic newspaper predicted, would move into the Sounds and beyond. If the development of farmed salmon in Puget Sound in Canada was any guide, the northern Marlborough waters would 'teem with purse seine boats'; thousands would be employed using 'high-class machinery'; and 'girls' could make good wages. Considerable taxes would allow the state to finance future endeavours that would feed considerable home consumption and exports of chilled salmon to Australia.[74] Fifteen years later salmon were occasionally seen in the Wairau River, but hopes for a further industry and employment, whether private or government-funded, had faded. For the small players, the financial loss and disappointment must have been considerable.

'The virgin forest harvest'[75]

In 1864 Dr James Hector, hired by the government, toured the country to secure exhibits for an international exhibition that would afford the colony a chance to demonstrate to the world 'the value of the internal resources of the Colony and its advancement in the arts of civilised life'. Marlborough had barely become a province

but Hector, noting its timber and the potential for deep-water facilities, had no doubt that 'an extensive timber trade', boosted by small settlements, would spring up. Havelock and Picton had good harbours, and a tramway could connect Picton and the Wairau. Both towns, he predicted, would have 'considerable importance'.[76]

Historian Rollo Arnold considered that 'few nineteenth century western communities owed more to the forest harvest than did colonial New Zealand'. New Zealand's timber was 'vastly more important' in the colonial than in the homeland economy.[77] The country's climate and abundant accessible forest saw wood unchallenged as a domestic fuel until the late 1870s, when railways began to distribute coal effectively.

Wood was needed, too, for roofing shingles, fencing, wheels, barrels, buckets, tubs, railway sleepers, ships — even cost-effective street paving. By the late 1870s the industry was more mechanised than Europe's. By 1881 settlers' per capita consumption of wood and timber was about seven times greater than that in Britain and, again on a per capita basis, almost twice as many men were involved in the colony's milling industries than in Australia.[78] As increasing numbers of settlers spread around New Zealand they depleted the local wood resources, leaving the 'water-based' industries on Banks Peninsula and in north Auckland, from where shipping was relatively easy, well positioned to take advantage of the demand for timber. So too were the Sounds, with their long, tortuous arms of land reaching far out into the sea, and from which millions of cubic feet of timber were cut.

As early as 1864 Sounds timber was being exported to Southland, to predictions that this might 'do much to advance the prosperity of the [Marlborough] Province'.[79] Over 1866–67, as the West Coast gold rushes stimulated 'brisk exports', over 100 ships were dispatched from Māhakipawa to the West Coast;[80] for a period, 'timber-laden vessels from the Sounds and Hokitika' fed demanding and profitable markets from Wellington[81] to Foxton and Wanganui. In 1876 the 16 mills in the top of the South Island — almost all in the Sounds — cut 15.5 million 'super feet' of timber (a super foot is a cubic measurement for timber that equals one foot (0.3 m) square by one inch (2.54 cm) thick. A year later 22 vessels were reported to be lying off Havelock's Cullen Point awaiting loading.[82]

Millers in the Sounds, as in the rest of New Zealand, cut selectively, carefully picking the better species and those trees large enough to be commercially valuable yet not so big as to make it too difficult to split the trunks. Destroying acre after acre in pursuit of the few commercially valuable trunks, they did not bother to cut second-rate timber or work difficult ground.[83] The areas over which they got licences to cut were not necessarily large,[84] but collectively they opened up considerable land for settlement — although 'opening up' has to be interpreted carefully. With huge forest trees cleared, farmers, increasingly aided by essential scrub-cutters, were left to tackle the tangled detritus of creepers, vines, shrubs and smaller trees as they battled to develop pasture. Many farmers were keen to sell not only their labour but also their standing timber, produce — including food for horses — and firewood.[85]

Most mills in the Sounds were small. Animal power hauled the logs to the small relocatable mills positioned where the logs, generally only roughly trimmed, could be easily shipped out. Mechanisation was minor: the men worked the pitsaws by hand; other saws were powered by steam. The 15.5 million super feet collectively cut in 1876 was a considerable achievement at the time; today it would represent only a small proportion of a single mill's annual cut.[86] (See Appendix 2a and 2b for a list of small millers operating in the Sounds, 1848–90 and 1900–05.)

Locals valued the work and the millers' custom but had to adjust to the industry leaving the district once the resource was gone. In the early 1880s there were indications that millers were facing shortages of particular timbers and were closing or moving their mills.[87] In 1885 most forest near the sea was milled out and production dropped to 9 million super feet.[88]

However, that same year work began on the Wellington end of the North Island main trunk railway line; later the South Island main trunk would be extended north to Hurunui and south to Bluff. This enterprise was the work of Premier William Fox's colonial treasurer, Julius Vogel, who, from the mid-1870s, made huge and ambitious investments in railways. The resulting New Zealand Railways had a sustained ongoing demand for beech and kahikatea for sleepers.

Railway officials were impressed by the durability and strength of the Sounds' black beech, and also with the contractors' work in cutting to specifications. The demand created something of a sellers' market and in 1901 settlers with abundant black beech on their property began to think about milling — shrewdly extracting government guarantees to take the whole output.[89] Sleepers initially sold at 2s 6d (minus a royalty of 3d for those cut on Crown land), but in the first years of the new century prices for sleepers from the Sounds' valued wood continued to increase. In 1907 New Zealand Railways called for tenders to cart 60,000 'Birch Sleepers' from Marlborough Sounds to Lyttelton.[90]

Impecunious settlers, suggests one historian, could, with a few simple tools and paying a miller's royalty of 6d per 100 super feet,[91] clear their land and turn the 'cleared logs to profit'.[92] That reads a little glibly when applied to the Sounds. Land holdings were mostly small and timber therefore quickly cleared; any profits probably made only a marginal difference. However, an assured market allowed settlers with even small stands of beech on their land to consider the proposition.[93]

The value of bushed land went up, especially in the small blocks where access to the sea and immediate transport out made them attractive propositions. As sheep prices rose, so too did farmers' need for more bush to be cut for pasture. In the first decade of the nineteenth century even settlers offering top wages had sometimes to wait for millers' services.[94]

The small local millers, moving around the bays, would also have provided valued employment, despite some millers being bit players (see Appendix 2a and 2b). But again, for the Sounds' very small, scattered and often struggling population, that small additional wage would have been a godsend.

BY THE LAST DECADE OF the nineteenth century the bigger firms milling in the Sounds were making considerable profits. Baigent and Sons, the big Nelson millers, exported 172,000 super feet of timber from 'Blackball Point' in 1891,[95] and would mill in Nydia Bay (towards the inner reaches of Pelorus Sound) for a period from 1907. In late July that year the steam at Baigent's mill in the bay was turned on for the first time, 'and the tintinnabulation of whistles, guns, kerosene tins, etc, was deafening'.[96] However, from the mid-1880s until 1915, it was William Ross Brownlee who dominated the Sounds milling scene. Only in 1907 did the Marlborough Timber Company, set up by Westland miller John Craig and Christchurch timber merchant Daniel Reese and cutting in Ōpouri Valley, emerge briefly as a comparable company.

Brownlee's milling career began unexceptionally. Following his start at Māhakipawa, he instigated various milling operations in Kaituna, Nydia Bay (where he cut 10 million super feet of timber from about 1000 acres) and in the upper arm of Kaiuma Valley.[97] At the beginning of the 1880 depression a milling consortium in which he was involved collapsed. Brownlee, combining his engineering skills and milling experience with an astute business sense, grasped a risky opportunity and established Brownlee and Co. In 1882 the company bought 500 acres (202 ha) of the best bush and positioned a big mill on the Pelorus River bank at Blackball, about 5 kilometres upriver from Havelock so that the coastal vessels could load directly from the mill. He began developing a railway line and imported railway machinery, engines and wagons and invested in costly new equipment.[98] The gamble paid off. By 1897 continually improving levels of mechanisation had increased the firm's annual output from 3 million to 4 million super feet, a huge output compared with the annual 120,000 super feet produced by the largest mill at Kaikōura.[99]

By 1912 Brownlee's buildings covered about 4 hectares and included a loft for the pigeons that were used to alert the firm of ships' impending arrivals (and bring back the returns from far-distant polling booths in national and local elections). The sawmill employed 120 men, and the site also boasted a port, 20 workers' homes and two breweries. Blackball was also the terminus for the 80 kilometres of the 'light railway construction' built to bring in the huge logs from Pelorus Valley forests and ship the milled sawn timber out.[100] Brownlee's operated four sailing ships, a scow (*Eunice*) and the tug SS *Pelorus*, from its wharves at Kaiuma and Māhakipawa, and used coastal steamers to get its timber out.

The risk-taking, the willingness to spend and the tight management that typified the Brownlee operation was shared by a later comer to the scene, the Marlborough Timber Company. John Craig and Daniel Reese and the eight business associates who established the firm got their opportunity when, in the early 1900s, Reese secured the contract for highly valuable milling rights in the neighbouring Ōpouri and Rongo valleys, in a major setback for Brownlee's.[101]

Nydia Bay, a long way from roads and with only a few families and a school, was transformed into 'the busiest centre of the Sounds' when the Marlborough Timber Company's railway arrived in 1907.[102] A settlement for the company's wharfies, truckers and yardmen developed on William Gould's farm near the wharf. Gould ran a store, his woolshed was used as a hall and he built a grass tennis court. Mr Craig, a mill manager in Brownlee's mould, worked men hard but paid fairly, and retained their loyalty for years. In 1905 a postal-note office was established at Nydia Bay and from then on the bay was included in a regular mail service. Then in 1908, a year after the Marlborough Timber Company arrived, a post office and a telegraph office were installed, a telephone line was cut into Kaiuma Bay, and lines were erected for Nydia Bay.[103]

Daniel Reese established an efficient two-way trade with Australia. Trans-Tasman ships such as the barque *Manurewa* took the company's timber to Sydney, returning with coal from Newcastle for Christchurch, or Australian hardwood timber for port expansions at Wellington and Lyttelton.[104]

The firm operated from 1907 until about 1919,[105] milling in the Ōpouri Valley

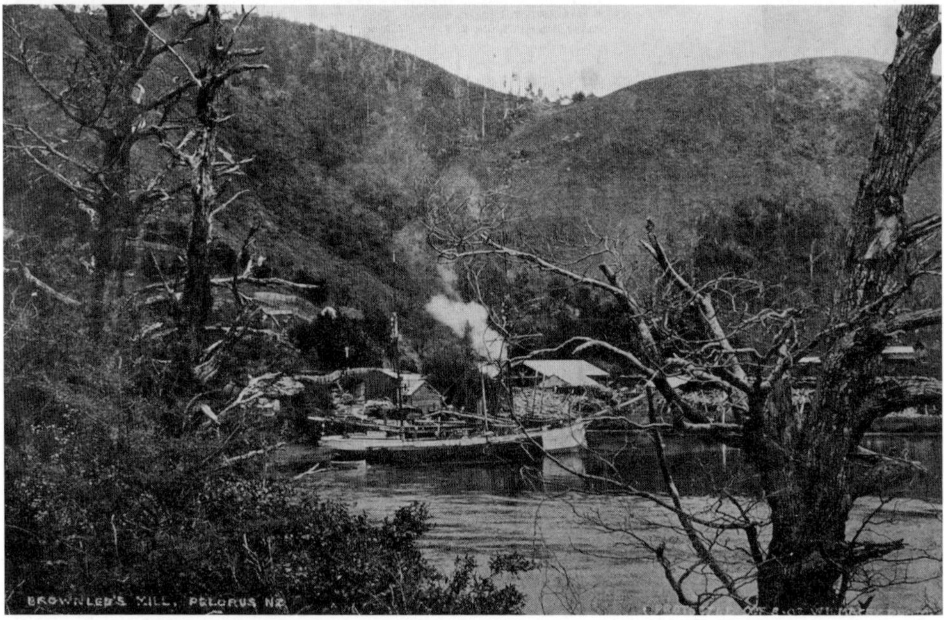

ABOVE Nydia Bay wharf, c. 1910, with great stacks of milled timber awaiting export. ALEXANDER TURNBULL LIBRARY, 1/2-066848-F

BELOW Timber being loaded at Blackball, the Brownlee port near Havelock. If the tide was low, the timber was freighted out to the ships. Today, silting that occurred after the river was declared a sludge channel (to accommodate the sediment that came down from the Wakamarina diggings) would prevent such ships getting so far up-river. W. H. MACEY, AUCKLAND LIBRARIES HERITAGE COLLECTIONS, AWNS-19050824-16-4

from where its audacious tramline over a 4572-metre range down to Nydia Bay enabled timber to be shipped out easily.

In 1901 only 1620 acres (655 ha) were cut in Pelorus Sound and 250 (101 ha) in Queen Charlotte Sound, suggesting a depleted resource.[106] In 1905 it was officially recognised that tōtara was very scarce; rimu, kahikatea and mataī were the main species milled; while beech was cut only for railway sleepers and bridges.[107]

Five years later the milling boom was over, the smaller mills closing down or running slowly.[108] In 1913 it was anticipated that cutting would last only into the early to mid-1920s. Brownlee's, having been in Havelock for 51 years, moved to Westland in 1915. His five mills in the Sounds had cut out all the available timber — 89 million super feet of rimu, kahikatea and mataī (not including the 100 million super feet milled from the Rai and Ōpouri valleys before the Marlborough Timber Company arrived.)[109]

Four years later the Marlborough Timber Company installed a box-mill, to turn a lot of the currently wasted timber into fruit or butter boxes.[110] By 1920 tōtara was effectively milled out, and timber generally was so scarce that 'every available tree is being sought after' and mills were 'being put into places that would have been scorned in pre-war days'.[111]

MILLING IN THE SOUNDS LASTED 50–60 years until the resource was exhausted. From the 1860s to 1909 some 35 mills had worked in the Sounds at various stages. Although the wisdom of such wholesale clearance would, from relatively early on, start to be questioned, the cumulative effect was huge. For the new settlers, for whom bush clearance was vital to survival, the 'sawmilling industry was their greatest boon'.[112]

Men like Brownlee and Reese, who made money from milling, could afford to pay their substantial, skilled workforce regularly, which had spinoff benefits.[113] In that climate, a small farmer like Orry Hope (see Chapter 7), for instance, could develop a small freighting operation;[114] Gould set up a store at Nydia Bay; and the Rutlands supplied chaff for their horse teams to Brownlee's at £5 a tonne.[115]

The mills created that important nexus of settlement, schools and confidence. Brownlee's workforce, able to afford supplies in the Brownlee store in Havelock's Lucknow Street, contributed to local retail businesses. (William Smith, the company's book-keeper and paymaster, ran the store, assisted by William Henry Orsman, whose son Harry would go on to compile the monumental and scholarly *Dictionary of New Zealand English* in 1997.)

By 1906 Havelock township had a population of over 300. It boasted a large primary school that the millers' children would have attended (a school established at Blackball in 1894 lasted only one year), three hotels, several churches, a post and telegraph office, a public library, stores other than Brownlee's, and a hospital. The *Pelorus Guardian* was published twice weekly, the regular Nelson–Blenheim coach service passed through, and a steamer sailed fortnightly between Havelock and Nelson.[116]

The stable workforce at Nydia Bay boosted the roll at the Nydia Bay school — such factors provided a crucial psychological underpinning for the dreams and aspirations of small Sounds communities.

The Havelock–Nelson steamer service, doubtless stimulated by Brownlee's business, would have been a godsend for those needing regular freight services; even the small milling operations would have created further opportunities for coastal shipping. Brownlee's own ships, carrying farm produce to outside markets, increased links to the outside world, while the constant columns of favourable newspaper reporting on milling brought the Sounds to the attention of the wider world.

Writing in the late 1930s, John Brownlee, William Ross's son, claimed that, with the possible exception of Perano's whaling business, Brownlee's was the single venture to make significant money out of the Sounds.[117] Probably the region's major shipper, sawmiller and employer, it has been argued that it was 'one of the most successful and progressive timber undertakings' in New Zealand.[118] Its efforts, business practices, fortunes and impact were constantly in local papers. With Brownlee's operating, the Sounds was seen as a region with a future.

'The mineral treasures of this wild locality'

In 1879 the single mining official in the Sounds was upbeat. Marlborough province had, he reckoned, 'a large tract of valuable mineral land [in which] either by accident or by the judicious employment of that very essential element, "capital", rich discoveries will yet be made'.[119] Such predictions were part of a wider pattern in the Sounds. Mining prospects were always promoted with 'an invariable optimism', and 'the possibilities of every find' exaggerated.[120] Money, plant and engineering were poured into antimony and goldmining in the district, but fickle overseas markets for antimony and inadequate and inaccessible gold resources[121] meant that the ventures ended in failure and the accompanying, unremarked human heartbreak.[122]

Antimony, extracted from stibnite (the chief ore containing antimony), was used in everything from printers' lettering to specula for telescopes and the pigment for dyeing women's eyebrows. When alloyed with metal or tin, it was used in large guns and armour plate.

The story of antimony in the Sounds began in a low-key way. The discovery of stibnite north of Resolution Bay in 1872 passed almost unnoticed.[123] But in September 1873 antimony was found in rocks in a landslide below Mount Stokes, possibly by John Ashworth, living with his family in Endeavour Inlet. This time the papers took note, the *Marlborough Express* immediately prophesying benefit from 'the mineral treasures of this wild and hitherto almost unknown locality'.[124] Ashworth obtained a lease from the Marlborough Waste Land Board. Further prospecting found a mineral belt tending north-west to Port Gore, and the ore contained gold as well as stibnite.[125]

The privately owned Marlborough Antimony Company was formed in 1874, with Ashworth and Charles and Fred Turner, of the Ravenscliff Run, among its owners. Internationally, antimony was in demand and success must have seemed assured.[126] No new techniques were needed to work the lodes; the material could be taken down the hill to the inlet for treatment. There was a good anchorage, flat land for a township, and a stream that could be used to drive the machinery. Abundant timber around the site would fuel three Nelson-made furnaces used to heat the iron retorts in which the ore was to be melted. The company optimistically estimated it could produce up to 100 tonnes a week of partly refined antimony, to be shipped direct to England and sold for £40 a tonne, four times the price paid for untreated high-grade ore.

Two more lodes were found and samples were dispatched to England for testing. By early winter of 1875 a small township had sprung up in the head of the bay, and in October the following year the first lot of antimony from the mine arrived in Wellington.

Hopes were dashed shortly after when it was found that the molten stibnite had eaten away the retorts, and no solution to this issue could be found. Attempts to sell the company failed, and antimony mining ceased — for a while. Ashworth and his family stayed on making sporadic attempts to smelt more ore. He once almost killed himself in the process[127] before turning his hand to more low-risk ways of wresting a living from the land.[128]

In 1883, with antimony prices in England close to record highs, a new syndicate was established, with Ashworth as mine manager, to mine in the high outcrops on the 1600-foot (487-metre) range between Endeavour Inlet and Port Gore. About 30 workers arrived and a considerable lode was identified. Three independent but connected tramways went in. Further prospecting found further stibnite, with samples displayed in the 1885 Wellington Industrial Exhibition and at the Colonial Exhibition in London.[129]

Having spent £5000 but needing more, the syndicate formed the publicly listed Endeavour Inlet Antimony Company in 1885 and set about introducing new furnaces and plant and employing experienced men. Jaketh Wearne, who had worked in Australia and Cornwall, replaced Ashworth as mine manager; Harold Ensor was appointed mine engineer (while managing a store and preaching on the side). Four hundred tonnes of an 'apparently unlimited supply'[130] of antimony was sent to London, where there were good prices. The little township developed, with 50 or so well-paid miners in company houses.[131] Some boys were employed, sorting out the ore before it was treated in the furnace. Wellington's *Evening Post* confidently calculated the profits.[132]

THE QUALITY OF THE MARLBOROUGH metal drew favourable international comment, but in 1887 the market collapsed. After negotiating in London, the company went into voluntary liquidation but continued to work the mine for the newly established and asset-holding London-based New Zealand Antimony Company (registered in 1887).

Extraordinarily, and explanations can only fall back on the optimism and visions of success that underlay this European settlement, once again there was considerable investment. New levels were opened up and connected to the main tramway. The crushing plant was expanded, the smelters improved; the company could now process 900 tonnes of ore annually. The workforce increased to 70, with 30 children attending the school.[133] But prizes in international exhibitions for the ore did not offset the fact that imported expensive and experimental equipment once again failed.[134] Relations with the New Zealand Antimony Company soured, and the London agent who was supposed to be representing and protecting the New Zealanders' interests proved disastrous. The plant slowed production in 1890 and went into voluntary liquidation again in 1892.

At this point another, largely Wellington, syndicate bought the company's assets and formed the Star Antimony Company, with Wearne again as mine manager. The workings were further developed, and more innovative equipment was installed. Prices failed to recover, however, and in 1896 the company suspended operations.

By 1904 the place was derelict and its debts were still being settled, but two years later Wearne, who had played a significant role in all but one of the various companies

Antimony mine, Endeavour Inlet, No. 1 paddock and dam. By mid-1886, and with the Endeavour Inlet Antimony Company well underway, the water-race provided the necessary water for the water tables and jiggers that separated out the ore from other matter. Water, too, drove the 1.8-metre Pelton wheel, itself something of a provincial landmark, that powered the entire plant. To the right is the timber 'paddock', where the mined rocks were tipped to await processing.
NELSON PROVINCIAL MUSEUM, TYREE STUDIO COLLECTION, 179104

since 1885, was behind a further huge and costly attempt at reopening the mine for business. A great deal of antimony was suddenly required for rebuilding in San Francisco after its disastrous earthquake of April 1906, and three months later a lode of antimony was discovered at Edgecombe Point in the outer part of Endeavour Inlet. Buyers took up expensive share options, and demand for housing in Picton exceeded supply as incoming miners jostled to settle their families there.

When further high-grade antimony was discovered in Resolution Bay the following year — thousands of tonnes of ore were, again, confidently anticipated[135] — the Resolution Bay Antimony Prospecting Company Ltd was formed and over-subscribed. Meanwhile there were hopes for new finds in Endeavour Inlet. Metal containing 60 per cent antimony was discovered on the hillside between Big and Camp bays, and prospectors were working around Pukekoikoi, out towards the entrance of the inlet.[136]

However, unstable ground hindered prospecting in the hills around the inlet and no large reef was ever found. Internationally, prices fell again and by the end of 1907 all antimony prospecting in the inlet and in Resolution Bay had finished. In 1910 the land around the inlet was subdivided and opened for selection — the government considered that it had greater potential for farming than mining.[137] Wearne, strongly opposed to this decision, committed suicide.[138] The Endeavour Inlet mine, New Zealand's largest antimony producer with a total output of 37,000 tonnes, was finished. More money had been spent than was ever recovered.[139] None of the subsequent brief flurries of renewed interest — in 1916, during the Depression in the 1930s, in the 1950s, or from 1961 into the early 1970s — ever got off the ground.[140]

At their peak in the mid-1880s to early 1890s, the Endeavour Inlet Company and New Zealand Antimony Company employed 50–75 skilled workmen. But most had been brought in; local involvement appears to have been limited to those few boys,[141] and perhaps a few Sounds men involved with installing the equipment or with construction around the mine. However, there were the same sorts of indirect benefit that came from milling. Mining engineer Harold Ensor, managing the store, sold supplies at just above cost price to the miners. He also preached to the little settlement and would later become Havelock's Anglican vicar. In 1885 a post office opened with John Ashworth as postmaster; Kenepuru settlers dispatched almost daily supplies over the saddle or brought them to the camp by boat; in the 1890s a slaughterhouse was set up in Slaughterhouse Bay (between Punga Cove and Deep Bay);[142] and a miner's wife ran a small bakery.[143] The Marlborough Education Board

ABOVE No. 1 paddock and dam, antimony mine, Endeavour Inlet. This provides something of a close-up of the top right of the previous image. Mined rock, brought down on the vertiginous railway, is being tipped down a shute into the paddock. The 35-feet-deep dam, excavated at the end of the 1880s from loose gravel in fast-flowing water, enabled the Pelton wheel to double the available horsepower going to the plant. NELSON PROVINCIAL MUSEUM, TYREE STUDIO COLLECTION, 179103

BELOW The entrance to the antimony mine, high in the hills above Endeavour Inlet. NELSON PROVINCIAL MUSEUM, TYREE STUDIO COLLECTION, 181917 built a schoolhouse, where a Mr Thistleton taught 30–40 pupils. In 1890, while the antimony mines were in full swing, Captain Henry Fisk in his elegant *Torea* supplied a weekly mail, goods and passenger service to the mines, one of a number of such runs and each providing an invaluable service to settlers, both Māori and Pākehā.[144] He would soon be joined by Captain Oscar Norgrove and the *Phoenix*.

Other little steamers also serviced the area. By 1888 the mine had become something of a tourist destination, drawing sightseers from Wellington and Christchurch. Sounds steamers like the Anchor Steam Shipping Company's *Huia* (7s 6d return, meals 1s 6d) would carry them up to the inlet. A night-time arrival was an adventure: 'Going up the Inlet it was dark . . . [and] almost impossible to say where the water and the land joined, so deep were the shadows,' one tourist wrote.[145] Once there, a 'bright little stream' ran into the sea. A tramway joined the wharf to the township. There, some tented and others rented out corrugated-iron workingmen's cottages at two shillings a week. Flower and vegetable gardens grew luxuriantly; cattle grazing on the flats produced milk and butter. Fish were plentiful, ducks and chickens roamed freely.

The real tourist drawcard was the mining plant, a marvel of ingenuity and innovation to which each company added. On the flats away from the village the Endeavour Inlet Company had erected an open wood-and-iron dressing-shed. There, washing tables and jiggers used water to separate out the ore from other matter; ore crushers and pulverisers were at work. Smelting, operational 12 hours a day, was carried out in three stages to achieve the highly refined mineral.

The New Zealand Antimony Company, sinking extraordinary money into additional development of the plant and mine, added other marvels. In 1888 its 75 employees were opening up new levels and drives and building additional tramways. These, sidling around the hill, got the ore to the main downhill tramway. New water-races were constructed, and a wharf that could accommodate a small steamer; 'a most complete laboratory [with] necessary appliances' was installed, the crushing plant was expanded, the smelters improved, and a large dam — built by excavating loose gravel to a depth of 35 feet (10.7 metres) in fast-flowing water — enabled the Pelton wheel to double the horsepower it provided.

Perhaps even more marvellous — and certainly more breathtaking — was the horse-tramway that ran from the wharf to the foot of the hill to access the lode at the top of the range. This three-rail tramway in three sections climbed steeply some 180 metres in about 800 metres. The tramway was self-acting — the full carts going down pulled the empty ones up — and each section was controlled by a double-band brake. Wet weather meant problems and derailments, but even in the best of conditions it presented 'a somewhat alarming mode of conveyance to a person at all troubled with nerves'.[146]

At the top of the third section, 53 metres below the summit, where there was a cold spring and where the foreman and miners lived, there was also the entrance to the main 244-metre tunnel. This gave access to a reef of varying width that contained ore of 60 per cent antimony at its centre. The tunnel, off which were many drives and interconnecting shafts,[147] emerged on the other side of the hill. From there, 400 metres above sea level, was 'one of the most beautiful views to be seen, even in this colony, where there are so many grand and beautiful views' — down into Port Gore and stretching out towards D'Urville Island and the long land running out to Cape Jackson, Queen Charlotte Sound.

THE EXCITEMENT AND RUSH THAT had accompanied the first gold finds in and around the Pelorus Valley in the mid- and late 1860s were declining when, in February 1872, the *Marlborough Express* announced that Charles Turner, Richard Nicholls and Charles Greenlaw had found gold in a reef that crossed the narrow spur between Waimatete Bay in Port Gore and Kempe Point on that long, bleak arm of land that runs north to Cape Jackson. Only one reef had been found, the paper stressed. As well, the country was difficult, landing was almost impossible, and water as well as food would need to be got in — the results 'could assuredly be nil'.

Despite the paper's rare downbeat tone, the provincial government, possibly to provide a legal title that would allow the men to develop the 'indications' they had spent three years finding,[148] proclaimed the 150 acres (60 ha) as the Ravenscliff Goldfield at Port Gore. Events quickened. By May 1872 tests had revealed that the quartz contained gold worth almost £4 an ounce and Greenlaw was in Wellington seeking investors.[149] A few months later, with further finds at Golden Point, Provincial Superintendent Arthur Seymour announced the Queen Charlotte Sound Gold Field, a vast area that (Māori reserves and freehold land excepted) spanned the area between Port Gore and Endeavour Inlet, rising up to Mount Furneaux (823 m) and Mount Stokes (1203 m). This was further expanded in September 1874, effectively to include the ridge bordering Queen Charlotte and Pelorus sounds, as far south at Torea Bay.[150]

Samples from the field sent to Wellington were of white crystalline quartz 'literally saturated with gold', and considerable quantities of gold were also found

The long arm of Te Taonui a Kupe Cape Jackson, jutting into Raukawa Moana Cook Strait, separates Tōtaranui Queen Charlotte Sound (on left) from Te Anamāhanga Port Gore (on right). In 1870, quartz reefs were found on the ridge running south-west from the cape. LLOYD HOMER, GNS SCIENCE, 24317

in specimens at the Ravenscliff Goldfield.[151] But the finds were in reefs, not alluvial deposits; any exploitation needed companies with substantial funding, not fortune-seekers with panning dishes. With Charles Greenslaw as manager and with major financial backing from many of the same individuals — Charles Turner, Richard Nicholls, Josiah Harris prominent among them — three companies (the Queen Charlotte Mining Company, the Port Gore Gold Mining Company and Turner Gold Mining Company) were rapidly established and licences applied for.[152] By late September 1873 nine claims or leases, such as the colourfully named Hit or Miss, Resolution, and Cook's Adventure, were being worked in three lines of three.[153] Charles Turner's cutter, *Florence*, ran repeated trips getting men and materials to the cape, while local boats took those indefatigable sightseers from Picton on what, again, seems to have become a well-trodden round of the Ravenscliff field.

From the 'substantial' wharf at Kempe Point a well-benched and graded road took visitors to the reefs. There, the Turner and Port Gore companies were jointly driving a tunnel in the Turner Mine. A further shaft, sunk to meet the tunnel, had unveiled a reef with visible gold, and a tramway and a chute sent the rock to the battery on the Port Gore claim. Its 10 heads of stampers were driven by a powerful stationary engine. Visitors could also view the smithy and the 12 or so solidly built miners' cottages, anchored to the ground by iron stakes to protect them against the wind (the miners' families probably lived in Picton).[154]

Nine months later and all was not well. In the Turner Mine the six men tunnelling around the clock had met with such hard rock that progress slowed to a foot a day; the gold quartz content was lower than expected; and the battery, without quartz to crush, lay idle. The Queen Charlotte Mining Company, whose miners had kept working only because they were shareholders in the company, suspended work. Activity on the Cape Jackson reefs was principally confined to the Turner and Port Gore companies.[155] The problem was (temporarily) deflected when the Port Gore Company found an apparently very rich vein and amalgamated with Turner's. The resulting vigorous development programme had the batteries going 24 hours a day, six days a week, but the richness of the quartz did not improve significantly.

IN MARCH 1875 A TERRIBLE storm swept away the equipment, the building that housed the battery, the wharf and coal supplies. Costly repairs were carried out and protective works were developed, but company finances remained poor.

Turner's attempt to raise money by mortgaging the company assets did not appease the shareholders expecting dividends, or stall those with dividends in arrears from pursuing the company through the courts. In July 1876 the company went into liquidation.[156]

In retrospect, the outcome was inevitable. Official reports of potential for gold were always guarded.[157] Turner's land was not evaluated before expensive capital work started. Moreover, when the strongly anticipated payable quartz was not found, the companies involved were inadequately financed to undertake further searches. The battery lay idle, tying up money that was then unavailable for crucial prospecting.[158]

Cape Jackson, however, had not seen the end of gold prospecting. The efforts of Turner and his family saw a new well-financed and strongly directed Ravenscliff Mining Company fitting new timber into the mineshaft, re-laying railway lines, repairing the wharf and buildings, and reopening the mine in 1879, its name changed from the Turner Mine to the Ravenscliff Mine.[159] Again, the story takes on fairytale dimensions. Miners found quartz so penetrated with gold that it 'appears to hold the stone together in some places and the latest specimens are rich as the most covetous shareholders would desire'.[160] Crowds flocked to see samples of what were proclaimed as possibly the richest finds in Marlborough. Expectations of English investment to finance other mines in the district ran high.[161] And still, uneconomic returns led to the inevitable difficulties, and in 1882 operations ceased. The following year the Ravenscliff Mine was auctioned off as a going concern — somewhat oddly considering that the company had recovered about 500 ounces of gold worth around £1825 (from which government levies and wages had to be paid), while it had spent about £20,000 searching for payable reefs.[162]

With the optimism that seems to have been essential to settlement in the Sounds, some retained hopes for the field. After the rich 1879 find, Jacob Plimmer briefly held rights to the Queen Charlotte Mining Company's original lease. Houston F. Logan, one-time manager of the New Zealand Antimony Company, and partner William Duncan were involved around 1885 with the same lease, clearing drives and rockfalls, retimbering and taking samples. The Antimony Company bought what was probably the Ravenscliff mine and Jaketh Wearne discovered some quartz studded with gold.

But in 1889 the company decided that antimony was a better bet, and goldminers again deserted Cape Jackson.[163] In 1890 Robert Ewing of Wellington took over the Ravenscliff Mine. As late as 1894 he still hoped for results, and with labour plentiful and cheap, opined the *Marlborough Express*, success was probable.[164] Ewing cancelled the leases in 1900. A final exploration in 1906 was no more successful.[165]

Elsewhere in the Sounds, subsequent finds of gold also resulted in the now-familiar high expectations and subsequent loss and disappointment. In late 1872 gold-bearing quartz was found on what is now Golden Point; the year the Golden Point Gold Mining Company (Turner, Nicholls and Greenlaw were all shareholders) obtained a lease to mine.[166] The initial promise was not realised, and when the Cape Jackson mines collapsed, so did the Golden Point venture. But in 1877, as the new finds at the Cape Jackson mines created a mild gold fever, Nicolls led the establishment of the Golden Point syndicate.

Claims were pegged out and, alongside a considerable amount of underground prospecting, the Golden Point Gold Mining Company was floated in January 1878. Dr James Hector found some leaders, but no true reef, and indications of silver.[167] That was enough for the *Wanganui Herald*, which reported gold 'of an exceptionally fine quality' and as a remunerative percentage of the quartz.[168] Another company was formed, and visitors and prospectors climbed from the wharf up a steep dray road to the houses, a smithy and other buildings set among the gardens and peach trees of an abandoned Māori village. Daniel Love and one of his men found a reef on Māori land at nearby Ruakaka Bay.

Two years after it began, and for all its careful management of costs,[169] the Golden Point Gold Mining Company collapsed. In yet another saga of hope emerging phoenix-like from ashes, shareholders formed the even shorter-lived Golden Fleece Company, then, in August 1880, the Golden Eagle Gold Mining Company. Men were employed and families arrived but a record of the parents' inability to pay a teacher indicates the familiar outcome. Despite back-breaking work in poorly ventilated conditions, and an ingenious pumping system that discharged water at 300 litres per minute, the reality was that the 20 tonnes of quartz eventually crushed yielded only 10 ounces of retorted gold and the supply appeared to have been exhausted. The company, its future dubious from 1883, wound up in 1887.

In 1873, about the same time as the Turner Gold Mining Company was taking up its leases on Cape Jackson, a sample of gold-bearing quartz found at the head of Long (Reef) Bay in Kenepuru Sound saw the formation of the small Pelorus Gold Mining Company. Further investigations were unpromising, and with the unfavourable outcomes at Golden Point and Cape Jackson, the venture ended.[170]

When compared with the other provinces, mining in Marlborough contributed

A relatively recent photo of Golden Point, opposite Picton, Tōtaranui Queen Charlotte Sound, showing the steep terrain up which heavy machinery had to be manhandled. LLOYD HOMER, GNS SCIENCE, 24005

very little to the local economy and in the Sounds even less. Nor did the Sounds' gold fields stimulate growth and development in the way the Wakamarina Gold Field in the Pelorus Valley had. Those rushes stimulated growth in Picton and transformed Havelock. They promoted track development around the Grove and attracted money for roading between Anakiwa and Havelock as well as for wharf development. In 1865 a mail run was established between the Grove (where a postmaster was appointed that year) and Picton, and also between Picton and Havelock.

Even so, the Queen Charlotte gold, like the antimony mining, contributed in a small way to the importance of Picton. Picton was, albeit briefly, the centre for the mines. It was where much of the capital originated for opening up the Cape Jackson mines; it was where tourists embarked to visit the Queen Charlotte Sound antimony and goldmines. Its growing prosperity and position as the jumping-off place for the Sounds may have been a good advertisement for those seeking opportunities there.

SETTLERS WERE ALWAYS ON THE lookout for new business ventures. Yet too often the industries failed, resources were exhausted, there wasn't enough capital or easy access to markets, or the businesses never properly got off the ground. Over time, newspaper statements became less aspirational, but what remains important is the hope and excitement that the perceived opportunities offered. And perhaps more.

The mills' wharves and plant, the miners' homes anchored on that bleak Kempe ridge, the whaling stations with their gruesome activity, the fish stations on cramped foreshores far out in the Sounds — all created visible structures, machinery and signs of settlement. Was this proof for apprehensive settlers and tourists that investment might pay off and that the country and its new inhabitants had a solid future?

At the antimony mines, settlers tucked their English cottages below the densely bushed range and grew English flowers. The flourishing gardens and orchards there and elsewhere in the Sounds may have reassured people that, even among these daunting hills, 'Home' could be created. In some psychological way these plantings were acts of possession. The continued investment in dubious ventures over some decades were evidence of the existence and importance of hope and belief as the newcomers (with little thought to the Māori whom they were dispossessing) settled in their new country.

5. Visitors by the Boatload

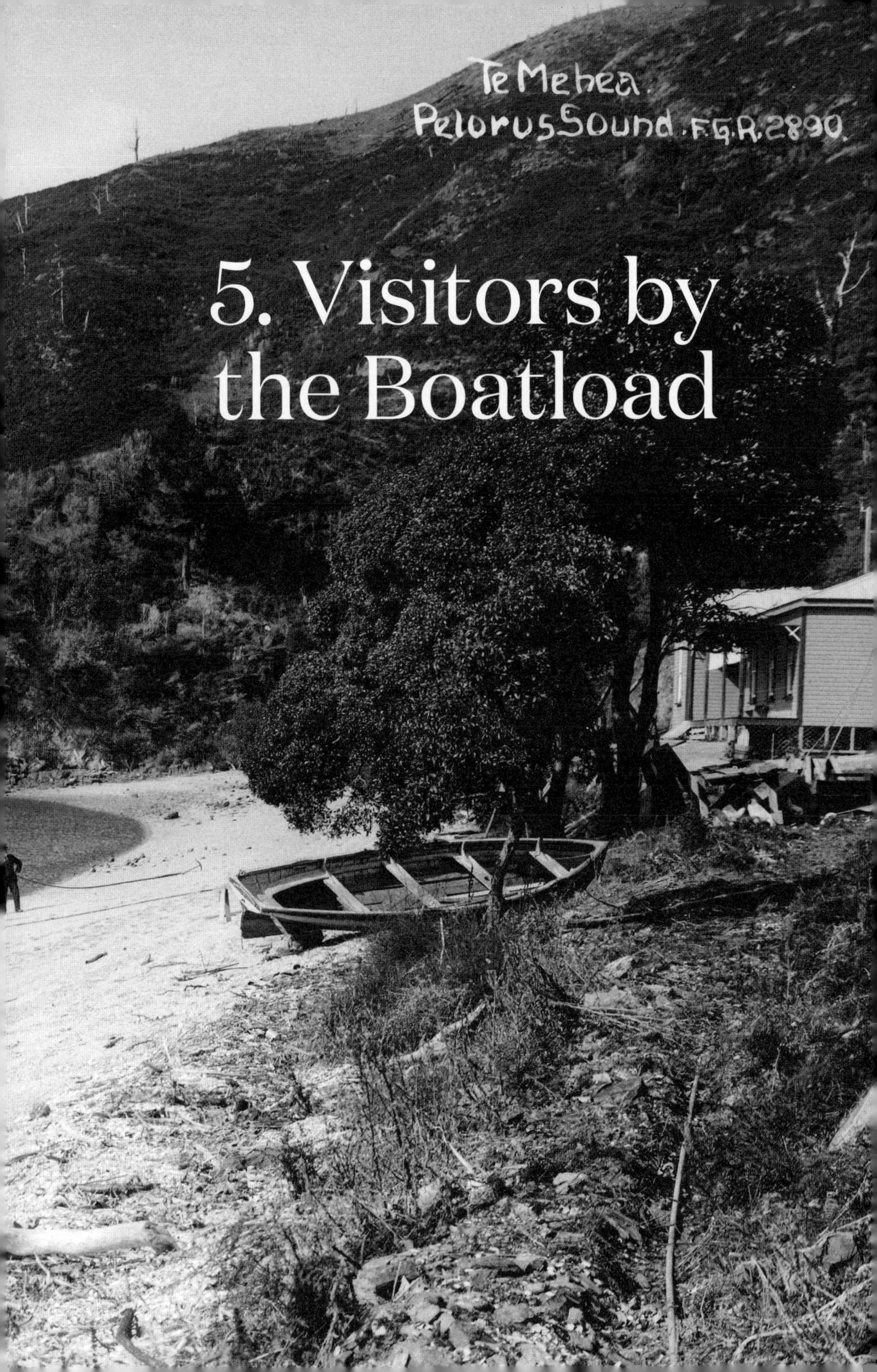

> Only 'a wooden man can gaze at a distant ridge without desiring to see beyond it', and the views and changing colours of a Sounds sunset created 'a desire to see it all at close quarters, to see it as the Maori and first Europeans first saw it'.

In mid-January 1859 the SS *Lord Ashley*, with 300 passengers aboard, set off on a long-mooted excursion to Queen Charlotte Sound. Hopes ran high for this first-time venture. But poor facilities on board, a late arrival at Picton that allowed passengers no time to go ashore, and a chaotic disembarkation once back in Wellington left *The Colonist*'s reporter with a distinctly jaundiced view of the whole affair, and, indeed, of the future of Picton.[1]

Fourteen years later, however, on 1 January 1873, no pleasanter or brighter morning could have been arranged for the 400 or so passengers on the New Zealand Steam Shipping Company's SS *Phoebe* for the day's excursion to Picton. The atmosphere was warm, the seas smooth, the refreshments ample, the scenery picturesque. There were one or two drawbacks. Four hundred passengers meant a very full boat and not enough seats. Picton sightseeing was limited to the hospital and the provincial government buildings, and the hotel meal was the worst the reporter had ever eaten. Generally, however, all 'went "as merry as a marriage bell"'. The 'happier, merrier, and livelier party [ever] yet seen afloat or ashore' was back in Wellington by 11 p.m.[2]

Not all travellers were so impressed by New Zealand's small steamers or the

Marlborough Sounds. A year or so before, G. T. Chapman, voyaging through the colony, recalled the general disagreeableness of the small, overcrowded steamers, of which *Phoebe*, at 585 tonnes, was one. Sailing across Cook Strait, they 'roll[ed] and tumbl[ed] enough to frighten one, and [made] small progress, unless the wind, for sport, gets behind them'. Far from picturesque, Chapman thought the land in Tory Channel looked scrubby and, notwithstanding Picton's kind, comfortable and hopeful inhabitants, the 'pretty' village looked 'as if it had been dropped there by mistake'. And it lacked road access to Blenheim.[3] Anthony Trollope's impressions of Picton's precarious prosperity when he visited New Zealand, albeit among beautiful scenery, were similarly double-edged.[4]

Perhaps the locals were accustomed to the vagaries of New Zealand travel. Certainly, the New Zealand Steam Shipping Company rapidly repeated its first success. From the mid-1880s other shipping companies organised increasingly extensive tours, local captains arranged local jaunts and individuals devised their own explorations. A European racing canoe, reportedly carrying an extraordinary 100 square feet (9.2 square metres) of sail, first crossed Cook Strait in 1890.

From 1894 'boating men', under sail or manning an oar, were discovering the beauties of the Sounds. Fish were there for the taking, though their variety and numbers were already diminishing. From 1882 the Marlborough Acclimatisation Society regularly notified the seasons for shooting deer, quail, pheasants and ducks and, until they were finally protected, native birds (often a staple of the Māori diet). Rabbits and hares were always fair game.

History created further attractions. The 'bold coastline of Marlborough' was easily visible from Wellington. Simply by clearing Port Nicholson Heads one was in waters 'that are as full of thrilling associations as the world Homer knew, and provocative of the most fantastic thoughts'. Only 'a wooden man can gaze at a distant ridge without desiring to see beyond it', and the views and changing colours of a Sounds sunset created 'a desire to see it all at close quarters, to see it as the Maori and first Europeans first saw it'.[5] Farmers were not always so pleased, but the creation from the 1880s of 'climatic reserves' (where bush was set aside to promote favourable climatic conditions, stop streams drying up, prevent floods and landslides, preserve healthy streams and rivers and prevent erosion and its undesirable consequences) fed this desire to see a past Sounds world.[6] Scenic reserves, which began to appear early in the twentieth century, had a similar effect.

As the shipping companies, promoters of the Sounds and settlers were realising,

Looking south-east from a high point in Tōtaranui Queen Charlotte Sound into the inner sound.
JOHN PASCOE, ALEXANDER TURNBULL LIBRARY, PACOLL-9765-09-69

there was money in them thar hills. The *Marlborough Express* and, to a lesser extent, the *Evening Post* ran article after article strongly promoting the Sounds — their scenery, the activities they offered. Promoters of the region worked hard along similar lines — promulgating the physical, energetic challenges of a Sounds holiday of fishing, rowing and swimming as well as the contemplative, regenerative vacations to recuperate from the stresses of modern life.

The timing was perfect for such development and promotion. New Zealanders (and they were not alone in this), worrying that 'the sturdy pioneers' of the past were being replaced by unhealthy factory labourers and sedentary clerks, passed the Physical Drill in Public and Native Schools Act 1901, providing that drill be taught in those schools to all children aged eight and over.[7] The Department of Tourist and Health Resorts was established in the same year to promote a growing leisure industry and develop a national and international tourist economy that contributed to the country's coffers.[8] Tourism fed into the coffers of Sounds communities too. The range of services provided, along with the money tourists spent, contributed towards breaking down the isolation of the Sounds and improving their economic viability. However, not everyone was keen: the tensions around land use, land conservation and financial gain that are still being played out in the Sounds were beginning to become evident.

But when, at the end of 1873, the New Zealand Steam Shipping Company rapidly followed its first initiative with another 'marine excursion' to Picton, the town 'looked as pretty and snug as ever', the scenery was breathtaking and the smooth Sounds waters (a long-used selling point) made for unbridled enjoyment.[9] By the mid-1880s, as visitor numbers began to grow and as the 'pleasure grounds' of the Sounds became better known,[10] the enthusiastic press reports got longer. The Union Steamship Company began running Christmas and Easter jaunts, as well as much-advertised long-weekend excursions. Carefully timed to fit in with the Blenheim–Picton train timetable, the itineraries quickly expanded beyond Queen Charlotte Sound to Pelorus, to the quiet beauty of D'Urville Island's Greville Harbour or to the remoteness of Port Hardy. Or passengers might opt for the excitement of being swirled and swept through the narrow waters of French Pass. 'Any of our young fellows who desire to spend a week or ten days' holiday at a cheap rate (our individual expense only amounted to £2 18s 3d) and see marvellous scenery should go to Pelorus', opined a *Marlborough Express* correspondent in 1893 — in fact, it was deplorable to live even as far away as Wellington and not give in to the lure of the Sounds.[11]

By then tourists could experience, without the accompanying inconveniences, the rigours of a frontier whose boundaries grew as their ships pushed into bays where no cruise ship had gone before. Destinations expanded to take in the remoter parts of Pelorus Sounds and World's End. Itineraries offered variety and affordable 'days of smooth water cruising, with plenty of fishing, and the enjoyment of beautiful scenery, to say nothing of complete freedom from business worries, and the fag of ordinary, every-day life'.[12] Wellington's reality could be postponed until early Monday morning.

INCREASED STEAMER SIZE AND FURTHER amenities created other drawcards. In 1911 the Union Steamship Company's 3502-tonne *Mokoia* took only 102 minutes from Wellington Heads to Tory Entrance; the 270-nautical-mile three-day round trip well down into each Sound took 22 and a half hours.

The feat and the successful cruise were widely reported. But speed was not the only criterion for success. The 240 passengers abroad the *Mokoia* reportedly made for genial company and, if quoits or deck billiards palled ('as they generally do'), guests could turn to cricket, cards or pillow fights. When boats landed at Tennyson Inlet, the ships' officers looked to their guests' comforts. With their 'floating home to hand', passengers could be assured that there was none of 'the makeshift of the camp . . . the risks attendant on untried boarding houses or hotels'.

Rather, there were two meal sittings (no overcrowding here), the 22 waiters were attentive, and there was 'operatic and other music at luncheon, dinner and at sundry other times. In fact music seemed to be going all day long, and sometimes far into the night. It was all part of the scheme.'[13] By the 1890s the Sounds' fame had reached an international market.

The Anchor Steam Shipping Company steamer *Murray* and the Wellington Steam Packet Company's *Stormbird* were not slow to offer competition. The little local trader *Waitapu* was launched on the excursion market about 1890, offering a four-day trip and 'exceptionally reasonable' fares.[14] In 1893 locally knowledgeable passengers, along with the ship's size and draught and the tide, gave the *Evening Post*'s reporter, 'Viator', and the party of Mikado Minstrels an adventurous perspective of a holiday where the stop-off places read like a list of must-see's of the area, and activities were thoughtfully tailored to passenger whim.

Once across Cook Strait (a 'lively' crossing that required Captain Westrupp and his officers to vacate their bunks for the passengers) and in Pelorus Sound, there was a race with another steamer carrying another party of Wellingtonians. *Waitapu* then anchored off the Archers' property in Tuna Bay; passengers paid their respects, and explored the estate. They went on a fishing expedition in the little rowing boats brought across for the purpose, they tussled mightily with a small shark, they had to row back to the steamer — she was grounded on a falling tide. (The Sounds were not surveyed until 1912 and there was no official information on Pelorus Sound's tides or their big tidal range.) Once floating again, *Waitapu* left in moonlight for John Mills' estate at Brightlands, then slipped through Hopai Bay's narrow entrance to Thomas Mills' comfortable 12-room residence, before calling in at Homewood. Sailing on down to Havelock they happened on the Nelson-bound *Lady Barkly*, out-of-date copies of the *Evening Post* were handed across, and the ships parted amid cheers and renderings of 'Home, Boys, Home' and 'Auld Lang Syne'. *Waitapu* grounded again on Havelock's notorious mudflats, but a fast-making tide had them soon afloat and at Havelock.[15]

Some locals were quick to cash in on tourist interests. In Queen Charlotte Sound in the early 1880s a number of boat owners were offering day trippers 'lovely trip[s] down the placid waters of the Sounds', the prospect of fishing, and moderate fares.[16] Overnight picnics, moonlight excursions, weekend trips and opportunities to stand inside whales' jaws at Te Awaiti were advertised; weekend trips were scheduled to allow Blenheim gentlemen to get back in time for work on Monday.

The antimony mines, even when not operating, were always a drawcard. In 1900 E. C. Perano acquired his first *Elsie*, licensed for 80 passengers and fitted with new boilers, seating and awnings.[17] A few years later his new trading and day-excursion boat, *Rob Roy*, offered tourists a commodious sundeck with canvas awnings and plenty of space for up to 260 passengers within river limits (rather fewer on the open sea). The main saloon alone held 18 berths; the ladies' cabin accommodated nine.[18] If such investments are indications of the money being made from tourism ventures, these were making money.

Union Steamship cruises flourished well beyond 1920, but the advent of the versatile, easily hired 'oil-launch' at the turn of the century, along with increasing numbers of roads and tracks, contributed to the demise of the little steamers' cruise trips.[19] Their arrival coincided with the building of summer homes in the more accessible Queen Charlotte Sound, together with accommodation houses advertising an ever-expanding list of local attractions. Camping became increasingly popular, and holiday houses offered bases for the men and women who, some more stalwart than

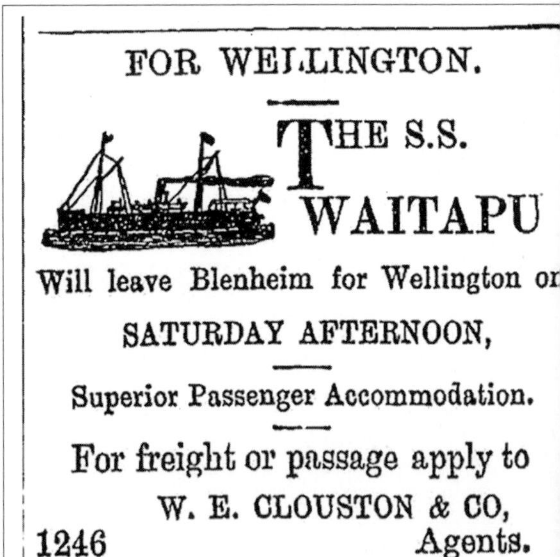

FOR WELLINGTON.

THE S.S. WAITAPU

Will leave Blenheim for Wellington on

SATURDAY AFTERNOON,

Superior Passenger Accommodation.

For freight or passage apply to

W. E. CLOUSTON & CO,

1246 Agents.

ABOVE 'Group on a boat, Picton Sounds', 1908. The launch glides to the beach in quiet waters – a lovely example of how the then developing Sounds leisure industry sought to promote itself. The image also illustrates the new-fangled 'oil-launch' that from 1902 began transforming life for many European Sounds settlers. ALEXANDER TURNBULL LIBRARY, 1/2-C-002535-F

RIGHT This image of the little steamer *Waitapu* accompanied many advertisements for its tourist and freight services around the Sounds. *MARLBOROUGH EXPRESS*, 22 AUGUST 1890

others, ventured into the hills, enjoyed the views and rendered their memories into prose lightly washed with Romantic overtones.

The small launches allowed holidaymakers to explore 'the most interesting' spots in Queen Charlotte — 'Whatamango, Maraetai, Anapua . . . Tauranga Kawau . . . the peninsula of Kaihinu, with its ancient Maori pa and its little sentry-islet Moioio'.[20] The launches took campers around Queen Charlotte Sound, their skippers equipped with nautical skill and local knowledge of where to pitch the tents.[21] Launches ferried holidaymakers to Torea and on to the delights of Kenepuru or Nelson.[22]

World War I impacted on this, but as early as 1917 launch trips were getting underway again,[23] and the Pelorus Motor Boat Club was established at the end of that year.[24] By mid-November 1918, along with the lists of returned soldiers, newspapers were again reporting that visitors could hire recreational vessels in the Sounds, and enjoy a day on the water and the many varied charms of the individual bays.[25]

A SOUNDS HOLIDAY OFFERED a variety of activities as well as stunning scenery. Swimming was always an integral part. (The cold water does not appear to have been a deterrent, perhaps because of the penchant of the time for invigorating cold baths.) Fishing and, less frequently, hunting were also on offer. Detailed knowledge had been amassed of the considerable variety of fish that might be found 'wherever the line was dropped'.[26] Some tourists, revelling in a boatload of fish taken with no regard to size or sustainability, went on to catch more. Within a few years the wastage from such parties and its deleterious impact on the fish stocks created at least one call for limits on catches.[27]

By 1893 hunting was sufficiently profitable for much of the Sounds to be presented as a sportsman's paradise.[28] Kākā and kererū (New Zealand pigeon) were plentiful, though stoats and weasels were reducing the number of California quail, and pheasants were rare. Red deer (numerous enough for fawns from the Sounds to be transferred to Waikaremoana and Dunedin) were increasing in the district and in the Pelorus and Wairau valleys. Hares and rabbits roamed widely.[29] By 1903 wild goats, sheep and pigs could be shot about Cape Jackson,[30] and a hunter might try for shags anywhere in the Sounds.[31] Those looking for a gentler sport might search for wild honey in the bush.

For some time, well-notified seasons for shooting birds (native and introduced) offered the only protection to native species. Specific protection of native birds was introduced only gradually (kākā in 1913, kererū and paradise duck in 1916). What difference such measures made to sportsmen far from the prospect of detection and long accustomed to shooting 'sackfuls' of birds[32] was questioned even at the time. Seasons were also introduced for deer shooting.[33]

Whaling provided a dramatic spectator sport. Locals had always taken an interest in the activity; now passengers on the Picton–Wellington run sometimes caught the thrill of the chase. In 1917 (the year the Peranos caught 17 humpbacks), government photographer S. B. Taylor shot 4000 feet of film of whaling at 'Te Awaiti' (probably Fishing Bay), much of it in a south-east gale, when the sea builds at the heads and rides in through the narrow entrance in great surges. The result was hailed as 'a valuable recording of a New Zealand industry which may truly be described as heroic'.[34] Locals, delighted with the promotion, proclaimed the film as 'one of the best advertisements that Marlborough has ever had, and a cheap one at that'. Few would 'see a whale hunt in reality . . . Now the whole of Blenheim can see it cheaply and with the comfort of an easy chair.' Tourist interest was boosted and international interest was surely in the offing.[35]

Individual tourists were doing their own exploring by water from the mid-1880s. In 1885 the *Marlborough Express* noted that four Wellington gentlemen (showing an enterprise not seen before) had their boat carried from Queen Charlotte Sound over Torea Neck. Nelson-bound, they were also seizing a chance to explore Pelorus Sound.[36] In 1890 Hokitika canoeists George Parkes and his brother, in what the *New Zealand Herald* termed a 'foolhardy voyage', braved delays, dramas, strong winds, currents and tidal rips to become the first to attempt, and succeed, to canoe Cook Strait.[37] Within the decade canoeing in the Sounds was attracting international attention[38] and, well in advance of today's intrepid adventurers, at least one couple spent their honeymoon in Kenepuru in a canoe.[39]

Today, recreational sailors in the Sounds have access to detailed charts, a widely available boating guide and long-amassed information from boating acquaintances. In 1890, however, George Parkes' account of his trip across the Strait, his journey to Picton and his subsequent trip through Pelorus Sound was possibly the first to furnish the recreational and general public with an itinerary through the Sounds and information on the sailing conditions he met: the williwaws 'roaring' down Endeavour Inlet and the calm reached beyond the mouth of the bay; the winds coming in great gusts down Pelorus Sounds' Northwest Bay, almost capsizing the canoe; and the 'fearful' south-east gale that 'swept the surface of the water with irresistible fury',

ABOVE J. Watson and W. Smith stand outside a picnic tent in 1911. Lunches were often laid out in such tents to keep the food cool. MARLBOROUGH HISTORICAL SOCIETY, 6392

BELOW No need to get your feet wet getting ashore. Here, a rowing boat tows passengers from the little steamer to shore in a punt. MARLBOROUGH HISTORICAL SOCIETY, 4554

Rob Roy Canoes, 1887. Over 4 metres long, these canoes were built of planks and, apart from a small central cockpit, were decked over. For sea voyages they could be rigged with sails. In this photo members of Wellington's Tainui Canoe Club, formed in 1870, are sailing in Tōtaranui Queen Charlotte Sound. ALEXANDER TURNBULL LIBRARY, 1/2-035133-G

leaving him little option but to furl sail and run before the wind under bare poles. But the storm, once it abated, left him in good stead. Parkes was able to round West Entry Point — and there we leave him in a freshening breeze and under full sail, making for Admiralty Bay, French Pass and Nelson.[40]

His solo expedition was a not inconsiderable achievement. Among the great Pelorus reaches whose hills and relentless bush hem in the sea, Parkes was alone in a tiny craft. He had no way of letting people know of any mishap. If he thought of such things he gave no indication. Instead, he wrote of camps in deep bays under the stars, of 'luxuriant' karaka in a bay on Kenny Isle (Pohuenui) and of early-morning swims only a few metres from where he had slept on 'warm soft sand'. There were big driftwood fires for boiling the billy, the screeches of kākā and tūī and the heavy beat of kererū wings. High points gave extensive views over the Sound and water like glass. Here was a 'retreat from care and worry' unequalled anywhere else in New Zealand.[41] And, as other Sounds' advertisements would state, the capital city was always close. The space the *Marlborough Express* accorded this account of his trip gave it considerable attention.

Parkes travelled in an area where settlement only touched the edges. Yet it was, in some ways, extraordinarily peopled. No sooner were he and his brother in Queen Charlotte Sound than they visited Jaketh Wearne at the antimony mine. In Pelorus Sound, Parkes fell into company with the crew of a fishing boat, and fished with her captain, the boat-builder Patrick (Patsy) McCauley. A Mr Pulman and family passed them at one point, and Parkes stayed the night with them at Crail Bay. He had barely left the next morning before he entered a 'snug little nook' owned by a Mr Palmer, an artist who was in his 'romantically picturesque' camp — 'a perfect paradise to a man of his taste'. He called in on the Macefields, and sailed or paddled quite a distance to see the Stuarts at Te Towaka in Cissy Bay and the Archers in Tuna Bay.

As he left the Sound, Parkes met up again with 'my friend Patsy' at the failed Bulwer fishing station. To slip into a bay where clearance and homes signalled human presence, friendliness, generosity and possible succour must have been comforting. For their part, the settlers, isolated from the world and deprived of company, would have welcomed his presence and the news he brought. Did such factors contribute to the otherwise economic imperatives that lay behind the development of the accommodation houses that settlers were establishing within the decade?

A COUPLE OF YEARS AFTER Parkes' memorable trip, members of Wellington's Star Boating Club (later the Royal Port Nicholson Yacht Club) cruised in the Sounds for the first time. Newspaper reports provide a picture not unfamiliar to Sounds sailors today — the rough trips home, being holed up in a bay for days at a time. But such accounts did not deter. *Syren* was there when, in 1895, along with the 9-tonne 'crack yacht' *Waitangi*, she was joined by *Muratai, Maritana, Kotiri, Atlanta, Ngaira, Kotiri, Wainui* and Alexander Turnbull's *Irirangi* and half-rater *Miru*. These were among the increasing numbers of yachts that returned season after season, to cruise and sometimes take part in the Picton regatta.

The crossings were fast, even by today's standards. Helped by a south-easterly, in 1899 *Waitangi* made the run from her Thorndon mooring to Tory Channel in four hours 35 minutes — then the fastest time ever made by a Wellington yacht.[42] Eight years later, in beautiful weather and under full canvas, *Syren* returned from Tory Channel in three and a half hours.[43] Then, as now, crossings were potentially dangerous: the occasional stories of near wrecks and near loss of life were widely syndicated.[44]

By the end of the 1890s, as long-distance coastal recreational sailing made its appearance, the odd pleasure yacht (sail and steam) arrived from Auckland or Christchurch. 'Pelorus Sound is a fine yachting ground,' declared a 1905 Tourist and Health Resorts Department report, predicting it becoming as important to Wellingtonians as the Hauraki Gulf was to Aucklanders. Seven years later, launches were crossing Cook Strait or coming up the coast from Sumner, sharing in those pleasurable retrospective frissons provided by shark sightings.[45] In Tory Channel one 'man-eating' shark 'with a reputation for fierceness' 'attack[ed] open boats and bit the oars', sending crews scuttling for the shore. *Waitangi*'s crew responded to one such reported attack, driving 'a ½ inch harpoon right through one of these monsters, which in its struggles struck the harpoon against the keel, and bent the instrument right over as though it had been a piece of wire'.[46]

However, the beauties of the Marlborough Sounds were becoming better known to more than yachtsmen (the term is used advisedly). In 1894 a party of seven Wellington gentlemen led by W. P. James, clerk of the Magistrate's Court, loaded their whaleboats and oars onto SS *Grafton* to be dropped off at Ketu Bay, Pelorus Sound. They camped one night on shore, and from there progressed from homestead to homestead, where the families welcomed them with hospitality and largesse. Gentlemen they may have been, but they were not averse to a tow from SS *Murray* 'right up' to the Bonds' station in Homewood Bay. The rest of the time they rowed — they covered 22 nautical miles one day from Manaroa to Kenepuru Sound and continued on, over a series of days, to reach Tennyson Inlet before heading for West Entry Point. From there they ran through to French Pass and Nelson under sail.[47]

The group left the Bonds' place (it was Christmas Day) to make a day trip to Hopai. After 'a very jolly time' they pressed on to Manaroa, where Mr Godsiff received them hospitably. In Kenepuru, McMahon 'placed a whare at their disposal' and all went to a musical evening at his house. John Mills' homestead at Brightlands was the next stop, before the Archers' welcome at World End. Heavy rain there forced them to abandon their tents and seek refuge in the house, where 'Mrs. Archer's kindness could not have been exceeded'. At Waihinau Bay, too, the McCauleys 'made them very much at home'.

The party would continue to meet such hospitality throughout the rest of their holiday. Whatever the weather (and it was indifferent), they returned home enthused with their accomplishments, their explorations and the Sounds' residents' hospitality.[48]

WITHIN THE SOUNDS, SMALL BOATS, with oars to beat the area's fickle winds, were best. In 1898 eight veterans of a similar venture the previous year left Wellington, their rowing boat *Toroa* slung on the davits of Union Steamship's *Rotorua*. The aim was to explore Queen Charlotte Sound. Accompanying them were 'an able and experienced officer' whom few could better for navigating or rowing, as well as a steward, chief cook and three able seamen.

Rotorua altered her course to drop them nearer the camp at Fly (now Ratimera) Bay in Ruakaka Bay and the party made its way north as far as Ship Cove. They used the ready-made campsite before rowing east into East Bay, then south to Picton. Serious effort was needed throughout, but they later relished memories of the great gusts of wind that blew their tents away, the 'torrent' of rain that wet their clothes and bedding, and their brief grounding on the rock just off Snake Point (today well marked on the charts).

They made an abortive search for shackles said to have been left by Cook, they swam, saw dolphins, relaxed after hard rowing, gazed at stars and moon, and generally had the satisfaction of hard-gained knowledge and of the beauty and romance of Queen Charlotte Sound, where each day seemed 'finer than the

Petone Naval Volunteers, Marlborough Sounds, 6 December 1906. ALEXANDER TURNBULL LIBRARY, 1/2-010394-G

one before it, and each place we went to seemed more beautiful than the one we had left'.[49]

Within a few years the Petone Naval Volunteers and other such groups were loading their cutter, tents, kits and provisions on the *Rotorua*, crossing the strait, and setting off from Picton to explore the Sound.[50]

Rowing and yachting trips generally involved men only — cramped quarters, the weight of the gear and social custom precluded women for decades more. As such, they provided a camaraderie enjoyed and abetted by the excitement and satisfaction of beating into bays under sail or with 'severe rowing'.[51] Cruising yachts or launches provided better opportunities than the steamers to get away from it all. Parties in rowing boats could get even further away by eschewing settlers and their homesteads or yachts and their bunks. Rowers found romance in having tents as the only shelter and appreciating 'the luxury of ferns' for bedding;[52] at Ship Cove the beaten-down tall English grass and mint growing among 'numerous cherry trees and willows and honeysuckle, all mixed in grand confusion with the different varieties of native trees' formed a comfortable substitute for the fern.[53]

Whether its smaller size was a factor, Queen Charlotte Sound seemed to offer a romantic dimension that Pelorus lacked. Certainly, there appear to have been fewer settlers to call on.[54] The historical associations of Ship Cove 'gave a licence to the imagination' and as the eye 'ranged over a vast forest, clothed with the identical tints which so delighted the members of his [Cook's] party' so one 'could picture the scene as it appeared . . . Cook's fine old ship at anchor in the bay, surrounded by canoes which had come from the neighbouring pahs, at that time filled with a multitude of savages.'[55]

MEANWHILE, MEN, AND SOME WOMEN, were setting out into the bush. In 1895, 'lovers of picturesque forest scenery' and especially the 'artist, the fisherman, the sportsman and the naturalist' who wished to gratify these 'outdoor and manly pleasures' were urged to climb Mount Stokes (1203 m) for 'one of the finest panoramic views to be seen anywhere'. There were routes from Kenepuru or Endeavour Inlet (each about six hours), and from Manaroa (two hours), reported 'Zenc' in the *Marlborough Express*. He and two others had left from Kenepuru early, taking the track towards Endeavour Inlet to the foot of the saddle. They left the track there to climb up the ridge. Sometimes they pushed 'through thickets with a dense undergrowth of supplejacks', sometimes 'glades'. At one point they followed a stream where 'impenetrable foliage' grew at intervals overhead. Above its pools were '[g]reat ferns, with shining fronds and delicate mosses dripping with spray . . . huge trees started from the crevices . . . dead trunks . . . and creeping ferns formed natural bridges'. Flocks of canaries (probably yellowheads), bellbirds, cuckoos, robins, parakeets and a range of smaller species darted about. At about 900 metres, close to the bushline, they had to force their way through a dense belt of *Oleria colensoi* (leatherwood) growing in its only Marlborough habitat. Then, above the bushline, they were in an area 'ablaze with shrubs and wild flowers' — pimelia, four new species of *Celmisia*, *Danthonia*, buttercups, *Bulbinella hookeri* and speargrass.

The trig and the top were only a short distance on. Beyond were the 'Pelorus hills rising tier upon tier, and range behind range . . . while the waters of the Pelorus and Manaroa Sounds appeared like great inland lakes'. To the south were the Kenepuru hills, to the east lay Queen Charlotte Sound, indented by inlets and punctuated by its scattering of small islands. Beyond that, Cook Strait, Kāpiti, Wellington Heads and the Rimutaka (now Remutaka) Range, to the north Cape Jackson, and to the south Cape Campbell. The adventurers came home by starlight and at the saddle, in true romantic fashion, 'glow-worms on the tree and bank illuminated the sides of the beaten path we must follow'.[56]

The shape of the future, however, was already apparent. The birdlife was still abundant but the trampers had seen tracks of a wild cow and calf, and pigs had 'literally furrowed [the ground] with their rooting'. They had shot a wild sheep at the summit. From the trig, a settler's homestead and clearing were immediately below them. Their views from the top of Mount Stokes were not of an untrammelled Eden.

A year later, in 1896, Professor Thomas Kirk of the Agricultural Department and a number of others — including, for the first time, women — climbed Mount Stokes; six months later nine women and five men set off on a two-day expedition. That party's enthusiasms for the views possibly exceeded Zenc's — they made two ascents to appreciate them fully, and they experienced, too, the drama of an unplanned night out and a storm. They came home with specimens to be 'planted or pressed and carefully preserved as souvenirs of the expedition'.[57]

The word 'tramping' was coming into vogue.[58] These long day or overnight excursions, today part of our tramping heritage, would lay the groundwork for subsequent expeditions, by men and women, up Mount Stokes and around the Sounds.

Tom Gullery with horse, cart and boat on the Torea–Portage road, inner Pelorus Sound.
MARLBOROUGH HISTORICAL SOCIETY, 016727

ABOUT THE SAME TIME ANOTHER, more sedentary, activity was being taken up. In January 1899 some 30 schoolgirls, with chaperones and a few 'Picton ladies', camped out at Endeavour Inlet. Excursions, euchre parties and a fancy-dress party helped fill the three to four weeks they were there.[59] By 1908, record numbers of campers were turning Portage into 'a miniature township of tents'.[60] Campers soon became more intrepid, hiring launches to take them and their tents to virgin bush still standing in part of Bay of Many Coves, or to Resolution Bay, Te Awaiti, Te Weka, Opua and Whatamango bays.[61] Mixed parties went out unchaperoned. Even into the first year of the war, local papers were full of the numbers of tourists and their activities.[62]

Options were also growing for those who did not fancy roughing it in boats or under canvas. In the mid-1880s the proprietor of Havelock's Masonic Hotel enterprisingly recognised that tourists travelling or fishing in the 'famed' Pelorus Sound needed somewhere to stay. In his establishment, guests would have 'every attention', he boasted, advertising wines and spirits of the best brands and good stabling and paddocks.[63] Thomas Gullery, who had lived in the district from boyhood, also launched into providing tourist accommodation. His property at Portage was ideally situated. It had easy access from Picton, Manaroa and Kenepuru, with the 'excellent' road over the saddle to Torea Bay taking a mere 20 minutes or so walking, and it possessed one of the few 'decent' beaches in the Sounds. In 1893 his newly enlarged farmhouse provided 'commodious' accommodation under a fine stand of trees.[64]

The Sounds, and Picton as their gateway, became increasingly accessible as the twentieth century progressed. More and more tourists were arriving on the Wellington–Picton and Nelson steamers. From around 1910 the social columns of the *Evening Post* featured increasing numbers of items on families, individuals or yachtsmen spending time in the Sounds. The roads were improving, and by 1915 Picton was a mere two-day drive from Christchurch.[65] The days of taking the Christchurch–Wellington steamer, then the Wellington–Picton steamer as the fastest way for Cantabrians to get to the Sounds were over.[66]

Daily services ran from Blenheim to Christchurch and, via Havelock, to Nelson. The Sounds tourism industry might have its pressure-points (there was the odd complaint about a shortage of good accommodation and launches, and the need for a faster Cook Strait ferry),[67] but here were all the signs of an embryonic tourism infrastructure. A growing choice of launches could run guests out into the Sounds to the bay of their choice. As Gullery's accommodation flourished, other settlers, particularly in Queen Charlotte Sound, launched themselves into the hospitality business, using existing rooms, enlarging their homes or adding a small annex to cater for paying guests.

In Resolution Bay, Robert Ewing first offered accommodation in 1900. In 1907 his new house still had the ubiquitous sacks hung from window frames (the windows were on their way), but even so it was booked out in mid-January.[68] By 1906 the Homewood Accommodation House was in full swing; Glenburn had been established (in some unidentified bay in Tory Channel);[69] the Baxters were set up for guests at Erie Bay in 1909; and in 1915 Miss Mary Norton at Te Awaiti offered a 'splendid place' to stay. There was accommodation on Blumine Island; from about 1909 Redheugh (also spelt Redhaugh), in Opua Bay, offered guests 'typical Sounds hospitality' and 'luscious peaches'; intending residents at Hugo and Leila (Eliza Jane) Terrill's place in Dryden Bay arrived in Bowden's steam launch, *Gannet.*[70]

The Boltons in 1910 offered accommodation in Kenepuru, by which time Crail Bay and Te Mahia also had boarding establishments. In 1920 Ethel Beauchamp Hazelwood had her first paying guests for the summer in the old farmhouse at Anakiwa, in which Craddock and Harriet Beauchamp had once lived.[71] However rough and ready, the places had a certain cachet. As early as 1906 D. W. Foote at Homewood Accommodation House reported 20 oil-launches regularly tied up at the Homewood wharf, bringing in some 500 tourists and settlers;[72] by 1914, Sounds' boarding houses were said to be 'well patronised', and, among those able to reach them, they retained their popularity during the war.[73]

Ethel Hazelwood, married and homesick for Anakiwa, overcame her husband's initial opposition and started the boarding house as a way of getting back to the Grove.[74] Others, burdened with low farm returns, took guests simply to keep the farm viable.[75] Facilities and attractions were initially, understandably, modest — and guests generally did not have high expectations. However, in 1897 a furnished cottage, in 'one of the pretty bays' not far from Havelock, offered good bathing, sailing, rowing boats, a good track to Picton, Blenheim or Havelock; the regular mail services direct from Wellington and Havelock got particular mention.[76] Such a list might be expanded by offers of hunting and fishing, the evocation of unique scenery and unequalled climate, all for a moderate tariff. Snappily worded advertisements became even snappier, and while the basics changed little, getting there and back got even easier. By 1915 most accommodation houses had their own launches, and from 1909, with phone connections to Picton or Havelock established in many bays, holidaymakers had no need 'to be long out of touch with the rest of the world'.[77] Importantly during the war, war news could be received daily by phone.[78]

The pattern of days at Anakiwa, representative of so many Sounds holidays, was leisurely and unpretentious. Guests might walk, picnic, hire the boats, play tennis. Fish caught was cooked by the host. There was no electricity, kerosene lamps lit the dining room, people gathered to sing after dinner. In the homestead guests had candles in their rooms, those in the tents placed over wooden platforms had lanterns slung on a pole, and everyone went to sleep to dogs barking in the woolsheds and moreporks calling from the gullies.[79]

'Water-side' cottages where families could 'camp', doing their own cooking and cleaning, became a further option from the early twentieth century.[80] Wellington residents were also building their own summer homes in Resolution Bay and in Endeavour Inlet.[81] Captain P. G. Howden and his wife, Elizabeth, had bought 1040 acres (420 ha) of bush-covered land and in 1904, to cater for friends and relatives, they built their 'beautiful summer residence', equipped 'with every modern convenience', below Mount Furneaux (823 m).[82] 'Well established' holiday homes and baches, too, were making their appearance in the more frequented Grove Arm.[83]

In 1849 Archbishop George Selwyn, being taken down Queen Charlotte Sound, had seen 'shoals of black fish and porpoises, their dark bodies contrasting strangely with the red light reflected from the sunset on the calm water from which they sprung into the air and fell back again'.[84] In Katherine Mansfield's short story 'The Voyage', a small girl accompanying her grandmother to the Sounds embarks on the Picton ferry. Amid the clamour of the Wellington wharf, the ferry was 'all beaded with round golden lights' looking 'as if she were more ready to sail among stars than out into the cold sea'. They arrived in Picton to a 'white mist that rose and fell and the sea still sounded asleep as slowly it rose and fell on the beach'.[85]

Many visitors, trying to convey a feeling and a sense of the Sounds, fell back on terms such as 'unequalled' or 'impossible to describe'. Others persevered, trying to re-create in words the world into which the Sounds transported them. There was not the West Coast's 'stern grandeur', but on a rough day,

> Great curtains of rain with many folds and pleats pass slowly across the view . . . the waters are agitated, white-capped waves race and wrangle noisily, winds war with tide and current. Whirlwinds scurry across the Sounds like gyrating ghosts, and all is restless, fractious, angry . . . Clouds

ABOVE Guests awaiting transport, Torea Bay, Tōtaranui Queen Charlotte Sound, c. 1900. ALEXANDER TURNBULL LIBRARY, 480501/2

BELOW Glenlee Accommodation House began offering accommodation in 1910–11. By the 1920s, when it was run by Bill and Nina McNabb, its promotional material, like that produced by other establishments, carried an ever-expanding list of available facilities. ALEXANDER TURNBULL LIBRARY, B-K-1435-PIC

> die, become spirits, invisible . . . long filaments of mist . . . curl out from the deep clefts in the hills and finally melt and disappear. The hills take on a deep blue tone . . . changing as the day grows older into violet . . . the bare headlands shine like burnished gold in the last rays of the sun. All the land merges into blackness with the night. The stars come out . . . reflected in the polished water. There is no sound but the far away call of a morepork, the distant bark of a dog, or the rhythmic moving of oars in their rowlocks a mile away. The Sounds seem to be asleep. One speaks in whispers.[86]

Into this pristine world, predatory mammals were released throughout the country from the early 1880s. Some 3000 weasels were set free in Marlborough alone in 1884.[87] Birds were immediately under threat. By 1909, at the antimony mines, 'every night . . . weasels kill[ed] the birds in the trees overhanging the house'; during the day weasels could be seen running at an extraordinary rate up supplejacks, chasing korimako (bellbirds), tūī and other birds in the tops of the mataī, and eating tūī eggs.[88]

The bush itself, as well as potentially valuable timber, was also destroyed in farmers' summer burns. In 1911, even as the *Marlborough Express* journalist quoted above reported on the world of water, winds, mist and stars, he recorded that farming in Queen Charlotte Sound and Tory Channel was

> baring or will bare every hill and dell of the bush. 'A good burn' means much to the settler, but it desolates the Sounds. All along Queen Charlotte and in Tory Channel are chains of treeless hills with great patches of monotonously [sic] green — sometimes with light brown pastures, and marked by slips revealing the skin of the earth itself.[89]

'Many thousands of acres . . . cleared and laid down in grass . . . will gladden the eye of the bucolic farmer, [but] there will be little left to enchant the artist', wrote one of a growing group of concerned travellers.[90] Tourists, too, as elsewhere in New Zealand, thoughtlessly vandalised the Sounds' 'scenic gems' to the extent that that there were fears for their future.[91]

Reservation for preservation

New Zealand has a long history of creating land reserves for various purposes. Nelson's provincial government in 1857 notified reserves of 'waste' land in the Sounds — areas of nine to 50 acres set aside 'for the purposes of public utility' in Pelorus and Queen Charlotte sounds. These were generally for watering or grazing, though land for public buildings in Picton was also set aside.[92] Such actions were commonplace. In 1864 more such utilitarian land designations were made in Queen Charlotte Sound — for such things as the signal and pilot stations on Blumine Island and on Ship Cove's foreshore, and the public utility reserve on Motuara.[93]

As early as 1874 the government of the day began receiving advice (and graphic pictures) on the effects of the destruction of forest cover around the world, and the consequent erosion, flooding, loss of pasture and damage to rivers. From 1881, eyeing the economy rather more than the scenery, the Department of Lands and Survey progressively gazetted thousands of hectares of New Zealand's indigenous forest as protection forest or climatic reserves. The area — 21,000 acres or 8500 ha — that the Department of Lands and Survey set aside in Marlborough in 1913 indicates how seriously the government took this initiative. The land in question was almost entirely on the upper slopes and peaks of the bushed ranges in Port Underwood and the Sounds areas, including Mount Stokes and Mount Robertson; further reservations were planned for the Richmond Range. Such blocks were large enough to regenerate after a fire. However, the department warned firmly against letting landholders take up burned-over areas — 'this would probably lead to the wilful destruction of tracts of reserved bush'.[94]

The reservation of scenic areas came later. In 1898, as debates raged about the possibility of a national park in the Pelorus and Ōpouri valleys, politician Charles Mills, fearing for the future of milling in the area, spoke for a large sector of public opinion when he robustly declared that 'the extensive interests of the present generation [should not be sacrificed] merely to study the sentimental feelings of prosperity'.[95] Many considered the bush doomed anyway as civilisation and progress marched across the country — burning bush, accidentally or intentionally, was part of the natural process of settlement.[96]

Such notions did not go unchallenged. During the 1890s and into the early 1900s New Zealand, according to historian Michael King, 'matured as a nation'.[97] As New Zealanders celebrated Dominion Day (26 September) in 1907 they were also marking the end of the colonial era; as 'new' New Zealanders, they increasingly appreciated their heritage of this country's scenery, flora and fauna.[98] The Animals Protection Amendment Act 1910 replaced a raft of somewhat piecemeal earlier legislation and, for a time at least, fully protected most native birds.[99] The Forest and Bird Protection Society (forerunner of Forest & Bird) was formed in January 1914 to 'protect and secure native forest reserves and bird sanctuaries'[100] and to interest particularly children in native flora and fauna and their protection. The Forestry League was formed in 1916 to promote the preservation of forest areas and the interests of forestry and educate the public, again in preservation and protection.[101]

Over these years and beyond, as elsewhere in New Zealand, a growing body of opinion attested to the value of the Sounds heritage, bush, plants and birds. Visitors deplored its destruction and the too-frequent clearance of land useless for farming. In a debate that would rumble on for decades, accusations flew of unimaginative, short-sighted philistinism and lack of aesthetic appreciation, fuelled by almost irrevocable destruction being wrought overseas in the name of 'progress'.[102] In 1893 members of the Marlborough Land Board sat down with the plans of Queen Charlotte and Pelorus sounds to select different blocks to be set aside to conserve the scenery.[103]

THE FIRST SCENIC RESERVES WERE created largely under the Land Act 1892. The first ones in the Sounds were in 1896: a total of about 670 acres (270 ha) covered by heavy beech timber on vacant Crown land in Deep Bay (Pelorus Sound), Tennyson Inlet and Cannibal Cove.[104] Two years later, land on Putanui Point was reserved for state forest purposes.[105] Numerous other reservations, scattered about the Sounds, followed. To single out just a few: in 1901 Motungarara Island, at the entrance to Queen Charlotte Sound, was reserved for the 'preservation of native flora and fauna';[106] Nukuwaiata Island (Inner Chetwode) was gazetted a scenic reserve in 1904.[107] (Only in 1934 would the Scenery Preservation Act 1908 provide similar protection to Te Kakaho Island, or Outer Chetwode. Until then it was deemed too valuable as grazing land because it had the only 'decent' landing and living place with a constant supply of fresh water. Little notice was taken then of Ngāti Kuia's long occupation.)[108] Weka Point, part of a bigger peninsula in Kenepuru Sound 'with one of the finest pieces of bush scenery to be met with-in the district' and needing protection from burning and clearing, was gazetted in 1902;[109] that same year, following a Nelson Land Board recommendation in 1899, a large area behind Garne Bay was set aside as a scenery preservation reserve.[110]

In 1896 a permanent historical reserve was created at Ship Cove, from the shore to the summit of the watershed,[111] thus ensuring that the cove and setting would be retained in its natural state. These reservations under the Land Act, however, offered only partial protection: individuals could appeal to the relevant land boards to clear and graze the reserves, and these requests were often acceded to, despite the potential risk of fire and cattle damage.[112] The Scenery Preservation Act 1903 provided the first real safeguard. Under this legislation, land unsuited to farming or development could be designated as a permanent historical, scenic or thermal reserve and fines of up to £100 were payable for any damage (including by stock) to the bush, or for allowing a fire on adjourning land to encroach into a reserve.[113] However, the Commissioner of Lands spelt out a significant qualification: '[N]o forest land . . . which is suitable for farm land [is] permitted to remain under forest.'[114]

The business of actually establishing the reserves got underway. The Scenery Preservation Commission held public meetings, heard individuals' recommendations and conducted visits. Henry Mathews, chief forester in the State Forest Department and member of the Scenery Preservation Commission, arrived in Marlborough in 1906. After seeing 40–50 scenic spots (including Ship Cove where he saw three enormous patches of ferns he deemed were 'probably unrivalled in any part of the Colony for their grandeur and beauty') Mathews was optimistic about the number of reserves the commission might want to establish in the Sounds.[115]

It turned out, however, that the Scenery Preservation Act 1903 was poorly drafted and its processes were slow. People became frustrated and inevitably disappointed when their suggestions for reservations were not adopted; farmers continued to worry about the 'wholesale' taking of land.[116] The Act was amended in November 1906, and 10 years later seven blocks of land in the Sounds (ranging from 65 to 1683 acres, or 26 to 681 ha) had been set aside as scenic reserves.[117]

A look at three of these indicates the sort of criteria that contributed to the commission's decisions. In 1908–09, following years of local agitation over J. W. Perano's avowed intentions to burn,[118] 600 acres (242 ha) of land rising to high, beech-covered hills in Kumototo or Double Bay was reserved. It was close to Picton, popular with campers, had good launching places for boats and 'now stands out in solitary beauty, for the once-covered hills of the Sounds are bare and dry, and the children of coming generations will find it hard to believe that once upon a time all were like Double Bay'.[119]

By 1910 areas of the reserve in Pelorus Sound's Deep Bay, created under the Land

The Ship Cove Monument. Sadly, Alexander Turnbull's suggestion of a simple inscription on a plain stone monolith, in keeping with 'the modest nature of the great navigator', was poorly realised. The site interpretation now has a strong Māori focus, but the squat structure, still standing today, remains inadequate for its task of commemorating either Cook or the aspirations of those who wished to remember him. ALEXANDER TURNBULL LIBRARY, 377941/2

Act 1892, had been burned, tracks had been cut through the bush and Mrs Campbell's cattle were wandering around in it. But the 'fine block of forest' was expected to regenerate well, and buying up her portion and the adjoining Archer land would ultimately give the country 'the most beautiful bay in the Sounds, with practically no one who could claim to light a fire and thus run the risk of destroying the bush'. Immediate action was needed if one of the 'most lovely spots in the Dominion' was to be preserved from destruction. 'We have a chance here, and one that we shall never have again, of preserving this whole Bay in its natural state; [or] for the want of a few hundred pounds let it go.'[120] The bay was reclassified as a scenic reserve under the Scenery Preservation Act in 1911.[121]

In the meantime, attention had turned again to Ship Cove. In 1906 Robert Ewing, who ran the boarding house at Resolution Bay, and John Moore, formerly a government stock inspector, suggested marking Cook's landing site in the cove. A 'creditable memorial', Ewing suggested, would provide something of a tourist mecca. Camping grounds could be developed, and the opportunity could be taken to protect flora and fauna. Public subscription lists were circulated throughout Marlborough, and Ewing led the way with a generous donation.[122] Harvey Turner on Motuara Island was appointed caretaker of Ship Cove, and Stephenson Smith, Commissioner of Crown Lands, visited to talk about the siting of the proposed monument, improvements for the existing camping facilities and a possible track to open vistas across Endeavour Inlet.

And there the matter stalled, for want of public interest and financial contributions. Finally, on 12 February 1913, as a crowd of two thousand massed on the narrow strand between the bush and the sea at Ship Cove, Governor Lord Liverpool and his wife arrived to unveil the concrete monument to Cook's visits.

Some attempts were made to recognise the Māori past in the Sounds. In 1910–11 Archdeacon Thomas Grace offered to find 'Native' names for Deep Bay, 'as the country is singularly destitute of recorded Native history and the original maps give no assistance whatever'.[123] This offer was part of a larger effort to recognise Ngāti Kuia and Ngāti Apa occupation at the time of Cook's visits, rather than use a 'modern name given by Ngati-awa and Ngati-toa'.[124]

In 1912 a Mr Neame made a number of attempts to have the scenic reserve at Putanui Point reclassified so he could 'fell, burn and use the land for settlement'. Lands and Survey, mindful of the area's strong historical links back to Māori settlement and the semi-fortified village of Hikapu, destroyed in Te Rauparaha's raids, responded by adding more land to the reserve (against which Neame would continue to protest).

The commissioner also cited the now 'glorious bush in Hikapu Reach. Neither should be sacrificed on [Neame's] plea of utility.'[125]

However, it is important to note that such reservations were made in line with European appreciations of scenery and land use, not Māori interests. In fact sometimes the opposite was the case. In 1907 the *Marlborough Express* reported that land for reserves in Queen Charlotte Sound would be from Māori reserves in Kumototo, Ruakaka, Miritu (Bay of Many Coves) and Endeavour Inlet 'which have been lying idle for years and of which the Natives have made no use whatever'.[126] As noted earlier, Tennyson Inlet was designated a scenic reserve instead of being used as a reserve for landless Māori.

Policing and enforcement were perennial problems in the new reserves. Reflecting attitudes and practices that persisted over further decades, a Mr Peillman in 1910 pointed out that his heavily bushed section adjoined a reserve and his lease conditions demanded he clear his section. Yet it was impossible, he claimed, to clear without burning, which risked damaging the reserve. He was highly sceptical, too, of claims that tourism brought money into the local economy. 'Now, I have been here ten years, and all I have had out of a tourist is one shilling, and my nearest neighbour a whole 2s 6d.'[127]

However, the Act did provide a measure of protection and, in a new and novel way, recognised that the land had values other than economic. Its 'scenic, scientific, historic and natural curiosity values . . . made it worth preserving for future generations'.[128] The Act thus contributed to a growing climate of opinion in which individuals and groups, official or otherwise, acted to protect the bush. There was a context, then, when in 1919 the Scenery Preservation Commission called for further reservations at 'well-known resorts, such as the Wanganui River, Marlborough Sounds, and the Hot Lakes districts' to ensure that 'the unique attractions of these localities' were 'retained and preserved for all time'.

That same year the commission sought to reserve the still-existing 'small scattered areas' containing 'scenery of outstanding beauty', as well as other similar spots, when virgin blocks were being opened up for settlement. [129] In the Sounds, the Act provided the legislative framework for a mass of further reservations from the 1920s to the 1970s. These linked scenic beauty to recreation (and financial gain). At that time, prescience would have been needed to see that the latter might jeopardise the former.

'In the Grove Arm of Queen Charlotte Sound, pushing off for another place.' In *Wind in the Willows* (1908), Grahame's characters loved 'messing about in boats'. Something of what those words imply is the essence of this and of many other Sounds boating photos – the just-ruffled sea, the bush, the play of reflected light. MARLBOROUGH HISTORICAL SOCIETY, 6702

Professionalising the promotion

If the scenery was so good, why weren't more arriving to ignite the opportunities that tourism offered? At the beginning of the twentieth century the promoters of the Sounds were struggling to attract the numbers to make a difference to the local economy. The many promotional features in the *Marlborough Express* and *Evening Post*, the social column spotlights on wealthier personalities visiting the Sounds, accounts of yet another sports team holiday or gubernatorial tour were widely syndicated. But the desired results did not eventuate. Were the Sounds too close to be fashionable, pondered the *Marlborough Express*, or were Marlborough people insufficiently enterprising and 'pushful'?[130] Whatever the reason, in 1910 *The Press* considered most New Zealanders were failing 'take in one of the most picturesque parts of New Zealand'.[131]

After the Department of Tourist and Health Resorts was established in 1901, there were more-direct efforts to bring in tourists. Professional promotional material was prepared on the Sounds and their attractions,[132] and the first tourist map of the Sounds was published in 1904.[133] A year later a new, considerably improved map allowed tourists to see 'at a glance' all the necessary information on coach, vehicle and steamer routes; tracks, telegraph and telephone stations and accommodation houses; as well as habitats of trout, deer and quail.[134]

In 1904 the Marlborough Industrial Exhibition, designed to showcase the region, exhibited 25 framed photos of the Sounds provided by the department,[135] which also produced a large advertisement for 'New Zealand's Great Scenic Routes and Pleasure Resorts' that was widely promulgated. The Sounds' 'splendid cruising waters, well sheltered and picturesque' and their 'excellent sea-fishing; steamers and oil launches' were duly listed.[136]

A handsome departmental publication, *The Marlborough and Nelson Districts*, appeared in 1909, drawing attention to the Sounds' beautiful scenery and their easily accessible, inexpensive health resorts so ideal for recuperation and recreation. The following year, the new Picton and Sounds Promotion Society also sprang into print.[137] Almost a decade later, in 1919, Edith Howes, that highly popular author of books such as *The Dream Girl's Garden*, *Wonderwings* and *Little Make-Believe and other stories*, produced *Marlborough Sounds: The Waters of Restfulness*, intended to 'help take the risk out of taking a holiday in the Sounds'.[138]

The Sounds Promotion Society, 'acting on the principle that Heaven, and possibly Government, will help those who help themselves', had been launched in March 1910 with local dignitaries Arthur Seymour and John Duncan MP as patrons. It aimed to improve Picton's image and preserve native birds and bush all over the Sounds.[139] What it did, beyond publishing a well-received booklet, is unclear; in 1914, it was adjourned indefinitely. In 1915 G. W. C. Moon, newly appointed as 'Government tourist agent' with responsibilities for the Marlborough district, arrived with promises to do all possible to ensure that Picton and the Sounds' 'exceptional claims as holiday places for city people and tourists' would become better known.[140]

By 1920 the Sounds, their easy access from Wellington and the shelter they could offer to small craft were constantly promoted as regional and local attractions.[141] The Marlborough Progress Committee was established to get the main trunk line (that long-anticipated magic wand for facilitating Sounds' settlement and development)[142] completed and a fast strait ferry operating. Picton's foreshore began to be developed to better advertise the province. The war was over, and it was hoped that new opportunities might help break down financial and 'parochial prejudice'. 'Marlborough the Golden' was the new catchcry — though how far it reached into the Sounds and those working to make a living there is a moot point.[143]

6. Moving Goods and Connecting People

> 'In some places the track runs through settlers clearings covered with stumps and logs, burned and charred; then through native shrubbery and tangled scrub of a very peculiar kind, and blown down forests which were something terrible to get through . . .'

IN 1862 AN *OTAGO DAILY TIMES* correspondent crossed Cook Strait from Wellington in the 'comfortable little steamer *Storm Bird*', one of 'the line of steamers' running between Wellington, Picton and Nelson. Once in the Sounds he was captivated by the 'complete protection' that Tory Channel offered — its 'blue still waters', the 'abrupt cliffs, now wooded hills with vegetation down to the water's edge and . . . snug little coves'.

Picton itself, with its 300 inhabitants, he found to be more extensive than immediately supposed. Its 18-metre wharf could accommodate large ships, its big receiving warehouse was close by and, as the town was looking to become the export port for the interior, efforts were going into roading to link the town with the Wairau.[1]

Almost two decades later another correspondent on the same journey enthused about the sea in the Sounds, which 'always bears the appearance of a lake'. Further afield, the Wairau, with its high yields of grain, was 'studded with homesteads'. Picton, too, was more than the 'mere village' that it seemed, its 800 residents 'far above the ordinary class of colonists'. The roads out of Picton and between the Wairau and Nelson were really only bridle tracks, and the Wairau River, more than a mile across, was a formidable barrier. But, with 'the trunk line of railway . . . completed from the south, [Picton] will become one of the most important towns in the colony'.[2]

Leaving aside the quality of Picton's citizenry, the two observations highlight issues that the Sounds settlers faced — access to and communication with the outside world, and within their own. Small coastal traders were in and out of the Sounds, but the picture of a 'line of steamers' was, at that time, a flight of fancy that ignored the maritime hazards of Cook Strait and its environs and the difficulties of developing a reliable and regular service.

Land access was also critical to settlement and to 'opening up' the Sounds.[3] While the main trunk line would not arrive in Picton until 1945, regional roads linking Picton, Blenheim, Havelock and Nelson were in place by the end of the nineteenth century. By the 1920s a remarkable network of meticulously surveyed and constructed smaller bridle tracks around a metre wide, begun in the latter part of the nineteenth century, linked settler with settler and with the outside world. These tracks allowed settlers to get produce to market or attend the red-letter boat days, collect their mail from post offices or the designated bays, and talk and socialise. Better communications technologies, too, facilitated the social links and networks so necessary for life in the Sounds. Telegraph, then phone services were gradually installed (as in the rest of rural New Zealand); and heavily subsidised mail boats delivered post, along with other goods ordered, generally once or twice a week. Settler life and living was becoming a little easier.

Rowing, sailing and motoring

In 1893 tourists arriving for the annual rowing regatta at Portage noticed a woman striding up to the ridge on her way to Queen Charlotte Sound. By the time they had made the top of the ridge she was about a mile out in Queen Charlotte Sound and rowing fast. 'To accomplish that feat . . . the lady must be a good walker, an excellent runner, and a magnificent sculler,' someone was reported as saying.[4]

To the Sound settlers, rowing was simply part of life. Oars powered the early Census delivery and collection, though it took a month to move through to all the households in Pelorus Sound and round to Croisilles Harbour. Frederick Fell towed timber for his whare for miles behind his rowing boat from Brownlee and Co.'s Havelock mill;[5] Beauchamp's mailman rowed out from Havelock to Beatrix Bay; and

The McMahon family on their property at Taradale, Kenepuru Sound, with a vital link to the outside world – their rowing boat. Tides and fickle or contrary winds meant that rowing, often done standing and facing forwards, was a necessary skill. PAULINE AND COLIN MCMAHON

William and Augusta Harvey's children, boys and girls, often rowed some 27 nautical miles (50 kilometres) to Havelock to trade butter and get flour (catching the tide allowed a same-day return). Oars got people to weddings, meetings and neighbours' houses. These trips were done in small craft, so any logs and detritus lying just below the surface posed significant hazards. Yet no one considered these feats, involving contrary tides, fickle winds and unseen obstacles, remarkable. If tide or weather impeded progress, settlers pulled their craft onshore, upended them for shelter if necessary, and camped, making do with fish or shellfish.

Rowing would not do, however, to get their products to the necessary wider market. George F. Day (his later title, Captain, was, as in many other cases, probably a recognition of experience rather than formal qualifications) arrived from Kent, England, with his parents in 1841. In 1846 or thereabouts, he bought the schooner *Flirt* and began trading between Wellington, the Sounds and Foxton.[6] There is no record of where he called, or what he carried, and little to suggest that many such steamers were plying up and down Pelorus Sound at that point. Only from 1864 does the ever-growing number of shipping notices and newspaper articles alert readers to the existence of the multiplying number of little Sounds traders and their trips. The fact that in 1896 Captain Fisk, official conductor of the Census around the Sounds, was using such a craft, indicates something of the importance of these traders to the area.[7]

In the mid-1860s gold rush, the *Moa*, adapted, like the *Lady of the Lake*, for trade between Picton and Havelock and enticed down those long Pelorus reaches for timber, brought in loads of 'well assorted' freight from Lyttelton. From the mid-1870s, newly established shipping firms began scheduling regular services. In 1875 the Union Steamship Company, later to extend its hold across all New Zealand shipping, instituted a weekly Wellington–Picton service. By the 1880s its expanded Wellington–Nelson–Picton service ran three times a week. The SS *Hawea*, the first of the company's fleet, was followed by ever-faster, bigger, more manoeuvrable ships, whose arrival in the country excited inches of enthusiastic newspaper comment.[8] By the beginning of the twentieth century, the company's Wellington–Picton–Nelson freight and passenger services were a lifeline to Sounds settlers.

By 1880 the trading routes of competing companies spider-webbed around the Sounds. The Anchor Steam Shipping Company (founded in 1880) ran the Picton–Nelson–Greymouth route carrying passengers and freight (few of the ships were larger than 150 tonnes).[9] Those ships also sailed between Wellington, Endeavour Inlet and Nelson during the antimony boom in the mid- to late 1880s, and for a brief period regularly called at Ketu Bay in outer Pelorus. From 1899 the Golden Bay Steamship Company steamer *Te Kapu* did the Wellington–Nelson–Golden Bay run via Tory Channel, Endeavour Inlet and French Pass.

Private coastal traders were also running the regular freight and mail deliveries so essential to the Sounds' development. N. Harvey and his schooner *Active* moved between Nelson and Wellington with posts, hop-poles and timber, and returned with cargo for the Sounds.[10] Captain Watts, well acquainted with Sounds waters through his trips between Nelson and Havelock on his scow *Goldseeker*, began scheduled trips to the Sounds in 1881 — 'a great boon' to many settlers despite the inevitable delays caused by wind and weather.[11]

As settlement expanded, and milling offered assured freight, local steamers continued to make a play for the trade. The ship that became a Sounds identity was the 78-tonne steamer *Manaroa*. She first arrived, newly built, in 1897 to trade between Wellington and Havelock.[12] By end of 1903, and in a pattern typical of such little steamers, she was on the government-subsidised mail run, trading regularly between Wellington, Havelock and bays in Pelorus Sound, and moving sheep between the sound and Wellington, Picton or Whanganui. Despite the occasional local plea for a larger vessel with passenger accommodation,[13] she continued trading until 1930.[14]

The growing web of activity broadened. In 1897 *Te Kapu* began trading between Wellington, the Sounds and Golden Bay for the Sounds–Golden Bay Steamship Company (employing men well acquainted with Sounds conditions). In 1900 growing trade between Wellington and the Sounds had well-known Auckland boat-builder R. A. Logan producing a 100-tonne steamer that could go at 11 knots and carry perishable cargo including sheep — by then Picton's freezing works was doing brisk business.[15] From the turn of the century until late March 1918, E. C. Perano's first and second *Elsie*s ran a well-advertised regular route between Picton and Pelorus Sound, taking in Kenepuru and Manaroa and carrying mail, passengers, timber, wool, sheep and any general cargo. In 1920, buoyed by increasing trade, Perano bought the large, fast, kauri-built Auckland steamer *Rob Roy*. The freight carried on a trip from Auckland — 25 tonnes of sugar, four tonnes of golden syrup, 60 doors, 10,000 super feet of kauri and 7000 empty sacks — indicates cargo capacity.[16]

By 1916 the success of the Picton freezing works saw 'well-known steamers' such as *Waimea*, *Regulus*, *Alexander*, *Kennedy*, *Calm* and *Breeze* (specially adapted to carry sheep) running between Picton and the Sounds for Lyttelton, Wellington, Petone or

ABOVE The long oars of these boats, and their sleek lines, made them efficient, elegant craft. Picton's freezing works are behind. PICTON HERITAGE AND WHALING MUSEUM, COURTESY PICTON HISTORICAL SOCIETY

BELOW Steamers did not carry all the freight. Coastal scows, such as this one sailing past Black Point, with Mahau Sound stretching away in the background, were tough, flat-bottomed, practical boats. They were used all over New Zealand to carry heavy freight, and contributed much to the opening up of the Sounds. MARLBOROUGH HISTORICAL SOCIETY, 6711

Whanganui;[17] two years later Perano, in partnership with Edward Zohrab, bought the 121-tonne *Admiral* for the Picton–Sounds trade and mail.[18]

However, a gradual fall-off in shipping to and from Queen Charlotte Sound illustrates well the symbiotic relationship between settlement and ships. As mining activity faded out and as the realities of farming in those western bays became more apparent, the population drifted away — Resolution Bay School, for instance, was eventually the only school in the outer part of Queen Charlotte, a considerable contrast to the tens of schools that continued to pop up throughout Pelorus. With fewer people in the outer sound towards the end of the first decade of the twentieth century, traders and mail boats called less frequently. Pelorus Sound was the 'working sound', not Queen Charlotte.

FROM THE END OF THE nineteenth century the oil-launch began to transform the lives of small traders, settlers and the boating public.[19] The launches appeared in the Sounds in 1902 and ownership took off, despite the £200 price tag (over $32,000 in today's money). Picton became the headquarters of the popular Fairfield, Hercules, White and Lozier engines. Petrol was seven shillings per eight-gallon case (30 litres) and was delivered in Picton in 100-case lots. Within less than a decade, newspapers claimed that almost all European settlers owned a launch.[20]

By 1909 E. R. Lane's flourishing boat-building shed in Picton was turning out high-quality launches for locals and others.[21] Long, beamy and shallow-draughted, and 'with curved hoods to shelter passengers and engine and to carry deck-loads of luggage', the launches were 'the life of the Sounds — tramcar, railway train and lorry all rolled into one'.[22] Their ease of handling and fuelling along with their versatility and convenience soon had them putting the little steamers out of a job.

By 1915, although the little steamboat *Gannet* still made regular runs to the Grove, Te Awaiti, and to as far north as Resolution Bay, it was launches that carried visitors from Picton to Torea Bay, from where a 'good cart track' took them to Portage to link with launches that carried them through or beyond the Sounds — to French Pass or Nelson.[23] Like today's water taxis, they were also available for casual hire between Picton and any of the Sounds bays,[24] opening the Sounds to the tourist trade as never before.[25]

In 1903 miller Tugoald Bratli's new 17-foot (5-metre) launch *Gitta*, able to go 7 knots into a stiff southerly, hooked up to the heavily laden scow *Magic* and the box-

The second *Elsie* at Grove Wharf, 1910. Tidal flats further down the Grove meant passengers disembarked at the wharf, then travelled by horse-drawn coach to Anakiwa (opposite) or across the Linkwater plain to Havelock. Both *Elsies* had checkered histories that demonstrate only too well the precariousness of trading in the Sounds. The first was destroyed by fire at Blackball in 1906. The second, after costly problems with her boiler (its top 'fell in' in 1909), sank after hitting a rock off Long Island, toward the northern entrance of Tōtaranui Queen Charlotte Sound.
MARLBOROUGH HISTORICAL SOCIETY, 4161

like pontoon she was towing for 65 minutes 'without a knock or missing fire once'.[26] Such powerful launches, much more convenient and versatile than the steam-powered boats that had towed the punts (barges) in the 1890s,[27] enabled the punting business — that backstay of Sounds transport — to flourish.[28]

WHERE SHIPS AND SHIPPING ARE an essential lifeline to the outside world, wind, weather and tides assume enormous significance. In the Sounds, the storms and swells that today see the Cook Strait ferries cancelled or delayed created a particular challenge. In 1879, in thick weather that had her captain thinking he was off Cape Palliser, *Swallow* was wrecked at the entrance to Tory Channel. No one had seen the coast early enough to prevent the ship being driven onto the rocks. *Chapman's Traveller's Guide through New Zealand* described the channel's eastern entrance as 'very narrow, and jammed up with sunken reefs. The water rushes through like a mill race, sweeping . . . vessel[s] . . . into the open strait.'[29]

Calm conditions in the Sounds can belie those outside; building seas and the strong currents at the entrance made coming or going hazardous. In December 1863 SS *Phoebe* was running her regular Picton–Wellington route through a smooth Tory Channel under Captain A. Kennedy. As they reached the entrance, 'furious' south-east gales were building up huge seas. In the constrained channel and dire conditions, turning back was impossible. The *Wellington Independent* reported:

> [T]he water near the channel boiled with agitation and the SS Phoebe could scarcely make headway from the dangerous rocks at our side. There were three men at the wheel . . . they stuck to their posts, and after two hours' trying against sea and wind, got into the Straits. For half-an-hour, when in the channel, the steamer did not make her own length from the rocks and the men at the wheel could scarcely retain their hold, from the waves and the heaving sea . . . The captain tried for five hours to make for Wellington . . .[30]

Only when the gale blew itself out did they get into port. Ten years later *Phoebe* was again approaching Tory Channel, at night and in the face of a strong spring tide. She initially failed to answer her helm. Only her strong engines going at full revs prevented the horror of a 'full shipwreck'.[31]

The Sounds and Tory Channel, long used as a 'shipping refuge',[32] were a haven to ships coming in from Cook Strait's often storm-driven waters[33] to shelter in Guards Bay, Port Gore or Waitata Bay in the outer Pelorus. Sometimes they would run under Queen Charlotte Sound's Long Island — though waves breaking on the shore sometimes 'sent the spray up in such clouds as to completely hide the land from view'.[34]

Perhaps it is unsurprising that from 1795 to 1970, 34 ships were wrecked in the Sounds, most before 1900.[35] Cloud or haze can obscure the hills; dense rain obliterates the land; fog and darkness blanket the geographical features so critical to navigation. Katabatic winds sweeping down the gullies in great squalls caused ships, particularly those in ballast, to capsize or founder; baffling winds left vessels unable to make headway and vulnerable to squalls or tide; navigational error and misjudgement led to strandings; ships sank when they hit uncharted rocks. The financial loss to small traders, especially, would have been hefty.

Few oil-launches were lost but sailing ships were especially at risk.[36] Nor were steamers immune.[37] On 30 June 1873 the 300-tonne steamer SS *Rangitoto* was lost after she struck a reef near Cape Jackson. All crew and passengers were rescued, including someone's prize pig.[38] On 1 September 1884, Shaw Savill Line's 1850-tonne SV *Lastingham* was wrecked about 150 metres from Cape Jackson, just inside Port Gore. In vile weather, visibility at Jacksons Head was terrible. Despite desperate crew effort, the ship, apparently off-course, failed to come about. 'The scene was one of indescribable confusion, wind howling, rain falling, people rushing about shouting and screeching, and the sea breaking over the ship's side.' In a huge sea, some managed to spring from the ship to the nearby rocks or float ashore. They spent a miserable night huddled together on the mainland. In the morning, three left to try to make their way along Cape Jackson's steep and exposed headland to find help. They were not seen again. Five steamers passed close to land, but none appeared to notice the survivors' signals. Days later, Captain Jensen of the *Agnes*, sailing between Pelorus Sound and Kaiapoi with timber, rescued them. Eighteen lives were lost,[39] and over £17,000 of merchandise.[40]

OVER TIME, REGULATIONS AND TECHNOLOGY contributed to a safer environment and increased certainty in the service so essential to Sounds settlers. Bigger ships, less reliant on sail and with stronger gear and engines, could keep to timetables. Officers' examinations and certifications, and ships' surveys, contributed to there being fewer wrecks and mishaps. To the considerable ire of launch captains, their craft were also caught up in the new safety regulations. These, together with sizeable penalties, were introduced and steadily tightened across the maritime industry.[41] From 1907 all launches had to carry life-belts (of a make now regarded as dangerous), buoys, lights and a fog horn (of a specified type); those over 5 tonnes were to have a certified master and engineer on board. As launch numbers increased over the next few years and as their utility went beyond pleasure to playing a critical role in settling the country, they became increasingly caught up in further requirements around qualifications, annual surveys and appropriate equipment.[42]

A range of other measures increased maritime safety and accessibility. Captain E. M. Chaffer's Tory Channel chart, published by the Hydrographical Office in London in 1839, was widely available within the decade.[43] James Heberley was appointed pilot for the north entrance to Queen Charlotte Sound in 1863[44] and signal station reserves were created at Cape Koamaru, Blumine Island and at Ship Cove a year later.[45] The stations themselves, however, were never built. Heberley was still named as pilot in 1869, though I found no accounts of his carrying out his official duties.

Over the years, government steamers systematically searched for reported dangers. Once identified they were gazetted, and hazardous places were identified and marked. Luke Rock, off Dieffenbach Point, Queen Charlotte Sound, 'the most dangerous point in the whole of our magnificent Sound', was buoyed in 1865.[46] Over time, surveys were carried out. Cape Jackson Passage was surveyed in 1896 after the *Lastingham* went down,[47] but only in 1912 was the Sounds area, and in particular that 'ships' refuge', Guards Bay, 'properly surveyed'.

Lighthouses, boosting commerce and settlement as well as maritime safety, were in demand.[48] A light for Tory Channel Heads was first officially mooted in 1863[49] and the pyramid-shaped leading lights (still used today) were finally first exhibited on 1 January 1882.[50] Ōkukari resident Charles Godfrey was the first keeper on a not insignificant annual salary of £90. Blind since childhood, he was later assisted by the boy Joseph Timms.[51]

Beacons (poles with distinctive topmarks) were installed over time.[52] By 1874 beacons identified the channel in Havelock Harbour, though sailors persisted in destabilising them by tying vessels and rafts to them, despite the considerable advertised penalties and rewards for information.[53] In 1883 the all-too-easily-damaged beacons were replaced by a new set that extended along the 5–6 miles (8–10 kilometres) of the tidal channel to Hikapu Reach.[54] These were improved in 1902,[55] but did not prevent even local masters getting grounded in the mud — sometimes for days.[56] Work to mark the channels better would continue for decades. In 1884 an unlit beacon was erected on Jackson's Rock, off the cape that snakes out to form the western extremity of Queen Charlotte Sound, but it was swept away in a storm. The still-standing solid concrete beacon replaced it.

By the beginning of the twentieth century, revolutionary and relatively cheap gas-powered automatic signal lights began to be installed around the Sounds. At Cape Jackson the Wigham continuous gas-light (which unfortunately did not live up to its name) was installed in 1903 and refuelled by Mr Norgrove on *Phoenix* (in 1904) and E. C. Perano on *Elsie* (1905). It was moved in 1911 to the considerably more accessible Dieffenbach Point, within the Sound, to mark a reef that was deemed 'a menace to navigation'.[57] In 1916 a reliable light was finally installed at the Cape Jackson beacon.

Yet even as regulation and navigational aids improved maritime safety and regular services increased, Picton lacked the infrastructure necessary to get goods to export ports. In 1866, five years after Picton had become a port of entry, the Railway Department built an 18-metre wharf on what is now Picton foreshore. Twenty years later it was decided that it was too short and offered few inducements to the Union Steamship Company to bring in the larger ships needed to achieve reasonable freight costs and build a direct Picton–Wellington trade.[58]

In 1886 the Public Works Department (PWD), on behalf of the Railway Department, completed the first 30-metre extension of the wharf, installed a goods shed and improved the sidings.[59] Periodic attempts to promote the port by stationing a naval base at Picton or within the Sounds achieved nothing.[60] By 1906 Picton's rotten and dilapidated wharf was again attracting complaints.[61]

The absence of an administrative structure in the Sounds caused myriad issues, one of which being that there was no harbour board to take the initiative over the wharf. Over the years and enjoying a captive market, Railways had derived considerable revenue in the district but showed little interest in developing the wharf itself. Charles Houghton Mills, advocating a fast ferry running from a custom-built wharf at Titahi Bay, just north of Wellington, to Picton via Queen Charlotte Sound's northern entrance, round the turn of the century, got nowhere.[62] Wharf charges were long a bone of contention,[63] and the department did not respond to the launchmen's requests for their own wharf and facilities at Picton.[64]

Complaints began to be aired about who should bear the ongoing costs of the small wharves the Marine Department had erected in various Sounds bays. Use of these was charged and Sounds settlers, already 'unfairly' burdened with the cost of track maintenance, long and doggedly maintained that they should not have to pay for wharf upkeep as well. Further charges, they argued, would be unfair and discriminatory. Such debates would remain alive for decades.

Finally, and after much local lobbying, the government paid for a new ferro-concrete deep-water wharf, started in 1911 and in use by 1915.[65] The *Evening Post* prophesied that the wharf and the recently opened freezing works had given rise to 'a new Picton'; the main-trunk railway line might be 'struggling' along at about one mile a year, but its eventual arrival at its Picton terminus[66] would open up the Sounds. However, there was no stock wharf,[67] improvements to various existing facilities were a way off, and the railway line was decades away.[68]

Elsewhere local marine infrastructure improved gradually. Havelock's first wharf, government-built for coastal traders and begun in 1883, was finished in 1884 at a cost of £441.[69] By 1906 the silting-up near the wharf combined with the half a metre lost at low tide reportedly made it 'a matter of chance whether a vessel gets past Cullen Point or snuggles into the mud for a few days' rest'.[70] Masters taking on goods at Havelock could choose between taking a full load and risking getting marooned, leaving before the tide got too low, or anchoring outside Cullen Point and having the rest of the cargo lightered out. In 1907 the newly established Havelock Harbour Board (1906–66) took charge.[71] Three years later a loan from William Brownlee enabled the significant dredging needed for vessels to come up the channel and moor independent of the tide (an appropriately celebrated milestone).[72] New beacons up the tidal channel to the town were installed in 1915.[73]

The Sounds also benefited from government assistance with facilities outside the little ports. Noting the expenditures under 'Roads and Bridges' in PWD annual reports, the government subsidised wharf construction and approaches for New Zealand's coastal settlements and those up navigable rivers. Extensive and expensive repairs indicate the importance of such structures.[74] The £289 spent on the Māhakipawa wharf was indicative of the sums spent on the Torea, Te Awaiti, Portage and Waitaria wharves. Moreover, by 1919 all but the Te Awaiti wharf were run by the Marine Department,[75] locals remaining unwilling to assume any responsibility. In a long-used line of sorry argument, the secretary of the Pelorus Road Board in 1917 informed the Marine Department that there was 'no chance of any local body taking over control of the Grove Wharf'. The cost of collecting the dues would 'render such a move next to impossible . . . it is only fair and just for the Marine Department to make

A private wharf in Onahau Bay in Tōtaranui Queen Charlotte Sound, just to the south-west of Picton. MARLBOROUGH HISTORICAL SOCIETY, 017529

the repairs as the district is isolated'. In that instance, Secretary Allport agreed to pay the cost of repairs up to £10. More generally, maintenance costs were subsidised, mostly on a £1 for £1 basis.[76]

Settlers and holidaymakers also built their own wharves. From the turn of the century the Marine Department, for a small fee, licensed the structures and the right to occupy the foreshore[77] — and gazetted the considerable penalties should a vessel collide with any unlicensed structure. Where private wharves were used by the official mail boats to bring in goods and tourists (thus making the wharves part of the official Sounds infrastructure), government assistance was available.[78]

DURING 1881–82, AND EVEN as some of the first Sounds tracks were under construction, the government announced further assistance to Sounds settlers. A boat canal cut between inner Kenepuru and today's Take in Bay would provide valuable sheltered waters in which to move around. Even more dramatic was the proposed cut, first mooted in 1882, through Piripaua Neck, the high ridge of land between Ōpouri Bay and Kawai Sound (today's Forsyth and Beatrix bays). But the 'much needed convenience'[79] that considerable engineering feat might represent pales into insignificance beside a much more ambitious plan — to link Queen Charlotte and Kenepuru sounds by a canal. Today the proposals form a fascinating case study of the confidence of engineers' ability to overcome natural challenges, notions of regional development and senior government MPs' expectations of considerable government expenditure for a fairly minimal benefit backed by unsubstantiated claims.

The Kaiaho Canal at Take in Bay was cut through the low headland during 1881–82 at a cost of £223. Sixteen years later, in 1898, PWD, tackling what must have been a longstanding intractable problem, began removing huge quantities of accumulated silt, building wing walls to prevent further silting, and further deepening the canal to allow passage at all times. Other, increasingly spasmodic, work was carried out until 1912, when all work apparently stopped. Small craft, however, still used, and valued, the canal to the mid-1940s.[80] Today it is dry at low tide, but shallow small craft can still use it with discretion.

The Piripāua Neck cutting, through 'a razor-backed ridge, 80 feet high and 145 feet wide from high water to high water', was a very ambitious project. Locals were credited with occasionally hauling their boats over the ridge but in 1898 the *Marlborough Express* noted that settlers, anxious to avoid '17 miles of rough water', had subscribed

ABOVE The Canal, Kenepuru Sound. Today, the canal is badly silted up, but its position was still marked on a 1982 map. HOCKEN COLLECTIONS UARE TAOKA O HĀKENA, UNIVERSITY OF OTAGO, BOX-305-007

BELOW Piripāua Neck, separating Forsyth Bay and Beatrix Bay in the outer Pelorus Sound. The marks of the attempted cut to allow sheltered passage between the two bays and, so it was claimed, facilitate the way to Havelock, are still visible. JOHN PASCOE, ALEXANDER TURNBULL LIBRARY, PACOLL-8765-08-77

'generously' to the project.[81] By then the ridge had been lowered by 12 metres. Further dramatic cutting planned for the following year would reduce it to 3 metres above high-water mark. Then, once 'some rough skids are laid down', it would be 'an easy matter to haul boats through'.

It was not an easy matter. In that first year, appropriately experienced men were difficult to recruit and many slips had to be cleared. However, some 300 cubic metres of earth and 600 cubic metres of rock were excavated. The following year, with nothing further achieved, Charles William Adams, the chief surveyor, recommended that the money would be better spent by advancing the Manaroa–Piripāua Neck track and buying a double-purchase winch and skids that would allow settlers to haul their boats over.[82] Further small sums were spasmodically spent on the project, perhaps to clear more rockfalls, until 1905.[83] Today, the promoted benefits seem dubious. The cut would have allowed vulnerable small launches and rowing boats to avoid the dangerous squalls and winds that swirl up the Waitata and Tawhitinui reaches, but the distance around would have been shortened by only about 4½ nautical miles, far from the frequently claimed 17.

However, even as the Piripaua Neck project lapsed, politician C. H. Mills, opening the Sounds Dairy Factory in August 1905, floated a far more ambitious undertaking: a launch tunnel between Onahau Bay and Te Mahia Bay that would put Havelock only two hours from Picton; perishable fruit and produce could then be profitably sent to Wellington.[84]

The idea took a few months to gain traction but by January 1906, as the results of a feasibility report were awaited, the list of envisaged potential benefits proliferated. The tunnel, 'a miniature Panama Canal', would cut 112 kilometres from the Picton–Nelson run, claimed the *Marlborough Express*, and Pelorus settlers would have readier communication with Picton. Picton's prosperity depended on the tunnel; it would give a fillip to trade and increase tourist traffic — and if it cost a lot, so had other schemes all around the country. Subscriptions began to be talked about, and pound-for-pound subsidies.[85]

In April 1906 the district road engineer, C. H. Williams, perhaps diplomatically, said he considered the idea 'quite feasible'. However, he also pointed out that high water at Te Mahia was over 3½ feet (1 metre) higher than at Onahau — the tunnel would have to be 10 feet (3 metres) higher than originally estimated to allow for the rise and fall in tides. This, he thought, might lead to heavy tidal flows in some seasons but should not interrupt traffic at half tide. (Two years later a newspaper report commented that without costly locks the channel would mostly be a 'mill-race'.)[86]

The tunnel would need lining to prevent cave-ins and the savings in distance, Williams pointed out, had been dramatically overstated. To get to the Chetwode Islands (as a point of reference on the Picton–Nelson route) via the tunnel and Pelorus Sound would save only 1.2 kilometres compared with the route via Queen Charlotte Sound. Moreover, the larger ships plying that Nelson route would need a tunnel that was 40 feet (12 metres) wide at the bottom. The project, too, he warned, would be expensive. A launch tunnel and approaches would cost around £35,855; a canal for steamers would come in at more like £1.1 million. Unless a similar tunnel was cut through the headland between Elaine Bay and Whakitenga Bay in Croisilles Harbour, 'the expenditure of such a large sum of money' merely to connect the two sounds 'cannot be considered', Williams said.[87]

However, given the project's value to the Sounds settlers, he proposed a funding model to help finance the large plant that would be needed, and the large contract and the engineering problems attendant with managing excavations, some of which would be underwater. A levy based on the size of landholdings would be, he thought, equitable and ascertain real interest.

The project refocused on the potential link to Havelock and the value to Pelorus settlers. Local support was not universal[88] but Mills and the Sounds branch of the Farmers' Union continued to pick away at it for the next six years, endlessly (and seemingly fruitlessly) citing farmers' stress, the desirability of channelling sheep to Picton's freezing works rather than Canterbury's, facilitating wool exports, minimising settlers' handling and freight costs, access and communications, cheapening timber supplies and politicians' belief in farmer contributions to the economy. In 1911, a new marine engineer's report quite unexpectedly dismissed almost all anticipated difficulties.[89] In 1912 the Marine Department made the necessary tidal observations.[90] Then, suddenly and with no reported local comment, there was no more discussion of the project — for the moment, the tunnel was dead in the water.

Tracks and roads

In 1901 the Census identified a population of 506 Europeans in Pelorus Sound — 280 men and 226 women. Queen Charlotte Sound lagged behind with only 184 people (99 men and 85 women).[91] By 1911 numbers had grown considerably — 1304 Pākehā in the whole Sounds district, and 214 Māori in Pelorus Sound and valley.[92] Such numbers were important. Numbers indicated prosperity, settlement and facilities; rising numbers would further boost settlement.

In 1901 the increase of 200 Pākehā settlers over the previous five years, the *Marlborough Express* opined, was because of the Department of Lands and Survey's 'wise policy' of forming tracks in the area.[93] The claim was in line with the thinking of the day: roads and bridle tracks, central government and the country's newspapers agreed, were the 'economic catalysts' needed to open up the land, promote settlement, end isolation and create essential access to markets and services.[94]

In 1870 Vogel's work scheme and his newly created Public Works Department had put the government centre-stage in creating land access to boost settlement. Twenty years later, and in the Sounds' densely forested country then being settled, government surveyors reported that 'unless tracks are previously made, the lands do not readily find selectors'. Serious work would be involved. Cart roads were needed, with by-roads formed as bridle-tracks 'rigidly on the permanent grades' that would be used if dray-roads were to be built in the future, and the price of such work should be added to the per-acre land cost, to reflect the advantage that each section got from its position.[95] With roads formed, wrote the *Pelorus Guardian* in 1893, farming, 'the real bone and sinew of all places', could get underway.[96] The government's obligation to settlers was reiterated over the next few decades,[97] though from 1910 on, in relation to the Sounds, the PWD was increasingly pointing out that settlers were enjoying the advantages but making no financial contribution to roading.

Road construction, then, was vital to settlement and prosperity. Regionally, the 1860s gold rushes in the Wakamarina Valley and, from 1881, the government's appreciation of the value of Pelorus Valley timber, saw some government spending on the district's transport infrastructure.[98] By 1890 the Blenheim–Havelock–Nelson road and its continuation to the West Coast were 'a major roadwork'.[99] Too often dangerously rutted or blocked by windfalls, it was, nevertheless, maintained (after a fashion) and slowly improved. In 1888–89 the government began constructing a dray road between Māhakipawa and the main road near Havelock to facilitate stock movement,[100] and building the Havelock wharf at which steamers could unload.

Rail contributed to that wider network. The line between Blenheim and Picton was built with money from Vogel's scheme and finally got beyond the swamp south of Picton to the banks of the Ōpawa River in 1875, to reach Blenheim in March 1880.[101] But not for decades would the Sounds settlers' hopes and aspirations for the 'Southern

Main Line' be realised with a terminus at Picton and a ferry to bridge Cook Strait and access markets further afield.[102]

However, even simple tracks could open up new opportunities for work, travel and keeping in touch. By 1908 Sounds settlers had made 'scores of formed tracks . . . through holdings',[103] cutting and chopping back to get from their bush clearings to a neighbour's, or to get to a ridgeline where travel was easier, or to the sea. But it would take a programme of official road- and track-making, carried out on a scale that individuals could not match, to provide vital reliable communication to the hinterland and with the wider world.

The Sounds road/track construction began in 1882. The geography presented formidable challenges, and there was a depression, during which central government had tended to direct money towards not roads but railways (particularly the North Island main trunk line).[104] The absence of a rating body and sundry other aspects of administrative infrastructure created additional problems in the Sounds.[105]

Yet from the mid-1890s until about 1912 a very considerable public works operation developed a network of well-engineered and well-constructed tracks in remote and challenging terrain in many parts of the Sounds. In 1882, £58 12s 5d was spent on the track from Kenepuru Sound to Crail Bay, and on the 1.2-metre-wide, 6.5-kilometre-long track from Kenepuru Sound to Manaroa. These were financed half out of parliamentary funds, half out of accrued thirds. (Under the Land Act, a third of the Crown land sales money was available to local authorities as long as the Land Board had approved their expenditure plans. A fourth of the leases on small grazing runs, disbursed for 15 years from when rent was first paid, was similarly available.)[106]

The intention to build another track, which would become a 2.4-metre-wide small road 'to progress' over the Torea–Portage saddle, and also to cut the Kaiaho boat canal and the canal through Piripaua Neck, were itemised as future projects.[107] It was a promising start, and over the next few years tracks were surveyed and graded according to government specifications to allow for later conversion to dray roads. However, expenditure was restricted, and construction often progressed painfully slowly.[108]

UNTIL AS LATE AS 1893 that climate of retrenchment prevailed.[109] The Sounds' lack of administrative structure for roading also continued to impede progress.[110] The Counties Act 1876 had created 63 counties, one of which was Sounds County.

These bodies could elect to take over responsibility for funding and constructing and maintaining their own roads, ferries and bridges, or they could contract with the PWD to have the work done. The necessary funding would be raised by rates, levies, loans, subscriptions, tolls, other money received by the council (for instance, gold revenue) and the thirds and fourths available to the local authority. Fifty-one of the 63 counties accepted this responsibility.

In practice, from 1876 to 1922 central government, wanting roads built, either gave county councils grants to do the work, or did the work itself then handed over the responsibility for ownership and maintenance to the local body.[111]

The Sounds and five other isolated areas were exempted from the Counties Act's provisions (possibly because they had no roads).[112] This meant that there was no body with which the government could work or to which it could pay the small amounts of thirds and fourths, and nor were rates levied to help fund roadworks.[113] Instead, the money accumulated in Treasury.[114]

Sounds residents favoured this rates exemption. They paid tax and customs duties like everyone else, they argued, but the nature of where they lived meant that they did not enjoy the same benefits from public expenditure as others — post offices were in private houses; there were no large schools or bridges and hardly any roads. If they started paying rates like everybody else they would be paying for a lot of infrastructure that did not benefit them.

From 1890 the government, under a certain amount of local pressure[115] and using funding from accrued deferred payments or from subsidies, put track-building in the Sounds back on its agenda. John McKenzie, whom the *Marlborough Express* credited with doing more than anyone else to open up the tracks in the district, was Minister of Lands.[116] A new cooperative scheme put an end to the PWD's perennial problems with unskilled contractors, unsatisfactory and uncompleted work, poor treatment of workmen and unpaid suppliers. The new scheme, which reflected the Liberals' support of the working man, let contracts directly to small groups of 10–12 men who used good-quality government-provided materials. Until the end of the century the government considered that it thus achieved quality control and the flexibility to expand or contract any project; small groups presented no negotiating difficulties.[117] In the Sounds, critically, the scheme provided work, mostly on tracks.[118]

By 1897 a huge public works programme of track construction was underway across the country, including in the Sounds.[119] With these works complete, Sounds settlers would no longer have to drive stock along rough beaches, they were in closer

A new, wide, well-graded track winds its way around Whatamongo Bay, one of Tōtaranui Queen Charlotte Sound's deep bays. Allports Island is in the distance. TYREE STUDIO COLLECTION, NELSON PROVINCIAL MUSEUM, 181932

touch for 'stock purposes' with Havelock and Picton, and no longer had to worry about river crossings or high tides.[120] Gangs at either end of a planned track cut and blasted their way into the bush, repaired winter damage, laid corduroy (placing small tree or punga trunks closely together to stop loads sinking into the mud), made fords, dug drains and built bridges. Most of the last were small, but a 15-metre suspension bridge was needed at the head of Kenepuru Sound, where half and high tides turned a small stream into something of a river.

A 2.4-metre-wide bridle track was being built from Tennyson Inlet to Rai Valley, as was a 1.2-metre wide, 34-kilometre stock-driving track from Nydia Bay to Havelock, intended to open up 8500 acres of Crown land. Contracts were let progressively, with sections finished before the next was set.[121] But whatever the shortcuts, the standard of work remained high. Even in land long reverted to bush, the contours of these old tracks can still be followed in open hill country, though tracks easily trod 40 years ago are now slipping badly or becoming lost to regrowth.

The distances were considerable. In 1898, for instance, and on the high, steep country that makes up Kenny Isle, a bridle road almost linked Richmond Bay with Ketu Bay; it would shortly reach the post office at the bay. Plans were afoot to take a branch road from near the Richmond–Ketu Bay saddle to connect as directly as possible with Beatrix Bay, where it would link to the Manaroa–Okoha road. With that complete there would be 'direct communication by land with bays in the Kenepuru and Pelorus Sounds for a distance of upwards seventy miles; and on the completion of the seven-mile section now in progress, from Portage Bay to Te Mehia [sic] the land-connection will be complete to Havelock, and the province generally'.[122] It was no mean feat.

The challenges in building the rather shorter Tory Channel–Whatamonga–Picton track were typical of those throughout the Sounds. In 1894 work began on a track rising from a bay opposite Te Awaiti to run along the 180- to 215-metre-high ridge to the Whatamonga–Port Underwood road.[123]

Earlier, tracks in the Sounds had to be 4–6 feet (1.2–1.8 metres) wide with at least 3 feet (0.9 metre), sometimes more, 'cut in the solid' — dug back into the slope of the hill to provide firm ground beneath the track. In 1898, on the Tory Channel–Whatamonga–Picton track, surveyor Charles Adams reduced the width where possible to 2 feet (0.6 metre) 'in the solid'. Such a change, he argued, would get the tracks completed and wide enough for horsemen, and any widening needed could be done later, as funds allowed.[124]

This track progressed by about 6.5 kilometres a year, with bush clearance running ahead of the track construction. Repairs were always needed after winter storms, and these could be substantial — flooding in June and July 1896 brought down 2000 tonnes of boulders and shingle close to the ford in the Waikawa Creek, which threatened to change the direction of the creek.[125] Waikawa Māori had erected a groin in the stream to hold it temporarily in check.

On the planned Tawhitinui–Rai Valley line that would link up that west/south-west side of Pelorus, the gangs cut a 10-metre-wide clearing in dense bush to create a 'cattle-drive' from Cregoe Point at the western end of Tawhitinui Reach to west of Section 4, Block V, Tennyson Inlet. Felling, clearing and stacking the undergrowth resulted in a little over 8 kilometres of cattle-drive being constructed.[126] Planning only just preceded construction. The way ahead on the planned dray road from the head of the Kenepuru Valley over the 564-metre saddle to the south-east of Mount Stokes was only partially explored by the time initial construction work began.

IN QUEEN CHARLOTTE SOUND EVEN basic roading was minimal. Money was needed to reform and metal the Picton–Waikawa road, and more if it was to progress from Waikawa Creek towards Picton. In the other direction, 2.4 kilometres of a dray road to link Picton with the Grove had been surveyed on the permanent grade and started at each end. But finance was tight, and progress was limited to a small sea wall at either end and about 1.6 kilometres of a sidling 1.8-metre-wide dray road, sometimes through rock. The intention was to create a track for pedestrians, horse traffic and cyclists until funding came through for the proper 3.6-metre-wide carriage road from Picton to the Māhakipawa and Wakamarina gold fields and thence to Havelock.

Visions stood in place of construction. The road, once completed, would be 'of great public utility [and] tourists', led on its winding route along the shores of the Sound, would find it 'a route of great beauty'.[127] It would be another 17 years before the first car drove over the completed Grove Road.

On Arapaoa Island settlers benefited more immediately from the considerable track work underway. Bridle tracks from the west side of the island to the saddle above Te Awaiti were to join existing bridle roads on the east side of the island. These, in turn, connected Onopopiti, Te Awaiti, Whekenui and Ōkukari bays.

From about 1880 to 1910 some £27,000 (over $5 million today), mostly from accrued thirds and fourths, was spend on roading in the Sounds.[128] In that sparsely

Jack Love, Morey Woods, Tapi Love and Martin and Jack Searle got the first car over the Picton–Māhakipawa road in four and a half hours, on 30 October 1915. In spite of local demands and petitions, it took 52 years after the first track was cut in 1862 to get a road suitable for vehicles.
MARLBOROUGH HISTORICAL SOCIETY, 1541

populated, difficult country, and in a pattern replicated nationally, the government invested and continued to invest in track development. In the Sounds, by 1898 'some hundreds of miles of tracks' had been built for the 'sparse' though 'loyal' inhabitants.[129] The French Pass track was begun in 1899 and finished about 1912, providing market access to the settlers on both sides of that steep, rugged, twisting peninsula. In 1905 tracks on the narrow, heavily bushed coastal strip were being pushed north from Nydia Bay to Fairy Bay, and on towards Tawhero Point to join with the Tawhitinui–Rai track. Smaller tracks, too, were on the books, to be constructed from Resolution Bay to Endeavour Inlet and from Endeavour Inlet to Titirangi, again over daunting country.[130]

OVER THE DECADES FROM THE mid-1880s, however, Sounds inhabitants not infrequently complained that Marlborough was not getting its share of public works,[131] that local bodies were disadvantaged by the funding arrangements,[132] and that the roading vote was underspent.[133] Not everyone agreed.[134] Without an economic analysis and complex comparisons of population numbers, time of settlement and relevant geographical challenges, such allegations are difficult to substantiate. Some would say the complaints came from settlers who failed to appreciate the engineering challenges the roads presented[135] and the fact that their battles over compensation contributed to delays in roadworks.[136]

It can also be argued that it was the settlers' fault for being unwilling to resolve the real issue — they were still making use of the exemption in the Counties Act 1876 to avoid having to form a local body, and remained reluctant to pay rates for infrastructure that did not benefit them personally. But that attitude may have indicated the poverty in which many Sounds settlers were living.

Nevertheless, tracks and track-making were transforming Sounds settlers' lives. Track-making meant employment. Even if not directly involved in track work, locals could earn extra income ferrying in mail, equipment, materials (timber and explosives) and people.[137] With the introduction of the cooperative contracts system in the mid-1890s, men and boys could take up contracts, either back to back or with breaks in between.[138] Farm work could be attended to between contracts. The cooperative scheme also provided small groups of men with a clear and practical way to join forces while enabling them to choose their workmates — skilled men chose each other, suggesting that they were maximising opportunities.[139]

All gangs were paid the same rate but the experienced men, the 'thorough experts', worked longer hours, earning up to five shillings a day more. On average Sounds men, working all weathers including through the worst of winter, made almost 8 shillings per eight-hour day — the standard wage for millworkers and bushmen.[140] (District surveyor Stephenson Smith admitted in 1898 that with no supervision, officials had no idea how long the men had actually worked.) Against this, the men had to pay for expensive stores to be brought in, with bread costing up to 9 pence a loaf, though meat was cheap.

Stephenson Smith also created opportunities for the 86 men he had working for him to save at least part of their wages by having money orders sent straight to the post office. Over 10 months from June 1897 to March 1898 a total of £2439 15s 2d was dispatched. The men found it saved them trouble at home, and some asked for more than half their salary to be sent as it could not get lost.[141]

The work, however, was hard and relentless, and made extraordinary progress considering. Road-maker Jonathan Brough's lively accounts of his gangs' work on the French Pass road in 1899 detail the more than 48 kilometres in seven months he and his men built in western Pelorus Sound, sometimes cutting and widening an existing track, sometimes putting down new track. The French Pass track, some 56 kilometres, was built in just two seasons, the achievement all the greater given the country it traversed. The French Pass–Garnes Bay section was typically tough country. Brough writes:

> In some places the track runs through settlers clearings covered with stumps and logs, burned and charred; then through native shrubbery and tangled scrub of a very peculiar kind, and blown down forests which were something terrible to get through . . . The men had some tough cutting and slashing through some of those dark supplejack gullies.[142]

Yet through often 'steep sidling country', working with pick, shovel, wheelbarrow and some blasting, Brough's gangs cut back mostly 3 feet (0.9 metre) into the solid, felled the bush back about 10 metres and achieved a good grade, though Brough pointed out that it was built for horsemen and drovers more than for 'bike men'.[143]

Blasting carried out by inexperienced crew resulted in two serious accidents during the 10 months covered by Stephenson Smith's report to Lands and Survey. (The men had been 'warned to be careful'.)[144] And two experienced boatmen were drowned bringing in mail from French Pass to Brough's camp in Savill Bay.[145] However, the benefits the tracks conferred on the settlers is difficult to overestimate. Brough noted that the French Pass track made 'a difference of £1 per head between driving heavy cattle out and shipping them, and in some places they had not been able to get their heavy cattle out for years'.

With the track in, that situation was turned on its head — it was reported soon after that '100 head of cattle had been driven in and out of French Pass this season'[146] (a statistic that gives some perspective on the scale of farming in the area).

Other benefits are less easily quantified. Being part of a work gang helped men 'relieve the monotony of their lives'.[147] Women, too, walking up from their homes to admire progress and walking along 'the track as far as it is made', miraculously found a measure of sociability. The Webber girls from French Pass were fairly constant visitors and once walked 70 kilometres to the end of the track and back. (One recorded her delight in the 'smell of the newly turned earth . . . the hoar on the broken ground . . . the exquisite glimpses of sea and landscape [that] made wonderful pictures of exhilarating beauty'.)[148]

TRACKS TRANSFORMED SETTLERS' social connections. From Northwest Bay to Worlds End, settlers 'during the last 20 years have been leading a life of dreary isolation through want of tracks,' Brough noted. 'The only way to get about was scrambling around and through almost impassable bush thickets or fallen trees, or by scaling some of the rocky headlands. The shores and beaches are strewn for miles with angular blocks of stone.'[149] With the track made, 'Mr Tiller who lives in Northwest Bay . . . has never once used his boat or rounded Stafford Point to Wilson Bay.'[150]

Given the drownings occasioned by wind and weather capsizing boats, it is not surprising that Arthur Tosswill at Garne Bay killed a 'fatted calf' when the track from French Pass reached his bay.[151] Tracks put an end to having to drive stock along tide-dependent, rough beaches (to the detriment of the animals' welfare); they placed better postal services and access to education for their children within settlers' reach.

Over time, usage scoured the tracks and weather caused slips.[152] As early as 1899 settlers were worried about the lack of maintenance on the Havelock–Nydia Bay track, which was not, they argued, a by-road but a main road (for which government had responsibility), used in one instance by 2000 cattle and 200 sheep.[153] Ten years on, their arguments were still falling on unsympathetic ears. At the beginning of 1911 the PWD agreed to carry out maintenance if funded from thirds and fourths, and only on tracks that were contiguous to the properties on which the thirds accrued. Money was being, and would be, expended on new works or track widening but the government would not do maintenance.[154]

Settlers who attended a 'mass meeting of settlers from Waitaria and Fitzroy Bays' were adamant they still did not wish to form a local body, with the responsibilities and financial obligations that entailed. Public works spending in the Sounds had been so minimal that since colonisation it amounted to only £500–600 a year.[155]

How representative those views were of the settlers of outer Pelorus is unclear.[156] The government of the day referred to the settlers' 'evident prosperity', and while over the next few years it voted thousands of pounds on the main link roads around the Sounds, considerably less was spent on tracks from accrued thirds and fourths.[157] The Farmers' Union pointed out in 1911 that £200 'was neither here nor there' spread over 400 kilometres of tracks.[158]

By 1916, expenditure on roads, bridges and railways was curtailed across the country.[159] Nevertheless, in 1920 the PWD reported that Sounds County tracks had been maintained and important ones repaired.[160] Over the next decades the department's responsibility for further road development and maintenance of existing tracks or roads would continue to be debated.

Post and phones

Mail services played a vital role in enabling people to maintain the important emotional and business ties that build and sustain settlement. The provision of postal services, reported the Post Office Department in 1865, was 'an important test of prosperity'. However, unusually among government departments at the time, while 'the freest communication . . . at least cost to the public' was desirable, the postmaster-general believed it was also desirable that the Post Office pay its way.[161] The ups and downs of getting the mail to the Sounds in the early days were a reflection of how successive governments balanced the provision of an essential service against its cost.

A Wellington–Picton mail service was established in 1856. By 1859 Picton had a postmaster. The gold rushes and Picton's becoming a port of entry meant that the volume of mail increased markedly in the early 1860s;[162] in 1863, post offices were established at the Grove, Māhakipawa and Havelock,[163] and to cater for miners' needs, Mr Liardet and his whaleboats worked the Picton–Havelock run.[164] But such services

ABOVE John Webber's view of the pā and open marae area on Cook's Hippah Island, 1778. ALEXANDER TURNBULL LIBRARY, B-098-011

BELOW A scene from Captain Cook's third voyage to New Zealand. Meretoto Ship Cove, Tōtaranui Queen Charlotte Sound, February 1777, to the right are astronomical observation tents, from which Cook and his second lieutenant James King made further calculations regarding latitude and longitude. Also shown are Māori fishing and drying fish, several waka and crew members of the *Resolution* and *Discovery*. JOHN WEBBER, ALEXANDER TURNBULL LIBRARY, B-098-015

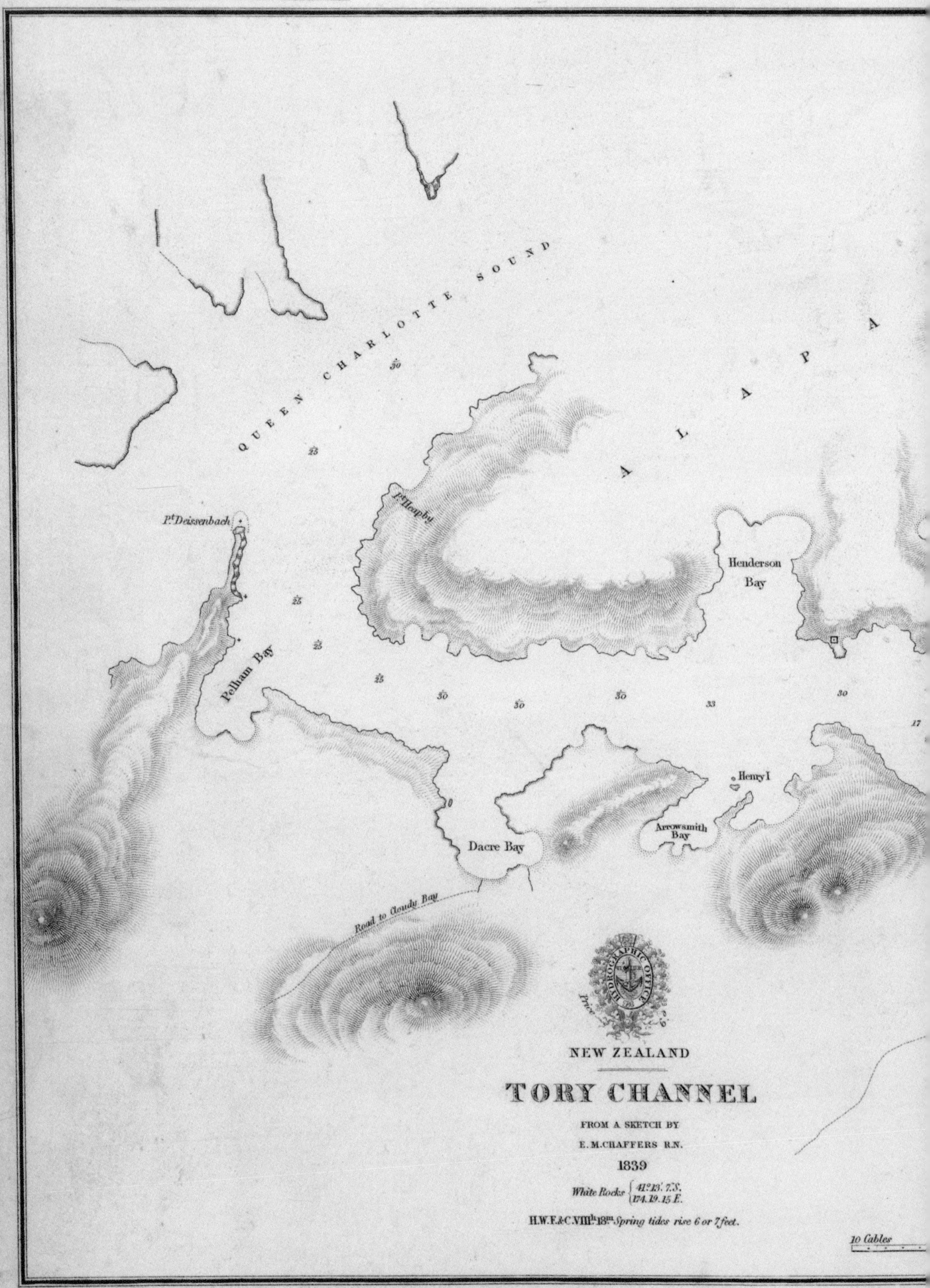

London Published according to Act of Pa
Sold by R.

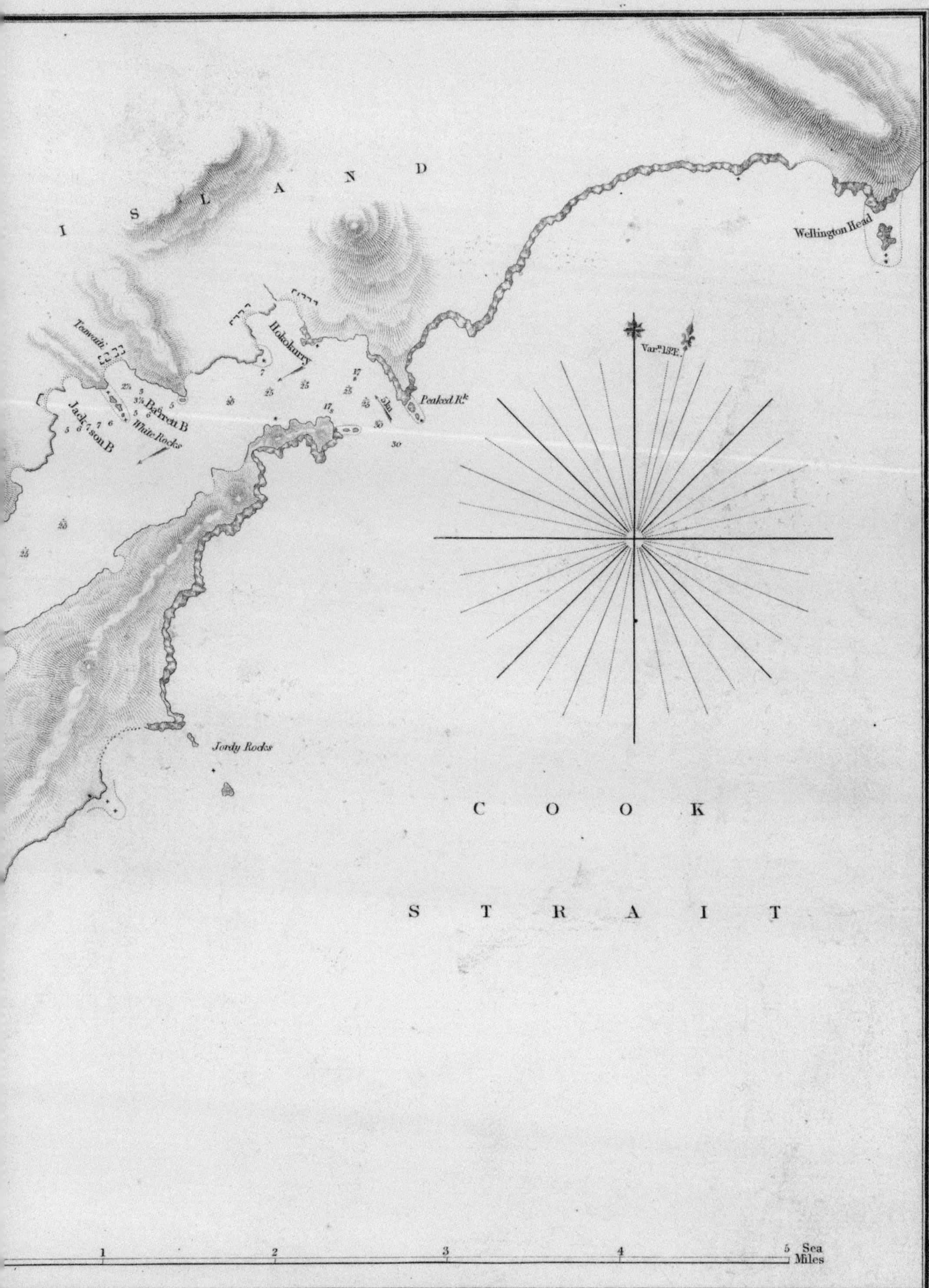

Engraved by J.&C. Walker.

ce of the Admiralty Decr 18th 1841.

s 21 Poultry.

1414

PREVIOUS PAGE E. M. Chaffers' sketch of Kura Te Au Tory Channel, 1839. Generally, the time and cost to develop these charts through the Hydrographic Office in England meant that in the early years especially it was local knowledge rather than Admiralty charts that guided ships around the coast. ALEXANDER TURNBULL LIBRARY, MAPCOLL 834.2AJ 1839

ABOVE Frederick Aloysius Weld, *Makapawa Bay, Pelorus Sound, 1861*. ALEXANDER TURNBULL LIBRARY, A-269-022

OPPOSITE An early and not very accurate plan of the island of Alapawa (Arapaoa), 1840. AUCKLAND LIBRARIES HERITAGE COLLECTIONS, AP 3802

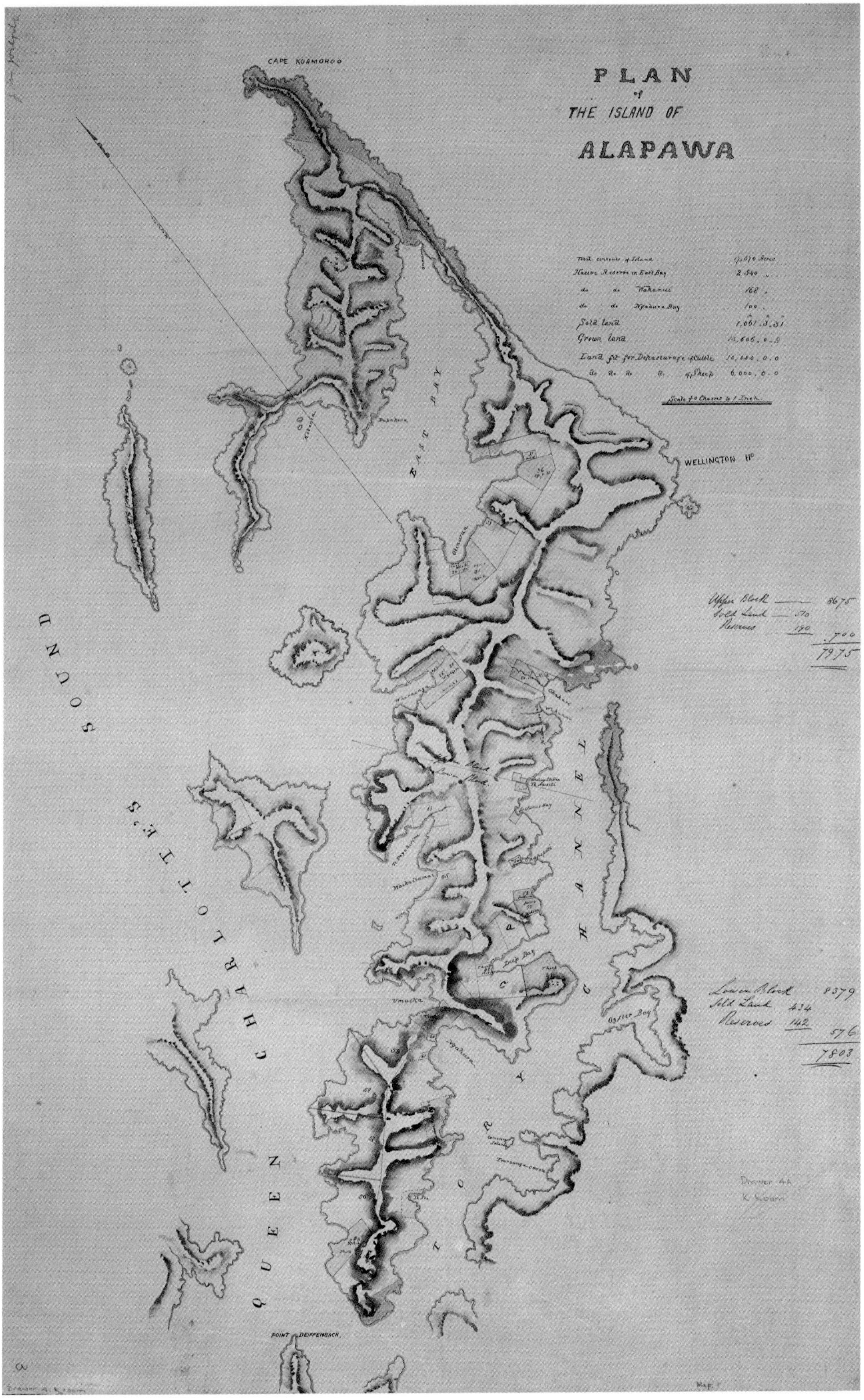
PLAN of THE ISLAND OF ALAPAWA
CAPE KOAMAROO
Total contents of Island 17,670 Acres
Native Reserve in East Bay 2,540 "
do do Wakanui 168 "
do do Ngakura Bay 100 "
Sold land 1,061.3.31
Crown land 13,606.0.9
Land fit for Depasturage of Cattle 10,000.0.0
do do do do of Sheep 6,000.0.0
Scale 40 Chains to 1 Inch
EAST BAY
WELLINGTON H°
Upper Block 8675
Sold Land 510
Reserves 190
700
7975
QUEEN CHARLOTTE'S SOUND
TORY CHANNEL
Deep Bay
Oyster Bay
Lower Block 8379
Sold Land 434
Reserves 142
576
7803
POINT DEIFFENBACH
Drawer 4A
K Room

Mapping the Sounds – both sea and land – was seen as vital to its development for settlement. Shown here are survey drawings for roads on Forsyth Island, 1911 (below), and a section of road between Fairy Bay and Tawhero Point, 1910 (right). The detail is indicative of the challenges of the terrain. ARCHIVES NEW ZEALAND TE RUA MAHARA O TE KĀWANATANGA, W5, BOX 1324 NO. 26706; BOX 1338, NO. 28340

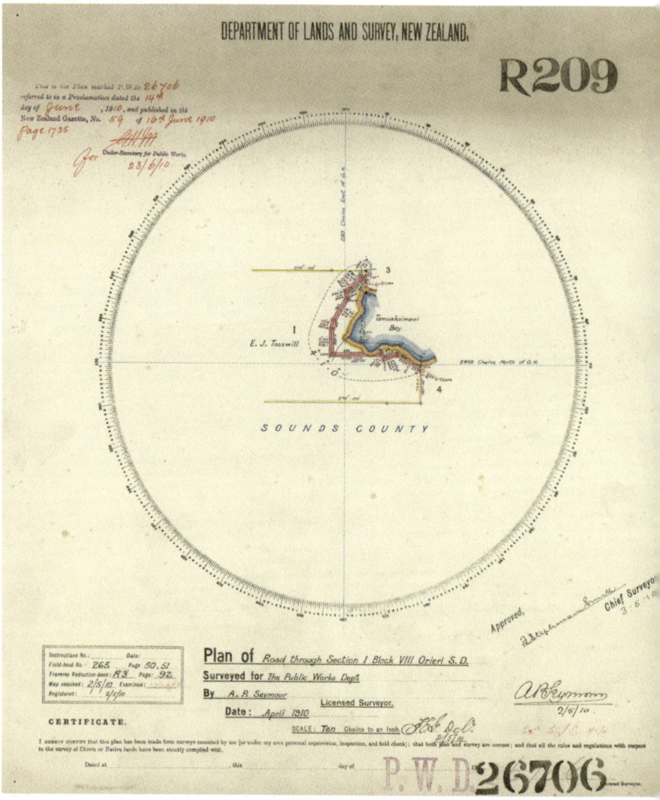

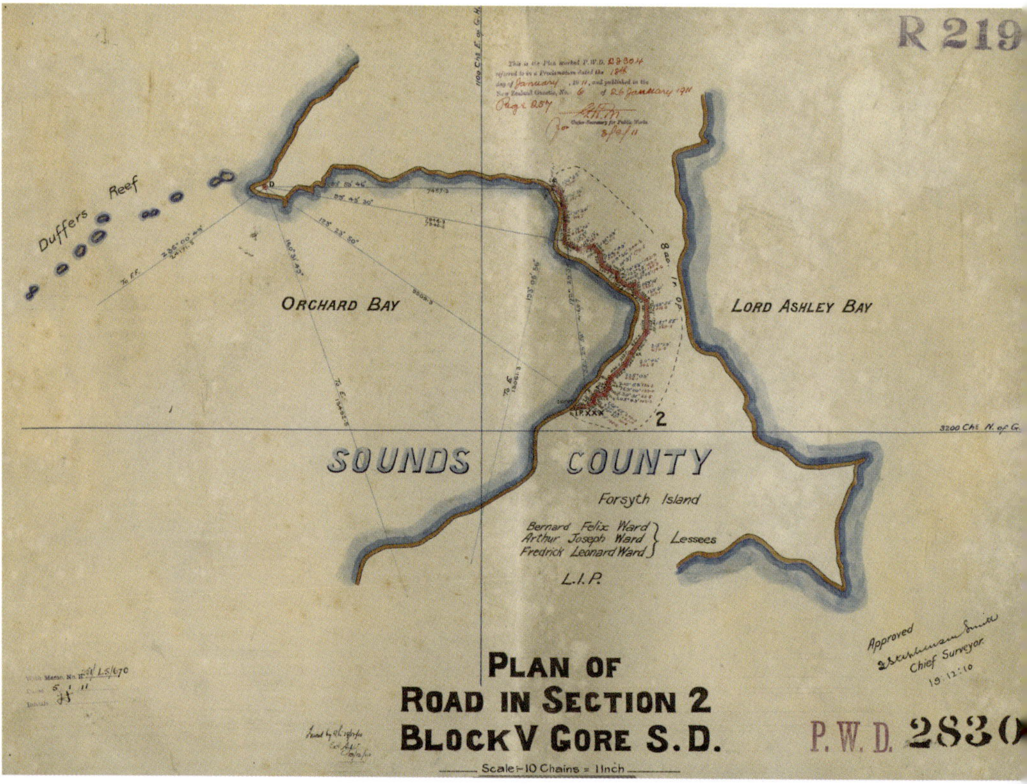

MARLBOROUGH SOUNDS
GOVT
TOURIST
DEPT
NEW ZEALAND

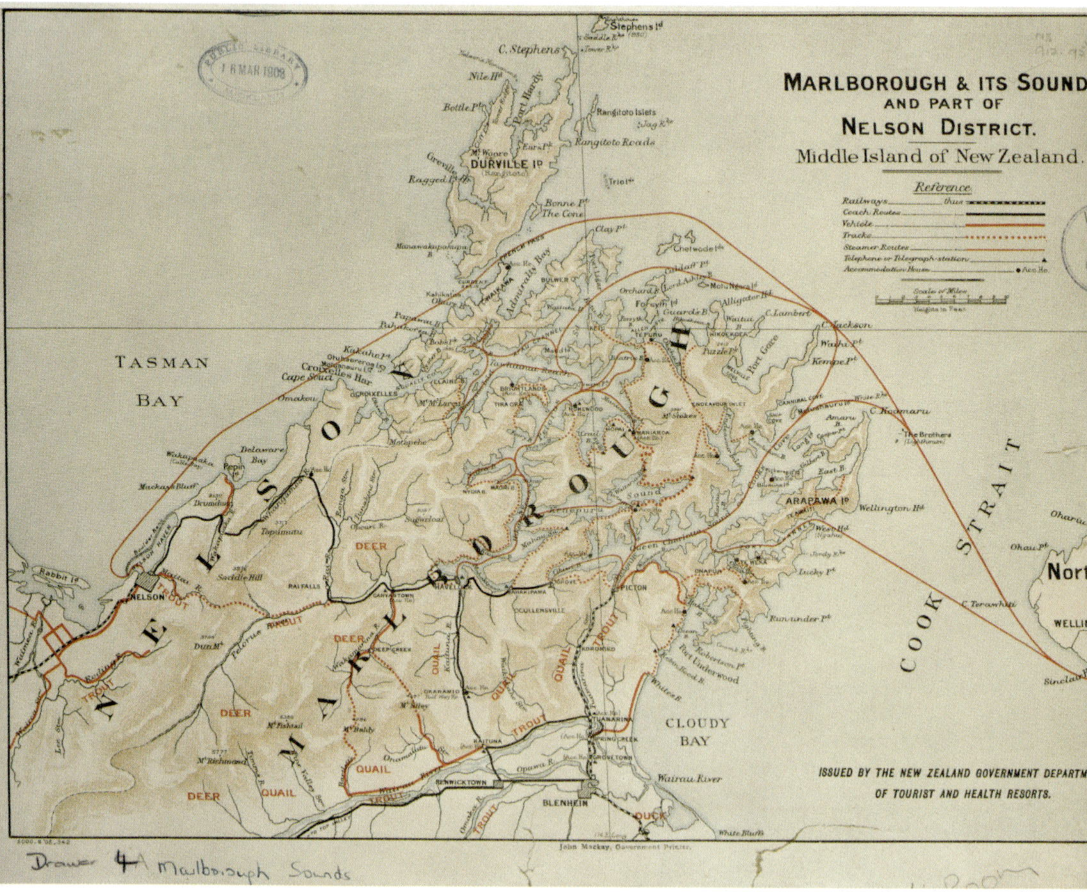

PREVIOUS PAGE In this poster advertising the Marlborough Sounds a steamer sails past a point in Kura Te Au Tory Channel. It was one of those marvellous images that the New Zealand Tourist and Publicity Department were putting out in in the 1930s. To Pākehā viewers at the time, those bare hills would have demonstrated settler ability to turn poor land into productive farms. ALEXANDER TURNBULL LIBRARY, EPH-E-TOURISM-1930S-03

ABOVE Even from its very early days, tourism was seen as an important source of revenue for the Sounds. This map, issued by the Department of Tourist and Health Resorts in the early twentieth century, shows the many transport and communication routes for visitors, as well as the hunting and fishing opportunities, including trout, deer and quail. AUCKLAND LIBRARIES HERITAGE COLLECTIONS, MAP 299A

did not come cheap. In 1868 the annual expenditure on the Picton–Havelock service (three days a week) was £244 8s, the revenue only £70 4s 4d.[165]

In the remote and sparsely settled Sounds, timetabled postal services were a difficult proposition. The Havelock–Homewood run in Pelorus Sound was instigated in 1869,[166] but for two decades more, settlers in the outer Pelorus depended on the vagaries of passing ships' timetables for their mail. Only in 1891 was James Cross and his steamer *Waitapu* awarded a fortnightly run between Wellington and Havelock, calling at specified bays in the outer Sounds — Māori Bay, Homewood, Maud Island, Ketu Bay — on both the inward and outward trips, and at other intermediate places as required.

Population was the problem — as this grew, services were consolidated. From 1882 post offices, sometimes as separate buildings, sometimes run from settlers' homes, and equipped with an ever-widening range of facilities, began to be dotted about the Sounds. That year Kenepuru and St Omer offices were opened, with official postal runs between Havelock and Kenepuru via St Omer; Picton and Torea via the Grove, St Omer, Crail Bay, Kenepuru and Torea.[167] In 1885, with antimony mining booming, Endeavour Inlet got a post office, and weekly mail services were established between Kenepuru, Kenepuru Heads and (by land over the hill) Endeavour Inlet; a mail boat also ran fortnightly between Picton, Whatamonga Bay and Port Underwood.[168] Manaroa, too, got a post office in the 1885–86 year.

With a post office established at Te Awaiti in August 1889, Heberley, then Captain Fisk (in 1891), were contracted for the fortnightly run.[169] From the early 1890s postal-note (transmission of money by post) and money-order facilities were available in some offices.[170] For those within easy reach of a post office, time-consuming journeys to transact day-to-day business were a thing of the past.

Sometimes services were cut. As the antimony venture floundered (again) in 1892, the mail service between Picton and Endeavour Inlet was reduced from twice to once weekly.[171] Within a few years, however, and on a national basis, the Post Office Department was using tendering and longer contracts to achieve better services and increase frequency.[172] Fortnightly runs, with different boats running alternative weeks, saw settlers in Pelorus Sound enjoying a weekly service from Blenheim via Havelock or from Wellington.[173] A further weekly mail left Picton for the Grove and Torea (from where mail for Kenepuru and Manaroa was taken over the hill twice weekly), and for Endeavour Inlet. A Wellington boat did a further fortnightly run to Hikoekoea and Ketu Bays, Brightlands, Homewood, Northwest

ABOVE Mail delivery, possibly in Tōtaranui Queen Charlotte Sound, c. 1900. ALEXANDER TURNBULL LIBRARY, 48049

BELOW 'The Torea at Tarwhite'. The big gathering, with everyone in their best clothing, illustrates the importance of the steamers' visits. PICTON HERITAGE AND WHALING MUSEUM, COURTESY PICTON HISTORICAL SOCIETY

Bay, Māori Bay and Havelock — with Mahau Sound included on the return trip.[174]

There were gaps. Settlers on the west side of Arapaoa Island, for instance, had no regular delivery until 1909 when, following sustained settler protest, a post office was set up in Wharehunga Bay. Mr Greensill from the long-established Sounds family was in charge; Perano's *Elsie* called in fortnightly on her Picton–Havelock run.

Delivery often involved small local launches, and frequent handling.[175] From around the turn of the century ships such as the Union Steamship Company's *Penguin* and *Wainui*, sailing between Wellington, Picton and Nelson, provided regularly notified mail services; the company's 222-foot (68-metre) *Mapourika* was still carrying Sounds mails in 1920.[176] The Sounds and Golden Bay Steamship Company's *Te Kapu* ran regularly between Havelock and the Sounds via Tory Channel, Te Awaiti, Picton, Endeavour Inlet and Kenepuru.[177]

In keeping with the wider experimentation with pigeons as carriers in the early twentieth century, Horace Norgrove (of the mail boats *Phoenix* and *Elsie*) tried them, unsuccessfully, for postal work. Only six of the 17 birds released returned.[178]

Over time, new routes took in further bays and many, particularly in Pelorus Sound, enjoyed weekly delivery. The complexity of the arrangements can perhaps be best appreciated in Charles Mills' reply to a complaint about missed mail at Te Puru in 1905. The *Manaroa*, Mills pointed out, did not call at Te Puru on the way from Wellington but on its way out from Havelock. He regretted that the settlers had not been advised of this. But, he stressed, the Te Puru mail was not a fortnightly service. It was a weekly service, managed with the Havelock and Wellington steamers each coming on alternate fortnights. The department had tried to get a steamer to serve Te Puru going in *and* out of Havelock, but

> the contractors were unable to agree to the vessel calling on the voyage from Wellington because of missing the tide at Havelock. They state there is a fair trade with Wakatahuri both from and to Wellington, whereas but little is done with Te Puru. A separate mail is made up at Wellington for Te Puru, and if the settlers prefer that it be landed at Wakatahuri, or kept on the *Manaroa* until she returns to Havelock, either course will be adopted. There is every wish on the part of the post office to meet the convenience of those served by the Te Puru office, so long as this can be done without interfering with the call at Wakatahuri.[179]

THE CHALLENGING CONDITIONS IN WHICH the mail ships often operated made any service remarkable. The smaller oil-launches might have to navigate their way into bays in strong winds amid which they could lose steerage among submerged rocks. They had to come alongside sometimes derelict wharves or anchor off. On the bigger vessels, cattle had to be loaded or pushed overboard to swim ashore. A huge variety of freight needed to be swung on, passengers had to be reunited with their luggage, the mail bags hurled on board. A *Pelorus Guardian* reporter on one of *Manaroa*'s fortnightly sailings in May 1908 found the trip packed with 'interest, variety and excitement'.

The *Manaroa* left Havelock 10 a.m. Friday, expecting to be in Wellington before dark on Saturday. In Mahau Sound the tide prevented the crew getting within cooee of homestead and wharf, so the mail was rowed ashore. In Hikapu Reach she dropped more bags at Whatanihi and Paradise bays before reaching Nydia Bay at 2.30 p.m. in the 'teeth of a heavy rainsquall . . . The nor'wester was fitful, and the bay was white with spume driven high by the willy-waughs.'

The 10,000 feet of timber that was to be loaded could not be punted out. By this time, and with the original timetable already gone by the board, the *Manaroa* anchored and spent the night in pelting rain and heavy wind. The following day the timber was loaded by 11 a.m. and, in a bitterly cold south-easterly, the *Manaroa* weighed anchor and battled to Northwest Bay, where, as 'the wind . . . nearly [took] charge of the vessel', goods and mail were loaded. At Homewood the mail was sent ashore hurriedly before the ship 'thrashed into Crail Bay in the teeth of the gale', again to drop off mail. She then pushed on to Eli Bay, dropped off the last of a consignment of 100 bags of grass seed on C. H. Mills' property, which, the reporter observed, would soon be well grassed. The *Manaroa* reached Hopai Bay at 4 p.m., where the fern at the northern end was noted to be recolonising, before making 'the comparative calm at Tosswill's place at Waimaru'.[180] There the account ended.

In the bays where there was no post office, men rowed out on 'mail day', the passing ship slowed, the mailbags were off- or on-loaded and the dinghy returned to land where settlers from the neighbouring bays would have gathered to wait.[181] Smaller launches possibly came closer in, much the way the tourist business on the Pelorus mail run operates today.

Rough and ready though it was, the Sounds mail service provided an economic lifeline to settlers, bringing and taking bulk items as well as perishable goods, the timing of which was critical.[182] But more than economics were involved. As isolated

ABOVE The little trader *Manaroa* pulling away from the Havelock wharf. Helped by a Department of Agriculture annual subsidy of £400, *Manaroa* called at 18 post offices on the trip to and from Havelock. Mrs Severn, the stewardess for many years and something of an institution, attended to the passengers' comfort.
HAVELOCK MUSEUM, HM1009

RIGHT A. Greensill in Bolton Bay, Mahau Sound, picking up deliveries. The big tidal rises and falls meant sledges were the best way of getting around the beach without dirty boots.
MARLBOROUGH HISTORICAL SOCIETY, 016708

ABOVE The official opening of the Tia Ora post office in 1914. MARLBOROUGH HISTORICAL SOCIETY, 5098

RIGHT Post office, Manaroa. MARLBOROUGH HISTORICAL SOCIETY, 0000.200.23

rural families found, delivery of mail and newspapers provided a vital psychological link with families and friends and the wider world — no wonder settlers were upset by changes in delivery schedules that could introduce a week's delay. Mail day also provided an opportunity for the Sounds communities in adjoining bays to stop work, boat or walk to the collection point, and to chat and share news. In 1913 a woman who was alone at home all day because her husband was away working and her children were at school looked forward to mail days. 'It was a thing I have to look forward to, to have a chat with one or another, and perhaps to see someone on board whom I knew,' she was reported as saying.[183]

From the turn of the century, all around the country, mail services thrived and the Post Office reported significant increases in revenue. In 1901 this was boosted by the introduction of the universal penny post, which 'would carry a letter to any part of the colony, to Great Britain, and to nearly any part of the Empire' as well as to a range of other countries. The move put New Zealand 'in the forefront of the civilised countries of the world'.[184] Across the country mail volume boomed. Money orders, postal notes and similar services were introduced from the 1890s, and an ever-growing number of telegraph facilities were installed in an ever-growing number of post offices. A receptive public and a climate of opinion gave rise to an environment in which central government saw its role as providing basic services.

Information about the level of subsidies for a significant number of postal services around New Zealand (and overseas) was first provided in 1893.[185] Sounds subsidies were predictably high; by 1920 the only subsidies that exceeded them were those for the routes from Wellington or Lyttelton to the Chatham Islands, from Bluff to Halfmoon Bay on Stewart Island, and from Westport north to Little Wanganui.[186] Sounds settlers had little reason to feel aggrieved.

TELEGRAMS AND TELEPHONES WERE SIMILARLY big business. In 1862 the Canterbury Provincial Council laid the country's first telegraph line, between Christchurch and Lyttelton; four years later a Cook Strait telegraph cable linked the two islands. Sending a telegram, revolutionary then, was, by today's standards, a somewhat cumbersome process. Messages had to be brief, translated into Morse Code, tapped into the telegraph network and, with a charge of a penny per word, dispatched. On arrival at the nearest telegraph office to the desired address, the message was decoded, written down, and the telegram physically delivered.[187] For some time the cost meant that businesses were the main users, but telegraph lines were steadily and significantly extended year by year, and the £79,537 earned in 1876 had become £110,000 by 1892.[188]

In 1866 telegraph cables from Wellington came into Whites Bay, Port Underwood, Picton, Havelock, and Nelson via the Maungatapu. A year later Havelock got a telegraph office,[189] and lines were criss-crossing the top of the South Island by 1876. The general practice was to erect telegraph, and then telephone, lines alongside roads or railway lines, which was of course a challenge in the Sounds at this time. Only at the beginning of the twentieth century were telegraph and telephone party lines (with distinctive rings for each household and the opportunity to eavesdrop on others' conversations) gradually set up, finally linking up the small groups of settlers with the wider world. Even then, comprehensive coverage was not achieved.

In 1901 Māhakipawa had a telegraph and telephone office with a money-order and postal-note office. Savings bank facilities were also available. A telegraph line went to Mahau.[190] The following year the government, which had a monopoly on developing and installing the country's phone system, began installing telephones in Pelorus Sound.

The value that phones brought to the economy saw lines across the country constantly upgraded for better service, with direct connections made to bigger and bigger exchanges. Telephony, sound miraculously transmitted by electricity, had been in New Zealand since 1877. Now you could talk directly to someone far away, now their response was immediate, now no one needed to learn Morse.[191] Public uptake of the new technology saw phone rents (phones were not owned) fall from the initial considerable charge. In line with his government's Liberal principles, Prime Minister Richard Seddon rejected the idea of paying for local calls, and the cost of a combined telephone/telegraph system was, innovatively, kept low by setting up small telephone offices around the country from where isolated settlers could phone their messages to the nearest telegraph office for onwards transmission.

However, while a significantly subsidised rural mail system (see Appendix 3) was seen as a legitimate government cost, there was not, for reasons on which we can only speculate, the same mindset around providing telephone lines into small rural communities.[192] The government, realistic about the economies of the exercise, often required there to be 30 subscribers before it would set up an exchange.[193] Requests for phone lines were vetted against installation and maintenance costs, the likely revenue from line rentals and the length of time it would take for a line to become self-supporting. Nor were businesses exempt from government scrutiny — the line to the freezing plant at Forsyth Bay, expected to cost over £5500, was turned down in 1902 because it was unlikely to be self-supporting within a reasonable time.[194]

Having tasted the new technology, Sounds settlers, prominent and otherwise, were only too aware of the 'terrible inconvenience' of having no phones during sheep sales, or during sickness, and the practical advantages and efficiencies of being able to signal a ship's approach (particularly if it were late and likely to miss the train connection to Blenheim).[195] They petitioned, they had questions asked in the House, they wrote to their local papers setting out the issues and possible resolutions, sometimes with guarantees that a line would pay its way.[196] The Farmers' Union and the Christchurch Meat Company added their voices.

Finally, from 1903, telegraph and party phone lines (which could serve up to 10 customers each) were installed alongside bridle tracks. That year, via telephone exchanges linked through to the various Pelorus Sound post offices, a telephone line connected to the main system ran out to Mahau, Portage, Kenepuru Head, Waitaria, Manaroa and Hopai, and was being extended to Elie and Crail Bays and Homewood.

These were the old single 'earth return lines'. Hooked on porcelain cups, they were strung on trees or taken along fencelines, with the fence itself serving as part of the circuit. Mānuka poles got them across estuaries. If they made contact with the ground at any point, or a fence or a tree, they were likely to break. Lines across estuaries got wet in high tides and short-circuited, and the signals at the destination were poor. As in many other rural areas, the 8 or 10 families on each party line had to patrol regularly (sometimes over miles of line) to clear branches, firm up posts and check the insulators. But even with this most economical approach the installation costs were not insignificant — the Mahau line cost £128 8s 11d, those in Pelorus totalled £1582 9s 2d.[197]

In 1906 a 'circuitous route' through Māhakipawa and Picton finally connected Havelock, Picton and Blenheim by phone. The outside world was coming ever closer.[198] That year, too, with construction costs by then significantly reduced and amid a general rural clamour for connections to the telegraph system,[199] lines finally began to be installed on the eastern side of Queen Charlotte Sound and in Tory Channel. After some years of representation a mile of cable was laid in Tory Channel to create a phone connection between Picton and various settlements in the channel,[200] and two years later a line was strung between Picton, Okukari and Wharehunga, with another extended from Wharehunga to Ōtānerau in 1910.[201]

The rugged terrain called for intrepid construction workers. Thousands of poles had to be unloaded from their transport and manhandled into place. The amount of telephone wire needed weighed tonnes. And, of course, there was the weather. Mr O'Brien, working on the Nydia and Paradise Bay line, had 'shown that it takes exceptionally rough weather to hinder his work', but the approaching winter definitely slowed his progress.[202] However, by 1919 phone lines finally snaked out to many inlets in Pelorus.[203]

The government, which owned the lines, took responsibility for upgrades. In 1901 it began what would become a 70-year process of installing new metallic lines. The insulated double wires laid were less liable to be affected by rain and wind and gave a good signal.[204] They were more expensive, of course. The amount of metal wire needed doubled, and the two wires had to be carried on poles, with new insulators and insulator pins. The wire used for the circuits between Havelock and Māhakipawa, and Picton, Māhakipawa and Manaroa, in 1913 weighed over 17 tonnes.[205]

Labour costs increased. Equipment, too, was upgraded — in 1908, some users in Pelorus Sound line were supplied with superior new phones that were specially designed for long-distance calling, and a condenser was installed so that ringing was not interfered with if someone on the line left the receiver off the hook — a useful modification for those still getting to grips with unfamiliar technology.[206] But such upgrades were far from being comprehensive or quick.

In that climate, some simply did it themselves. In 1909 C. H. Harris ran a 7-kilometre wire between his homestead at Pohuenui and Whakatahuri. He found it particularly useful during wool and sheep sales, and the cost was not prohibitive.[207] A decade later, Post and Telegraph began encouraging this approach and established an early version of a layby scheme to encourage settlers to erect their own private connections to the nearest telephone office (at no cost to the government). The department sold the materials to settlers, at cost, with payments made twice a year. The interest rate (5–6 per cent) depended on prompt payment and the sum was to be paid off within 10 years. A postwar shortage of materials restricted the scheme's implementation, but not the government's hopes to extend it as soon as possible.[208]

The comment on the 'wonderful distinctness'[209] of the Havelock–Blenheim connection in 1906 is a sharp reminder of the hazardous nature of phone communications at the time. Dial-up systems and manual connections made 'Are you there?' a thoroughly relevant initial response to a call. But despite the inevitable minor squabbles about some overuse of party lines, those who were connected luxuriated in the new convenience. In 1916 the committee organising the Endeavour Inlet Patriotic Picnic — Mr Aikma, of Endeavour Inlet, Messrs Jones and Ewing of Pukekoikoi, and Mr Reeves of Punaruawhiti — talked over the phone line that they had themselves installed. Night trips in launches to committee meetings were a thing of the past. In the comfort of their homes they organised a 'patriotic picnic, sale of work, etc . . . to take place at the Inlet on Boxing Day . . . [T]he committee has the affair well in hand now, and great results are hoped for.'[210]

7. Carving Out New Lives

'Our greatest want has been, as usual, food. Fanny and I had two days upon tea only, and then another day upon milk and water. No bread, no flour, no meat, no sugar or honey . . .'

By the 1870s the English, along with large groups of Scots and Irish and small groups of other Europeans, were settling in New Zealand, that 'Britain of the South'.[1] They had come to better their lives. They worked at making a living with extraordinary perseverance, effort and optimism. As they set down roots, they established communities; some fifty years on the first of their number were growing old and dying. Theirs is an extensively documented world in which, even as the struggles are acknowledged, the successes in transplanting old-world institutions, loyalties and patterns of living into a new world are widely recorded.

The situation for Māori stands in stark contrast. By this time they were a very small part of the population. Across the country Māori were outnumbered by Pākehā from 1845, and the Māori population did not significantly increase until the latter half of the twentieth century. In the Sounds area in 1881, while 404 Pākehā were living in Queen Charlotte and Pelorus sounds,[2] only 127 Ngāti Awa were in Queen Charlotte Sound, and 83 Rangitāne and Ngāti Toa lived in Pelorus Sound and Valley.[3] Both populations were scattered in small groups, with most on the reserves established at the time of European purchase. These reserves, as elsewhere in Te Tau Ihu (the top of the South Island) did not provide an adequate base for Māori to either engage effectively with the Pākehā economy or maintain their traditional hunter-gatherer practices.[4]

Māori feature little in any contemporary newspaper reporting in the Sounds: the official snippets of information in reports compiled largely by European observers provide information only on their economic, health and welfare status.[5] A picture builds of a people impoverished by the loss of their lands and then further impoverished by government policy and practice. But if details of the pattern of day-to-day living remain elusive, it is possible to infer something of the resilience and strength gained from customary practice and the enactment of core Māori values that physically and culturally kept their communities alive.

WE LEFT WILLIAM AND AUGUSTA HARVEY and their four children in Clova Bay, housed in tents until the bush was sufficiently cleared to build a small house. They would have brought basic supplies with them — flour, potatoes, salt, treacle, sugar, tea, sufficient homemade soap to last for a while, kerosene, a yeast plant, possibly some jam, a round or two of cheese, perhaps a handful of vegetables to eat and for seed.[6] They, like subsequent settlers, would have supplemented that food with what they could find and hunt. They possibly ate fernroot, and the flowers of the kiekie, known as tāwhara, could be peeled back to a base that reportedly tasted something like honey-flavoured watermelon.[7] Fuchsia berries were good for pies and puddings, though currants were needed if the result was not to be insipid. Fish were (mostly) there for the taking, the delicious green-lipped mussels grew in the rocky and soft-sediment intertidal areas,[8] and the bush was 'alive with birds, parrots were as numerous as flies, eating the seeds on the pepperwood trees'. Kererū, tūī, weka, the shining cuckoo or pīpīwharauroa (the end of its long, distinctive call as mellifluous as its Māori name) in spring, and kākā (not much liked as food but unprotected until 1913) were 'a great source of food'. These doubtless fell to Augusta's hand as well as William's — women were often good shots. Wild cattle roamed the bush from the 1840s, goats and more pigs were introduced; from the 1890s deer, though protected, were fair game, and wild honey — with massive combs from just one hive filling two to four kerosene tins — could be found into the 1930s and 1940s.[9]

The Harveys' first home was a thatched lean-to with a sail slung across to a tree to provide a storage area, and there was an outside cooking fire. Their 'real' two-room house was built with sawn timber and its unsatisfactory thatch would be replaced by tōtara shingles, split with a wide axe-head into centimetre-thick slabs, and a large fireplace in one room afforded the luxury of cooking inside.[10]

We have to imagine the details of how the family survived the initial years, the precariousness of their life when fish and game became scarce, the worry over precious days' work on the land lost when William travelled to Nelson to replenish basic supplies. (What would become Havelock was then a pā at the junction of two Māori trails.[11]) We can only speculate, too, on what Augusta felt whenever William left her and the children and sailed out of the bay, taking with him their one link to the wider world; nor do we know whether their hopes of making a home and a livelihood in this new world ever wavered.

Their experience typified the considerable ingenuity and versatility that Sounds life demanded for decades — the effort of breaking in the difficult land, obtaining timber to build (the women sawing alongside the men), the need to develop skills in carpentry, hunting, boating, animal husbandry, droving, gardening . . .[12] Getting things growing and farming the land had to be balanced against making enough cash to survive in an isolated country where communications were poor, there was effectively no formal health care, and access to schools, a critical ingredient of parents' hopes for a better life for their children, was not easily achieved.

Keeping up the necessary ingenuity, resourcefulness, strength and determination was not always easy, and sometimes impossible. In 1861 Edward Hope went to Australia 'to try to get something better to do than could be done in New Zealand . . . We are really tired of New Zealand now, for we can never get money enough together to enable us to invest it in anything payable, and the colony is too old now for men of no means, however industrious and willing to better themselves.'[13] Although, for want of a better option, he eventually returned, he was not alone in finding the settler dream misrepresented and his fortitude faltering.[14] But for all his disillusionment, Edward then stayed, and his family's letters and a diary provide a valuable insight into what settling in the Sounds meant.

JANE HOPE ARRIVED IN NELSON with her three sons, Edward, Richard Johnson (known as Johnson) and Orry, in 1853. Like most immigrants at that time, she had come from England;[15] atypically, the family initially had a bit of money to fall back on. However, by 1860 the boys were working at whatever they could find and Jane

ABOVE Donald McCormick, Whatamonga Bay, Queen Charlotte Sound. By the time this photograph was taken, in the early twentieth century, many of the older generation of those first Pākehā settlers had passed away. MARLBOROUGH HISTORICAL SOCIETY, 015495

BELOW William and Augusta Harvey and two of their children pose for a photo outside their cottage at Clova Bay. The cottage was well sited for maximum winter sun. Family history has Augusta on one end of the saw when they built the first little place, but says nothing about her involvement with this iteration. The fireplace, with its chimney of split logs layered in clay, was a luxury. The Godsiffs at Titirangi in 1865, by contrast, used an oven built into a bank of earth. This was warmed by radiated heat from stones heated by fire. PICTON HERITAGE AND WHALING MUSEUM, COURTESY PICTON HISTORICAL SOCIETY

depended on them for rent — the parson for whom she kept house, she claimed, had not paid her wages. Her attempts to sell valuables such as brooches, chains, boots, satin slippers and silk stockings in Nelson's then considerably straitened circumstances failed — other settlers could not afford them. In 1861 Jane was living in an unheated box-like structure that the local doctor had built for his books. '[D]irty, unkempt and poverty stricken', she was admitted to a local asylum under restraint.[16] There is little documented over the next few years but we do know that Orry, by then in his thirties, had signed the pledge (not to drink alcohol), though he continued to have 'bad days'. He had married and started a family; Edward had found (but did not entirely keep) the Lord.

By 1876 Edward, who had been bankrupted, had found work in a flax mill in Blenheim; in 1878 he was working on contract at Māhakipawa. With no continuity of employment and little to fall back on, and wanting to pay his creditors and get ahead, he fixed upon owning land as the magic solution to his problems. He had heard of grazing land on Forsyth Island — 'when Allen [presumably a previous owner] had it he sent a lot of wool from there'. A few months later, Edward was hoping to get a £100 loan at 10 per cent interest — he knew of land that was carrying 'about 400 sheep now, in its unimproved state, it could soon be rendered capable of carrying a thousand sheep'. This, he reckoned, would quickly enable him to repay his debts. He had heard, too, of the terms on which Martin (thought to be a Māori chief at Wakapuaka) would 'let or dispose of the Chetwood [sic] Island, the nearest one to the mainland. Orry heard it had been offered for £5 a year rent. Don't talk to anyone else about it.'[17]

In 1877, prior to the government's early moves to open up land for settlement in the Sounds,[18] Orry and family were at Port Ligar. He had leased land from Crichton, a Havelock storekeeper whose other holdings in the 1880s included further land in Port Ligar and on the Chetwodes. He enjoyed a sense of new-found freedom: 'As I am finding my own tucker I can have anyone I like to stay with us.' He got wages from Crichton, too, apparently for work on Crichton's other holdings.[19] The fact that his nearest neighbour was 5 nautical miles (8 kilometres) away did not seem to diminish Orry's liking of the place. The *Waitohi* and other steamers on the Havelock–Nelson route passed about 2.6 nautical miles (5 kilometres) off and could be signalled if necessary.

There is no description of what he was living in, but family history has him building solid wooden structures. His knowledge of animal husbandry, building, hunting and butchering were all in demand. About half of the 500 sheep he was to look after had been 'so much neglected that it will take me a long time to get them quiet, as there are a lot of wild sheep in the bush, and the tame ones get mixed with them'.[20] Fences were needed to avert the constant danger of tutu poisoning, and he planned to build a sty to house the three wild pigs he had caught and wanted to fatten and kill. As well, 'I find what I learned about boats long ago is very useful to me now, as there is a great deal of boat work to be done here.'

Orry's letter is alive with optimism. With the dogs' help, 'I hope to get everything straight in time. Lizzie [his wife] and the children like the place very much and little Edward [his son, named after his brother and generally referred to as Ebb] is very fond of going with his Dadda in the boat when it is fine weather.'[21] A couple of weeks later, winter, accompanied by a very cold sea breeze, had set in but there were no frosts, and Lizzie judged that what with hunting, the stores they had bought, and the goats in milk, they would have plenty to eat.

AS SO MANY OTHER SETTLERS found, however, the land did not generate sufficient income to support a family. Within five months of arriving at Port Ligar, Orry was shearing on the Chetwodes for Crichton, his hands so sore from thorns that he could not hold a pen. A month later he was mustering and shearing at the Harris brothers' property in Ketu Bay. Such work, of course, took him away from developing his land, and wet weather meant no work and no payment. Crichton had not sent his wages, and even if he had, 'we had to draw so much in advance to bring us to Port Ligar,' his wife wrote, 'and there is all the stores that we have had since we have been here. Orry thinks there will be very little if anything coming to him.'[22]

Throughout New Zealand, families at the time struggled with unpaid wages. Strapped for cash, they bought only necessities, were threatened with legal action for non-payment of bills, and were constantly juggling resources to pay debts. On a number of occasions Orry had to clear debts to Crichton, or struggled with other payments because Crichton failed to pay him on time. Two years after they had arrived, Orry had to repay money owed to Crichton before Lizzie could get the children some badly needed clothes, and he had to sell his new guns to get money to buy a cow. In 1884 Lizzie wrote:

> '[p]oor Orry has not been paid for his mustering and shearing at Port Ligar yet, so we must try and be more economical in case he does not get it, which will be a great loss . . . It may be alright . . . but if it does not come

> soon he must go up and see Mr Crichton about it. I hope he will not have to go up to Havelock, but we have not a penny in the house at present.[23]

This hovering on the verge of impecuniousness and disaster is a constant theme throughout the family's letters. Edward and his wife Fanny, after a family tragedy, had moved to Port Ligar in 1878 and Edward was apparently contracting at the Harris brothers' Ketu Bay property. A month later Orry helped out with potatoes and sugar, but Fanny could not pay for the raspberries she wanted because 'we have not heard anything of the two pounds Edward sent for stores, and two pounds is all the money we have got . . . I hope something else will turn up as soon as Edward is finished here, but we must put our trust in God.'[24]

In late 1882 a bag of lamb's wool and a calf skin were the only assets that Orry and Lizzie had left to sell — 'the hide will pay the freight [for the flour], one shilling. We got the flour with my butter money.'[25] Lizzie's tiny home industry/barter arrangements were obviously essential. On 1 January 1884, six years after they had come to Port Ligar, Lizzie finally had more than one cup in the house. In 1888 she lamented that they were 'very hard pressed' and could not send her mother-in-law, Jane, the steamer fare for a visit. Hammond was wanting his money for Orry's boat, *May*, which they had bought to freight timber and to get around the Sounds, 'but we cannot raise any of it', and though Orry was 'taking the timber to try and clear off what he owes to Mr Crichton, he has been so long, owing to bad weather' that he was afraid others would have already taken it.

In November the same year Edward, by then in Deep Bay (Admiralty Bay), wrote to his mother:

> Our greatest want has been, as usual, food. Fanny and I had two days upon tea only, and then another day upon milk and water. No bread, no flour, no meat, no sugar or honey, and James fished all day and could not catch even a cod. No vegetables, the only eatable thing being some small green gooseberries.[26]

Clothing was another constant drain. The children's clothes and everyone's boots, so essential for working and getting around, were always wearing out and being outgrown. Lizzie cut down adult cast-offs, mended and darned — and Orry 'growled' at the waste if she trimmed the children's undies with pretty braid.[27]

Meanwhile, in Nelson, Jane had found work in 1867 in Nelson's Trafalgar Hotel and was coping well. She acted as something of an agent; sent her sons much-appreciated clothes and household equipment, arranged for sales of produce, organised money matters and dealt with creditors. (She would keep up this role until at some period she moved to live with Orry and Lizzie at their farm in Admiralty Bay until she died in early 1901.)

By May 1889 Orry and family were living on their own land in Dora (now Pukatea) Bay (Admiralty Bay), but the daily pattern of work that Lizzie Hope recorded in her diary would have been very similar to that in Port Ligar. Apart from the times when Orry went on the booze (the social and economic impact of drinking, especially when families were barely managing financially, has never been quantified), the list of steady work was constant. Firewood had to be cut and brought in, calves driven home and sheep mustered. They cut wood (though whether for sleepers, firewood or a mill is not specified) and Lizzie was sometimes involved pitching the felled trees down the hill. Orry went fishing once, and he and Ebb 'took a bee tree'. An animal died and a day was spent skinning it. Lizzie's butter had to be delivered to one of the little traders, *Darby* and *Dauntless*, that plied between Nelson and Havelock, and three head of cattle loaded on the other. Orry visited the neighbours to resolve issues of straying stock and dogs and organise to borrow a boat. He also went to French Pass to collect 300 pounds (136 kilograms) of flour and a bag from Jane that Lizzie hoped would contain children's clothes and boots. Ebb, by then 15, helped. Ebb went pig hunting with his father or on his own, and cut and pitched wood. There was no break on Sundays.

Lack of capital made unanticipated misfortune all the greater. At Māhakipawa on 1 July 1878, Fanny, heavily pregnant, was woken by the crash of the roof of their house falling in and found herself and her three children surrounded by flames. Fanny, her head badly burned, managed to rescue her son and one daughter, but the other child perished in the flames and the rescued daughter died of her burns a few days later.[28] Any fire in such an isolated environment could and did bring similarly devastating consequences.[29] What caused the Hope fire was not established. (The family claimed there had been no fire or ashes in their wooden chimney at the time.) Quite apart from the trauma (almost untouched on in the letters), that disaster further blighted them financially for years.

Other mishaps seem almost trivial by comparison, yet they too carried financial implications. A storm ruined garden produce; a cow fell over a cliff and broke her back so they had to buy another; a second cow died from eating tutu; honey could not be sold; Lizzie's butter, left standing in the sun on the local trader, was spoiled; in 1888 the *May* broke her anchor chain in a sudden gale, the rudder was carried away and she sprang leaks. 'Orry says it will take about £15 to put her to sea in going order,' Lizzie wrote, 'and he is going away shearing or something to earn some money.'[30]

The 'or something' carries a note of disillusionment, disenchantment or desperation that others must have shared. Yet these were rarely evident in the Hopes' letters, although Lizzie and Orry's early optimism is replaced by matter-of-fact stoicism that was particularly marked whenever the family discussed health matters. Fanny hoped that the wound on her head from the fire, still discharging five months later, would be healed better by the air than by ointment. In 1882 'all the [French] Pass children are very ill, something the matter with their lungs . . . it is as much as they can do to breathe'.

Later Lizzie reported that everyone was ill with dysentery. In the absence of professional medical care or access to hospital they fell back on Holloways Pills (an extremely popular patent medicine whose ingredients of aloe, myrrh and saffron can hardly have done much for the range of complaints for which they were used),[31] liniments tried on a hit-and-miss basis, and whatever Jane could find in Nelson. Childbirth brought its own perils. There were no midwives. Husbands and local women did what they could. Lizzie was clearly relieved when Fanny, who 'was very bad indeed', was, once again, safely delivered.[32]

IT WAS LESS EASY TO be stoical about the unpredictable sea that was so much part of their lives. 'Every bay, gully and headland seems to have squalls and whirlwinds of its own . . . down gullies and bays, through those necks and tongues of land,' wrote road-maker Jonathan Brough in *The Colonist*. The very names the settlers gave the winds indicate treacherousness. In Pelorus Sound the 'shandy gaffers' (whirlwinds) of 'Manaroa Reach . . . come walking out of every bay and all over the place, and make clouds of water spray, and white foam dance high in the air'; 'snarlers and snorters' swept up Northwest Bay, the 'black busters' of Stafford Point and the 'fore-and-afters' of Tawero Point each carried their own dangers. Similar winds swept Queen Charlotte Sound, where 'even the most skilful men have been drowned and most of the settlers have been upset at times'.[33]

Any unplanned absences caused anxiety. In 1877, when Orry Hope had been away shearing for an unplanned four days at Ketu Bay, Lizzie tried to attribute this to

Scrubcutters (from left) Jack Christensen, Ted Eden(?), Crink Gilchrist and Jack Johnson in a quiet moment at Momorangi Bay, Queen Charlotte Sound, 1907. Their work would have been as arduous as any in the Sounds. From the mid-1880s, when skilled men (and boys) had largely replaced family labour, such men, using well-honed techniques, swung 1.8-kilogram axes day after day from dawn to dusk, each able to fell 1.6 hectares a week. MARLBOROUGH HISTORICAL SOCIETY, 4227

the foul weather delaying the shearing. Later (with perhaps more experience of the Sounds and their weather) she was 'afraid to see Orry go out in the boat now, the weather changes so suddenly'. Her fears were not groundless. In August 1888 'Tike Turner got capsized at Hammond Point and the fishermen picked him up. You know how he used to sail about in such bad weather.' A decade later young Charlie Stuart (the Stuarts were then running what is now Te Towaka) was drowned in Fitzroy Bay. His brother and another young man had drowned earlier, after their boat capsized somewhere off Maud Island. 'We have much to be grateful to God for his great goodness in preserving our boys in the great dangers they are continually running in the boats,' Lizzie wrote.[34]

The Hope family letters open up a microcosm of much of Sounds life. Getting a farm established was so precarious that Arthur Beauchamp's son Harold (Katherine Mansfield's father), at the age of 11, worried about the wool lost to brambles and bush-lawyer as he helped muster.[35] As we have seen, most settlers supplemented their income with contract work in roading gangs, shearing or fencing. (Fencing or shearing contracts at the Harris brothers' Pohenui Station were welcome into the 1930s.)[36]

Others turned their hands to a range of other ventures. From 1890 to 1898 Benjamin McCauley, who was by then getting established in Bulwer and already doing the exhausting work of running sheep on two blocks of land some distance from each other, used the coastal knowledge he had gained as a fisherman to take up the French Pass–Stephens Island mail run.[37] Other small commercial ventures — Lizzie Hope's butter-making, Orry's freighting and wood-cutting; Harcourt Williams' small smithy at Kaiuma in which he repaired machinery and shod horses; tourist accommodation — all were part of that wider, long-extant pattern.

Lizzie's frequent reports of her children's achievements and charms certainly evince the pride and love she and Orry had. But children's unpaid contributions to household income were also vital in helping keep families afloat, and even after the Education Act 1877 made primary education compulsory, busy periods on the farm caused absences. Jane, aged 15 and beyond primary school, worked for a family at Waikawa in the Current Basin, probably milking, making butter and doing general farm work.[38] Ebb Hope, in his mid-teens, went pig hunting and burned bush. He was also involved in the difficult, dangerous and exhausting work of keeping cattle together as they were driven through a tangled mess of rātā, supplejack and kiekie, pushed along rough tracks or swum around headlands. Dougal, only 10, was away for days at a time fishing with his brothers around D'Urville Island. Brother Dick, a year younger, helped his father with cutting and threshing the harvest.

The boys also filled their father's role when he was away on the 10-day trip to Nelson. Most Sounds boys left school young to work at home or take up contract jobs, cutting scrub on D'Urville Island or sowing grass seed in the Bay of Many Coves.[39] What time was there to acknowledge the small, inevitable human tragedies they incurred? Holding in his arms a dying dog that had been trampled by the cattle he was helping Peter Archer bring out, young Charlie Leov was in tears.[40]

'The boys are splendid boatmen, and very well up in stock and all kinds of bush-work, and they are first-class axemen[,] . . . good rifle shots and they seem to get about the hill-sides like deer . . . they look as wiry and as tough as a wire fence.' As with his description of the 'comely girls', road-maker Jonathan Brough's report in 1900 reflects and contributes to that ideology of the superiority of country over town life.[41] However, boys doing men's work needed men's skills and stamina. The long sweep of a scythe only looks effortless, the machines used to harvest cocksfoot grass seed had wildly swinging arms that constantly threatened their operators, the great stacks of silage had to be built in such a way that they did not slide down in a heap, the stooks of oats had to be dragged from the lofts where they had been stored and cut with a chaff cutter — it was hard, hot, dusty, noisy work.[42] Driving horses that were pulling specialised farming equipment was skilled in itself, quite apart from the animals' jibing, hard mouths or sheer bloody-mindedness. The Williams family at Kaiuma fondly remembered their horse Tige and his propensity to bolt:

> There used to be . . . the great contrast of Jack North driving up the country road between his properties in his dray with his faithful steed 'Prince' whom he used to encourage regularly with 'Get up Prince' (evidently to stop Prince going to sleep on the job) and Tige going down the dray track across the valley flats while his driver yelled 'Whoa' and he galloped.[43]

Sheep, cows, dogs and horses all demanded care. Fence posts had to be dug and wires strained, sheep mustered and dipped, bush felled and burned, grass sown on the burned hills, sheds built, hay scythed and pitched into stacks, land ploughed and harrowed. Unmarried men, working early and late and catering and caring for themselves, had to be meticulously organised, having a basic meal ready when they came in at night. Sundays could go in bread-baking, washing and, in season, making jams and preserves from fruit from the orchard.

YET, IN SPITE OF THE unremitting cycle of work, as we have seen, returns were often small, and the result was often debilitating intergenerational poverty. Among a considerable number of 'illiterate whalers, fishermen, and heavily mortgaged small sheep farmers', some of them third-generation settlers whose children had little knowledge of the outside world,[44] other families were also just hanging on.

By the end of 1898 a small, non-contributory, state-funded old-age pension became available to both Māori and Pākehā over 65 and 'of good moral character'. Leaving aside its tight and subjective eligibility criteria, the requirement to collect the payment from set places created access difficulties for some, particularly isolated Sounds-dwellers.[45] Some were possibly not even aware of their entitlement. Certainly, quite dire poverty persisted. In 1911, for instance, a family of dirty, destitute and uneducated children were found living in Penguin Bay (Pelorus Sound) in a whare with their illiterate mother. She owned nothing and only neighbours' generosity kept them afloat.[46]

The unsung heroes of this world were the women, most of whose lives are not well recorded. They followed their husbands, moving, like Elizabeth Guard, from the close-knit society in which they had grown up to homes too often in 'dreary isolation'.[47] A sad picture builds of men working all hours and women left alone in dingy, inadequate homes, bearing the brunt of responsibility for sometimes many children,[48] in isolated settings. Men's work afforded them social contact but the women could go for weeks without contact with another woman — or indeed with anyone in the outside world.

In the midst of raising large families, women often also had full responsibility for growing vegetables. Soap, candles and butter were all made at home in time-consuming processes.[49] Carefully maintained standards meant that piles of sheets, towels and nappies had to be frequently boiled in the copper, then rinsed in the nearest creek; mud-encrusted trousers and garments stained with grass, sawdust or ash had to be hand-washed — or attacked vigorously with a yard broom.[50] There was endless darning, mending, cooking, baking, scrubbing, and few or no mod cons. Hannah Godsiff, who died in 1920, was far from alone in never having 'anything but hardships, no luxuries, no conveniences in the house . . . [she] carried water all her life.'[51]

Cut off as they were, women hungered for letters. Atypically, the Arthur Beauchamps at Beatrix Bay had their mail delivered to and collected from Havelock fortnightly, which could involve two days' rowing and an overnight camp somewhere along the way.[52] Deprived of that level of luxury, Sarah Archer at Tuna Bay wrote to her sister Harriet that she had 'been waiting for 2 years to hear from you . . . I thought I would just drop a line to you to let you know that we are alive and doing very well.' Had Harriet received her last letter? 'I entrusted it to a man to post that called here.'[53]

'You must not neglect writing . . . your letters are all we look forward to,' Lizzie Hope told Jane in 1877, but there might be no mail for six weeks at a time, and the disappointments created by such irregular schedules were compounded when bad weather prevented the men rowing out to the traders. Even when letters were safely on board, delivery was not guaranteed. 'I hear sometimes,' Edward wrote to his mother, 'should the Mail Bag happen to be sealed up, and only a few odd letters posted, they are just put on board loose and might easily become mislaid.'[54]

Aided, perhaps, by proximity to Picton, the women at Te Awaiti whaling station enjoyed one or two luxuries denied to others. Twice a year a carrier pigeon would be dispatched with a note to the Picton merchants of what the camp needed.[55] The itinerant peddler 'Peter the Syrian' would sometimes arrive with packages carefully wrapped in waterproof canvas bags. Inside were 'gaudy clothes, work clothes, jewellery, hardware, cosmetics, bolts of dressmaking materials'. £100 might go on half a year's supplies.[56] Otherwise, women in the Sounds led lives constrained by domesticity. Any break was welcome. 'I must not forget to tell you of my new accomplishment', Lizzie Hope wrote of her new way to avoid cabin fever. 'I can take the boat out when the weather is fine and pull round the bay for wood. The children sit in the bottom of the boat and we have a trip by ourselves.'[57]

Yet only rarely do the Hope women's letters suggest the unhappiness or the loneliness that must have been a part of their lives. Occasionally Lizzie allows herself a note of exasperation: 'the weather is dreadful, raining in torrents and blowing a gale. Yards up to your ankles in mud, and kitchen almost the same, children talking in my ear and shaking me all the time.'[58] In 1878, not long after the tragic fire, Fanny was alone with the new baby and young James and enjoying reading *God's Glad Tidings*, 'for it is very lonely here in the bush, while Edward is away. I get thinking till I get so sad, I do miss my two dear lost ones, or rather not lost, only gone before.' She, James and the baby later 'went with Edward . . . into the next bay where he is at work, it is so very lonely by myself all day long, for Edward does not come back till night.'[59]

It was raining when Mrs Macefield first arrived at Manaroa's log-strewn beach in 1889. She, uncharacteristically, burst into tears.[60] That was an unusual reaction. In a world with no such thing as counselling and the churches able to offer only intermittent solace,[61] settlers adopted a code or ethic of 'enduring positively' to help them cope with 'the climate of risk' in which they lived. Elizabeth Beauchamp, motivated perhaps by loyalty and duty, shared her husband's 'vicissitudes with uncomplaining courage'. Settlers had 'a dourness, almost a contempt for people who found the life too hard . . . It was not seemly to fuss'; those who showed emotion received little sympathy.[62]

In writing to others away from the Sounds, putting a good face on life was a coping technique. Work, too, was prescribed as a treatment in the face of loss. Into the twentieth century, those who stayed on 'were so busy surviving there was no time to mourn'.[63] The lucky ones 'had private means of support — good understandings with their husbands or wives, they enjoyed and loved their children'.[64] When the emotional balance was fragile, they sometimes did the same as others who were struggling in isolated areas and used humour as a bulwark against disaster.[65] They told stories well about 'little amusing things . . . that made life bearable . . . Laughing at ourselves to keep up our morale. We needed something.'[66] Over the years the pull that the Sounds themselves exerted possibly helped people bear disasters and distress with fortitude.[67] The place, so much a part of their lives, was part of them, and leaving the Sounds was unthinkable.

Forging communities

There is little of the world described above in the newspapers of the day. Instead, the columns are full of weddings, parties, welcomes to new neighbours and farewells to old, of community and sporting events, of political and community meetings that brought people together. Contributions to the many war funds during World War I and locally organised farming assistance further defined the small, often tightly knit communities. These emerged from the practical help that families and neighbours provided in emergencies, at busy times on the farm, and in getting their children educated.[68]

However, pent-up irritations and frustrations could be a volatile mix, especially when alcohol was added. And disputes could endure. E. G. Cousins at the Hill and Teasdel property in Resolution Bay in 1912 left in a fury having had a row with Mrs Florence Clift over whether or not he had left the garden gate open; he did not return until he was an old man, in the 1990s.[69] Quarrels could turn violent — two 'mad drunk' men being ferried to Port Ligar began fighting, lurched overboard and, despite searches, were never seen again.[70] Social conservatism gave rise, too, to some terrible situations, such as that of the 18-year-old mother whose illegitimate baby was born healthy but found dead half an hour later; or poor Alice Green, found guilty of procuring and using an instrument to cause a miscarriage.[71]

Yet common needs and interests were a social glue, generally creating and nourishing the social networks vital to the success of the settlement. The Hopes' annoyance with the Turners over fences and straying cattle never got beyond irritation, and Hector Martin of Motuara Island dissipated anger with a widely publicised retraction for his hasty words uttered one day at Pig Bay.[72]

The patterns of mutual assistance and obligation were reinforced by sometimes complex familial relationships. Aunts, daughters or nieces looked after children or families where a parent had died, sons stayed on the farms their fathers had started. The links within the Wells family at Whakatahuri, Pelorus Sound, are a splendid example of these interwoven relationships. They were related by marriage to the Hocquards, the McManaways and the Harveys.

Thomas Dalton McManaway came to the Marlborough Sounds in the 1870s, and married Jane Hocquard from Warwick Beach, just through Allen Strait. The McManaways went to live at Boarding House Flat, where the Climos owned and ran a boarding house for the Okoha mill hands. (Farmer Isaac Harvey had set up the mill between 1860 and 1870.) Jane McManaway became ill and was looked after by Isaac Harvey's wife, Lizzie. When Jane died, Lizzie looked after her two children, and the widower Thomas married Augusta Harvey, Lizzie's sister. At some point Isaac Harvey sold the mill and moved to Saratoga, just over the hill from Whakatahuri. Thomas and Augusta McManaway moved to Whatakahuri, where McManaway, Isaac Harvey and Phillip Hocquard (Jane's brother) became joint shareholders in the short-lived fish-freezing works. Phillip married Frances Harvey, bought neighbouring Saratoga from Isaac, and lived there. Another McManaway son, Tom, married Dolly Harvey, so that the grandfather, son and brother-in-law were all married to three of the daughters of William and Augusta Harvey.[73]

Even as those familial roots were going down, business, social and political connections were forging wider communities. Captain William Henderson, one-time proprietor of the Grove Hotel, for instance, had long-lasting business networks that reached across various business/social communities and generations. He successfully contracted for the mails between Picton and Blenheim before leaving the Grove, probably in the early 1870s, to become headman at Alex Duncan's timber mills on

9700 acres (3926 ha) at the head of Kenepuru Sound and including two smaller areas in Portage and Endeavour Inlet. The steam tug *Alfie* at Waitaria Bay towed punts and carried goods around the Sounds. Henderson looked after the punts and was responsible for the timber being shipped by scow. His son, John Daniel Henderson, subsequently owned a Goulter Bay property and lived there with his wife while farming at Waitaria. He also owned a passenger and stock punting business.[74]

In Tuna Bay in 1889 a lonely Sarah Archer wrote, '[W]e see people some times but they are like angels visits few and far between and when they do come it is in a rush. There was no less than 6 boats here and a vessel at our landing 3 weeks ago and at christmas we had 27 diggers here.'[75] Even when the first recreational steamer came into the bay in 1893, few, if any, women would have been aboard.[76]

However, towards the end of the nineteenth century, as farms and families became better established, socials, regattas, picnics and gatherings provided valuable opportunities for family and neighbours to meet, relax, gossip and cement friendships. At Jane Turner's house in the late 1880s,

> dozens gathered every Sunday and often through the week . . . we all went for a walk or we danced all the evening and it was heavenly. Willie Couper, Ernest Hensen, Jim Kellor, all the Rutland tribes, Forests, Smiths, Jones, Andersons, several nieces McKenzie from Howick, Louis, Stuart, and members of the Archer family from Tuna.[77]

The amount of work that went into organising such opportunities, whether social, political or sporting, indicates their importance in the lives of isolated Sounds families — a value perhaps expressed in the building of Waitaria Hall in Kenepuru in 1912, and the Homewood Memorial Hall in 1953.

FROM THE 1890S, LOCAL NEWSPAPERS regularly reported on social gatherings that suggest relative prosperity and leisure. In 1898, after rain had caused the cancellation of an earlier do,[78] Kenepuru residents gave a surprise party for the McMahons at Taradale. The band, dancing, songs, cards and other 'drawing-room games' suggest a sedate affair — but it didn't break up till four in the morning. In April 1903, with 'the joys and frivolities' of Easter having come and gone, the families at Crail Bay organised a cooperative picnic in Pig Bay. The Sounds cricketers were roundly

ABOVE As things got easier, gatherings for picnics and parties became a significant part of Sounds life. The McCormack family, friends and neighbours arrive by rowboat to a beach picnic. Picnics, along with parties, piano-playing and singing, games of football and cricket and boxing matches, brought people together to relax and socialise. PICTON HERITAGE AND WHALING MUSEUM, COURTESY PICTON HISTORICAL SOCIETY

BELOW Rounders on the Greensill lawn, Bolton Bay, Mahau Sound, c. 1912. MARLBOROUGH HISTORICAL SOCIETY, 016698

beaten by the Havelock team, and there was a chance to toast a newly married couple. 'Shure we had a grand toime, entoirley,' the *Pelorus Guardian* reported.[79]

In 1907 the little Endeavour Inlet community organised a highly successful sports day and dance that lasted until 'broad — very broad — daylight did appear'. The occasion's success suggested that an annual event was warranted. At Endeavour Inlet, too, a model yacht club was formed; its annual regattas (in which Māori were involved) were widely attended.[80]

From all over the Sounds, guests arrived by foot, boat or horseback for family occasions, twenty-firsts, weddings and funerals. Formal clothes and any presents were carefully packed to survive the journey. By the turn of the century some families could afford to celebrate weddings expansively. Miss Clara Bright's marriage to Isaac James Landall of Dieffenbach, at Punaruawhiti Bay, Endeavour Inlet, was a typically splendid affair where flowers were used in the bride's dress — a 'cream satin-stripe, trimmed with cream satin gimp and chiffon, a tulle veil and sprays of orange blossom'.

Her 'shower-bouquet [was] of native clematis with foliage of native jessamine' and her three bridesmaids were similarly decked out. The Picton contingent arrived by the oil-launch *Union* to 'a veritable bower' of native greenery and clematis festooning the house, with clematis decorating the lunch table. Hours later, guests cheered as a 'gaily decorated launch' glided out of the bay, carrying the groom and the bride in her going-away dress of navy-blue serge with a hat to match.[81]

With Sounds women as 'fully alive to the importance of the franchise and prompt to use it' as their men,[82] political gatherings drew in the crowds and created further opportunities for men and women to socialise; Charles Houghton Mills, the Sounds' long-time Liberal MP and a farmer like themselves, was well known and liked.[83]

At a local political level, branches of the Farmers' Union (later Federated Farmers) played a critical role in Sounds affairs. The non-partisan national body, set up in 1899, had broad-ranging objectives around protecting and promoting members' interests consistent with the Liberal tenet: 'The more prosperous the farmer the more prosperous the towns.'[84] In January 1902 the *Pelorus Guardian* announced the intention to set up a Pelorus branch to cover Māhakipawa, Kaituna and Pelorus. The first meeting of the group, possibly following amalgamation with another sub-branch, was in October that year.[85]

From its beginning, the Pelorus branch battled over noxious weeds, telephone connections, the uncompleted Picton–Blenheim railway line, wharves, the ever-pressing problem of assistance for country schools, and stock facilities at the Picton port or freezing works.[86] With no county council to raise, coordinate and represent local interests, the branch played a particularly significant role in addressing, in a practical and largely apolitical fashion, the issues that affected local farmers.[87]

Yet the union's value went beyond local politics. 'Every farmer and farmer's wife and daughter', reported the *Marlborough Express*, was encouraged to join.[88] However, meetings remained very much male territory — women attended only if race meetings were scheduled. The importance of Farmers' Union meetings to men can be judged by the effort sometimes involved in getting there. Members rode up to 40 miles (70 kilometres) along tracks or travelled similar distances by boat, knowing that hours of rowing would be needed if engines broke down. Membership, unrestricted by social barriers, grew. Union branch meetings brought farmers, farm workers and bushmen from all over the Sounds together to talk over common problems. Family picnics brought whole families into the fold.

SPORTING EVENTS AND REGATTAS WERE much-anticipated occasions at which the communities could gather, gossip and compete. The small regatta in Picton, held on 19 November 1862 to mark the third anniversary of the creation of the province, was the first of many, each larger than the one before, drawing entries in rowing and sailing from across the region. In 1862 the Te Awaiti whaleboats and locally designed and built sailing boats took many top honours. The almost annual rowing successes of the Jacksons peaked in the 1930s, as that generation competed nationally and internationally.[89] Cricket, too, was played and keenly watched, while the Peranos and, for a time, the Loves were part of a highly competitive rugby team. From 1911, Sounds men competed nationally and internationally in rifle-shooting.[90]

From about the mid-1880s, smaller regattas in various Pelorus Sound bays began attracting teams and spectators from all over the district and beyond. By 1893 Portage could be easily accessed from Picton over the 'excellent road' from Queen Charlotte's Torea Bay, and from Manaroa and Kenepuru; the Wellington boat could get there in about eight hours; and Thomas Gullery had enlarged his accommodation house. Day-trippers from Havelock arriving on the 40-tonne *Waitapu* (willing to tow — and charge — small boats) found the bay 'alive with [brightly painted] rowing craft of all descriptions' as well as well-designed yachts and boats. Picton's *Tarara-boom-de-aye* had been carted over the hill from Torea Bay for the occasion.[91] The 1900 Boxing Day sailing and rowing regatta at Wilsons Bay attracted 400 people, and for the Pelorus

ABOVE Lilliput Club's first Model Yacht Regatta, East Bay, Arapawa (Arapaoa) Island, 1909. That year, Jack Love's yacht won the race for the club. People came from all over the district, and competition among the beautifully built boats was keen. The regattas ended with the advent of World War I. PICTON HERITAGE AND WHALING MUSEUM, COURTESY PICTON HISTORICAL SOCIETY

BELOW Moetapu Regatta at Moetapu Bay, Mahau Sound, 1914. PICTON HERITAGE AND WHALING MUSEUM, COURTESY PICTON HISTORICAL SOCIETY

Motor Boat Club's inaugural annual regatta at Moetapu in 1905 the Sounds steamers *Elsie* and *Pelorus* were laid on to carry visitors from Havelock to Moetapu. Some 750 turned up. One early return sailing was scheduled to cater for farmers who had evening milking to do.

Regattas evolved. With the women 'as good as the men' at rowing and capable of 'hand[ling] the oars with great skill', their races often attracted much interest.[92] The Eli Bay regatta included sailing, an oil-launch race, and a range of rowing races for both sexes. The schedule was soon widened to include children's events.

The 1901 Māhakipawa athletics, 'the event of the district', offered not inexpensive prizes for both men and women; the Waitata Bay sports day in 1912 included widely graded, handicapped axe events, launch races, the ladies' nail drive, and luncheon. A year later, the Sounds Hacks Sports Club held their annual meeting at Waitaria on Boxing Day. Sports competition was always taken seriously — it was not unheard of for disagreements to end in free-for-all brawls.[93]

ON 5 AUGUST 1914 NEW ZEALAND entered World War I. The country's considerable war propaganda machine had not got underway before local volunteers left the district amid lusty renditions of patriotic songs, the national anthem and assurances that they would 'be a credit to the expeditionary force and would give a good account of themselves'.[94] Even as their men marched away, Sounds communities began supporting the war effort. In late August, after a two-day canvas, Sounds settlers contributed over £262 to the recently launched Marlborough War Fund; some three months later Pelorus, Queen Charlotte and Tory Channel settlers donated another £152, a significant sum. The Sounds Patriotic Fund rapidly became a prominent item at Farmers' Union meetings.

As the deaths and destruction of the war intensified, the helplessness of these little communities may have been eased by such contributions. Published lists, identifying individuals and the amounts donated, rewarded those who had given (and shamed those who had not). Local fundraising bodies ran dances, games and bazaars; Māori men performed haka, 'anciente and modern battle-cry and dances', while women did poi; the religious leader Haimona Pātete arranged a 'monster Maori festival' in Picton in aid of the Belgium Relief Fund.[95] The not inconsiderable £310 donated in 1915 to the large number of other fundraising efforts[96] typified most local communities' steady contributions to the war effort.[97]

Axemen's Carnival in 1910, Waitata Bay, outer Pelorus Sound. The popularity of this celebration of the woodchoppers' skills is evident. MARLBOROUGH HISTORICAL SOCIETY, 0000.200.22

Children were also involved. Within a few months of the war starting, the nation's children had donated £2000 to the school ambulance fund; the *Marlborough Express* and *Pelorus Guardian* indefatigably published details of individual children's donations of hankies that they had hemmed or small sums of money. Sounds children, Māori and Pākehā, were also caught up in nationwide propaganda efforts that sought to turn their involvement with the war effort into a vehicle for teaching them wider loyalties — 'the real meaning of love of country [and the Empire] and of personal sacrifice'.[98]

Nor were 'our own wounded soldiers' and their comforts ignored.[99] In February 1915 Sounds women (and some men) joined the rest of the country in knitting army socks, balaclavas, mittens. By June, locals were sending socks, towels, hankies, pyjamas, vests, pillowslips, combs, cushions and nightshirts to the hospital ships to carry overseas; sales of buttonholes, tray cloths and produce, and competitions and 'coin afternoons' raised further funds.[100]

Meanwhile, farms had to be kept going. Initially, when the men joined the Expeditionary Force, farms might be sold or leased. In 1915, however, the various branches of the Sounds Farmers' Union opened registers of those who were willing to help bring in the region's harvest or assist in an emergency. It was a generous move, given the burden that the remaining, usually older men, and women and children were already carrying.

The real impact of the war, however, was the inevitable common tragedy. On the overseas fronts, 65 Sounds men (Māori and Pākehā) fought, of whom 25 died. Some families lost multiple members. Many more were wounded. This death rate reflected that of many New Zealand districts, but in small communities the tragedies reverberated. A war memorial to the Sounds dead, sited on the Torea–Portage saddle, was unveiled in 1920.

Education provision: Small beginnings

'[O]ur children . . . are a proper lot of dunces, Ebb the worst, for they cannot even read, we cannot attend to them properly,' Lizzie Hope wrote to her mother-in-law in January 1886. She returned to the issue of education at the end of the letter: 'At present we are living very hard . . . if the children were only getting taught, I should not mind, but it seems dreadful such a lot of dunces.'[101]

Unlike many of the new settlers, Lizzie herself was literate.[102] Like most parents in isolated rural areas, she wanted her children educated, not fighting 'Life's Battles' 'in ignorance' and left facing social and economic disadvantage.[103] In this, the Pākehā parents at least were fortunate in the direction of government education policy, and particularly lucky with their Education Board. Most of their children attended at least primary school. Māori parents at Waikawa and Okoha made similar if not greater efforts to get schools for their children, but the government's response, particularly at Okoha, was markedly different.

The country's first Education Act was passed in 1877. It provided for an elementary secular education, compulsory to age 13, free to age 15, in schools established and run by each of the regions' education boards and paid for by a government-funded capitation grant. Attendance was critical to getting the full capitation — schools where attendance was poor or there were insufficient children on the roll had only some of their costs covered and parents might have to make up the teacher's salary.[104]

Interestingly, nine years after the Act had been passed, Lizzie appeared unaware of its provisions. Where people did know about it, the response was positive. 'The "standards"' (the classes through which children progressed) are 'household words from the remote inlets of the Sounds to the plains of the Wairau', reported the Education Department inspector for the Marlborough Education District in 1878. He went on: 'The people are beginning to know and comprehend the work of each standard, and to share the aspirations and successes of their children,' who were themselves wanting to do well.[105]

Prior to the abolition of provincial governments in 1876, the Marlborough Provincial Council had established a number of schools in the district, though most would not have been available to the Sounds population.[106] Arthur Penrose Seymour, chair of the new Marlborough Education Board 1877–1903, had been heavily involved with the provincial council. Over the years, his reports as board chair stress the determination to ensure that the children of 'the very class that is doing so much towards the opening-up and the close settlement of the waste places of this colony' would not go entirely uneducated.[107] The board, convinced that it 'would be wanting' if it did not help the isolated settlers and therefore 'cannot for a moment contemplate' refusing to grant aid,[108] spearheaded an initiative that constituted what the *Marlborough Express* described much later as 'probably the most generous scheme of "back-blocks" provision in the Colony'.[109]

Using the provisions of the 1877 Education Act, the board over its lifetime systematically set up a considerable number of 'aided' or household schools (the names appear to have been used interchangeably). These Grade 0 schools were officially described as small schools 'started by private enterprise [almost always parents] in outlying districts in which it would be premature or inconvenient to constitute school districts'.[110] Unofficially, they were schools established in small, isolated situations where the per capita grant would not cover their costs and for which parental contributions were unlikely to be adequate.[111] Provisions allowed roll numbers up to nine (above that and the school became a Grade 1 school) and salaries varied but were always lower than for more highly graded schools. In 1902 the lowest salary in a Grade 0 school was £3 15s, in contrast to Grade 1 schools, where the lowest salary that year was £34 10s and the highest, at Te Awaiti, was £67 17s 6d. Despite the pressure these 'financially unproductive' household schools put on the Marlborough Education Board, they would become the vehicle of almost all educational provision in the Sounds.[112]

Some of this provision was informal to a degree. Nola Leov's memories of her schooling in the early 1930s at Te Towaka are of a teacher boarding at someone's home, teaching what few local children there were (and sometimes a few who boarded — for a sum).

> A family room was used . . . there was a collection of books, which had come from another household school which had closed down . . . We didn't have any books that were used for the actual classes. Not at all. The teacher wrote things on the board. We did have copy books for writing.

An inspector came once a year, and the impending visit might produce a flurry of formal learning in English and arithmetic.[113]

Aided schools at Kaiuma, Kenepuru and Hopai, all in Pelorus, were opened in 1880; Anakiwa (1882), Te Awaiti (1884) and Manaroa (1885) followed. From then until 1920, new schools were opened at the rate of two to four a year.

Some had high expectations for what these schools might achieve.[114] More realistically, they were probably the only way to get education within reach of children in remote districts.[115] The Marlborough board also used the provisions of the Act to open half-time schools, and, from the start, pushed for an average daily attendance to count towards full capitation.[116] It fell back, too, on the system of pupil-teachers — older children, mostly female, who were paid 'a pittance' for teaching younger

Te Awaiti, showing the school building at back left with a small building behind it. James Norton's house, with a thatched roof, is to the right. The Norton family, along with the Jacksons and Keenans, provided competition to Charlie and Jo Perano almost until 1920. PICTON HERITAGE AND WHALING MUSEUM, COURTESY PICTON HISTORICAL SOCIETY

ones.[117] This arrangement was not ideal, but again, the scheme was a valuable expedient.[118] Even as the Marlborough board was about to be subsumed into the Wellington Education Board in 1916, it retained its commitment to the small, 'thinly-attended, comparatively costly' aided or household schools that prevailed throughout the Sounds.[119]

These children would not have been educated at all without a united parental front. Indeed, parental educational aspirations can perhaps be judged by the costs, direct and indirect, faced in getting schools established, maintained and staffed. In order to get a school established, parents, unlikely to have had many prior dealings with bureaucracy, had to get their neighbours involved. They had to make a case to the Marlborough Education Board for a school, propose or offer a site, and either offer an existing building that could be used or agree to build one free of charge. They had to form a school committee that was responsible for the school's day-to-day operation. Those seeking an aided school had to provide the teacher's board and lodging — and pay their wage. By 1908 this was £25 (compared with the £64 salary of a state-employed teacher at a bigger school)[120] — a significant sum for parents who were not well off.[121]

Once a government-funded school was operating, the Marlborough Education Board stepped in to provide books and the capitation grant (as long as attendance levels were reached).

Did the children get the education their parents hoped for? Ernest Rutherford went to Havelock School and went on to split the atom; in 1919, under her father's tuition at Havelock, my mother, Elsie Barrowclough, gained a national junior scholarship with the highest marks in the Wellington education district, and was seventh in New Zealand.[122] However, such achievements were unlikely to be matched in the small Sounds schools. Some inspectors' reports (their perspectives were generally positive, even enlightened) highlighted teacher enthusiasm — a quality we now know is critical to good learning. In 1911 some schools were commended for the standard of writing, arithmetic and 'neat work'; in geography, where the inspector was partly looking for 'the study of man' and 'his reaction to his environment' rather than memorised names of capes and headlands, 'the quality and vigor [sic]' of the Māori Bay teacher ensured a high rating. At Bulwer, Arbor Day was carried out enthusiastically.[123] Growing library size was sometimes commended.

FEW INDIVIDUAL TEACHERS EMERGE TODAY from the many who taught in the system. Harriet Beauchamp, teaching in her Anakiwa house and later at the Grove School, used whatever skills and education were given to clergymen's daughters in England. Sylvanus Budge also taught in his own house in the early days of the Tahuahua (Blackwood Bay) School. His speech, dress and manner marked him as a well-educated Englishman with, possibly, a colourful past.[124] Yorkshireman H. L. Twisleton had arrived in New Zealand as a young man, was 'prominent' in milling circles, was 'an inveterate pedestrian and mountaineer' and, until age caught up with him, an 'oarsman of some repute'. His eulogists remembered more: a pastoral poet of 'a musing temperament', '[h]is extreme conscientiousness was everywhere recognised, and his ability and thoroughness everywhere proved . . . He was all his life a student, and had a profound knowledge of English literature and English history.'[125]

How this went down in the schools at Waitohi, Endeavour Inlet or Te Awaiti we have no way of knowing. More often than not, and despite some inspectors' high aspirations, teaching probably consisted of 'the monotonous drudgery of grinding away at the bare rudiments'.[126] The small, unattractive salaries paid by the tiny aided schools were little inducement, and those attracted were possibly only 'moderately competent'.[127] The difficulties of getting a teacher or maintaining adequate roll numbers forced many schools into educationally disruptive patterns of temporary or permanent closure. Household schools were particularly affected — in 1901, for instance, nine closed, each for a quarter-year, because of no teacher.

In that environment, government efforts to improve teacher supply and quality could make little immediate impact. The untrained pupil-teacher system was barely operative before, in 1882, Marlborough introduced its own board exam questions for prospective teachers to 'safeguard against absolute incompetence'.[128] These exams later became compulsory, and all teachers were under pressure to get qualified.[129] From 1905, government-run holiday or weekend schools and, later, correspondence lessons provided training to all Marlborough teachers, though 10 years on, their impact was questioned.[130]

From the 1900s the government also tried to improve teacher supply by addressing salaries, superannuation and funding to school boards. From 1905, country service was introduced, whereby teachers' college students had to have one placement in a country school to progress up the educational career ladder.[131]

Again, in Marlborough, none of those measures — nor the drawcard of free board and lodging — led to a dramatic improvement in teacher numbers. The isolation, lack of professional guidance, discipline problems and lack of assistance in private study often meant that the young (mostly female) teachers did not even last the year. Some ended up living in households where they became 'like something of a household drudge',[132] or being physically or aggressively confronted after taking disciplinary action in school against one of the children.[133] In 1913, only 40 of the 120 adult teachers in the board's employ were certificated and almost two-thirds were women.[134] Two years into the war, the nation's small rural schools often had no option but to appoint 'almost any fairly well qualified person'. Fewer than half were certificated and they were overwhelmingly female.[135]

From 1908 the Education Department developed a free textbook scheme for the first three years of schooling, and progressively expanded the supply of other educational material.[136] But could fancy new school publications overcome the issues of remoteness and (often) poor teaching? What achievements really lay behind the huge range of subjects taught: reading, spelling, writing, composition, arithmetic, geography, drawing, history, singing, needlework, moral instruction, recitation, arts and crafts ('handiwork') and drill — posture, breathing exercises ('already the narrow-chested boy is beginning to disappear')?[137] At the turn of the century the *Marlborough Express* reported that the small aided schools in the Sounds 'have with very few exceptions fully justified their existence, by producing as good results as it is reasonable to expect'.[138]

Māori battle poverty and prejudice

Kurahaupō peoples had seen their chiefs killed or scattered, their populations decimated, their pā destroyed. Land, pā, kāinga, landing places, cultivated gardens, urupā and strategic headlands — places critical to their history and identity — were by now in individual Pākehā or government ownership. Māori were largely confined to reserves whose acreage was steadily eroding and whose quality was always poor. Moreover, from the 1880s, their economic opportunities were diminishing.

Pākehā settlement increasingly restricted any traditional foraging. The reserves were too small to develop as economic units, and over time the Pākehā pattern of cultivation — along with a failure or unwillingness to understand the situation or needs of Māori — contributed to the development of a negative response to the prospect of any further land allocations to Māori. Māori were left competing, sometimes 'fiercely', with Europeans for seasonal employment,[139] and often had to leave the district to get work.

In the 1880s we find Waikawa men working on the Māhakipawa gold field; some children were mustering and shearing in Queen Charlotte Sound, others had accompanied their parents to the whaling station for what were largely unproductive seasons. In 1891 the community went shearing, leaving a few children behind. In 1893 a number of parents were at Havelock cutting flax; a year later, after two consecutive crop failures ruled out much contract work, the children helped with the wheat harvest; there was sometimes work picking hops.[140] On at least one occasion Māori fished for Sullivan's fish factory, hauling in considerable catches.[141] The Waikawa community also continued to work their own lands in the Sound and in Tory Channel, struggling, as did Māori on the other reserves, to make the poor land productive. They suffered, too, from perennial agricultural problems: crop failures and flooding that destroyed land and animals. In 1906 a nationwide potato blight resulted in another food shortage.

On the 'useless' and inaccessible land at Okoha, once a favoured camp spot for Māori, people were so poor that in the 1880s and 1890s officials, finally convinced of the gravity of the situation, disbursed emergency food supplies.[142] Yet those at Okoha trying to mill their own timber were stymied by bureaucratic stalling and incompetence. The community's attempts to set up a mill and get a better financial return and fuller employment for its own people were repeatedly frustrated. A 1904 Land Board decision came down heavily in favour of Richard Climo and a Mr Fawcet, who had applied for 7 acres (2.8 ha) of supposedly vacant land on which they wanted to build a mill. No matter that the Crown Land ranger had stated that Māori saw the land as common, and that it had been excluded from the reserve for that purpose and Māori had cleared, grassed and built on it[143] — these arguments did not sway the Land Board.

In 1906, as Māori were dealing with Climo on rights to mill, as well as their royalties as landowners and Māori employment at the mill, Climo undercut negotiations by transferring the milling rights to someone else. In 1908, government approval for Ngāti Kuia to cut 7 acres (2.8 ha) of timber from the bush at the head of the bay was never formally notified to them.[144] In 1920 Ngāti Kuia at Okoha were able to negotiate a 10-year lease to cut and mill a 5-acre site but it fell through because operations did not begin within the stated time. Few Waikawa Māori were able to benefit from what remained of the milling boom, and sheep farming remained the community's main occupation, uneconomic though it was.[145]

The situation was only marginally better at Waikawa. 'The Māori are not so well off as they used to be or they would subscribe to pay one of their number to remain here to look after and keep the children at school while they themselves were away bushfalling [sic] or putting in their crops,'[146] the Waikawa schoolteacher reported in 1892. In 1915 Waikawa Māori were living on bread and tea; they had no dairy cows and were growing neither potatoes nor maize.[147] The government had donated seed potatoes and food in 1906, and a decade on, European officials were wont to attribute the lack of settled farming and fishing to moral failings.[148]

Sounds Māori, like others in Te Tau Ihu, were often living in the most remote spots, beyond easy government reach. A pattern of government response developed. If it was 'sometimes willing and able to alleviate their distress, policy generally, as revealed by either action or omission, told tangata whenua that they either come to terms with the problems of this new order — often substantially at their own expense — or face the continuing decline in their conditions.'[149] At a systemic level, official responses were denying the assistance that would have strengthened communities and well-being.

IN 1852 GOVERNOR GREY HAD established a 'civil list' to provide food, pensions and medical care for 'indigent' Māori who were not beneficial owners of the Native Reserves Fund (known as the Tenths Benefit Fund after 1897).[150] Hospitals and schools were to be built and maintained, chiefs' services recognised and Māori well-being and advancement promoted;[151] subsidies were offered to fund native medical officers who were required to treat indigent Māori,[152] welfare payments were available for 'indigent and infirm Natives'. Money from Governor Grey's civil list and the Native Reserves Fund should have been available to alleviate economic hardship.

That money, however, was frequently administered and disbursed to Māori disadvantage. On paper, resident magistrates or, at their behest, police, schoolteachers, ministers or native agents investigated cases and granted pensions and aid where they considered it appropriate. However, as Ngāti Kuia at Okoha found, even in times of pressing need such investigations caused lengthy delays, and perceptions of Māori as lazy, dirty, unclean, drunk and 'communistic' usually resulted in judgemental and mean responses.[153] Local officials almost always awarded an amount below that of the old-age pension, and disempowered Māori by awarding the funding to local shopkeepers or suppliers for food items rather than to Māori themselves. Other necessities such as transport and footwear were not funded.[154]

Moreover, the way the tenths funding revenue was used raises questions around why it, rather than government money, was used to finance social services for Māori in Te Tau Ihu. The government used the Native Reserves Fund to provide for the welfare and medicine of individual beneficiaries of the fund (who were also eligible for state old-age pension when it was introduced in 1898). Elderly beneficiaries of the fund could sometimes get emergency assistance from whatever was left after the tenths rental income had been disbursed, but the amounts were so small that payments were made only every six months.[155] Again, the amount paid might have been pennies, but to those living on the economic margins it was a lifeline, perhaps funding a desperately needed doctor's appointment.

In 1892–93 the Land Court identified those deemed to be individual beneficiaries of the tenths trust, and Ngāti Kuia and Rangitāne were excluded, which must have been a considerable blow.[156] At the same time destitute Europeans, for whom the list had not been intended, were sometimes given welfare payments from the Native Reserves Fund.[157]

WHEN THE OLD-AGE PENSION WAS introduced in 1898, the problems of eligibility and access meant that take-up by Māori in the Sounds was almost non-existent. Māori did not have to register births, so proving you were 65 could be problematic.[158] If eligibility were somehow established, access to land counted as income for this means-tested benefit, irrespective of the paucity of that income. European officials generally assumed that Māori would spend the pension on alcohol, not food, and were quick to refuse or reduce payment 'because the natives have all the use of lands, which if they choose, they may cultivate for their own benefit'. In 1902 only two Māori at Picton and one at Oruapuputa in the Māhakipawa Arm received an old-age pension — and even these were insecure because of officials' mistakes and inconsistences.[159]

The same pattern of misuse of specialised funding can be seen in medical care. Early colonial governments appointed native doctors to give free medical care to Māori, and during the 1850s unspecified 'medical expenses' were sometimes paid from the tenths rental income. In 1865 five doctors were appointed in Te Tau Ihu, including in Queen Charlotte Sound.[160] By 1894 half of the then 27 native medical doctors in the country were in the South Island, treating a considerably lower Māori population than in the north, a disproportion that continued through to the 1930s.[161] But in the Nelson–Marlborough region, funding came from reserves income, not the civil list. While coverage was remarkably comprehensive, the poor health of those at Okoha illustrates the issues around small, isolated Māori communities not having continuous access to accessible subsidised care.[162] (These issues began to be resolved only when the Labour government introduced universal health care in the 1930s.)[163]

Government use of revenue from the tenths reserves fund to help finance Māori welfare raises fundamental questions. From 1840 (though the Sounds area did not receive any funding until later) until 1939 when the Social Security Act provided universal health care in New Zealand, the fund subsidised Māori medical and welfare services across Te Tau Ihu. In this period there were few government-provided social services, such expenditure was not inconsistent with the fund's purpose and the Trust money resulted in a greater provision of health care than in other regions. But proceeds from the fund were partially replacing, not supplementing, government funding; government was paying less. This did not happen elsewhere in the country. Apart from one repayment in 1879, the fund continued to cover medical expenses without reimbursement until the 1940s.[164] Effectively, state-provided social services available to Māori elsewhere were, in Te Tau Ihu, 'partly funded by a trust owned by the recipients themselves' and yet controlled 'paternistically and often parsimoniously' by government.[165]

NATIVE MINISTER JAMES CARROLL'S ATTEMPTS to introduce a measure of self-government did not assist. Under the Maori Councils Act 1900 a network of local councils consisting of appointed tribal members[166] could administer by-laws, take responsibility for sanitation and health and offer welfare assistance within their own communities. In 1905, the Arapawa District Maori Council was established for the huge region of Marlborough, Buller and Nelson, its members a roll-call of the significant families in the area.[167]

While, as with the various road boards, a lot of time went into dog licensing, the Māori Council did address health/welfare matters at both Okoha and Waikawa.[168] It dealt with drunkenness, and it granted money to the Okoha Maori Village Committee to help the village build a footbridge so that schoolchildren could cross safely when the stream was flooded. It dealt with assistance to the elderly and infirm, worked to find ways of improving the Waikawa Village drinking water[169] and tried to find ways to limit alcohol consumption. But national politics modified the councils' powers and funding and interest soon waned.[170] In 1909 only 20 from a possible roll of 400 voted at Blenheim,[171] and most Māori councils had ceased to exist by 1910.[172] Although revived nationally again in 1919, they remained relatively powerless.

That, then, is the framework. For the communities at Waikawa and Okoha the impact was devastating. For decades, inadequate housing and poor sanitation contributed to poor health. During the 1890s and into the new century, Māori adults and children at Waikawa suffered from chickenpox, skin problems, measles (which could keep children away from school for weeks)[173] and fever epidemics; whooping cough struck in 1895 and again in early 1896; serious influenza hit the community in 1892, 1894, 1902 and 1903.[174]

Māori could not afford better sanitary arrangements or the safe water supplies they needed. Typhoid, around the turn of the nineteenth century an all-too-common illness internationally, returned repeatedly to devastate Māori communities.[175] The 'low fevers[s]' in 1875 in the damp, low-lying locations in Pelorus Valley and Queen Charlotte Sound and at Waikawa in 1879 were probably typhoid.[176] In the middle of 1892, in what would prove to be almost two years of illness, Waikawa schoolteacher John MacDonald reported that what he called 'the plague' was increasing alarmingly, affecting 'every house in the district'.[177] By November, old whalers William Keenan and Isaac Love were reported seriously ill and, with the disease breaking out in Port Underwood and Te Awaiti, other Māori in the Sound were suffering. Three weeks later James Keenan at Hitaua Bay died from the disease — the sixth within three to four months. Others were dangerously ill.[178]

Further outbreaks occurred into 1894, and typhoid was back in 1896 and again around the turn of the century.[179] An urupā for those who died in a smallpox epidemic lies towards the mouth of Mahau Sound — the disease was there, too.

Amid the overcrowding and malnutrition, tuberculosis and bronchitis often led to pneumonia, the incidence of which was far greater for Māori than for Pākehā.[180] In 1915 the Waikawa settlement was 'full' of tuberculosis, and 'many of the children [had] it in latent form'. In the first decades of the twentieth century respiratory diseases, and especially tuberculosis, would continue to devastate Māori health, in the Sounds as elsewhere.[181]

Māori generally had little immunity to Western illnesses and were unfamiliar with — and sometimes unwilling to take — Pākehā medicine or advice. Where they did seek help at Picton or Blenheim hospitals, they faced hospital boards reluctant to accept 'outside' patients — a response probably informed by race.[182] While the number of South Island native doctors suggests that iwi or hapū members' petitions to the four Māori MPs for medical assistance did not go unheeded, the isolated Māori communities faced difficulties that were hard to surmount. The consequential health impacts were 'disastrous'.[183]

The European response at times seems to have been wilfully indifferent, if not callous.[184] While the *Marlborough Express* daily informed its (largely European) readership how to prevent typhoid during the 1892–94 epidemic, government officials were fully aware that the village people were drinking polluted water. Yet it took months for anyone to suggest they put banks around the wells and boil all drinking water.[185]

During the 1896 epidemic a schoolteacher, reported that 'no steps have been or are being taken to stamp it out'.[186] The local chemist, F. Shaw, alone appears to have acted with compassion and care. The villagers' public testimonial acknowledged that at a time when the mortality had been 'painful to chronicle', Shaw had dispensed kindness and free treatment and that while he was helping not a single person had died.[187]

The school inspector's response to the dire poverty in which Waikawa Māori were living in 1915 stands in grim contrast. There were plenty of fish to catch, he judged; all they needed to do was to go and catch them. But they were too likely to go off to live with relatives in the Sounds, unlike the Wairau Māori, whom she considered 'a better class' and less migratory.[188]

In 1904 Kipa Whiro, who after his father died took up a senior leadership role in the Ngāti Kuia–Rangitāne community,[189] and Maka Kiharoa from the Okoha community eloquently represented the plight of their people to the government:

> We and our children suffer from many ailments; but in as much as we have no doctor provided by the Government we feel it is a very heavy burden to pay for both medical aid and the conveyance of our sick by launch to Havelock — and you will understand that we are 47 miles by sea from Havelock. Thus we feel heavily the expense incurred in taking our sick to Havelock together with the actual cost of healing and maintaining the patients so much so that we are afraid to take our sick to the doctor lest we should be unable to meet the costs of his services and medicines.[190]

In June 1906, following decades of poor health and low birth rates among Ngāti Kuia at Okoha, a Dr Bartlett in Havelock was appointed as the Māori medical officer.[191] But he had heard rumours of alcoholism, and did not think he was paid enough to treat 'exacting natives'.[192] He decided he would only visit outside a 16-kilometre radius of Havelock in emergencies. The following year he was replaced by a Dr Williams, who made no charge for his care and gave 'more general satisfaction here than any medical man has done for many years. He is clever and attentive and what is almost of equal importance sober.'[193] However, Dr Williams wanted the acutely ill to come to his Havelock surgery, arguing that they would need treatment there or at the nearest hospital. He also wanted to avoid making the 41-nautical mile (75-kilometre) trip to Okoha unnecessarily.[194] But for Māori, Dr Williams' 12-hour launch trip was a three-day row.[195] Thus the doctor's stance meant that many cases of tuberculosis in the community remained undiagnosed for some time.[196]

In Nelson, a Māori hostel had long been used as a base for Māori patients, but in Havelock no such venue existed. Ngāti Kuia coming from the outer sounds faced Havelock hoteliers who blatantly refused to lodge Māori. In 1905 Tahuaraki Meihana, in a dignified letter to the *Pelorus Guardian*, set out the facts — only the offer of a place in a boathouse meant that sick relatives gained shelter from the rain and averted possibly fatal consequences.[197] The Nelson hostel was far from satisfactory, but in 1904 Ngāti Kuia petitioned for a similar hostel at Havelock. In 1905 an unsatisfactory building was agreed on and funded (inadequately, some argued) from reserves funds. Increasing numbers used it, especially after Dr Williams replaced Dr Bartlett. But petty official harassment seemed to assail the initiative, and issues of overcrowding and resulting further illness were not addressed until the 1930s.[198]

In 1919 an annual subsidy of £10 10s became available for doctors to underwrite the cost of visits to outlying Māori patients,[199] but until the reforms made by the first Labour government, Okoha Māori unable to make the trip to Havelock depended for their medical care on local schoolteachers and the medicines provided by the native medical doctors.[200]

Meanwhile, questions of eligibility of access to native medical doctors had become increasingly complicated. Māori leaders were themselves divided on whether the free medical care was only for trust beneficiaries, for all Māori, or only for the 'indigent'. Such issues were compounded by intermarriage and spouses' eligibility.

THE HISTORIES OF THE NATIVE Waikawa School and Okoha School can be read as further instances of the absence of health and welfare building blocks for Māori. But they are also testament to a singleness of purpose demonstrated as those communities, often ill and always impoverished, worked with extraordinary resilience to equip their children for living in the new environment.

By 1860 mission schooling had given Māori a higher standard of literacy in te reo Māori than European settlers had in English.[201] The Native Schools Act 1867 was one thrust of an assimilationist policy developed after the land wars to break down Māori collective behaviours — in this instance by promoting secular, state-controlled, English-language primary schools for Māori communities.

Reflecting a rationale that Māori were most likely to use and support schools that they had requested and contributed to, the government imposed onerous financial and other conditions that had to be met before a native school could be established. In a two-part process, applicants for a school had to demonstrate backing from a 'considerable number' of Māori men within the district, put their request in writing, donate at least an acre of land, pay a quarter of the teacher's salary and half the cost of the buildings (for which standards were set) and teacher's residence, pay half the maintenance and provide the schoolbooks.[202]

A legislative change in 1871 removed the need for communities to help pay the teacher's salary and the building costs. When the Education Act 1877 made primary education free and compulsory, those provisions did not apply to native schools, though Māori children were entitled to attend the free schools (if any were accessible).[203] Two years later native schools were transferred to the Education Department. The rules (for example regarding attendance) were tightened. In 1894 schooling became compulsory for Māori children, and attendance provisions were further tightened in 1901.[204]

Although the changes to the Native Schools Act in 1871 heralded a significant increase in native schools and pupil numbers,[205] in many parts of the country Māori were still unlikely to get an education unless they were close enough to attend a free government school.[206] Official reports suggest that in the early twentieth century only six 'mainstream' schools in the Sounds had Māori pupils, although the Europeanisation of Māori names on school rolls makes it difficult to establish that number with certainty.

Two native schools were established in the Sounds where there were significant Māori populations: at Waikawa in 1878 and at Okoha in 1900. (Schools inspector James Stack, reporting in 1878, mentioned a third school in Pelorus, where 11 children were present when he visited,[207] though subsequent reports make no mention of this.) In 1901 hopes for another school, requested by a Hitaua Bay resident, fell victim to the constantly changing Māori education policy, although an Education Board

Okoha school pupils and teachers. The image is undated, but in 1901, a slip forced the school to relocate closer to the village, a job the church undertook and the government belatedly and reluctantly reimbursed. This unresponsive attitude to the Okoha villagers' needs was demonstrated again when the government refused to meet the costs of enlarging the school room to cater for the growing school population. With the notable exception of the appointment in 1912 of Mrs Sarah Wilson (nee Hemi), who herself had been a student at the school, unmarried women were appointed as teachers over the next three decades. N. BAIGENT COLLECTION, NELSON PROVINCIAL MUSEUM, 315921

school, which Maori sometimes attended, very briefly operated there.[208] The school at Tahuahua was not 'native', as it was sometimes described.[209]

Although £562 was spent on building the Waikawa schoolroom, it and the teacher's house were badly sited and built. The school was barely habitable in winter and unpleasantly hot in summer. A further £100 had to be spent within the first year to make it habitable. Such difficulties, along with landslides and blocked drains, persisted. Repairs were effected but only after parents contributed half the cost[210] — an extraordinary imposition to place on an impoverished community. The school committee, its members not well versed in bureaucratic practice, for years had to battle the delays caused by the widely spaced inspectors' visits and their requests to the Education Department to get issues resolved.[211]

The Waikawa school teachers were well paid by the standards of the day — a handsome £150 was voted from government estimates for the first teacher's salary, but a number of teachers were paid only £100, and there were some considerable fluctuations.[212] Some teachers seem to have risen above the often variable quality of the time, and number spoke te reo Māori (not a requirement).[213]

Stack in his initial inspector's report on Waikawa School did not hold back on Māori 'moral shortcomings', their 'ignorance and vice' and the potential for European children to be endangered 'by the unrestrained viciousness of the Maori youth'.[214] A later report piously hoped that Māori would be 'further educated by the example of thrifty settlers'.[215] But such men eventually stopped visiting and the tone of inspectors' reports changed over time. Some evinced an interest in and sympathy with the pupils and the difficulties that schooling involved for them and their beleaguered community.

Year after year, inspectors' reports noted that many pupils passed exams with good marks. In 1895, after an epidemic lasting 20 months, exam results were deemed 'satisfactory'; in 1897 an abnormally long whaling season had caused extended absences, but traces of 'honest, useful work were readily discoverable'.[216] That year, too, Eva Henry, a Pākehā brought up in a Māori family, was awarded, slightly irregularly, a native scholarship to go to secondary school. Timoti Tahuaroa Watson and Mihimete Watson were each awarded a scholarship in 1905.[217]

These were no mean achievements, particularly given the problems of absenteeism that the 'alarming, disruptive and devastating impact of ill-health and disease' created at Waikawa, compounded by the adults' itinerant employment patterns.[218] Repeated efforts were made by parents and teachers alike to get around

Mihimete (Amy) Watson, who attended Waikawa School, holding the McLean Scholarship Award, 1905, allowing her to attend Hukarere Girls' College, in Hawke's Bay. PICTON HERITAGE AND WHALING MUSEUM, COURTESY PICTON HISTORICAL SOCIETY

Pupils attending the relocated and so-called Okoha Second School, c. 1902–03. Back row (from left): William Hemi, Winnie Blutcher and Martha Mason. Middle row: William Walker, Harry Wells, James Isaac, Nellie Walker, Hemi Walker, Polly Blutcher, Hilda Walker and Bert Climo. Front row: Henry Hemi, Empson Mason, May Hemi, Hipa Walker, Charlotte Hemi, Lena Walker, Frank Wells and Reece Hemi, and an unnamed child. PICTON HERITAGE AND WHALING MUSEUM, COURTESY PICTON HISTORICAL SOCIETY

such difficulties. Teachers sometimes closed the school during the harvesting season, or altered school terms to facilitate attendance (and ensure capitation). In 1890 the Waikawa parents applied, unsuccessfully, to the Education Department for a small grant to pay one of them to look after the children while the rest were away working. In 1897 some 20 children were left with teacher George MacDonald while their parents went down the Sound to whale. In 1898, Keepa, the school committee's chair, had the school terms changed, and (fruitlessly) personally guaranteed children's attendance.[219] The strenuous but sadly largely unsuccessful efforts to tackle absenteeism do not appear to have been matched by any real departmental interest in addressing the basic issues that underlay the incompatibility of Māori employment patterns and Pākehā educational demands.

In 1908, as part of a wider decision about the future of all South Island native schools, the Waikawa native school was closed and taken over by the Marlborough Education Board.[220] Māori would continue to attend, but it was no longer a native school.

UNTIL 1900, eucation options for children at Okoha were effectively non-existent. For children from Okoha, D'Urville Island School and Whangarae School in Croisilles Harbour, established in 1890 and 1898, respectively, were nominally in the vicinity.[221] But both involved difficult, lengthy, even dangerous travel by boat.

In 1899 the Anglican Church, concerned about the growing impact of Mormonism,[222] acted on behalf of Ngāti Kuia and asked the Education Department to help establish a school at Okoha. There were by then an estimated 16 schoolchildren. The department agreed, but under conditions that suggested it had little regard for its statutory obligation to provide free and compulsory education for Māori children. For each beneficiary, the Native Reserves Fund was to pay £1 5s. Further, the Okoha people were to provide a building, and if the school proved 'fairly' successful in its first quarter, the Education Department would provide (a low) £3 15s capitation and school materials. Supply of a building would be considered after a year and a satisfactory inspector's report.[223] The school opened in September 1900 under two church-appointed teachers, Miss B. Baigent and her assistant, Miss Byles.

Though denominational, the school was listed as a 'subsidised' or 'South Island assisted' native school and was regularly inspected and examined by the Education Department.[224] Attitudes to the use of Māori language in school would harden from 1905, but in 1901, a teacher sympathetic to the enlightened views of James Pope

(Inspector of Native Schools 1885–1909) on the need for Māori language in schools encouraged its use, and pushed the boys to study to get into Te Aute College in Hawke's Bay.[225] By 1903 there were 21 children in attendance, more were expected, and the inspectors' reports were favourable. Nevertheless, the department turned down a request to enlarge the building. By this point, however, the parents had become concerned about the extent of religious instruction, and in 1905 the department declared that Okoha School, like five other schools in the area, had become 'beyond all doubt, denominational in character' and withdrew all subsidies.[226]

With some state (via the Marlborough and Nelson education boards), some church, and some reserves funding, Okoha School kept going in its somewhat irregular status and, because board funding was linked to pupil attendance, with teachers not always paid properly. By 1913 numbers had dropped to 10 as parents moved away to find jobs in farm work, felling and fishing. Then in 1915 the Public Trustee withdrew the reserves funding and the Education Department closed the school. The church continued to offer voluntary support, and teaching limped along for a while.[227]

Okoha children now had to attend Canvastown School, days of rowing away. Their educational needs forced their parents away from their reserve lands, jeopardising vital language retention and creating further ruptures in their community.[228]

An attempt to reopen Okoha School in 1921 failed because the government considered South Island Māori 'more or less completely Europeanised'.[229] Its future operation (see Chapter 9) depended on church and local initiative.

What is again noteworthy in the Okoha School history is the tenacity with which the parents, like those at Waikawa, worked to get their children educated. In the midst of the deadly epidemics and against all manner of other odds, they generally got their children to school. Yet both villages faced an Education Department failing to deliver on its statutory obligations.

Native schools had been established to aid assimilation, in part by teaching in English. When, by 1905, Māori in the South Island were considered to be speaking English well, officials saw no further need for the native schools, judging them to have achieved their purpose.[230] The schools had always been underfunded and underresourced, offering education of whose lesser quality Māori were aware.[231]

AROUND THE TURN OF THE century, as the established churches' increasing focus on Europeans left a spiritual gap and a communal need, Māori were developing

Haimona Pātete (1863/64–1921), Māori activist, advisor, minister and founder of the Church of the Seven Rules of Jehovah. ALEXANDER TURNBULL LIBRARY, PACOLL-5549-3

their own responses to Christianity, trying to find a church that would minister to their needs and address their particular situation in this new world. Mormonism had something of a broad appeal and may have reached Ngāti Kuia in the 1890s via their relations on D'Urville Island, but it did not seem to have the same impact in the Sounds. Instead, some took comfort from Te Hāhi o te Ruri Tuawhitu o Ihowa, or the Church of the Seven Rules of Jehovah, founded by the impressive Haimona Pātete of Ngāti Kuia and Ngāti Koata, who emerged in the 1890s as a political and religious leader.

Pātete hoped that this 'one church' would minister to Māori spiritual needs and unite all denominations and tribes. It was not intended as a threat to the Anglican Church; rather it contained elements of Māori and English spiritual practice. The church's robes, services and hierarchical structure and its recognition of the English sovereign as head of state and church reflected many aspects of Anglicism, although there was no communion because of Māori views about eating a body and the destruction of its mana. Adherents were expected to live their lives along seven guiding principles: life, goodness, love, knowledge, strength, trust and authority.

It never became the Māori people's one true church, although it was particularly strong in the Wairarapa, and committed congregations also met regularly at various places in Marlborough, including Waikawa.[232] It would decline in the 1920s under the impact of Rātana, but at the turn of the century Waikawa Māori were united in being 'very much taken up with and believ[ing] in' Pātete.[233]

THROUGH ALL THEIR DIFFICULTIES, MĀORI in the Sounds continued to practise their rights 'as people of the place' to use the customary foods and maintain the knowledge and practice of the previous generations.[234] Whakapapa continued to be handed down, old narratives and values were sustained and learned across generations. Those born in the 1930s learned practices and ways of thinking from their elders, so that Bosun (Stephen) Huntley could write about the concept of 'the Sounds as our Mother . . . and Kura Te Au is the mother's womb . . . they called the highest Maunga in this area Rahotia [penis] to fertilise the womb!'[235] And Laura Bowdler knew that in the first decades of the twentieth century, 'the whanau groups would go around to the Love whares . . . in Kura Te Au to gather fish and Kaimoana to preserve and store to help carry them over the winter months'. Her father called it 'subsistence living, that no one seemed to have much in the way of money but there was never any shortage because our people were so good at providing food not just for our own whanau but also for the old people of their whanau in Waikawa'.[236]

The kaitiakitanga handed down also involved tapu and other practices to ensure sustainability. Bosun Huntley, recalling the inherited knowledge and traditions of kaimoana and fish habitats of the bays in Tōtaranui and Kura Te Au, the history of the raupatu (confiscation) there, and the spiritual significance of land around Te Pungu, the sheltered part of Tory Channel, wrote that the area

> has always been regarded as prime real estate, not just by us but by the old people in times gone by . . . [In Te Weu Weu] in the past the kehua [spirits] have chased folk out of there and my grandfather refused to fish in there because of Tapu. [His family] always steered clear of Moioio Island because of the kehua. We were told that after the Raupatu there were three hundred slain on the island. The ferry wash is still washing ko iwi [human bones] out of the banks. This is where Ngaitahu had their first foothold in Te Waipounamu and was where the famous Te Atiawa fighting chief Te Hureiwhenua lived out his final year.[237]

By 1916, settlers were said to be in every bay in the Sounds. The land was milled and burned and fenced, the new people took food from the land with little knowledge or care for what or how much they needed. As early as the 1880s, imported fish introduced by acclimatisation societies (and protected by legislation) were having a deleterious effect on native species. Europeans took eels irrespective of season.[238] They shot native birds as game. The very nature of the reserves to which Māori had been relegated, as well as the steady allocation of land to the new settlers, saw them severely restricted in the wide-ranging foraging they had carried out for centuries. They could no longer run pigs or sheep as they once did.[239]

Settlers' bush clearance brought about massive deforestation and a consequent loss of plants and birds. Tragically and ironically, Māori at Okoha milled timber to provide employment for their people, thereby further destroying bird habitat.[240]

Māori increasingly lost opportunities to collect mahinga kai and kaimoana. And yet, as time went on, the paucity and poverty of their reserves made them more and more reliant on the traditional food-gathering methods they were losing.[241] Without them, Māori in the Sounds, like those on reserves elsewhere, would at times 'literally have starved'.[242] Well into the twentieth century, mahinga kai was all that was 'standing between [Ngāti Kuia] and starvation'.[243]

8. Depression, War and Making a Living

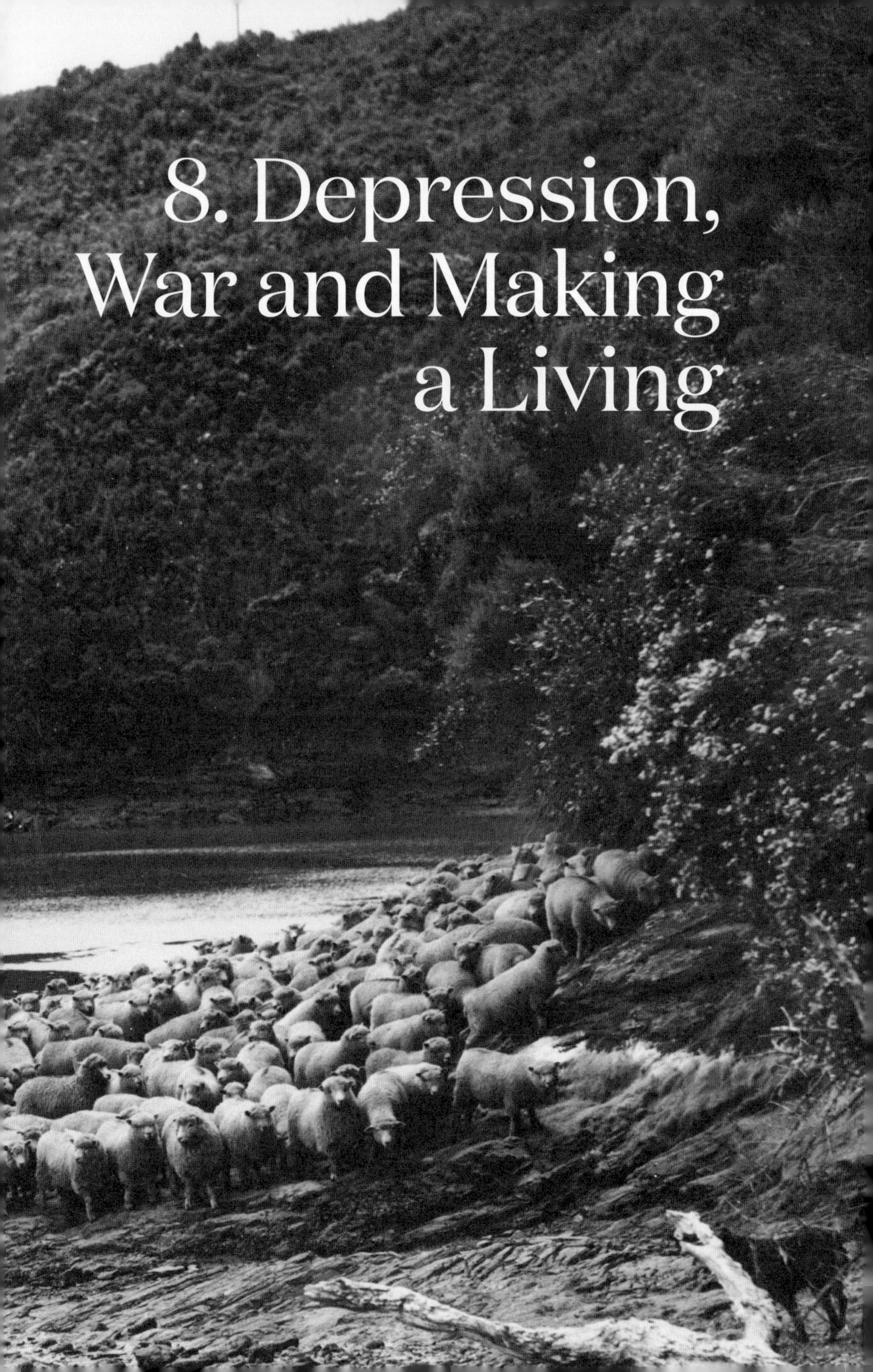

> 'He is a family man, hard working, but his vessel is old, and beset with seemingly continual mechanical troubles which retard his efforts . . . In other words, he is not an economic unit, but by crikey!, he tries hard.'

On 27 March 1920 the *Pelorus Guardian* editorial addressed its readers: 'It has been a long, weary struggle during the horrible world war, and the aftermath has proved too powerful for the weakened frame. We have done our best in the interests of the district and the Dominion.'[1] With that, the paper closed its doors.

That eulogy in many ways set the tone for the next five decades. Farming was the Sounds' economic mainstay, but from the early 1920s the population dwindled[2] as farms failed and land reverted to scrub or was sold for scenic reserves.[3] International tensions during the Korean War in the 1950s saw the US buying up large amounts of wool, creating 'the greatest wool boom in New Zealand's history'.[4] But this proved to be only a brief respite after the economic slump of the 1920s–30s, the Great Depression and World War II.

Moreover, it was becoming increasingly clear that while some areas of the Sounds were 'eminently suited to farming', much was not.[5] Too often farming methods, as well, lagged behind developments elsewhere. Post-World War II agricultural mechanisation, new soil management and farming methods were followed by a commodities boom in the 1950 to mid-1960s, yet the benefits to Sounds farmers were largely restricted to the few remaining bigger Pelorus farms. Even there, profitability was still achieved by relentlessly hard work relieved only by Sundays.[6]

That profitability was dramatically and suddenly hit by a 40 per cent drop in wool prices from 1966 until the early 1970s that reduced sheep numbers and export revenue. When agricultural profitability picked up nationally from the mid-1970s,[7] most of the small, uneconomic units in the Sounds had gone. Nor could the other traditional Sounds industries — milling, fishing, whaling — provide a viable economic lifeline to permanent residents. Perano's closed its whaling operation in 1964.

By then, a different exploitation of the land and its scape had begun. The Lands and Survey Department's steady acquisition of 'picturesque Sounds scenery' from the late 1920s[8] had fed into a growing public interest in conservation. The establishment of the Outward Bound School at Anakiwa in 1962 further propelled the Sounds and their environment into the nation's consciousness. Farmers' guesthouses offered distinctive and popular holidays. By the 1960s road construction (the most significant of infrastructure developments) finally began to put farmers and other Sounds' permanent residents 'on the main roading network of New Zealand'; 'local people [could] . . . produce more . . . and . . . transport what they produce'.[9]

As goods went out, tourists came in, their numbers boosted by the advent of the roll-on-roll-off ferry in 1962. New, faster water-taxis whizzed holidaymakers from bay to bay; bach numbers and little holiday communities — developed for pleasure rather than profit — were growing; increasing numbers of boaties were discovering the delights of the cruising grounds. When plans and planting for big commercial *Pinus radiata* forests looked to transform the landscape, and mussel farms began to be anchored around the shoreline, new voices — including the growing number of holiday residents whose families, in boats or baches, had long been in the Sounds and who felt they had a stake in the area's future — began to enter the debates about the future of the Marlborough Sounds.

Farming: The long decline

In 1931 the Great Depression was deepening. One farmer near Havelock had six bales of wool and 100 sheep in poor condition to sell on an unreceptive market.[10] Survival on such small, uneconomic, essentially subsistence farms was almost impossible.[11]

Harold Leov was one who weathered the Depression. He had a wealth of practical experience, relatively fertile land at Te Towaka and a sympathetic mortgagee. He cut posts and became a sub-agent for a farming agency, buying and selling sheep locally. He survived partly because he was so in debt to his farmhand that he eventually handed the farm over in lieu of overdue wages. The farmhand, 'a decent sort of bloke', soon similarly fell into arrears and offered it back; thereafter, ownership moved between the two.

When the Depression ended, Harold happened to own it. He had firmly believed in continuing to work the land because 'the day might come when it might turn enough to restore the fences and buildings'.[12] A reading man, he was, too, perhaps more open to new ideas than some farmers around him.

Some weathered the 1920s and 1930s using unpaid family labour.[13] Others found enough money to open accommodation houses, or they cleared bush, fenced, cut scrub on contract or went fishing at French Pass. But things got harder: gangs tended to be hired only for the essential shearing and at French Pass fishing became so popular that returns were reduced.[14] Self-sufficiency was essential, but even that demanded 'a large orchard, vegetable garden, cows to milk' and supplementing your 'own meat [with] fish and mussels off the beach'.[15]

The Depression did not have a uniform impact across the Sounds. At Anakiwa the Challises were among a group of farmers benefiting from the Linkwater Dairy Company's continued operation. Until 1953, when it succumbed to the inefficiencies of small-scale production, the company operated as a creamery where farmers could deliver their milk daily, have it weighed and separated and take a share of the whey home to feed their pigs. There was a modest prosperity, aided by the careful husbandry typical of the time.[16] While no one was particularly wealthy, only a few possibly 'had holes in their clothes' and some, in later years, had enough money for an inexpensive annual holiday.[17]

Most in the Sounds, however, did not enjoy even marginal prosperity. The land continued to go back. In 1933 Henry Robb's Skiddaw farm was covered with tauhinu and mānuka well over a metre high; only 200 of its 300 sheep could be mustered. From 20 bales of wool, Robb got £63. His wethers sold at the works for only 3s each.[18] Other farmers simply walked off, with nothing to show for years of effort on over-capitalised land. In 1939 the Armstrongs in Fairy Bay had 800 acres (324 ha). There was a formed track, useful for driving and other access, as well as houses, a shed, fences, an orchard, dips and yards, all valued at £800. They ran 20 sheep, 6 dairy cows, 13 young cattle and 6 sows. On the land's unimproved value of £120 they paid £4 16s annual rent. Wool sales, the sole farm income, had brought in £2 2s. Mr Armstrong got paid another £120 for contract work but there was nothing else.[19] They were gone within a decade.

The effects of the 1920s slump and the Great Depression were felt in the Sounds long after they officially ended. The total acreage under grains and pulses, never a large part of the Sounds economy, fell from 178 acres in 1922–23 to 50 in 1940–41.[20] Stock numbers dropped between 1920 and 1945: dairy cattle by 30 per cent; breeding ewes from 168,030 to 97,437; only beef cattle numbers grew slightly.[21] As the 1930s moved into the 1940s, the mechanisation that could improve production was mostly unaffordable. Draught-horses and manpower continued to be widely used; stumping, draining, hay-making and spreading lime fertiliser were all done by hand.[22]

The few milking machines milked only a fraction of the cows, and even farmers with flocks of 600 sheep had only two-stand machine plants for shearing.[23] Although the first electrical shearing plant (powered by a Pelton wheel) was set up in 1932,[24] contract shearers, brought up using blades, did not always learn to use the new equipment even as diesel-powered electricity arrived in the 1950s.[25]

World War II further disrupted production. The Sounds, as elsewhere, faced labour shortages. Over 100 young men (and a few women) of the 1060 people registered as being in Sounds County and French Pass left to join the armed forces. Others were manpowered outside the district, into the war effort. Men who did not join up were generally in the Home Guard. Many critical items such as fencing material, work trousers and boots were either unobtainable or in short supply; fuel was heavily rationed. As men left the district, women and children did what they could; but without the labour to keep the tauhinu and mānuka constantly in check, land quickly reverted.[26]

American stockpiling of wool during the Korean War (1950–53) saw the wool price in New Zealand jump from 6d per pound to 14s, then £1 a pound. Prices would fall rapidly again when the war was over, but in the meantime the Heberleys at Ōkukari found that plucking wool from the fences made good sense.[27] Although Harold Leov could not immediately afford to replace the two ex-army Bren guns he used as tractors,[28] farm machinery, part of the postwar agricultural revolution that would transform New Zealand farming practice,[29] was becoming within reach.

Small bulldozers came on the market. From the mid-1950s young John Harvey, in downtime from his and his brother's milling, used their new Caterpillar tractor, complete with the hydraulic arms then coming into vogue, to begin a new era in roading contracts.[30] The 'roading going on all round the Sounds from the 1950s into the 60s when most roading had been completed' meant that in really heavy rain, 'mud and clay were washed off and turned the whole Sounds yellow'.[31] Harvey pushed through farm access tracks and county roads, opening up farms to new fences, fertilisers and Land Rovers that saved hours once spent packing heavy fencing equipment from the beach up 300-metre hills.[32]

Fences and fertilisers saw stock numbers increase. New veterinary practices had lambs treated for worms, though 'in those days, the treatment was basic, some[times] diabolical'. They used it in the hope 'it'd kill the worms before it killed the lambs'.[33] Soil research arrived and with it, in 1949–50, molybdenum, one of the seven essential trace elements applied for pasture growth and to treat acid soils. One of Harry Leov's sons spelt the name out in pasture, its remarkable effects (and his wrong spelling) soon apparent to all.[34]

The advent of fertilisers was accompanied by revolutions in applying it. Gone was hand-sowing with lime (done from the 1920s); in came blowers. These 'were tricky to handle until you got roads', and terrain always limited their range.[35] The 'big innovation' was aerial topdressing,[36] but for many farmers, concerns around price and the rugged terrain meant that it was often seen as unviable.[37] Some with access to the few airstrips in the Sounds used it from the mid-1950s;[38] for others, as we see below, the question was whether they used *any* fertiliser, however it was applied.

IN MANY WAYS, HOWEVER, THE approach to farming in the Sounds had changed little, partly because of the absence of roads until the middle of the century. In the early 1920s an unmetalled road ran between Te Mahia and Onahau (the need for constant maintenance, said the PWD in 1929, made metalling it 'out of the question').[39] And during the war the military significance of the Torea–Portage link had attracted a £320 grant.[40] In 1940, in the French Pass–Kenepuru area, the only road ended at Okiwi Bay. Into the 1950s the Picton–Linkwater road was so bad that stock were punted, not driven, to Picton from the Grove, and Geoff Challis, farming just south of Anakiwa, preferred to row to Picton rather than go by road. Linkwater itself was generally accessed from the Havelock end.[41]

Elsewhere, the government-constructed tracks that the non-rate-paying settlers were expected to maintain were regularly used for droving, mustering and farm work.[42] (As late as 1976 there was still no clear delineation between government and county control and consequent responsibility for formed or unformed roads.)[43] But track maintenance took the men away from more pressing work on their own farms at a time when depopulation, particularly in the outer Sounds during the war, meant a reduction in manpower.

However, by the late 1940s officials considered that since, post-Depression, launch owners Wal Orchard, the Johnsons and the Kennys had invested in more reliable launches and in punts for lighter stock and freight in the Sounds, tracks were being used less. Government money for extraordinary maintenance was given only reluctantly. (Launches and punts of course carried their own hazards. Considerable seamanship was needed to ensure heavily laden punts did not overrun the launch, and in any weather the buildup of carbon monoxide in enclosed cabins was a real threat.)

By 1949, after no government expenditure on tracks for over a decade, and with official expectations of permanent residents doing the track maintenance clearly not being realized, the government assessed that extensive work and capital expenditure were needed to clear slips, stop scouring, and move loose rocks that reduced the width of the tracks.[44]

Yet, even as the tracks slipped away, for some their value had not eroded. At the Okoha settlement, landowner E. Mason wrote to the Minister of Public Works in 1940. He lived about 4 kilometres from the wharf where the mail launch called. Over half the track, he wrote

> is almost unuseable . . . I have to get through mud and slush to their some time cant get their at all could I get some help from your department to make this road useable at all time as it is very necessary to get our goods away . . . for instance to get 1 ton of manure to my place I have to sledge it at two bags a time were as if I had a decent road I could take it up in two loads with my truck . . .[45]

Nor did all Sounds residents own launches (few if any Māori did), and, as always, tide, wind and weather could make reaching destinations very difficult.[46]

Launches and tracks might mitigate the problems posed by distance but could not eliminate them. Wal Orchard began punting the Titirangi cattle to the Picton

Port Ligar, looking back at E. J. Shand's house and woolshed, c. 1944. The farm covered the whole of the Port Ligar Bay area. The port itself opens out into the mouth of Te Hoiere Pelorus Sound and Raukawa Moana Cook Strait. MARLBOROUGH HISTORICAL SOCIETY, 0000.200.4

saleyards in 1949, ending the traditional Patersons' annual cattle drives. For decades, the Patersons had driven hundreds of cattle over the tracks put down at the beginning of the century to Havelock, then a further 700 kilometres — first through rough, often untracked country down the Wairau Valley and over the Rainbow Road to Hanmer, and then on main roads (and from 1948 by train) to Christchurch.[47] Pelorus sheep and lamb were freighted out, first by local steamers or scows, then by Wal Orchard's or the Johnsons' punts.

Water transport was certainly faster, but it carried hidden costs. Martin Shand recalled that having to punt animals from the outer Sounds to Havelock meant dispatching them two days to three days beforehand. Too often they lost condition en route and 'you got what you could for them. It was too expensive to hire grazing or bring them home. You were vulnerable to agents not working on your behalf, you were a price taker for everything, taking whatever you could get.' Desperate farmers sometimes accepted prices that barely paid the freight.[48] In 1973 the branch road from the French Pass road finally reached the Shand farm and, weather and road conditions permitting, stock could be trucked out with less manhandling and less stress and taken straight to the saleyards or the Nelson freezing works.[49]

QUITE APART FROM THE ENVIRONMENT in which they were operating, poverty, which nourished conservative farm practices, limited many farmers' land management techniques. Ash from burning off would provide a short-lived fertility but the fires destroyed the humus, the vital organic matter in the soil, in which the imported improved grasses and cultivars could grow. What's more, in the fires' aftermath, weeds and the grey-blue tauhinu would be everywhere.

Good seed, fencing to control weeds so as to allow close cropping, rotating the stock — all the practices that Isaac Harvey had advocated decades before — allowed the Shands at Te Kopi to get ahead. Those who had little or no fencing and who could not afford decent seed fell back on frequent burning as the only economic (but short-term) way to improve fertility and destroy weeds. Martin Shand remembered that in the 1960s it was nothing

> to see whole areas — hundreds of acres — black. They'd burn in the autumn with the idea of getting the grass away when the lambs dropped. Amazing. Some blocks where the fern had got away for a couple of years,

rather than leave it they'd just burn it all off. Huge fires burned everything, sometimes including the sheep.[50]

In Queen Charlotte Sound in particular, fires got into some reserves, leaving only 'shrivelled, blackened trees'; slips scarred the land. [51]

Reluctant to take on potentially expensive experimentation because of the cost of borrowing for fencing and better-quality grass seed, many kept burning and 'kept the land clear for no good purpose' instead of moving forward.[52] Time-honoured methods tended to prevail. Only those 'who have learnt the best method of [farming the country] through years of experience' should be listened to, was a common response.[53] Martin's father Jack Shand, farming at Port Ligar, was 'a very particular farmer.'[54] But farming 'wasn't really his forte,' Martin said, 'so he struggled with it, tried to take on board' what he could do about introduced weeds and getting roads put in. He focused on 'the things he could do, the things he knew he could manage'. Farmers' children were not involved in decision-making; they mostly just did what they were told.[55] People relied on practicality and 'common sense, really. Always watch your neighbours. But not very progressive.'[56]

Just how unprogressive farming techniques were in the Sounds became apparent in 1949. Perhaps aware of new Australian approaches to land management,[57] that year J. A. Paterson at Titirangi published a letter on the value of 'rotational grazing that allowed the land to recover between grazings, [doing] all that burning does without its harmful effects'.[58] The vociferous, sometimes almost unpleasant, defence of traditional Sounds practices that followed suggests an unreceptive audience, unwilling to engage with the fact that the only things flourishing on their properties were *Danthonia*, fern and exotic weeds — foxgloves, St John's wort, rat's tail and *Heracleum*, and, later, small outbreaks of prickly pear.[59]

In the late 1940s and early 1950s many farmers were refusing to acknowledge the visible and clearly documented erosion around them. At a time when a dramatic decline in kill at the Picton works indicated considerable land deterioration,[60] farmers steadfastly denied that carrying capacity was reducing or that farm management techniques should be changed.[61] They rejected an opportunity to address animal pest control, and also government assistance with fencing, topdressing and freight for supplies in order to control indiscriminate burning.[62] They rejected the idea of a Weeds Board to control weeds because of cost implications.[63] They did not agree to a soil conservation committee (catchment board), despite evidence nationally that these led to improved land management as well as acting as vehicles for valuable subsidies for specified farming activities.[64]

A decade on, attitudes (and most farmers' economic situations) had not changed. In 1968 a topdressing demonstration was finally organised because of Federated Farmers' concerns about poor farming outcomes and falling land prices in the area. Evidence of the value of 'molybdic super' (molybdenum) in encouraging grass growth and of the close grazing that controlled tauhinu, the 'No. 1 weed',[65] and raised land productivity was spectacularly visible. '[A] depleted hill farm' in Kenepuru could, 'with improvements and the injection of reasonable capital, become a profitable concern,' an official wrote to M. E. Robb of Kenepuru Sound.[66] Yet the demonstration was poorly attended and the farmer involved thought he'd 'mark time'.[67]

Some, however, did keep up with new farming practices. Harold Leov, reading the Department of Agriculture journal, developed an interest in trace chemicals and worked with Percy Begg, a Marlborough Department of Agriculture adviser, and he and his neighbours began to trial different types of grass and fertiliser. He talked to other farmers.[68] At Waitaria, Frank Godsiff's move to Romneys significantly improved lambing rates and returns on wool; his shelterbelts won prizes; and he spread huge amounts of molybdic super and lime with DC3s.[69]

Despite the general conservatism and falling population, pastoral farming would remain a mainstay in the Sounds, continuing into the late 1970s to 'significantly [contribute] to the economic and general welfare of the Sounds' permanent population'.[70]

Others, without that mainstay, looked to various ingenious money-making ventures. During the war, surprisingly good money could be obtained for goat or deer skins. These were put in aeroplanes' fuel tanks, where the skins swelled to seal any bullet hole.[71] Goats and pigs were shot as pests and, with pelts or pig snouts and tails dispatched as evidence for payment, brought in useful bounties.[72] During the 1950s Mary Kirk Williams and her family of seven, living a straitened existence in Ngaruru Bay, sold the nautilus shells that washed up on Tory Channel beaches for a dollar apiece.[73]

BY THE MID-1940S A FURTHER process of consolidation or sale for scenic reserves was underway.[74] Some 45 farms had once been worked in Pelorus. By the 1950s, five with the better 'Ketu' soils in the outer Sounds, Te Rawa in Northwest Bay, and Brightlands, with its big cleared areas, were the only ones of any consequence.[75]

Those in the better soils were Port Ligar, Okoha, Titirangi, Te Towaka and Pohuenui. Flora Robb (née Godsiff) and her husband George Robb bought a farm in Four Fathom Bay in the early 1950s. Its situation is indicative: there were no proper fences, the land was covered with scrub and tauhinu on which the sheep made a poor living, though the cattle did well on fernroot and native trees. There were no roads and the only tracks were pig tracks under fern and scrub.[76]

Even official records paint a picture of a population dwindling away, family by family. In the Bulwer/Fitzroy Bay/Worlds End area in 1950 the Burke and McCauley families made up the little Bulwer settlement — yet Colin McCauley, like many of his contemporaries, was seeking opportunities elsewhere.[77] The Browns were still at Elaine Bay,[78] and war-damaged R. A. Archer remained in Tuna Bay. At Canoe Bay, R. C. Harvey had died and no one else was likely to come in. F. D. Hope at Titoki Bay was intending to move and live in Homewood; his home at Port Ligar would probably be demolished. Like Clunies-Ross of Garne Bay, who had become a fisherman, M. Johnson of Savill Bay was there for only six months a year.[79]

The end of the 1960s heralded a further exodus. 'Quite a lot' of 'prominent people left — the Hocquards, for instance, who had previously bought up uneconomic farms in the outer Pelorus, [and] the Patersons [who sold up in 1976] who had done a lot of work to improve their farms'.[80]

A similar process of movement from the land was at work in Queen Charlotte Sound. From the early 1950s land in Tory Channel and the sound was progressively sold for baches or for pine forests,[81] or to the government as reserves.[82] By the end of the 1960s, weekenders in Queen Charlotte Sound outnumbered the mostly retired 150 or so permanent residents.[83] By 1970 the Bucklands had spent two decades building up yards and outhouses, making tracks, running sheep, growing vegetables and trying flowers. That year they sold their land in Deep Bay (Endeavour Inlet) back to the Crown. The sheep were punted out or killed, the woolshed was dismantled.

Māori, too, were affected. From the end of World War II 'a steady exodus' of Māori families left from all over the Sounds — Port Gore, Croisilles, Canvastown — for larger urban centres.[84] In 1970 Milly and Vern Watson sold their farm at Ōnauku and left the bay 130 years after Milly's great-great-grandfather, Rihari Tahuaroa, had first arrived there.[85] For these small Māori and Pākehā landholders it was the end of an era.

Depleted resources

For a period from the 1920s, stories of fish, drama and plenty pepper reports on the Sounds. A shark attacked launches; a huge sunfish, caught on a line and impervious to bullets and thrusting knives, towed a launch around the bay; another fish — or perhaps an octopus — brought a launch to a standstill.[86] Ten years on, and perhaps as an antidote to war, *The Pilchard Fishermen*, the National Film Unit's beautifully atmospheric 1945 film, reworked the narrative of bounty and beauty — the one little fishing boat that the government had not commandeered leaving Picton at dusk, scanning under dark cliffs for the phosphorescence that betrayed where a shoal of sardines (young herring) teemed in the deep water close to the shore, laying, then hauling in the encircling net and steaming home. Less atmospheric frames moved to Brown Barrett's Picton canning factory where some 60,000 fish — 3 tonnes — were canned, sterilised and shipped out every day, mostly for troops overseas. Māori 'girls', to whom, the film explains, 'the preparation of food from the sea comes naturally', were chiefly employed.[87]

A single sheet in a government file describes how, in 1967, commercial quantities of mackerel were pouring into Tory Channel and Queen Charlotte Sound's northern entrance. In the channel, members of the three families involved were stationed on the hills as spotters to alert the beach seine-net parties of approaching shoals. Where there were no hills, men rowed, silently searching out the fish by boat, their oars barely touching the water, to secure sightings. The file note mentions big takes in 1964, and an eager local and Nelson and Auckland market. In 1966 there is mention of using the fish for other than bait. Similar quantities of fish were in Port Ligar, but as the travelling time to Picton in open sea conditions was six to seven hours, fishermen were not interested.[88]

In 1927 even Auckland papers deemed newsworthy the value (some £425) of a haul of about 2000 fish from a new hāpuku ground in Cook Strait, about an hour's run from Tory Channel.[89] Other, more profitable reefs were expected to be found. In the 1950s the country's developing taste for crayfish meant big money and opportunities to leave the Sounds for work in the Nelson and Wellington fisheries and beyond.[90]

The Fishburn operation, begun in 1942 when Sounds newcomers Jim and Albie Fishburn and their wives Flo and Ethel began line-fishing out of Dryden Bay in Queen Charlotte Sound, was an exceptional success. Investment in new boats and, by the 1960s, a radio-telephone and echo-sounder, then cutting-edge technologies, dramatically improved profit margins, as did a new freezer, product innovation and export sales.[91] The venture remained a going concern into the 1980s, with its wharf, its generators going day and night, and its lights acting as unofficial navigational aids to those feeling their way past White Rocks and down into the sound after dark.[92]

But such success stories notwithstanding, the overall state of fishing in the Sounds was in decline, as everywhere, due to declining fish stocks. Barrett's factory suffered the fate of so many Sounds' initiatives, closing in 1950 because of badly declining catches and because the firm lacked the capacity to deal with the vagaries of the ocean-going herring, whose distribution varied locally and seasonally and whose movements were unpredictable.[93]

AT THE END OF WORLD WAR II fish all around the country were 'harder to catch', despite new, more effective techniques being adopted. Sounds fishermen could not afford the mechanised and well-equipped fishing boats that moved faster, stayed out longer and travelled further to compete in fishing grounds where traditionally they had not fished.[94]

By 1940 motor-trawlers, and motor-vessel set-net or line-fishing, out of Picton, Havelock and French Pass had replaced the rowing boats used during the Depression years.[95] But even in the more established Picton industry about half of the Sounds fishermen were part-time, and the new vessels were still often too small to go the distance needed to land a good catch.[96] If weather made a poor catch likely, the men stayed put. The demands of their farms meant that they could not often work the longer fishing hours needed to benefit from efficiencies of scale.[97] At French Pass, from where Sounds fishermen often worked, the three boats that worked year-round in 1937 averaged seven landings a month, the rest no more than two a month.[98] In 1950 almost half of the Sounds fishermen showed profit margins lower than the annual median income of £203.[99]

Catches, from a decreasing number of species, fell or remained static.[100] In 1951 the four men with trawlers licensed to work the tight four-month season in the inner reaches of Pelorus Sound had to take up other work or 'just tie their boats up'.[101]

Fish stocks, too, were declining. Between 1920 and 1950 only those fishing out of Picton made any profit, and only there was any local employment generated. The policy of the Fisheries Division of the Marine Department over the decades was to do research, to regulate accordingly and to attempt to enforce.[102] In an effort to

A fisherman and his son at Whakatahuri, Forsyth Bay, outer Pelorus Sound, in 1949. JOHN PASCOE, ALEXANDER TURNBULL LIBRARY, PACOLL-8765-09-71

protect fish stocks it progressively introduced bans on various fishing methods and restrictions on commercial and recreational fishing alike.[103]

Their research demonstrated that the highly efficient seine-netting was the most injurious aspect of the Sounds fishery. The department therefore banned it in the inner reaches of Pelorus Sound and in Queen Charlotte Sound below Dieffenbach Point. Fishing was permitted for only four months a year, between April and August, to minimise interference with fish spawning. A minimum mesh size was regulated to ensure that only good-sized fish would be caught, and a maximum time was stipulated for nets to be in the water. Regulations became increasingly stringent over the years.[104]

The intention was to make the fishery economic. The new regulations would restrict fishing to those who partly depended on it for a livelihood, as well as tourists. It would also rectify imbalances, because particular species 'are in an overstocked condition . . . and will benefit from being thinned out'. It would not affect tourist catches, as Danish seine fishermen did not fish for cod, groper or snapper.[105]

Settlers, the Havelock Town Board and Harbour Board and the Sounds Branch of the Farmers' Union mounted a barrage of criticism: the regulations would still allow too much of the Sounds to be seine-netted; the whole thing was against the advice of those who knew; they predicted dire effects for both the price of fish and the state of the fishery. Local MP Tom Shand foresaw fishermen out of business and trawlers depleting a valuable tourist asset, taking the blue cod that drew in the amateurs.[106] Allowing any seine netting and trawling would, the locals claimed, imperil the blue cod fishery, the fishing industry, the fishermen themselves and the tourist industry. Facts — that blue cod were caught by lines, not nets; and that only four trawlers were operating in the area, with marginal impact — did nothing to dampen decades of vociferous local opposition.

Enforcement was also problematic. In 1934 local Fisheries staff considered that Sounds fishermen were in a 'really desperate position and practically the only way to get profitable catches is to operate in what are at present sanctuaries'. Perhaps unsurprisingly, reports of illegal trawling, widespread after the Depression,[107] continued into the 1970s. The attempts at enforcement leave an impression of something of a maritime Wild West. Fishermen, at times apparently with the connivance of their local MP, fished without licences, used illegal nets and lines, took undersized fish and sold them illegally.[108]

Only in the mid-1960s, when guesthouse owners and tourism operators banded together to see fishing regulations enforced[109] and the Fisheries Division became better resourced, did penalties start to be imposed. Until then, fishermen and tourists alike appear to have had little compunction about taking undersized fish and too many of them.[110]

In 1968 the situation of Mr Hawkins typified that of many Sounds fishermen. He relied on the permitted seasonal trawl fishing for a major part of his annual income:

> [From] time to time, over the past ten years other commercial fishermen have also spasmodically worked this fishery only Hawkins has been consistent; he is a family man, hard working, but his vessel is old, and beset with seemingly continual mechanical troubles which retard his efforts due to his hopelessly increasing cost factors. In other words, he is not an economic unit, but by crikey!, he tries hard.[111]

Tom King-Turner was one who continued to fish, working around D'Urville Island and taking crayfish off Kahurangi Point on the West Coast; in the 1980s he chartered for research bodies. Yet by the 1960s it was becoming clear that the future for Sounds fishermen lay not in the Sounds, learning the trade from their fathers, but in seeking professional qualifications that opened the way for themselves or some of their children to fish, consult or teach all over the world.[112]

'PERANOS MUST COME FIRST' READ the sign in Cuddon's engineering factory in Blenheim, which from the 1950s provided vital technical skills and much of the Perano equipment and its finessing.[113] By then, Perano commercial acumen and adaptability had seen their Tory Channel operation develop into an important regional and local industry. Shrewd business sense and pragmatic decisions would continue to characterise the firm. By 1956 it was a well-managed limited liability company, J. A. Perano Whaling and Company Ltd. An associated company, Whekenui By-products Ltd., was established in 1957.[114]

Back in 1918, after the right whale catch had declined and humpbacks had become the whale of choice, profits and tonnage of oil grew exponentially. In 1920 seven humpbacks yielded 235 tonnes of whale oil with a value of £8225; in 1950, 139 whales yielded 973 tonnes of oil valued at £36,000. The company had also been turning out bone dust for fertiliser from 1920 and in 1950 produced 100 tonnes.

The firm was little affected by the Depression, and as an essential industry and with

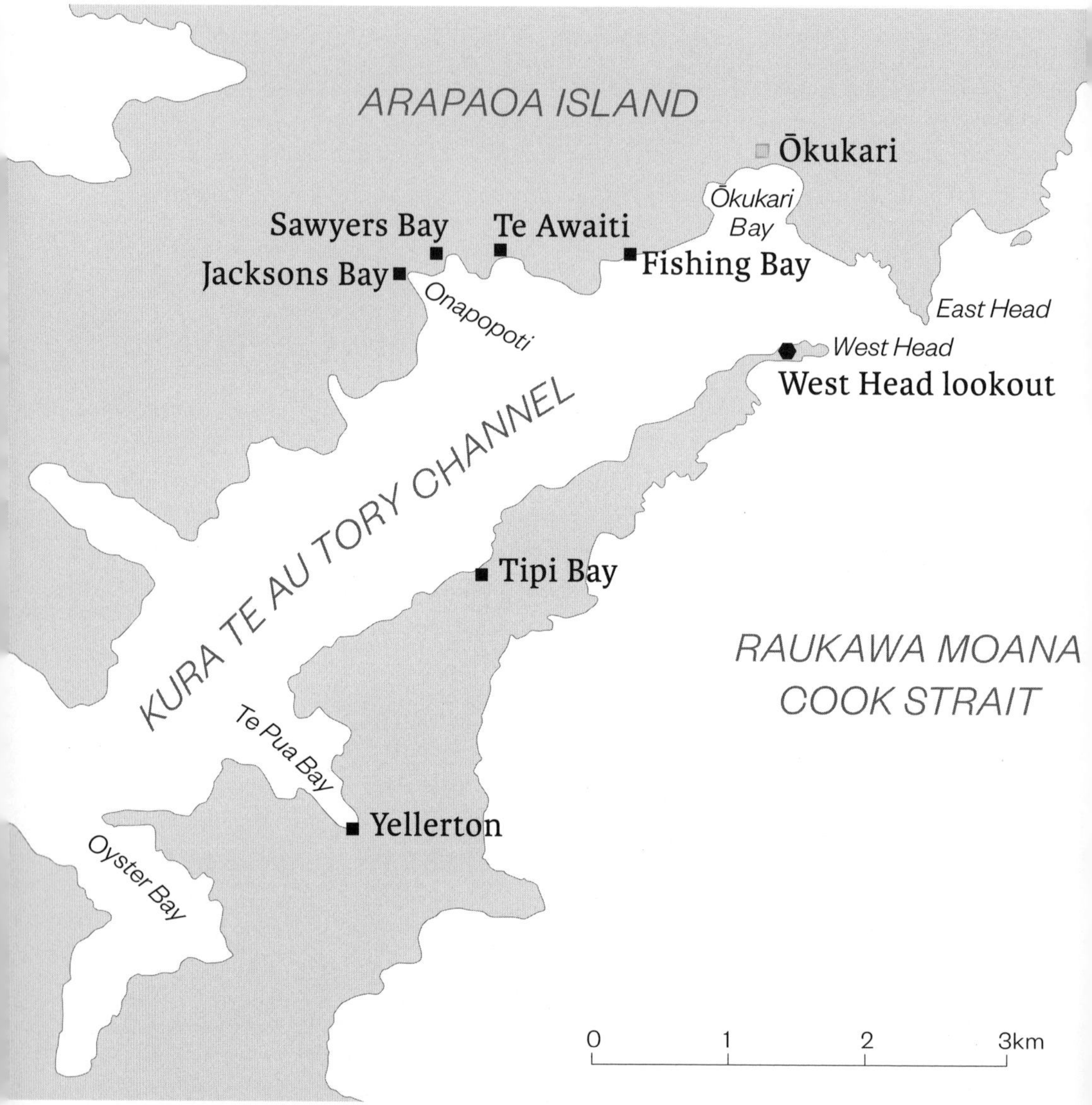

A map of the Kura Te Au Tory Channel whaling stations. In 1923, Joe Perano pulled out from the partnership with his brother Charlie and began whaling in Whekenui; Charlie continued at Tipi Bay. Fierce fraternal rivalry ended in a court case and costs to Charlie he could not afford. He closed the Tipi Bay station in 1928, and a lot of the machinery was shipped across to Whekenui, by then the sole Tory Channel whaling operation. ADAPTED FROM NIGEL PRICKETT, THE ARCHEOLOGY OF NEW ZEALAND SHORE WHALING (WELLINGTON: DEPARTMENT OF CONSERVATION, 2002)

'every gallon of oil' needed for New Zealand or Australian defence forces or other vital operations, Perano's did well out of World War II.[115] This meant that the company had the money to diversify. By 1950 it was producing 300 tonnes of canned whale meat.[116]

The canned whale meat venture began just after the war. In 1945, as a 'protein-starved world' emerged from a punishing war, the secretary of the Marine Department tried to convince a somewhat suspicious New Zealand public that they had a moral obligation to eat the highly nutritious and tasty new protein source. If the general public was not convinced, Sounds locals had no such qualms. Florence Trotter remembered 'Ma Walding' and her business partner at Picton's Federal Hotel

> used it to make pies and did all different things with the whale meat. It was really very nice. It used to go black because they'd hang it out and then when you were ready to eat it, you cut the outside off and then you got nice pink-red meat inside. ... We used to have quite good steaks.[117]

Brown Barrett's Picton canning factory also began experimenting with canning whale meat mixed with onions, parsnip and carrots.[118] In 1946 Perano's established a joint initiative with Brown Barrett and started exporting whale meat to the UK. The British were delighted because the highly nutritious meat was not rationed; demand grew to exceed what the Peranos could supply. Then in about 1949 new regulations changed the canning process, the tins blew their lids, and the venture collapsed overnight.

Locals continued to buy unprocessed whale meat for their dogs and the Fishing Bay works continued to turn out processed whale meat, frozen and bagged as pet food, to be sold across the country. Florence Trotter remembered that when Richard Keenan fed it to his hens, he 'got the most beautiful yellow eggs'. The Perano recipe was kept very carefully under wraps — marketing whale by-products was then extremely competitive and industrial piracy was not unknown.[119]

In 1962 a sudden dearth of humpbacks resulted in the decision to hunt sperm whales until the humpback whaling recovered.[120] The firm had the financial flexibility to make the necessary adjustments, including another re-equipping to ensure ships with an adequate range and seagoing capacity, a spotter plane and the identification of new goods and markets. With its employment of local people and the direct and indirect benefits to the economy accruing from its operations, Perano's must have seemed a permanent and important firm to those in and around the Sounds.

The company's capacity to adapt to new conditions and remain competitive was continually demonstrated by its timely investments in new equipment and plant. In 1920 three specially built launches were used in whaling.[121] The fast chasers *Miss Liberty* and *Miss Whekenui* were equipped with the latest killing technology.[122] The tug *Tuatea* was redesigned to make her more efficient and powerful.[123] Over time, too, the plant was updated and improved. A primitive shelter on Lookout Hill, probably dating from the late 1930s, was given a wooden floor, a wood stove and a viewing window; lockers and facilities for making hot drinks were installed — a far cry from the early huddling in whatever shelter the men could find. Signal flags were replaced in 1936 by radio-telephone communication; lookouts trained the bright light of an Aldis lamp on the boats to signal when they needed to turn on their radios for advice on the whales' movements.[124]

There was a record season in 1950 after a more efficient plant had increased the station's handling capacity. There were no more bottlenecks of killed whales decomposing while awaiting processing, and the new, 'cigar-shaped' tanker *Hinunui* meant efficient trans-shipping of its 163 tonnes of whale oil to Dutch cargo ships anchored in the stream at Whekenui.[125]

Speed and efficiency continued to be sought. By the early 1960s Perano's had invested hundreds of thousands of pounds to achieve a small but sophisticated, highly mechanised and surprisingly quiet factory (although its motors generated enough power to light up all of Picton).[126] Winches, rams, mechanised saws and the rotating steam-powered Norwegian Kværner pressure-cooker that extracted the oil[127] with such efficiency meant that from the 1960s Perano's largely met international regulations requiring that whales taken be 100 per cent used.

It was a messy business. Two or three hours after loading the cooker, only the 'grax' or frothy residue from the cooking process was left. When this was periodically blown out to clear the valves, the sea, already stained by red-brown patches, would be covered with grey scum in which blind hag eels writhed and swarmed.[128]

The success of the 1963 season (119 sperm whales)[129] was short-lived. Competition was fierce, and the climate around whaling had changed. Back in 1931 New Zealand had signed the International Whaling Convention to limit whaling; in 1935 it developed legislation to help implement the convention's principles around conserving the species and regulating the industry.[130] Annual licences were introduced for shore-based whaling in 1937–38 and whaling was almost completely banned across the world in 1986.[131]

Yet in 1963 whaling was still a global industry. Russian and Japanese factory ships were operating intensively around New Zealand, and the Russian ships, we now know, were falsifying their returns to the Whaling Commission and catching banned species.[132] They also dumped their oil on the international market.[133] Perano's, even with government assistance, could not compete. On 21 December 1964 Perano's *Orca* harpooned its last whale. Only when the men received their pay cheque did they realise that their jobs, and the Perano whaling operation, the last to close in New Zealand, were finished.[134]

With it went an enterprise that had helped put Marlborough and the Sounds on the map. In an environment quite different from today's, whaling added a point of difference to what other tourist destinations might claim. If newspaper articles are anything to go by, there was little sympathy for these massive creatures, about which so little was known, even though they were 'rapidly being hunted to extinction'.[135] As late as 1964 the National Film Unit's *North-east Corner* matter-of-factly filmed the sighting, chase and death-throes of a great sperm whale.[136] Whaling, while it lasted, was a tourist drawcard.

When the whaling disappeared, so too did vital opportunities for seasonal employment. In 1930 Perano's had employed 19 men (8 at sea and 11 onshore). This rose to 50 in 1946 (36 at sea and 14 onshore) and 54 two years later (40 at sea, 14 onshore).[137] Into the 1940s the men were not well paid (11 days of working 12 hours were needed to pay a £5 grocery bill),[138] but over time the opportunities for employment grew and diversified — masters, gunners, chaser-drivers, whale spotters, engineers, firemen, wireless operators, boiler attendants, digester attendants and factory hands.

Alan Hall, teaching at Whekenui School in 1963, observed clear differences between the skilled European workforce at Perano's and the Māori workforce living at Fishing Bay. The two groups had little social contact.[139] The Peranos had built a hall there, and Florence Trotter, whose father and husband were both whalers in the 1950s and 1960s, recalled that the Peranos had provided 'adequate' baches for the workers with which residents could do what they wanted — 'you painted them, you made them how you liked'.[140]

'It was hard to get a job [at the whaling station]', Florence Trotter remembered.

> It was good money, everybody wanted to work there. You had to wait for a vacancy . . . having connections helped. They knew you, they knew the family, and if a vacancy came up, you didn't get preference, but if you were in line, you'd get the job.[141]

Many Māori in Picton and in Queen Charlotte Sound worked at the Picton freezing works and seasonally at Perano's. When Perano's stopped operating, the loss of that pattern of regular work would have hit hard.

THE VERY NATURE OF MILLING meant that once an area was milled over, the activity ended: the millers and their mills left. By 1924, with Brownlee's and Craig and Reese no longer in the district, the milling industry in the Sounds seems to have been almost moribund. In Rocky, Paradise and Mud bays in Hikapu Reach (Pelorus Sound) earlier milling had left, in challenging country, an estimated 6 million super feet of good-quality timber.[142] Two millers, the Prentice brothers, developed ambitions plans to mill this, including building 500 metres of tramway to get the timber to the mill and a large wharf for shipping to Wellington.

The likely costs of extraction and the Forest Department's insistence on a publicly competitive tender appear to have stymied the initiative.[143] Two years later, in 1926, in the three or four lines then accorded to the timber industry in Marlborough in its annual report, the Crown Lands Department recorded that there was one small mill working in Pelorus Sound and several small mills in pine plantations.[144] Little remained of a once burgeoning industry in the area.

In the late 1940s Hylton and John Harvey, descendants of William and Augusta, aged 19 and 17 respectively, began developing a mill at Tōtaranui, at the back of Clova Bay. Theirs is a compelling story begun out of economic necessity and demonstrating extraordinarily hard work and adolescent determination.[145] Harvey Timber Company, up and running in 1950 and cutting on their father's 1300-acre (526-hectare) block, was one of only three mills then operating in the Sounds. The Okoha mill, at the top of Anakoha Bay where two previous mills had operated, cut beautiful timber from the rimu that grew to about 300 metres above sea level, its dark honey-coloured sap timber a different colour to that growing on the shadier side above Tōtaranui. The very small Roadley mill worked on the steep land behind Northwest Bay.[146] Some milling was also going on in Queen Charlotte Sound, to make way for baches, not farms as in the past.

By the early 1960s the Harvey brothers had financed equipment upgrades and moved the mill to ensure efficiencies. That John was using downtime between orders to build roads for the county (ensuring that their employees — local lads — had work) was an early indication of the inevitable. Timber was in short supply. The old-man

The Perano whaling station in Whekenui, south of the Kura Te Au Tory Channel entrance, 1967. Today, much of the early infrastructure has gone, but heritage noticeboards draw visitors' attention to the bay's history. AUCKLAND LIBRARIES HERITAGE COLLECTIONS 1207-2010

pine in the area had been felled, the few newer plantations would not be ready to mill for another decade or so, and the native bush in Crail, Nydia and Four Fathom bays had run out. Views on milling native timber were changing, too, and it was harder and harder to get permission from Lands and Survey to mill timber on Crown land.

By 1952 they were cutting some 6000 super feet annually, but by 1965 John, increasingly made ill by diesel fumes, could see the writing on the wall. He and his wife Denise reluctantly left, with £10,000 to show for 20 years' of work. In 1974, the year the government cancelled all milling rights to native timbers, Hylton sold the mill to a Christchurch syndicate, which closed it. After almost 100 years of milling in the Sounds, the last functioning mill, which had operated for 28 years to provide a living for its few employees as well as its owners, was gone.[147]

Conservation reserves come into their own

From the 1920s the Department of Lands and Survey made extensive land purchases to protect the area's scenic values. Air and ferry services brought in holidaymakers in increasing numbers. Accommodation houses provided creature comforts and organised activity, and trampers moved through the area. Baches, many still owned today by the families whose predecessors built them, saw small formal and informal communities grow up. In isolated bays, yachts and launches swung quietly at anchor or from moorings.

Such habitation was giving rise to a new phenomenon. A wave of new long-term, intermittent 'settlers' — the bach-owners nestled in Queen Charlotte Sound's little bays and the loose fraternities of yachties — was emerging. Increasingly strong ties to the area developed during frequent visits, sometimes over generations, meant that they felt at home there, and were anticipating that their children and grandchildren would inherit that landscape.

They also had views on how the area in which they holidayed should be developed. By the end of the 1970s this new wave of settlers was bringing a different edge to earlier laments on the destruction of a unique environment in the interests of 'progress'.

'Nature Notes', penned in Wellington's *Evening Post* during the 1930s by R. H. D. Stidolph, 'field naturalist', noted ornithologist and honorary scenic inspector,[148] created something of a litany of species loss. Shooting parties on yachts did not care if they were shooting a protected king shag (endemic to the Sounds), a spotted shag or a common black, white-throated, little black or pied shag.[149] By 1939 the migratory sand plover, the piopio (New Zealand thrush) and the bush canary (mōhua or yellowhead) had vanished from the Sounds;[150] the pihoihoi or pipit was rarely seen by 1940.

Loss of birdlife was not the only sign of environmental degradation. Foreign plants and animals continued to be introduced into the area with little thought about their possible impact.[151] New Zealand fur seals were so rarely seen at the time, due to intensive hunting, that a sighting off the Marlborough Sounds in 1939 led to reports of a 'strange sea creature'.[152] Over the war years, with many hunters away in the armed forces, pigs were 'absolutely ruining' the Sounds area, destroying any new growth. The problem had gone beyond individual management — any attempts to clear them out saw the animals simply moving on to the next property.[153]

'Nature Notes' and other records, however, reach beyond their narrative of decline or loss or 'holding on'. Their observations were part of a growing national consciousness of New Zealand's natural world and its value, fostered by tramping clubs, government and other groups, which led over time to a raft of legislation intended for species preservation and the creation of reserves.[154] At the end of the 1960s a proposal to raise the water level of Lake Manapouri in the southern South Island to create cheap hydro-electricity for an overseas-owned aluminium smelter propelled an enormous environmental protest — New Zealand's 'green awakening'.[155]

This interest in the natural environment was reflected in the Sounds. The country's papers were bursting with letters and articles on the continuing destruction of bush in the Sounds to gain essentially worthless land, on the failure to learn from the past, and the jeopardy being visited upon the next generation's heritage. The Forestry League, which during the 1920s and 1930s worked to educate a public little interested in fire prevention, was one of the advocates of a national park in the Sounds in the late 1930s.[156] The Ship Cove and Queen Charlotte Sound Reserves Board (into which the early Ship Cove Board morphed in 1938), the Grove Arm Domain Board (formed in 1935), the Pelorus and Kenepuru Reserves Board (1961) and the Croisilles–French Pass–D'Urville Island Reserves Board (1962) comprised interested, enthusiastic, knowledgeable farmers, launch owners and local-body representatives who, along with other volunteers from boating and Rotary clubs, did an enormous amount of conservation work.[157] By 1972 the Ship Cove and Queen Charlotte Sound Reserve Board alone was involved with 16,618 acres (6725 ha) of reserve land.[158]

Land was gifted for reserves, too. In 1930 Wellington solicitor Robert Machlan

Macaliser donated a considerable amount of land he had bought in Tahuahua to be added to the Ruakaka Reserve; a further donation a little later created a public utility reserve, where bush has since regenerated.[159] In 1933 R. C. Bruce, founder of the Bruce Trust, collaborated with the Forestry League to buy, then reserve for the public, 217 acres (88 ha) of beautiful bush land behind Bulwer that was about to be cut. 'So much of the scenic Sounds country [had] been so ruthlessly destroyed' that the gift was doubly attractive, the *Evening Post* commented.[160] In 1970 John Shand, who had already created a private scenic reserve on his Port Ligar farm, gifted the part of Maud Island where the Stephens Island frog, the 'rarest of the three primitive endemic New Zealand frogs', was in the largest concentration, as a private reserve with restricted access.[161] In 1971 it became a flora and fauna reserve, to be known as the T. P. Shand Reserve in memory of John Shand's cousin and local MP Tom Shand.[162]

THE STEADY ACQUISITION OF LAND for reserves would transform the Sounds. By the late 1920s, as the holiday population grew, Lands and Survey Department officials continued to conserve 'picturesque' scenery.[163] The earlier, careful caveat was still in force: a reserve could be created only where it did not impact adversely on settlement, and as long as claims for reimbursement were not 'unreasonable'.[164]

By the 1970s, even as land continued to be acquired to protect existing reserves, consolidate them or create new ones,[165] new thinking was needed. Given the impacts of forestry, mussel farming and bach development, how was the relationship between development, recreation and conservation best managed in the cumulatively vast area of the reserves in the future?

In the late 1930s farmers around the country were flooding Lands and Survey with offers to sell their unproductive land.[166] In the Sounds the department acted imaginatively to build an ever-increasing number of reserves. Satisfactory financial settlements were reached and grassy slopes were swapped for shady bushed or reverting land.[167] Regenerating bush became a permitted land use and farmland was bought for the purpose.[168] The department acquired the 'rugged coastline of steep slopes and massive exposed rocks at Cape Lambert', which it 'recognised as important to acquire'[169] along with the hundreds of acres of steep, east-facing forest of beech, fern, mānuka and introduced scrub in Nydia Bay that completed the Tennyson Inlet Reserve and further protected it from fire.[170]

In 1960, against vociferous local opposition (not in evidence in 1890, when the riparian strip was taken from Māori), the Marlborough Land District was the first to regularise adjoining owners' historical occupation and encroachment on the Sounds foreshores. A very considerable amount of land was reserved for scenic, historical, foreshore and landing purposes and protected against further exploitation. Over the years, Lands and Survey's further acquisition and administration were hotly contested;[171] today, views on the taking of Māori reserves land for public reserves are changing.[172]

Protection was not always immediate. In 1948, not only were king shags declining but Ship Cove was also heavily infested with goats and pigs; the remains of small sheep pens on the only flat land on Little Chetwode attested to the island's agricultural past.[173] But a decade later, wildlife officer Brian Bell, subsequently a renowned bird scientist and conservationist, recorded that native plants were returning on the Chetwodes. On Motuara much of the vegetation had become almost impenetrable.[174] On Edgecombe Point the once densely massed supplejack, other vines and highly varied bush had, by 1961, matured into a 'luxuriant area of native forest of podocarps and hardwoods'.[175] A decade later a tall closed forest had regenerated on Long Island and the bush on Motuara was flourishing; an old homestead chimney still stood on the eastern side of Pickersgill Island, but kohekohe was emerging from regenerating scrub and bracken was giving way to tall kānuka. Kohekohe was flourishing on Blumine Island, too, and the bush on Allports Island, just out of Picton, was regenerating well.[176]

From the late 1950s islands in the Sounds were supporting burgeoning bird populations. The Chetwode Islands, by 1948 'a successful natural sanctuary', hosted a huge abundance of South Island robins (toutouwai), a large number of parakeets (kākāriki) and other native birds.[177] On Motuara in 1972 small numbers of kererū (pigeons), warblers (riroriro), fantails (tīrairaka pango), bellbirds (korimako), chaffinches (pahirini), silvereyes (pihipihi), kingfisher (kōtare) and introduced birds flourished; bellbirds were doing well on Blumine Island.[178]

The 1970s heralded the ecologically critically important translocations of wildlife to island sanctuaries. The Wildlife Division in the Department of Internal Affairs attempted, unsuccessfully, to settle the threatened South Island saddleback (tīeke) on Big Chetwode;[179] and in 1972 juvenile toutouwai were transferred from the Chetwodes to Motuara.[180] The role of the Sounds islands in species preservation would be further enhanced after the dramatic reduction of rats that followed one of 'the only eradication attempts on islands anywhere in the world' at that point, on Awiti and Tawhitinui Islands in the early 1980s.[181]

Yet even in the mid-to-late 1960s, wide-scale burning continued to threaten the reserves. Fire protection across the geographically challenging area was patchy. Tighter regulation from the mid-1950s on, and the appointment of eight permanent residents as fire officers (the radios that came with the job were handy for ordering groceries, catching boats going past, getting weather reports or help, or advising of breakdowns), could only do so much. Annual training sessions were established in 1977. It took the decline in farming, a growing public awareness of fire, technology — helicopters, floatplanes, efficient fire-fighting pumps — and a willingness to prosecute to greatly reduce fire risk.[182]

BY 1969 THE DEPARTMENT OF Lands and Survey was responsible for 88,000 acres (35,612 ha) of reserves, 9750 acres (3946 ha) of vacant Crown land and 16,300 acres (6596 ha) of state forest reserves.[183] By then the question of how this estate should best be administered was the subject of constant discussion. National park status was (again) rejected[184] — the reserves were considered too scattered between pockets of privately owned land.[185] And, particularly in Pelorus, these pockets were farms on which people lived, and which formed a significant part of the local economy.[186]

Might the newly established Hauraki Gulf Maritime Park provide an effective model for simultaneous development in farming, forestry, tourism and recreation?[187] The idea was mooted and public support was crucial for the concept to proceed. A meeting at Homewood on 8 February 1969 was the first of a series to talk the idea over with a range of users. Meanwhile, the Minister of Lands discussed the details with farmers who were often opposed or at least sceptical,[188] and carefully crafted papers helped explain and develop the concept. In July 1971 an historic meeting in Havelock, attended by some 200 people, set out the almost finalised framework.

This was about managing the reserve land, not private holdings. It was recognised that part of the Sounds' attractions lay in the co-existence of potentially conflicting uses across natural and manmade landscapes. Commercial uses would sit alongside recreational. As in the past, 'only land best used as a reserve would be included'; land below the foreshore was to be excluded to minimise potential for conflict with the fishing industry; proposed power or roading development would not be affected; planning and tracks would obviate tensions between holidaymakers, farmers and those in the fishing industry. Nor would scenic values be compromised for tourism.

Overdevelopment and sophisticated facilities 'in every bay and associated with every beach' were not intended.[189]

There was no opposition and in 1972 the 30,000-ha Marlborough Sounds Maritime Park was created. Like the Hauraki Gulf Park, it aimed 'to protect the flora and fauna, and ensure public access to the park'.[190] An advisory board (used in national parks and considered an excellent way of involving locals) represented a large cross-section of the community.[191] Private members were unpaid, 'but the new board attracted a more realistic level of funding'.[192] Chaired by the local Commissioner of Crown Lands, the board met all around the Sounds. This was a shrewd move. People could not easily leave; issues, as far as possible, had to be resolved.

Ian Mitchell, who followed George McMillan as chair of the board from 1976 to 1985, considered it an effective body. Improved funding saw several new campsites established with improved facilities. The Momorangi Bay Motor Camp acquired a new shop/caretaker's residence and a revamped water and sewage system. Local bodies gave valuable assistance. The Marlborough Harbour Board constructed new jetties at Motuara and Ship Cove about the time of the Cook bicentenary, and the Marlborough County Council helped with new campsites alongside the Kenepuru road. Over time, the board brought tracks up to a better standard.[193]

But perhaps the greatest achievement was the huge increase in the park's size, over time, from 30,000 ha to almost 51,000 ha. By 1986, 104 separate reserves 'scattered amongst forestry operations, farms and private baches' stretched from Croisilles to D'Urville Island in the north to Whites Bay in the south-east.[194] Ian Mitchell's 'wheeling and dealing' on unproductive lease-in-perpetuity land was behind this expansion. His intensive negotiations opened up deals for the acquisition of land that previously could only be swapped or have boundaries adjusted.[195] Purchases included the whole catchment above Wharehunga and the 'gem' of Mistletoe Bay; in the late 1970s Lands and Survey agreed to the Titirangi purchase whose long sandy beach, recreational potential and ease of access to the outer sound made it perhaps the most important purchase Mitchell's board recommended.[196]

The board relied on Lands and Survey to survey these holdings. Post-purchase, as everywhere else in the country, the Forest Service carried out pest control. The board also worked with the Wildlife Service, becoming 'almost a taxi service' in getting Wildlife staff to the islands. It benefited enormously, too, from the work of Kerry Johnson, a widely skilled local and chief ranger, a man 'whom you couldn't help liking', who was respected locally and who helped create a climate of partnership

St Omer House, tennis court, and beach, Kenepuru Sound, c. 1923–28. The dinghies, for rowing or local fishing, the long, sandy beaches bordering the relatively warm sea, and the tennis court all helped draw guests back year after year. ALEXANDER TURNBULL LIBRARY, PAN-1723-F

and goodwill.[197] Mitchell recalled that board members, although unpaid, were hard-working locals of considerable integrity, who were 'devoted to enhancing the Sounds' and put in their own machinery and resources to achieve that.

In 1976 a Lands and Survey-led consultative process produced what would become known as *The Strategy for the Conservation and Development of the Marlborough Sounds*. The first of its kind in New Zealand, it sought 'the balanced use and protection [of the Sounds'] sea and coast as a public domain'.[198] Judgements on the strategy's success or otherwise in resolving tensions between commercial exploitation and protection imperatives lay in the future — and that future would change dramatically when, in 1987, the Maritime Park Board was disestablished and a new Department of Conservation, replacing the Department of Lands and Survey, was charged with conserving and protecting all Crown land.

'Marlborough the Golden'

Early September 1920. 'Goodbye, Marlborough the Golden,' shouted Captain Euan Dickson amidst intense excitement and above 'the song of the exhaust'. His historic first flight across Cook Strait completed, he and his 'Avro machine' were on their way back to Christchurch.[199] Within just over a decade, aero club members (significant players in the development of New Zealand's aviation industry) were calculating how cheap holiday flights could reach the Sounds from Wellington within the hour; what were the 30–40 minutes needed to reach Manaroa or Waitaria where a landing strip could be (and was) developed, when it took eight or nine hours to get there by boat?[200] Additionally, in 1926 the comfortable and fast *Tamahine*, 'one of the latest examples of British naval architecture', began her daily dedicated Wellington–Picton service.[201] Well-subscribed Sounds excursions on the *Tamahine, Wahine, Marama* or the even faster, innovatively designed *Rangatira*, able to carry 600 passengers, remained good copy into the 1940s.[202]

The arrival of *Aramoana* in 1962 revolutionised Cook Strait crossings. The completion of the Picton–Christchurch railway in 1945 had created an opportunity to develop a rail ferry to compete with conventional shipping. Yet the Union Steamship Company failed to replace the ageing *Tamahine*. When, in 1958, the Cook Strait Transport Enquiry Committee determined that a roll-on-roll-off ferry (to take train carriages) was the best option, the company had no interest in building or operating such a service. So the government commissioned and built the ship, and, to ensure sufficient and adequately experienced officers and crew, contracted Union Steamship to operate the service. (New Zealand Railways and its subsequent iterations took over the service in 1971.)

The new service was a revelation. The 'near-seamless link in the national railway and road network' experienced none of the delays or double-handling associated with the earlier ships. The *Aramoana* was followed in quick succession by the *Aranui* (1965–84), *Arahura* (significantly bigger, purchased 1983), *Arahanga* (a largely cargo ferry, 1972–2001) and *Aratika* (1974–99). Railways' success was partly a matter of timing — they were bulk people carriers operating before the massive discounting of airline tickets. Being first also created a considerable competitive advantage. Union Steamship's attempt to develop a roll-on-roll-off service with the *Wanaka* and *Hawea* did not last a decade.[203]

IN 1936 THE OLD ATTRACTIONS of the Sounds still held. There one found a landscape 'of primaeval forces, where Man, in his scattered homes in the darkness [of Tory Channel] seems but a puny thing in these fastnesses' . . . the 'solitary figure by the wharf or on the beach as the vessel approaches . . . looks pygmy against the steep, towering background, the fickly, uncertain foreground'.[204]

Eleven-kilogram snapper could be caught; eerily beautiful 180- to 220-kg stingrays could be scattered by throwing stones into the water. The Sounds' '[h]alycon days . . . in the beautiful bush-clad districts' were 'something different' from the ordinary holiday.[205]

Tourists came, even if not always in the numbers the local Chamber of Commerce wished for. Toc H, the international Christian organisation, began holding annual camps, mostly at Resolution Bay where the cottages lasted long after the organisation's visits ceased. During World War II petrol and travel restrictions made holidaying in the Sounds highly attractive; postwar, the Youth Travel Association was not alone in discovering the educational and social values of Sounds' holidays, along with reasonable prices.

Labelled only 'Dorothy and her snappers', this photo shows why the Sounds was such a popular fishing destination. JOHN PASCOE, ALEXANDER TURNBULL LIBRARY, PA1-O-1308-58

From the early 1920s, trampers further explored the Sounds, with ever-greater numbers after the war ended. Some 500 people walked from Northwest Bay to the junction of the Nydia Bay–Tennyson Inlet track in 1949 — 'a good summer use'.[206] By the mid-1960s a growing network of tracks opened up prospects of better tramping. The hundreds of walkers through during the 1967–68 summer encouraged D. B. Brown at the Resolution Bay Boatel to enlist voluntary workers to open up the old Resolution Bay/Endeavour Inlet track. (Locals had already, with Lands and Survey's permission, cleared the Resolution Bay/Ship Cove track.)

The Marlborough County Council was forming a track from Camp Bay to Okoha Saddle. With the three reserves boards interested, aspirations grew. In May 1968 Chief surveyor Trevor Thomas Bright discussed plans for a network of tracks over whole area of Okoha, Titirangi, Port Gore, Cannibal Cove, Ship Cove, Resolution Bay and Endeavour Inlet, with buildings to provide overnight accommodation.[207] Plans to extend the old Nydia Bay track from Tennyson Inlet to Kaiuma[208] and the development of a multimillion-dollar industry around the 71-kilometre Queen Charlotte Sound track were still to come.

An unprecedented eight yachts anchored in Cockle Cove in 1930. As the yachting fraternity grew, the Waikawa, Mana and Pelorus boating clubs were established over the next 40 years. From the early 1970s, lighter gear and young, enthusiastic parents increasingly made family boating a reality. Better yachting facilities helped.

The Marlborough Harbour Board was formed in 1958. Within 10 years, as 'a wealthy Local Body deriving a steady income from the NZ Railway operated ferries', it helped develop a new modern marina at Picton and built 'extensive boatsheds at Picton itself'.[209] The long-awaited harbour board marina at Waikawa (about which Māori had rather different views) was finally completed on 7 October 1988.[210]

Over time, the rough and ready facilities and swing pile moorings at Havelock were transformed. Wharf amenities were upgraded in the 1950s, and periodic dredging meant that the passage was no longer dependent on launch propellors digging out the channel. In 1966, reflecting the general trend towards amalgamation of small local bodies throughout the country, the Havelock Harbour Board merged with the Marlborough Harbour Board. In 1970, after considerable local pressure, further dredging ensured the wharf was useable at all tides. Better channel markers were put in over the next decade or so, and in the marina in the early 1980s the wooden pontoons secured to old mussel buoys and floating at all tides were installed, presaging today's high-quality recreational and industry facilities.[211]

Tourist reading a map, 1945. The sea was not the only drawcard for recreation, with many exploring the bush-clad hills and enjoying the spectacular views. JOHN PASCOE, ALEXANDER TURNBULL LIBRARY, PACOLL-5926-50

With the marina, locals and boaties from Wellington, Christchurch and as far south as Dunedin had accessible, secure boating facilities and ready access to the Sounds or to the more distant waters of the Chetwodes, Rangitotos and D'Urville Island. By 1965 the first of the club moorings that now dot the Sounds were laid in Hitaua Bay and Charlies Bight, where deep water close to the shore made anchoring challenging;[212] annual cruises and picnics helped build members' knowledge of their sailing grounds in a supportive and informed environment.

Clubs, too, kept their members informed of new developments such as the prohibition on dumping rubbish at sea in the early 1980s. In 1979 Keith Murray and Baron Ralph von Kohorn, vice-commodore and former commodore respectively of the Mana Cruising Club, published the authoritative *A Cruising Man's Guide to the Marlborough Sounds and Tasman Bay*. Even as the groundwork for a larger boating fraternity was being laid, older generations were returning year after year with the next, slipping (or battling against katabatic gusts) into favoured bays. Their occupation was temporary and intermittent, but they, like the earlier settlers, were building intergenerational memories, associations and emotional responses about the world into which they were privileged to be moving.

BOAT-BUILDING VENTURES CONTINUED TO PROVIDE boats and services. At Whakatahuri, Claude Wells continued building boats until 1950.[213] In his later years, and until he died in November 1949, Picton's Ernie Lane crafted dinghies (though not larger boats).[214] After World War II, Peter Jorgensen, a sponsored immigrant, launched what has become a very successful intergenerational boat-building business at Snake Point in Queen Charlotte Sound that he later moved to Picton.[215] About the same time qualified boat-builder Cyril Carey established his yard in Picton, and from around 1944 until 1958 Ted Swanson at Tahuahua built 17 boats, many with his characteristic hull, and maintained, remodelled and repaired others. After his death in 1958 his son took the business to Picton.[216] Until the end of the 1990s Harold Saunders, in Jacksons Bay, built a lot of boats, many of them still around.[217]

From about 1946 until at least the late 1970s, and alongside their meagre livings from fishing, boat repair and engineering, the resourceful, individualistic and 'non-conformist' Allan (known as Francis) and Tom Wells (Claude's sons) set up the Sounds Wrecking Company, their unregistered ship-breaking business in Whakatahuri, a bay with

> a stony beach . . . littered with rusty iron and nonferrous metals . . . and chandlery strewn all over the place . . . Ships might remain anchored off the bay . . . until remembered as containing some needed fitting. Or they might be used as bulk storage for scrap metal until they too were torched or in other ways became useful.[218]

After the kauri hull and fittings were taken from the three-masted scow *Southern Isle* (83 tonnes), the remains of her hull were used for foreshore control at Whakatahuri. The operation was remote and out of sight of officialdom; the Wells brothers' somewhat unorthodox deals put them only just on the right side of the law.

AFTER THE WAR, FAMILIES COULD again dream of building a bach, and farmers were happy to sell considerable tracts of unprofitable land for subdivision. Developers' expectations were high. F. E. Musgrove, envisaging a modern hotel and subdivisions that catered for over 1400 families, in 1945 bought up a chunk of land in Queen Charlotte Sound that stretched 13 kilometres from Karaka Point to Curious Cove.[219] A year later, the erstwhile air force convalescent camp at Curious Cove and its 33 hectares offering 50 'high-priced residential sections' was on the market.[220] By the early 1960s baches were 'really mushrooming', particularly in the more easily accessible Queen Charlotte Sound. The 20 baches in the Bay of Many Coves in 1952 had more than doubled by 1963 and more were going up all the time, apparently in a rush to get in before the impending district scheme could impose any restrictions, and before any more government purchases for reserves.[221]

Growing up in New Zealand's relatively egalitarian environment of the 1950s, some believed that the Sounds baches were the prerogative of the rich. Yet there was nothing fancy about most of these dwellings — boathouses doubling as living spaces, tents providing additional accommodation, indoor or outdoor cooking depending on the weather, and washing up requiring tank water to be heated. Kerosene lamps hung from walls, the kerosene tins made excellent buckets. Butter was cooled in creeks or in safes set into cliffs, meat-safes hung in trees, lavatories were long-drops or large buckets filled with chemicals that were emptied in specially dug holes or carried out into the Sound. Families swam, fished, collected mussels, boated, or joined in the life of the little holiday communities that were developing, and to which they returned year after year, often generation after generation.

Day boat tours or longer excursions for the casual tourist had long been on offer. The Depression slowed the pace of cruising holidays, but in January 1934 the 815 people away in one fortnight suggests that purse strings were being loosened. For those wanting longer stays, professionally produced printed brochures offered 'standing canvas camps'. Here 'the joys of camping [came] with none of the drawbacks . . . Fairylands to roam in . . . FUN for everyone.' Guests needed to bring only blankets, sheets and towels.[222] The Curious Cove holiday camp was established in 1945. In 1950 A. C. Manning turned its somewhat pokey little cabins and hall into the still-operating resort where, in the 1950s and 1960s, university students held their annual student congress. Harry Heberley's Te Pangu Fishing Lodge in Tory Channel was 'a gem in the blue'.[223] In the early 1960s, in Queen Charlotte Sound, Robert and Colleen Gilkinson developed The Gem Resort and offered cheap and cheerful accommodation.

Farmers' guesthouses in Queen Charlotte Sound, Tory Channel and Kenepuru from the 1920s to the 1950s (20 places were operating in Pelorus and associated sounds)[224] further developed that unique Sounds attraction. Many guests booked year after year for the same period, to meet up with the same group of people and, from the Godsiffs' St Omer House, to depart to the same haka and the emotional strains of 'Now is the Hour'.[225]

These places were initially developed to offset falling farm incomes. Even if profits were negligible,[226] a few accommodation houses would go on to become the mainstay of some farmers.[227] At St Omer, modest facilities were, over time, upgraded. Apart from the occasional weka stew, the early plain and unadventurous fare reflected typical New Zealand tastes. Menus broadened from the mid-1970s on to include the fancy new coq au vin or lamb cassoulet.

St Omer guests could swim, read, walk and mess about in boats. Fishing excursions, moonlight picnics (very popular), sightseeing trips to Havelock and Pelorus Bridge were organised, and the evenings were filled with enthusiastic conviviality. Music came from one communal battery-powered radio; board games and cards or the latest dances (and hairdos) were highly popular. Ping-pong (table tennis) was introduced, singing could be risqué — 'As soon as I touched my seaweed, I knew it was going to be wet' was long a favourite; men's ballet, in decorative toilet-paper tutus, sprang across the stage.[228]

The staff, often daughters of friends, enjoyed the sociability as well as gaining employment, good training and valuable work experience.[229] However, by the 1950s

ABOVE A bach at Lochmara Bay, Grove Arm, in 1948. This was typical of baches in the Sounds (and throughout New Zealand), until the 'MacMansioning' of the 1990s saw large, ostentatiously expensive homes being built in the Sounds and many older places improved to realise today's expectations of a holiday home. PICTON HERITAGE AND WHALING MUSEUM, COURTESY PICTON HISTORICAL SOCIETY

BELOW 'Off on a holiday cruise at Pelorus Sound', probably in the 1930s. MARLBOROUGH HISTORICAL SOCIETY, 0000.200.10

Baden Ewart's Momorangi Bay Store, which he ran through the 1950s and early 1960s. Ewart also drove the County Council grader. PICTON HERITAGE AND WHALING MUSEUM, COURTESY PICTON HISTORICAL SOCIETY

the country's increasing economic prosperity provided a challenge. Motels, boosted by growing car ownership, started to dot the country (Picton's first arrived in 1951 or 1952).[230]

Tourist expectations appeared to be changing. There was too little 'de luxe' accommodation, one official thought in 1954, and the guesthouses sported too many small, sometimes dark rooms that needed a paint, antiquated furniture, insufficient single rooms and pebbly beaches.[231] Like the few 'boatels' built in the 1960s in Queen Charlotte Sound, the accommodation houses faced challenges on all fronts. Their income over the traditionally limited holiday period precluded large amounts of capital development. Well-established guesthouses like St Omer House and Raetihi Lodge continued to attract the numbers, but the boom in the Sounds' tourist accommodation houses did not last into the 1970s.[232]

Other sources of income could be gained from tourism, however. From the 1920s Picton businesses began to organise themselves for holiday services, dispatching weekly orders to baches. Farmers delivered milk or vegetables; bach-owners took delivery in their dinghies or waded out.[233] The annual brochure *Pelorus Sound, New Zealand's Playground*, which listed the attractions and transport on offer, was updated and reprinted into the 1950s to help visitors negotiate their way through and around the little-roaded Sounds. Bigger, faster, better launches catered for Sounds' tourists and passengers.[234] Mail launches and various other launch services took passengers to the 'real beauty spots such as Worlds End'. The popular and informative drivers were accomplished at jacking up accommodation and providing that valued ingredient of New Zealand holidays: the opportunity to get chummy with the locals.

The Outward Bound School built on the old Beauchamp property at Anakiwa in 1962 brought more welcome publicity. Established on somewhat militaristic lines to foster self-reliance and self-discipline among the nation's young men (women were admitted a decade later), the school was long associated with the popular, sporting (and homophobic) Governor-General Lord Cobham, who spearheaded its establishment.[235] Photos, films and news reports created broad interest. Participants from varying backgrounds lived in 'pioneer conditions'.[236] The National Film Unit's widely shown *Pictorial Parade No. 135* beautifully depicted the landscape as the attendees tramped, swam or plied, with greater or lesser skill, up and down Queen Charlotte Sound in the school's elegant whaleboats.

New ventures and conflicting priorities

During the 1970s three further developments had the potential to impact considerably on the Sounds' landscape and its commercial exploitation. And a significant and broad public debate around the co-existence of commercial development and conservation began.

There is a certain irony that the Harvey mill closed just as pines were again being planted in parts of the Sounds. In the early 1920s, New Zealand had shared in the long-held international concerns about a timber famine. Perceiving a 'rapidly diminishing native forest resource', the Director of the Forest Service, MacIntosh Ellis, ambitiously planned for large-scale planting of exotics to ensure that New Zealand was self-sufficient in wood.[237] From about 1925 to 1935, after Forest Service inspection and speculation on commercially viable afforestation in the Sounds that would provide beauty with profit,[238] some 12,355 acres (5000 ha) were planted, mostly with *Pinus radiata*.[239]

In 1935 round-the-world yachtsman Francis Chichester and Geoffrey Goodwin, partners in planting pines and real estate in Upper Hutt, planted Farnham Forest — 600 acres (242 ha) of *Pinus radiata* on Snake Point, Queen Charlotte Sound. In the late 1930s a further burst of interest in afforesting the Sounds' denuded hills was accompanied by visions of aerial sowing, hills clad in exotic forest, erosion control and commercial milling.[240]

However, the various proposals spawned for Crown land that locals advanced lacked the scale and commitment the Forest Service had hoped for,[241] and by the mid- to late 1940s it had concluded that most of the Sounds land was unsuited to forestry.[242] In the early 1950s local bodies and various speakers (the Harveys among them) at Federated Farmers meetings encouraged farmers to plant cooperatively and extensively, but only five plantations eventuated.[243]

Those were planted by locals presumably envisaging profit and local employment. But during the Forest Service's second planting boom in the early 1960s the Service began thinking about planting big forests in the Sounds.[244] Whether permanent residents might have any role in these big forests planted and harvested by outside contractors is a matter of speculation. Then, in January 1971 the owners of Farnham Forest on Snake Point had the timber cut — without a permit.

Bay of Many Coves' residents (mostly bach-owners) formed the Bay of Many Coves Environmental Association, to protest against the cutting.[245] They did not want

Miss Pelorus on the mail run, 1970s, while a small child messes about in a boat, unencumbered by parental anxieties. ALEXANDER TURNBULL LIBRARY, PA12-5560-153

logs gouging their way down slopes or bark choking their beaches and ruining the fishing and scallop beds for years.[246] Also, exotic afforestation, the association argued, created erosion when the steep slopes were clear-felled; escaped 'sinkers' from the rafts of logs being towed into Picton were dangerous to big and small craft, commercial and recreational vessels alike. There was noise, the 'barren and unattractive' forests changed the Sounds' aesthetics; and 'wilding pines' were seeding themselves all over the Sound.[247]

The issues were complex, involving rules around subdivision, zoning and water classification, logging-out methods, road access, how recreation was managed where the coastline was in private ownership, and water pollution.[248] With planning in vogue from the 1950s, a coordinated approach was the logical way to resolve the issues, but the Marlborough County Council had no district plan. In its absence, and under a new director who was promoting forestry all over the country, regardless of its impact, the Forest Service concluded in 1974 that exotic forestry should be an 'important factor' in the Sounds' future development. (Education and cooperation, they suggested, would get the public alongside.)[249]

By then over $1 million worth of Forestry Encouragement loans made available under the Forestry Encouragement Act 1962 had enabled big forestry companies to buy up thousands of acres.[250] The Forest Service was also exploring how to get more land designated as suitable for commercial forestry.

The Department of Lands and Survey, which was buying available land for reserves and wanting such acquisitions to continue,[251] reached an agreement with the Forest Service: the northern side of Queen Charlotte Sound would be left to revert to bush, while forestry could take place on the sound's southern side, on Arapaoa Island and in Tory Channel.[252] Work on implementing this scheme began in Tory Channel in early 1975; the pines were planted by midwinter.[253]

About then, too, a Forest Service proposal to plant exotics from Port Underwood to D'Urville Island became widely known. Research strongly criticised the proposal,[254] and the opposition from bach owners and other individuals, the Nature Conservation Council, the Wildlife Service, Forest & Bird and the Bay of Many Coves Environmental Association was so considerable that an inquiry was established.[255]

The scheme did not go ahead. But the opposition then and earlier signalled a new environment. *The Strategy for the Conservation and Development of the Marlborough Sounds* was published by the Ministry of Works and Development in 1977. Treating the Sounds as 'an integral area', it suggested ways to accommodate 'the different types of land and water management ensuring that natural, cultural and recreational values are conserved and enhanced while also providing for viable commercial forestry, fishing and marine farming and the welfare of the Sounds permanent population'.[256] Native forest and regenerating bush were to be preserved, the high conservation values of visually prominent headlands and coves were to be recognised.[257]

And yet within the year, almost half of the total area of the Sounds had been identified as suitable for commercial planting,[258] and further, even more ambitious plans were in the offing.[259] That third wave of new settlers were not afraid to inject their voices and values into the debate around conservation and commercial exploitation. By the early 1970s, this was extending into issues of aquaculture.

'WORLD'S FASTEST-GROWING MUSSELS ARE IN the Sounds,' the *Marlborough Express* told its readers on 12 August 1969. The Sounds' sheltered, clean waters provided good nutrition and both the blue and green mussels reached maturity in a year. Investment was already flourishing but, as more mussel farms were established, environmental issues were coming to the fore.

Māori, as well as later Sounds settlers had long picked the New Zealand green-lipped mussel *Perna canaliculus*, the Mediterranean blue mussel (*Mylitus galloprovincialis*), the fan mussel (*Pinnidae*) and the horse mussel (*Atrina zelandica*) — for food or profit. A small number of mussels were first harvested commercially in the Tasman/Marlborough area in 1958.[260] Four years later the green-lipped mussels (neither blue nor horse mussels have been grown commercially) were dredged for the first time. As the dredges ploughed through the mussel grounds, they harrowed the 'crust' of mussels from their anchors in the mud bottom, irreparably damaging the beds.[261]

In 1969 the mussel beds in the Hauraki Gulf, well appreciated by Auckland's Greek community among others, were dwindling, victims of over-dredging.[262] Attention focused on the Sounds and Tasman Bay. By 1968 up to 11 boats, mostly from Nelson, were dredging there. Landings rose from 3.5 tonnes in 1962 to 392 tonnes in 1968.[263] Regulations failed to prevent the exploitative harrowing and the beds' inevitable collapse.[264] By 1969 only 350 hectares of mussel beds remained, mostly in inner Pelorus, Kenepuru Sound and Hikapu Reach. In many of the beds the mussels were small or undersized.[265]

Hand-picking would continue well into the 1970s.[266] However, in 1968, inspired by harvests at Vigo, Galicia, in Spain (that 'Mecca for mussel-farming'), the Associated Fishermen of Nelson (briefly) and the Fisheries Industry Board (in it for the long term) sponsored ground-breaking research by PhD students David Flaws and Philip Tortell, who were studying under Victoria University of Wellington marine biologist Dr Richard Bevis Pike. In various bays in Pelorus Sound over 1971–72, large rafts were set up with rope long-lines suspended below them and the researchers began looking at how to get mussel spat to settle on the ropes.[267]

By the early 1970s seven applications for mussel farms were awaiting Marine Department decisions, initially in Kenepuru and later in Pelorus and Queen Charlotte sounds.[268] But fouling organisms were as keen as the mussels to attach themselves to the long-lines beneath the rafts. It took further research to discover that black polypropylene rope (developed as a substitute for No. 8 fencing wire but rejected by farmers) attracted only mussels and not other unintended and unwanted organisms. The mussels particularly liked fibrous, fraying rope ends, and Tortell's 'Christmas tree' rope with crosspieces of the same material 'proved highly successful as a collector of mussel spat'.[269]

However, reseeding the ropes from naturally occurring spat gave unpredictable harvests. Because no one knew when mussel larvae were in the water, settlement varied between years. Attaching locally found larvae in onion bags was labour intensive and costly. The problem was partly resolved in 1974 when abundant mussel spat attached to seaweed was found on Ninety Mile Beach, Northland.[270] Spat was air-freighted to Marlborough by the bucketful. But the critical question of how to encourage it to attach to the ropes remained. In 1978 it was found that cheap tubing made from biodegradable cotton fabric would protect the immature mussels. Seeding contractors set themselves up. When in August that year the 'first purpose-built mechanical harvester plucked mussels from the long-lines at a rate of five tonnes a day', it was a 'quantum leap forward'.[271]

The local response was enthusiastic. In the early 1970s retirees had begun to sink their savings into industry, and such investment would continue into the following decades as farmers sought to diversify and supplement income sources. By 1972, the numbers of 'substantial rafts . . . in bays fronting Scenic Reserves' in Pelorus and Charlotte Sounds and Tory Channel were increasing.[272]

Once again, however, a changing environment meant that what would once have been an acceptable development had to face questions relating to sustainability and environmental degradation. Lands and Survey worried about haphazard development of farms 'whose nature was not fully spelt out and the impact of whose harvesting techniques were not identified',[273] their impact on 'holiday values' and on what we now term visual pollution.[274] The various Sounds scenic boards worried that the provisions of the Marine Farming Act 1971 were being deliberately circumvented.[275]

However, the Ministry of Transport, the licensing body, refused to address these objections. It firmly maintained that its interest only extended to safeguarding the 'freedom and safety of navigation' and ensuring the rafts' strength, the adequacy of their moorings, and navigational warnings.[276]

With so many competing interests expressing their views, the waters became well and truly muddied. *The Strategy for Conservation* had provided that mussel farms had be away from good anchorages and beaches, but what did that actually mean?[277]

Lands and Survey continued trying to balance the reserves' scenic and recreational values against commercial development.[278] At times their decisions reflected the situation of the time;[279] later, as a plethora of government and local bodies became involved, 'a random mix of decisions' too often resulted in undesirable outcomes.[280]

As boaties and bach owners watched rafts being moored around the coastline and plans for significant expansion were notified, strong feelings about the future of the Sounds would be voiced by people concerned with safety and conservation, and who wanted a different world from that in which commercial expansion was the only priority.

9. Towards the New Century

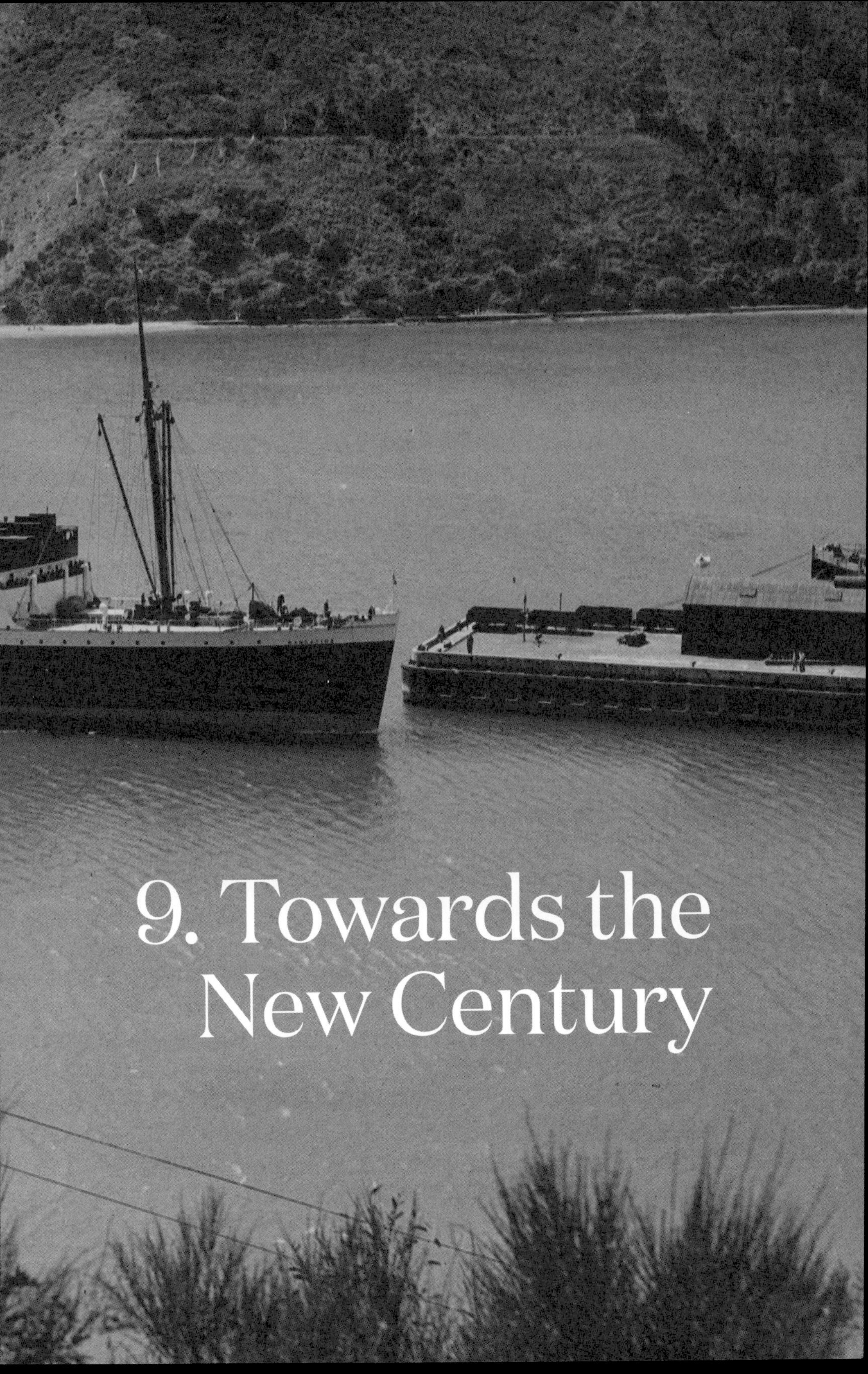

> 'Absolute freedom, and independence, total independence . . . If I need to go somewhere, I can get in the car and go . . .'

HARRY CHRISTIAN, LIVING AT TE RAWA from around the 1920s, had no wish to leave. Mail arrived twice weekly, the news more promptly by radio, there was fishing and 'sea-bathing', the Sounds' 'luxurious' climate grew grapes, oranges and lemons. Services supplied by plane would, he thought, only increase as aviation took off. All that was needed was a deep-water port at Te Puru for the summer's tourists. Then, with reasonable boosting to realise their unlimited potential, the Sounds would become 'the Honolulu' for Wellingtonians.[1]

Others might have found that idyll less easy to imagine. As in isolated areas elsewhere, the hard work demanded for the initial Pākehā settlement in the Sounds continued. Growing up in the 1930s and 1940s, Nola Leov saw her family putting 'everything they had into it' to survive — or do a little better than surviving.[2] Not for nothing did John Harvey, great-grandson of the first European settlers in Pelorus, entitle his memoir *Where There's a Will There's a Way*. The situations that sprinkle Shirley Buckland's lively recollections of Sounds life from the mid-1930s into the 1980s demonstrate that determination, resilience and ironic humour remained critical ingredients of permanent Sounds residence.

The isolation in which Nola Leov had grown up and which had left her thinking that Sounds children grew up in a 'closed, very badly off community' continued decades into her adulthood.[3] When Debbie Moleta arrived at Waitui in the outer Pelorus in 1981 the isolation, and the frugality and constant care required with money, made her feel as if she 'had gone back in time'. Old appliances and old domestic patterns persisted well after they might have in urban areas.[4] Yet there were changes. Houses were improved and mod cons helped, schooling and medical services became more accessible, the advent of roads down to Titirangi (the last finished in 1979) made the wider world accessible in a way that the earlier settlers had not experienced. Life became easier. If they had to leave, Sounds residents, richly and intimately knowledgeable about the extraordinary world in which they lived, found that it took them years to get over the departure.

IN 1928 THE LEOV FAMILY house at Te Towaka was in a 'shocking' state. Built only a couple of decades before, its inferior materials were so riddled with borer that Mrs Leov's sewing machine once sank through the floor. The roof leaked extensively, the windows did not shut properly. The only form of heating was the usual wetback wood stove. While this was effective if you stood near, no one at the time heated more than a single room. 'If you felt cold, you put on more clothes or blankets,' Nola recalled. There was a bucket toilet. Light was provided by two kerosene lamps and candles.

Some houses were better built and, from 1932, the first Pelton wheel in the Sounds powered not just one but two family homes.[5] But almost everyone lived in much the same circumstances,[6] and those circumstances were reflected, in varying degrees, throughout the country's housing stock at the time.[7]

Over the decades from the 1930s, better homes, electric power, improved health services and education provision made Sounds life easier. Harold Leov, after about 1935, 'when wool prices took a little leap for the better', installed a flush toilet.[8] Hylton Harvey's house on the other hand, built in the mid-1940s when he had little money, had no such luxury. For the first year there was no money for a water pipe so the daily ration was fetched, a four-gallon tin at a time, from the creek 20 metres below the house and poured into a 44-gallon drum on the roof.[9] In the 1950s many families were still rinsing their washing in nearby creeks.[10]

Electricity arrived, in one form or another, but not quickly enough for some. Pelton wheels installed in convenient streams from the 1930s were creating sufficient electricity to run small shearing plants and homes,[11] though people switched to candles in the late evenings. The Depression, then the war, stymied government attempts to push reticulated power right around the country; even in late 1967, after years of representation and 'agitation', much of the Sounds was still 'a no-man's land electrically'.[12] The 150 or so permanent residents depended on fuel-hungry diesel or petrol generators.

The difficulty was the problem posed by the holiday baches. As in other rural areas, those wanting electricity had to pay for an agreed amount of use; reticulation costs would then be shared between the Marlborough Electric Power Board and users. But bach owners, who were 'by far the largest number of possible electricity users', were designated minimal users and were thought unlikely to agree to the costs, which they would likely consider high for their limited use. (Though there is no record of the Marlborough Board being asked, power boards had by then a lot of experience of unneighbourly disputes over such matters.) Many parts of the Sounds, particularly in Queen Charlotte Sound, were not therefore included in the reticulation scheme.[13]

However, on 31 January 1966 an order-in-council brought the unreticulated area of the Sounds under the control of the Marlborough Electric Power Board. The board got a firm commitment on cost sharing from the Rural Electrical Reticulation Council, a body that could grant funding in situations where the intending subscribers were being asked to accept prices that were too high for them.[14] Over the next 20 years power was slowly extended throughout the Sounds. Many baches, built to take advantage of shelter, sun and seclusion, were hard to link up; concerns about the aesthetics of the placement of power lines and other legislative requirements had to be resolved. Occasionally a helicopter was necessary in more challenging terrain, which added expense. In 1973, at a time when local bodies or central government generally absorbed such costs, bach owners were asked to pay for the power line to be extended from the Elaine Bay substation to Tennyson Inlet. The Marlborough Electric Power Board had exhausted its funds.[15]

Further developments in infrastructure

'Minister praises Sounds settlers' self-help' proclaimed the *Marlborough Express* on 15 May 1972, two days after the final major road to be built in the Sounds — a road. R. J. Paterson had first advocated for in 1956 — was completed. Serving only a few families, the road ran for 22.5 kilometres from Kenepuru Heads to Titirangi Saddle, connecting farms in Waitui and Guard Bays to the country's roading system.[16] It climbed from sea level to 701 metres, at times cutting through reserves.

The Patersons, over a number of years, had worked out the line of the road. Even so, its construction was dogged by issues. Because there were no local rates, local contributions were expected, and in the end the Paterson family paid the entire local cost of $13,000; they knew that the settlers had to be seen to be helping themselves in order to attract funding from the minister's discretionary Assistance to Isolated Settlers Fund. A detailed case also had to be made, taking into account government policy. The Patersons argued the deleterious effects of distance, sea travel and associated freight, the need for topdressing, labour and high costs of farm production, and the tourism potential of the area.[17]

Why was it so difficult? We have already seen that Sounds development was held back in many ways because for so long there was no rates collection body that could assume responsibility for infrastructure. Instead, the Sounds Branch of Federated Farmers, working to a mandate from its members, 'handled any problem in the area' — be it goat, pig or weed control or roading proposals. Where a mandate was not forthcoming, initiatives lapsed.[18]

In relation to roads, from the 1920s to the 1950s years went into negotiating government subsidies, generally on a £1 for £1 basis. PWD policy was to construct and improve roads only for settlement purposes;[19] money for maintenance was not willingly granted.[20] Settler benefits and costs were carefully scrutinised and officials were ever wary of creating precedents.[21] Occasionally, where tourist interests were identified, the Tourist Department would represent the Sounds settlers' or Kenepuru Road Board's interests or give a grant.[22]

Only in 1965, when the old Sounds County, the Kenepuru Road Board and the French Pass Road Board merged into the Marlborough County Council, did a local body covering the whole area emerge.

Four factors conjoined to bring roads to the Sounds in the early 1950s. The Marginal Lands Act 1950 exemplified a new focus on primary production and developing and improving marginal lands. In its 1951 election policy, too, the Holland government called for 'modern tourist services to tourist resorts' and for the '[c]ompletion of roads giving access to scenic attractions'.[23]

Second, even as postwar shortages remained, booming wool prices meant that New Zealand was better placed to catch up on the backlog of construction work, including its public roads.

Third, particularly in parts of Kenepuru and Pelorus, a number of farmers could afford to invest in bulldozers, in which they (or their sons) pushed out farm access roads. Others hired in bulldozers. (The skills gained here would often be used in creating feeder roads to a main route. Today, on the French Pass road, these are public roads providing access to various bays.)[24]

On 12 November 1952 the French Pass Road Board, chaired by Harold Leov, won a government grant from the Minister of Works' discretionary Assistance to Isolated Settlers Fund to build a road from Okiwi Bay to French Pass. Pushed by board member Alan Woodman, the road board had levied 'an annual rate of ¼ of a penny in the pound on the capital value of properties in the district'. Stan Goosman, a former roads contractor and Minister of Works, had been impressed with the settlers' willingness to help with construction. The £80,000 (a nine-to-one subsidy) was an unparalleled amount for those used to rather stingier handouts.[25]

The road was finished in July 1957, exactly 100 years after Arthur Elmslie, the first European settler in the district, had settled at French Pass. The feeder roads to Elaine Bay and Deep Bay went in later. In 1955 the board was focused on developing roads on D'Urville Island and out to Bulwer (what became known as the Te Towaka–Port Ligar road). This, funded in part by John Shand's contribution of £300 towards the local share of the costs, was opened on 9 August 1968 (initially with a farm road leading down to Port Ligar itself and later extended to Bulwer).[26] These roads would be progressively upgraded.

The fourth factor that helped realise roads in the Sounds was that officials began to realise the area's tourism potential. From that point on, roading grants (slowly and cautiously) began to be approved. In November 1946 and in 1954, further subsidies were ticked off for the Torea–Portage road, 'the main route for settlers and the travelling public'.[27] From 1957 to 1969 successive sections of the standard 3.6-metre-wide Ohinagaro–Kenepuru Heads road won subsidies, opening up 'all the internal roading within the Kenepuru Road District'.[28] But even in the new funding environment, each proposal was carefully considered in terms of numbers and size of farming operations likely to benefit, and the funding of public roads as against feeder roads developed by private contractors was carefully demarcated.[29]

However, even in this climate, not all infrastructure proposals went ahead. In the mid-1940s to early 1950s, local farmers' plans to cut through Piripāua Neck and build the Onahau Cut created a temporary distraction. Their unwillingness to contribute to the expensive Piripāua Cut ended that project about 1950, some two years after it had been revived.

The Onahau Cut fared only marginally better. Federated Farmers gave it a boost in December 1949: might this tunnel not be one way to help rectify the drop in production from the wars and slumps, and the isolation that was keeping the young away? 'We ask for British fairplay, after nearly 100 years of toil and sweat. We have played our part.'[30]

Local perceptions of government obligations to provide, appeals to the value of the tunnel to yachtsmen's wives (who liked only calm water) and similarly not-always-accurate statistics saw a committee of inquiry set up in 1949, but a cost–benefit analysis did not support the project.[31]

Roading, however, as in the past, continued to be a valuable source of local income. John Harvey contracted to the Kenepuru Road Board during the mill's downtime to pay off both his roading and his milling equipment. He worked on the roads in the late 1950s, cutting back to 3 metres in the solid ('you couldn't count any fill on the outside edges'; it had to be solid ground underneath on the Manaroa–Waitaria and the Crail Bay–Eli Bay roads, and blasting through rock to create a four-wheel-drive road on the Waitaria Hill. He also opened up a number of 'well-graded' bridle tracks made over 50 years before.[32] Harvey recalled:

> There's quite a lot besides just making a road. You've got to get all the culverts in, trim all the banks, keep everything tidy. A young man used to come in and help with all those sorts of jobs. You wouldn't read about it today, but he used to go along the top, trimming all the banks by hand because it was a lot quicker than me doing it, fiddling around trying to do a neat job [with the blade]. Peter North, he was.[33]

These were back-country roads, built to lower specifications than might otherwise have been used.[34] When, within a few years, some of the Kenepuru roads were assessed for use as bus routes, officials visiting the area were amazed that they had been considered safe for school transport. '[T]hey are extremely narrow and winding; the surface has little or no metal . . . a shower of rain is sufficient to create a hazard for conventional type vehicles', the Education Department transport manager reported in 1967. The Waitaria–Nopera Bay road was 'incomplete' and his vehicle had had to be left about a mile short of the school.

A local resident advised him not to use his car to get into Manaroa, so he was driven the 5.6 kilometres between Manaroa and Waitaria Bay School in a locally

A 1971 view of the French Pass road, which had finally reached its destination only 15 years earlier, showing a north-east-bound tide surging through the pass. The photo illustrates the steep terrain up which any feeder roads in the Sounds had to be built. V. C. BROWNE & SON, 13317, 13373

owned vehicle with chains. The road was 'extremely steep, narrow, and winding and rises to about 1200 ft at the summit, dropping down to a paper road in the valley below'. The final stretch was across a paddock.[35]

The French Pass road had its own set of hazards — heavy rain combining with a lack of metal made for 'massive ruts and wallows' of mud and being blown off some of the high ridges was a real risk — one grader driver always drove with a window open in case his grader was blown over.[36]

But what mattered to the residents was that they were no longer dependent on launches, punts and weather for their loads of superphosphate, and for the wool, timber, stock and, more recently, mussels they sent out.

Tourists began to flock to the area (though, as always, numbers were relative), and Sounds women could get out and about more easily. The completion of the French Pass road (like the Whatamongo–Port Underwood road from Queen Charlotte Sound) 'has shown how isolation can be eliminated', wrote Commissioner of Works Frederick Hanson in 1958.[37] 'Roads give you a sense of freedom,' said Joy Redwood, thinking of the pleasures of the road down to the farm in Titirangi Bay for which her husband Tony had been responsible for in 1979.

> Absolute freedom, and independence, total independence . . . If I need to go somewhere, I can get in the car and go whereas even with the now substantially built and powered boat, a) you had to have a man, b) you had to have the right tide to put the boat in, c) the weather had to be right. We've had occasions where we were going to dos, that sort of thing, and had to cancel because of the weather. It is very seldom that the road is out . . . so it is that sense of freedom and independence totally and being able to do things with the children, for the children and now the grandchildren. You spend time getting ready, you're two hours 10 minutes into town, you've got to be organised, you've got to have appointments, you end up waiting. One-day trips are very tiring, you're spending four and a half hours just driving on the road, other than driving in town, but that's what you do because the opportunity is there and that's the way we live. The really annoying part is when you're back late and it's dark and blowing a southerly and you're opening the gates at the wharf . . . and you come back to a cold house. I know the boating days, I remember, and this is wonderful by comparison.[38]

Two other significant roading projects were completed in the 1960s and 70s. Roy Archer, grandson of Tuna Bay settler Peter Archer, wanted to sell holiday sections but his small farming business disqualified him from receiving roading assistance. So he formed a company with bach owners in adjacent bays and made a road out of the old 1890 bridle track. It was completed in December 1962, without government subsidies. For a time, tolls were charged for maintenance, and the Marlborough County Council took over the road in the late 1960s.[39]

In 1979 Tony Redwood in Anakoha Bay worked with the Maritime Park Board, the county council and others in the bay who contributed their time and bulldozers to turn the bridle track, built at the end of the Depression to connect settlements to Endeavour Inlet, into what was essentially a private four-wheel-drive road providing very limited access to the new Titirangi road.[40] Redwood did more than half the work 'for love because he could see it was . . . an opportunity to get the road, to transform our lives and it did'. Two years later, 'the county council had money to spend on roading'.

Redwood, practical, experienced in bulldozing and with a good understanding of roading and water control, was in charge. Within two months, a public council-standard road with culverts and a good width was in place. The value of individuals' initiative, experience and labour was, as always, critical. 'If we hadn't taken that first step,' said Joy Redwood, 'we wouldn't have had a road now. Roads and technology have made a monumental difference to life in the Sounds.'[41]

IN 1949 TWO PORT GORE settlers, Dawkins and Smith, climbed 450 metres once a fortnight to pick up their mail bags from Endeavour Inlet. The open and often hazardous sea conditions, the Post Office judged, made a direct service impossible. Juggling the cost of delivery against the number of householders who benefited, the department also concluded that even a fortnightly service would be 'far in excess' of what could be provided to get mail through to two settlers.[42]

From whatever perspective they were viewed, mail deliveries were contentious. The Post Office wanted a financially viable service. The settlers constantly worried that their existing deliveries might be curtailed.[43] Deliveries twice weekly, they argued, were inadequate for Correspondence School materials, freighting out fresh produce and servicing the tourist trade.

The Johnsons, mail contractors doing three runs of 105, 100 and 90 nautical miles at times in open waters, considered that the service they provided was under-subsidised and only profitable because they ran a passenger and freight service as well. They were also under considerable time pressure, they argued, as Havelock's tidal mudflats allowed daylight trips only. Tidal streams at Kenepuru Head, where 'the mail boat makes about half a dozen calls [meant that] the Head call must be worked on a reasonable tide, otherwise it can only be worked under difficulty'.[44] Having to run engines hard against the tides incurred further expense.[45]

A meeting of settlers and officials called by Federated Farmers in December 1948 saw the issues well aired. Officials acknowledged the lack of an increase over 12 years, that settlers had issues with Correspondence School mail, getting perishable goods in and out, the constant use of their launches and that better services might slow the flow of young from the area. While such matters were outside Post Office policy, they said, '[T]he matter should not be considered solely from a mail point of view.'[46]

Nothing changed. For the next three decades the Orchard Brothers, W. Hutchinson, M. North and E. Johnson all contracted for the twice-weekly Pelorus service;[47] Mervyn Kenny's Red Funnel launches did the Queen Charlotte Sound run until the early 1950s, when the business went under and independent contractors picked up the work.[48]

EVERYWHERE, EVEN INTO THE 1950S, '[t]elephones were still relatively rare ... there was approximately one (landline) phone for every five people. Many country districts were served by party lines, with up to 10 customers each.'[49] In the Sounds, overcrowded lines permitted only brief conversations, while manual exchanges going down at night prevented emergency calls. In a few places, cables carried the lines underwater,[50] but for the most part, the old 'earth return' lines were still in place and needing constant patrolling.[51]

Metallic circuits were generally only installed from the mid-1970s, as automatic exchanges were built. Only when automatic switching arrived were the old lines phased out. In some places party lines persisted into the twenty-first century, making the Sounds one of the last places in the country to have them.[52]

THE ARRIVAL OF PUBLIC HEALTH facilities had also lagged behind their provision in urban areas. Twenty years after a system of public health nurses was set up in 1948, Carol King-Turner arrived as the Sounds' first district nurse, based in Havelock.[53] Her vigorously written memoir records the dramatic changes when she brought the postwar medical world to the Sounds. Gone were the once-widely-used hot bread poultices for infected splinters, and fluid from boiled koromiko leaves for diarrhoea or dysentery.[54] She dispensed from her cornucopia of new postwar medicines to treat everything from palms jagged by fishhooks to angina to poverty-related ailments like boils.[55]

Some health issues King-Turner was not qualified to deal with. Pregnant Sounds women had to come in to Picton or Havelock's maternity unit a fortnight or so before they were due to give birth — being on the safe side meant facing the boredom and expense of a prolonged wait. In an emergency, even into the 1950s, Pelorus patients coming to Havelock by boat would have to wait not only for the right tide to get in along that long narrow channel across tidal mudflats, but then again until the Blenheim ambulance arrived. Nor could King-Turner summon an ambulance; only doctors could do that.

However, King-Turner's appointment certainly brought a faster professional nursing response. Using family connections and acquaintances, she hitched rides with fishermen, casually filleting fish along the way to pay for her ride; braved sea conditions others might not have risked;[56] and kept up an unrelenting schedule, dealing with accidents, emergencies and inoculations. Neighbours rallied with their ever-more efficient launches to help. Health nurses continued to visit the Sounds until the early 2000s, but until air-lifts arrived, King-Turner's successors, lacking her extensive network of Sounds connections, largely depended on the inadequate roading system to reach their patients.[57] Critical patients had to wait for Picton's Dr Smythe to arrive by sea via Cape Jackson, then submit to a six- or seven-hour return journey by road.

In 1946 the 'god-sent' and now almost legendary Dr Vic Jacobson arrived in Havelock.[58] Responsible for the maternity hospital, road accidents in the vicinity and for general practice in the Pelorus Sound area, he provided an unprecedented service to locals, Māori and Pākehā, for some 30 years, in a round of regular visits on Wednesdays and Saturdays. 'Preferably you had your accident on those days,' Joy Redwood pointed out. Summoned by phone and combining 'a passion for medicine with a passion for fast boats',[59] Jacobson would take on any seas — and did, often first glimpsed in a cloud of spray as he dashed to a crisis.[60]

His belief in home visits and his willingness to keep an eye on older people allowed many to continue to live in the Sounds when otherwise they might have had to leave. Always ready to use his boat (and boating skills), he was happy to evacuate

The mail boat pulling up at Te Rawa farm wharf in Wilsons Bay, Hikapu Reach, Te Hoiere Pelorus Sound. Neil Foote receives a package from the wife of the boat's skipper, Sonny Johnson. The Johnson family had the mail-delivery contract for the inner sounds from 1924 until the 1970s.
MARLBOROUGH HISTORICAL SOCIETY, 0000.900.1046

people to specialised care, and in his later boats he installed a surgery and a stretcher for emergencies. Dr Jacobson retired in the early 1980s, his trips to the outer Sounds by then less necessary. Modern emergency evacuations were possible from the early 1960s, when the Manaroa airstrip was licensed for the Marlborough Aero Club to fly passengers, and from the 1970s helicopters provided an even more flexible service.

Meanwhile, in 1978, Tony Redwood and his neighbours had used heavy machinery to put in the access road, and the council widened this a couple or so years later.[61] But earlier technologies continued to prove their worth. Where they remained, party lines continued to enable people to answer their phones from others' houses and respond to emergencies.[62]

THE DRIVE TO ENSURE THEIR children's education continued to be a parental priority. In 1922 the New Zealand Correspondence School was established 'to assist settlers in remote districts where the number of children is too small to justify' establishing a school.[63] Uptake in the Sounds paralleled the national response.[64] The distinctive green school envelopes containing lessons material arrived and were mailed back, Correspondence School radio programmes broadcast from 1937 to 1997, and mornings dedicated to lessons were integral to many primary-aged Sounds children's lives. Equally valued were the books that, from the 1950s, were sent to them by the National Library Service.

That take-up was all the more remarkable given the burdens the system imposed on mothers in particular. Supervision was time-consuming, relentless and unpaid. Noel Moleta recalled: 'Mum had too much to do. I didn't want to sit at a desk, so after the initial excitement with the new things from school, I soon decided it was a bit boring and wanted to go outside . . . I'd just go.'

Supervising the next generation of Moletas in the 1980s, Noel's wife Debbie remembered: 'There were times when Noel would come home and we'd all be in tears. But there were good days as well. I think of that song, "Some days were diamonds and some days were stone."'[65] She was not alone in such feelings, and the huge commitment and pressure of home-schooling via Correspondence School could easily create a sense of failure.

Mothers also worried that time spent supervising their children's correspondence lessons meant time away from working on the farm and contributing to the family income. In Queen Charlotte Sound around the 1960s, mothers' intensive representations to the Education Department on this issue, and their then identifying an available room and sufficient numbers of local eligible children, saw mothers being appointed as 'supervisors'. There was no payment until the late 1980s, but over-stretched mothers found this development a god-send because they all took turns, and no one was watching their children all day. Morning greetings had a particular Sounds twist: Shirley Buckland would say, '"Good morning, children." A response of "Good morning, Mum — Auntie Shirl or Mrs Buckland" echoed forth.'[66]

The absence of school committees ruled out one avenue for socialising. But new opportunities came with, for instance, the popular Pelorus branch of the national Correspondence School Parents' Association. Joy Redwood, whose children were on correspondence at intervals from 1983 to 1993, remembers that they met at Homewood Hall, shared lunches, and parents met the teachers and watched them interacting with the children — all experiences that made the long journeys by car or boat worthwhile. 'School days', which ran from 1957 to mid-1999, provided another social occasion. Organised by the resident Correspondence School teacher and attended by a couple of teachers from Wellington, these were held at the hall 'once a term, three times a year. Children went, generally with both parents in tow, because few women could operate a boat.'[67] The days allowed parents to observe, socialise, chat and relax with other members of an increasingly dispersed community, while the children thrived on meeting others outside their own family.[68]

Meanwhile, the bricks-and-mortar schools that remained still faced long-standing problems. From the 1920s, more of the country's teachers became qualified;[69] and from 1938 the 'country service' provision required teachers aspiring to grades above a certain level to spend a year in a country school, which ensured these schools a better supply of experienced teachers. Yet teacher turnover remained high in the Sounds.

Other longstanding problems of small rural schools persisted into the 1960s, including indirect costs to parents such as long drives; uncertified or incompetent teachers; teachers who resorted to corporal punishment against which parents, who so needed the teachers, had little recourse; classrooms converted from boatsheds or henhouses; and isolation.

At Whekenui School in Tory Channel in 1962 (its final year), teacher Alan Hall's enthusiasm, focus and contemporary approach to teaching were much valued.[70] Hall remained concerned that what he saw as the national acceptability of failing at school was exacerbated by the Sounds' environment further limiting educational aspirations.

Children at Whekenui School, 1951. Keen that a school be established, Gilbert Perano had given assurances about the facilities that would be available, but in spite of these, Whekenui School, housed in a converted World War II shed that had once been a hen house, had no drinking or washing facilities and the students used a stick to frighten the blowflies from the outdoor long drop. But Ian Kidman's recollections and photographs from his year spent teaching there in 1951 indicate a happy time. He took the children, some of whom are shown here, down to the beach, did nature study, played sport; self-deprecatingly he recalled that 'occasionally we'd read and write'. A new building arrived in 1961, but in 1962, the sole teacher, Alan Hall, was reassigned to a Rai Valley school and Whekenui School was closed. PICTON HERITAGE AND WHALING MUSEUM, COURTESY PICTON HISTORICAL SOCIETY

Boarding with the Peranos introduced him to another facet of rural life: he shared a room with one of his pupils in the crowded house. 'Good morning, sir', the boy said each morning as they dressed, each standing beside their respective beds.[71]

By the mid-1960s schools began to be amalgamated, and the question of which schools would join forces and where threw up all sorts of issues.[72] Roads might need reconstruction or metalling for the school bus, and any moves might impose significant additional transport and time costs on families getting their kids to the bigger school. Would some families revert to Correspondence School, so that the newly amalgamated school became unviable? The departmental files, full of parental suggestions, clarifications and complaints, are testimony to the effort that Sounds parents continued to put into their children's education.[73]

THE TENOR OF SOUNDS LIFE changed remarkably little. Vegetable plots remained essential, endless fruit bottling a fact of life. Mutton, a staple, was sometimes varied when wild pigs coming down to eat the lambs were shot; a cattlebeast might occasionally be shared out around the neighbours. Chickens were kept for their eggs, which, into the 1950s, were coated in preservative. Fish was a regular part of the diet. If Sounds farming families had the basis of a better diet than some urban dwellers, the food was pretty basic, and sometimes still in short supply, having to be eked out among large families and farm helpers.

As a child in the 1930s Nola Leov remembers eating 'mutton and 27 vegetables'. The Harvey family, at much the same time, ate 'mutton, spuds, bags and bags of peas — you'd buy bags of dried peas, boil them up. They went a bit mushy but they were pretty good. You'd feed the pigs on that today.' Another Harvey favourite was bits of bread pulled away from its first rise and thrown into 'a pan of hot fat or lard . . . we called them floaters and we ate them with golden syrup. Beautiful.'[74] Over time, the ingredients remained the same but some Sounds housewives of the late 1970s, like their urban counterparts, tried out the fashionable quiches, salads, soups and pizzas. But the emphasis remained on food that made the best use of big and well-tended vegetable gardens. In 2014 Joy Redwood told me, 'I grow wonderful leeks. In summer I have the usual things — beans, silverbeet, carrots, zucchini; in winter I have broccoli, cabbage, leeks, carrots and silverbeet, and potatoes go right through.[75]

Her fruit and flower gardens, which she works in around the demands of the farm, maintain that cornucopia of produce and beauty that the old Sounds farms nurtured. Some of the fruit trees go back three generations, there are spring bulbs in the orchard, and the hydrangeas, agapanthus, fuchsia and pungas that do well in the Sounds give her flowers all year round.[76]

In the mid-century, children, as before, had their own — often gendered — tasks. Boys split wood, kept the woodbox full and helped scald the bristles off a newly killed pig; girls helped with the washing. Nola Leov's father would not take the girls lambing. Both sexes were involved in the endless grubbing of mānuka and tauhinu, filling the lamps and emptying the chamber pots (the least popular job). The community ethos of helping others was extended to children. Shirley Buckland (aged 14) and her brother (12), taught to take their responsibilities seriously, once spent a month at Port Gore on their own looking after the neighbours' domestic animals and milking the cows. Sometimes they would walk the old, steep tracks back to Furneaux Lodge, where they lived, for the day.[77]

Yet the children had a leisure seemingly denied to the earlier generation — cooking potatoes and newly caught fish on the beach, fossicking among the endless variety of things found there, foraging for blackberries, bird-nesting, playing games with grasses, sailing little boats made of flax stalks and wide-leaf sails, collecting cicada shells. In 1927 intrepid trampers Lorna Orchard, clad in long bloomers and strapped shoes, and her new teacher, Miss Fryer, left Whakatahuri to climb the untracked Mount Kiwi, only 180 metres short of Mount Stokes. Young Harry Williams visited 'old Wirewhiskers Joe Heaton and his dog' to get advice on sailing toy sailboats. About 1939 John Harvey and his brother Hylton, in their very early teens, pushed through untracked bush to the summit of Mount Stokes. They got home after nightfall, lighting their way with improvised torches of 'nigger-head' ferns and dry leaves.[78]

UNTIL AT LEAST THE 1950S, life for their parents 'was physically demanding and the tasks endless. Without electricity, enormous amounts of firewood had to be cut weekly; without refrigeration, meat had to be kept fresh; there was fishing and gardening. People worked hard from dawn to dusk, women worked on after dusk.'[79] By the 1950s, although some farming families had more money there were still the 'constant small children' to keep an eye on, Correspondence School to be supervised, the drudgery of housework and the 'cooking, endless cooking' that kept the house running.[80] A relentless pace was essential to get everything done. In the 1960s, 'at five in the morning, [Mrs Paterson at Waitui] would be click, click, click in her plastic

Te Towaka farm, January 1959, with Mount Sherwell rising steeply behind. As life got easier, some children had jobs that were more adventures than chores. The young John Harvey went with his father to find wild hives and collect honey; it is from high in these hills at Te Towaka that Nola Leov retained some of her 'loveliest memories of going out in the dark during a muster and waiting for the dawn light'. JOHN PASCOE, ALEXANDER TURNBULL LIBRARY, PACOLL-8765-03

sandals round the house. She was an amazing worker, an amazing worker! Running round the house — very fast clicks.'[81] For Debbie Moleta the absence of electrical appliances even in the early 1980s left her feeling 'as if I had moved back in time'.[82]

Denise Harvey, who married John in 1959, said, 'There were good days and bad days — days in which no one did anything right and you were at screaming point [and] you just had to think, "tomorrow will be better". And if tomorrow wasn't, then the day after.' She found it stressful when John was logging. 'It was a dangerous job. I can still hear them felling trees away over in the bush and I'd hear the old power saw roaring away and I'd hear the crack as they came over and I'd hold my breath until I heard the saws start up again, and I'd think, that's OK!'[83]

Those marrying into tightly knit, often familial communities found that it was vital to acquire tolerance. 'Adaptability, accepting that, however unreasonably, it is the way it is . . . And maturity helps you accept things . . . [I]t's better not to worry about some things you can't do anything about,' Joy Redwood, who came to the Sounds in 1986, recalled in 2014. She also wanted to be part of a wider world, wanted to know 'what's happening in the world outside', not be 'blindly accepting. I listen to National Radio, of course — you don't want to shut yourself off. [It's important to] be thinking about what's happening in politics, how it is going to affect your living out here and the way you've got to do business.'

The casual sociability and support network that work often occasioned for men was generally still not part of women's lives. Getting away from a Sounds farm, however briefly, demanded a lot of organisation and planning, Joy Redwood remembered. Into the 1970s many women were 'isolated with a capital 'i' because [you were] dependent on the male of the family to take you everywhere in a boat. The thinking in most of the Sounds was that women didn't take the boat, the men operated it.' The one woman who came into the Sounds and took a boat herself up to Havelock was 'quite something'.[84]

Those essential trips into town provided opportunities to go shopping and have a sense of 'people around you'. They were a rare chance, too, to dress in good clothes — in the 1960s, Sounds residents visiting Picton, Havelock or Blenheim could always be identified by their clothes.[85] The travelling time (then and now), however, could often be quite disproportionate to that spent in town. John and Denise Harvey and family would spend hours on their monthly boat and bus trip to Blenheim from Manaroa and back. Little time was left to attend to the carefully itemised shopping, let alone for the longed-for browsing. Nor was there money to waste on luxuries like condensed milk.[86] Debbie Moleta remembered that farmers in the Sounds made 'everything from scratch', and put most of the money back into the farm, leaving nothing for non-essentials.[87]

BUT EVERYONE ELSE WAS DOING it tough too, and the vividness and verve with which lives in the Sounds are remembered today show the deep, lasting attachment people formed to the place they grew up in. Harry Williams' memoirs of the 1930s and 1940s shape the shoreline and the bays of Kaiuma, Mahau Sound and Hikapu Reach with settlers and illuminate a closely populated world of strong and valued family and social connections. Life might have been dominated by tides and cows, but that world, with its picnics, regattas and personalities, formed an identifiable community in which the neighbours were as memorable as the excitement of John Brownlee's speedboat competing in the Masport Cup at Motutapu.

The Pickerings, for instance, ran 'a few stock and pigs' at Black Point from the mid-1940s. She was 'a very large and imperturbable lady with a very large family' who used to row into Havelock, Williams wrote. The Williamses would give them a tow if they met them. Dick and Marion Fell owned a small house on the eastern side of Hikapu Reach. 'Old Dick was a very fine old gentleman with a very forward thinking approach to the world' whose Pelton wheel supplied the house and workshop. Mrs Fell was diabetic. In those pre-insulin days she maintained a strict diet of cabbage three times a day to control her condition.

Everyone knew that the Eli Wells family always cut barracouda free rather than bring them aboard. Everyone, too, knew Horrie and Kate White who ran the Havelock taxi and service car in the 1930s and 1940s. They always went far beyond the call of duty, delivering shopping for customers and giving children a ride home. Kate, a demon driver, had an 'expressive vocabulary'; Horrie, fat and squeezed between the steering wheel and the back of his seat, would warn his women passengers as he changed gear, 'Mind your knee, lady, sometimes my hand slips off this knob.'[88]

Social events and gatherings continued to bring the little Sounds communities together. Dances, attended by Māori and Pākehā alike, were long the 'big thing' and the Loves' 'orchestra' played at all manner of functions throughout the area from about 1915 into the 1950s. With 'only a squeezebox for music [they] really enlivened up the dances all round the Sounds'.[89] In the 1920s the Terrills in Dryden Bay had a boatshed floor specially sprung for dancing, and decorated the room with streamers, foliage and lifebuoys. Ladies arrived with a long ball dress, carefully packed for the trip, and a plate. They drank tea, the men drank beer.[90] In the 1930s and 1940s the house of one of the Love whānau had a marvellous dance floor, and dances were held at Whakatahuri whenever a boat was launched.[91] The shed floor would be meticulously scrubbed, strewn with sawdust and boric acid, the shed decorated, and kegs of beer were always in good supply. 'We didn't think it a real hulie unless there was at least one fight, and someone was left snoring it off under one of the seats,' wrote Lorna Orchard.[92] Distance was no deterrent to attendance. Trekking over the saddle from Port Underwood to Maraetai Bay and hitching a boat ride to Dryden Bay was not unknown, and around the 1940s two young men rowed from Port Gore to Picton in a clinker-built dinghy whose leaks were caulked with mutton fat.[93]

Weddings, farewells and funerals continued to provide opportunities to socialise even as the little communities were losing residents to more populated areas. In Pelorus Sound, the Homewood Memorial Hall, built by volunteers and opened on 11 April 1953, became an important social centre. Federated Farmers meetings were held there, and a glance at some of the items in their agendas shows the importance of the organisation as a de facto local body — they discussed and made representations on the mail service, conservation and burning, the proposed Te Mahia–Onahau and Piripāua cuts, a night line for the doctor, repairs to the Homewood and Havelock wharves, a better allowance for Dr Jacobson, hydatids control and county amalgamation.[94]

ON 1 SEPTEMBER 1939 GERMANY invaded Poland and two days later New Zealand declared war. On 7 December 1941 Japan attacked Pearl Harbor — a 'serious attack on New Zealand' was envisaged as a real possibility.[95] The Sounds' extensive anchorage, it was thought, made the Nelson–Blenheim–Picton area a possible direct target for invading troops and 'a jumping off place from which to seize Wellington'.[96] New Zealand's defence depended on it having command of the sea, maintaining 'the strongest possible naval forces in the ANZAC area and [providing] these forces with secure Naval bases', it was argued by some, and air and sea routes between the US, Australia and New Zealand needed be kept open at all costs.[97]

On 9 June 1942 the War Cabinet signed off on extensive restrictions to boat movements, prohibiting certain anchorages and evacuating some residents.[98] A month later the defence of the Nelson–Blenheim–Picton area against potential

Japanese invasion was considered 'a moral and physical necessity'.[99] Launchman Clunies Ross, for one, was unimpressed with the restrictions and failed to respond as he should have to a challenge when he was working in restricted waters. 'Silly fools,' he said, 'they know who we are.'

By then coastal gun emplacements were largely in place.[100] Within a year, war signal stations were under construction on West Head and in Te Iro Bay (both in Tory Channel), at West Bay (now Lochmara Bay), and on Wedge Point. The planning for an anti-submarine station on Long Island was well underway.[101]

The US made its first official enquiry about using Queen Charlotte Sound as a deep-water anchorage in April 1942.[102] Further initiatives for defending fuelling and servicing the fleet were soon identified.[103]

However, from mid-1942 naval victories against Japan saw the focus shift from possible defence against that power to housing the US fleet in New Zealand.[104] Restrictions on various facilities were revised or lifted.[105]

At the end of September 1943 work on the coastal gun emplacements was halted and the guns were dismantled and shipped out.[106] Home Guard units were effectively stood down from 13 December 1943 and evacuation plans were abandoned.[107] Within Queen Charlotte Sound and Tory Channel the restrictions on boat movements were modified a year after being imposed and removed in mid-December 1944.[108]

As the country entered 'the greatest conflict ever to engulf the world, and one in which New Zealanders gave their greatest national effort',[109] Sounds residents, as in World War I, responded promptly. Some 112 men, including Māori for whom enlisting was optional, saw active duty; 10 were killed. Three women were involved in auxiliary corps.[110] Those under age helped many of the district's older farmers with farm work — and accounts.

Locals contributed financially to the war effort, produced food for England, and spent evenings winding big skeins of wool into balls so that women could knit the jerseys, scarves, balaclavas and socks that were sent off in huge bales to the soldiers.[111]

Manpower regulations introduced in 1942 required everyone aged between 18 and 40 to work where they were directed. Some women had to leave the area but others stayed, doing 'men's jobs' driving launches or working on as 'land girls'. Yachts and launches were requisitioned for use as navy patrol boats.[112]

On 2 August 1940 the Cabinet approved a national Home Guard, a community-based local body open to all men not in the armed forces. By 1941 this had morphed from a body tasked with ensuring capacity to deal with national emergencies into a guerrilla force capable of defending their localities.[113] In the Sounds 147 men, often a number from the same family, enlisted in the Home Guard — a similar proportion to the response in the country at large.[114] Their training and duties naturally further eroded an already drained local workforce.

In 1941 the government requisitioned rifles for Home Guard use. While many farmers who already had one to protect flocks from deer and pigs sometimes held on to their own,[115] some quite inadequate 'elderly' rifles might be handed out. One Sounds man 'was entrusted with a Hotchkiss machine gun without ammunition,' Nola Leov recalled, 'with which he was to defend, if required, the entrance to Pelorus Sound'.[116]

There can be no doubting the dedication of those who rowed, hitched a ride in a passing launch or walked to join the regular Saturday training sessions held in key spots around the Sounds. Hylton Harvey was 17 or 18 when he joined in about 1943. By then, fear of a Japanese invasion had been scaled back. Even so,

> we dug trenches . . . We'd do drill, hand-grenade throwing, rifle-shooting . . . Quite a few of us did quite a few weeks at Woodbourne camp, [using] their rifle-range . . . We had marches every day. I can remember those days, beautiful mornings, frosty and cold. But everyone belonged . . . we had camps in the weekend . . .

It was 'the most sociable time' he remembered. David Leov's memories of the time suggest a peculiarly relaxed approach to training. He recalled assorted weapons, mostly .303s of World War I vintage, some from the Boer War, as well as some .22s. Later on, Bren guns became available and the men formed a machine-gun unit. The boys later dug out the spent bullets — they were 'excellent' ammunition for slingshots.

Boys came along for training with their fathers and had a turn at shooting practice when the adults finished. Some became fairly proficient. The men did the minimum amount of drill possible but they all enjoyed manoeuvres, which were occasionally (unintentionally) somewhat sabotaged by the boys.[117]

Public Works staff and contractors built the military fortifications but locals were involved in developing sewerage and water plants, building jetties, installing power generators and bulldozing the feeder tracks in the Sounds' high, steep and difficult terrain. Some local launches, such as E. C. Lawrence's very large *Gilda*, or *Charmaine* and *Miss Picton*, had not been requisitioned and in them men like

ABOVE Royal Marines from the aircraft carrier HMS *Indefatigable* on exercise in the Marlborough Sounds in December 1945. NATIONAL MUSEUM OF THE ROYAL NEW ZEALAND NAVY, OC319

RIGHT A woman knits for the navy in January 1945 as the mail launch takes her to her destination. JOHN PASCOE, ALEXANDER TURNBULL LIBRARY, 1/4-045918-F

Lawrence and the Kenny Brothers and F. E. Musgrove braved often atrocious weather towing punts or lashing them alongside, bringing in shingle and other materials, including construction equipment and machinery.[118]

Their considerable seamanship and knowledge of the area were critical to the work. Land-based work, too — loading and discharging gravel, sleepers, cement, lorries, tractors, or hauling bulldozers out of mud — was heavy and relentless. When the guns were dismantled for shipping out once the scare was over, a new set of challenges arose. Their weight posed the potential for disaster if the punts overrode the towing launch, or the load slid overboard.[119]

Payment for that work was not always prompt, but by the end of the war some farmers had done well financially from military use of their land. As wartime buildings were dismantled and the fittings removed, the Defence Department negotiated with Sounds farmers to determine levels of compensation for land used by the army (and therefore out of productive use). Discussions were often protracted — while the department did not want to short-change them, many farmers hung out for what they considered their due reward.

Not all buildings were removed. The Peranos were invited to 'supervise' (i.e. use) the military buildings left behind at Tory Channel entrance. Other assets were sold to farmers — for wharves, huts, use of a submarine cable to the mainland until it was removed, barbed wire, army buildings.[120] The Peranos, who paid £450 for the 42 small buildings making up Whekenui Camp and other buildings at Fishing Bay, were able to massively update their facilities there.[121] Only on Blumine Island and at Maraetai Bay and Ketu Bay were the concrete gun redoubts left to stand.

YET AS THE WAR ENDED, that world of intimate communities bound by common circumstance and relationships was eroding. Families were leaving, the physical remnants of their lives increasingly lost under encroaching vegetation. The institutions of that older world remained, but not unchanged. The unpaid labour of children could no longer be counted on as school claimed more of their time, particularly secondary-school-age children. Others sought paid work. Church services relaxed into more of 'a social occasion, something of an attraction'.[122]

Some fixtures remained: by the 1950s the Kenepuru annual combined church garden party had become a keenly anticipated event for many around Pelorus. But the highly popular Motutapu Bay regatta lapsed in the 1930s, and the famous Sounds

Axeman from the Sounds at the Hopai Beach Sports Day in January 1959. These events were enormously competitive and demanded considerable skill. Richard Bradley recalled that 'my grandfather, Uncle Tane and Uncle Bill, who were axemen by profession, used to go to the A&P shows and give chopping displays and enter the competitions for extra money. Uncle Tane and Vern Stafford used to have competitions with their big cross-cut saw racing a chainsaw. Sometimes they competed against Sounds man Geoff Hoquard, one of New Zealand's chainsaw champions. And Uncle Tane and Vern always established the rhythm that got them through and ensured they always won.' JOHN PASCOE, ALEXANDER TURNBULL LIBRARY, PAI-O-1308

dances appear to have ended towards the end of the 1950s. The Te Towaka and Hopai sports days are still occasions for considerable conviviality and competition today, and holidaymakers and local bach owners increasingly attend.

Boat-shops, carrying farm goods around Pelorus for purchase into the mid-1960s, continued to provide excellent opportunities to socialise. In 1964 A. S. Paterson from Blenheim brought out plastic goods still new on the market, showed farming films and demonstrated new farming chemicals.[123] The old delivery mechanisms may have lingered on, but they were delivering new material to support new approaches.

Institutions, too, were changing. Federated Farmers had long been a male bastion but the first women's divisions were formed in 1925, in response to backblock women's pleas of loneliness and the need for help.[124] When women's divisions were finally established in the Sounds in the mid-1950s they gave women new opportunities to get together away from their homes. The Queen Charlotte Sound Division (formed 1953) organised visits from Father Christmas and other events for children in the outer sound, regardless of membership. Such meetings were lifelines for women trying to hold families together as their husbands worked all hours, often away from home. They were also opportunities to develop organisational and financial skills — even if they focused around the inevitable fundraising raffles and produce sales whose items the women had slaved to provide.[125]

Involvement in the Correspondence School Parents' Association provided similar opportunities. Women had 'to be vocal because we were the voice of the CS [Correspondence School] and our children's education'.[126] Mothers became proficient at dealing with officialdom on such matters as changes in funding and the way lessons were taught (and would continue to advocate into the late 1990s as cutbacks set in.)[127] Invaluable transferrable skills were learned.

The Sounds was never an easy environment, but humour often enlivened difficult days. In 2004, Deirdre Mackay captured various fishermen's memories. Des McManaway served Bill Burke a breakfast of scallops and eggs 'and all I got from Bill was a gruff "Salt!" I plonked a can of Ajax in front of him [but] he didn't register and put it on his food, and was soon spitting mad.'[128]

Des's brother Allan remembered: 'You had to be on the ball with food when Bernie [Wells] tied up next to you. One of his favourite quips as he took the last piece of cake was "You've got to be quick!" . . . Bill and I once doctored a Marmite sandwich especially for him with the foul-tasting stuff people used to paint on their nails to stop them biting them . . . Bernie was in quick but . . . ended up spitting it over the side . . .[129]

And for all the difficulties, fond memories remain among the old-timers. Bernard Wells found that fishing 'gave him the freedom he wanted'.[130] As an old man in his early eighties he said,

> I am missing [fishing]. I still feel in my body that if I had a crew member like my daughter, Joy Marie, I could still do it. I miss the challenge — of deciding where to be, listening to the forecast and heading for the appropriate place . . . On some days I'd set out ten nets and didn't make a bin of fish, but if I lived my life over again I'd be glad to have the same mate and the same life — I'd love to do the whole thing over again.[131]

Māori and the 'oppression of subsistence'

There were continuities in the way in which Pākehā lived in the Sounds, even as the communities in which they lived changed. On some levels, Māori lived their lives alongside Pākehā. They fought in the same war (or were involved in the same Home Guard), they did Correspondence School, they attended the same dances, competed in the same sports. They were subject to the same Depression from the 1930s.

But Māori, who were poor already, suffered additionally from the depletion of access to traditional food sources as land was increasingly alienated. Many moved from the Sounds into the regional centres, but with a sense of deep 'heart-wrenching' loss of connection to pāpakainga tūturu (original home) and whanaungatanga (sense of kinship).[132] Yet a small core remained, operating a 'Māori economy', though in a reduced form determined by circumstance,[133] and maintaining ahi kā, keeping the home fires burning and the rights 'as people of the place' to mahinga kai and the knowledge and practices of previous generations.[134] The lives Māori lived in the Sounds through the middle and later part of the twentieth century had qualitative differences from those of Pākehā.

If Pākehā residents were poor, Māori were poorer. The huge cumulative loss of Māori land from the occupation reserves dominates this period. Between 1920 and 1929, 60 per cent of land was sold. Most sales were a result of Māori being forced to give up on uneconomic blocks of largely unfarmable land. During the 1930s Depression more owners sold their interests or simply left the district in search of work. Many never returned. In the 1950s Māori were also pressured to sell land for scenic reserves.

In Ngaruru Bay they were permitted to keep only a small portion of the land in a bay they repeatedly and strongly argued they needed to retain to make their living;[135] Whatamango Bay Māori also lost land, despite wanting to keep for it for fishing.[136]

Further surges of sales in the 1960s, 1970s and 1980s mean that today some 86 per cent of the original reserved lands is no longer in Māori ownership.[137] In the 150 years since they were created, eight of the nine occupation reserves in Queen Charlotte Sound have been entirely alienated, all but one sold to private individuals. Most were sold in blocks larger than 50 acres.[138] Of the remaining reserve, the 2135-acre (864 ha) Ruakaka reserve (once the largest), only about 60 acres (24 ha) remain in Māori ownership.[139] Sales of reserve land in Tory Channel in 1945 and 1970–90 reduced Māori holdings to about 28 per cent of what was originally designated as Māori reserve.[140] Of the Port Gore reserves, only 365 acres (148 ha) from the larger block and one 5-acre section remain in Māori ownership.[141]

At Okoha between 1908 and 1930 the loss of some 435 acres (176 ha) reduced the amount of land iwi farmers had to feed their growing population.[142] Moreover, Māori now own less than 500 acres of the small amounts of land they inherited from Pākehā fathers. (This had been gained from small town reserves or bought in Queen Charlotte Sound, mostly on Arapaoa Island.)[143] The loss was all the greater because the land they were selling was reserve land given as compensation for land taken under the Waipounamu Purchases. With every piece of land sold, Māori suffered further loss from whatever compensation they had received.

If land sales are the dominant feature in the story, loss of access to valued sites, through either sales or land modification, are part of it. With Māori denied almost all opportunities to participate in government or other agencies making land-use decisions,[144] land was drained, its use changed, waste was dumped near areas where kaimoana was collected. In the 1920s, for instance, sewage from houses leased on land at Waikawa was piped out directly into the sea in front of Māori properties. Effluent from the freezing works contaminated shellfish beds in Shakespeare Bay from the 1890s right through until 1984; a sewer built in 1960, when kaimoana was still a vital food, added further pollution.

The building of the marina in Waikawa Bay in the 1970s destroyed 'at least two-thirds of the most active kaimoana beds and estuary area', once the 'largest and most productive estuary in Queen Charlotte Sound'.[145] Fast ferries, operating in the early 1990s, caused 'catastrophic damage' to pāua and kina beds in Tory Channel and disturbed urupā.[146]

More and more fishers with their new fishing technologies and faster boats

ABOVE Okoha residents, 1959. JOHN PASCOE, ALEXANDER TURNBULL LIBRARY, PACOLL-8765-01-29

BELOW Arapawa Māori Boating Club (the long white building to the right) in Waikawa Bay, Picton, c. 1956. Māori members of the community continued their involvement and successes in the local rowing scene. PICTON HERITAGE AND WHALING MUSEUM, COURTESY PICTON HISTORICAL SOCIETY

were having a marked impact on fish stocks available to Māori by the 1970s. For those dependent on kaimoana (i.e. Māori all over Te Tau Ihu)[147] this was a serious concern that the following decades would only heighten. By the early twenty-first century, recreational fishing in particular would challenge Māori ability to pass down concepts and practice of sustainable fishing.[148]

FROM THE 1950S, SOME LEGISLATIVE changes helped protect Māori land, but at the same time other legislation, such as the so-called 'Uneconomic Interests' legislation (the Maori Affairs Amendment Act 1967),[149] resulted in further land alienation. Economic necessity, however, continued to drive most of the sales. Rangitāne had tried to exchange their unsuitable and isolated Endeavour Inlet reserve for more fertile centrally located land in 1910 and again in 1920, but without success. Nor did a suggestion in 1964 for compensation ever get traction.[150]

Māori who were already badly off were further disadvantaged because blocks owned by multiple individuals were not eligible for development capital.[151] Rising birth rates and hereditary successions often increased the number of owners on each title, exacerbating the situation.[152] Pockets of land, too, were so scattered that, with little or no capital, working them economically was highly problematic.[153] Too often caught in what has been aptly phrased 'the oppression of subsistence', iwi could neither develop nor keep their interests in their resources or their lands.[154]

By the 1930s, Māori were not farmers but farm labourers living off kaimoana and fisheries, garden produce, wild pigs and cash from seasonal work.[155] During the Depression those living in small centres distant from employment opportunities were over-represented in unemployment statistics. The inequities of the unemployment relief schemes (the authorities, still rationalising that Māori were better able to live off the land than Pākehā, paid Māori only half of the Pākehā rates)[156] resulted in reduced living conditions that should have given rise to official alarm.

Lack of money and housing shortages forced Pelorus Māori into the Nelson or Havelock hostels that functioned as a base for Māori needing to come to town. In Nelson, the authorities failed to address long-represented concerns about tuberculosis in the hostel;[157] it closed in October 1949, after a decade of official concerns around overcrowding — a move that did nothing to solve the problem of accommodating people who needed it.[158] The Havelock hostel, still operating into the late 1930s, was poorly maintained, overcrowded and a focus for local Pākehā prejudice.[159]

Such conditions, and arguably worse, were not unknown elsewhere. Richard Bradley recalled the conditions in which his older whānau lived:

> Rakautara or Aniseed was a public works camp established during the Depression on the east coast of the South Island. Both my parents grew up there while the government was putting the railway through. The Depression provided a good excuse for doing the work because all these people on the dole, they'd go down there in atrocious working conditions and they could put the railway in — rain, hail or snow, the rail will go through. They lived in unlined railway shacks, and hey, it didn't matter if you had 11 kids, that was your house. So you parked some of them up with your cousin who only had two kids or you shifted some of them off to D'Urville Island with our relations down there and that was it.

From 1935 the first Labour government introduced pay parity on government relief schemes, and new contract work schemes operating with Native Affairs Department oversight attracted the same levels of paid relief as Public Works schemes.[160] Local work under the Native Affairs contract scheme saw the Stokes track between Okoha and Endeavour Inlet built sometime in the mid-1930s.[161] But any large-scale, significant material difference created by that scheme is difficult to discern — poverty remained widespread. Richard Bradley remembered that 'Mum used to say we had it tough. But everyone had it tough and it's relative to what your aspirations are. But I get a sense that some people by the 1930s knew what their lot was and you made the best of it.'

When the Depression ended, the situation improved only marginally.[162] 'At that point,' Bradley said,

> many like my grandparents and my great-grand uncle Jack MacDonald moved back to the Wairau Reserve or back down the Sounds. Those in the outer Sounds were sustained in much the same way that Tūhoe are sustained at the moment — you need the government contract to keep the road open even though no one's using it, because that's the only form of cash that's coming into the shop to attract newspapers twice a week. Fishing was pretty much subsistence or for swap. On the commercial fishing side — you'd go and catch the fish and give them to someone else to sell.

By the 1940s and 1950s employment during the winter increasingly became available only in the provincial towns.[163] These factors, and parents' wish to improve their children's educational opportunities, all contributed to increasing Māori migration away from the Sounds and environs and the associated emotional cost.

DURING THE 1930S AND 1940s tuberculosis was known as 'the Māori disease'. The name says much about the extent to which it and other diseases associated with overcrowding, poor housing and malnutrition attacked Māori communities, and with which Māori families in the Sounds were all too familiar.[164] Unsurprisingly, in 1938 a survey of Māori housing needs in Havelock and Canvastown found 'hardly habitable' homes with poverty-stricken inhabitants who could afford only old houses or shared accommodation and who needed help with rehousing.[165] In the Sounds, the little Okoha community was neither immune[166] nor alone.[167]

Access to medical care did improve with the Labour government initiatives in the late 1930s.[168] Miss Craig, the first district nurse in the area, working out of Picton from 1937, began regular weekly visits to Waikawa and the Wairau, fortnightly visits to Havelock and Canvastown and less frequent visits to the Outer Sounds.[169] She provided 'preventive work, particularly in infant welfare'.[170] The Sounds communities in the outer Pelorus were no longer dependent on health care coloured by prejudice and government inaction,[171] or on the Māori Mission House at Anakoha to procure medical supplies.[172]

The Social Security Act 1938, too, brought in free health care, disability benefits, and a universal old-age benefit from 60; in 1944 the family benefit (means-testing ended in 1946) boosted Māori families' income considerably.[173] But the poor housing, even then recognised as impacting on health, remained a festering sore. In the 1950s a 'significant and successful effort' went in to reducing disease among Māori, but the Waitangi Tribunal recently concluded that cultural marginalisation still plays a part in the significant disparity between Māori and Pākehā life expectancy.[174]

EDUCATION PROVISION WAS STILL FAILING Māori children, and the Correspondence School model, a lifeline for Pākehā in isolated situations, did not always work for Māori families. On Poihere White's farm on the western side of Hitaua at the entrance to Tory Channel, neither the dogs nor their master spoke English,[175]

The little school at Okoha and its pupils, c. 1950. The school's position had long been precarious. Government funding was withdrawn in 1921, but the church kept the school running as an Anglican school until the mid-1930s, when the falling population saw the mission itself closed. The Redwoods and the community then kept a school on the Redwoods' property until government funding again became available, in about 1950. During the 1950s, even its roll of about 15–20 Māori and Pākehā pupils did not solve the perennial problem of securing qualified and committed teachers in a remote community. Again, those problems probably contributed to Māori families moving from Okoha to Nelson. The school closed in 1966, although two untrained teachers stayed on for a short time. PICTON HERITAGE AND WHALING MUSEUM, COURTESY PICTON HISTORICAL SOCIETY

a fact that suggests no meaningful link to educational institutions or aspirations. Moreover, Richard Bradley remembered,

> Lots of those Sounds kids were reliant on Correspondence School while they were helping on the farm and fishing for a living. So lots of guys like my cousin John, Uncle Jack Hemi's son from Ōtānerau, they were what they'd call illiterate now, I guess. The Army saved my Uncle Walter Watson from being stuck down the Sounds. After he came back from Malaya, he became a qualified builder. This helped the families too. He could fix up the old family homestead at Onauku down at East Bay, and keep the old launches in the water.[176]

However, Waikawa School, exceptional because it was located in a primarily Māori community, offered — as it still does — a state education to both Māori and Pākehā children. Increasingly since the 1980s, state primary schools nationwide have been, to at least some degree, teaching Māori language and culture. The remote Okoha School continued to be plagued by problems. After the government refused further funding in 1921 the Anglican Church kept the school running as a mission school into the late 1930s, when the mission itself was closed because of the falling population.

It is not clear what educational provision there was, apart from Correspondence School, until the late 1940s. However, with whānau help, financial input from the mill and the generosity of the Redwoods, a new school was built on the Redwood property and finished in 1949. Its 51 pupils, including the Redwood children, were fronted by teachers, some of whom were trainees, working in the state system. The school functioned until 1966, when those Māori families that remained moved to Blenheim or Nelson to continue their education.[177]

FARMLAND IN THE SOUNDS WAS always too poor for small holdings to be profitable. Over time it gave way to a tourist playground — with an economic base built on the alienation of Māori land. Poignantly, each parcel of land taken reduced iwi ability to sustain themselves on the reserves. This slide was accelerated by increasing environmental modification and degradation — milling, exotic afforestation, the further development of marginal lands, draining, dumping and pollution. It was not just the decreasing availability of food. Not many 'decreases in the amount of fish and other seafood, and/or difficulties over access to traditional fishing sites [were needed to] affect the quality of life and help to tip the scales in favour of moving to a more populous district'.[178]

As Māori left, so the costs they bore — costs too little recognised by developers — increased. Stephen Huntley's evidence given in 2012 against the King Salmon farm proposal reflected the losses experienced earlier — of fish and kaimoana and the places that entwined his people and their cultural traditions with the land and the sea.

> We have lost two very important cultural iconic sites to salmon farms in Kura Te Au, Te Punga (beak of Te Wheke o Mururangi). Te Punga is also the name given to the spiral design carved onto men's Ihu (noses) with tamoko, and signifies the natural design of the Nautilus shell that the cuttle fish breed in, these are regularly washed up on beaches in Te Punga Bay.
>
> This place used to be a very prolific kina bed . . . it was sheltered, a very good place to harvest . . . [About] 50 local Maori shareholders . . . used to camp there over the summer. No one goes down there anymore because the beach has got that shallow with black stinking mud . . . This bay used to have great habitat, for fish and kaimoana, not any more . . . This is an insatiable industry . . . the best sites for them are our most valuable kaimoana gathering sites. Don't let them have any more — they shouldn't be able to privatize our garden: 'Enough is enough.'[179]

'It breaks our hearts' to think of a fish farm in such a place, wrote Arthur Huntley.[180]

Because 'so few of the tangata whenua could remain on their whānau land' they 'were severed from their tūrangawaewae . . . [and] other very important things were lost — the support of whanaungatanga, knowledge of whakapapa, knowledge of history, knowledge of tikanga, and the very heart of our culture, te reo itself'.[181]

Yet households at Waikawa, Okoha and in scattered places around Queen Charlotte Sound continued to hand down, if sometimes in inevitably attenuated forms, the old narratives, values and traditions that would help bind their generation to the next. We see this process in the accounts of the seemingly idyllic childhoods of Laura Bowdler, Florence Trotter and Richard Bradley, who grew up respectively in the 1940s, 1950s and 1960s in Queen Charlotte Sound.

Laura Bowdler's grandfather, Riwai, was adopted by one of the Loves but retained his Keenan surname. Her mother was Lilian May Keenan, née Boulton. Her father was

James Henare Kura Te Au Keenan, his middle name embodying the importance of Tory Channel to the whānau. There are Love whānau urupā at the head of Hitaua Bay, where the family have extensive holdings; tīpuna lie in the burial islands at the head of Anatohia.[182]

Florence Trotter's whakapapa links her to the Loves, the Heberleys and the Arthurs. Her grandfather was Tukurangi Keenan, who married Te Hera Love; her great-great grandfather, William Martin Keenan, was married to Sarah Heberley. Her mother was the daughter of John Arthur III and his wife, Miro Amelia Love.

Family, community and communal activities and care were integral to Florence and Laura's childhoods. In the 1950s Florence's father, Richard Keenan, 'a hard worker', was employed in the freezing works and at the whaling station. Taking advantage of the seasonal employment opportunities, he went 'spud picking, just anything. It might have been hard, but there was always something.'

Florence remembers poverty in Waikawa Bay. 'Some children, even when it was very cold, came to school with no shoes, things like that.'[183] Yet, '[g]rowing up in Waikawa Pa was absolutely wonderful.' The Māori Affairs houses, owned by the occupants, were two- or three-bedroom 'substantial-looking homes'. The communal life reinforced the community and its values. No one locked their doors. Her father had a 'massive garden and chooks [and] anyone was welcome to help themselves'. She and the other kids loved the swimming hole just under the bridge; out in Waikawa Bay they would climb on the boats lying at anchor. Their grandfather, Johnny Arthur, lived above where they swam and kept an eye on them — 'you could hear him: "Get off those boats!" We did — "There's Uncle Johnny Arthur, He's watching us!"'

The children fished for cockabullies and collected cockles in the lagoon where the marina now is. 'We'd fish, go out in in the boat. I remember our dad — he'd row for miles in a long narrow dinghy that you had when you couldn't afford a launch. Mum and Dad would load all of us and any cousins who wanted to come into the boat and we'd row out as far as Curious Cove.' There they caught cod or tarakihi that 'you'd just cook on the hot stones. Everything else was considered rubbish.' They scavenged in the hills for cape gooseberries that her mum made into jam, and in the bush for konini berries. 'Dad would show us the flax, the kiekie, because they used to eat the inside parts of the kiekie when they were children.'

Florence, her sister and brother helped on their grandfather's farm at Waikawa and the families went to the whaling station in the holidays. There were visits to Anatohia, where the Loves and Keenans farmed.

The Love whānau owned land in Tory Channel and in East Bay, and whānau members also built elsewhere in Queen Charlotte Sound.[184] Hector Love's big house at the Anatohia homestead remains in whānau ownership in 2021. In a bay 'called Papakura or Silvery Park' (Sylvia Park) in Ōnauku Bay, another branch of the whānau owned what Laura remembered as

> one of the finest houses in the Sounds, and the only one that we knew of that had an inside toilet! It also had a ballroom . . . [with] a proper sprung floor, high ceilings with plaster mouldings and chandeliers. The kauri bi-fold doors used to open the room onto the lounge where the Maori band played. It had the biggest kitchen table I have ever seen, it would seat 15 people.[185]

In Waikawa Bay another Love house, 'Top House . . . was a beautiful home'. On the hill above the bay, Love family members had also built Arapawa towards the turn of the nineteenth century; in the mid-twentieth century, and with its top storey removed, it remained in whānau ownership.

Richard Bradley described the net his whakapapa cast. His mother

> was a MacDonald and MacDonalds form a sort of tribal dynasty for Rangitāne of the Wairau. You are either a MacDonald or a Te Mete (Smith) and they're heavily intermarried into the Huntleys, Aldridges and Masons so it doesn't matter. By comparison, if you move to Pelorus, you're a Hemi, or a Mason, who intermarried as well. They're all Ngāti Kuia and Rangitāne. So that's how I connect to the Pelorus and Queen Charlotte area — through my mother.

The Smiths, MacDonalds, Huntleys, Loves, Riwakas, Matangis, Keenans and Watsons all intermarried. Further linking Rangitāne to the Sounds was the granting of 'one of [the government's] Landless Native reserves' in Endeavour Inlet — it was one of those places 'for which some of our people still had affinity'.

Few Māori beyond Waikawa shared in whatever wealth the improved economic conditions of the 1950s created. 'My family in Endeavour Inlet went everywhere in boats,' Bradley said.

> But they were rowing boats, not launches. I don't hear too many people talking about cracking it. The people that did better — there was that

> difference, even in my time — were people who got rents from what are now called the land incorporations. These were blocks of land that were really good grazing blocks that the Pākehā leased and the Māori Trustee collected the rents paid out for them. At the Wairau Pā, you could see the difference between the Ngāti Rārua whānau who got annual cheques and grants from the Māori Trustee or Wakatū Incorporation, and the Rangitāne people who didn't get rents from their lands and just worked.
>
> My father was Pākehā, so when we went to the beach with Dad we went swimming, walking or 'recreational' fishing, or just sitting around having a picnic. When we went with my grandparents or aunties, it was business. We went collecting shellfish, whitebaiting or fishing and it was not recreational fishing. We were catching stuff we needed to eat. So they were the sorts of differences.

TĪTĪ HAVE ALWAYS BEEN A major food source for Māori. Te Ātiawa did some muttonbirding in Tōtaranui,[186] but killing, preserving and eating them was particularly important for Ngāti Kuia. Over time, however, their rights to harvest tītī were eroded. In 1901 Nukuwaiata, Te Kakaho (the Chetwodes) and Motungarara (Tītī Island) were made reserves to protect native flora and fauna.[187] In 1918 Ngāti Kuia were given conditional rights to land to take fish, kōura, karaka berries and tītī from the islands (with officials suggesting that settler farmers grazing stock there 'keep an eye' on Māori).[188]

In the mid-1930s the Department of Lands and Survey made trustees responsible for the muttonbirding and for organising the day or two it was to occur (generally in March). Traditional methods were to be used. Initially, the sheer difficulty and logistics of getting agreement within the required tight timeframes made this a difficult and demoralising process for those involved. However, the practice (further islands were included subsequently) went on into the 1950s.[189]

'The people from my side of the Wairau,' Richard Bradley recalled,

> would go muttonbirding down at Tītī Islands and they'd hire the mail boat, either the *Miss Onahau* or the *Miss Portage*, and . . . they'd argue down there who was getting muttonbirds and they'd come back. Everyone was waiting at the wharf because when the boats came in they'd have all the

> birds hanging on the rail — that's what made all those old boats last so long — all the oil dripped into the timber and preserved it.

From the end of the 1950s, conservation of the species triumphed over Māori harvesting rights. In 1966, after a five-year closed season, muttonbirding did not resume.[190]

THE COMPLEX WEB OF RELATIONSHIPS reached across to D'Urville Island. Within Queen Charlotte Sound,

> My mother's sister married a Watson, and the Watsons in East Bay had slightly better land — enough flat land for sheep. And the farm had been operating for two, three generations. In the late 1950s, early 1960s, we'd stay with Uncle Walter Watson and his family — they had three substantial houses there, they had their own launch with a decent motor in it, and they could afford to go to Picton, as well as buy groceries and other luxuries. I liked going with those uncles because they were drinking on the boat and I got to steer. It'd be in the dark. 'Oh, just follow that ridgeline and when you see it drop, just turn past that.' So we'd go all the way up and tie up by the Red Funnel launch wharf, which was right across from Oxleys and the Federal hotels. Walk straight out, hop on the boat and off you'd go, chug, chug, chug.
>
> We also stayed with Uncle Walter. You'd get to ride a horse, which was really good, because town kids don't do that, and Uncle Walter had a clinker dinghy and it had a British Seagull outboard engine. This was 1961. We'd go across to this rough area of the farm and when we got there, he'd take the propeller off and make some connection and it was a scrub-cutter and he'd be able to cut through all of this mānuka. I was impressed with that!
>
> We often went to Uncle Jack's at Ōtānerau in East Bay. It was different because it was more of a subsistence farm. He had a small house and we all had to sleep in one room. Uncle Jack was a Māori Battalion veteran. He came back a captain, but he didn't get the same deal as other captains who returned. He got this steep, crappy, leftover piece of land in Ōtānerau Bay because [they said] all Māori could live off the land and so they didn't need so much land. The Māori know how to survive — hell, they can live off the land, go up the creeks and eat.

Looking down on Watson's farm, Ōnauku, in East Bay, Arapawa (Arapaoa) Island, 1949. Twenty-one years later, in 1970, Vern and Milly Watson gave up their attempts to wrest a living from the land that even in the late 1950s was described as running 20 to 30 sheep to the acre. ALEXANDER TURNBULL LIBRARY, 39021

To get money most of my uncles worked at the Picton freezing works and the whaling station. During the whaling season they'd be away for months. My uncle Jimmy MacDonald used to say, 'We worked in the freezing works, we'd get covered in lamb fat and boils and it was hard to get a girlfriend.' Then they'd head off down to the whaling station for three months, get covered in whale blubber and the stink made it almost impossible to get a girlfriend! So he'd come home from the whaling station and by the time the whale blubber smell had worn off, they were back off to the freezing works.

Mum said that her grandfather, Peter Hohua MacDonald, sat up late at night talking politics with his brothers — Tuiti MacDonald, the MP for Southern Māori, and Hoani. They only spoke in Māori when they didn't want the kids to know what was going on.

Richard revelled in opportunities to listen to his grandfather — 'and this is how I got interested without realising'.

[My grandfather would say,] 'Oh, yeah, your mother's land is over here and so you've got some interests over there.' From about the age of six or seven I would go with my mother to tangihanga of our relations. There were no marae in Blenheim as such in those days, so you'd go to people's houses and the women would be in the room doing all the stuff that women do supporting the whānau and the men would be outside cooking and talking politics. At night-time there would be a short church service and speeches from the different families who came in support, and there were all sorts of political issues getting discussed on those occasions.

That small boy, listening to his elders, would grow up to play a role in critical Treaty negotiations to help provide a way forward for his people.

10. New Directions

> 'We don't have a freight run, which is a difficulty . . . Someone said to me it takes twice as long and costs twice as much and you have to work twice as hard if you live in the Sounds.'

SINCE EARLY PĀKEHĀ SETTLEMENT, FARMING, fishing and a sprinkling of other activities have provided a pattern of economic exploitation in the Marlborough Sounds. The trends towards over-development and environmental over-exploitation related to those activities, observable from the beginning of the 1980s, continue to play out today, though in an increasingly complex environment.

The most recent Census, in 2018, listed 3909 permanent Sounds residents, a considerable rise since 2006, when it stood at 2043.[1] Most of the population is of European descent, though the growing population of Māori now totals 11.3 per cent. Kenepuru Sound, more easily accessible than some Sounds areas, provides a particular population snapshot. It hosts something of a permanent population — tradespeople, those working online, retirees, with seasonal workers at the lodges swelling the population over summer. Only five families' children attend Waitaria Bay School. It would be hard to generalise this pattern into the rest of the Sounds.

For decades, farming was the economic backstay of the Sounds. Today, Kenepuru's 13 farms have stock units that range from 150 to 3000. Today, Heberleys' is the sole working farm in Kura Te Au Tory Channel.[2]

In Tōtaranui Queen Charlotte Sound, East Bay was still a working farm in the 1980s; today, the land is largely scrub.[3]

Nor is there new permanent settlement at Okoha, in Te Hoiere outer Pelorus Sound. By 1966, Joy and Tony Redwood explain, and prior to the school closing,

> some of the population had already left to get employment elsewhere . . . The removal of the mill at the head of the bay to Renwick in 1968 was the final blow. Those who worked in the mill left as well, although a couple of Māori families who didn't have children did stay on for some years doing casual work and farming in the area. Today, [there are seven houses left and] successive generations of the same families continue to visit. However . . . there have been no permanent residents there for at least 20 years or more. One family continues to run some stock, albeit at a distance, at the head of the bay.[4]

Of the remaining seven large farms in outer Te Hoiere, part of the Shand farm at Port Ligar was sold in 2018 and the rest remains in family hands. The 1471 hectares at Waitui, where the Moleta family has farmed for 45 years, is one example of the constant rethinking and ingenuity that the Sounds demand of their farmers. Noel and Debbie Moleta and their family farm today for profit, not productivity. Almost 20 years ago they began crossbreeding sheep to improve growth rates and fertility. Then they went organic, and subsequently diversified into mussel farming. More recently they have bought more land in the Tasman district to breed and fatten sheep and lambs and to grow hops.

With several of their children working in the family business, Noel and Debbie have now retired more than 300 hectares at Waitui, more than 170 hectares of which they are planting in trees, mostly from their own nursery, in the One Billion Trees programme. 'The IBT programme,' says Noel,

> has helped Waitui move forward into a new environmentally conscious time. It aims to protect our biodiversity and make it an even more picturesque place to live. A small reduction in production will be countered by fewer native weed pests seeding into pasture in future. We will have a green belt of native bush around the coast with pastures above. Room for all . . .

From a high point above Harris Bay on the Raukawa Moana Cook Strait side of Port Ligar, looking across to Tītī Island. Nukuwaiata Island, the bigger of the Chetwode Islands, is at back left.
SHELLIE EVANS

Meanwhile, the Tapawera venture gives them a perspective on Sounds farming. 'The 28ha planted in hops at Tapawera grosses more income than the whole of Waitui.'[5]

At Okoha, Tony and Joy Redwood continue to develop their farm, breaking in new land, putting in new fencing and building a new house for the son who is now working there — the fifth generation of Redwoods on the property. They, like the Moletas, have also invested in new property — in the Redwoods' case, just out of Havelock, on which they can finish off ewes and lambs from the farm.[6] But distance from the regional towns still has to be taken into account, Joy said in 2014:

> We don't have a freight run, which is a difficulty, so any large item we have to take a tandem trailer or work it out somehow — timber and those sort of things. It's quite an exercise, whereas if you're in town the trailer comes round, it happens. Someone said to me it takes twice as long and costs twice as much and you have to work twice as hard if you live in the Sounds. It was quite a good summation, I thought.[7]

A third forestry planting boom, in the mid-1990s, resulted in 17,000 additional hectares of the Sounds going over to forestry in 2016–17,[8] with the industry contributing $8.96 million to the Picton and Sounds economy in 2016.[9] With existing forests able to be replanted[10] and with the current domestic and international demand for timber, the industry looks set to continue, with owners and contractors with good infrastructure and management confident of good prices.[11]

Is forestry the future for the Sounds? Local body regulations that tie into national legislation and standards on how forests are to be cut, ongoing concerns about runoff and sedimentation, particularly in Te Hoiere,[12] and increases in ocean freight costs since Covid-19 will all affect the future profitability of isolated blocks of *Pinus radiata*.[13]

Longtime internationally qualified forester Dallas Hemphill believes that mixing it up might be in order. 'Most private land is already covered either in pines or in native regeneration, of which some could benefit from underplanting native canopy trees.' Might carbon forestry mixed with high-value species such as oak, eucalyptus and native species sustainably farmed to maintain a continuous canopy be an option?[14] Current government assistance for planting only applies to land not already regenerating, and the carbon economics of native forest are not always viewed positively.[15]

The release of the final report of the Climate Change Commission in June 2021, and unknowns about future carbon prices and economic incentives add further complexities. However, it does seem that forestry has an important role in carbon capture and mitigation and the commission has asked the government 'to encourage additional carbon capture on smaller blocks of trees on farms'. A grant scheme 'may help assist "mosaic" landscapes of smaller forest blocks interspersed with other land use'.[16] What should be planted — indigenous forest of introduced pine — is increasingly debated.

As in the past, the decline in farming has seen land moving into Crown ownership. Public reserves now cover 60 per cent of the Sounds. Elsewhere, bush is regenerating, aided and abetted by Department of Conservation (DOC) work on the reserves, and by a range of voluntary community restoration groups. Working to protect and restore heritage values and ecosystems, they run trapping lines and bait and monitoring stations to eradicate cats, mustelids and possums; a few work on educating the general public through greater engagement with conservation and the wider issues of the survival of rare and endangered species.[17]

Those groups are also involved with the nationwide problem of wilding pines, a big issue in the Sounds. These self-sown 'weed trees' are a legacy of the conifers, mostly *Pinus insignus*, planted about 100 years ago as shelterbelts. From the 1990s on they began springing up on burnt-off pastures and former paddocks, on roadsides, on spurs with light bush cover, on coastal escarpments and along power tracks. Slips, fire, pig-rooting and wind damage offered — and offer — further opportunities to get established. DOC, recognising early the threat to the Sounds' unique landscape, began work on its own land, and from 2007 the Marlborough Sounds Restoration Trust has developed an impressive community-led wilding pine programme in Tōtaranui Queen Charlotte Sound.[18] The stark trunks that today stand against the skyline, and the hillsides covered by skeletal trees are evidence of regenerating bush, not its destruction.[19]

VISITORS CONTINUE TO BE ENTICED into the Sounds, with their purchases contributing substantially to the $394 million visitor spend in the Marlborough region in 2019.[20] There are wrecks to dive, eco-tours to take. About 30,000 people a year walk or mountain-bike some or all of the well-maintained 71-kilometre Queen Charlotte Track, on their own or with guides. Extensive community and sector consultation and

A punt heavily laden with timber (above) and a mussel boat bringing sacks of mussels in for processing (below) are typical scenes of industry in the Sounds. However, the employment opportunities generated are largely in the wider Marlborough region. SHELLIE EVANS

industry knowledge and expertise have produced splendidly illustrated and layered information to inform visitor choices.

Tourists arrive by road, by air or on the regular Interislander and Bluebridge ferry sailings from Wellington, their speed inside Kura Te Au and Tōtaranui restricted since 'fast ferries' in 1995 caused destructive swells. The holidaymakers head to baches, eco-lodges, luxury accommodation, backpacker lodges, tent sites or hired craft. Until Covid the number of cruise ships visiting Tōtaranui over the summer season was growing, sometimes disgorging twice the population of Picton into its town centre — a boon to local businesses if not local inhabitants.

Baches in inner Tōtaranui and Kura Te Au, all easily reached by boat from Picton, are in almost every bay or on every headland. The recent sale of ex-forestry land for lifestyle blocks in nearby Port Underwood, too, may herald more such development.[21] The Pelorus Sound mail run, a favourite with tourists, brings in goods and mail to rather fewer Pelorus baches — a valuable service to those still lacking road access.

The now sealed French Pass and Port Ligar road and the still largely unsealed feeder roads have provided for growing visitor numbers and access to baches sprinkled around in outer Te Hoiere. On the west side of Tōtaranui, tourists drive and haul boats, caravans and trailers over the tortuous, winding Titirangi road as far as Anakoha and Titirangi bays. Information on cruising, anchoring and sea conditions is available online, albeit subject to patchy cellphone coverage. It is a far cry from the days when those early recreational sailors and rowers slipped into a bay and hoped for a quiet night.

The Covid-19 pandemic and resulting international border closures have created uncertainties for Sounds tourism operators, as they have everywhere. Marlborough, says Jacqui Lloyd of Destination Marlborough, is a 'lucky region'. It is centrally located, and domestic visitors to the Sounds have always outnumbered international tourists. The future, however, remains 'opaque'.[22]

THE AQUACULTURE INDUSTRY IN THE ecologically rich area of the Sounds, begun in the 1970s, continues to thrive. The initial focus on mussels has expanded to include king salmon, Pacific oysters, pāua, kōura and seaweed. All ventures are run and serviced from Picton and Havelock. The impact is significant: 590 marine farms covered 2600 hectares of the Sounds in 2021 and provided 65 per cent of the country's mussels, 1 per cent of its oysters (most still came from Bluff), and 56 per cent of its salmon. In 2020 the aquaculture industry, nationally, earned an estimated $653 million.[23] The contribution to the local economy is not insignificant. In 2016, 108 businesses created over 769 jobs in marine farming and seafood manufacturing, earning Marlborough $63.1 million.[24]

In 2012 a board of inquiry looked at New Zealand King Salmon's proposal to open nine new salmon farms within the Sounds. The company and the industry body (which, while it claims to aim for constructive partnerships with iwi, does not instance any such partnerships) argued that this was a green, sustainable, profitable industry offering employment in remote places. Opponents argued the risk to fish species from intensified and harmful algal blooms and salmon faeces; visual pollution created by the large farms; and water and seabed pollution from 40,000 tonnes of fish-feed being released annually.[25] Second- and third-level effects identified included salmon attracting seals, which attract sharks, which eat the protected Hector's dolphin.

Māori argued that the proposed long leases allowing exclusive use might exclude them from traditional fishing and kaimoana sites. Piecemeal developments and supposedly minor changes in the past, they argued, had damaged the Sounds ecosystem, possibly irrevocably.[26]

In February 2013, after a hearings process substantively criticised by many,[27] the board approved four of the nine proposed farms; up to 12 farms may now operate in the Sounds. Conditions around consents allow 19,000 tonnes of additional salmon feed to be discharged into the Sounds in each of the next 35 years.

In 2016 the Marlborough District Council identified concerns about 'the negative consequences of intensive fish farming'.[28] Are King Salmon's initiatives another instance of a now historical pattern of unsustainable Pākehā development for short-term economic gain? The company, one commentator states, has not been obliged to ensure that the economic benefits they identified are realised. The region is therefore left with uncertain economic benefits from a polluting industry that is offering only a small number of low-level jobs. Higher water temperatures are already negatively affecting profitability.[29]

Moreover, the decision is likely to have set a precedent for future aquaculture for Tōtaranui. In the past, in that Sound, recreational and industrial activities had been 'clearly separated'. Now, any decision to allow further such development would inevitably adversely affect the opportunity to convert the sound into one big marine reserve, or to have it listed as a UN Heritage Site, or develop it for eco-tourism.

'MILFORD WAS GRAND, BUT PELORUS was beautiful,' a reporter on a parliamentarians' tour of the Sounds wrote in 1892. He went on to record the 'fairyland' of bush and water and the 'charm altogether indescribable, resting upon bay, and islet, inlet, and jutting point, gentle undulation and precipitous cliff and hillside'. Yet no attempts, he noted, were being made to save Sounds from burning and stocking. In America,

> this Sound would have been converted into a national park . . . in Europe it would have been jealously guarded . . . here the most beautiful wooded points are being sold, and the bush burnt off them to carry sheep. Every lover of the beautiful, and everyone with a spark of national pride in the beauty of his country, and of patriotism in his soul, should protest against this vandalism.[30]

The Sounds' role in re-creation, as well as recreation, has captured imaginations for over a hundred years. For decades, tourism was heralded as a way to profit from and protect the environment, a critical part of the visitor experience.

Today, environmental consciousness, and with it the requirements of the Resource Management Act, have imposed restrictions on local bodies' planning, requiring greater sensitivity to the impact of our activities on the environment. This is apparent in the tightly regulated recreational fishing in the Sounds, and in the creation of two marine reserves — one in Tōtaranui and the other in Te Hoiere.

With this consciousness has come a host of attendant responsibilities for councils — education activities, planning and monitoring (sometimes reflecting responsibilities under national policy statements since 2010), to mention a few. The Marlborough District Council has developed curriculum-linked programmes for schools and school-age children; it sponsors the biennial Cawthron Marlborough Environment Awards to showcase businesses, community and individuals taking laudable environmental initiatives. The council and DOC oversee the Te Hoiere/ Pelorus Catchment Restoration Project, carried out in conjunction with Ngāti Kuia, which is working to establish holistic land management of the area.

Ships' wakes have been monitored since 1995, water quality since 2012, and the information fed into Land Air Water Aotearoa's national database. Several baseline scientific studies are underway. An initial monitoring report in 2011 identified 129 ecologically significant and widely varied marine habitats in the Sounds and invited the public to nominate further such sites.

A 2017 publication from the National Institute of Water & Atmospheric Research (NIWA), *A 1,000 Year History of Seabed Change in Pelorus Sound/Te Hoiere, Marlborough*, provided an historical context within which to understand changes within the Sound, and recommendations for how best to plan to ensure 'beneficial environmental outcomes for seabed habitats'. However, soaring visitor numbers in the recent past raise additional questions about the sustainability of the Sounds' 'unspoilt' nature. Even in the outer Te Hoiere and beyond, to the Rangitoto Ki Te Tonga D'Urville Island area, the increasing numbers make it hard to capture a sense of 'the remote'. Constantly improved charts, electronic navigation and fish-finding equipment are putting further pressure on a marine environment already seriously compromised by, and still suffering from, the damage from past land management, overfishing and destructive shellfish-gathering practices.

Over the years, hundreds of thousands of cubic metres of soil and clay have slipped into the sea from roads in Tōtaranui and Kenepuru, as well as those giving access into Te Hoiere.[31] The new farming — aquaculture — adds more pressure, as of course does global climate change. 'To destroy is easy while to restore is difficult, perhaps impossible. So it is common sense to preserve before it is too late,' wrote one of those late nineteenth-century reporters.[32]

But what might such preservation look like? Was that reporter thinking of some idyllic pre-contact landscape? Scenic reserves now cover a very considerable part of the Sounds land, but for Māori one result has been continued reduction of access to mahinga kai, now set about with prohibitions or restrictions that accompany Pākehā notions of conservation. The Marlborough District Council, like all local bodies, has obligations under the Treaty of Waitangi to involve local iwi in developing indicators of the health of the coastal environment, but to date such initiatives have not been marked by success.

MĀORI HAVE HAD LITTLE (if any) power to affect the significant environmental damage that today continues to restrict their ability to exercise the rights they enjoyed before Pākehā arrived in the Sounds. The language contained within statutes today in regard to Treaty obligations ('having regard to', for instance, as opposed 'to giving effect to') greatly influences the degree of consultation carried out. Councils may be more willing to adhere to the letter of the law rather than embracing its spirit.

The Marlborough District Council has developed a coastal monitoring policy to look at how iwi can be involved in planning;[33] in its 2018–28 long-term plan it noted that a review of its current Māori engagement policy is 'likely to result in a dedicated Māori engagement policy'.[34] However, in 2021, a review of proposed aquaculture rules saw five of the nine iwi making a range of charges around the failure of the council to consult adequately with iwi, including incompetence and preferential access to non-iwi farmers.[35]

Moreover, the sheer volume of consultation required, and iwi under-resourcing, mean that there are serious questions round the council's ability 'to make full account' of submissions from Māori. Critically, the Waitangi Tribunal notes, an institution's culture ultimately determines the importance that things Māori are afforded.[36]

Generational shifts also affect efforts to retain traditional practices. In 2008 the Waitangi Tribunal noted that tangi, hui and sporting events were bringing iwi together and strengthening cultural resources, though to a lesser extent than previously. Changing expectations and lifestyles, and movement from tribal lands and traditional food gathering have all contributed to a loss of traditional knowledge, and a growing group of rangatahi 'who would rather eat out at McDonald's or Kentucky Fried Chicken not having experienced delicacies such as smoked tuna and watercress'.[37] Most claimants blamed the destruction of resources for this, not social change.

The 2008 Waitangi Tribunal report noted Treaty breaches and grievances in Te Tau Ihu — loss of ownership, loss of access to and control of mahinga kai, forests, customary fisheries, waterways and other natural resources. Iwi argued that reserves policy moved Māori onto land whose size did not permit a traditional or European way of life yet lacked the resources to enable iwi to progress as a tribe. Nor, without rangatiratanga (the right to exercise authority) over fisheries, harbours, seabed and foreshores, and given the significant environmental and damaging changes, were iwi able to exercise any meaningful kaitiaki function or provide for cultural or economic needs.[38] The very things, Māori argued, that gave iwi their mana and standing were eroded.

In 2010 and 2012 deeds of settlement for the Te Tau Ihu iwi were assented to, and were enacted in August 2014. The main provisions of the iwi-specific settlements include a Crown acknowledgement of wrongs done, an apology and cultural and financial redress. This last, recognising each iwi's 'traditional, cultural and spiritual association . . . with places and sites owned by the Crown within their rohe', provides for iwi and the Crown to work together 'to protect and enhance the conservation values associated with these sites'. Land was vested in or transferred to iwi as redress. Māori place names have been restored, some new ones added.

Recent annual reports and Ngāti Kuia's more regular *Pānui* newsletter attest to the iwi's intention to rebuild a tribal base for the next generation in an effort to restore what has been lost, including the fundamental values of whanaungatanga, manaakitanga and kaitiakitanga. For Rangitāne and Te Atiawa, fishing companies are returning funds that ensure future business success and good returns to shareholders; Ngāti Kuia are exploring ways of offering whānau support to establish collectives, researching organic certification of whānau blocks, and developing an export market for organic products including kānuka tea and honey.

Even as an outsider, I get a sense of renewal and hope. In the March 2019 *Pānui* the Ngāti Kuia chairperson wrote: 'Since our last pānui there has been plenty of mahi completed and there's a lot that's about to begin. A distinct Ngāti Kuia flavour is being felt throughout Te Tauihu.'

I talked to Richard Bradley in 2014 when the Rangitāne Treaty settlement was close. His narrative — of land, legend and belonging, and of the past and presentness of history — carries the seeds of a new future.

> One particular uncle, Frank MacDonald, knew all about Rangitāne whakapapa and history and also that of other iwi. When, in 2003, the Department of Conservation was wanting to upgrade Cook's landing site at Ship Cove to better reflect the Māori side, it piqued my interest. So before we were ready to do the project I picked up Glynn Barratt's book because that seemed to be the latest book on the Sounds. Of course I saw some of Uncle Frank's whakapapa in there, and Tipene O'Regan talking about . . . the culture and history of the Sounds.
>
> So I thought of the Te Ātiawa–Taranaki–Ngāti Apa connections in our whakapapa. Some of our people have different names — Uncle Tuiti MacDonald is named after Tuiti Amaru, one of the Ngāti Apa tīpuna. So all of us involved in the Ship Cove project go down there and this Cook monument is all there is. DOC wanted to paint it taupe, so it didn't stand out. I said, 'Hang on a minute, that's like a symbol of the Raj — the British Empire. You can't allow that. What you have to do is add a component, not tone one down.' People say they're the wrong cannons. Well, who cares? Our issue, we had to argue, is not that Rangitāne were there and Te Ātiawa are here now. Neither of us is here. The Department of Conservation is here.
>
> We worked through those mana whenua/tangata whenua historical relevance arguments and finally decided that the representation should

be about the time of Cook's arrival. We didn't want to try to reinterpret the whole Treaty thing. We decided that what we all had in common was the shaping of the Sounds, and that focus, which meant talking about Kupe, should be a principal one.

All the discussions that people have had about that key story — that Te Ātiawa have today, that we Rangitāne have had — are the stories of how Kupe fought Te Wheke and how that battle shaped the land. That giant octopus is still lying there in Anatohia, that long headland leading south out of the bay, that's the big tentacle, the lead tentacle. Kupe's names are all round D'Urville Island, and they come all the way round the outside of the Queen Charlotte Sounds, all the way, and then stop at that particular landmark, Nga Taumanu o Te Matahourua or White Bluffs. We understand that the names are based on our knowledge of that time. I can add my experience, but that is of a tohu or sign.

The last things to be put in at the Ship Cove upgrade were the pouwhenua, one depicting Rangitāne, one depicting Te Ātiawa and one depicting Kupe. We were standing on the beach, myself for Rangitāne, and Joe Puketapu, chairperson of Te Ātiawa marae, and DOC, and they were lowering the final pouwhenua into the hole in the ground. As soon as it went in, there was an earthquake! I looked around at Joe and he looked around at me and we both never said anything. And then two of the DOC guys said: 'Wow! Did you feel that earthquake!' And I said to Joe, 'Thank Christ for that, mate. Until they said that I thought it was one of those Māori bullshit events!'

When that man Kupe went back into the earth, that is the first manifestation in my lifetime that I've seen of Kupe, as in the stories of shaping the land. Uncle Frank and his generation carved Kupe as the kaitiaki of Omaka Marae. His friend Ngahue is on the top of the meetinghouse and he has his foot on a piece of pounamu. Kupe is the figure at the bottom of the front post when you walk into the wharenui — he's the tekoteko, or guardian, for want of a better name.

The two people who designed the first carved wharenui in the top of the south were my Uncle Frank and Tipene O'Regan. So that's why, when you look at that wharenui, you see that it represents how we saw Te Waipounamu — the Ngāi Tahu tīpuna Marukaitatea on one side and

The largest of the three tōtara pouwhenua at Meretoto Ship Cove carved by Reg Thompsett (Tainui, Ngāti Māniapoto), depicting Kupe, his birds Rupe (a kererū) and Te Kawau-a-Toru (a kawau pāteketeke or king shag), and the octopus Whekenui, which Kupe fought and killed, staining Kura Te Au Tory Channel with its blood. Two smaller pouwhenua, representing the historical mana whenua status of Rangitāne, Ngāti Apa and Ngāti Kuia and the present mana whenua status of Te Ātiawa, also stand at the site. MIKE YARDLEY, NEW ZEALAND HERALD

Te Huataki of Rangitāne on the other side. The maihi or outstretched arms are all the Ngāti Mamoe and Waitaha ancestors connecting both iwi to the tekoteko. Kupe is the celebrated ancestor where you go into the whare and Ngahue is standing with him. Uncle Frank and Tipene O'Regan wove all that history together both inside and outside in the mahau or verandah by carving all of those ancestors who lived in and around the Marlborough Sounds.

So I grew up with these relationships in a familiar setting and that was the start of my political awareness. Each one of those ancestral names is not just a name, it is a connection. Tarakaipa, he lived on Tarakaipa Island and he's half Ngāti Apa and Ngāti Tara. He married Te Hewi, of Rangitāne, Ngāi Tara and Ngāti Mamoe and that connects up with the Ngāti Mamoe living on the other side of the Clarence River. Through those relationships, our influence extended on one side of the river, and the Ngāi Tahu influence was on the other side. The intermarriages between the two iwi allowed for travel in the contested land.

I'm the only one in my family that's witnessed a random earthquake when a pouwhenua went into the ground! That's become a legend. Everyone talks about it. My kids can say, 'Oh, yeah, I remember Dad telling us about that! He one of the fellas that was there!' I think that's important to hook into the story because you could argue that if I didn't belong there or didn't have a connection to that place, I wouldn't have witnessed that event.

I named my granddaughter Atapō. First, of course, because it's that particular time, after midnight, but before dawn when the sky is just beginning to redden and the birds are starting to stir. Te Atapō. But it's also the name of that point in Endeavour Inlet that sticks out on Edgecombe Point. I remember Uncle Walter saying when we were going past the entrance to Endeavour Inlet on the way to Ōnauku, 'Oh, well, boy, that's where your Rangitāne crew is! But now you're with us.' I found out later from Atapō's other grandmother, who had a bach in Camp Bay, that that's the point where you can look out into the northern entrance of the Sounds. Atapō is my first grandchild and my first granddaughter and I thought at the time, 'It's a new horizon.' So that's why I named her that. I often thought that, in the end, this is how this is done.

Appendices

Appendix 1a: Pākehā settlement 1864–69

News on the Marlborough Sounds and its Pākehā residents was fairly sparse in the early years of Pākehā settlement. The material in these three appendices is taken from various sources to indicate the extent and places of European settlement at various point in time. The first of these provides a baseline against which subsequent population spread can be noted.

In Queen Charlotte Sound records from this period mention James Heberley, then living on Long Island, where presumably he had a small subsistence farm, being appointed pilot (elsewhere, he was identified as 'farmer Tory Channel'); Arthur Beauchamp's brother Craddock buying 100 acres in 1863; Scott Duncan, sawyer, occupying the Grove Saw Mill, Picton; Courtney Kenny, Commissioner of Crown Lands, and sheep farmer Donald McCormick owning 3000 and 600 acres respectively; sheep farmer Robert Woodgate owning 300 acres in Wharehunga Bay; and in 1865 George and Charles Turner being awarded the first grazing licence for the Ravenscliff Run, which would reach from Cape Jackson to below Mount Furneaux in Endeavour Inlet. They built a house in Cannibal Cove. George left, but Charles and his wife farmed and raised a family.[1] Phillip Homes farmed 50 acres in Queen Charlotte Sound, as did whalers James Jackson, William John snr and William Keenan; Joseph Toms held 30 acres.

In 1862 Patrick McMahon was the first European to settle in Pelorus Sound, at Kenepuru (on the 'Taradale Estate').[2] William Adams, clerk, owned a section in Beatrix Bay; while farmers Alexander William Harvey and George Rutland occupied 50 acres and 150 acres respectively in Pelorus Sound. David Wells, sawyer, owned 50 acres in Kenepuru Sound; sheep farmer Robert Blaymire owned 1000 aces in Pelorus, Tahuahua, and Kenepuru (no mention is made of his holding at Blumine Island).[3]

In 1865, following the surveying done for Captain J. Halliday around the flat areas of Titirangi Bay, Alligator Head and in the western bays of Port Gore, Hannah and Henry Godsiff settled at Titirangi to manage the place for Halliday. William McManaway and brother-in-law William Campbell settled in Hikoekoea Bay, just north of Titirangi Bay, and began farming there about 1870.

Recorded only by his last name, Smith, 'a seafaring man', and his Māori wife settled on the lower slopes in Port Gore, built a house and woolshed and grew wheat in blocks in and around Melville Cove.[4] At some stage in the 1860s William Stuart settled in Burnside Bay (renamed Te Towaka Bay in 1908 by Post and Telegraph),[5] and in 1869 the Godsiffs moved to the Manaroa run.[6]

Appendix 1b: Pākehā settlement 1881

This section creates an impression of the numbers and places of settlement in the Picton electoral district as identified in the 1881 Census.

Although by the 1880s Māhakipawa Valley, Linkwater and the Grove area were largely milled out,[7] there were 70 people at Māhakipawa and 42 at Anakiwa. Curiously, despite the flat land at its head and its proximity to Picton, Lochmara Bay had only one resident. There were seven at The Rocks (in Double Bay, across from Picton) and 10 at Waikawa.

Mining activity had also created pockets of settlement — Golden Point, off Kumototo Bay, where gold was found in the early 1870s, registered 23 people; Endeavour Inlet seven; Ravenscliff four; Jackson's Head (Cape Jackson?) 36; and Turners Bay (now Anaho Cannibal Cove) 13. Elsewhere, Queen Charlotte Sound appears virtually unpopulated. Boat builder and serial bankrupt Henry Berg, who built the fast Wellington yacht *Xarifa*, which would visit the Sounds, was (briefly) among 10 people at Ship Cove. Eight people lived on Arapawa Island (now Arapaoa Island); among the 37 in Tory Channel were three at Ōkukari Bay and nine at Jacksons Bay.

Six people were wresting a living in the highly tidal Mahau Sound, while Pelorus Sound could boast only about one settler for every 40 kilometres. In the handful of bays of about 10–200 acres and 'famous'[8] for their pasture, there are bigger groups of people — 113 in Kenepuru Sound, 14 at Hopai, 41 at Wet Inlet, five at Homewood; while the 39 at Clova Bay were clustered where the Harveys had established their home in 1849 and where Henry and Elizabeth Godsiff had arrived at Manaroa in 1869. Milling accounted for the 31 at Nydia Bay and probably the 14 at Black Point.

The outer Sounds were sparsely populated: one person lived on Forsyth Island (legal title to the island was sold only in 1898);[9] there were 12 at Ketu Bay where the Harris brothers, William Sumpter and Edwin Headley would develop their station, Pohuenui. Six were at Akaroa, in Anakoha Bay.[10]

Appendix 1c: Pākehā settlement by mid-1890s

The King-Turners had arrived at Waitata Bay in the outer Sounds in about 1876; Peter Archer, from Denmark, and his wife Sara bought their section in Tuna Bay, Tennyson Inlet, in 1880. (Mill hands working for the Duncans, appalled at the remoteness of Tennyson Inlet, named it Worlds End).[11] John (Jack) Fell, one of three brothers who had been 'given' three freehold sections in Nikau Bay, in Pelorus Sound, his wife Janet and architect brother Dick (who had had to leave London for health reasons) were also there, as was another brother, Fred, who had taken up his land in about 1887.[12] The Wells family was at Four Fathom Bay (the next bay north); the Maud Brothers, Bertrand, Arthur, Rowland, as well as another unidentified settler were farming just north again, in Yncyca Bay. (The Indian name, meaning 'home', may have been given by a Reg Kidd, who had worked in British Columbia.)[13]

Thomas Hearn Mills (who had taken over the Hopai, Homewood and Crail Bay runs acquired in an earlier partnership with his brothers Charles Houghton, already a Liberal politician, Alfred and John)[14] was living and raising a very large family at Hopai; another brother, Harry, appears to have spent some time at Elie Bay. Henry and Hannah Godsiff were by then at the Peninsula Run adjourning Manaroa; Henry had also bought land in Waitaria Bay, Kenepuru Sound, about 1879, which a son, David, took over when Henry died in 1898. Tom Clifford and family were on Maud Island; John Mills, who owned land in Kenepuru, was living at Brightlands, across Tawhitinui Reach from Maud Island; while Sarah, daughter of William and Augusta Harvey, the earliest settlers in outer Pelorus, appears to have been on the island itself. There, too, Thomas Mills ran 200 of the 1600 sheep he was running in the Sounds. Mr Tosswill, a young Canterbury bachelor, was sheep farming in Fitzroy Bay; the Browns were in Tennyson Inlet, at Fern Flat (now Elaine Bay); a number of fishing families were based at Bulwer; William Stuart was at Te Towaka Bay, where it was easy access over the hill to the Elliots in Admiralty Bay; and Arthur Elmslie was at French Pass, where he had arrived about 1857.[15] Mr Creighton had an 'extensive' holding at Port Ligar;[16] a Mr Jackson lived alone on Forsyth Island; the Redwoods had a fine 350-acre sheep run in Anakoha Bay, and in Ketu Bay; Captain Harris had 6000 acres. Francis Digby Neave amalgamated local farms and, with the exception of some Māori reserves, had taken all the densely bushed land below 600 metres between Anakoha Bay and the head of Port Gore.

In Queen Charlotte Sound, Richard Eames Bowden, who had previously worked for timber merchants and Luke's Foundry in Wellington and whose brother was the well-known captain of the trader *Gannet*,[17] had the Scarborough Run, 'a nice piece of sheep land' in or around Dryden Bay.[18] Further north, Mr Turner's presence in Cannibal Bay, where, as noted the principal house for the Ravenscliff Run was built, was noted.[19] In 1896 William Baldick, (related to the Jacksons by marriage) had small holdings on Blumine Island and had replaced the original two-room whare with an eight-room house that was used by Sounds workers.[20] (He farmed there until his death in the early 1940s.)

Appendix 2a: Small timber mills 1848–96

DATES	MILLER	LOCATION	QUANTITY OF TIMBER	ADDITIONAL INFORMATION
1848	Family records of milling activity	Mahau Sound		This may have preceded the Harvey settlement
1861	Alexander Duncan	Grove	Initial cut 8000 super ft* daily	
Early 1860s	Bradshaw	Tennyson Inlet	Unknown	Exported timber from Tuna Bay
	Harvey family milling at Harvey Bay		Unknown	
1864	Herbert Gaby, William Evans Dive	Māhakipawa	Cutting rights to 1000 acres	Such mills provided reasons for freighters to call
1866	Alexander Brown & Alexander Petrie Inglis	'Anakeewa' (Anakiwa)		Land leased from Capt. Hood. Partnership dissolved 1872, but Brown milled until 1872
1867	Cornfoot, Robinson & Co	Parkers Arm, first arm in Kaiuma Valley	Unknown	This operation was short-lived
1870s	Richard, James & Samuel Climo	Oruapuputa side of Māhakipawa Arm	Unknown	Timber was rafted to Capt. Dive's mill at Hood Bay
1870–79	Capt. Dive	Relocates to Hood Bay, Mahau Sound	1870–78: 12 million super ft	
	Alex Duncan	Took over father's right to 7000 acres, Tennyson Inlet	8 million super ft	Harveys, without a licence, withdrew

188–87	Alex Duncan	9700 acres, Kenepuru Run; small areas in Portage Bay & Endeavour Inlet	16 million super ft	Used machinery he had shipped from Dalton's Koromiko mill to Waitaria Bay
1860	Isaac Harvey	Okoha		One of five mills to operate there over 100 years
Late 1860s	Harvey & Henry Godsiff in partnership with Arthur Beauchamp & Fredrick Suisted	Manaroa		
1875	Turnbull & Sons	Ketu Bay		
1876	Unidentified operator	Ketu Bay	39,000 super ft	
1887	Henry Godsiff	20 acres in Grants Bay		
1896	Richard & James Climo	Harveys Bay		

* A square foot of timber of a specified thickness, usually 1 inch.

NOTE: These names and locations have been drawn from a range of sources. They are unlikely to identify all milling operations in the Sounds, or their various sites. Remnants that can still be found today in the Sounds suggest that small mills were scattered everywhere, often operating within a kilometre or so of each other.

Appendix 2b: Small timber millers 1900–05

DATE	MILLER	LOCATION	ADDITIONAL INFORMATION
1900	Harvey Brothers[21]	Clova Bay[22]	At this point this is the only mill in the Sounds
1901	Richard Climo buys milling rights from settlers	Nydia Bay. Buys large area of rimu, birch & mataī expected to last 15 years	Mill established and large wharf put in[23]
1903	Ward & Sons from Omamalutu	Nydia Bay. Land bought from local settlers	
1903 1905	Pugh Bros (8hp)	Nydia Bay	160,000 super ft timber for Picton market, employed 5–6 men and 3 hands
1903	Tugoald Bratli (8hp)	Taranui Mill, Crail Bay	Employed 9 men, including Bratli, cutting some 9000 railway sleepers, 20,000 super ft of mixed timber
1903	Beech Bros	Head of Kenepuru Sound	
1903	E. Pullman	Resolution Bay	Cutting about 150 railway sleepers a week, employed 5 including proprietor
1905	Pullman & Bryants (12hp)	Started 1902[24] Resolution Bay	3 hands, cutting 200,000 super ft for railway sleepers. Mill to close shortly
1905[25]	Pullman & Sons	Crail Bay mill	6 hands, 400,000 sleepers
1905	Kenepuru Sawmill Co. (12hp)		8 hands, 240,000 super ft used locally, 240,000 super ft sleepers
1905	Climo & Fawcett's (17hp)	Okoha	10 hands, 320,000 super ft exported from district

Appendix 3: Subsidised mail services

SERVICE	ANNUAL SUBSIDY AND FREQUENCY OF SERVICE	MILES OF COMPLETE VOYAGE	COST PER MILE (SHILLINGS & PENCE)
	1905		
Wellington, Ketu Bay, Homewood, Māori Bay (and all other offices), Havelock	£700 for 43 trips Dec 1891–Dec 1906	210	1.018
Havelock and Bulwer	Fortnightly service	210	1.018
	1910		
Wellington, Ketu Bay, Homewood, Māori Bay (and all other offices), Havelock	£600, fortnightly service	183	10.44
Picton, offices in the Sounds, Havelock	£120 increased to £122 when in 1909 Ōtānerau (Arapaoa Island) and Wharehunga added	164	6.84
	1915		
Wellington, Whakatahuri, Homewood, other offices, Havelock	£440, fortnightly service	300	11.56 (fourth-highest subsidy in New Zealand)
Picton, offices in the Sounds, Havelock	£330, fortnightly service	330	9.23
Picton, Grove Wharf, Te Awaiti, Resolution Bay	£185 increased to £192 10s when subsidy increased Sept 1914. Thrice-weekly service	88	3.36
Picton and Portage	£60, monthly service	14	3.3
Portage and Kenepuru Head	£70, 6 days a week	46	3.51
Portage and Crail Bay	£137 increased to £147 when subsidy increased Sept 1914. Weekly service	106	6.4

NOTE: The information presented in the annual reports does not always allow uniformity.

Notes

Abbreviations

AJHR *Appendix to the Journals of the House of Representatives*
ANZ Archives New Zealand (Wellington)
ATL Alexander Turnbull Library (Wellington)
CCL Commissioner of Crown Lands
CLD Crown Lands Department
Compendium Alexander Mackay, *A Compendium of Official Documents Relative to Native Affairs in the South Island*, 2 vols (Wellington: Government Printer, 1872–73)
DNZB Dictionary of New Zealand Biography
DOC Department of Conservation
EDAR Education Department annual reports
EDIR Education Department inspectors' reports
HC Hocken Collections Uare Taoka o Hākena, University of Otago
L&S Department of Lands and Survey
L&SAR Department of Lands and Survey annual reports
MDAR Marine Department annual reports
ME *Marlborough Express*
MSMP Marlborough Sounds Maritime Park
MOW Ministry of Works (1948–73)
MWD Ministry of Works and Development (1974–)
NENZC *The Nelson Examiner and New Zealand Chronicle*
P&T Post and Telegraph Department
PWD Public Works Department (1870–1947)
PWDAR Public Works Department annual reports
Te Ara Te Ara: The Encyclopedia of New Zealand
TPD Department of Tourist & Publicity (incl. Dept of Tourism and Health Resorts up to 1951)

Introduction

1 Waitangi Tribunal, *Te Tau Ihu o te Waka a Maui: Report on Northern South Island Claims* (Wai 785), vol. 3 (Wellington, 2008), p. 1210
2 Rachel Buchanan, *Ko Taranaki Te Maunga* (Wellington: Bridget Williams Books, 2018), p. 103
3 Danny Keenan, quoting Justice Eddie Durie in 'The trouble with the NZ wars', *The Dominion Post*, 4 July 2019.

1. Settling the Land

1 I. B. Campbell & M. R. Johnson, 'Nelson and Marlborough', in J. M. Soons & M. J. Selby (eds), *Landforms of New Zealand* (Auckland: Longman Paul, 1992), pp. 430–32.
2 Jonathan Brough, 'Tracks', *The Colonist*, 31 December 1900, p. 4.
3 Hilary and John Mitchell, *Te Tau Ihu o te Waka: A History of the Māori of Nelson and Marlborough*, vol. 1: *Te Tangata me te Whenua / The People and the Land* (Wellington: Huia Publishers, 2004), pp. 18–19.
4 Ibid., pp. 32–36; Stephen O'Regan, 'Queen Charlotte Sound: Aspects of traditional Māori history', in Glynn Barratt (ed.), *Queen Charlotte Sound New Zealand: The Traditional and European Records, 1820* (Ottawa, Canada: Carleton University Press, 1987), p. 144. O'Regan also discussed the links with these names with wider cultural traditions (pp. 142–45).

5 Mitchells, *Te Tau Ihu o te Waka*, vol. 1, pp. 41–42.
6 Ibid., p. 37.
7 Reg Nicol, pers. comm., May 2017.
8 O'Regan, 'Queen Charlotte Sound', pp. 145–46.
9 I am indebted to Professor Richard Walter, University of Otago, for the date of arrival.
10 Waitangi Tribunal, *Te Tau Ihu o te Waka a Maui: Report on Northern South Island Claims* (Wai 785), vol. 1 (Wellington, 2008), p. 27.
11 Ibid., p. 20. Re 'original peoples' or the groupings with whom they had merged see p. 27.
12 Ibid., 27–28. For their relationship with Ngāi Tahu see p. 96.
13 Ibid., p. 94.
14 R. J. Paterson, *The Sea Was Our Boundary: The Titirangi / Waitui Story of the Patersons 1929–1977* (self-published, 2011), p. 15. Paterson notes the finding in Titirangi Bay of a North Island greenstone patu and greenstone from Pelorus River suggests trading links beyond Pelorus Sound.
15 J. C. Beaglehole (ed.), *The Journals of Captain James Cook*, vol. 1: *The Voyage of the* Endeavour, *1768–1771* (Cambridge: Cambridge University Press for the Hakluyt Society, 1955), p. 250. Cook found that traded items had travelled some 135 nautical miles up the North Island east coast to at least Cape Kidnappers.
16 Michael M. Trotter, *Marlborough Sounds Archaeological Survey 1974*, Canterbury Museum, Christchurch, 1974, pp. 8–18.
17 Barry Brailsford, *The Tattooed Land: The Southern Frontiers of the Pa Maori* (Auckland: Reed, 1981), p. 4.
18 Michael Hoare (ed.), *The* Resolution *Journal of Johann Reinhold Forster 1772–1775*, in four volumes (London: Hakluyt Society, 1982, vol. 2, p. 301) provides a more recent estimate than Cook's – see Beaglehole (ed.), *The Voyage of the* Endeavour, p. 247.
19 Trotter, *Marlborough Sounds Archaeological Survey*, p. 5; Michael M. Trotter, *Titirangi Archaeology: An Interim Report* (Christchurch: Canterbury Museum, 1977), pp. 4, 9; Michael M. Trotter, 'Settlements, sites and structures around Ship Cove', in Barratt (ed.), *Queen Charlotte Sound, New Zealand: 1820*. On p. 126 Trotter provides further evidence of sites used by both the 'moa-hunting' and 'classical' people.
20 Mitchells, *Te Tau Ihu o te Waka*, vol. 1, p. 172.
21 J. C. Beaglehole (ed.), *The Journals of Captain James Cook*, vol. 2: *The Voyage of the* Resolution and Adventure, *1772–1775* (Cambridge: Cambridge University Press for the Hakluyt Society, 1961), part 1, Appendix IV, Extracts from Officers' Records, Furneaux's Narrative, pp. 738–39.
22 Ian Barber, 'Early contact ethnography and understanding: An evaluation of the Cook expeditionary accounts of the Grass Cove Conflict', in Alex Calder, Jonathan Lamb & Bridget Orr, *Voyages and Beaches: Pacific Encounters, 1769–1840* (Honolulu: University of Hawai'i Press, 1999), pp. 168–69.
23 Beaglehole (ed.), *The Voyage of the* Resolution *and* Discovery, part 1, p. 60.
24 Trotter, *Marlborough Sounds Archaeological Survey*, p. 3; Trotter, *Titirangi Archaeology*, p. 1.
25 Trotter, *Titirangi Archaeology*.
26 Hilary & John Mitchells, *Te Tau Ihu o te Waka: A History of Maori of Nelson and Marlborough*, vol. 2: *Te Ara Hou / The New Society* (Wellington: Huia Publishers, 2007), p. 163.
27 Beaglehole (ed.), *The Voyage of the* Resolution *and* Discovery, part 2. p. 811. Anderson's comment on the difficulty of catching the birds echoes the comment that Forster made on the previous voyage – see Hoare (ed.), *The* Resolution *Journal of Johann Reinhold Forster*, part 2, p. 302.
28 Beaglehole (ed.), *The Voyage of the* Resolution *and* Discovery, part 1, p. 67.
29 For the quote see Hoare (ed.), *The* Resolution *Journal of Johann Reinhold Forster*, vol. 3, p. 426.
30 Brailsford, *The Tattooed Land*, pp. 44–45.
31 Trotter, *Titirangi Archaeology*, p. 12.
32 Louise Furey, *Māori Gardening: An Archaeological Perspective* (Wellington: Department of Conservation, 2006), p. 19.
33 Trotter, *Marlborough Sounds Archaeological Survey* (p. 7) suggests the probability of a garden there. Brailsford (*The Tattooed Land*, p. 51) states unequivocally that there was one.
34 Brailsford, *The Tattooed Land*, p. 55.

35 Michael M. Trotter, *Archaeological Site Survey of East Bay, Arapawa Island* (Christchurch: Canterbury Museum, 1978), pp. 2–4.

36 Michael Trotter, pers. comm., 25 February 2014. Janet Davidson (pers. comm., July 2014) also noted her experimental kūmara gardening in the area with horticultural experts and quoted comments from North American experts on the mound method – see M. Burtenshaw, G. Harris, J. Davidson & F. Leach, 'Experimental growing of pre-European cultivars of kūmara (sweet potato, *Ipomoea batatas* L. Lam.) at the southern margins of Māori horticulture', NZ *Journal of Archaeology* 23 (2001). Ian Barber, 'Molluscan mulching at the margins: Investigating the development of a South Island Maori variation on Polynesian hard mulch agronomy', *Archaeology in Oceania* 48 (2013), p. 49.

37 Janet Davidson, pers. comm., July 2014.

38 Ernst Dieffenbach, *Travels in New Zealand, with contributions to the geography, geology, botany, and natural history of that country* (Capper reprint, 1974: Early New Zealand Books: enzb.auckland.ac.nz), p. 25; 'Sketch of an excursion . . .', *NENZC*, 29 March 1845, p. 13.

39 Brailsford, *The Tattooed Land*, p. 8.

40 Mitchells, *Te Tau Ihu o te Waka*, vol. 1, p. 171.

41 James King, *Journal* (untitled), Doc. no. 55/116, February 1777, Public Record Office, London, quoted in Mitchells, *Te Tau Ihu o te Waka*, vol. 1, p. 173.

42 Beaglehole (ed.), *The Voyage of the* Resolution *and* Discovery, part 1, p. 71 and p. 71 n.1.

43 J. C. Beaglehole (ed.), *The Endeavour Journals of Joseph Banks: 1768–1771*, vol. 1 (Sydney: Trustees of the Public Library of New South Wales in association with Angus & Robertson), 1963, p. 462.

44 James Kenneth Munford (ed.), *John Ledyard's Journal of Captain Cook's Last Voyage* (Corvallis: Oregon State University Press, 1963), February 1777, p. 13.

45 Mitchells, *Te Tau Ihu o te Waka*, vol. 1, p. 184.

46 Ibid., p. 172.

47 Trotter, 'Settlements, sites', p. 123.

48 Anon., *A Journal of a Voyage round the World* (London: T. Becket, 1771), quoted in Brailsford, *The Tattooed Land*, p. 26.

49 Brailsford, *The Tattooed Land*, pp. 52–54.

50 Trotter, *Titirangi Archaeology*, p. 16.

51 Trotter, 'Settlements, sites', p. 124.

52 Beaglehole (ed.), *The Voyage of the* Endeavour, p. 157n, quoted in Trotter, 'Settlements, sites', p. 114.

53 Beaglehole (ed.), *Banks's* Endeavour *Journal*, vol. 1, p. 460, n.2.

54 Brailsford, *The Tattooed Land*, p. 27.

55 Beaglehole (ed.), *Banks's* Endeavour *Journal*, vol. 1, p. 460; Brailsford, *The Tattooed Land*, p. 7.

56 *William Anderson's Journal* in Beaglehole (ed.), *The Voyage of the* Resolution *and* Discovery, part 2, p. 810.

57 Ibid., p. 811.

58 Trotter, 'Settlements, sites', p. 130; Janet Davidson, pers. comm. in relation to preferred styles of warfare.

59 Beaglehole (ed.), *Banks's* Endeavour *Journal*, vol. 1, pp. 452–53.

60 Ibid.

61 Beaglehole (ed.), *The Voyage of the* Endeavour, p. 247.

62 Beaglehole (ed.), *Banks's* Endeavour *Journal*, vol. 1, p. 457.

63 Ibid. (p. 454) and Beaglehole (ed.) *The Voyage of the* Endeavour (p. 235, n.3) give slightly different accounts of this incident, in which it would appear that Cook behaved aggressively. Cook recorded that he was worried because the *Endeavour* was being that careened, and the English were therefore more vulnerable.

64 William Anderson was generally more critical of – or disenchanted with – Māori behaviour, social organisation and customs. See *William Anderson's Journal* in Beaglehole (ed.), *The Voyage of the* Resolution *and* Discovery, part 2, pp. 813*ff*.

65 Beaglehole (ed.) *The Voyage of the* Endeavour, p. 240.

66 Beaglehole (ed.), *Banks's* Endeavour *Journal*, vol. 1, p. 459.

67 J. C. Beaglehole, *The Life of Captain James Cook* (London: Hakluyt Society, 1974), p. 525.
68 Beaglehole (ed.), *The Voyage of the* Resolution *and* Discovery, Introduction, p. xxxviii.
69 Beaglehole, *The Life*, p. 525.
70 Beaglehole (ed.), *The Voyage of the* Resolution *and* Discovery, part 1, p. 59.
71 Anne Salmond, *The Trial of the Cannibal Dog: Captain Cook in the South Seas* (London/Auckland: Allen Lane/Penguin, 2003/2004), pp. 315–16.
72 Beaglehole (ed.), *The Voyage of the* Endeavour, pp. cclxxxii–cclxxxiii.
73 Andrew David, Rüdiger Joppien & Bernard Smith (eds), *The Charts and Coastal Views of Captain Cook's Voyages, vol. 1, The voyage of the* Endeavour, *1768–1771* (London: Hakluyt Society, 1988), pp. 239–45.
74 Beaglehole (ed.), *The Voyage of the* Resolution *and* Adventure, p. 575.
75 Beaglehole (ed.), *The Voyage of the* Endeavour, p. 243. Beaglehole, in a footnote, clarifies the confusion created by the old man referring to Arapaoa Island and the English thinking it referred to the South Island as a whole.
76 Beaglehole (ed.), *Banks's* Endeavour *Journal*, vol. 1, p. 452.
77 Quoted in A. Charles Begg & Neil C. Begg, *James Cook and New Zealand: The Voyage of the* Endeavour, *1768–1771; the Voyage of the* Resolution *and* Adventure, *1772–1775; the Voyage of the* Resolution *and* Discovery, *1776–1780* (Wellington: Government Printer, 1969), p. 122. In relation to the flax seeds see Glynn Barratt, *Bellingshausen: A Visit to New Zealand, 1820* (Palmerston North: Dunmore Press, 1979), p. 38.
78 Quoted in Begg, *James Cook and New Zealand*, p. 143.
79 Waitangi Tribunal, *Te Tau Ihu o Te Waka a Maui*, vol. 1, pp. 28–29; Mitchells, *Te Tau Ihu o Te Waka*, vol. 1, p. 86.
80 Barratt, *Bellingshausen*, pp. 120–21.
81 Ibid., pp. 44, 55.
82 Ibid., pp. 81, 83.

2. New Arrivals

1 Angela Ballara, 'Customary Māori Land Tenure', p. 24 in Waitangi Tribunal, *Te Tau Ihu o te Waka a Maui: Report on Northern South Island Claims* (Wai 785), vols. 1, 2 & 3 (Wellington, 2008).
2 Ibid., p. 41
3 In relation to Te Rauparaha's movements see Hilary and John Mitchells, *Te Tau Ihu o te Waka: A History of the Māori of Nelson and Marlborough*, vol. 1: *Te Tangata me te Whenua / The People and the Land* (Wellington: Huia Publishers, 2004), p. 86; Roger Smith, 'Marlborough Sound NZ', cartographic material (Wellington: Geographx, 2010).
4 Stephen O'Regan, 'Queen Charlotte Sound: Aspects of Maori traditional history', in Glynn Barratt (ed.), *Queen Charlotte Sound, New Zealand: The Traditional and European Records, 1820* (Ottawa, Canada: Carleton University Press, 1987), p. 140.
5 Re the numbers of Te Rauparaha's men see S. P. Smith, 'History and traditions of the Taranaki coast: The South Island raids', *Journal of Polynesian Society* 18, no. 4 (1909), pp. 186–87. For the route and details of destruction see Smith, 'Marlborough Sound NZ'.
6 James Heberley's diary, Picton Museum, quoted in Oliver Sutherland, *Arthur Elmslie, Whaler and Gentleman, and Anaru, the Farm at French Pass* (Nelson: self-published, 2006), p. 29.
7 Smith, 'History and traditions of the Taranaki coast'.
8 Edward Jerningham Wakefield, *Adventure in New Zealand from 1839 to 1844 with Some Account of the Beginning of the British Colonization of the Islands* (London: John Murray, 1845) (ebook), pp. 58, 59.
9 Mitchells, *Te Tau Ihu o te Waka*, vol. 1, p. 139.
10 Ibid. For the settlements of Rangitāne and Ngāti Kuia see Hilary & John Mitchells, *Te Tau Ihu o te Waka: A History of Maori of Nelson and Marlborough*, vol. 2: *Te Ara Hou / The New Society* (Wellington: Huia Publishers, 2007), p. 20.

11 Waitangi Tribunal, *Te Tau Ihu*, vol. 1, pp. 90–95; 153–64; Mitchells, *Te Tau Ihu o te Waka*, vol. 1, p. 139.
12 Stephen O'Regan, 'Tōtaranui: Aspects of Māori traditional history', in Barratt (ed.), *Queen Charlotte Sound New Zealand*, p. 140.
13 Barry Mason, closing statement [2004], doc B20(a), p. 1, cited in Waitangi Tribunal, *Te Tau Ihu*, vol. 2, p. 1013.
14 https://collections.tepapa.govt.nz/topic/1001
15 Mitchells, *Te Tau Ihu o te Waka*, vol. 1, pp. 231–32, 236.
16 Jock Phillips, 'Whaling – Ship-based whaling', Te Ara: www.TeAra.govt.nz/en/whaling/page-2
17 Ibid.
18 Ibid.
19 Mitchells, *Te Tau Ihu o te Waka*, vol. 2, p. 28.
20 Robert McNab, *The Old Whaling Days: A History of Southern New Zealand from 1830 to 1840* (Auckland: Golden Press, 1975 [1913]), pp. 4–13. For the Sydney prices see Wakefield, *Adventure in New Zealand* (p. 16). By 1833 the volume of business the shore-based whaling stations and the overseas ships visiting Port Underwood generated during the whaling season was so great that Hobart businessmen wanted a colony to be established to handle it – see W. A. Chambers, *Samuel Ironside in New Zealand*, quoted in Sutherland, *Arthur Elmslie* (p. 25).
21 Phillips, 'Whaling'.
22 Sutherland, *Arthur Elmslie*, p. 27; Carol Dawber, *The Jacksons of Te Awaiti* (Picton: River Press, 2001) pp. 28–29.
23 Mitchells, *Te Tau Ihu o te Waka*, vol. 2, p. 29.
24 McNab, *The Old Whaling Days*, p. 297; Ernst Dieffenbach, *Travels in New Zealand, with contributions to the geography, geology, botany, and natural history of that country* (Capper reprint, 1974: Early New Zealand Books: enzb.auckland.ac.nz), p. 49.
25 Wakefield, *Adventure in New Zealand*, p. 49.
26 Tony Walzl, *Ngāti Rarua Land Issues 1839–1960*, in Waitangi Tribunal, *Te Tau Ihu*, vol. 1, pp. 18–19.
27 See the individuals' respective biographies in DNZB, Te Ara: https://teara.govt.nz/en
28 Hilary and John Mitchells, *Te Tau Ihu o te Waka: A History of the Māori of Nelson and Marlborough*, vol. 4: *Ngā Whānau Rangatira o Ngāti Tama me Te Ātiawa / The Chiefly Families of Ngāti Tama and Te Ātiawa* (Nelson/Picton: Ngā whānau rangatira o Ngāti Tama me Te Ātiawa, 2014); Wakefield, *Adventure in New Zealand*, p. 14.
29 Sutherland, *Arthur Elmslie*, p. 30; Dawber, *The Jacksons*, p. 21.
30 Richard Boast, 'Te tango whenua – Māori land alienation – Pre-Treaty transactions', Te Ara: www.TeAra.govt.nz/en/te-tango-whenua-Māori-land-alienation/page-2
31 Mitchells, *Te Tau Ihu o te Waka*, vol. 1, pp. 241–42.
32 Ibid., pp. 247–48.
33 Dieffenbach, *Travels in New Zealand*, p. 49.
34 Dawber, *The Jacksons*, p. 33.
35 Ibid., pp. 11–23, quoted in Sutherland, *Arthur Elmslie*, p. 28.
36 Dieffenbach, *Travels in New Zealand*, p. 49.
37 McNab, *The Old Whaling Days*, pp. 9–10; Dawber (*The Jacksons*, pp. 149–50) gives details of the overnight stays, suggesting that the men would climb the cliffs and make their way back to the station, get their gear, return and cut up the blubber on the spot. Unable to see how they could then have moved the sheer quantity of blubber back to the station, I have omitted that detail.
38 Wakefield, *Adventure in New Zealand*, p. 46.
39 McNab, *The Old Whaling Days*, p. 349.
40 L. S. Rickard, *The Whaling Trade in Old New Zealand* (Auckland: Minerva, 1965), p. 73, quoted in Sutherland, *Arthur Elmslie*, p. 37.
41 Wakefield, *Adventure in New Zealand*, p. 48.
42 Ibid., p. 237; Mitchells, *Te Tau Ihu o te Waka*, vol. 2, p. 185.
43 Ibid. (vol. 1), p. 233.

44 Ibid., pp. 236–37.

45 Ibid., pp. 238, 241; Mitchells, *Te Tau Ihu o te Waka*, vol. 2, pp. 193–94.

46 Ibid. (vol. 2), p. 28; re Whekenui and Ōkukari see Dieffenbach, *Travels in New Zealand*, p. 104.

47 Nigel Prickett, *The Archaeology of New Zealand Shore Whaling* (Wellington: Department of Conservation, 2002), p. 76.

48 Sutherland, *Arthur Elmslie*, pp. 16, 38.

49 A. D. MacIntosh, *Marlborough: A Provincial History* (Christchurch: Capper Press, 1977), pp. 41–42, quoted in Sutherland, *Arthur Elmslie*, p. 38.

50 Dieffenbach, *Travels in New Zealand*, quoted in Sutherland, *Arthur Elmslie*, p. 37.

51 Quoted in McNab, *The Old Whaling Days*, p. 336.

52 James Coutts Crawford, Papers, quoted in Sutherland, *Arthur Elmslie*, p. 41; Wakefield, *Adventure in New Zealand*, p. 44.

53 Dieffenbach, *Travels in New Zealand*, quoted in Sutherland, *Arthur Elmslie*, pp. 35–36; Wakefield, *Adventure in New Zealand*, quoted in Sutherland, *Arthur Elmslie*, p. 29.

54 Dieffenbach, *Travels in New Zealand*, quoted in Sutherland, *Arthur Elmslie*, p. 32.

55 Wakefield, *Adventure in New Zealand*, p. 50.

56 Dieffenbach, *Travels in New Zealand*, quoted in Sutherland, *Arthur Elmslie*, p. 37.

57 Mitchells, *Te Tau Ihu o te Waka*, vol. 4, p. 287.

58 Don Grady, 'Guard, Elizabeth', DNZB, Te Ara: https://teara.govt.nz/en/biographies/1g23/guard-elizabeth

59 Dawber, *The Jacksons*, pp. 60–61.

60 *NENZC*, 'Sketch of an excursion . . .' 29 March 1845, p. 13.

61 Dawber, *The Jacksons*, p. 32.

62 Ibid., p. 80.

63 Don Grady, 'Jackson, James Hayter', DNZB, Te Ara: https://teara.govt.nz/en/biographies/1j1/jackson-james-hayter

64 Ibid.; Dawber, *The Jacksons*, pp. 83, 85.

65 Sutherland, *Arthur Elmslie*, pp. 40–48.

66 *Papers Past* reports on shipping movements 1842–44 regularly list the names of passengers carried on the *Nelson Packet*.

67 Cathy Marr, 'Crown–Māori Relations in *Te Tau Ihu*: Foreshores, Inland Waterways and Associated Mahinga Kai'. Report commissioned by the Treaty of Waitangi Research Unit on behalf of the Crown Forestry Rental Trust, 1999, in Waitangi Tribunal, *Te Tau Ihu*, vol. 3, p. 1060.

68 Mitchells, *Te Tau Ihu o te Waka*, vol. 2, p. 20.

69 McNab, *The Old Whaling Days*, p. 20.

70 *NENZC*, 'Sketch of an excursion . . .'.

71 Mitchells, *Te Tau Ihu o te Waka*, vol. 1, p. 37.

72 Dieffenbach, *Travels in New Zealand*, p. 68.

73 Mitchells, *Te Tau Ihu o te Waka*, vol. 2, p. 249.

74 Wakefield, *Adventure in New Zealand*, p. 17.

75 MacIntosh, *Marlborough: A Provincial History*, quoted in Sutherland, *Arthur Elmslie*, p. 34; re the population estimates, pp. 35–36.

76 Sutherland, *Arthur Elmslie*, p. 36.

77 Wakefield, *Adventure in New Zealand*, p. 7.

78 Mitchells, *Te Tau Ihu o te Waka*, vol. 2, p. 271.

79 John Wallis Barnicoat, *Journal*, quoted in Mitchells, *Te Tau Ihu o te Waka*, vol. 2, p. 155.

80 In relation to the widening society see Mitchells, *Te Tau Ihu o te Waka*, vol. 2, p. 173; in relation to the broadening of the Māori diet and adoption of European dress see p. 182; in relation to alcohol and tobacco see pp. 184–87.

81 Re the small traders from Māhakipawa see *NENZC*, 'Government notices, Sailing directions, Pelorus Estuary', 6 January 1855, p. 3. The date is vague because the report says the trade was already existing. In relation to the fall-off in trading see Mitchells, *Te Tau Ihu o te Waka*, vol. 2, p. 272.

82 Peter J. Lineham, 'Missions and missionaries – Missionaries from Britain', Te Ara: www.TeAra.govt.nz/en/missions-and-missionaries

83 Geoffrey Gorer, 'The pornography of death', *Encounter*, October 1955, pp. 49–52 in Lachy Paterson & Angela Wanhalla, *He Reo Wahine: Māori Women's Voices from the Nineteenth Century* (Auckland: Auckland University Press, 2017), p. 269.

84 McNab, *The Old Whaling Days*, pp. 342–42. Julie Kennedy also suggests a school was established there then (*Picton and Queen Charlotte Sound: A Chronology* (Picton: Picton Historical Society, 2013, p. 11).)

85 http://nzetc.victoria.ac.nz/tm/scholarly/tei-MacOcta-t1-body1-d18-d5-ft5.html. McNab (*Old Whaling Days*, p. 342) also suggests, with his reference to 'rival denominations', that competition was now welcomed.

86 Sutherland, *Arthur Elmslie*, pp. 34–35; McNab, *The Old Whaling Days*, p. 341.

87 Re the size of these congregations see the population estimates in Waitangi Tribunal, *Te Tau Ihu*, p. 355; Mitchells, *Te Tau Ihu o te Waka*, vol. 2, p. 470ff.

88 Mitchells, *Te Tau Ihu o te Waka*, vol. 2, pp. 74–76.

89 John V. Broadbent, 'Garin, Antoine Marie', DNZB, Te Ara: https://teara.govt.nz/en/biographies/1g4/garin-antoine-marie; Mitchells, *Te Tau Ihu o te Waka*, vol. 2, p. 106. The Mitchells give the date of his arrival as 1844.

90 Paterson & Wanhalla, *He Reo Wahine*, p. 265.

91 Archdeacon Salisbury, quoted in Ethel Beauchamp Hazelwood, *Life at Anakiwa: The First 100 Years 1863–1963* (Anakiwa: self-published, 1974?), p. 3.

92 J. C. Crawford, *Recollections of Travel in New Zealand and Australia* (London: Trubner, 1880), quoted in Sutherland, *Arthur Elmslie*, p. 35.

93 G. Clarke, Missionary Register, vol. 22, 1833, p. 468, quoted in J. M. Barrington & T. H. Beaglehole, *Māori Schools in a Changing Society: An Historical Review* (Wellington: NZ Council for Educational Research, 1974), p. 26.

94 McNab, *The Old Whaling Days*, p. 337.

95 Samuel Ironside, *Journal*, 21 January 1841 (Wesleyan Archive, Christchurch), quoted in Mitchells, *Te Tau Ihu o te Waka*, vol. 2, p. 82.

96 Barrington & Beaglehole, *Māori Schools*, p. 28.

97 Kennedy (*Chronology*, p. 11) gives details of the numbers of the attendees at Te Awaiti School and details of the school in Tōtaranui.

98 Mitchells, *Te Tau Ihu o te Waka*, vol. 2, pp. 82, 114.

99 F. W. Smith, 'Samuel Ironside and the Cloudy Bay Mission': www.methodist.org.nz/files/docs/wesley%20historical/11(1)%20samuel%20ironside%20.pdf, p. 13.

100 Mitchells, *Te Tau Ihu o te Waka*, vol. 2, p. 82.

101 Ibid., pp. 114–15.

102 Samuel Ironside diary, quoted in Thomas E. Simpson, *Kauri to Radiata: Origin and Expansion of the Timber Industry of New Zealand* (Auckland: Hodder & Stoughton, 1973), p. 384.

103 Mitchells, *Te Tau Ihu o te Waka*, vol. 2, p. 192.

104 W. A. Chambers, 'Ironside, Samuel', DNZB, Te Ara: https://teara.govt.nz/en/biographies/1i3/ironside-samuel

105 Waitangi Tribunal, *Te Tau Ihu*, vol. 1, p. 194.

106 Ibid., pp. 194– 96; Wairau Affray: www.theprow.org.nz/Māori/wairau-affray/#.YQiL05MzbMU

107 Waitangi Tribunal, *Te Tau Ihu*, vol. 1, pp. 198–99.

108 'The Methodist conference', *Evening Post*, 8 March 1905, p. 2.

109 Ibid.

110 Mitchells, *Te Tau Ihu o te Waka*, vol. 2, pp. 106–10.

111 Ibid., p. 108.

112 Ibid., pp. 109–10.

113 Barrington & Beaglehole, *Māori Schools*, p. 31.

114 Mitchells, *Te Tau Ihu o te Waka*, vol. 2, pp. 124–27.

115 McNab, *The Old Whaling Days*, p. 20.

116 Wakefield, *Adventure in New Zealand*, pp. 12, 17.
117 'Barnicoat, John Wallis': http://demo.recollect.co.nz/nodes/view/168
118 Barnicoat diary, 19 March 1843, in Mitchells, *Te Tau Ihu o te Waka*, vol. 2, p. 37.
119 W. Barnicoat, letter to the editor, 'Queen Charlotte Sound', *NENZC*, 12 April 1845.
120 *NENZC*, 29 March 1845, p. 13.
121 The quote is from the New Zealand Company Twenty-fourth Report, in A. D. MacIntosh, *Marlborough: A Provincial History*, quoted in Henry D. Kelly, *As High as the Hills: The Centennial History of Picton* (Picton: Cape Catley, 1976), pp. 12–13.
122 Frank W. Ponder, *A Labyrinth of Waterways: The Forgotten Story of New Zealand's Marlborough Sounds* (Wellington: Wenlock House, 1986), p. 30.
123 Mitchells, pers. comm., June 2015.
124 Wakefield, *Adventure in New Zealand*, p. 21.
125 Ibid., p. 18.
126 McNab, *The Old Whaling Days*, p. 350.
127 *NENZC*, 'Government notices, *Government Gazette*, Province of Nelson, 30 November 1854, Sailing directions, Pelorus Estuary', 6 January 1855, p. 3.
128 Ibid.
129 Ponder, *A Labyrinth*, p. 70.
130 'Government notices', *NENZC*, p. 3. Unfortunately the typescript of extracts of the Jolliffe journals held in ATL do not contain any of the material on the Pelorus visit.
131 Boast, 'Te tango whenua'.
132 Ibid.; Rāwiri Taonui, 'Te ture – Māori and legislation – Laws affecting Māori land', Te Ara: www.TeAra.govt.nz/en/te-ture-Māori-and-legislation/page-2. Nationally, any settlers' extravagant pre-Treaty claims were generally dismissed or the land they had was considerably reduced. However, under the ordinance, the Crown could keep the difference between 'land claimed and land awarded to the Europeans'. This provision was relaxed by Governor Fitzroy in 1844, allowing settlers to purchase directly. The 'dubious' methods included threats; targeting individuals instead of recognising Māori collective ownership of land; dealing with 'non-owners'; promising land for reserves which, even if provided, were often unsuitable or inadequate.
133 Mitchells, *Te Tau Ihu o te Waka*, vol. 1, p. 356.
134 Waitangi Tribunal, *Te Tau Ihu*, vol. 1, p. 182.
135 Old Land Claim papers, 410 & 410a, ANZ, quoted in Dawber, *The Jacksons*, p. 53.
136 Dawber, *The Jacksons*, p. 53.
137 Waitangi Tribunal, *Te Tau Ihu*, vol. 1, pp. 170–71. The evidence given to the tribunal does not date Jackson's claim.
138 'Government notice', *New Zealand Gazette and Wellington Spectator*, 7 May 1842, p. 5. See also Waitangi Tribunal, *Te Tau Ihu*, vol. 1, pp. 173–75; Mitchells, *Te Tau Ihu o te Waka*, vol. 1, p. 266.
139 Ballara, 'Customary Māori Land Tenure', in Waitangi Tribunal, *Te Tau Ihu*, pp. 143–44.
140 Waitangi Tribunal, *Te Tau Ihu*, vol. 1, pp. 178–79.
141 Kelly, *As High as the Hills*, p. 16.
142 Waitangi Tribunal, *Te Tau Ihu*, vol. 1, p. 320.
143 Mitchells, *Te Tau Ihu o te Waka*, vol. 1, pp. 360–61. In 1845 Māori at Waitohi were anxious about 'white men' living there and said they planned to leave to settle elsewhere in the Sound. Ropoama, in early 1849, worried about inadequacy of 300 acres being offered for 58 people – a marked contrast with 201 acres in the company's settlement scheme (p. 362).
144 Mitchells, *Te Tau Ihu o te Waka*, vol. 1, pp. 360–63. For Ropoama's involvement see Mitchells, *Te Tau Ihu o te Waka*, vol. 4, pp. 200–04.
145 Waitangi Tribunal, *Te Tau Ihu*, vol. 2, p. 538.
146 Mitchells, *Te Tau Ihu o te Waka*, vol. 1, p. 363.
147 Waitangi Tribunal, *Te Tau Ihu*, vol. 2, p. 538.
148 Quoted in Mitchells, *Te Tau Ihu o te Waka*, vol. 1, p. 362.
149 Waitangi Tribunal, *Te Tau Ihu*, vol. 2, p. 539.

150 Ibid., p. 539.
151 Dawber, *The Jacksons*, p. 83; re the MacDonalds see Mitchells, *Te Tau Ihu o te Waka*, vol. 2, pp. 27, 33.
152 Kelly, *As High as the Hills*, p. 16.
153 Waitangi Tribunal, *Te Tau Ihu*, vol. 1, p. 344.
154 Ibid., pp. 317, 320.
155 Mitchells, *Te Tau Ihu o te Waka*, vol. 1, p. 362.
156 From 1840 to 1865 land was sold only to government, often at very low prices. Alienation was also achieved by confiscation after the New Zealand Wars, and that land used for Pākehā settlement. In addition, the Native Land Court might convert customary title to freehold; further losses of land often resulted. Boast, 'Te tango whenua'.
157 Waitangi Tribunal, *Te Tau Ihu*, vol. 1, p. 395 re McLean attributed to Ngāti Toa.
158 Ibid., p. 316.
159 Ibid., pp. 371, 375.
160 Mitchells, *Te Tau Ihu o te Waka*, vol. 1., p. 376.
161 Ngāti Toa Deed of Settlement, *Compendium*, vol. 1, p. 308, in Waitangi Tribunal, *Te Tau Ihu*, vol. 1, p. 399.
162 Mitchells, *Te Tau Ihu o te Waka*, vol. 1, p. 371.
163 Waitangi Tribunal, *Te Tau Ihu*, vol. 1, pp. 394–404.
164 Ibid., p. 402.
165 Mitchells, *Te Tau Ihu o te Waka*, vol. 1, p. 372.
166 T. Brunner to the CCL, Nelson, 13 January 1855. In *Compendium*, vol. 1, 1873, pp. 297–99 in Mitchells, *Te Tau Ihu o te Waka*, vol. 2, pp. 372–73.
167 Mitchells, *Te Tau Ihu o te Waka*, vol. 1, pp. 371–74.
168 Ibid., p. 372.
169 At about ¼ of a penny, of which there were 240 in the pre-decimal pound, the farthing would be worthless today.
170 Crown purchases of *Te Tau Ihu* interests, 1853–1860, Mitchells, *Te Tau Ihu o te Waka*, vol. 1, p. 375.
171 Cybèle Locke, *'The Poorest Tribe under the Heavens': Ngati Kuia's Socio-economic Circumstances, 1856–1950*, research report commissioned by Crown Forestry Rental Trust, Wellington, 2002, p. 8.
172 Mitchells, *Te Tau Ihu o te Waka*, vol. 1, pp. 372–73; re 1853–1860 Crown purchases of *Te Tau Ihu* interests see p. 375.
173 Waitangi Tribunal, *Te Tau Ihu*, vol. 2, p. 561.

3. New Agriculture

1 J. B. Condliffe, *New Zealand in the Making: A Study of Economic and Social Development* (London: Allen & Unwin, 1963), p. 117.
2 *NENZC*, 18 March 1857, p. 2.
3 Arthur Willis, Gann & Co., *The New Zealand Handbook, or, Guide to the 'Britain of the South': A description of the provinces of . . . together with the latest information on every subject needed by the capitalist-emigrant and the working man* (London: E. Stanford, 1862), p. 40.
4 Rollo Arnold, *The Farthest Promised Land: English Villagers, New Zealand Immigrants of the 1870s* (Wellington: Victoria University Press, 1981, p. 4) discusses the impact of water transport on land-based transport systems.
5 Judith A. Johnston, 'New Zealand bush: Early assessments of vegetation', *NZ Geographer*, April 1981.
6 Jonathan Brough (*The Colonist*, 31 December 1900, p. 4) writes in these terms of the Sounds children whom he observed during a stint of roadmaking in the area, citing 'invariably good-looking daughters . . . [who] are good workers, can milk cows, make butter and do all kinds of farm work' while the boys were 'splendid boatmen, and very well up in stock and all kinds of bush-work and they are first-class axemen' . . . [are] good rifle shots and they seem to get about the hill-sides like deer, and they look as wiry and as tough as a wire fence.'

7 Tom Brooking, *Lands for the People? The Highland Clearances and the Colonisation of New Zealand, a biography of John McKenzie* (Dunedin: Otago University Press, 1996), pp. 82–83. In relation to the biblical beliefs underlying land development see Tom Brooking, 'Use it or lose it: Unravelling the land debate in late 19th-century New Zealand', *NZ Journal of History*, vol. 30, no. 2 (October 1996), pp. 141–45.

8 *AJHR*, 1879, Session 2, C.–7, System of selection of land on deferred payments, p. 1.

9 Willis, *Handbook*, p. 83.

10 Arnold, *The Farthest Promised Land*, p. 261.

11 Ibid.

12 Quoted from Graeme Wynn, 'Destruction under the guise of improvement? The forest 1840–1920' in Eric Pawson & Tom Brooking (eds), *Making a New Land: Environmental Histories of New Zealand*, 2nd edn (Dunedin: Otago University Press, 2013), p. 127.

13 Sean Handley, 'The history of benthic change in Pelorus Sound (Te Hoiere), Marlborough', prepared for the Marlborough District Council (National Institute of Water and Atmospheric Research, February 2015), p. 8.

14 Frank Sargeson, *Once is Enough* (London: Brian & O'Keefe, 1973), pp. 52–56.

15 'Advertisements', column 3, *The Colonist*, 19 April 1859, p. 2.

16 Government notices, *The Colonist*, 15 July 1859, p. 2.

17 Norman Brayshaw, 'No. 59 – Kennys Isle', manuscript notebook, pp. 2–5, Marlborough Historical Society Archives.

18 'Advertisements', column 2, *The Colonist*, 10 March 1863, p. 2.

19 *NENZC*, 6 October 1863, p. 2.

20 *NENZC*, 23 August 1864, p. 2.

21 Ibid.

22 Shipping intelligence, *NENZC*, 8 December 1868, p. 2.

23 Flora Robb (*St Omer House: Family Life in the Guest House and some Sounds History* (Nelson: self-published, 2013, p. 24) notes that her paternal grandfather, David Godsiff, and George Wheatman, who carried out surveys for individuals, helped Goulter and his son in their surveying.

24 *AJHR*, 1886, C.–1A, Surveys of New Zealand, p. 8.

25 *AJHR*, 1885, C.–1A, Report on the surveys of New Zealand, p. 13. For the quote see pp. 3–4.

26 *AJHR*, 1885, C.–1A, Report on the surveys of New Zealand, pp. 3–4.

27 *AJHR*, 1892, Session 1, C.–1, L&S, Appendix 1, Marlborough, p. 6.

28 *AJHR*, 1881, Session 1, C.–4, Surveys of New Zealand, p. 12.

29 *AJHR*, 1885, C.–1A, Report on the surveys of New Zealand, pp. iii, 13.

30 *AJHR*, 1891, Session 2, C.–1A, L&S, Appendix, p. 12.

31 *AJHR*, 1894, Session 1, C.–1, L&S, Appendix 2, surveys, p. 29.

32 *AJHR*, 1883, Session 1, C.–1, CLD, p. 2.

33 *AJHR*, 1885, C.–1A, Report on the surveys of New Zealand, p. 1.

34 *AJHR*, 1883, Session 1, C.–1, CLD, p. 1.

35 *AJHR*, 1878, Session 2, C.–1, CLD, p. 3.

36 *AJHR*, 1881, Session 1, C.–5, Crown lands for future settlement, p. 3.

37 Jim McAloon, 'Land ownership – Centralisation after 1870', Te Ara: www.TeAra.govt.nz/en/land-ownership/page-4

38 *AJHR*, 1890, Session 1, C.–1. CLD, p. 3.

39 For the notice of application by Baxter and Davenport see 'Marlborough Land Board', *ME*, 9 March 1887, p. 3; for Landall's see 'The Land Board', *ME*, 5 April 1887, p. 3; for the results of the auction see 'Local and general news', *ME*, 2 June 1887, p. 2.

40 'Local and general news', *ME*, 27 March 1888, p. 2. Re the value of the small grazing run scheme to the Sounds see *AJHR*, 1892, C.–1, L&S, p. 7.

41 'Local and general news', *ME*, 27 March 1888, p. 2; 24 April 1888, p. 2; 31 July 1888, p. 2.

42 'Marlborough Land Board', *ME*, 6 June 1893, p. 2 notes that land in Tennyson Inlet, shut up for two years, was to be opened up because of settler desire; re 'land hunger' see 'Unlock the land', Letters to the editor, *Evening Post*, 16 June 1898, p. 6. See also 'The general election', *ME*, 31 October 1902, p. 2.

43 For instance, 'Unlock the land', Letters to the editor, *Evening Post*, 16 June 1898, p. 6.

44 'Crown lands in the Sounds', Letters to editor, *Evening Post*, 14 July 1890, p. 3. 'Settling the Sounds', *ME*, 3 September 1884, p. 2 also provides evidence of settler anger at perceived inequities.

45 'Marlborough Waste Lands Board', *ME*, 7 April 1884, p. 2.

46 *AJHR*, 1874, Session 1, C.–5, L&S sold to new settlers and others.

47 'The Pelorus Sound', *Nelson Evening Mail*, 23 September 1880, p. 4.

48 'Agricultural statistics', *ME*, 8 April 1883, p. 2.

49 M. D. Laffan, 'Soil research in the Marlborough Sounds', in M. D. Laffan, B. K. Daly & J. S. Whitton, *Soils of the Marlborough Sounds* (Nelson: Soil Bureau, Department of Scientific and Industrial Research, 1987), p. 4.

50 Brooking, *Lands for the People?*, p. 57.

51 Ibid., pp. 15–18, 85, 95.

52 *Pelorus Guardian*, 7 February 1893, quoted in Nola M. Leov and Margaret J. Turner, *Marriages Have Been Arranged: Life in Carluke, Autumn 1893* (Nelson: self-published, 2011), p. 24.

53 'Mr Macalister interviewed', *ME*, 11 June 1892, p. 2.

54 McAloon, 'Land ownership'.

55 Condliffe, *New Zealand in the Making*, p. 209.

56 *AJHR*, 1894, Session 1, C.–1, L&S, Extract of reports from CCL, Marlborough, pp. 9–10.

57 For example, *AJHR*, 1894, Session 1, C.–1, L&S, Crown lands available for settlement, table p. 10. Second-class land at 10s an acre was available in Tennyson Inlet (5000 acres), Nydia Bay (3800 acres), Paradise and Mud bays (1300 acres) and Crail Bay (800 acres). In 1895 some 2300 acres from Te Mautau a Maui Bay to Crail Bay was available (*AJHR*, 1895, L&S, C.–1, Appendix 1, Administration, Marlborough, Crown lands available for settlement, p. 14. In 1898, 7000 acres was to be opened up in Queen Charlotte Sound (*AJHR*, 1898, C.–1, L&S, Appendix 1, p. 17. By the early 1900s, most land suited to 'profitable occupation and development' throughout the country had been opened up – see *AJHR*, 1903, C.–1., L&S, p. 1.

58 *AJHR*, 1906, C.–1, L&S: Appendix 1, Marlborough, p. 29.

59 'Mr Macalister interviewed'; 'Ministerial speech', *ME*, 24 February 1893, p. 2.

60 'Marlborough Land Board', *ME*, 1 September 1884, p. 3.

61 *AJHR*, 1897, C.–1, L&S, p. iv; *AJHR*, 1892, Session 1, C.–1, L&S, p. 7; *AJHR*, 1897, C.–1, L&S, p. iv.

62 *AJHR*, 1907, C.–1A, L&S, pp. 13 & 14.

63 *AJHR*, 1909, Session 2, C.–1, L&S, Appendix 1, Marlborough, p. 33.

64 For demand exceeding supply see *AJHR*, 1911, C.–1, L&S, Appendix 1, Marlborough; for the slowing of uptake see *AJHR*, 1913, L&S, Appendix 1, p. 14; for the land in the Sounds see ibid., Surveys, p. 16.

65 M. D. Laffan and B. K. Daly, 'Soil resources of the Marlborough Sounds and the implications for exotic production forestry. 1. Soil resources and limitations to exotic forest growth', *NZ Journal of Forestry* 30, no. 1 (1985), p. 55.

66 Bishop Sadlier, letter to Dr Mullins, 12 April 1916, Letterbook 1271, pp. 365–67.

67 Frank W. Ponder, *A Labyrinth of Waterways: The Forgotten Story of New Zealand's Marlborough Sounds* (Wellington: Wenlock House, 1986), p. 70.

68 For the list of plants I used Nola M. Leov & Margaret J. Turner, *The Making of the Bridle Track to French Pass: A Salute to an Early Roadmaker, Jonathan Brough* (Nelson: Copy Press, 2015), pp. 10–11 and Handley, 'The history of benthic change', p. 8. However, those Leov & Turner describe were growing on the ridge above Te Towaka in 1899, and the authors' comment on the varied nature of the Sounds bush should be noted. Ponder (*A Labyrinth of Waterways*, p. 80) comments on the size of the tōtara. See also 'A jaunt in the Hinemoa', *Evening Post*, 24 September 1892, p. 1 for some of the detail that struck early Sounds visitors.

69 Nola M. Leov, pers. comm., August 2014.

70 Harry Williams, 'Life at Kaiuma Bay in the Pelorus Sound, Collingwood', August 1998, private papers, pp. 1, 18.

71 Helen Beaglehole, *Fire in the Hills: A History of Rural Fire-fighting* (Christchurch: Canterbury University Press, 2012) chapters 1 & 2 provide accounts of burning, the techniques used, and the

attitudes settlers brought to the job. 'Local and general news', *ME*, 31 August 1892, p. 2 refers to the 1200 acres Mills was clearing on his two properties at Hopai and Homewood, along with a large area already cleared by local settlers.

72 'Captain Cook's rendezvous', *ME*, 2 March 1906, p. 1.

73 'The Pelorus Sound', *Nelson Evening Mail*, 23 September 1880, p. 4.

74 *Pelorus Guardian*, 4 December 1894.

75 Soil Conservation Survey: Sounds area: Interim report, 24 January 1950. AATE, W3396, 889, Box 1, 76/3, Marlborough Sounds Soil Conservation District 1946–61, ANZ.

76 'Picton', *The Colonist*, 10 February 1882, p. 3.

77 Hope family letters, p. 49.

78 'Last week's floods', *ME*, 13 November 1916, p. 3.

79 'Agriculture Department', *Manawatu Herald*, 24 August 1893, p. 3; 'School of Music', *The Colonist*, 26 February 1894, p. 3; Nola Leov, oral history; 'Marlborough news', *The Press*, 5 February 1910, p. 4. The destruction of native birds is dealt with in Chapter 8.

80 'Local and general news', *ME*, 14 August 1913, p. 4.

81 Harvey, Hylton, oral history.

82 Williams, 'Life at Kaiuma Bay', pp. 3, 14.

83 Ibid., pp. 12–13.

84 'Marlborough Land Board', *ME*, 11 January 1910, p. 5; see also 'Local and general news', *ME*, 15 December 1914, p. 4.

85 'Noxious weeds', Letter to the editor, *ME*, 6 July 1911, p. 6.

86 Ibid.; see Ian Popay, 'Weeds of agriculture – Weeds in pasture, crops and forestry', Te Ara: www.TeAra.govt.nz/en/weeds-of-agriculture/page-2

87 Williams, 'Life at Kaiuma Bay', pp. 10, 11.

88 'Marlborough Land Board', *ME*, 11 January 1910, p. 5.

89 See, for instance, 'Sounds Farmers' Union', *ME*, 10 May 1913, p. 6; 'Farmers' Union', *ME*, 8 September 1913, p. 3; 10 June 1914, p. 3.

90 Correspondence, 5 May 1910, 23 May 1910, Head office, Marlborough Sounds Maritime Park – Scenic reserve – Deep Bay 1910–85, AANS W5951 25421, Box 66, MSM–0113, L&S, ANZ.

91 Beaglehole, *Fire in the Hills*, pp. 23–70.

92 *Pelorus Guardian*, 14 February 1913.

93 'New Zealand', *The Star* (Christchurch), 12 May 1880, p. 2.

94 Beaglehole, *Fire in the Hills*, pp. 19–42. See 'Fire in forests', *Bay of Plenty Beacon*, 24 May 1939, p. 5 as illustrative of the abandon with which fire was used as an agricultural tool.

95 Robb, *St Omer House*, p. 27.

96 *Pelorus Guardian*, 28 February 1908.

97 Beaglehole, *Fire in the Hills* (Chapter 2 looks at the economic effects of uncontrolled burning on the small farmers).

98 Nola M. Leov & Margaret J. Turner, *Changes: Rai Valley, 1901–1902* (Nelson: self-published, 2014), p. 62.

99 'Grassing hilly fern land', *The Press*, 17 March 1898, p. 3. The reply by 'Manaroa' I have assumed is from Isaac Harvey's grandfather, although a Mr William Branson, who also corresponded with the *ME*, was living at Manaroa in 1891 – see 'The Sounds as sheep producing country', *ME*, 16 May 1891, p. 4.

100 'Grassing hilly fern land'. For other material on ploughing in the Sounds see 'Ploughing fern hills', *ME*, 6 November 1913, p. 6 and, on the hillside plough see Williams, 'Life at Kaiuma Bay', p. 12.

101 *AJHR*, 1906, C.–1. L&S, Appendix 1, p. 29.

102 'Grassing hilly fern land'.

103 Leov & Turner, *Changes*, p. 61.

104 Hylton, oral history. The suggestions in 1906 advocating precisely the opposite – burning annually, stocking lightly and letting native grasses get a hold and choke out the fern – are indicative of the more popular and time-honoured tradition. See 'An interesting letter', *ME*, 15 March 1906, p. 1.

105 'Farmers' Parliament', *The Dominion*, 17 July 1913, p. 10.

106 *AJHR*, 1898, C.–1, L&S, p. iii comments on the need for large holdings in 'forest-clad country which can never be ploughed', a description that could suit the Sounds.

107 Ponder, *A Labyrinth of Waterways*, p. 81.

108 'Advertisement', 29 June 1875, in James Wallace, Timeline, Resolution Bay, Wallace Family papers.

109 This may have been shrewd investment. The Beachville Estate at Bulwer, said *The Colonist*, was 'all that can be desired by those wishing to build where health and convenience are great considerations', but sections hung fire (and would until at least 1901, when the Nelson Land Board resolved to sell them 'at an early date' ('Nelson Land Board', *The Colonist*, 17 July 1901, p. 3.)

110 www.waterfallbay.co.nz/history.html. In 1915 Arthur Tosswill, a retired sea captain from Whanganui, bought Port Ligar, then sold it to Phillip Shand in 1923–24. It has remained in the Shand family since, though, as stated, some was sold in 2018.

111 'Agricultural and pastoral', *Otago Witness*, 11 May 1893, p. 12 stated that Neave had £12,000 to spend on the property and planned a road in over the Mt Stokes saddle. 'The Marlborough Sounds, How the Census is taken', *Evening Post*, 9 May 1896, p. 1 gives Neave's achievements. See also R. J. Paterson, *The Sea Was Our Boundary: The Titirangi/Waitui Story of the Patersons 1929–1977* (self-published, 2011), pp. 16 & 18. He states that Neave's son Digby ran 22,000 sheep. However, Rabone's 1899 directory recorded the flock numbers as 6500 (Nola Leov, pers. comm).

112 'District news', *Nelson Evening Mail*, 21 January 1902, p. 2.

113 'Thursday', *ME*, 23 June 1881, p. 2.

114 'Local and general news', *ME*, 25 May 1881, p. 2.

115 Heather Heberley, *Riding with Whales: Stories of Great Sounds Women* (Picton: Cape Catley, 1999), p. 45. For where the seed was grown see Donald Furness, *Tahuahua: The Story of Blackwood Bay, Queen Charlotte Sound* (Blenheim: self-published, 1974), p. 46. Carol Dawber, *The Jacksons of Te Awaiti* (Picton: River Press, 2001, p. 105) reports one of two Italian families growing cooksfoot in Ngaruru Bay. 'The Marlborough Sounds', *ME*, 19 January 1909, p. 5 reports Italian fishermen in Maraetai Bay doing the same. Given the geographical inaccuracy of accounts at that time, it is possible that the references are to the same people.

116 Williams, 'Life at Kaiuma Bay', pp. 12–14.

117 See respectively, 'Local and general news', *ME*, 23 February 1906, p. 2; 'The Marlborough Sounds,' *ME*, 19 January 1909, p. 5; 'Getting in early', *Feilding Star*, 8 August 1913, p. 2.

118 Re the comment on markets see *AJHR*, 1906, C.–1, L&S, Appendix 5, Clarence Valley lands, p. 85; re the varieties see Williams, 'Life at Kaiuma Bay', p. 10; G. J. C. Harvey, *Where There's a Will There's a Way: Memories of My Childhood and Sawmilling Days in the Marlborough Sounds* (Blenheim: self-published, 2008), p. 12.

119 'The silent Sounds', *Evening Post*, 22 May 1915, p. 10.

120 'Kenepuru', *ME*, 1 May 1916, p. 7; re the oats see 'The silent Sounds'.

121 Harvey, *Where There's a Will*, p. 12.

122 'A delightful holiday trip', *Evening Post*, 22 April 1893, p. 1 (supplementary).

123 *Pelorus Guardian*, quoted in Nola M. Leov & Margaret J. Turner, *Highs and Lows: Changes in the Lives of the Turners of Carluke, and improving access to the outside world, 1892–1893* (Nelson: self-published, 2011), p. 12. The Pelorus district would soon be 'a little pocket borough from whence the butcher will be able to draw fat stock at the critical time of year when most needed', the paper predicted.

124 'Advertisements', column 2, *ME*, 7 May 1914, p. 8; 'Advertisements', column 4, *ME*, 23 January 1915, p. 4.

125 *Pelorus Guardian*, 15 December 1891, quoted in Leov & Turner, *Marriages Have Been Arranged*, p. 43.

126 Hope family letters and Elizabeth's Diary, p. 33; 'The dairy industry in the Sounds', *ME*, 6 February 1906 p. 2.

127 'Notes for brazier and dealer', *The Press*, 18 February 1893, p. 2.

128 Re the credit system and the Department of Agriculture see Tony Nightingale, 'Government and agriculture – Formation of the Department of Agriculture', Te Ara: www.TeAra.govt.nz/en/government-and-agriculture/page-4

129 Nola M. Leov & Margaret J. Turner, *Intermezzo: The Fortunes of the Turner Family and the Evolution of Rai Valley, 1885–1892* (Nelson: self-published, 2011), p. 10.

130 'The dairy industry in Marlborough', *ME*, 15 November 1902, p. 4.
131 'The Hon. C. H. Mills at Havelock', *Evening Post*, 17 January 1901, p. 5.
132 Hugh Stringleman and Frank Scrimgeour, 'Dairying and dairy products – Cooperatives and centralisation', Te Ara: www.TeAra.govt.nz/en/dairying-and-dairy-products/page-3
133 'Opening of the Sounds dairy factory', *ME*, 21 November 1905, p. 2.
134 'Local and general news', *ME*, 30 January 1907, p. 2.
135 Re the support see *Pelorus Guardian*, 20 November 1908; for a description of the launch see 'Dairying in the Sounds', *ME*, 19 December 1909, p. 4.
136 'Butter factory returns', *The Dominion*, 19 August 1912, p. 9.
137 'The dairy industry in the Sounds'.
138 *Pelorus Guardian*, 13 September 1910.
139 Arthur Fell, talking to Rev. David Gribble, 1973.
140 'Blenheim dairy factory', *ME*, 16 September 1914, p. 2.
141 Harry Williams, 'Outward-bound from Havelock', undated, private paper, p. 3; Williams, 'Life at Kaiuma Bay', p. 16.
142 Williams, 'Life at Kaiuma Bay', pp. 20–21.
143 'Advertisements', *ME*, column 6, 7 December 1910, p. 5. By 1911, 198 people in the Sounds owned 185,463 sheep – a big increase from 172,037 the previous year.
144 In 1911 only two farmers owned more than 10,000 sheep and only one more than 5000 – see 'Advertisements', *ME*, column 6, 7 December 1910, p. 7. That pattern persisted. Robb, *St Omer House*, p. 6, in her list of the sheep held by settlers at Manaroa and in Kenepuru paints a similar picture. Of the 27 farmers listed, 13 held fewer than 500 sheep, eight had between 500 and 1000 and six had over 1000, including W. T. Masefield, who had 2950 sheep.
145 *AJHR*, 1905, C.–1, L&S, Appendix 1, Marlborough, p. 14.
146 *Pelorus Guardian*, 20 December 1907, noted a rise of 16,000 from the previous year.
147 'Sheep returns', *ME*, 18 October 1913, p. 5; re shipping to Wanganui see 'Commercial', *Wanganui Chronicle*, 18 March 1915, p. 7; re Picton Works see 'Shipping space', *ME*, 12 April 1915, p. 2.
148 'The Sounds as sheep producing country', *ME*, 16 May 1891, p. 4.
149 'News and notes', *Hawera & Normanby Star*, 21 September 1892, p. 2; 'Splendid lambing in the Sounds, *Pelorus Guardian*, 3 October 1905, p. 4.
150 *Pelorus Guardian*, 3 October 1905.
151 Nola M. Leov, pers. comm., June 2015.
152 'News of the day', *The Colonist*, 14 April 1871, p. 3.
153 Hugh Stringleman and Robert Peden, 'Sheep farming – The refrigerated meat trade', Te Ara: www.TeAra.govt.nz/en/sheep-farming/page-5
154 'Agricultural notes', *The Press*, 24 November 1891, p. 6.
155 In 1880 William Nelson had put up what rapidly became the huge works at Tomoana in Hawke's Bay – see Jane Tolerton, 'Agricultural processing industries – Freezing works, 1880s to the 1970s', Te Ara: www.TeAra.govt.nz/en/agricultural-processing-industries/page-7
156 'The Sounds as sheep producing country'.
157 See Agricultural Notes', *The Press*, 24 November 1891, p. 6 for the quote; 'The Sounds as sheep producing country'.
158 'Gear Meat Company', *ME*, 5 June 1891, p. 2.
159 'The Tyser Line Limited', The Cyclopedia of New Zealand [Wellington Provincial District]: http://nzetc.victoria.ac.nz/tm/scholarly/tei-Cyc01Cycl-t1-body-d4-d63-d89.html
160 See Julie Kennedy, *Picton and Queen Charlotte Sound: A Chronology* (Picton: Picton Historical Society, 2013, pp. 26–28) for details on the shipping of frozen meat. The shipment of meat in 1891 did not go direct, as additional frozen cargo was picked up at Gisborne and possibly other ports – information from Loreen Breuhart, October 2015.
161 Kennedy, *Chronology*, p. 32.
162 'The sheep market', Letter to the editor, *ME*, 31 May 1900, p. 3.
163 'Commercial', *Wanganui Chronicle*, 18 March 1915, p. 7.

164 Henry D. Kelly, *As High as the Hills: The Centennial History of Picton* (Picton: Cape Catley, 1976), p. 83. Kelly's account of the freezing industry in the preceding pages are also used.

165 Stringleman & Peden, 'Sheep farming – The refrigerated meat trade'; in relation to the demand for new breeds see 'Sheep returns', *ME*, 10 August 1886, p. 2.

166 Robb, *St Omer House*, p. 23.

167 'Local and general', *ME*, 20 October 1892, p. 2.

168 Re the Ravenscliff Run Halfbreds see 'Advertisement', 29 June 1875, in Wallace Family papers; for general comment on Leicester-cross sheep see 'Sheep breeding in New Zealand', *The Press*, 20 September 1898, p. 6.

169 'The sheep market', Letter to the editor, *ME*, 31 May 1890, p. 3.

170 'Farm notes', *Bay of Plenty Times*, 11 March 1912, p. 6; 'Prime Marlborough', *The Dominion*, 30 September 1911, p. 16.

171 'Picton notes', *ME*, 16 February 1903, p. 3.

172 'Sheep on passenger boats', *Poverty Bay Herald*, 22 March 1910, p. 5.

173 'The scrub pest', *ME*, 15 June 1901, p. 5; 'Goats as scrub-clearers', *Nelson Evening Mail*, 20 June 1901, p. 2; 'Notes on the Angora goat', Letters to the editor, *ME*, 9 November 1901, p. 4.

174 'Motuara Island', *ME*, 6 March 1906, p. 1; 'Personal items', *ME*, 5 July 1906, p. 2.

175 'Angora goats', *Evening Post*, 2 December 1907, p. 8; 'Angora goats', *The Dominion*, 4 December 1907, p. 5; re potential meat market see 'News of the day', *The Press*, 26 July 1907, p. 6.

176 AAFA W1633 4ll, Box 99, O. & L.07/73, 1909–11, ANZ. The improvements were in the land, fencing, yards, dip, orchard, outbuilding, shelter shed, cottage.

177 'Ministerial visit', *The Dominion*, 30 March 1908, p. 6.

178 Re the unsuitability of the island see 'Ministerial visit', ibid.; re the goat transfer see 'Local and general', *Feilding Star*, 20 October 1910, p. 2; re the reserve see *Nelson Evening Mail*, 26 May 1913, p. 4; re sanctuary see 'A week in Picton Sounds', *Hawera & Normanby Star*, 19 April 1915, p. 2.

179 'A delightful holiday trip', *Evening Post*, 22 April 1893, supplement, p. 1.

180 'In the Sound', *Pelorus Guardian*, 11 September 1894.

181 Re the homestead see 'Manaroa – Mr. William Taylor Macefield', Cyclopedia of New Zealand, vol. 5: http://nzetc.victoria.ac.nz/tm/scholarly/tei-Cyc05Cycl-t1-body1-d2-d28-d8.html; re his sailing see 'Travels in a canoe', *The Press*, 26 June 1890, p. 2.

182 Robb, *St Omer House*, p. 23.

183 'News and notes', *ME*, 29 January 1904, p. 1.

184 *AJHR*, 1906, C.–1. L&S, Appendix 1, p. 29.

185 *AJHR*, 1908, C.–1, L&S, Settlement of Crown lands: Nelson, p. 34. (The comment applies to Waimea and Sounds counties.)

186 'Advertisements', column 3, *ME*, 15 August 1911, p. 8. A similar advertisement ('Splendid Sounds property', *ME*, 2 May 1911, p. 8) also indicates the substantial properties available.

187 'News of the day', *The Colonist*, 1 June 1916, p. 4.

188 Leov & Turner, *Changes*, p. 61.

189 'Our industries', *ME*, 3 June 1893, p. 2.

190 'Possibilities of Marlborough', *ME*, 19 September 1908, p. 2.

191 'The Marlborough Sounds: A week in Arcadia', *ME*, 19 January 1909, p. 5.

192 'Farming in the Sounds', *The Dominion*, 6 January 1913, p. 8.

193 Picton & Sounds Promotion Society, *Picton and the Marlborough Sounds: The finest holiday resort in the Dominion of New Zealand: A descriptive booklet containing views and descriptive matter designed to set forth in a compendius [sic] form the attractions of this picturesque country* (Picton, 1910–11), p. 19.

194 'The land of the level road', *ME*, 7 June 1910, p. 6; re the Alymers see Furness, *Tahuahua*, pp. 38, 46.

195 'The Marlborough Sounds: A week in Arcadia', *ME*, 19 January 1909, p. 5; re the *Torea* see Loreen Brehaut, 'Sounds mailboats': www.theprow.org.nz/enterprise/Sounds-mailboats/#.VTAwcSgVrHg

196 Picton & Sounds Promotion Society, *Picton and the Marlborough Sounds*, p. 13.

197 *Lyttelton Times*, 16 February 1865, p. 3; 'Travels in a canoe', *The Press*, 26 June 1890, p. 2; 'Local and general, Picton carnival', *ME*, 24 December 1890, p. 2.

198 Waitangi Tribunal, *Te Tau Ihu o te Waka a Maui: Report on Northern South Island Claims* (Wai 785), vols. 1, 2 & 3 (Wellington, 2008), vol. 2, pp. 962–63.

199 Waitangi Tribunal, *Te Tau Ihu*, vol. 2, pp. 562–64.

200 Hilary and John Mitchell, *Te Tau Ihu o te Waka: A History of the Māori of Nelson and Marlborough*, vol. 1: Te Tangata me te Whenua / The People and the Land (Wellington: Huia Publishers, 2004), p. 412.

201 Ibid., p. 641.

202 Ibid., p. 672.

203 Waitangi Tribunal, *Te Tau Ihu*, vol. 2, p. 561.

204 Ibid., pp. 564–65. Re the Waitangi Tribunal's comments on the need for large-scale farming see p. 641; re the European action see p. 658.

205 Waitangi Tribunal, *Te Tau Ihu*, vol. 2, p. 563.

206 Alexander Mackay to Native Minister, Compendium, vol. 2, 6 December 1865, p. 312, quoted in Waitangi Tribunal, *Te Tau Ihu*, vol. 2, pp. 564–65.

207 Re loss of land see Waitangi Tribunal, *Te Tau Ihu*, vol. 2, p. 571.

208 Ibid., p. 574.

209 Ibid., pp. 668–69 re the Buller issue; pp. 665–66 describes the land laid out around Croisilles Harbour; pp 657–58 mentions the West Coast scheme.

210 Cybèle Locke, *'The Poorest Tribe under the Heavens': Ngati Kuia's Socio-economic Circumstances, 1856–1950*, research report commissioned by Crown Forestry Rental Trust, Wellington, 2002, p. 8 discusses these expectations and promises.

211 'Petition of Teone Hiporaiti and 20 Others', 7 July 1884, quoted in David Alexander, 'Landless Natives Reserves in Nelson and Marlborough', report commissioned by the Crown Forestry Rental Trust, 1999, p. 14, quoted by Waitangi Tribunal, *Te Tau Ihu*, vol. 2, p. 658.

212 Ibid., p. 659

213 Waitangi Tribunal, *Te Tau Ihu*, vol. 2, p. 658.

214 Brooking, *Lands for the People?*, p. 154.

215 Editorial, *Pelorus Guardian*, 3 July 1894, quoted in Nola M. Leov & Margaret J. Turner, *Slough of Despond?* (Nelson: self-published, 2013), p. 32.

216 Waitangi Tribunal, *Te Tau Ihu*, vol. 2, p. 660.

217 Alexander, 'Landless Native Reserves' p. 659; re the cut-off point see Waitangi Tribunal, *Te Tau Ihu*, vol. 2, p. 661.

218 Richard Bradley, interview, January 2015.

219 Leov & Turner, *Slough of Despond?*, p. 32.

220 Richard Bradley, interview, February 2015.

221 Waitangi Tribunal, *Te Tau Ihu*, vol. 2, pp. 665–68.

222 Peter N. Meihana & Cecil R. Bradley, 'Repatriation, reconciliation and the inversion of patriarchy', *Journal of the Polynesian Society* 127 (2018), p. 311.

223 Richard Bradley, interview, January 2014. Re the numbers in Big Bay see Waitangi Tribunal, *Te Tau Ihu*, vol. 2, p. 667.

224 Richard Bradley, interview, February 2015.

225 *Pelorus Guardian*, 25 March 1910.

226 James MacDonald, brief of evidence on behalf of Rangitāne, 10 March 2003 (doc M10), p. 5, quoted in Waitangi Tribunal, *Te Tau Ihu*, vol. 2, p. 667.

227 Waitangi Tribunal, *Te Tau Ihu*, vol. 2, p. 663.

228 Ibid.

229 Ibid.

230 Ibid., p. 661.

231 *AJHR*, 1881, G.–8, Alexander Mackay to under-sec, Native Department, 6 May 1881, p. 16, noted in Waitangi Tribunal, *Te Tau Ihu*, vol. 2, p. 642.

232 Ibid. in relation to the land deemed appropriate for Pākehā farmers; and Waitangi Tribunal, *Te Tau Ihu*, vol. 2, p. 661 for the Maori-specific numbers.

233 Leov & Turner, *Slough of Despond?*, p. 33.
234 Ibid., pp. 93–94.
235 Waitangi Tribunal, *Te Tau Ihu*, vol. 2, p. 551.
236 Ibid., pp. 548–52.
237 Ibid., p. 566.
238 Ibid., p. 563.
239 Re loss of land see ibid., p. 571.
240 Ibid., pp. 575–76.
241 Alexander Watson, brief of evidence on behalf of Te Ātiawa, 30 January 2003 (doc I1), p. 25, quoted in ibid., p. 548.
242 Anthony Keenan, brief of evidence on behalf of Te Ātiawa, January 2003 (doc I7), p. 9, quoted in ibid., p. 548.
243 Waitangi Tribunal, *Te Tau Ihu*, vol. 2, pp. 541–48; re the Crown's failure to actively protect Māori land ownership see p. 675.
244 Ibid.
245 Riwai Love and 14 others to Minister of Public Works, 24 May 1920 (Alexander, David, Report commissioned by the Crown Forestry Rental Trust, 1999, 'Reserves of *Te Tau Ihu*', vol 1, pp. 350–51, quoted in Waitangi Tribunal, *Te Tau Ihu*, vol. 2, p. 570. See also Waitangi Tribunal, *Te Tau Ihu*, vol. 3, pp. 1093–97. The description of the landowners protesting the licence to occupy the public reserves as Pākehā is mine.
246 Alexander Mackay to Native Secretary, Compendium, vol. 2, 3 October 1863, p 138, quoted in Waitangi Tribunal, *Te Tau Ihu*, vol. 2, p. 961.
247 Mitchells, *Te Tau Ihu o te Waka*, vol. 2, p. 232.
248 *AJHR*, 1874, G–2c, p. 2, A. Mackay to under-sec., Native Department, 24 June 1874, quoted in Waitangi Tribunal, *Te Tau Ihu*, vol. 2, p. 692.
249 'Marlborough Land Board', *ME*, 10 February 1904, p. 4. Settlers Climo and Fawcett were milling in the area in 1904 and wanted a five-year lease on 7 acres at Okoha for grazing their bullocks. Tuiti MacDonald and Crown Lands ranger A. Kenny advised the Land Board that because the iwi had considered the land as common it had not been included in the Okoha reserve survey, and that they had cleared, grassed and built on it. The board granted an annual lease to the Europeans on the condition that they fenced it (thus preventing any common use). Kipa Whiro had to move his house within the month.
250 Waitangi Tribunal, *Te Tau Ihu*, vol. 2, p. 966.
251 Ibid., p. 969.
252 Ibid., p. 966.
253 David Young, *Māori Society and the State in Colonial and Post-colonial Te Tau Ihu, 1880–1960: A Survey of Official Archives* (Wellington: Crown Forstry Rental Trust, 1999), pp. 15–16, quoted in ibid. 2, p. 978.
254 Waitangi Tribunal, *Te Tau Ihu*, vol. 3, p. 1035.
255 Waitangi Tribunal, *Te Tau Ihu*, vol. 2, pp. 660–61.
256 Locke, *'The Poorest Tribe'*, p. 102.
257 Waitangi Tribunal, *Te Tau Ihu*, vol. 2, pp. 961–64.
258 Waitangi Tribunal, *Te Tau Ihu*, vol. 3, p. 1068.
259 Danny Keenan, quoting Justice Eddie Durie in 'The trouble with the NZ wars', *The Dominion* Post, 4 July 2019.

4. Whales, Minerals and Fish

1 Helen Beaglehole, *Lighting the Coast: A History of New Zealand's Coastal Lighthouse System* (Christchurch: Canterbury University Press, 2006), p. 79.
2 'A jaunt in the *Hinemoa*', *Evening Post*, 24 September 1892, p. 1.
3 'The Picton fish curing works', *ME*, 22 September 1886, p. 2.

4 Re the European rowing dinghies see Frank Ponder, *A Labyrinth of Waterways: The Forgotten Story of New Zealand's Marlborough Sounds* (Wellington: Wenlock House, 1986), p. 128.

5 Evidence of Laura Bowdler (née Keenan) for Tahuaroa-Watson Whanau, Board of Inquiry, New Zealand King Salmon proposal, undated, p. 3. Mike Taylor (Picton) was able to date Keenan's work as a boat-builder.

6 Deirdre Mackay, *Voices from the Sea* (Motueka: self-published, 2007), p. 201; Paul Mulcock, 'The New Zealand branch of the Mulcock family', pt 3: 'The story of Bulwer farm in Pelorus Sound' (unpublished), p. 3. Mackay identifies the boat-builder as Benjamin McCauley but, as both authors associate him with the *Ark*, I am presuming confusion over the name.

7 'Local and general', *ME*, 29 March 1893, p. 5.

8 For Keenan's family relationships and boat-building see Evidence of Laura Bowdler (née Keenan) to Board of Inquiry, New Zealand King Salmon proposal, p. 3; re Nixon see 'A reply to Mr Fisher', *Evening Post*, 25 November 1896, p. 6; re Lane see 'Picton', *ME*, 17 December 1907 and 'Picton', *ME*, 6 December 1909, p. 5. For information on E. R. Lane see Chris Bowe, 'The legacy of Picton boat-builder Ernie Lane': www.cleanweb.co.nz/abode/708/documents/Ernest%20Richard%20Lane.pdf and https://waitematawoodys.com/tag/ernie-lane/

9 Lorna Orchard, *Time and Tide Waits for No Man* (Blenheim: Yvonne Fell, 2004), pp. 20–21, 29–31, 50.

10 'Whaling off Te Awaite', *ME*, 29 August 1893, p. 2.

11 'Young adventurers', *The Star* (Christchurch), 1 November 1907, p. 4.

12 'Picton', *ME*, 29 October 1907, p. 5.

13 *AJHR*, 1910, H.–15, MDAR, p. 7.

14 'The land of the level road', *The Press*, 21 May 1910, p. 11.

15 Ibid.

16 *AJHR*, 1909, Session 2, H.–15, MDAR, p. 6.

17 Don Grady, *The Perano Whalers of Cook Strait, 1911–1964* (Wellington: A. H. & A. W. Reed, 1982), pp. 21–25.

18 The first reported capture of a humpback is in the *Otago Daily Times*: 'Omnium gatherum', 20 June 1892, p. 4. Thereafter, until 1916, newspapers report them being caught, but not until 1917 were they described as the whale of choice – see 'Whalers', *ME*, 17 October 1917, p. 6. See also Grady, *The Perano Whalers*, Appendix 3.

19 In relation to *Waitohi* see Grady, ibid., pp. 24, 55; re the harpoon see p. 29; re the boats see pp. 27, 30–31, 50; re Tipi Bay Station see p. 33.

20 Grady, *The Perano Whalers*, p. 220.

21 Ibid., p. 31.

22 'Picton notes', *ME*, 16 February 1903, p. 3.

23 '"There she blows"', *Horowhenua Chronicle*, 1 December 1913, p. 4; 'Whalers', *ME*, 15 November 1918, p. 3. Re the workings of the gun see Jack L. McSherry III, 'The harpoon gun': www.arcticwebsite.com/WhaleHarpGun.html. Once dead, the whale was winched in, then pumped full of air when alongside the boat to keep it afloat as it was towed in to the factory.

24 Grady, *The Perano Whalers*, Appendix 3.

25 Ibid., pp. 127–28.

26 Ibid., pp. 1–2, 158.

27 Ibid., pp. 33, 35, 38, 93.

28 Heather Heberley, *Riding with Whales: Stories of Great Sounds Women* (Picton: Cape Catley, 1999), pp. 28, 29.

29 *Lyttelton Times*, 3 July 1865, p. 2.

30 On the absurdity of the imports and the need for local industry see 'Local industries', *ME*, 2 October 1884, p. 2; re the money spent on imported fish see 'Fish canning', *Evening Post*, 11 May 1939, p. 5.

31 'Local and general', *ME*, 1 May 1874, p. 5. A further report ('A run through the Marlborough district', *ME*, 19 May 1881, p. 2) provides a good description of his plant.

32 'Launch of the "Unity"', *ME*, 19 February 1873, p. 2.

33 'A run through the Marlborough district', *ME*, 19 May 1881, p. 2.

34 'The Picton fish curing works', *ME*, 22 September 1886, p. 2.

35 Ibid.

36 'Advertisements', column 4, *ME*, 30 July 1888, p. 2.

37 'Local and general news', *ME*, 26 May 1896, p. 2.

38 For the initial notices see 'News of the day', *The Colonist*, 14 April 1871, p. 3; 'Provincial and general news', *North Otago Times*, 5 May 1871, p. 3. Re the drownings see 'Havelock', *Wanganui Herald*, 19 October 1880, p. 2.

39 'Parliamentary papers', *Taranaki Herald*, 3 July 1885, p. 2. The places Rutland nominated were in Queen Charlotte Sound: he thought Arrowsmiths Bay (on the south side of the entrance to Erie Bay) and Resolution Bay were the best places. In Pelorus Sound he suggested Tawa Bay, near Tennyson Inlet, and another bay on the north side of Apuau Channel; Orchard Bay, Forsyth Island (a refuge in southerlies); and an unnamed bay in Ketu Bay (considered a safe anchorage in all winds though possibly open to the north).

40 *Lyttelton Times*, 'Malborough', 3 July 1865, p. 2.

41 'Notes from the Wairau', *Nelson Evening Mail*, 5 June 1886, mentions a proposed canning venture in the Sounds. This would fit with the Bulwer initiative.

42 Re the bailiff's action see 'Advertisements', column 3, *ME*, 23 July 1887, p. 2; re the bankruptcy see 'Advertisements', column 4, *ME*, 21 October 1892, p. 2.

43 'Waimea-Picton election', *ME*, 13 August 1887, p. 3.

44 'Local and general', *ME*, 10 May 1888, p. 2.

45 'The Marlborough Sounds: How the Census is taken', *Evening Post*, 9 May 1896, p. 1.

46 'Advertisements', column 1, *Evening Post*, 23 August 1902, p. 5; 'Our fish supply', *Wanganui Herald*, 30 August 1902, p. 2; 'Local and general', *The Star* (Christchurch), 4 September 1902, p. 3.

47 'News items', *Poverty Bay Herald*, 9 May 1905, p. 4. This article also seems to hint at difficulties not reported elsewhere. Re Sullivan's business title, acquisition and plans for a tourism venture see AECB 8615 TOI/38, 1902/154, Marlborough Sounds scenery 1902–09, ANZ, F. J. Sullivan to T. E. Donne, Tourist Dept., 25 September 1905.

48 *Pelorus Guardian*, 8 September 1905.

49 *Pelorus Guardian*, 5 May 1911; Orchard, *Time and Tide*, pp. 20, 21, 26.

50 *AJHR*, 1915, H.–15, MDAR, p. 70.

51 June Hope, pers. comm., June 2018.

52 *AJHR*, 1910, H.–15, Marine Department, p. 6; Hope, pers. comm., June 2018.

53 *AJHR*, 1917, H.–15, MDAR, Table showing the number and type of vessels employed in fishing, number of fishermen and others employed in the industry for year ended 31 March 1917; *AJHR*, 1920, H.–15, MDAR, Table showing the number and type of vessels employed in fishing, number of fishermen and others employed in the industry for year ended 31 March 1920.

54 *AJHR*, 1913, H.–15, MDAR, p. 6; *AJHR*, 1915, H.–15, MDAR, p. 15; 'Local and general news', *ME*, 3 July 1913, p. 4.

55 *AJHR*, 1921, H.–15, MDAR, p. 15.

56 Hope, pers. comm., June 2018.

57 'The fishing industry', *ME*, 3 April 1914, p. 3; Mackay, *Voices from the Sea*, pp. 113–14.

58 *ME*, 'Local and general news', 9 January 1895, p. 2.

59 'Advertisements', column 6, *ME*, 4 March 1890, p. 3.

60 Legislation to prevent the destruction of the oyster beds included the Oyster Fisheries Amendment Act 1874, which imposed a closed season in Auckland province (*AJHR*, 1875, H.–31). The Fisheries Conservation Act 1884 allowed for closed seasons for taking oysters and minimum sizes (*AJHR*, 1885, H.–13, p. 4) and closure of the Tory Channel beds until 1892 (*AJHR*, 1889, H.–31, p. 4). The Oyster Fisheries Act passed in the previous session put an export duty on oysters and provided for the leasing of the foreshore to allow oyster beds to be formed, although the regulations on export duty and licensing people did not apply to the South Island (*AJHR*, 1893, H.–31, p. 3). Amendments of the Sea-fisheries Act 1894 in 1896 and 1897 made selling of oysters in a closed season an offence,

empowered the government to fix areas of the seashore to be included in oyster-bed leases, and, in 1897, enabled the regulation and protection of mussel and other shellfish beds.

61 *AJHR*, 1889, H.–31 MDAR, p. 4.

62 *AJHR*, 1895, H.–29, MDAR, p. 3.

63 Re licences see *AJHR*, 1896, H.–15, MDAR; *AJHR*, 1897, p. 4; 'Oyster culture', *ME*, 7 August 1895, p. 4; *Pelorus Guardian*, 10 May 1895.

64 *Pelorus Guardian*, 10 May 1895, p. 2.

65 *AJHR*, 1898, H.–15, MDAR, p. 6. 'Oyster culture in the Pelorus Sound', *ME*, 12 October 1898, p. 4 provides a fuller, if somewhat conflicting, account of Maule's works.

66 M1 118, 2/7/46, Pt. 1, Oysters – Cook Strait and Marlborough Sounds, 1908–48, ANZ: Sec. Marine to John Connolly, 25 August 1914; re local advice see Ayson to John Connolly, 9 October 1915.

67 'Advertisements', *Auckland Star*, 25 November 1915, p. 7; 'Local and general news', *ME*, 9 December 1916, p. 4; 'Port of Onehunga', *Auckland Star*, 13 December 1916, p. 4. The departmental accounts are considerably less expansive.

68 M1 118, 2/7/46: NZ Trawling & Fish Supply Co. Ltd. to Minister Marine, 12 July 1915.

69 *AJHR*, 1915, H.–15, MDAR, p. 16 referring to £32 16s being spend on replanting of oysters in Cook Strait; *AJHR*, 1918, H.–15, Marine Department, p. 5.

70 M1 118, 2/7/46: Ayson to Sec. Marine, 18 December 1920, ANZ; on the water temperature see *AJHR*, 1930, H.–15, MDAR, p. 21.

71 M1 118, 2/7/46 Pt. 1: Oysters – Cook Strait and Marlborough Sounds, 1908–48, ADOE 16612, ANZ.

72 'An important industry', *Thames Star*, 18 August 1916, p. 4.

73 'Great possibilities', *ME*, 12 July 1917, p. 3.

74 Ibid.

75 This subtitle is taken from Rollo Arnold, 'The virgin forest harvest and the development of colonial New Zealand', *NZ Geographer* 32 (1976), pp. 105–26, which has provided a fascinating and useful framework for much of what follows in this section.

76 'Report of Dr Hector to the Royal Commissioners of the New Zealand Exhibition', *Otago Daily Times*, 17 September 1864, p. 10. See also 'West Coast', *Otago Daily Times*, 25 March 1864 for a similar statement by J. W. Sullivan, attached to the *Fawn* expedition. He reported on the 'excellent quality' of the timber 'and in the future of the development of the resources of the Middle Island [it] cannot fail to become of the greatest value'.

77 Arnold, 'The virgin forest harvest', p. 105.

78 Ibid., pp. 105–06 provides the information for this paragraph except where otherwise attributed.

79 'Marlborough commercial', *Southland Times*, 11 August 1864, p. 2.

80 Arnold, 'The virgin forest harvest', p. 108.

81 *Wellington Independent*, 11 June 1874, p. 2.

82 J. O. Ross, *Pride in their Ports: The Story of the Minor Ports* (Palmerston North: Dunmore Press, 1977), pp. 138–40, cited in Joy Stephens, 'Havelock': www.theprow.org.nz/places/havelock/#Main_content

83 A. D. MacIntosh, *Marlborough: A Provincial History* (Blenheim: Marlborough Provincial Historical Committee, 1940), p. 277.

84 The following was reported in the *ME*. In 1884 Brownlee bought 500 acres 'of the best bush in the Pelorus Valley'; in 1887 Henry Godsiff was granted a licence to mill 20 acres in Nydia Bay; in 1901 a rise in sheep prices meant demands for greater clearance and the following acreages were to be felled in and around the Sounds: Pelorus Sound 1620 acres, Queen Charlotte Sound 250 acres, Pelorus Valley 810 acres, Kaituna Valley 220 acres, Waitohi Valley 150 acres. Note that most of the reporting relates to cutting, not clearance.

85 Arnold, 'The virgin forest harvest', pp. 122–23.

86 Dallas Hemphill, pers. comm., August 2021.

87 *ME*, 25 May 1878, p. 5 discusses millers' probable movements out of the district; 'Local and general', *ME*, 5 October 1882, p. 2.

88 Arnold, 'The virgin forest harvest', pp. 109–10.

89 'Wellington items', *The Star* (Christchurch), 8 June 1901, p. 6.

90 'Advertisements', *ME*, 5 May 1902, p. 3.

91 Brian R. Paton, 'Sawmill pioneers in the Pelorus', unpublished dissertation, Lincoln College, 1892, p. 12.

92 Arnold, 'The virgin forest harvest', p. 122. In the 1880s in South Canterbury settlers were paid £4 a cord for firewood. (A cord is 3.6 cubic metres.)

93 'Wellington items', *The Star* (Christchurch), 8 June 1901, p. 6; 'Advertisements', *ME*, 5 May 1902, p. 3; *Pelorus Guardian*, 23 October 1903.

94 Re the demand for millers see *Pelorus Guardian*, 26 July 1907.

95 'Local and general, Timber export', *ME*, 3 February 1891, p. 2. I have not been able to identify where this is.

96 *Pelorus Guardian*, 26 July 1907.

97 John Brownlee, 'A brief history of the sawmilling industry in the Pelorus Sound district' (unpublished, 1939): www.peloruspeople.org.nz/havelockmuseum/index.mvc?ArticleID=2); Harry Williams, 'Life at Kaiuma Bay in the Pelorus Sound, Collingwood', August 1998, Williams private papers, p. 1.

98 'Day dreams', *The Colonist*, 14 November 1884, p. 3; Don Grady, *Still More Grady's People: Still More Unforgettable Characters in the Top of the South Island* (Nelson: Nikau Press, 2004), p. 97.

99 'Information about Marlborough', *ME*, 2 November 1897, p. 4.

100 Grady, *Still More Grady's People*, p. 89; Brownlee, 'A brief history of the sawmilling industry', pp. 3, 4.

101 Grady, *Still More Grady's People*, pp. 101–03.

102 *Pelorus Guardian*, 22 May 1908.

103 Re postal note service see *AJHR*, 1905, F.–1, P&TAR, p. viv; re mail service see p. xvii; re telegraph offices see *AJHR*, 1908, F.–1, P&TAR, p. xxv.

104 John Orchard, 'A short history of sawmilling in the Nydia Bay area', *Journal of the Nelson and Marlborough Historical Societies*, 2, no. 1 (1987): http://nzetc.victoria.ac.nz/tm/scholarly/tei-NHSJ05_01-t1-body1-d4.html

105 Ibid.

106 'The timber industry', *ME*, 18 April 1901, p. 4.

107 'The timber industry', *ME*, 25 October 1905, p. 3.

108 *AJHR*, 1910, C.–1, L&S, Appendix 3, 'Report on the timber industry in the Auckland and Marlborough Land districts', p. 41.

109 From 1864 to 1915 the firm shipped out the following timber: Māhakipawa (1864–69) 12 million super ft; Kaituna (1870–85) 40 million super ft; Havelock (1871–75) 9 million super ft; Nydia Bay (1876–80) 10 million super ft; Kaiuma Bay (1880–87) 18 million super ft; Blackball (1885–1915) 100 million super ft (Brownlee, 'A brief history', p. 4).

110 *AJHR*, 1917, C.–1, L&S, Appendix 1: Settlement of Crown Lands: Marlborough, p. 14.

111 *AJHR*, 1920, C.–3, Forestry Department, p. 33.

112 Arnold, 'The virgin forest harvest', p. 123.

113 Brownlee, 'A brief history', p. 5; re the standard logger's wage see Nola M. Leov & Margaret J. Turner, *And They Lived Happily Ever After: W. H. Turner's Family 1867–1871* (Nelson: self-published, 2010), p. 40.

114 Hope Family letters, p. 58.

115 Grady, *Still More Grady's People*, p. 86.

116 Paton, 'Sawmill pioneers in the Pelorus', p. 20. *The Cyclopedia of New Zealand (Nelson, Marlborough & Westland Provincial Districts)* (Christchurch: Cyclopedia Company Ltd, 1906), p. 406 provides the information on William Orsman: http://nzetc.victoria.ac.nz/tm/scholarly/tei-Cyc05Cycl-t1-body1-d2-d28-d14.html

117 Brownlee, 'A brief history', p. 4.

118 Geoffrey Whitefield & Faith Barber, Submission to Historic Places Trust for registration of the Brownlee homestead, 1994–95.

119 *AJHR*, 1879, Session 2, H.–11, 'The goldfields of New Zealand', p. 13.

120 Cited in Mike Johnston, *Gold in a Tin Dish: The Search for Gold in Marlborough and Eastern Nelson*,

vol. 2: *The History of the Eastern Marlborough Goldfields: The Northbank, Mahakipawa and Queen Charlotte Sound* (Nelson: Nikau Press, 1993), p. 405.

121 Zealandia information panel. As we shall see, the Sounds, like the province, yielded little gold. The following figures indicate the provinces' total gold entered for duty exportation 1857–95: West Coast 5,581,128 oz, £22,177,748; Otago 5,195,817 oz, £20,544,464; Auckland 1,940,147 oz, £7,316,702; Nelson 249,075 oz, £98,618; Marlborough 83,724 oz, £326,052; Wellington, 273 oz, £1044; Canterbury 48 oz, £192.

122 Johnston, *Gold in a Tin Dish*, p. 405.

123 Ibid., p. 349.

124 'The Marlborough reefs', *ME*, 20 September 1873, p. 6.

125 Johnston, *Gold in a Tin Dish*, pp. 349, 351.

126 Ibid., pp. 352–53; 'Untitled', *ME*, 21 July 1875, p. 3.

127 Johnston, *Gold in a Tin Dish*, p. 353.

128 Ibid.

129 Ibid., p. 354–55.

130 *Thames Star*, 25 November 1884.

131 Johnston, *Gold in a Tin Dish*, pp. 359–60.

132 'Advertisements', column 6, *Evening Post*, 13 November 1886, p. 2.

133 Johnston, *Gold in a Tin Dish*, p. 366.

134 *AJHR*, 1889, Session 1, C.–2, 'The mining industry' (p. 106) has officials' early comments on this difficulty.

135 'Antimony discovery', *Bay of Plenty Times*, 17 April 1907, p. 3.

136 Johnson, *Gold in a Tin Dish*, pp. 370–73.

137 Ibid., pp. 373–74.

138 'Supposed suicide', *ME*, 17 July 1907, p. 5.

139 Johnston, *Gold in a Tin Dish*, p. 375.

140 'Antimony mining in the Sounds', *The Colonist*, 19 April 1916, p. 1; 'Antimony mining', *Evening Post*, 28 July 1932, p. 14; Shirley Buckland, *Reflections on a Lifetime* (Nelson: Shirley Buckland, 2007) mentions a Christchurch company that had men working in a mine between Furneaux Lodge and The Pines in Endeavour Inlet in the 1950s. Re the 1960s–70s interest see 'Antimony mine at Endeavour Inlet', *ME*, 28 October 1961; 'Antimony mining in Q.C. Sound', *ME*, 14 October 1970; 'Close control on Endeavour Inlet prospecting work', *ME*, 8 August 1972; 'Mining Co. makes its position clear', *ME*, 18 August 1972; 'Antimony in the Sounds?' *ME*, 21 August 1972; 'Public apology over mining activities in Sounds', *ME*, 21 August 1972; 'Mining company's plans for Endeavour Inlet', *ME*, 6 August 1973.

141 'Advertisements', column 5, *Evening Post*, 13 November 1886, p. 2; re the number employed see *AJHR*, 1887, Session 2, C.–1, 'Mines report', p. 9. However, job losses accompanied the downturns. In 1890, when the New Zealand Antimony Company was in trouble, the workforce was halved. See *AJHR*, 1890, C.–3, 'Goldfields etc.', p. 94.

142 Buckland, *Reflections*, p. 93.

143 'The New Zealand Antimony Company', *Evening Post*, 27 February 1888, p. 4. Unless otherwise stated, the source for the following few paragraphs is the *Evening Post*. By the time this article was written the Endeavour Inlet Company was no longer in existence. However, apart from a few details, I have assumed that the work described was what it had done, and occurred before the major expansion described below, undertaken by the new New Zealand Antimony Company.

144 Julie Kennedy, *Picton and Queen Charlotte Sound: A Chronology* (Picton: Picton Historical Society, 2013), p. 28. See also 'Advertisements', column 6, *ME*, 10 August 1891, p. 3.

145 'The New Zealand Antimony Company', *Evening Post*, 27 February 1888, p. 4.

146 Ibid.

147 Ibid.; Johnston, *Gold in a Tin Dish*, p. 362; *AJHR*, 1888, Session 1, C.–2, 'The mining industry', p. 3. I am indebted to Mike Johnston, who provided the following clarification of mining terminology: Most people, wrongly, refer to any more or less horizontal mine working as a tunnel. However, a *tunnel* is a horizontal passageway open at both ends. A more or less horizontal passageway with only one entrance

is a *drive*. It is synonymous with *drift* and *adit*, although a drive (and adit) usually follow a mineralised zone or some other feature of interest to the miners. A passageway that intersects the zone of interest at roughly right angles is a *crosscut*. A *level* is usually a roughly horizontal passage used for working a reef or mineralised zone. In steeply dipping reefs they are commonly 30 metres apart vertically, but this not a universal rule. Miners work from a level to extract the ore, which is then conveyed along the level either directly out of the mine to a tramway or to a shaft for raising the ore to the surface above. Where possible, miners work up from a level so that the ore can be dropped by gravity down to the level, and also any water encountered can be readily drained from the working face.

148 'Local and general', *The Star* (Christchurch), 16 February 1872, p. 2.

149 *Evening Post*, 13 May 1872, p. 2.

150 Re boundaries of the first Queen Charlotte Sound Goldfield see Johnston, *Gold in a Tin Dish*, p. 349; re its expansion see 'Proclamation', 'Advertisements', column 1, *ME*, 16 September 1874, p. 1.

151 'Local and general news', *ME*, 16 August 1873, p. 4.

152 For the Queen Charlotte Mining Company and the Port Gore Mining Company see 'Advertisements', column 2, *ME*, 29 January 1873, p. 4; for the Turner Gold Mining Company see 'Advertisements', column 1, *ME*, 19 February 1873, p. 3. The Turner company had £388 in hand at the time of registration. That, however, was better than the Port Gore Gold Mining Company, which, by 1874, had £97 cash in hand.

153 'The Marlborough reefs', *ME*, 20 September 1873, p. 6.

154 Ibid., Johnston, *Gold in a Tin Dish*, pp. 129, 133.

155 'Marlborough gold fields', *ME*, 27 June 1874, p. 7 reports on the official warden's report.

156 Johnston, *Gold in a Tin Dish*, pp. 134–39; re the mortgagee sale see 'Advertisements', column 1, *ME*, 25 December 1875, p. 3.

157 'Marlborough', *Grey River Argus*, 13 June 1873, p. 4. The official report on the Sounds goldfield was hedged with 'ifs': 'Marlborough gold fields', *ME*, 27 June 1874, p. 7 reports Warden Whitehorn who noted that while results were satisfactory, 'at present all that can be said [on the future] is merely conjectural'.

158 Johnston, *Gold in a Tin Dish*, p. 139.

159 Ibid., p. 140; *AJHR*, 1879, Session 2, H.–11, 'The goldfields of New Zealand', p. 13; 'Advertisements', column 2, *ME*, 10 July 1878, p. 3. In relation to the name change see 'The auriferous reefs in Queen Charlotte Sound', *Evening Post*, 14 August 1879, p. 2.

160 'Untitled', *ME*, 23 November 1878, p. 5.

161 Johnston, *Gold in a Tin Dish*, pp. 140–41.

162 'Advertisements' column 2, *ME*, 12 December 1883, p. 2; re the company's finds and expenditure see Johnston, *Gold in a Tin Dish*, p. 143. In the district in 1883 gold was selling at £3 13s an ounce, so that sum is at best approximate.

163 Johnston, *Gold in a Tin Dish*, p. 143; 'New Zealand Antimony Company', *Evening Post*, 11 January 1889, p. 3.

164 'Local and general news', *ME*, 23 November 1894, p. 2.

165 Johnston, *Gold in a Tin Dish*, p. 145. The *ME* at the time also reflects the falling away of activity.

166 'Extracts from the Provincial Government Gazette', *ME*, 29 January 1873, p. 4.

167 Johnston, *Gold in a Tin Dish*, pp. 150–51.

168 'The gold discovery at Picton', *Wanganui Herald*, 18 February 1878, p. 4.

169 *AJHR*, 1879, Session 2, H.–11, 'The goldfields of New Zealand', p. 13. Warden Allen pointed out that the company was developing resources before incurring heavy machinery costs.

170 Johnston, *Gold in a Tin Dish*, pp. 158–59.

5. Visitors by the Boatload

1 'Excursion to Queen Charlotte Sound', *The Colonist*, 28 January 1859, p. 3.

2 'New Year's Day', *Evening Post*, 2 January 1873, p. 2.

3 G. T. Chapman, *Chapman's Traveller's Guide Through New Zealand: A Picture of New Zealand, Geographical, Topographical and Statistical* (self-published, c.1872), p. 93.

4 'Mr. Trollope on New Zealand', *The Press*, 2 June 1873, p. 3.

5 'Loch and fell', *ME*, 7 January 1911, p. 3.
6 Helen Beaglehole, *Fire in the Hills: A History of Rural Fire-fighting* (Christchurch: Canterbury University Press, 2012), p. 63.
7 Caroline Daley, *Leisure & Pleasure: Reshaping and Revealing the New Zealand Body 1900–1960* (Auckland: Auckland University Press, 2003), pp. 4–8.
8 *AJHR*, 1902, H.–2, Department of Tourist and Health Resorts annual reports, pp. 2–3.
9 *Evening Post*, 30 December 1873, p. 2.
10 'Local and general news, The Sounds', *ME*, 31 August 1892, p. 2. The article suggests that the prosperity brought about by bush clearance had contributed to the Sounds' growing reputation.
11 'Local and general', *ME*, 10 April 1893, p. 2.
12 'Marlborough Sounds excursion', *Wanganui Herald*, 1 April 1909, p. 5.
13 'In smooth water', *Evening Post*, 3 January 1911, p. 6.
14 'Advertisements', column 5, *Evening Post*, 1 April 1890, p. 2.
15 'A delightful holiday trip', *Evening Post*, 22 April 1893, Supplement, p. 1.
16 'Local and general news, Fishing', *ME*, 13 September 1888, p, 2.
17 'Cheap excursions', *ME*, 28 December 1900, p. 3.
18 'A new steamer', *ME*, 3 April 1906, p. 4.
19 'The land of the level road', *ME*, 7 June 1910, p. 6.
20 James Cowan, *New Zealand: The Marlborough and Nelson Districts* (Wellington: Department of Tourist and Health Resorts, 1909), p. 10.
21 'The Marlborough Sounds: A week in Arcadia', *ME*, 19 January 1909, p. 5.
22 'District news', *Nelson Evening Mail*, 21 January 1902, p. 2.
23 'Local and general news', *ME*, 11 January 1917, p. 4.
24 'Local and general news', *ME*, 5 September 1917, p. 4.
25 'Holidays in the Sounds', *The Dominion*, 27 December 1920, p. 6. For comments on the beauties of the bays see 'Marlborough's modesty!', *ME*, 11 April 1902, p. 2.
26 'A cruise in the historic waters of the Marlborough Sounds', *NZ Illustrated Magazine*, 1 January 1905, p. 257; 'Marlborough's modesty!', ibid.
27 'Untitled', *Manawatu Standard*, 16 April 1910, p. 8.
28 'Advertisements', column 4, *Evening Post*, 12 April 1887, p. 2.
29 'Local and general news', *ME*, 7 June 1893, p. 2.
30 'Marlborough's modesty!', *ME*, 5 September 1902, p. 2.
31 'Local and general news', *ME*, 25 August 1903, p. 2.
32 Nola M. Leov and Margaret J. Turner, *Why Carluke? The Turners and their English cousins, 1881–1882* (Nelson: self-published, 2010), p. 27.
33 'Regulations for shooting red deer', *ME*, 12 March 1913, p. 7.
34 'Whalers', *ME*, 17 October 1917, p. 6.
35 'At our very doors', *ME*, 12 February 1919, p. 4.
36 'Local and general', *ME*, 30 December 1885, p. 2.
37 'A foolhardy voyage', *NZ Herald*, 27 February 1890, p. 5; 'Travels in a canoe', *The Press*, 26 June 1890, p. 2. *The Press* spelt their name 'Parks'. However, as papers of the day tended to exercise a certain laxness in relation to spelling, I have adopted the spelling used in Te Ara.
38 'Local and general: *Sail and Paddle*', *ME*, 2 July 1899, p. 2 reported that New York's monthly aquatic journal had an article on canoeing in Queen Charlotte Sound.
39 'An Easter trip', *The Colonist*, 26 April 1893, p. 3.
40 'Travels in a canoe', *The Press*, 26 June 1890, p. 2.
41 'Marlborough's modesty', *ME*, 11 April 1906, p. 2.
42 'Advertisements', column 1, *Evening Post*, 13 March 1899, p. 6.
43 'Trade of Timaru', *Evening Post*, 8 January 1907, p. 7.
44 'Sensational yachting experience', *ME*, 5 April 1898, p. 2.
45 'News of the day', *The Press*, 18 March 1913, p. 6; 'Local and general news', *ME*, 11 March 1913; re the Sounds' reception see 'Local and general news', *ME*, 28 March 1914, p. 4.

46 'Sharks in the Sounds', 'Advertisements', column 5, *Evening Post*, 10 March 1902, p. 4.
47 'Christmas in the Sounds', *Evening Post*, 9 January 1894, p. 2.
48 Ibid.
49 'A holiday in Queen Charlotte Sound', *Auckland Star*, 22 July 1898, p. 6.
50 'A cruise in the historic waters of the Marlborough Sounds', *NZ Illustrated Magazine*, 1 January 1905, p. 257.
51 Ibid.
52 'A holiday in Queen Charlotte Sound'.
53 'A cruise in the historic waters of the Marlborough Sounds'.
54 Ibid. The article provides a picture of settlement in the outer sound at that time. A sheep farmer lived in Cannibal Cove (Anaho); in Resolution Bay Mr Ewing had built his house on the only flat land. On the other side of the sound, at Wharehunga, bush had been burned and the Radcliffe family were camping, waiting for a further burn before building their home. Among the 'ruin and neglect' of the antimony mine in Endeavour Inlet were Mr Seagar, his family with him for the holidays, and acting mine manager Mr Murray, along with, possibly, a residual workforce. At Fly (Ratimera) Bay, though not in the outer sound, the party found a Māori whare, a small garden and a few fruit trees. A shark was hung out to dry but at the time they visited, no one was there.
55 'A cruise in the historic waters of the Marlborough Sounds'.
56 'A trip to Mt Stokes', *ME*, 2 February 1895, p. 3.
57 For the brief mention of Kirk's expedition see 'Cabled topics', *Evening Post*, 22 January 1896, p. 2; for the other rather lengthier account see 'A trip to Mount Stokes', *The Star* (Christchurch), 23 July 1896, p. 4.
58 Shaun Barnett & Chris Maclean, *Tramping: A New Zealand History* (Nelson: Potton & Burton, 2014), p. 15.
59 'Local and general news', *ME*, 11 January 1899, p. 2. The time taken was subsequently reported.
60 'Local and general news', *ME*, 15 December 1908, p. 4.
61 'The Marlborough Sounds: A week in Arcadia', *ME*, 19 January 1909, p. 5.
62 Ibid.; 'Local and general news', *ME*, 24 December 1910, p. 4; 'Local and general news', *ME*, 20 January 1914, p. 4; 'Local and general news', *ME*, 3 February 1915, p. 4.
63 'Advertisement: Masonic Hotel, Havelock', *ME*, 16 January 1886, p. 1.
64 'A delightful holiday trip', *Evening Post*, 6 May 1893, supplement, p. 1.
65 'Marlborough Sounds', *ME*, 10 March 1915, p. 6.
66 'News of the day', *The Colonist*, 23 January 1911, p. 2.
67 'Marlborough Sounds, tourist possibilities', *ME*, 15 January 1908, p. 5.
68 *ME*, 29 September 1900, p. 1; 'Picton', *ME*, 17 January 1907, p. 2.
69 'Advertisements', *ME*, 13 December 1906, p. 3.
70 'Marlborough Sounds', *ME*, 10 March 1915, p. 6; re Redheugh and the date of its use as a boarding house see 'The Marlborough Sounds', *ME*, 19 January 1909, p. 5; re Terrills see Heather Heberley, *Riding with Whales: Stories of Great Sounds Women* (Picton: Cape Catley, 1999), p. 21. By 1924 the Terrills were also advertising good accommodation, bathrooms, and fishing at Endeavour Inlet.
71 Julie Kennedy, *Picton and Queen Charlotte Sound: A Chronology* (Picton: Picton Historical Society, 2013), p. 43.
72 Re the number of launches see 'Marlborough Sounds scenery 1902–09', D. W. Foote, to C. H. Mills, 26 July 1906, AECB 8615 TOI/38, 1902/154, ANZ. C. H. Williams, District Road Engineer to Engineer of Roads, 19 November 1906, reported the tourist numbers.
73 'Local and general news', *ME*, 20 January 1914, p. 4.
74 Ethel Beauchamp Hazelwood, *Life at Anakiwa: The First 100 Years 1863–1963* (Anakiwa: self-published, 1974?), p. 15.
75 Flora Robb, *St Omer House: Family Life in the Guest House and some Sounds History* (Nelson: self-published, 2013), p. 31.
76 'Advertisements', *ME*, 18 November 1897, p. 3.
77 Cowan, *New Zealand: The Marlborough and Nelson Districts*, p. 10.

78 'Marlborough Sounds', *ME*, 10 March 1915, p. 6.

79 Hazelwood, *Life at Anakiwa*, p. 16.

80 'Local and general news', *ME*, 13 January 1906, p. 2.

81 'Marlborough's modesty!', *ME*, 11 April 1906, p. 2.

82 Shirley Buckland, *Reflections on a Lifetime* (Nelson: self-published, 2007), p. 6. This was part of the old Ravenscliff Run. Re the comments on the house see 'Picton', *ME*, 17 January 1907, p. 2; 'Marlborough Sounds', *ME*, 15 January 1908, p. 5.

83 Don Furness, *Tahuahua: The Story of Blackwood Bay, Queen Charlotte Sound* (Blenheim: self-published, 1974), p. 71.

84 'The Bishop of New Zealand's visitation to the southern island in 1848', *The New Zealander*, 27 September 1849, p. 3. I am grateful to the Mitchells for providing Hohepa Ngapaki with his Māori name.

85 Katherine Mansfield, 'The Voyage', *Selected Stories* (London: Oxford University Press, 1953), pp. 306, 312.

86 'Loch and fell', *ME*, 7 January 1911, p. 3.

87 'Nature notes', *Evening Post*, 29 November 1930, p. 17.

88 'Stoat and weasels', *The Dominion*, 26 July 1909, p. 8. The article was written by R. C. Bush, one-time engineer at the antimony mines, then Marlborough's agricultural inspector. He established the Bush Trust, which spent money buying and conserving land in different parts of New Zealand. The time Mr Clouston was at the mines, and when he wrote to Bush, is unrecorded.

89 'Loch and fell'.

90 'An Easter trip', *The Colonist*, 26 April 1893, p. 3.

91 Re the general population's propensity to destroy see Beaglehole, *Fire in the Hills*, p. 24; within the Sounds the following reports all provide examples of tourists' destruction: 'News and notes', *ME*, 14 January 1903, p. 1; 'Local and general news: Marlborough scenery' (which includes the quote), *ME*, 27 February 1904, p. 2; 'Topics of the day', *Evening Post*, 20 February 1904, p. 12.

92 'Government Gazette', *NENZC*, 27 May 1857, p. 2 identified these reservations as islands in the Pelorus River, about 100 acres (40 ha) on the neck of land between Pelorus Sound and Croisilles Harbour; a block of land between Kenepuru and Mahon Cove; about 9 acres (3.6 ha) at Waikawa Bay; about 150 acres (60 ha) between Ruakaka Bay and Blackwood Bay; about 80 acres (32 ha) on Ōnauku, East Bay, for watering; the promontory between Milton Bay (Picton) and Waikawa; and the land in Picton (then Cromwell).

93 *Nelson Provincial Govt. Gazette*, 1864, p. 132.

94 'Lands and Survey', *ME*, 17 September 1913, p. 3.

95 'National park petition', *ME*, 21 March 1898, p. 3.

96 *ME*, 25 May 1878, p. 5; 'An Easter trip', *The Colonist*, 26 April 1893, p. 3. These views were common at that time – see Beaglehole, *Fire in the Hills*, p. 57.

97 Michael M. King, *The Penguin History of New Zealand* (Auckland: Penguin, 2003), p. 79, cited in Colin Miskelly, 'Legal protection of New Zealand's indigenous terrestrial fauna: An historical review', *Tuhinga* 25, p. 73.

98 'Our flora and fauna', *Mataura Ensign*, 13 January 1914, p. 5.

99 Miskelly, 'Legal protection' – his assessment of the Act is on p. 31.

100 'Forest & Bird Protection Society', *The Press*, 24 February 1915.

101 *Rules and Objects of the New Zealand Forestry League Inc.* (Wellington: Watkins, Tyer, & Tolan, 1916).

102 'A jaunt in the *Hinemoa*', *Evening Post*, 24 September 1892, p. 1. Those views were reflected in other comments. On the national scene see the trenchant criticism of Edward Phillips Turner, then Inspector of Scenic Reserves, in 1911: 'It is our scenery that makes this Dominion one of the most delightful countries in the world . . . no nation with purely utilitarian ideals ever reached real greatness in its highest sense.' He continues with reference to 'our unimaginative settler' and contrasts New Zealand practice with that of England and Europe. See Beaglehole, *Fire in the Hills*, p. 64. For further local comment making international comparisons see, 'State forests', *The Daily Telegraph* (Hawke's Bay), 26 January 1893, p. 2.

103 'Local and general: Sounds scenery', *ME*, 18 January 1893, p. 2.

104 *New Zealand Gazette*, no. 66, 27 August 1896, p. 1360; re Cannibal Cove see L. W. McCaskill, *Scenic Reserves of Malborough* (Wellington: L&S, 1981), p. 42. ANZ has no files for that period on Cannibal Cove.

105 *NZ Gazette*, 15 September 1898, p. 1457.

106 *NZ Gazette*, no. 92, 24 October 1901, p. 2034.

107 *NZ Gazette*, no. 73, 1 August 1904, p. 2119.

108 Reserves, Marlborough Sounds Maritime Park, Chetwode Islands 1918–66, AANZ W5491 7613, Box 591, RES 8/8/52, Pt. 1, ANZ. Re Te Kakaha's reservation see *New Zealand Gazette*, no. 22, 5 April 1934, p. 878.

109 J. H. Mathews, chief forester, Forestry Dept, to surveyor-general, 20 November 1901, AANS W5951 25421, Box 69, MSM – 0157, Marlborough Sounds Maritime Park – Scenic reserves – Weka Point, 1901–82, ANZ; *NZ Gazette*, no. 103, 18 December 1902, p. 2697.

110 Marlborough Sounds Maritime Park, Garne & Saville Bays SR, 1900–2002, AANS W5942 7613, Box 139, Res/8/83/61, L&S, ANZ; McCaskill, *Scenic Reserves of Marlborough*, p. 32.

111 In relation to the historic reserve see Reserves and Crown Lands Enabling Act 1896, cl.13, 'Reserve in memory of its occupation by Captain Cook'. This specific mention of the reserve required that it be 'retained in its natural state as nearly as may be'. (I am indebted to Steve Bagley, DOC, Nelson, for this information.) 'Local and general news' *ME*, 29 March 1913, p. 4 reports that 2011 acres (814 ha) of Ship Cove had been taken as a sanctuary for native and imported game, but there appears to be no official gazetting of this.

112 Re the reserves and the damage by fire see 'Local and general news', *ME*, 14 January 1903, p. 1. Re land use applied for using reserves, in 1903 the board considered applications to clear and occupy part of Miritu and Ruakaka Reserve to graze cattle as a way of keeping down noxious weeds, to fell scrub on the Torea Reserve, and to burn fern on the foreshore of property in Queen Charlotte Sound and Kenepuru. The proposed usages were acceded to, though any burning was to be at the applicants' risk – see 'Marlborough Land Board, *ME*, 15 January 1903, p. 4.

113 Mike Roche, 'Edward Phillips Turner: The development of a "forest sense" in New Zealand 1890s to 1930s', Proceedings of the 6th National Australian Forest History Conference, Augusta, WA, 12–17 September 2004, p. 2, cited in Beaglehole, *Fire in the Hills*, p. 64.

114 CCL, 'Suggested Scenic Reserves – D'Urville Island', 30 August 1910, Patete, supporting documents, doc OY, p. 1 in Waitangi Tribunal, *Te Tau Ihu*, vol. 3, p. 1106.

115 'Scenery Commission', *Evening Post*, 28 March 1096, p. 2.

116 For ensuing frustrations as well as statements to soothe farmers' fears of 'wholesale taking of land' see 'Scenery preservation', *ME*, 24 August 1907, p. 5; re disappointment see 'Preservation of Forest Scenery', *ME*, 15 February 1906, p. 3. The Scenery Preservation Commission was itself conscious of their lack of momentum – *AJHR*, 1906, C. L&S, Scenery Preservation, C.–6, p. 2.

117 'Local and general news', *ME*, 21 March 1916, p. 4.

118 Tourists resorts – Marlborough Sounds – General, 1905–57, AECB 8615 TO1/135, 20/21 Pt 1, ANZ.

119 'A Marlborough beauty spot', *The Dominion*, 27 January 1908, p. 5.

120 CCL, Blenheim, to Sec. L&S, 23 May 1910, AANS W5951 25421, Box 66, MSM-0113, L&S head office – Marlborough Sounds Maritime Park – Scenic reserve – Deep Bay, 1910–85, ANZ.

121 *NZ Gazette*, no. 87, 1911, p. 3267.

122 'Captain Cook memorial', *ME*, 17 February 1906, p. 2; 'Ship Cove', *The Dominion*, 30 March 1909, p. 3.

123 L&S, head office – Marlborough Sounds Maritime Park – Scenic reserve – Deep Bay, 1910–85, AANS W5951, 25421, Box 66, MSM-0113, ANZ. Re Phillips Turner, 14 January 1910; re Mrs Campbell, CCL Blenheim, to Head Office, 23 May 1910, F. Ward, Ranger to CCL, Blenheim, 5 May 1910, F. Stephenson-Smith, L&S , to Sec. Scenery Preservation, 24 August 1911; re the Archdeacon's efforts, 13 October 1911, *NZ Gazette*, no. 87, 2 November 1911, p. 3267.

124 Ibid. With no name forthcoming, Skinner, CCL Blenheim, wrote to Sec. L&S, Wellington, 28 December 1911. The name agreed to at the time has obviously not stuck.

125 Scenic reserve, Putanui Point, 1910–86, AANS W5951, 25421 Box, 68, MSM-0141, L&S-Ho, ANZ. Re the claims of historical importance and the siting of Hikapu semi-fortified village see CCL, Blenheim, 19 March 1912. He instances *Memoirs of the Polynesian Society*, no. 1, p. 424, a reprinted account of the battle contained in S. P. Smith, 'History and traditions of the Taranaki coast: The South Island raids', *Journal of the Polynesian Society* 18, no. 4 (1909), p. 186. However, the description in that account of Hikapu being 'situated at the junction of Kenepuru Sound with that of Pelorus' does not adequately locate the site. For the gazetting of Putanui Point as a scenic reserve see *NZ Gazette*, 16 May 1912, p. 6113.

126 'Beautiful Marlborough', *ME*, 28 August 1906, p. 3.

127 'Scenic reserves and settlers', Letter to the editor, *The Dominion*, 26 January 1910, p. 5.

128 Ministry of Culture and Heritage, 'Scenery preservation in New Zealand': https://nzhistory.govt.nz/culture/scenery-preservation

129 *AJHR*, 1919, C.–6, Scenery Preservation Committee, p. 2.

130 'Local and general news', *ME*, 6 November 1908, p. 4; 'Marlborough's modesty!', *ME*, 11 April 1906, p. 2.

131 'The Marlborough Sounds', *The Press*, 26 March 1910, p. 8.

132 'The Tourist Department . . .' *ME*, 10 March 1902, p. 2.

133 Locals were critical – see Marlborough Sounds scenery 1902–09, Min. C. H. Mills to Superintendent of Tourist and Health Resorts, 9 April 1904, AECB 8615 TOI/38, 1902/154, ANZ. No replies to this correspondence were filed. On the local reception see also *ME* articles, 7 October 1904 and letters following.

134 'Local and general news', *ME*, 1 July 1905, p. 2. Lithographic reproduction ensured the attractive price – see 'Local and general news', *ME*, 7 June 1906, p. 2. Re the local advice see Marlborough Sounds scenery 1902–09, correspondence 20 February 1905, 27 February 1905, AECB 8615 TOI/38, 1902/154, ANZ.

135 'Table talk', *Auckland Star*, 4 April 1904, p. 4; 'Picton', *ME*, 13 July 1906, p. 3.

136 'Advertisements', supplement column 1, *The Free Lance*, 17 December 1904, p. 9.

137 'New publications', *ME*, 19 December 1910, p. 8.

138 'Literary notes', *Evening Post*, January 1919, p. 11.

139 'The Marlborough Sounds', *The Press*, 26 March 1910, p. 8.

140 'Local and general news', *ME*, 9 February 1915, p. 4.

141 'At our very doors', *ME*, 12 February 1919, p. 4. As noted previously, the film on the Tory Channel whaling industry and its shots of Sounds scenery was hailed as 'one of the best advertisements that Marlborough has ever had, and a cheap one at that'.

142 'Notes of the day', *The Dominion*, 30 September 1911, p. 13.

143 '"Onward Marlborough"', *ME*, 29 May 1920, p. 3.

6. Moving Goods and Connecting People

1 'Pencillings by the way', *Otago Daily Times*, 4 March 1862, p. 6.

2 'A visit to Picton', *NZ Herald*, 26 February 1881, p. 6.

3 'Notes of the day', *The Dominion*, 30 September 1911, p. 13.

4 Re women's prowess at rowing see 'A delightful holiday trip', *Evening Post*, 6 May 1893, p. 1; on their challenging men see 'Where is the snobbery?, *Evening Post*, 3 November 1892, p. 2; on the woman rower see 'An Easter trip', *The Colonist*, 26 April 1893, p. 3.

5 Nola M. Leov & Margaret J. Turner, *Best Laid Plans: Life in Carluke 1893–1894* (Nelson: self-published, 2011), p. 10.

6 'Personal matters', *Evening Post*, 26 August 1909, p. 7.

7 'The Marlborough Sounds: How the Census is taken', *Evening Post*, 9 May 1896, p. 1.

8 Re the *Maori* see 'Local and general news', *ME*, 2 January 1908, p. 4; re the information on the other of the company's ships associated with the Sounds see 'The ships list, Union Steam Ship Company of NZ': www.theshipslist.com/ships/lines/unionnz.shtml

9 NZ coastal shipping: www.nzcoastalshipping.com/anchor.html. Ships like *Stormbird, Huia, Charles Edward, Kennedy, Murray* and *Wallace* were regulars on this run.

10 Harry Christian, 'Sounds reminiscences or 40 years in Pelorus Sounds territory', Allan family papers, unpublished, c.1920s, p. 5. Christian does not date this service.

11 'Sailed', *Nelson Evening Mail*, 25 May 1881, p. 2.

12 'News & notes', *ME*, 21 April 1897, p. 1.

13 'Local and general news', *ME*, 27 May 1911, p. 4.

14 Christian, 'Sounds reminiscences', p. 5.

15 'Sounds–Golden Bay Steamship Company', *Hawke's Bay Herald*, 9 May 1900, p. 1.

16 'A new steamer', *ME*, 3 April 1906, p. 4.

17 'Advertisements', column 2, *ME*, 28 November 1916, p. 1.

18 'Mail notices', *The Dominion*, 12 January 1920, p. 8.

19 'Oil-launches' are first mentioned in Papers Past in 1896. They burned 'gasoline'. However, 'Wolfe's schnapps', *Bay of Plenty Times*, 29 August 1898, p. 2 refers to a scow that was fitted with twin screws worked by steam engines, not by 'oil motors'.

20 'Local and general news', *Nelson Mail*, 24 June 1908, p. 2; 'The land of the level road', *ME*, 7 June 1910, p. 6; re Picton's engine agencies and the fuel price see Christian, 'Sounds reminiscences', p. 2.

21 'Picton', *ME*, 6 December 1909, p. 5.

22 'The silent Sounds', *Evening Post*, 22 May 1915, p. 10.

23 Ibid. See also 'District news', *Nelson Evening Mail*, 21 January 1902, p. 2 (and for quote).

24 'Marlborough Sounds', *ME*, 10 March 1915, p. 6.

25 'The New Hebrides settlement', *Evening Post*, 8 May 1902, p. 6; 'Marlborough Sounds', *ME*, 10 March 1915, p. 6.

26 *Pelorus Guardian*, 19 February 1904.

27 'Local and general: Gear Meat Company', *ME*, 5 June 1891, p. 2.

28 'In the Sounds', *The Dominion*, 17 July 1913, p. 4.

29 G. T. Chapman, *Chapman's Traveller's Guide Through New Zealand: A Picture of New Zealand, Geographical, Topographical and Statistical* (self-published, c.1872), p. 92.

30 'Local intelligence', *Wellington Independent*, 17 December 1863, p. 2.

31 'Shipping telegrams', *Wellington Independent*, 30 January 1874, p. 2.

32 'Chamber of Commerce', *ME*, 15 June 1912, p. 5. The term was particularly used in relation to Guards Bay but was true of all of the Sounds, though for small craft the safety of different bays is dependent on wind direction.

33 For one account of the disruption to shipping in the area see 'Untitled', *ME*, 9 April 1920, p. 8.

34 'Local and general news', *ME*, 17 August 1903, p. 2.

35 C. W. N. Ingram, *New Zealand Shipwrecks, 1795–1970* (Wellington: Reed, 1974), cited in Michael M. Trotter, *Marlborough Sounds Archaeological Survey 1974* (Christchurch: Canterbury Museum, 1974), Appendix 1, pp. 23–24.

36 'Local and general news', *Nelson Evening Mail*, 24 June 1908, p. 2 refers to few launches being lost over the previous decade.

37 Details of the following three further incidents are taken from the reports on wrecks in the relevant Marine Department annual reports. In 1910 the barque *Hippaloa* (299 tonnes), struck Walker Rock, foundered, was under tow, but sank off Blumine Island, unable to make Picton. In 1912 the 77-tonne *Lizzie Taylor*, carrying timber, was dismasted and suffered damage when a sudden squall carried away much of her rigging. In 1914 the 200-tonne schooner *Maroro* missed stays and went on the rocks in Pelorus Sound.

38 'Wreck of the SS *Rangitoto*', *Wellington Independent*, 1 August 1873, p. 2.

39 'Eighteen lives lost', *Manawatu Times*, 5 September 1884, p. 2; 'Untitled', *Poverty Bay Herald*, 5 September 1884, p. 2. The quote is from 'The chief officer's story', *Manawatu Times*, 5 September 1884, p. 2. The *Poverty Bay Herald* article also describes another instance of a captain's misapprehensions of position. In 1880 the captain of the *Northumberland* thought Stephens Island was Kāpiti Island, and was only within a few miles of Nelson when he realised he was

not approaching Wellington. The size of the vessel is given elsewhere as 1143 tonnes ('Dreadful shipwreck and loss of life in Cook Strait', *The Colonist*, 6 September 1884).

40 'The insurances', *The Star* (Christchurch), 6 September 1884, p. 3.

41 'Launch owners complained vigorously about "obnoxious regulation"', *Pelorus Guardian*, 1 November 1907; 'Oil launches', *ME*, 29 November 1907, p. 6.

42 *AJHR*, 1914, H.–15 Marine Department, pp. 1, 11. Engineers of steamers or mechanically powered vessels sailing within restricted limits had to hold a third-class seagoing engineer's certificate, and ships had to be surveyed and carry specified equipment: *AJHR*, 1915, H.–15 Marine Department, p. 68.

43 It was, for instance, advertised in the *The New Zealander*: 'Complete sets of the charts', 'Advertisements', column 2, 23 May 1849, p. 1. To what extent masters with growing coastal knowledge took them up at that stage is unknown.

44 *Marlborough Press*, 27 December, 1863, in Julie Kennedy, *Picton and Queen Charlotte Sound: A Chronology* (Picton: Picton Historical Society, 2013), p. 19.

45 Scenic Reserves – Marlborough Sounds scenic reserves, 1928–32, attached to Deputy CCL to Sec. L&S, 19 May 1928, AANS W5491 6095, Box 1035, 4/539, ANZ. The Cape Koamaru and Ship Cove reservations were gazetted in the *Marlborough Provincial Gazette*, 22 December 1864. For Blumine Island the relevant notices are *Marlborough Provincial Gazette*, 22 December 1864, p. 132 (the 150 acres) and *Marlborough Provincial Gazette*, 13 April 1865, p. 35 (the 737 acres).

46 'Shipping', *Otago Daily Times*, 14 August 1865, p. 4.

47 *AJHR*, 1893, H.–31, MDAR.

48 Helen Beaglehole, *Lighting the Coast: A History of New Zealand's Coastal Lighthouse System* (Christchurch: Canterbury University Press, 2006), p. 79. 'Shipping intelligence', *The Colonist*, 30 September 1864, p. 2 reported that the *Marlborough Press* considered a light was needed on the northern end of Cape Jackson and another on Long Island, for safety of shipping coming into Queen Charlotte Sound.

49 *AJHR*, 1863, D.–2, Fourth report of the Postal Service of NZ, 1852–63, p. 10. Picton by then was a port of entry (see Kennedy, *Chronology*, p. 17) and for a time the rush for gold in the Wakamarina Valley in 1864 and the ships, miners and mail flocking through the channel made it all the more relevant. However, the sheer danger of the channel and the wisdom of encouraging masters to take their ships through it, and the declining returns from the goldfields, soon allowed other priorities in lighting New Zealand's coast.

50 A light for Tory Head was first ordered in 1874 as part of a lighting scheme for Cook Strait. The delays were around the appropriateness of lighting the channel entrance, changing priorities in determining lighthouse locations and, possibly, the planned inauguration of the Union Steamship Company's weekly service in 1875. See Beaglehole, *Lighting the Coast*, pp. 24, 25, 53–54, 73–55ff, 301–02.

51 Kennedy, *Chronology*, p. 26.

52 *AJHR*, 1869, E.–4 MDAR, p. 5 reports replacing a small beacon there which had been knocked over; Beaglehole, *Lighting the Coast*, p. 152; 'A beacon washed away', *Grey River Argus*, 17 March 1885, p. 2.

53 'Advertisements', column 3, *ME*, 2 May 1874, p. 4.

54 'The Pelorus Sound', *ME*, 19 June 1883, p. 2.

55 For instance in 1902, the Marine Department installed new beacons – *AJHR*, 1902, D.–1, PWDAR, PWD Statement, p. 63.

56 'News items', *Poverty Bay Herald*, 18 June 1902, p. 4.

57 Beaglehole, *Lighting the Coast*, pp. 152–54; *AJHR*, 1906, C.–1A, L&S: Surveys, p. 11. 'Jackson Head light', *ME*, 5 April 1910, p. 2 describes the second Pintsch light and the arrangements made to service it; 'Shipping', *Evening Post*, 24 February 1911, p. 6 deals with the second acetone acetylene light installed February 1911.

58 'Picton wharf', *ME*, 26 April 1887, p. 2.

59 *AJHR*, D.–1, PWDAR, Index to tables, p. 35.

60 The 1862 *New Zealand Handbook* first suggests this (Willis, Arthur, Gann & Co., *The New Zealand Handbook, or, Guide to the 'Britain of the South'* (London: E. Stanford, 1862). 'Untitled', *Nelson*

Evening Mail, 12 February 1897, p. 2 was the next to raise it. In 1898 J. W. Perano expounded on the attractions of the Sound as a naval base – 'Queen Charlotte Sound as a naval station', *ME*, 30 September 1898, p. 4. Other references promote the Sound as a naval base: Tomorrow's services . . .', *Evening Post*, 1 March 1902, p. 6; 'The best naval base', *ME*, 7 February 1910, p. 4; 'Local and general news', *ME*, 5 August 1911, p. 4; 'Naval training ship', *ME*, 20 February 1914, p. 5; 'Havelock', *ME*, 28 January 1919, p. 4.

61 'Picton's progress', *Evening Post*, 4 April 1906, p. 2; 'The minister's visit', *ME*, 20 November 1906, p. 3.

62 Re Mills' proposal see 'A ferry across Cook Strait', *Evening Post*, 12 January 1901, p. 5 and 'Local and general news: Picton Harbour Association', *ME*, 5 July 1902, p. 2. Re its squashing see 'Mr Millar in Marlborough', *ME*, 14 May 1908, p. 5. The minister said he could not discuss the scheme until Picton terminus was reached in another 10–12 years.

63 'House of Representatives', *Wanganui Chronicle*, 29 August 1903, p. 7. Mills was reported as hoping for a 20-knots-an-hour ferry.

64 'Roads and bridges', *The Dominion*, 4 June 1909, p. 6.

65 'Not a local matter', *Evening Post*, 16 July 1913, p. 8; Henry D. Kelly, *As High as the Hills: The Centennial History of Picton* (Picton: Cape Catley, 1976), pp. 151–52.

66 'The silent Sounds', *Evening Post*, 22 May 1915, p. 10; re the pace of building of the main trunk line see 'Roads and bridges'.

67 'Local and general news', *ME*, 22 August 1917, p. 4. A month later a relatively senior member of the Department of Agriculture's Livestock Division was reported as promising departmental assistance in getting better facilities ('Handling of stock', *ME*, 27 September 1917, p. 8). However, although a number of private and commercial wharves were built by 1925, a substantial new wharf was not built until 1957 (Kelly, *As High as the Hills*, pp. 153–54).

68 'Notes of the day', *The Dominion*, 30 September 1911, p. 6: 'Probably the procrastinating policy of the Government with regard to building the railway has had a deterring influence on the settlement of the lands. Marlborough has always suffered, and suffers still, from the lack of internal communication.' And again, 'The greatest need', suggested the *The Dominion* (30 September 1911, p. 13), 'was getting the main trunk line finished; with that done, the Sounds would be open to many.' Rollo Arnold, 'The virgin forest harvest and the development of colonial New Zealand', *NZ Geographer* 32 (1976), pp. 105–07, indicates the importance of rail at that time for settlement and exploitation.

69 *AJHR*, 1885, D.–1, PWDAR, Table 3, p. 7.

70 *Pelorus Guardian*, 26 July 1906.

71 *AJHR*, 1907, H.–15, MDAR, p. 53.

72 'The Havelock Harbour', *ME*, 18 June 1910, p. 8. The Marine Department contribution to PWAR, *AJHR*, 1910, p. 68.

73 *AJHR*, 1915, H.–15 MDAR, p. 68.

74 *AJHR*, 1898, C.–1, L&S, Appendix 3, Roads, p. 77.

75 Harbours, works, Torea Wharf, 1899–1981, AAPR, W3964, Box 3, 43/5/9/9, Pt 1, ANZ.

76 Other significant spending was: 1901 – £282 spent on the Torea wharf and shed, a considerable addition to the £7 spent before 1900 and £250 spent on the Te Awaiti wharf (*AJHR*, 1901, D.–1, PWDAR, p. 62); 1906 – £353 to the Portage and Waitaria bays wharf (*AJHR*, 1906, D.–1, PWDAR, p. 19). Smaller sums were: 1898 – £88 on the Grove wharf and shed (*AJHR*, 1898, D.–1, PWDAR, p. 40); 1906–10 the approaches to the Waitaria wharf were funded with small grants of anything from £18 to £42; 1910 – £4 went to the Homewood wharf; 1912– £12 was spent on the Elaine Bay wharf.

77 Examples of such work are *AJHR*, 1916, H.–15, MDAR, p 65 – G. S. Clouston's wharf and occupation at Whenuanui [sic] Bay, Queen Charlotte Sound; *AJHR*, 1917, H.–15, *MDAR*, pp. 69 & 70 respectively – Ebenezer Hay and Thomas Allport for wharfs and occupation in Titirangi and Endeavour Inlet respectively. A private wharf at Te Rawa was approved: *AJHR*, 1918, H.–15, *MDAR*, p. 14.

78 D. F. Foote to C. H. Mills, 26 July 1906, Marlborough Sounds scenery 1902–09, AECB 8615 TOI/38, 1902/154ff, ANZ.

79 *AJHR*, 1882, D.–1, PWDAR, Appendix 1, p. 59. *AJHR*, 1899, C.–1, L&S, p. 273 reported that in 1882 the channel was cut through Kaiaho Neck to save the upper Kenepuru settlers three-quarters of a mile

of land-cartage. Minimising rowing times in sometimes difficult water may also have motivated the construction.

80 Christian, 'Sounds reminiscences', p. 14.

81 'Local and general news', *ME*, 15 March 1898, p. 2. *AJHR*, 1899, C.–1, CLDAR, p. 86 also states that the distance saved by the cutting would be 17 nautical miles. Assuming that the cutting would be used by settlers around Whakatahuri, today the measured distance from there to Manaroa is 16.7 nm. However, going through the cut to Manaroa is 7.7 nm.

82 *AJHR*, 1900, C.–1, CLDAR, p. 87.

83 For those sums see the relevant PWD annual reports in *AJHR*, D.–1, in 1901, p. 62; 1902, p. 17; 1905, p. 16. No further expenditure appears in the reports, though additional work was confidently championed by the owner of Pelorus Refrigerating and Fishing Co., F. J. Sullivan. He wanted it to boost 'the tourist traffic which I am certain has a big future in these Sounds' – see Marlborough Sounds scenery, 1902–09, F. J. Sullivan to T. E. Donne, Superintendent, TPD, 25 September 1905, AECB 8615 TO1/38, 1902/154, ANZ. For the departmental response see TPD to F. J. Sullivan, 10 November 1905 (ibid.).

84 'News and notes', *ME*, 30 August 1905, p. 1.

85 'Local and general news', *ME*, 25 November 1905, p. 2; 'Local and general', *The Star* (Christchurch), 15 December 1905, p. 2 links the tunnel to Picton's prosperity; 'Local and general', *Star*, 16 January 1906, p. 2 compares the project to the Panama Canal, discusses the project's size and lists additional benefits.

86 'Is there something wrong?', *Taranaki Herald*, 2 June 1908, p. 4.

87 'The Marlborough Sounds', *ME*, 6 April 1906, p. 1.

88 See, for instance, 'The Onahau tunnel', *ME*, 27 July 1911, p. 7; 'Picton Borough Council', *ME*, 13 September 1906, p. 2; 'Mr Millar in Marlborough', *ME*, 14 May 1908, p. 5.

89 'News of the day', *The Press*, 15 August 1911, p. 6.

90 *AJHR*, 1912, H.–15, MDAR, p. 18.

91 'Census returns', *ME*, 14 May 1901, p. 4. Children are not mentioned as such and there was no Māori census that year: See Hilary and John Mitchells, *Te Tau Ihu o Te Waka: A History of Maori of Nelson and Marlborough*, vol. 2: *Te Ara Hou / The New Society* (Wellington: Huia Publishers, 2007), Table 11.1, Estimates of Population, 1830–1916, p. 470. The following pages provide a valuable discussion on population numbers, estimates and import.

92 Re the Pākehā numbers see 'Advertisements', column 5, *ME*, 11 November 1916, p. 4; re the Māori census see Mitchells, ibid.

93 'Census returns', *ME*, 14 May 1901, p. 4.

94 Carl Walrond, 'Roads – Funding road construction', Te Ara: www.TeAra.govt.nz/en/roads/page-2

95 *AJHR*, 1890, C.–5, Surveys of NZ, p. 3.

96 *Pelorus Guardian*, 7 February, 1893, quoted in Nola M. Leov and Margaret J. Turner, *Marriages Have Been Arranged: Life in Carluke, Autumn 1893* (Nelson: self-published, 2011), p. 24.

97 *AJHR*, 1904, C.–1, L&S, p. ix. Re the reiterations see *AJHR*, 1898, D.–1, PWD statement, p. ix; *AJHR*, 1901, D.–1, PWD statement, p. ii; *AJHR*, 1908, D.–1, PWD statement, p. xiv.

98 Re the road as an 'important line' see *AJHR*, 1881, C.–5, CLD, p. 13.

99 Rosslyn J. Noonan, *By Design: A Brief History of the Public Works Department, Ministry of Works, 1870–1970* (Wellington: Government Printer, 1975), p. 57.

100 *AJHR*, 1889, D.–1, PWD, p. 37.

101 Kennedy, *Chronology*, entries pp. 22–25.

102 'Local and general news', *ME*, 2 July 1884, p. 2.

103 *AJHR*, 1908, C.–1A, L&S, p. 2; *AJHR*, 1909, C.–1A, L&S, p. 11.

104 Carl Walrond, 'Roads – Why roads were built', Te Ara: www.TeAra.govt.nz/en/roads/page-2

105 *AJHR*, 1890, C.–5, Surveys of NZ, p. 3.

106 *AJHR*, 1902, C.–1, L&S, p. xv.

107 *AJHR*, 1882, D.–1, PWD, Table 5, p. 9; ibid., Appendix 1, p. 59. For the specific information on paying for the Kenepuru–Manaroa track and the finished width of the Torea–Kenepuru track see *AJHR*, 1890, C.–5, Surveys of NZ, Appendix 1, p. 32.

108 For example, *AJHR*, 1885, D.–1, PWD statement, Table 3, p. 7 indicates that £1 13 6d was spent on tracks in the Sounds; *AJHR*, 1886, D.–1, PWD statement, Appendix 1, pp. 37–38: 52 chains of bridle track cut from Torea Bay to Portage summit, 1 mile 56 chain cut from Clova Bay towards Waitaria; *AJHR*, 1888, C.–1A, p. 9, Report of the Survey of NZ, for forming a track from Te Mautua-a-Maui to Wet Inlet (Crail Bay) grading and specifications done.

109 *AJHR*, 1893, D.–1, PWD statement.

110 Walrond, 'Roads – Funding road construction'.

111 Ibid. County boundaries could mean there was no local body responsible for some of the roading. In 1884, for instance, the Kaituna road was so badly rutted that coaches lurched dangerously and passengers were reportedly almost thrown from their seats ('Local and general news', *ME*, 22 May 1884). In 1890 the *Pelorus Guardian* noted the 15 km or so of road for which no local body had responsibility, leaving locals to cut out fallen trees and move branches. The mail coach got stuck at various times during the summer (Nola M. Leov & Margaret J. Turner, *Highs and Lows: Changes in the Lives of the Turners of Carluke, and improving access to the outside world, 1892–1893* (Nelson: self-published, 2011, pp. 4, 6). Large chunks of vacant Crown land did not attract the revenue on which local bodies relied for road maintenance ('In Havelock', *ME*, 9 July 1909, p. 5). There was little money. Lack of detail makes it difficult to assess the adequacy of any grants for road maintenance received by the Pelorus Road Board, though we may note the £1 for £1 subsidy given in 1890 for gravelling and minor road formation on the Grove Road (*AJHR*, 1890, C.–5, Surveys of NZ); the £100 granted to Pelorus Road Board for forming, gravelling, clearing water tables and so on for Pelorus and Rai Valley Road (*AJHR*, 1892, C.–1, L&S), or the £109 18s 7d granted, with the board authorised to pay out £20 in each of bush-clearing, scrub-cutting and formation and £21 on maintenance (*AJHR*, 1902, C.–1, L&SAR, Table 41, p. 159). What there was, Sounds people argued, was distributed inequitably. They had failed to realise the advantages of having numbers of boards. In 1902 Marlborough's four road boards (Wairau, Pelorus, Picton, Kaikōura) received a total of £657 11s 2d. With the exception of Westland, other provinces (with literally dozens of boards) got thousands in total. Westland, worse off than Marlborough, got only £131 10s 6d that year (*AJHR*, 1902, C.–1, L&S, Table 41, p. 156).

112 Ken Berry, *Scrutiny on the County* (Blenheim: Marlborough County Council, 1986), pp. 21–22.

113 In relation to Marlborough Province's income from thirds and fourths see, for instance, *AJHR*, 1890, C.–5, Surveys of NZ, Table 8, which indicates that the huge province got only £7 10s. *AJHR*, 1891, C–1A, Survey Department, Road surveys, p. 30 notes that no thirds or fourths were paid out to Marlborough local bodies as 'the amount payable . . . [was] too small to expend advantageously'.

114 'Election intelligence', *ME*, 2 September 1887, p. 3 – Seymour comments on the money accumulating in Treasury.

115 See, for instance, 'Election intelligence', ibid; 'Local and general', 2 November 1887, p. 2; 'A road to the Sounds', *ME*, 24 January 1891, p. 2; 'The supplementary estimates', *ME*, 23 October 1894, p. 3. This last notes that some of the votes in the estimates were only got 'after forcible and persistent representations on the part of Mr Mills, who considered his district had not been fairly treated in the general estimates before'.

116 'Local and general news: Tracks in the Sounds', *ME*, 23 June 1894, p. 2.

117 Noonan, *By Design*, pp. 71–80.

118 'Current topics', *ME*, 7 September 1898, p. 4.

119 *AJHR*, 1897, D.–1, PWD statement, p. xi. In the 1896/97 year, for instance, PWD spent £208,694 building 787 km of carriage roads and 711 km of horse-roads, and maintaining 1894 km of carriage roads and 1041 km of horse-roads for ordinary traffic, and foresaw the need to continue such activity if settlement were to continue at the same rate.

120 *AJHR*, 1898, C.–1, L&SAR, Appendix 3, p. 75.

121 Re the Tennyson Inlet road see *AJHR*, 1889, Session 1, C.–1, Report of the Survey of NZ, p. 11; re the Nydia Bay road see ibid., L&S, p. 56.

122 *AJHR*, 1898, C.–1, L&S, Appendix 3, Roads, p. 76.

123 *AJHR*, 1895, C.–1, L&S, Appendix 3, Roads, p. 65.

124 *AJHR*, 1898, C.–1, L&S, Appendix 4, p. 75.
125 *AJHR*, 1898, C.–1, L&SAR, Appendix 3, pp. 75–77.
126 Survey road, Linkwater district, F. E. Greenfield and W. J. Elvy, July 1917, Original 159.6–9, Marlborough Museum and Historical Society.
127 *AJHR*, 1898, C.–1, L&S, Appendix 3, Roads, p. 77; 'Marlborough Sounds', *ME*, 1 August 1899, p. 4.
128 'Sounds local government', *ME*, 22 September 1910, p. 6.
129 'Allocation of public money', *ME*, 18 October 1898, p. 4.
130 'Public Works estimates', *ME*, 20 October 1906, p. 3.
131 Re the inequitable funding see 'Prospects of the Pelorus', *ME*, 19 January 1886, p. 2; 'The supplementary estimates', *ME*, 23 October 1894, p. 3; 'Wedding in the Sounds', *ME*, 21 December 1906, p. 2. On the political weaknesses see 'Local and general news', *ME*, 21 May 1907, p. 4. This last instances a fairly short-sighted refusal to contribute to progress the railway line beyond Seddon. A similar attitude would delay roading in the outer Pelorus in the 1970s.
132 'In Havelock', *ME*, 19 July 1909, p. 5.
133 'Marlborough votes', *ME*, 23 September 1908, p. 5. The article suggests that many of the track items had been previously listed (and therefore were not done) and that spending elsewhere was similarly instructive: £40,000 voted for the Blenheim–Waipara section of the railway, £29,000 spent; of the £5000 voted for the Picton railway wharf, only £946 spent.
134 'Political jottings, *Nelson Evening Mail*, 12 October 1898, p. 2. The paper claimed that analysis of public works expenditure province by province suggested that Marlborough was second only to Westland in terms of expenditure per head of population, getting £2 1s 11d per head of population against Westland's £9 7s 11 or, at the other end of the scale, Otago and Southland's 16s – information easily represented as a Liberal sweetener.
135 'The frozen meat trade: Tracks in the Sounds', *ME*, 29 June 1897, p. 2. This point was expressly made in relation to the Picton–Grove road. It is unlikely that it was the only instance.
136 'Marlborough Sounds', *ME*, 4 August 1899, p. 4. This article contrasts the behaviour of C. Y. Fell in refusing to allow a road to go over his property without compensation with his ready support for the road once the land had been bought by the Christchurch Meat Co.
137 Nola M. Leov and Margaret J. Turner, *The Making of the Bridle Track to French Pass: A Salute to an Early Roadmaker, Jonathan Brough* (Nelson: Copy Press, 2015), p. 20.
138 Ibid., pp. 20–21.
139 *AJHR*, 1898, C.–1, L&S, Appendix 4, pp. 97–98.
140 Leov & Turner, *The Making of the Bridle Track*, p. 16.
141 *AJHR*, 1898, C.–1, L&S, Appendix 4, p. 98
142 Leov & Turner, *The Making of the Bridle Track*, p. 42.
143 Ibid., pp. 41–42
144 *AJHR*, 1898, C.–1, L&S, Appendix 4, p. 98.
145 Leov & Turner, *The Making of the Bridle Track*, pp. 21–22.
146 Ibid., p. 44.
147 *AJHR*, 1898, C.–1, L&S, Appendix 4, p. 97.
148 Leov & Turner, *The Making of the Bridle Track*, p. 21.
149 Ibid., p. 44.
150 Ibid., p. 43.
151 Ibid., p. 20.
152 'Local and general news', *ME*, 24 January 1906, p. 2; on maintenance see 'Advertisements', column 3, *ME*, 17 March 1906, p. 3; *Pelorus Guardian*, 9 June 1903 refers to a long and considerable thunderstorm that damaged the tracks between Manaroa and Hopai, making them impassable for horses, and suggested that metalling should be part of road-making.
153 'Pelorus Road Board', *ME*, 11 March 1899.
154 'Tracks in the Sounds', *ME*, 26 April 1910, p. 3.
155 'Sounds local government', *ME*, 22 September 1910, p. 6.
156 'Sounds county', *ME*, 5 July 1910, p. 2. Hon. Roderick McKenzie, Minister of Public Works,

considered that 'the majority of settlers . . . will shoulder their obligations, and be a share of the expense in maintaining the tracks'.

157 'Public Works estimates', *ME*, 17 October 1911, p. 5 indicates that a total of £1200 was spent on the Havelock–Kaituna road (£200), Havelock main road (£299), Mahikipawa–Havelock road (£200), Picton–Grove road (£500), while some £600 was spent on Sounds tracks. 'Public Works estimates', *ME*, 19 October 1912 reports that apart from the Mahau Sound and Onahau Bay wharves' subsidy of £50, the vote for spending on link roads in the Sounds area included the Picton–Grove road funding of £3000. The £1300 voted for the tracks was much less. The schedule of proposed funding for roads in Sounds County was: in 1913, £75 ('Crown lands', *ME*, 15 October 1913, p. 3); in 1916, £1648 – from thirds and fourths accrued over the period 29 January 1910 to 31 January 1916 ('Land Board', *ME*, 16 March 1916, p. 3); £65 the following year ('Public Works Department 1917–18 estimates', *The Colonist*, 13 October 1917, p. 3). From 1918, proposals to spend such accrued sums were printed regularly in the *ME*.

158 'Sounds Farmers' Union', *ME*, 3 November 1911, p. 6.

159 *AJHR*, 1916, D.–1, PWD statement, p. xi; Appendix B, p. 18.

160 *AJHR*, D.–1, PWD statement, p. 30.

161 *AJHR*, 1865, D.–1, Postal Service of NZ report, p. 3.

162 See, for instance, *AJHR*, 1869, E.–1, Table 14, p. 9.

163 Geoffrey Wilson, *Linkwater: A History* (Linkwater: Linkwater Settlers' Association, 1962), p. 55; re Havelock see *AJHR*, 1864, D.–1, Postal Service of NZ report, Appendix, p. 11 (the report is for the 1863 year).

164 Loreen Brehaut, 'Mailboats in the Sounds': www.theprow.org.nz/enterprise/Sounds-mailboats/#.VTAwcSgVrHg

165 *AJHR*, 1869, E.–1, Postal Service of NZ report, Table 24, p. 15.

166 Ibid., Table 25.

167 I have not been able to determine a date for the opening of the Grove. Re its closure see *AJHR*, 1881, F.–1, P&T, p. 3; re the 1882 services see *AJHR*, 1882, F.–1, P&T, p. 3.

168 *AJHR*, 1885, F.–1, P&T, pp. 5, 6.

169 Kennedy, *Chronology*, p. 28; 'Advertisements', column 6, *ME*, 10 August 1891, p. 3.

170 See *AJHR*, 1892, F.–1 P&T, pp. vii–viii re the introduction of these services in other parts of the country; re some Sounds offices see Re Elaine Bay, *AJHR*, 1901, F.–1, P&T, re Māhakipawa see *AJHR*, 1902, F.–1, P&T.

171 *AJHR*, 1892, Session 1, F.–1, P&T annual report, p. xii.

172 *AJHR*, 1897, F.–1, P&T annual report, p. xv.

173 Mail for Havelock, Mahau, Māori Bay, Northwest Bay, Homewood, Brightlands, Ketu and Anakoa Bays left Blenheim once a fortnight. Further runs, operating on alternate fortnights, were established from Wellington to Havelock. One dropped off mail to Hikoekoea, Anakoha and Ketu bays, before running down into Tawhitinui Reach to Brightlands and Fern Flat in Elaine Bay, then back to Homewood, Northwest Bay, Māori Bay, into Mahau Sound and thence to Havelock. This service returned the way it came. The second did much the same route, but only on the return trip from Havelock did it call at Hopai, Beatrix and Nydia bays and Mahau Sound.

174 'Advertisements', column 2, *ME*, 17 August 1896, p. 3.

175 Christian, 'Sounds reminiscences', p. 6.

176 'Mail notices', *The Dominion*, 12 January 1920, p. 8.

177 'Political jottings', *Nelson Evening Mail*, 12 October 1898, p. 2; 'Marlborough Sounds', *ME*, 4 August 1899, p. 4; 'Advertisements', column 4, *ME*, 15 March 1900, p. 3; 'Local and general news', *ME*, 3 November 1903, p. 2.

178 'Local and general news', *ME*, 3 November 1903, p. 2. For another example of the attempted use of pigeons in NZ see Beaglehole, *Lighting the Coast*, p. 156.

179 *Pelorus Guardian*, 25 July 1905.

180 *Pelorus Guardian*, 22 May 1908.

181 Nola Leov, pers. comm., November 2015.

182 For the Endeavour Inlet settlers' need for well-timed service to get their perishable goods to Picton and then to Wellington see 'News of the day', *The Colonist*, 1 August 1913, p. 4.

183 'In the Sounds', *The Dominion*, 17 July 1913, p. 4.
184 *AJHR*, 1900, F.–1, P&T, p. 3; *AJHR*, 1901, F.–1, P&T, p. iv. See also Tim Shoebridge, 'Mail and couriers – Mail in the 20th century', Te Ara: www.TeAra.govt.nz/en/mail-and-couriers/page-3
185 This is the first time the P&T annual reports mention them.
186 *AJHR*, 1916, F.–1, P&T, Subsidized sea mail-services, p. 16. Similar tables can be found in the annual reports for the preceding years.
187 A. C. Wilson, 'Telecommunications – Early telegraphy and telegrams' (see map), Te Ara: www.TeAra.govt.nz/en/interactive/21998/telegraph-spreads
188 *AJHR*, 1876, F.–1, P&T, p. 1; *AJHR*, 1892, F–1, P&T, p. xviii.
189 *AJHR*, 1866, E.–5, Electric Telegraph Department, p. 5.
190 *AJHR*, 1902, F.–1, P&T, Table 22, p. 27.
191 Wilson, 'Telecommunications'.
192 Was it easier to equate the activity generated by small passenger and freight steamers with economic output than it was for phone lines, where fewer people were directly involved and the immediate returns on line rental were inevitably small?
193 Wilson, 'Telecommunications'.
194 'News and notes', *ME*, 5 August 1903, p. 1. Other instances are the rejection of telephone communications for the French Pass, Croisilles and Sounds settlers in 1902 because of anticipated loss of about £2000; rejection of a line from Tory Channel to Picton via Ocean Bay, Port Underwood, because of the anticipated expense of installation and maintenance (*ME*, 17 April 1905) and the refusal to install a phone link between Endeavour Inlet and Dryden Bay because the expense of maintenance would not justify the cost ('Local and general news', *ME*, 13 July 1909, p. 4).
195 'Telegraphic communication', *ME*, 19 January 1905, p. 3.
196 *Pelorus Guardian*, 20 February 1912. F. D. Neave, a Titirangi settler, wrote of the concern at closure of the telegraph office at Whakatahuri, his nearest office, after the proprietor died. The letter is an interesting example of the issues involved, practical suggestions made to ensure the office reopened, and the value of outlying offices for shipping. Neave noted the 'terrible inconvenience' when sheep sales were on, and always in cases of sickness. Taking the telegraph line to Te Puru, he suggested, was an extra mile but it was 'a fine sheltered bay for boats' and 4 miles closer to Titirangi 'for this end of the district and Port Gore; for all the shipping that lie on Guard's Bank in rough weather, or waiting for the bar at Wanganui; besides the large Maori settlement at Okoha'. The Redwoods at Okoha, the Ward Brothers on Forsyth Island and he himself, Neave wrote, were willing to give £25 guarantee 'that new line will pay its expenses', and P. Hocquard, at the post office at Te Puru, was willing to have the telephone office at his house.
197 *AJHR*, 1903, F.–1, P&T, pp. xxvi, 31.
198 'Telephone connection with Havelock', *ME*, 26 February 1906, p. 3.
199 *AJHR*, 1905, D.–1, PWD, p. xi.
200 'Telegraphic communication', *ME*, 19 January 1905, p. 3; 'Chamber of Commerce', *ME*, 31 October 1903, p. 4; *ME*, 17 April 1905; 'Local and general', *ME*, 27 April 1906; *AJHR*, 1907, F.–1, P&T, p. xxxiii.
201 *AJHR*, 1909, D.–1, PWD statement, Table 6, p. 24; *AJHR*, 1911, D.-1, PWD statement, Table 6, p. 36.
202 *Pelorus Guardian*, 24 May 1907.
203 'Marlborough Sounds', *ME*, 10 March 1915, p. 6.
204 Donald Furness, *Tahuahua: The Story of Blackwood Bay, Queen Charlotte Sound* (Blenheim: self-published, 1974), p. 110.
205 *AJHR*, 1914, D.–1, PWD statement, 1914, Table 6, p. 46; *Pelorus Guardian*, 14 January 1913.
206 *AJHR*, 1909, Session 2, F.–1, P&T, p. xvi. The bigger ohms wire allowed a greater current through without damaging the wire.
207 *Pelorus Guardian*, 21 December 1909.
208 *AJHR*, 1920, F.–1, P&T, p. 11; *AJHR*, 1921, F.–1, P&T, p. 17.
209 'Telephone connection with Havelock', *ME*, 26 February 1906, p. 3.
210 'Local and general', *Wairarapa Daily Times*, 9 October 1916, p. 4.

7. Carving Out New Lives

1 Arthur Willis, Gann & Co., *The New Zealand Handbook, or, Guide to the 'Britain of the South'* (London: E. Stanford, 1862) was a handbook for settlers published as emigration got underway.

2 'The Census', *ME*, 27 May 1881, p. 2.

3 Waitangi Tribunal, *Te Tau Ihu o te Waka a Maui: Report on Northern South Island Claims* (Wai 785), vol. 2 (Wellington, 2008), pp. 957–58. Hilary & John Mitchells, *Te Tau Ihu o Te Waka: A History of Maori of Nelson and Marlborough*, vol. 2: *Te Ara Hou / The New Society* (Wellington: Huia Publishers, 2007), p. 470 give the same figure but state that the 63 Ngāti Toa and Rangitāne were spread across Pelorus Sound and Valley.

4 Waitangi Tribunal, *Te Tau Ihu*, vol, 2, p. 950.

5 Ibid., p. 967.

6 Nola M. Leov and Margaret J. Turner, *Why Carluke? The Turners and their English cousins, 1881–1882*, (Nelson: self-published, 2010), p. 22. This list of goods to take was given out to intending settlers in 1888, but I have assumed that the Harvey's pioneering experience would have led them to take similar items.

7 Iris Wilkinson (Robin Hyde), 'On the road to anywhere', *NZ Railways Magazine* 10, no. 3 (1 June 1935).

8 Sean Handley, 'The history of benthic change in Pelorus Sound (Te Hoiere), Marlborough', prepared for the Marlborough District Council (National Institute of Water and Atmospheric Research, February 2015), p. 13.

9 Leov & Turner, *Why Carluke?*, p. 25. This account comes from Janie Turner in the Rai Valley, but see below for similar information from Harold Beauchamp. The detail re fuchsia berries is from Hope family letters and Elizabeth's diary, Hope family papers, p. 41; re the honey see G. J. C. (John) Harvey, *Where There's a Will There's a Way: Memories of My Childhood and Sawmilling Days in the Marlborough Sounds* (Blenheim: self-published, 2008) p. 26.

10 Frank W. Ponder, *A Labyrinth of Waterways: The Forgotten Story of New Zealand's Marlborough Sounds* (Wellington: Wenlock House, 1986), pp. 75, 76.

11 Ibid., p. 65.

12 Flora Robb, *St Omer House: Family Life in the Guest House and some Sounds History* (Nelson: self-published, 2013), p. 13 lists shallots, potatoes, 60 cabbages, 89 cauliflower, 20 lettuces, radishes, peas, beans, pumpkins, melons, cucumbers, marrows, carrots, gooseberries (later a considerable number), peaches and cherries grown by the Godsiffs at Manaroa in the mid-1890s.

13 Hope family letters, pp. 15–16.

14 Rollo Arnold, *The Farthest Promised Land: English Villagers, New Zealand Immigrants of the 1870s* (Wellington: Victoria University Press, 1981), p. 78.

15 The European population in New Zealand in 1861 was 94,983. Apart from the 26,487 born in the county, 50 per cent were English, 23 per cent Scottish, 12 per cent Irish, barely 1 per cent Welsh. There were also Australians and a few of European stock (Ken Berry, *Scrutiny on the County* (Blenheim: Marlborough County Council, 1986)). More particularly, Arnold, *The Farthest Promised Land*, p. 45, writes of the predominantly English immigrants arriving in Picton in 1871.

16 Hope family letters, pp. 11–15. The quote is on p. 15.

17 Ibid., pp. 34, 36, 37.

18 *AJHR*, 1879, Session 2, C.-12, CLDAR, 'Lands disposed of on deferred payments', p. 2. This is the first departmental report of land being offered unsurveyed.

19 For the quote see Hope family letters, p. 30; re the wages, June Allen, pers. comm., November 2014. The nature of Crichton's tenure is not clarified in the letters or diary.

20 Hope family letters, p. 30.

21 Ibid.

22 Ibid., p. 33.

23 Ibid., p. 51.

24 Ibid., p. 41.

25 Ibid., pp. 45–46.

26 Ibid., pp. 63–64.

27 Ibid., p. 48.
28 Hope family letters, pp. 37–40.
29 Heather Heberley, *Riding with Whales: Stories of Great Sounds Women* (Picton: Cape Catley, 1999), p. 70. Ida Scott (née Tosswill) recounts how she was the only child rescued when their house was burnt down.
30 Ibid., p. 63.
31 http://web.uvic.ca/vv/student/medicine/holloway.htm
32 Hope family letters, p. 54.
33 Jonathan Brough, 'Tracks', *The Colonist*, 31 December 1900, p. 4.
34 Hope family letters, pp. 50, 61, 65. 'Items of interest', *ME*, 20 December 1899, p. 4 identifies the man as Charlie Stuart and gives the family history.
35 Harold Beauchamp & Ethel Broughton Hazelwood, *Reminiscences and Recollections* (New Plymouth: T. Avery, 1937), pp. 39–40.
36 Robb, *St Omer House*, pp. 29–30. Robb lists Kenepuru names such Henderson, Borck, McManaway; later there was Johnnie Kawhau, Robb, and a variety of Godsiffs. The primary work was shearing, but Charlie Godsiff and another won a contract to fence a huge block at Pohueni after a burn (pp. 29–30).
37 Deirdre Mackay, *Voices from the Sea: The Stories of Some Nelson and Marlborough Fishing Families* (Motueka: Talley's Group, 2004): 'Mosquito fleet: The McCauley family', pp. 199–201; Paul Mulcock, 'The New Zealand branch of the Mulcock family', pt 3: 'The story of Bulwer farm in Pelorus Sound', unpublished, p. 11.
38 Brough, 'Tracks'.
39 Robb, *St Omer House*, p. 480.
40 Nola M. Leov & Margaret J. Turner, *Marriages Have Been Arranged: Life in Carluke, Autumn 1893* (Nelson: self-published, 2011), p. 43. Nola M. Leov & Margaret J. Turner, *Intermezzo: The Fortunes of the Turner Family and the Evolution of Rai Valley, 1885–1892* (Nelson: self-published, 2011), pp. 9–15 provides the detail of the dog on a drive to Kaikōura and beyond. It could well have happened in the Sounds.
41 Brough, 'Tracks'.
42 Harry Williams, 'Life at Kaiuma Bay in the Pelorus Sound, Collingwood', August 1998, Williams private papers, pp. 12–14.
43 Harry Williams, Kaiuma Bay, Pelorus Sound, panorama photo, c.1925, Williams private papers.
44 R. Bester (ed.), *Harvest of Grace: Essays in Celebration of 150 Years of Mission in the Anglican Diocese of Nelson* (Nelson: Standing Committee of the Diocese of Nelson, 2010), p. 24.
45 £18 per year (equivalent to $3200 today) was available to those with an annual income of no more than £50 ($8800). Proof of age and fulfilment of residency requirements were needed: https://nzhistory.govt.nz/old-age-pensions-act-passes-into-law
46 *Pelorus Guardian*, 24 November 1911.
47 Brough, 'Tracks'.
48 'In the Sounds', *The Dominion*, 17 July 1913, p. 4.
49 Leov & Turner, *Marriages Have Been Arranged*, p. 26; Williams, 'Life at Kaiuma Bay', p. 22 discuss the soap and candle-making; on p. 20 he describes butter-making.
50 Nola M. Leov & Margaret J. Turner, *Changes: Rai Valley, 1901–1902*, (Nelson: self-published, 2014), p. 37.
51 Muriel Washington, 'The Hannah and Henry Godsiff family: Early settlers in the Pelorus Sound', undated, private papers, p. 24.
52 I am indebted to Tony Redwood (pers. comm., October 2021) for information on the length of the row.
53 Elizabeth K. Parkes, *Better Prospects: The Parkes Family History* (Nelson: self-published, 1986), p. 83.
54 Hope family letters, p. 49.
55 Don Grady, *The Perano Whalers of Cook Strait, 1911–1964* (Wellington: A. H. & A. W. Reed, 1982), pp. 159–161, 40.
56 Ibid., p. 69.
57 Hope family letters, p. 42.

58 Ibid., p. 62.
59 Ibid., pp. 40, 41.
60 Washington, 'The Hannah and Henry Godsiff family', p. 24.
61 Anglican, Methodist and Roman Catholic clergy worked with extraordinary dedication and few resources. However, the Sounds' 225 named bays in highly indented coastlines that stretched over some 1500 km meant that visits and services were few and far between.
62 Nola Leov, pers. comm., August 2015.
63 Nola Leov, pers. comm., November 2014.
64 Ibid. I am indebted in this discussion to Nola Leov's considerations and understanding of how her parents survived mentally. Given the few changes in social conditions in the Sounds during the preceding decades, Nola considered that her comments were also likely to be true for earlier periods.
65 Jane Stafford, in 'Literary cartography and the backblocks: Mary Scott's Barbara stories', a talk at the National Library (Wellington, 8 June 2016), identified the ironic humour that Scott's characters used to manage hardships and disasters.
66 Harold Alexander Leov, 'The story of my purchase of Te Towaka and some of the doings that followed', Leov family papers, p. 6.
67 Hope family letters, p. 65. In 1899 Edward, in Nelson and dying of bone cancer, was 'very wistful' to come back to the Sounds – Nola Leov, pers. comm. Her father, Harold Leov, stayed on at Te Towaka longer than his own condition really permitted because his wife did not want to leave. Hylton Harvey reckoned it took him 10 years to get over leaving Pelorus Sound.
68 *Pelorus Guardian*, 24 November 1911.
69 E. G. Cousins in 'Personalities', Wallace family papers.
70 'The drowning fatality', *The Colonist*, 30 December 1908, p. 2.
71 Re the illegitimate baby see 'Local and general news', *ME*, 15 December 1913, p. 4; re the abortion see 'Rex v. Green', *The Colonist*, 15 March 1917, p. 2.
72 'Advertisements', *ME*, 18 March 1903, p. 3.
73 Lorna Orchard, *Time and Tide Waits for No Man* (Blenheim: Yvonne Fell, 2004), pp. 38–40; Mackay, *Voices from the Sea*, 'High spirits: The McManaway family', p. 191.
74 A. H. Reed, *Marlborough Journey* (Auckland: A. H. & A. W. Reed, 1963), p. 125.
75 Parkes, *Better Prospects*, p. 83.
76 'A delightful holiday trip', *Evening Post*, 22 April 1893, Supplement, p. 1. This account notes that the *Waitapu* was the first steamer the Archer children had seen.
77 Parkes, *Better Prospects*, p. 81.
78 'Local and general news': Surprise parties at Kenepuru', *ME*, 31 August 1898, p. 2.
79 *Pelorus Guardian*, 24 April 1903.
80 'Local and general news', *ME*, 5 August 1907, p. 4; 'The main trunk railway', *Evening Post*, 16 December 1912, p. 9.
81 Re the Borcks see Ada Elizabeth Grace Hetherington Godsiff private papers, p. 119; re the 21st see 'More or less personal', *ME*, 24 January 1906, p. 2; re the wedding see 'Local and general news', *ME*, 1 October 1903, p. 2. 'Wedding', *Evening Post*, 13 February 1911, p. 2 carries an account of munificent presents at the Kenny-Bowden wedding (both well-established Sounds families) suggesting generosity backed by money.
82 'The women's franchise', *Auckland Star*, 13 February 1894, p. 2.
83 'The Member for Wairau', *ME*, 25 October 1900, p. 2.
84 'Public meeting', *ME*, 2 June 1902, p. 4.
85 Leov & Turner, *Changes*, pp. 69–70.
86 Ibid., pp. 66–86.
87 Ibid., p. 70.
88 'Public meeting', *ME*, 2 June 1902, p. 4.
89 Carol Dawber, *The Jacksons of Te Awaiti* (Picton: River Press, 2001), p. 197.
90 'Pars about people', *Observer*, 14 March 1914.
91 'A delightful holiday trip', *Evening Post*, 6 May 1893, Supplement, p. 1.

92 Ibid.

93 'A disgraceful scene', *The Press*, 9 January 1914, p. 2 reports one sporting brawl; Orchard, *Time and Tide*, p. 33 suggests disagreements that were generally pretty short-lived.

94 *Pelorus Guardian*, 14 August 1914.

95 'Notes', *ME*, 13 May 1915, p. 5.

96 By 1915 the Department of Internal Affairs was accepting donations for the Belgium Relief Fund, NZ War Relief Fund, Red Cross Fund, NZ Red Cross Fund, Serbian Relief Fund, No. 2 Hospital Ship Fund, Relief of Belgian Children, Polish Relief Fund, Prince of Wales Fund, Montenegrin Relief Fund, Convalescent Homes in NZ Fund, Overseas Tobacco Fund, NZ Expeditionary Forces Tobacco Fund, Anaesthetics Fund, Mayor's Patriotic Fund, Wounded Soldiers' and Sailor's and Dependents' Fund, Christmas Shilling Gift Fund.

97 The Nydia Bay population and some Kenepuru settlers reportedly believed the Belgian relief issue 'a matter for taxation' ('Sounds Patriotic Committee', *ME*, 7 April 1915, p. 2), and a 'good few . . . openly def[ied] [the Marlborough recruiting board's efforts] to get them to enlist' ('Marlborough recruiting board', *ME*, 8 July 1916, p. 6). Rollo Arnold ('The virgin forest harvest and the development of colonial New Zealand', *NZ Geographer* 32 (1976), pp. 122–23) argued that stable communities and regular hours provided opportunities for Pākehā who had come mostly from 'virtual servitude in homeland villages' to participate in their communities and broaden their outlooks and attitudes, and that millers as a class notably contributed to this process.

98 *AJHR*, 1916, E.–1, EDAR, p. 3. In relation to Māori see John Barrington, *Separate But Equal?: Māori Schools and the Crown, 1867–1969* (Wellington: Victoria University Press, 2008), p. 114. He reports inspector Bird's comments on the 'important part' native schools played in creating feelings of patriotism and loyalty in young Māori and even among the adults, the 'magnificent efforts the people as a whole have made in response to the appeals made for patriotic purposes', and the willingness of Māori to volunteer.

99 'Relief funds', *ME*, 16 June 1915, p. 2.

100 'Advertisements', column 7, *ME*, 20 December 1915, p. 5.

101 Hope family letters, pp. 59, 60.

102 Nancy Swarbrick, 'Country schooling – Getting an education: 1800s', Te Ara: www.TeAra.govt.nz/en/country-schooling/page-1. Swarbrick estimates that in the 1850s about 25 per cent of Pākehā could neither read nor write, with another 14 per cent able to read only. Thirty years on, when Elizabeth Hope was writing, levels of literacy would still have been low.

103 Helen Beaglehole, *Always the Sound of the Sea: The Daily Lives of New Zealand's Lighthouse Keepers* (Nelson: Potton & Burton, 2009), p. 57ff. This details lighthouse keepers' concerns with their children's education, concerns that Sounds parents, with similar backgrounds, are likely to have held.

104 Nancy Swarbrick, 'Country schooling – Getting an education: 1800s'.

105 *AJHR*, 1878, H.–1, EDAR, Inspector's report, Marlborough, p. 69.

106 'Marlborough public schools', *ME*, 13 June 1874, p. 7 indicates that the following schools were established in the wider district: Picton Town School, Blenheim Boys' and Blenheim Girls' schools, Big Bush School, Marlboroughtown School, Tua Marina School, Spring Creek School, Renwick Town School, Kaituna School, Havelock Town School, Waitohi or Picton Town School, Grove School, Mahakipawa School, Wairau Valley School. However, both the Grove and Mahakipawa schools closed because of lack of children – another perennial problem of small rural schools dependent on itinerant families.

107 *AJHR*, 1905, E.–1., EDAR, Report of Marlborough Education Board, p. 84 cites the number of children involved in the small schools; for 'the worthy settlers' and household schools, see 'Educational items', *ME*, 15 April 1897, p. 2. For 'the very class that is doing so much' see *AJHR*, 1901, E.–1., EDAR, Report of Marlborough Education Board, p. 73.

108 *AJHR*, 1895 E.–1, EDAR, Report of Marlborough Education Board, p. 77.

109 'Topics of the day', *ME*, 15 December 1904, p. 1.

110 *AJHR*, 1879, Session 1, H.–2, EDAR, p. 3; The Education Department refers to the Act's provisions under s. 88 in *AJHR*, 1878, H.–1, EDAR, p. 2. In 1913 the report refers to household schools as those with fewer than nine children – *AJHR*, 1913, E.–02, p. xiv.

111 *AJHR*, 1882, Session 1, E.–1, EDAR, p. vii.

112 In 1885 the Education Department did not list any Sounds schools as aided but a comment in the school board report suggests they almost certainly were. Essentially from 1891 almost all schools were aided and this situation still prevailed in 1917, when the Wellington Education Board, referring to the school board report, notes the small, mostly household schools in Marlborough (*AJHR*, 1917, E.–2, EDAR, Primary education, p. 8). There is also some slight confusion surrounding the words 'aided' and 'household'. In the early 1890s the department refers to 'one-family aided schools'. However, from 1894, and though the statistics on Westland schools distinguish household and aided schools, in Marlborough the two descriptors seem to have been used interchangeably (*AJHR*, 1898, Appendices, Table 8, p. 40). Departmental statistics, when not specifically naming household schools as such, identified them as Grade 0.

113 Nola Leov, interview, 2014.

114 See, for instance, *AJHR*, 1882, Session 1E.–1B, Education Department, Reports of inspectors, p. xv, where Inspector W. C. Hodgson described them as 'almost the only humanizing and refining agent'.

115 *AJHR*, 1879, Session 1, H.–2, EDAR, p. 3.

116 *AJHR*, 1878, H.–1, EDAR, Report of Marlborough Education Board, p. 42.

117 Nancy Swarbrick, 'Primary and secondary education – Teachers', Te Ara: www.TeAra.govt.nz/en/primary-and-secondary-education/page-8

118 'Education in the backblocks', *Wanganui Chronicle*, 26 April 1906, p. 5.

119 Re the quote see *AJHR*, 1887, Session 1, E.–1B, Reports of inspectors of schools, p. 19. *AJHR*, 1917, E.–2, EDAR, Primary education, p. 8 identifies the large number of small household schools in Marlborough; 'Aided schools', *ME*, 24 July 1916, p. 3 writes on the importance of the new Wellington board dealing with the 'acute', 'important and complex' problem of maintaining the Sounds' aided schools.

120 *AJHR*, 1908, E.-01, Education: Country primary schools, return of schools where parents contribute to upkeep of school . . .

121 *AJHR*, 1904, E.–1, EDAR, Report of Marlborough Education Board, p. 81.

122 'Local and general news', *ME*, 29 March 1919, p. 4. The accompanying list of scholarships from the Marlborough district was not entirely unusual.

123 'Marlborough schools', *ME*, 4 May 1911, p. 3.

124 Donald Furness, *Tahuahua: The Story of Blackwood Bay, Queen Charlotte Sound* (Blenheim: self-published, 1974), pp. 39–41.

125 'Obituary', *ME*, 26 August 1905, p. 4; 'Obituary', *Otago Witness*, 6 September 1905, p. 40.

126 *AJHR*, 1881, Session 1, E.–1B, EDAR, Reports of inspectors of schools, p. 16. In 1881 Inspector W. C. Hodgson considered there was not even a 'remote contingency' that the children would be 'over-taught'. They needed relief from teachers who could not teach beyond those subjects, he thought, who had no place in the public system.

127 *AJHR*, 1894, E.–1, EDAR, Marlborough Education Board report, p. 74.

128 *AJHR*, 1882, Session 1, E.–1B, EDAR, Reports of inspectors of schools, p. xv. Re skill levels see *AJHR*, 1885, Session 1, E.–1B, Reports of inspectors of schools, p. 28; re ability to progress pupils see *AJHR*, 1882, Session 1, E.–1B, EDAR, Reports of inspectors of schools, p. xv; re pupil-teachers' use of the scheme see *AJHR*, 1893, Session 1, E.–1, EDAR, Nelson Education Board report, p. 72. I have presumed the situation was not unique to Nelson.

129 *AJHR*, 1904, EDAR, Marlborough Education Board report, p. 86. In relation to the push for qualifications see *AJHR*, 1908, E.–1, EDAR, Appendix C, Inspectors' reports, Marlborough, p. 121. The inspector suggested that advertised positions should be stressing required qualifications.

130 *AJHR*, 1915, E.–2, Education: Primary. While few appear to have been successful, Appendix A, Marlborough Education Board report, p. xi, noted keen participation and teachers' desire to improve their status; for the inspector's comment see ibid., Appendix C., Reports of inspectors of schools, Marlborough, p. xvii.

131 Nancy Swarbrick, 'Country schooling – Wider options: 1900s–1930s', Te Ara: www.TeAra.govt.nz/en/country-schooling/page-2

132 *AJHR*, 1910, E.–2, Education: Primary education, Appendix C, Inspectors' reports, Marlborough, p. 121.

133 *AJHR*, 1893, Session 1, EDAR, Nelson Education Board report, p. 72; 'Marlborough Education Board', *ME*, 14 April 1908, p. 7; 'Local and general news', *ME*, 28 July p. 4.

134 *AJHR*, 1913, E.–1, EDAR, Marlborough Education Board report, p. xiii; *AJHR*, 1918, E.–2, p. 7.

135 *AJHR*, 1915, E.–2, Education: Primary, p. 18.

136 By 1911 standard four children were provided with supplementary material, arithmetic books, atlases, and historical and geographical readers; a year later discretionary spending on school library books was permitted, and the scheme continued to be tinkered with to best meet its objectives. In 1908 the *School Journal*, that extraordinary publication that delighted and informed for decades, was first issued to some acclaim – parents did not have to buy a second reader and information could be easily updated – see *AJHR*, 1908, E.–1b, EDAR, Inspectors of schools, p. 23 on the *School Journal*.

137 *AJHR*, 1908, E.–1B, EDAR, Inspectors of schools: Marlborough, p. 28; re the pupil involvement in the full curriculum see 'The Marlborough Schools', *ME*, 15 March 1902, p. 4.

138 'The Marlborough Schools', *ME*, 15 March 1902, p. 4.

139 Ibid., p. 23.

140 Mitchells, *Te Tau Ihu o te Waka*, vol. 2, pp. 341–42.

141 *Pelorus Guardian*, 8 September 1905.

142 Waitangi Tribunal, *Te Tau Ihu*, vol. 2, p. 974; Locke, *The Poorest Tribe*, p. 41.

143 'Marlborough Land Board', *ME*, 10 February 1904, p. 4.

144 Ibid. This decision was not atypical; see Locke, *'The Poorest Tribe'*, pp. 66–67.

145 Locke, *'The Poorest Tribe'*, pp. 93–94.

146 G. MacDonald to Secretary of Education, 20 September 1892, Waikawa School, BAAA, 1001/671B, ANZ, cited in Mitchells, *Te Tau Ihu o te Waka*, vol. 2, p. 341.

147 Waitangi Tribunal, *Te Tau Ihu*, vol. 2, p. 974.

148 Ibid.

149 David Young, *Māori Society and the State in Colonial and Post-colonial Te Tau Ihu, 1880–1960: A Survey of Official Archives* (Wellington: Crown Forestry Rental Trust, 1999), p. 123.

150 This money was derived from rental money accumulated from the Nelson Tenths Reserves land in Nelson township and the Motueka district that was owned by the descendants of the original Te Ātiawa (a different group from those in Queen Charlotte Sound), Ngāti Koata, Ngāti Rarua and Ngāti Tama owners, but which the Māori trustee had required to be leased (Waitangi Tribunal, *Te Tau Ihu*, vol. 2, pp. 968–69).

151 Locke, *'The Poorest Tribe'*, p. 24.

152 Waitangi Tribunal, *Te Tau Ihu*, vol. 2, pp. 969–70.

153 Locke, *'The Poorest Tribe'*, pp. 41–42; Waitangi Tribunal, *Te Tau Ihu*, vol. 2, p. 970.

154 Mitchells, *Te Tau Ihu o te Waka*, vol. 2, p. 379; Locke, ibid., details the various departments involved in administering the fund, pp. 24–25.

155 Waitangi Tribunal, *Te Tau Ihu*, vol. 2, p. 976.

156 Locke, *'The Poorest Tribe'*, pp. 6, 43, 49, 68. The decision was made on the basis that Ngāti Kuia had been 'conquered' by the northern iwi claimants. The Waitangi Tribunal has since found that decision a breach of Kurahaupō rights.

157 Mitchells, *Te Tau Ihu o te Waka*, vol. 2, p. 379.

158 Furness, *Tahuahua*, pp. 50–51.

159 Waitangi Tribunal, *Te Tau Ihu*, vol. 2, p. 977; Mitchells, *Te Tau Ihu o te Waka*, vol. 2, pp. 379–82. The quote is from Registrar Old Age Pensions to deputy registrar Havelock, 17 October 1905, ANZW2756 9/9/1, Pt 2, Maoris, general, 1904–37, ANZ, quoted in Mitchells, *Te Tau Ihu o te Waka*, vol. 2, p. 382.

160 Waitangi Tribunal, *Te Tau Ihu*, vol. 2, p. 968.

161 Locke, *'The Poorest Tribe'*, p. 74.

162 Waitangi Tribunal, *Te Tau Ihu*, vol. 2, p. 969.

163 Ibid., p. 970.

164 Ibid., p. 970; Mitchells, *Te Tau Ihu o te Waka*, vol. 2, p. 373.

165 Waitangi Tribunal, *Te Tau Ihu*, vol. 2, p. 970.

166 Ibid., pp. 979–80; Ngapare Hopa, 'Ngā rōpū – Māori organisations – New Māori organisations, early 20th century', Te Ara: www.TeAra.govt.nz/en/nga-ropu-Māori-organisations/page-2. Hopa states that though elected locally, the councils were government controlled.

167 Members were Rore Pukekohatu (briefly chair, representing the Wairau kāinga), Pou Hemi Whiro, Watene Hemi Whiro and Tiemi Waaka (representing Okoha); Wi Taku Love, Wiremu Keepa and Karira Tahuaroa (representing Waikawa). Representatives for Havelock and Croisilles were also elected.

168 'Arapawa Maori Council', *ME*, 11 February 1907, p. 3.

169 Ibid.

170 Anthony Pātete, 'Pātete, Haimona', DNZB, Te Ara: www.TeAra.govt.nz/en/biographies/3p14/Pātete-haimona; Waitangi Tribunal, *Te Tau Ihu*, vol. 2, pp. 979–80; Locke, *'The Poorest Tribe'*, pp. 87–89.

171 'The Arapawa Council', *ME*, 20 February 1909, p. 5; Locke, *'The Poorest Tribe'*, p. 88 discusses the work of the marae committees.

172 Locke, ibid., p. 88.

173 Locke, ibid., p. 65.

174 Mitchells, *Te Tau Ihu o te Waka*, vol. 2, pp. 342, Mike Taylor, *The History of Waikawa School, Queen Charlotte Sound* (Christchurch: self-published, 2012), p. 32; Waitangi Tribunal, *Te Tau Ihu*, vol. 2, pp. 967–68, 981.

175 Young, *Māori Society*, p. 64, quoted in Waitangi Tribunal, *Te Tau Ihu*, vol. 2, p. 981.

176 Waitangi Tribunal, ibid., pp. 967–68. Re the 1879 outbreak see Taylor, *The History of Waikawa School*, p. 32.

177 G. MacDonald, 19 December 1892, BAAA, 1001/ 671B, Waikawa School 1893, ANZ, cited in Mitchells, *Te Tau Ihu o te Waka*, vol. 2, p. 342.

178 'Local and general news', *ME*, 21 November 1892, p. 2; 'New Zealand telegrams', *Taranaki Herald*, 15 December 1892, p. 2.

179 Mitchells, *Te Tau Ihu o te Waka*, vol. 2, pp. 341–42; Taylor, *The History of Waikawa School*, p. 32.

180 Locke, *'The Poorest Tribe'*, p. 80.

181 Waitangi Tribunal, *Te Tau Ihu*, vol. 2, pp. 1002–03.

182 Mitchells, *Te Tau Ihu o te Waka*, vol. 2, pp. 375–76; on hospital boards see also Locke, *'The Poorest Tribe'*, pp. 82–83.

183 Locke, ibid., p. 75.

184 Re the callous responses see 'Advertisements', column 1, *Evening Post*, 23 November 1892, p. 3.

185 Mitchells, *Te Tau Ihu o te Waka*, vol. 2, p. 342.

186 G. MacDonald to Pope, inspector, 13 June 1896, BAA, 671c, Waikawa School, ANZ, cited in Mitchells, *Te Tau Ihu o te Waka*, vol. 2, p. 342.

187 'Local and general news', *ME*, 10 February 1893, p. 2.

188 Waitangi Tribunal, *Te Tau Ihu o te Waka a Maui: Report on Northern South Island Claims* (Wai 785), vol. 3 (Wellington, 2008), p. 1093.

189 Millennium Art Gallery, Blenheim, *Remembering the Kurahaupo Settlement*, curated by Peter Meihana, June–August 2018.

190 Kipa Whiro, Maka Kiharoa to the Government, 22 October 1904, J 1 1904/1619, cited in Locke, *'The Poorest Tribe'*, p. 75.

191 Locke, ibid., p. 27.

192 Locke, ibid., p. 127.

193 Smith to Public Trustee, 13 July 1907, cited in Locke, ibid., p. 76.

194 Locke, ibid., p. 77.

195 Tony Redwood, pers. comm., October 2021, advised on the rowing times.

196 Locke, '*The Poorest Tribe*', p. 127.

197 Tahuaraki Meihana, 'A Native's grievance', Letters to the editor, *Pelorus Guardian*, 19 May 1905.

198 Waitangi Tribunal, *Te Tau Ihu*, vol. 2, pp. 981, 969; on Tahuaraki Meihana's letter on the accommodation of sick children, and subsequent action see Locke, *'The Poorest Tribe'*, pp. 86–87.

199 Locke, ibid., pp. 76–77.

200 Raeburn Lange, 'Te hauora Māori i mua – History of Māori health – Health improves, 1900 to 1920', Te Ara: www.TeAra.govt.nz/en/te-hauora-Māori-i-mua-history-of-Māori-health/page-3
201 http://en.wikipedia.org/wiki/Native_schools. As a consequence of missionary schools, in 1860, 75 per cent of Māori could read in Māori, 66 per cent could write in their own language. Where the government subsidised such schools, English had to be taught, so Māori attending must also have had some literacy in English.
202 Barrington, *Separate but Equal?*, pp. 15–16, 21.
203 Ministry for Culture and Heritage, 'Education Act passed into law': https://nzhistory.govt.nz/page/education-act-passed-law
204 Waitangi Tribunal, *Te Tau Ihu*, vol. 2, pp. 971–72 Ross Calman, 'Māori education – mātauranga – The native schools system, 1867 to 1969', Te Ara: www.TeAra.govt.nz/en/Māori-education-matauranga/page-3; Locke, *'The Poorest Tribe'*, p. 42.
205 Taylor, *The History of Waikawa School*, p. 1.
206 Ibid. The Mitchells' figures across the *Te Tau Ihu* region reflect the situation in the Sounds.
207 *AJHR*, 1878, Session 1, G.–7, Papers relating to Native Schools. Rev. J. W. Stack, Enclosure no. 2, p. 12.
208 In 1901 a Mrs White requested what would have been an aided native school at Hitaua Bay off Tory Channel, 20 km from Waikawa School. The department tentatively agreed to paying £6 capitation and providing inspection. But views were changing on the desirability of aided native schools, the lack of any policy for them, and their need, given that South Island Māori were better assimilated than in the North Island and spoke better English. Mrs White's initiative went no further. However, a board school was re-established in Hitaua Bay in 1907 and operated intermittently with rolls under 10 until 1914. Māori children at times attended.
209 'Personal', *ME*, 9 February 1915, p. 5 mentions a native school at Tahuahua (Blackwood Bay), but records and reports indicate that it was an aided Education Board school. The children of those designated in 1889 as owners of the Māori reserves in the bay (Furness, *Tahuahua*, pp. 26–30) would have been a dominant presence.
210 Taylor, *The History of Waikawa School*, pp. 11–12, 27–28.
211 Barrington, *Separate but Equal?*, p. 81.
212 Taylor, *The History of Waikawa School*, pp. 13, 30.
213 For instance, on Henry Nickless see *AJHR*, 1876, I.–1, vol II, Native Schools (Reports of Inspecting Officers), Mr Woon RM to Under Secretary Native Affairs, p. 8; re MacDonald and Greensill see Taylor, *The History of Waikawa School*, pp. 32 and pp. 33–35 respectively; *AJHR*, 1891, Session 2, E.–2, Native schools, p. 8.
214 *AJHR*, 1877, Session 1, G.–4, Papers relating to Native schools, p. 15.
215 *AJHR*, 1880, Session 1, Report from officers in native districts, G.–4, Enclosure No. 2, p. 1.
216 *AJHR*, 1895, E.–02, Education: Native Schools, p. 7 re epidemic; *AJHR*, 1897, E.–02. Education: Native Schools, p. 7.
217 Taylor, *The History of Waikawa School*, pp. 31, 35–36.
218 Morrow, 'Legacy of Loss', p. 113, quoted in Waitangi Tribunal, *Te Tau Ihu*, vol. 2, p. 972.
219 Mitchells, *Te Tau Ihu o te Waka*, vol. 2, p. 341; Taylor, *The History of Waikawa School*, pp. 17 and 33 comment on the teacher's efforts.
220 *AJHR*, 1907, E.–2, Education: Native schools, p. 8; *AJHR*, 1908, EDAR, p. xxxiii; 'Marlborough Education Board', *ME*, 6 April 1909, p. 5.
221 Locke, *'The Poorest Tribe'*, p. vi.
222 Canon David Gribble (pers. comm., February 2014) stated that in the 1890s the Anglican synod grew increasingly concerned with the arrival of Mormons in Nelson, their focus on Māori, their teaching that Māori were one of the 10 lost tribes, and their apparent lack of interest in education. Anglicans, Gribble said, developed a strong focus on education and health care to counter this.
223 Locke, *'The Poorest Tribe'*, p. 62.
224 *AJHR*, 1901, E.–2, Education: Native schools, p. 16.
225 Ibid., p. 12; re the teacher's efforts in Māori see Barrington, *Separate but Equal?*, p. 61.
226 *AJHR*, 1905, E.–2, Education: Native schools, p. 3. Locke, *'The Poorest Tribe'*, pp. 64–65, 70 discusses

prior departmental and church disagreements and the parental reaction to the apparent imposition of church teachings.

227 Locke, *'The Poorest Tribe'*, pp. 71–72.

228 Ibid., pp. vi, 52.

229 H. F. Ault, *The Nelson Narrative: The Story of the Church of England in the Diocese of Nelson, New Zealand, 1858 to 1958, with an account of the years 1842 to 1857* (Nelson: Standing Committee of the Diocese of Nelson, 1958), pp. 219–22, cited in Waitangi Tribunal, *Te Tau Ihu*, vol. 2, p. 984.

230 Mitchells, *Te Tau Ihu o te Waka*, vol. 2, p. 377.

231 Maxine Stephenson, '"Making do": The politics and pragmatics of the use of temporary spaces in New Zealand schools', *History of Education Review*, vol. 2, no. 2 (2003), pp. 15–29, cited in Barrington, *Separate but Equal?*, p. 21; Locke, *'The Poorest Tribe'*, statement of Thomas Walker (Tame Waaka), p. 52.

232 Pātete, 'Pātete, Haimona'.

233 G. MacDonald to Inspector of Native Schools, BAA, 100, 1/671c, Waikawa School, 1893–98, 22 July 1897, ANZ, cited in Mitchells, *Te Tau Ihu o te Waka*, vol. 2, p. 132.

234 Ibid., p. 1053.

235 Stephen (Bosun) Huntley, Evidence for Tahuaroa-Watson whānau, Board of Inquiry, King Salmon proposal, 2012, para. 68.

236 Laura Bowdler, Evidence of Laura Bowdler (née Keenan) for Tahuaroa-Watson whānau, Board of Inquiry, New Zealand King Salmon proposal, 2012, pp. 4–5. The Waitangi Tribunal, *Te Tau Ihu*, vol. 3, pp. 10450 provides similar instances of traditional patterns and management being used into the twentieth century.

237 Stephen (Bosun) Huntley, Evidence, paras 65–67.

238 Ibid., p. 1063.

239 Ibid., pp. 1061–63.

240 Waitangi Tribunal, ibid., pp. 1077–78.

241 Ibid., p. 1192.

242 Ibid., pp. 1048, 1110, 1131.

243 Ibid., p. 1192.

8. Depression, War and Making a Living

1 'Exit – the *Pelorus Guardian*', *The Press*, 27 March 1920, p. 8.

2 *Evening Post*, 'Marlborough Sounds', 29 January 1924, p. 9. In 1916 the Sounds had a European population of 1304 (735 men and 569 women) and a Māori population of 400 ('Advertisements', column 5, *ME*, 11 November 1916), 200 in Queen Charlotte Sound and Tory Channel, and the other 200 in Pelorus Sound and valley (Hilary and John Mitchells, *Te Tau Ihu o Te Waka: A History of Maori of Nelson and Marlborough*, vol. 2: *Te Ara Hou / The New Society* (Wellington: Huia Publishers, 2007), p. 470.) In the 1926 Census the total population including Māori in the Sounds was 935. There were 489 European men and 358 European women (total 847); and 59 Māori men and 47 Māori women (total 106) (*Maori Population Census 1926*, Sounds County).

3 'Marlborough Sounds', *Evening Post*, 29 January 1924, p. 9.

4 Ministry for Culture and Heritage, 'Impact of the war': https://nzhistory.govt.nz/war/korean-war/impact

5 Marlborough Land District – Marlborough Sounds canal project – cut at Onahau between Queen Charlotte and Pelorus Sounds – Also Havelock Harbour and control of Pelorus Sounds foreshore, 1951–58; Marlborough Sounds Soil Conservation District, 1947–61, Sounds Branch, Federated Farmers, W3396 889 Box 1, 76/2, ANZ; Memo, Preliminary report on the Marlborough Sounds area, 30 March 1949; ibid., MOW to Chairman, Soil Conservation Council, Wellington, Interim report – Soil Conservation Survey – Sounds area, 24 January 1950, ibid. The quote comes from Memo, Preliminary report, ibid.

6 R. J. Paterson, *The Sea was our Boundary: The Titirangi/Waitui Story of the Patersons 1929–1977* (self-published, 2011). Extracts from the Titirangi farm diary indicate a constant round of

mustering, dipping, shearing, crutching, drenching. Scrub was cut week in week out, year after year, though by 1949 gangs were hired in; ragwort was pulled out with almost the same frequency. Firewood had to be collected and sawn (in 1950 they used the tractor for the first time), occasionally before the mid-1950s they slashed and burned, farm tracks demanded attention, fences had to be run over the great flanks of hill (though from the mid-1950s, internal farm roads facilitated that work). Sundays provided the only rest day.

7 Brian Easton, 'Brexit: How New Zealand might cope': http://pundit.co.nz/content/brentry-how-new-zealand-coped

8 Deputy Commissioner L&S to Under-sec L&S, 'Proposed scenic reserves, Sounds County, 16 January 1928, Scenic Reserves – Marlborough Sounds Scenic Reserves, 1928–32, AANS W5491 6095, Box 1035, 4/539, ANZ.

9 Paterson, *The Sea was our Boundary*, p. 141; Percy Allen, Minister of Works, on opening the Titirangi Road, May 1972, quoted in ibid., p. 149.

10 Letter to Hon. E. A. Ransom, Box Inner Pelorus Sound, Photos/clippings, 21/F/5B 15, Marlborough Archives, Marlborough Historical Society.

11 CCL to Under-Sec. L&S, 'Fires in scenic reserves, Queen Charlotte and Pelorus Sounds', 11 April 1933, Scenic reserves– Sounds County (Marlborough Sounds), AANS W5491 6095 Box 325, 4/539, ANZ.

12 Harold Leov, 'The story of my purchase of Te Towaka and some of the doings that followed', Leov family papers, pp. 2–4, 5.

13 John Harvey, interview, August 2016.

14 Tony and Joy Redwood, pers. comm., October 2016; Leov, 'The story of my purchase', p. 5.

15 Redwood, ibid.

16 Geoff and Ted Challis, who started off on a 100-acre (40-ha) block, bought a second in the mid-1940s. Although that made the farm an economic unit for the two families, they were careful. They had 'chooks, generally only one sow that lived on whey from the factory, household scraps and fallen apples from the orchard'. The apples, with typical care, had been collected and covered with straw until being fed out (Christopher Challis, interviews, July & August 2016).

17 Re the characteristics of creameries see Hugh Stringleman and Frank Scrimgeour, 'Dairying and dairy products – Cooperatives and centralisation', Te Ara: www.TeAra.govt.nz/en/dairying-and-dairy-products/page-3; re the Linkwater factory see Geoffrey Wilson, *Linkwater: A History* (Linkwater: Linkwater Settlers' Association, 1962); David Young, *Maori Society and the State in Colonial and Post-colonial Te Tau Ihu, 1880–1960: A Survey of Official Archives* (Wellington, Crown Forestry Rental Trust, 1999) pp. 131, 130–38.

18 Flora Robb, *St Omer House: Family Life in the Guest House and Some Sounds History* (Nelson: self-published, 2013), p. 483.

19 Memo, 20 September 1939, L&S, MSMP – Scenic reserves – Chance and Penguin Bays 1932–2002, AANS W5951 25421, Box 66, MSM-0111, ANZ. Re the prior sale see Memorandum to CCL, Blenheim, 22 June 1939, ibid.

20 Census and Statistics Office, Agricultural and Pastoral Production of the Dominion of NZ – see relevant years.

21 *Soil Conservation Survey: Sounds area: interim report*, 24 January 1950, Marlborough Sounds Soil Conservation District 1946–61, AATE, W3396, 889, Box 1, 76/3, ANZ.

22 Kerry Neal & Nola M. Leov, *The Price of Vigilance: The Building of the Gun Emplacements in the Marlborough Sounds, 1942* (Nelson: self-published, 1999), pp. 29–30.

23 Shirley Buckland, *Reflections on a Lifetime* (Nelson: self-published, 2007), p. 134; Leov, 'The story of my purchase'.

24 G. J. C. (John) Harvey, *Where There's a Will There's a Way: Memories of My Childhood and Sawmilling Days in the Marlborough Sounds* (Blenheim: self-published, 2008), p. x.

25 Hylton Harvey, interview, 2013.

26 Nola M. Leov, *The Sounds in Wartime: A celebration of the contribution to the war effort made by an isolated New Zealand community 1939–45* (Te Towaka 50th Anniversary Home Guard Sports Committee, 1996), p. 12.

27 Heather Heberley, *Riding with Whales: Stories of Great Sounds Women* (Picton: Cape Catley, 1999), p. 36.
28 Nola Leov, interview, October 2013.
29 Wilson, *Linkwater*, pp. 136–38.
30 Harvey, *Where There's a Will*, p. 101.
31 Martin Shand, interview, August 2016.
32 Paterson, *The Sea was our Boundary*, pp. 25, 59.
33 Martin Shand, interview, August 2016.
34 Nola Leov, pers. comm., September 2016.
35 Nola Leov, interview, October 2013.
36 Ibid.
37 Memo, Preliminary report on the Marlborough Sounds area, 30 March 1949, Marlborough Sounds Soil Conservation District, 1947–61, AATE W3396 889 Box 1, 76/2, ANZ.
38 Nola Leov, interview, October 2013; Redwood, pers. comm., October 2016. Re the first topdressing in 1954 in Māhakipawa and the Grove see Wilson, *Linkwater*, p. 158.
39 L. May to Permanent Head, 10 July 1929, Marlborough Road District – Onahau to Te Mahia, Sounds County 1917–63, ADKK, W4357, 889, Box 189, 43/144, ANZ.
40 R. Lancaster, resident engineer, Memo 15 July 1946, Marlborough Road District – Torea Bay to Portage road – Roads and tracks – Kenepuru Roads Board, ABKK, W4357, 889, Box 189 43/157, Pt 2, 1939–60, ANZ.
41 Christopher Challis, interview, 7 July 2016.
42 Leov, *The Sounds in Wartime*, p. 11.
43 CCL to District Commissioner of Works, 7 May 1976, Marlborough Road District – Government roads in Marlborough Sounds 1975–77, AAQU, W3428, 889, Box 66, 43/400, ANZ.
44 Marlborough Road District – Port Underwood Road and Sounds tracks, AAKB, W4357, 889, Box 189, ANZ; regarding Tory Channel see R. H. Bell, CCL, to DG L&S, 17 July 1949; regarding Brightlands see senior engineer, MOW, to resident engineer, MOW, Nelson, 20 October 1949, ibid.
45 E. Mason, Anakoha Bay, to Minister of Public Works, 22 July 1940, Marlborough Road District – Torea Bay to Portage Road – Roads and tracks – Kenepuru Roads Board, ABKK, W4357, 889, Box 189 43/157, PT 2 1939–60, ANZ.
46 Ibid.
47 Paterson, *The Sea Was our Boundary*, pp. 75–81.
48 Martin Shand, interview, August 2016.
49 Martin Shand, pers. comm., October 2021.
50 Martin Shand, interview, August 2016.
51 R. H. Bell to Conservator, Forests, 'Burning and resowing', 1 August 1952, Historic and scenic reserves – forest fires on scenic reserves & CLD Nelson and Marlborough – Refund of cost of fighting, fire protection – Sounds, fire on scenic reserves, AANS 6095 W5491/9, 4/543, ANZ; 'Blackened hills abounding' and 'Fire-swept hillsides Sounds burns more extensive than ever', Marlborough Sounds Soil Conservation District 1946–61, AATE, W3396, 889, Box 1, 76/3, ANZ. The originating newspapers are not identified.
52 Martin Shand, pers. comm., August 2016.
53 These responses were taken from letters and papers following two meetings – see 'Meeting to discuss formation of Soil Conservation Council in Marlborough Sounds area, 23 June 1949', Marlborough Sounds Soil Conservation District 1946–61, ANZ; 'Report of meeting held . . . 18 August 1950', ibid; 'Soil conservation: What is best for Sounds?', *Evening Post*, 16 August 1950.
54 Harvey, *Where There's a Will*, p. 117.
55 Martin Shand, interview, August 2016.
56 Denise Harvey, interview, August 2016; John Harvey, interview, August 2016.
57 'Erosion survey: Victorian minister's visit to Marlborough, 4 April 1950', Marlborough Sounds Soil Conservation District 1946–61, ANZ (newspaper not identified).
58 'Soil Conservation', 23 July 1949, ANZ (newspaper not identified).

59 Hylton Harvey, interview, September 2013; Denise Harvey, interview, August 2016.

60 Memo, 'Sheep carrying capacity – Sounds area', undated notes stating that the kill of lambs, wethers and ewes at the Picton freezing works from the Sounds and D'Urville Island declined from 19,941 in 1941–42 to 9463 in 1948–49, Marlborough Sounds Soil Conservation District 1946–61, ANZ.

61 Marlborough Sounds Soil Conservation District 1946–61, ANZ; re erosion see Preliminary report on the Marlborough Sounds Area, 30 March 1949, ibid.

62 Soil conservation survey, Sounds area, interim report, 24 January 1950', ibid. A higher cattle to sheep ratio was needed in some places and so was an intensive drive for better pasture on flatter country. Both were dependent on better freight services and better pest control of deer and pigs. By then the Marlborough Sheepowners' Federation was concerned about the way these and goats were devastating the Sounds. Individual attempts to clear the animals simply saw them moving on to the next property ('Bushland pests', *Auckland Star*, 12 November 1943, p. 2).

63 Paterson, *The Sea was our Boundary*, pp. 108–09.

64 Re work of conservation boards see Paul Gregg, 'Soil erosion and conservation – Legislation and catchment boards 1940s–1950s', Te Ara: www.TeAra.govt.nz/en/soil-erosion-and-conservation/page-5. The councils worked to ensure land was used in a way that would enhance soil conservation and reduce or prevent erosion; subsidies were available for specified farming activities such as fencing, windbreaks. For the Sounds' response to the idea of establishing one see 'Meeting to discuss formation of Soil Conservation Council in Marlborough Sounds area, 23 June 1949', Marlborough Sounds Soil Conservation District 1946–61, ANZ.

65 Noel Moleta, interview, February 2014.

66 Memo to M. E. Robb, Co-operative demonstration farm, Kenepuru, 4 March 1968, AAFZ W1709 7174, Box 12, 31703 ANZ; 'From nought to 7 e.e. after tauhinu cleared', *Marlborough Press*, 3 October 1970. Co-operative demonstration area – A. G. Young, Marlborough Sounds, AAFZ, W31726, Pt 1, 1968–70, ANZ, also provides useful background.

67 Farm demonstration, M. E. Robb, Kenepuru, Marlborough Sounds, AAFZ, W1709, 7174, Box 12, 31703, ANZ.

68 Harold Leov, Te Towaka, to Chair, Soil Conservation Council, Wellington, 28 June 1949, Marlborough Sounds Soil Conservation District 1946–61, ANZ. Leov wrote on his experiences with different fertiliser. Nola Leov, interview, October 2013, discussed his work with Begg and his communication with others.

69 Robb, *St Omer House*, p. 257.

70 MWD, *The Strategy for the Conservation and Development of the Marlborough Sounds* (Wellington, 1977).

71 Hylton Harvey, interview, October 2013; Nola Leov, interview, October 2013.

72 Buckland, *Reflections*, p. 82.

73 Heberley, *Riding with Whales*, p. 109.

74 John Harvey, in Denise Harvey, interview, August 2016.

75 Martin Shand, interview, August 2016.

76 Robb, *St Omer House*, p. 257).

77 Deirdre Mackay, *Voices from the Sea: The Stories of Some Nelson and Marlborough Fishing Families* (Motueka: Talley's Group, 2004), 'Mosquito Fleet: The McCauley Family'.

78 Martin Shand, pers. comm., September 2016.

79 DG, P&T to Sec. Marine, Havelock launch service: E. A. Johnson, 8 March 1950, Shipping – Specific services – Marlborough Sounds steamer & launch services 1949–81, ABPL W4932 7457 Box 175, 49/1/10, ANZ.

80 John Harvey, interview, August 2016.

81 For this process at work in Endeavour Inlet see Buckland, *Reflections*, pp. 92, 131.

82 Donald Furness, *Tahuahua: The Story of Blackwood Bay, Queen Charlotte Sound* (Blenheim: self-published, 1974), p. 102.

83 NZ Electricity Dept to Nature Conservation Council, Electric power reticulation: Marlborough

Sounds, 9 October 1967, Transmission and telephone lines, Marlborough Sounds, 1964–86, AAZU W3619 Box 4, 8A/9/66, ANZ.

84 Peter N. Meihana and Cecil R. Bradley, 'Repatriation, reconciliation and the inversion of patriarchy', *Journal of the Polynesian Society*, 127 (2018), p. 315.

85 Heberley, *Riding with Whales*, p. 51.

86 Harry Christian, 'Sounds reminiscences or 40 years in Pelorus Sounds territory', Allan family papers, unpublished, c.1920s, p. 15–16.

87 *The Pilchard Fishermen*, National Film Unit, 1945, sourced from ANZ: www.youtube.com/watch?v=CBPGSPWFHxE. There is a certain irony that this film was made even as the industry was beginning to fail. But it was one the NFU had wanted to do, and they justified it as part of the war effort.

88 General: fishing matters – Trawling, Marlborough Sounds and Bays, 1955–73, AAFZ W2253 7910 Box 61, 42/24/7, Pt 1, ANZ.

89 *AJHR*, 1924, H.–15, MDAR, p. 15 first notes the existence of the grounds; 'New fishing grounds', *Auckland Star*, 12 September 1927, p. 17 provides the detail of catch and value.

90 Mackay, *Voices from the Sea*, pp. 117–18.

91 Heberley, *Riding with Whales*, pp. 134–37.

92 Keith Murray, pers. comm., October 2016.

93 *AJHR*, 1944, H.–15, Marine Department, p. 8.

94 *AJHR*, 1945, H.–15, MDAR, pp. 10–12.

95 *AJHR*, 1940, H.–15, MDAR, pp. 28–29.

96 There are no records of how many were locals. *AJHR*, 1928, H.–15, MDAR, p. 29; *AJHR*, 1929, H.–15 MDAR, p. 27; *AJHR*, 1936, H.–15, MDAR, p. 15 comments on the problems faced by those fishing out of French Pass and the lower Pelorus Sound; see also *AJHR*, 1937, H.–15, p. 23.

97 *AJHR*, 1935, H.–15, MDAR, p. 13.

98 *AJHR*, 1937, H.–15, MDAR, p. 23.

99 The 1956 Census, vol. 8, p. 68 gives the median income for all males as £203, though for all males aged 29–49 it was £548.

100 *AJHR*, 1950, H.–15, MDAR, Table II shows approximately the total quantities of fish and shell-fish landed at the various ports for the year ended 31 December 1949. See p. 45 in relation to French Pass, Havelock, Picton.

101 Inspector of Fisheries to Sec. Marine, Trawling in the inner reaches of Pelorus, 19 September 1951, Marlborough Sounds and bays 1913–54, ADOE 16612 M1/162, 2/12/13, Pt 1, ANZ.

102 *AJHR*, 1937, H.–15, p. 31.

103 *NZ Gazette*, 5 July 1922, p. 2157; 'News of the day', *Evening Post*, 6 July 1928, p. 8. Using Danish seine or purse-seine nets, with lines across the entrance to Pelorus Sound from West Head to East Head, anywhere in Tory Channel, or from Cape Komaru to Cape Jackson and to Harding Point attracted a £20 penalty; *NZ Gazette*, 12 October 1922 notifies the banning of trawling inside either Pelorus or Queen Charlotte sound; 'Sounds fishing', *Evening Post*, 14 April 1936, p. 10 reports the restrictions on catches of commercial and recreational blue cod fishing in both Sounds. By 1947 the restrictions were widened to cover other flat fish (flounder, lemon sole) and round fish such as butterfish, hāpuku, moki, snapper, trevally.

104 The regulations were updated over the years – see Minister of Marine to C. H. Jones, 14 July 1972, AAFZ, W2253 7910 Box 61, 42/24/7, Pt 1, General: fishing matters – Trawling, Marlborough Sounds and Bays, 1955–73, ANZ. By 1972 the trawl line was not to be more than 9 metres long, the net mesh not more than 115 mm, and there was to be no more than an hour between shooting out the nets and hauling them in again. Trawling was not permitted in Queen Charlotte Sound.

105 Minister of Marine to Pelorus District Farmers' Union, 3 May 1934, Marlborough Sounds and bays 1913–54, ADOE 16612 M1/162, 2/12/13, Pt 1, ANZ.

106 'Sounds fisheries', *ME*, 10 April 1934. (See Question in the House, attached to papers 28 March 1935, Marlborough Sounds and bays 1913–54; longtime farmer on Blumine Island Mr Baldick was given column inches for his views on the subject.

107 E. A. Hefford to Sec. Marine, 5 March 1934, ibid.

108 District Inspector of Fisheries to Chief Inspector of Fisheries, 31 May 1946, ibid. This file at ANZ repeatedly deals with similar issues.

109 MP Tom Shand to Sec. Marine, 9 February 1966, General: fishing matters – Trawling, Marlborough Sounds and Bays 1955–73, AAFA W2253 7910 Box 61, 42/24/7, Pt 1, ANZ.

110 Minister Marine to S. I. Verco, editor *ME*, 13 September 1949, Undersized fish – Marlborough Sounds and vicinity – prosecutions 1932–49, ADOE 16612 M1/211, 2/12/519, Pt 1, ANZ; 'Marlborough Sounds', *The Press*, 18 March 1938.

111 District Inspector of Fisheries, Nelson, to Sec. Marine, 20 September 1968, General: fishing matters – Trawling, Marlborough Sounds and Bays 1955–73.

112 Mackay, *Voices from the Sea*, pp. 101–05.

113 Don Grady, *The Perano Whalers of Cook Strait, 1911–1964* (Wellington: A. H. & A. W. Reed, 1982), pp. 80–81.

114 For details on the changing management structure see Grady, ibid., pp. 49–59; the change from family partnership to the limited liability company is detailed on pp. 149–50.

115 Notes for meeting, 29 April 1942, Prohibited places – Marlborough Sounds, 1942–45, AATY 8490 N1 514, 1742, ANZ.

116 *AJHR*, 1950, H.–15, Marine Department, p. 34.

117 Florence Trotter, interview, November 2014.

118 Heberley, *Riding with Whales* p. 59.

119 Re local use see Buckland, *Reflections*, p. 171; re the factory product see Grady, *The Perano Whalers*, pp. 153–57.

120 Grady, ibid., pp. 173–74.

121 *AJHR*, 1920, H.–15.

122 Re *Miss Liberty* see Grady, *The Perano Whalers*, p. 54; re *Miss Whekenui* see 'Modern whaling launch,' *Auckland Star*, 18 May 1926, p. 9, and Grady, *The Perano Whalers*, p. 52. Grady dates the advent of the chaser as 1925; re the chaser that arrived in 1938 see Stephen Gerard, *Straits of Adventure* (Auckland: A. H. & A. W. Reed, 1938), quoted in A. H. Reed, *Marlborough Journey* (Auckland: A. H. & A. W. Reed, 1963), p. 106.

123 Grady, *The Perano Whalers*, p. 71.

124 Ibid., pp. 1–4, 8–9; re radio telephone see p. 93. The quote is on p. 1. Re Pattie's involvement see p. 159.

125 *AJHR*, 1950, H.–15, p. 34; Grady, *The Perano Whalers*, pp. 71, 78.

126 Reed, *Marlborough Journey*, p. 103.

127 Martin Cawthorn, pers. comm., August 2014. Grady also provides an account – see pp. 73–78.

128 Martin Cawthorn, pers. comm.; Heberley, *Riding with Whales*, p. 59 has the details on the hag eels.

129 Grady, *The Perano Whalers*, p. 221.

130 *AJHR*, 1935, H.–15, MDAR, p. 11. The most important provisions created heavy penalties for taking pregnant or right whales, immature whales or females with calves; licensing of whaling ships and factories; using all the whale carcass; keeping records of catches and forwarding them to the appropriate authorities; appointing inspectors; and restricting whaling in Antarctic waters during 1935–36.

131 *AJHR*, 1938, H.–15, MDAR, p. 24.

132 Jez Weston: http://envirohistorynz.com/2011/06/18/the-end-of-whaling-in-new-zealand-the-soviet-factor

133 Martin, Cawthorn, pers. comm., August 2014.

134 The Great Barrier Island station at Whangamumu had closed in 1932, when prices for oil dropped; Charlie Heberley had managed a new station on the island at Whangararapara, established in 1956 and closed in 1962; the Kaikōura station at South Bay closed in 1921 (Jock Phillips, 'Whaling – Modern whaling and whale watching', Te Ara: www.TeAra.govt.nz/en/whaling/page-5; Grady, *The Perano Whalers*, p. 199.

135 'Research work', *Auckland Star*, 24 September 1938, p. 11. This article voicing concern was the only such one I found.

136 *North-east Corner*, National Film Unit, 1964, sourced from ANZ: www.youtube.com/watch?v=2Gm7bsRTz9I
137 See the relevant years in *AJHR*, H.–15, MDAR.
138 Heberley, *Riding with Whales*, p. 28.
139 Alan Hall talking to Loreen Brehaut, 12 May 2007, Picton Museum.
140 Ibid.; Florence Trotter, interview, November 2014.
141 Florence Trotter, interview, November 2014.
142 L&S to Mr Douglas, Forest Ranger Nelson, 16 June 1924, Nydia Bay Forest MSMP, 1924–29, ABMN W4096 7496 Box 7, 6/24, Pt 1, ANZ.
143 Forest Ranger R. B. Steele to Conservator, State Forest Service, 8 April 1924, ibid.
144 *AJHR*, 1926, C.–1, CLD, p. 16.
145 Harvey, *Where There's a Will*.
146 Harvey, interview, September 2016; re the colour of the sap timber see Harvey, ibid., p. 89. Tony Redwood provided the information on the number of mills there.
147 Harvey, *Where There's a Will*, pp. 172–74.
148 J. M. Cunningham, 'Obituary, R. H. D. Stidolph, Some reminiscences', *Notornis* 27 (1980), pp. 160–64. Re his honorary status as scenic inspector see Under-Sec. L&S, to CCL, Blenheim, 7 January 1939, Scenic reserves – Scenic reserves – Sounds County (Marlborough Sounds), AANS W5491 6095 Box 325, 4/539, ANZ.
149 'Nature Notes', *Evening Post*, 20 February 1932.
150 'Nature Notes', *Evening Post*, 18 February 1939, p. 17.
151 'News of the day', *Evening Post*, 21 June 1928, p. 10.
152 'News of the day', *Auckland Star*, 4 August 1939, p. 6.
153 'Bushland pests', *Auckland Star*, 12 November 1943, p. 2.
154 The Native Bird Protection Society was formed in 1923 and renamed the Forest & Bird Protection Society of New Zealand in 1935. The Wildlife Act 1953 (still in force) sought to provide extensive protection for flora and fauna. The Wildlife Branch (retitled Wildlife Service in 1974) was set up within the Department of Internal Affairs in 1945 to oversee 'native and some introduced species (but not the land they lived on)'. The Reserves and Domains Act 1953 repealed the Scenery Preservation Act but created strong provisions for protecting the land and maintaining it as reserves. It also provided a legislative base for existing practice, placing the very considerable amount of New Zealand's reserve and domain land under L&S management.
155 Forest & Bird, 'Manapouri: A Green awakening', www.forestandbird.org.nz/what-we-do/publications/forest-bird-magazine/articles-archive/manapouri-green-awakening
156 Re fire education see 'News of the day', *Evening Post*, 21 June 1928, p. 10, and 'Forestry League, *Evening Post*, 3 September 1928, p. 11; re national park see 'Forestry League', *Evening Post*, July 1937, p. 4.
157 Ship Cove and QCS Reserves AANS Board – Minutes and annual reports – Marlborough Land District 1968–72, W5491 6095, Box 319, 4/446/1, ANZ.
158 'Sounds Reserves Board holds final meeting', *ME*, 11 September 1972. The extent of reserves 'managed' by the boards is also found in Historic and scenic reserves – MSMP, 1962–71, AANZ W5491 6095, Box 279, 4/270, ANZ. Note that the boards are at times described as controlling/administering/managing their areas; the reality, says former Crown commissioner Ian Mitchells, was that they 'they kept an eye on things, doing needed work themselves and using their own boats for water transport. There was a so-called ranger.' Financing came through L&S grants made following specific applications. In the early 1960s, for instance, the Pelorus and Kenepuru Board asked for financial assistance to install toilets and fireplaces and get a motor mower to keep down 'the rank growth' to reduce fire hazards. A mower would cost £40, the facilities £120, it couldn't pay its members meeting fees even though distance created travel costs for some. It also had administration fees of £8 5s, yet, apart from £4 10s accrued from leasing the open areas of some the reserves, the board had no money. Within a few days the department granted £200. In 1967 the government grant across all boards was $10,191 (see ibid., papers, early 1969).
159 Furness, *Tahuahua*, pp. 73, 77–78.

160 'Green monuments', *Evening Post*, 6 February 1933, p. 13 notes Bruce's actions. Re the fate from which he saved the bush see 'Bird protection', *Evening Post*, 14 April 1932, p. 9.

161 Maud Island in Pelorus Sound – Tom Shand Flora and Fauna Reserve 1935–73 – Marlborough Land District, AANS, W5941, 6095, Box 332, 4/733, ANZ. Re the description of the frog see Sec. Internal Affairs to DG L&S, 17 January 1968. The initial gift was gazetted on 13 August 1970 (*NZ Gazette*, no. 40, p. 1441). Access was limited to public servants involved with the frogs or those checking the condition of the bush.

162 Memo, DG L&S to L&S, Blenheim, 26 April 1971, Maud Island in Pelorus Sound – Tom Shand Flora and Fauna Reserve 1935–73 – Marlborough Land District. The reserve's altered status and name was gazetted on 16 September 1971 (*NZ Gazette*, no. 69, p. 1929).

163 Deputy CCL to Under-sec. L&S, Proposed scenic reserves, Sounds County, 16 January 1928, Scenic Reserves – Marlborough Sounds Scenic Reserves 1928–32, AANS W5491 6095, Box 1035, 4/539, ANZ.

164 'Two ideals – Forest: Firewood, Lands Department and League', *Evening Post*, 7 July 1932, p. 6.

165 In 1962, for instance, over 718 acres (290 ha) owned by W. C. Gullery were bought for £810 (the land had been just valued at $1100) to create a further reserve in the Bay of Many Coves. Some of the country was steep, south and easterly facing, some already in good bush and another 300 acres (121 ha) included regenerating bush or native grass with scrub and small clearings. There were no buildings. The minister approved the purchase on 31 July 1963 (*NZ Gazette*, 7 December 1962, p. 2234). The area, placed under the control of the Ship Cove and QCS Reserve Board, was part of a significant amount of land running up from the shore of Aratawa Bay towards Cockle Cove reserve. A further 22 acres (9 ha) were bought from G. H. Hunt in Aratawa Bay in 1963, and in 1973 Cockle Cove and the Bay of Many Coves reserves were amalgamated. In 1982 this was classified as the Bay of Many Coves Recreational Reserve (L&S – Head office – MSMP – Scenic reserve – Bay of Many Coves 1924–82, AANS W5951, 25421, Box 65, MSM-0104, Pt 1, ANZ.

166 Scenic reserves – Scenic reserves – Sounds County, AANS W5491 6095 Box 325, 4/539, ANZ.

167 Because land swaps entailed no financial commitment, L&S was concerned that reserves money, specifically allocated to purchase reserves, was not being used and such acquisitions could threaten the money given in subsequent years (R. R. Johnson to CCL, Blenheim, 12 January 1973, Department of L&S – MSMP – Scenic reserve – Kenny Isle 1935–91, AANS W5951 25421, Box 67, MSM – 0126, Pt 1, ANZ).

168 Instances of such policies at work are Pickersgill Island, where Stidolph first suggested land could be retired for a reserve and the owner be given other land (Under-Sec. L&S to CCL, Blenheim, 7 January 1939, Scenic reserves – Sounds County (Marlborough Sounds), AANS W5491 6095 Box 325, 4/539, ANZ; CCL to Under-Sec. L&S, 3 February 1939, ibid. A similar sort of process helped create the Kauauroa Bay reserve (AANS W5951 25421, Box 67, MSM – 0126, Pt 1, ANZ).

169 L&S – MSMP – Scenic reserve – Cape Lambert 1953–82, AANS W5951 25421 Box 66, MSM – 0110, Pt 1, ANZ. The quote is from the Reserve Inspection Report, 1969.

170 DG L&S to Minister L&S, Addition to Nydia Bay Scenic Reserve, 4 December 1962, L&S – MSMP – Scenic Reserve – Nydia Bay 1938–84, AANS W5951 25421, Box 68, MSM – 0136, ANZ; on price see DG L&S to Minister L&S, May 1967, ibid. The fire danger to the bush had been increased when the Tennyson Inlet road, largely locally constructed to enable land to be subdivided, was pushed through.

171 *NZ Gazette* Notice, 'Declaration that lands shall be subject to Reserves and Domain Acts 1952', 18 February 1960, no. 9, p. 196, Foreshore reserves – Sounds County – declarations that lands be subject to section 17 of the Reserves and Other Lands Disposal Act 1955 – Marlborough Land District 1959–75, AANS W5491 6095, Box 432, 22/3028/25/1, ANZ; ex-ranger Kerry Johnson, pers. comm., March 2017.

172 DG L&S to Minister L&S, 19 December 1973; Minister Maori Affairs to M. MacDonald, 13 February 1974, Marlborough Land District – Town planning – Marlborough County district scheme – Also Marlborough Sounds 1956–80, ABWN W5021 6095 Box 714, 25/743/74, Pt 1, ANZ. L&S had designated MacDonald's land in Endeavour Inlet as reserve land, to be later added to the new maritime park. When MacDonald asked to have the designation removed, the Minister of Maori Affairs told him he had recourse under the Town and Country Planning Act or the Town and Country Planning Appeal Board. Other farmers protesting against the new designation had been

told the same, but the fact that the land under question had been set aside as part of the landless natives' reserve in Endeavour Inlet (a fact of which L&S was ignorant) was given no weighting at all.

173 R. A. Falla, director Dominion Museum, Report on visit to the Sounds 10–13 September 1948.

174 File note, 'Marlborough Sounds, October 1–15, 1959', Wildlife Service – Islands in and adjacent to Marlborough Sounds – general file 1959-68, AAAC W3179 Box 13, 46/29/8, ANZ. In the late 1960s A. Charles and Neil C. Begg (*James Cook and New Zealand: The Voyage of the* Endeavour, *1768–1771; the Voyage of the* Resolution *and* Adventure, *1772–1775; the Voyage of the* Resolution *and* Discovery, *1776–1780* (Wellington: Government Printer, 1969), p. 69 provides a similar picture.

175 L&S – HO – Scenic Reserve – Edgecombe Point 1910–85, AANS W5951 25421, Box 66, MSM-0114, Pt 1, ANZ. Phillip Turner created his list on 4 January 1910; the second record of growth is in 1961.

176 J. A. D. Flack, Robin research island survey, Queen Charlotte Sound. 11 July 1972, L&S – MSMP – Scenic Reserve – Pickersgill Island 1969–86, AANS W5951 25421, Box 68, MSM – 0139, ANZ.

177 R. A. Falla, director Dominion Museum, Report on visit to the Sounds 10–13 September 1948.

178 J. A. D. Flack, Robin research island survey.

179 Paterson, *The Sea was our Boundary*, p. 159.

180 DG Internal Affairs to DG L&S, 12 September 1972, L&S – MSMP – Scenic Reserve – Pickersgill Island.

181 'Five-year study mapping Sounds birds', *ME*, 29 July 1983 provides information on the extent and spread of predators at the time. 'Report on visit to Tawhitinui and Awiti Islands, 15 February 1983, L&S – Head Office – Scenic reserve – Tarakaipa and Tawhitinui Island 1913–85, AANS W5951 25421, Box 69, MSM-0147, ANZ. The other eradication programmes being run at the time were the Wildlife Service's programme on the Hauraki Gulf's Motuhoropapa and a small island in the Galapagos group.

182 Historic and scenic reserves – forest fires on scenic reserves & CLD Nelson. Re the value of prosecutions see W. M. Groombridge to DG L&S, Protection of State areas, 11 March 1964.

183 On the amount of land involved in the proposal see L. H. Russell, CCL Blenheim, to DG L&S, Marlborough Sounds Reserves, 3 January 1969, Historic and scenic reserves – MSMP 1920–71, AANZ W5491 6095, Box 279, 4/270, ANZ.

184 R. M. Velvin, CCL Blenheim, to DG L&S, 'Marlborough Sounds reserves', 18 August 1967, ibid. This suggestion was not new. It had first been canvassed in 1932 (Memorandum, Scenic reserves in the Marlborough Sounds, 10 February 1930, Scenic Reserves – Marlborough Sounds Scenic Reserves 1928–32, AANS W5491 6095, Box 1035, 4/539, ANZ); Marlborough Progress League to Minister L&S, 5 February 1932, ibid.; and again in 1962, when farmers' trenchant opposition and lack of funding saw it shelved.

185 DG L&S to Sec. Marine, Sounds Maritime Park, 13 July 1971, L&S background paper to the Havelock meeting, General: fishing matters – Trawling, Marlborough Sounds and Bays, AAFZ W2253 7910 Box 61, 42/24/7, Pt 1, 1955–73, ANZ.

186 MWD, *The Strategy for the Conservation and Development of the Marlborough Sounds* (Wellington, 1977).

187 DG to CCL, Blenheim, Marlborough Sounds reserves, 15 February 1968, Historic and scenic reserves – MSMP 1920–71. From fragmented management, no coordinated programmes, no material about the park and inadequate staff, the new Hauraki Gulf Park had moved to 'unified control, overall planning well underway', regularised finance, better staffing, the development of brochures etc, and the board working 'in harmony' with its neighbours. The only criticism being voiced was the lack of money (DG L&S to Sec. Marine, Sounds Maritime Park, 13 July 1971, L&S background paper to the Havelock meeting).

188 Duncan McIntyre, Minister L&S, response to R. J. Paterson, 9 September 1970 (Historic and scenic reserves – MSMP 1920–71). This response was typical of the diplomatic way in which the proposed development was being run. McIntyre referred to the Sounds' unique waterways and the variety of ways in which they were used, and pointed out that the value of Hauraki Gulf model was its provision for multiple uses. It was unlikely, he told Paterson, that creating the park would impact negatively on farmers – to the contrary, good farming was 'complementary to the concept of the Park, and the provision of adequate roading and other facilities as necessary' for it to be fully used.

189 DG L&S to Sec. Marine, Sounds Maritime Park, 13 July 1971, L&S background paper to the Havelock meeting.

190 Craig Potton, *The Story of the Marlborough Sounds Maritime Park* (Blenheim: Marlborough Sounds Maritime Park Board, 1986), p. 149. The booklet states that the park was established in 1973. However, I am indebted to Kerry Johnson for advising me that the first meeting of the new board (on 20 October 1972) was reported in the *ME*, 21 October 1972.

191 Kerry Johnson, pers. comm., February 2017. Represented on the board were L&S, local iwi, local community organisations, the Marlborough County Council, the Picton Borough Council (briefly), Federated Farmers, the Nelson City Council (because the northern part of the park was in the Nelson land district) and the Waikawa and Mana boating clubs.

192 Kerry Johnson, pers. comm., March 2017.

193 Ibid.

194 Potton, *The Story of the Marlborough Sounds Maritime Park*, front pages.

195 Ian Mitchell, pers. comm., February 2017.

196 Kerry Johnson, pers. comm., February 2017.

197 Roy Grose, pers. comm., February 2017.

198 Potton, *The Story of the Marlborough Sounds Maritime Park*, p. 149. Was this the strategy for *The Strategy for the Conservation and Development of the Marlborough Sounds* (Wellington: MWD, 1977)?

199 'Captain Dickson leaves Blenheim', *Evening Post*, 6 September 1920, p. 8.

200 Peter Aimer, 'Aviation – An aviation industry', *Te Ara:* www.TeAra.govt.nz/en/aviation/page-3; Nancy Swarbrick, 'Aerial recreation – Flying powered aircraft', *Te Ara:* www.TeAra.govt.nz/en/aerial-recreation/page-2; 'Cheaper flying', *Evening Post*, 17 December 1932, p. 11; 'Airport for the Sounds', *Evening Post*, 14 August 1933, p. 8.

201 'By air to Sounds', *Evening Post*, 19 October 1933, p. 14. 'In smooth waters', *Evening Post*, 11 January 1962.

202 NZ Maritime Record: www.nzmaritime.co.nz/r301.htm

203 Kevin Ramshaw & Bettina Maniatis (eds), *Interislander: A Ferry Tale: Connecting New Zealand for 50 Years, 1962–2012*: https://issuu.com/inflightpublishing/docs/interislander_50th_mag, pp. 10–11.

204 E. P. Dawson, 'The spirit of the place', *Auckland Star*, 21 November 1936.

205 'The Sounds: A lure for tired business men', *NZ Truth*, 4 December 1930, p. 12.

206 Senior engineer MOW to Resident engineer, MOW Nelson, 20 October 1949, Marlborough Road District – Port Underwood Road and Sounds tracks, ABKK, W4357, 889, Box 189, ANZ.

207 Minutes, 27 May 1968, Ship Cove and QCS Reserves Board – Minutes and annual reports – Marlborough Land District 1968–72, AANS W5491 6095, Box 319, 4/446/1, ANZ. Buckland (*Reflections on a Lifetime*) discusses the voluntary input – scrubcutters and grubbers were organised, women fed them and, with Outward Bound assistance, the track was formed to Kenepuru Saddle.

208 Kerry Johnson, pers. comm., March 2017; Roy Grose, pers. comm., February 2017.

209 R. M. Velvin, CCL, Blenheim to DG L&S, Wairau Harbour Board, 28 April 1967, Historic and scenic reserves – MSMP 1920–71, AANZ W5491 6095, Box 279, 4/270, ANZ.

210 Tony Fitzgerald, *It's Our Life: An Imperfect History of the Waikawa Boating Club Inc., 1950–2017* (Blenheim: Waikawa Boating Club, 2017), Chapter 8.

211 Paterson, *The Sea was our Boundary*, p. 105.

212 Keith Murray, pers. comm., 2021. Moorings such as those at Hitau Bay and Charlies Bight in Tennyson Inlet were in place by then.

213 Yvonne M. Fell, *Boats for a Lifetime*, 3rd edn (Blenheim: self-published, 2008), pp. 18–21.

214 Chris Bowe, 'The legacy of Picton boat-builder Ernie Lane': www.cleanweb.co.nz/abode/708/documents/Ernest%20Richard%20Lane.pdf

215 Lorna Mason, *Cockle Cove: Marlborough Sounds Haven for Four Generations* (Picton: Cape Catley, 2000), p. 142.

216 Furness, *Tahuahua*, pp. 95–96, 98, 100.

217 Graeme Moore, interview, July 2016.

218 Martin Berthold, 'Sounds Wrecking Company: Shipwreckers, breakers and recyclers, Wakatahuri [sic], Outer Pelorus Sound', *NZ Marine News*, vol. 56, no. 3 (60th anniversary issue, 2009).

219 *ME*, 14 December 1945, quoted in Ken Berry, *Scrutiny on the County* (Blenheim: Marlborough County Council, 1986), pp. 194–95.

220 Curious Cove, March 1946, Tourists resorts – Marlborough Sounds – General 1905–57, AECB 8615 TO1/135, 20/21 Pt 1, ANZ.

221 P. M. Berrill to Surveyor-General, Marlborough Sounds subdivision and planning, 23 August 1963, Marlborough Land District – Town planning – Marlborough County district scheme – Also Marlborough Sounds 1956–80, ABWN W5021 6095 Box 714, 25/743/74, Pt 1, ANZ.

222 Brochure, 1925, Tourists resorts – Marlborough Sounds – General 1905–57.

223 Newspaper clipping, 4 September 1951, ibid.

224 Robb, *St Omer House*, pp. 32, 463, 479.

225 In Kenepuru Sound alone, in the 1920s, there were seven guesthouses. By the 1930s the following were in business: Te Mahia (run by Mr and Mrs Cecil Bay); The Portage (Lawrences); St Omer House (Frank and Margaret Godsiff); Nopera Bay (Charles Godsiff); Crail Bay (McNabbs – generally accessed from Nopera Bay with a horse and dray to take guests and luggage over the hill); Bay View, where there was a post office (Ellen Orchard); Te Mara (Bowrons); Bell View, burnt down, rebuilt and named Raetihi Lodge in 1934. Post office facilities were available at Portage (Lorna Orchard, *Time and Tide Waits for No Man* (Blenheim: Yvonne Fell, 2004), p. 63). From 1943 to 1958 the Martins ran a guesthouse at Te Mara (Robb, *St Omer House*, p. 479); Robb provides the detail on the ceremony around departing guests, p. 251).

226 Heberley, *Riding with Whales*, p. 25.

227 Report of meeting held . . . 18 August 1950, Marlborough Sounds Soil Conservation District 1946–61, AATE, W3396, 889, Box 1, 76/3, ANZ, reported Mr A. H. Godsiff denying that tourists helped the Sounds because revenue from farms would far exceed that from tourism.

228 This account is taken from Robb, *St Omer House*, pp. 75–76, 120, 237–38, 251 but would reflect the type of holiday in any of the accommodation houses, if not the detail.

229 Julia Millen, pers. comm., September 2016.

230 Eric Pawson, 'Cars and the motor industry – A motorised society', Te Ara: www.TeAra.govt.nz/en/cars-and-the-motor-industry/page-1

231 Memo to General manager, TPD, Official Inspection Marlborough Sounds, 16 November 1954, Tourists resorts – Marlborough Sounds – General 1905–57.

232 Robb (*St Omer House*, p. 363) provides the following figures extrapolated from advertising in the Tourist Bureau pamphlets: 1939: 14 accommodation houses offering total of 435 beds, 12 cottages, 13 launches for hire, 19 campsites; 1950: 13 accommodation places, 500 beds, 4 cottages, 10 launches, 9 campsites. There were also some unadvertised establishments. 1970: 5 accommodation houses, 5 cottages or motels, no campsites; 1986: Raetihi Lodge, Hopewell and Portage were the principal places in Kenepuru; there were also a few baches and campsites advertised. By the mid-1990s there were 14 guesthouses in Pelorus, and 13 in Kenepuru.

233 Mason, *Cockle Cove*, p. 43.

234 'Passenger boat for Marlborough Sounds', *Auckland Star*, 7 December 1933, p. 8. The economics of the venture are interesting. In 1932, still in the Depression, Steele had paid £2000 for the Auckland-built *Tinopai*, able to carry 80 passengers ('Modern launch', *Auckland Star*, 15 November 1932, p. 9). She was uninsured when she was burned at anchor ('Launch burnt', *Auckland Star*, 22 December 1932, p. 8). *Miss Picton* replaced her (Memorandum, 1947, Tourists resorts – Marlborough Sounds – General 1905–57).

235 Ian McGibbon, 'Cobham, Charles John Lyttelton', DNZB, Te Ara: www.TeAra.govt.nz/en/biographies/5c27/cobham-charles-john-lyttelton; re his response to being asked to be patron of the Wolfenden Association, formed in 1967 to work for homosexual law reform, see https://nzhistory.govt.nz/culture/homosexual-law-reform/setting-the-scene

236 *Pictorial Parade*, No. 135, National Film Unit production, 1963, ANZ; Outward Bound: www.outwardbound.co.nz/about-us

237 Helen Beaglehole, *Fire in the Hills: A History of Rural Fire-fighting* (Christchurch: Canterbury University Press, 2012), pp. 71–72.

238 'Man-planted trees', *Ashburton Guardian*, 14 July 1921, p 6; 'Trees and land', *Evening Post*, 18 November 1921, p. 4; 'Grow redwood!', *Evening Post*, 4 May 1922, p. 7; 'City telescope', *Evening Post*, 11 September 1926, p. 10; 'In need of trees', *Evening Post*, 25 November 1925, p. 6; 'Planting trees in Marlborough Sounds', *Evening Post*, 1 December 1925, p. 6.

239 M. D. Laffan, B. K. Daly & J. S. Whitton, *Soils of the Marlborough Sounds* (Nelson: Soil Bureau, Department of Scientific and Industrial Research, 1987), pp. 54–55.

240 'Denuded hills', *Evening Post*, 9 September 1938, p. 10; 'Trees and social value', *Evening Post*, 10 September 1938, p. 8.

241 See, for instance, N. Paton to Conservator of State Forests, 7 February 1939, Policy and administration – Proposed afforestation projects – Marlborough Sounds 1925–73, ADSQ 17639 F1W3129/16, 1/1714B Pt 1, ANZ. Paton wanted to exchange a small amount of potential forestry land for grazing land. In a further example, in 1934 the department rejected out of hand an application to afforest Blumine Island as 'ludicrous' scheme quite unrelated to what the department was envisaging and creating only 'a handsome profit for the original speculator' – see Director of Forestry to Under-sec. L&S, Blumine Island – Queen Charlotte Sound, 24 January 1934, Scenic reserves – Sounds County (Marlborough Sounds). The Sounds settlers were described as 'impossible' to deal with, preferring to sell their land for baches.

242 Conservator of Forests, Nelson, to Director of Forestry, Proposed Marlborough Sounds afforestation scheme, 29 October 1946, Policy and administration – Proposed afforestation projects – Marlborough Sounds 1925–73; Courtney Biggs, Conservator of Forests, Nelson, to Director of Forestry, 10 March 1947, ibid.; Director of Forestry to Commissioner of Works, Afforestation in Marlborough Sounds, 15 September 1947, ibid.; Inspector, Note for file, 28 June 1949, ibid.

243 Robb, *St Omer House*, pp. 224–25. Hylton Harvey recalled that by the early 1960s he and John had planted 70,000 seedlings in Crail Bay. Further plantations went in at Eli Bay, Homewood and Skiddaw (all now milled but with little replanting), and one in Four Fathom Bay (only now ready for cutting).

244 A. Poole, DG Forestry, Afforestation Marlborough Sounds, 29 January 1963, Policy and administration – Proposed afforestation projects – Marlborough Sounds 1925–73; Report, 6 April 1963, ibid.

245 Mason, *Cockle Cove*, pp. 145–46.

246 David Collingwood, 'Snake Point forestry', in Mason, *Cockle Cove*, p. 231.

247 Nature Conservation Council, Minutes of meeting, February 1974, Afforestation – Marlborough Sounds 1968, AAZ W3619 Box 6, 6C/8/68, ANZ; Report on inaugural meeting of Forestry Advisory Committee . . ., 26 May 1975, Marlborough Land District – Town planning – Marlborough County district scheme – Also Marlborough Sounds 1956–80, ABWN W5021 6095 Box 714, 25/743/74, Pt 1, ANZ.

248 'Joint committee for the Sounds', *ME*, 23 September 1971.

249 Memo, Report on inaugural meeting of Forestry Advisory Committee . . ., 26 May 1975.

250 Afforestation – Marlborough Sounds 1968, ANZ. 'Public invest in big Marlborough Forest plans', *ME*, 24 July 1974 instances Dalhoff and King Holdings Ltd which, in a partnership scheme with subsidiary Sylvan Developments Ltd, was to establish 20,000 acres (8094 ha) through the Sounds at a minimum rate of 1000 acres (404 ha) per annum. Some 750 acres (304 ha) had already been established at Linkwater.

251 Groombridge to DG L&S, 13 August 1963, Marlborough Land District – Town planning – Marlborough County district scheme – Also Marlborough Sounds 1956–80.

252 Minutes of meeting . . . and the future of forestry development, 17 September 1974, Notes on L&S's position, Afforestation – Marlborough Sounds 1968.

253 Keith Murray, pers. comm., 17 February 2017.

254 D. A. Fields, Joint Centre for Environmental Studies, Canterbury University, 'The implications of exotic forestry for other resource uses in the Marlborough Sounds', 23 June 1975.

255 David Collingwood, 'Forestry in the Sounds', in Mason, *Cockle Cove*, pp. 233–34.

256 MWD, *The Strategy for the Conservation and Development of the Marlborough Sounds* (Wellington, 1977), Summary.

257 Potton, *The Story of The Marlborough Sounds Maritime Park*, p. 149.

258 Marlborough Harbour Board, 'Sawmill/processing plant: Picton', Afforestation – Marlborough

Sounds 1968. This was a summary of a larger study, 'The potential of Marlborough exotic forests for a large capacity sawmill/processing plant at the port of Picton'.

259 Native Forests Action Council, 'Save the Sounds campaign needed again', 6 July 1983, ibid.

260 Sean Handley 'The history of benthic change in Pelorus Sound (Te Hoiere), Marlborough', prepared for the Marlborough District Council (National Institute of Water and Atmospheric Research, February 2015), pp. 13, 14. The 1958 harvest was 21 sacks, though this was for the Nelson/Marlborough area.

261 Ibid., p. 14.

262 Raewyn Peart, *The Story of the Hauraki Gulf: Discovery /Transformation /Restoration*, (Auckland: David Bateman/Environmental Society, 2016), p. 244.

263 Marine Department, *A Preliminary Survey of Mussel Stocks in Pelorus Sound*, Fisheries Technical Report 61, (Wellington, 1968–69), p. 2.

264 General: fishing matters – Trawling, Marlborough Sounds and Bays 1955–73, AAFA W2253 7910 Box 61, 42/24/7, Pt 1, ANZ. Mussel dredging had been regulated under the Fisheries Amendment Act 1963. Those wanting to sell shellfish had to have permits, which imposed standard provisions, including not dredging in a harbour. In Pelorus Sound, the definition of harbour included Poupere Reach, Hikapu Reach and Mahau Sound (but not Kenepuru Sound). Dredging was permitted only in open waters towards Pelorus Sound entrance, including Tawhitinui and Waitata reaches. Dredging, too, involved trawling, which was subject to the four-month limit. In Queen Charlotte Sound substantial areas again fell within harbour limits where commercial fishermen could only take mussels by hand-picking.

265 Handley, 'The history of benthic change', pp. 14, 34; Marine Department, *A Preliminary Survey*, p. 13.

266 Handley, ibid., p. 14.

267 Philip Tortell, pers. comm., December 2016. Tortell acknowledged particularly the support of Peter Yealands, now a major Marlborough winemaker, and Jim Jenkins on the Fisheries Industry Board; *ME*, 12 August 1969.

268 MSMP – Scenic reserves – Weka Point 1901–82, AANS W5951 25421, Box 69, MSM – 0157, ANZ.

269 Philip Tortell, 'Investigation into settlement behaviour of mussels and the hydrology of a selected area with a view to farming the shellfish', PhD thesis, Victoria University of Wellington, 1976, p. 125. Tortell (pers. comm., December 2016) also speculated that the better attraction may have been due to colour but more probably due to the polypropylene black film's ultramicroscopic pits.

270 Biotechnology Learning Hub, 'How mussels are farmed in NZ': www.biotechlearn.org.nz

271 Carol Dawber, *Lines in the Water: A History of Greenshell Mussel Farming in New Zealand* (Picton River Press for NZ Marine Farming Association, 2004), pp. 101–13.

272 G. McMillan, CCL Blenheim, to Dir. Fisheries Management Division, 28 September 1972, MSMP – Scenic reserves – Weka Point 1901–82.

273 DG L&S to Sec. Marine, 16 September 1969, ibid.

274 Minister L&S to Minister Marine, 'Shellfish farming', undated, ibid.

275 G. McMillan, CCL Blenheim, to Dir. Fisheries Management Division, 28 September 1972.

276 Ministry of Transport, 6 September 1972, ibid.

277 Potton, *The Story of The Marlborough Sounds Maritime Park*, p. 149.

278 See, for instance, MSMP Board to Min. Ag and Fish, Application for Marine Farming Lease – Fairy Bay . . ., 19 July 1973, L&S head office – MSMP – Scenic reserve – Jacobs Bay 1909–86, AANS W5951 25421, Box 66, MSM – 0122, Pt 1, ANZ; L. H. Russell, CCL Blenheim, Mussel farming Chance Bay, 24 February 1970, L&S – MSMP – Scenic Reserve – Chance, Penguin and Fairy Bays 1932–2002, ibid.

279 Ibid. The farm was granted with little appreciation of the value of the all-weather bay to increasing numbers of boats. The mussel raft, approved on the basis of it being the same construction as existing rafts in Kenepuru, long took up a particularly useful spot for anchoring. In February 2018 it was no longer there, perhaps because of unnaturally warm water.

280 Handley, 'The history of benthic change', pp. 23–24.

9. Towards the New Century

1 Harry Christian, 'Sounds reminiscences or 40 years in Pelorus Sounds territory', Allan family papers, unpublished, c.1920s, p. 17.

2 Nola Leov, interview, October 2013.

3 Ibid.

4 Debbie Moleta, interview, February 2014.

5 G. J. C. Harvey, *Where There's a Will There's a Way: Memories of My Childhood and Sawmilling Days in the Marlborough Sounds* (Blenheim: self-published, 2008), p. 56.

6 Nola Harvey, interview, October 2013.

7 Until the 1950s heralded in the beginnings of a greater prosperity, a lot of people in small towns all over the country lived with nightwatchmen and few facilities, and children almost always shared rooms.

8 Nola Harvey, interview, October 2013.

9 Harvey, *Where There's a Will*, p. 68.

10 Carol King-Turner, *Pioneer Nurse in the Marlborough Sounds* (Rai Valley: self-published, 2004).

11 Harvey, *Where There's a Will*, p. 56. In 1967 an NZED official noted that there were '[a]bout 3 private generating plants' in the Sounds, with the rest dependent on generators for electricity. I have assumed that the private generators were Pelton wheels.

12 NZED to Nature Conservation Council, Electric power reticulation: Marlborough Sounds, 9 October 1967, Transmission and telephone lines – Marlborough Sounds 1964–86, AAZU W3619 Box 4, 8A/9/66, ANZ.

13 Transmission and telephone lines – Marlborough Sounds 1964–86.

14 A. H. McLintock (ed.), *An Encyclopaedia of New Zealand*, 'Distribution of Electricity by Local Authorities', Te Ara: www.teara.govt.nz/en/1966/power-resources/page-5

15 'Planning authority to study power lines in scenic areas', *ME*, 7 September 1966; N. G. Krebs, Sec. Nature Conservation Council, to CCL Blenheim, 18 October 1966, Transmission and telephone lines – Marlborough Sounds 1964–86; CCL Blenheim to Sec. Nature Conservation Council, Power lines in scenic areas, 12 June 1967, ibid.; E. C. Rollo, Sec. Nature Conservation Council, to Chief Engineer Marlborough Electric Power Board, 16 October 1968, ibid.; Marlborough Electric Power Board to Sec. Nature Conservation Council, Tory Channel – Arapawa Island reticulation, 9 September 1981, ibid.; Nature Conservation Council, meeting 9–10 February 1982, ibid. Re Tennyson Inlet and Elaine Bay see ibid., reports 1973ff.

16 R. J. Paterson, Waitui Farm, to F. M. Hanson, Commissioner of Works, 7 November 1956, Marlborough Road District – Torea Bay to Portage road – Roads and tracks – Kenepuru Roads Board 1961–67, ABKK, W4357, 889, Box 189 43/157, Pt 3, ANZ.

17 R. J. Paterson, *The Sea was our Boundary: The Titirangi/Waitui Story of the Patersons 1929–1977* (self-published, 2011), p. 149 for the description of the road, its cost etc; pp. 139–41 for the Paterson's early survey work; pp. 145–46 for the case they made to the government.

18 Re the MWD administration, W. W. M. Groombridge, Proposed regional plan – Marlborough Sounds, 4 June 1963, Marlborough Land District – Town planning – Marlborough County district scheme – Also Marlborough Sounds 1956–80, ABWN W5021 6095 Box 714, 25/743/74, Pt 1, ANZ; re Federated Farmers' role see Paterson, ibid., pp. 102, 108.

19 Furkert, Engineer-in-Chief PWD, to TPD, 17 July 1931, Marlborough Road District – Onahau to Te Mahia, Sounds County 1917–63, ADKK, W4357, 889, Box 189, 43/144, ANZ.

20 R. H. Bell, CCL, to DG L&S, 17 July 1949, Marlborough Road District – Port Underwood Road and Sounds tracks, ibid. Bell identifies the notion of settlers' maintenance work as rates equivalent, but the response from the inspecting engineer MWD to the engineer-in-chief of 7 December 1949 suggests the subsidy be given for grants to carry out track repairs where there was no alternative transport and the repairs would enable stock to be got to market.

21 See, for instance, Furkert, Engineer-in-chief PWD, to TPD, 17 July 1931, Marlborough Road District – Onahau to Te Mahia, Sounds County 1917–63; Resident engineer to district engineer, 29 October 1946, ibid.; Semple to E. P. Meachen MP, 6 December 1946, ibid.; R. Lancaster, Resident engineer PWD, to Under-sec. Hutchings, 15 July 1946, Marlborough Road District – Torea Bay to Portage road

– Roads and tracks – Kenepuru Roads Board.

22 Re TPD assistance see correspondence, 6 February 1931, Marlborough Road District – Onahau to Te Mahia, Sounds County 1917–63; TPD correspondence, 1951, ibid. For an instance of a TPD grant see memo, TPD to PWD, September 1946, Marlborough Road District – Torea Bay to Portage road – Roads and tracks – Kenepuru Roads Board.

23 Newspaper cutting, unidentified, dated 6 October 1952, in Marlborough Road District – Onahau to Te Mahia, Sounds County 1917–63.

24 Ian Dougherty, *The Making of the French Pass Road in the Marlborough Sounds* (Auckland: No Ordinary Life, 2008), p. 4. Feeder roads were built in a number of places. Apart from those discussed below, Vogel had built a private access road from the Te Mahia–Portage road to a house in Ohahau Bay that is much used today by those getting to the bay – see correspondence, 30 November 1964, Marlborough Road District – Roads along foreshore of Sounds . . . 1934–74, ABKK, 889 W4357/190 43/248 Pt.1, ANZ.

25 Dougherty, *The Making of the French Pass Road*, pp. 3 & 4. Re the road board's application for £40,000 see p. 4.

26 Ibid., pp. 12, 16.

27 Authorisation of requested £460 (approved on a three-to-one subsidy as long as it was not seen as setting a precedent), 28 November 1946, Marlborough Road District – Torea Bay to Portage road – Roads and tracks – Kenepuru Roads Board; Kenepuru Roads Board to Tom Shand MP, 18 November 1953, ibid. (The approval took almost a year to come through.)

28 Secretary, MWD, to Commissioner of Works, 25 March 1963, ibid.

29 Ibid. The approvals for funding were as follows – 1957: £480 on a four-to-one subsidy for the Waitaria Bay–Kenepuru Heads road. 24 June 1958: a similar subsidy was awarded to the Kenepuru Road Board for the Manaroa–Waitaria Bay section. 2 July 1959: St Omer–Crail Bay–Hopai road was approved. 16 May 1960: Ohinagaro–Kenepuru Heads road approved on an eight-to-one subsidy (reflecting the one given to French Pass and the meagre state of the Kenepuru Road Board finances).

30 Sounds Branch, Fed. Farmers, to Min. Agriculture, re Onahau Canal, 18 October 1950, Marlborough Land District – Marlborough Sounds canal project – cut at Onahau between Queen Charlotte and Pelorus Sounds – Also Havelock Harbour and control of Pelorus Sounds foreshore 1951–58, AWBN W5021 6095 Box 629, 22/4995, Pt 1, ANZ.

31 Re Piripaua Cut see Paterson, *The Sea was our Boundary*, p. 107. Re Onahau Cut see p. 104. Paterson records that Brian Greensill of Broughton Bay revived this matter over 1947–52. However, see Semple to E. P. Meachem MP, 6 December 1946, Marlborough Road District – Onahau to Te Mahia, Sounds County 1917–63. When considering upgrading the routes from Portage and Te Mahia, Paterson notes 'the possibility of the [Onahau] Canal or tunnel which would no doubt supersede both routes'. I was not able to find out what occasioned this comment. See also Federated Farmers' petition, Launch services in the Marlborough Sounds, Pt 1, 1949–50, AAFZ W5704 412 Box 380 Ag. 84/13/185 ANZ. The petition set out the benefits to locals and the economy, the advantage to yachtsmen – yachts could move from one sound to the other without 'the anxiety [to] yatchsmen's wives and families . . . These brave fellows have fought in two terrible wars and they and their offspring have earned this short cut'. Similar sentiments about debts due to returned servicemen appear elsewhere. Letters 4 July and 18 July 1950 spell the end of the canal plan. See also Marlborough Land District – Marlborough Sounds canal project – cut at Onahau between Queen Charlotte and Pelorus Sounds.

32 Harvey, *Where There's a Will*, pp. 105–06; John Harvey, interview, August 2016.

33 Harvey, interview, August 2016.

34 Malt, District Commissioner of Works, to Commissioner of Works, 16 May 1960, Marlborough Road District – Torea Bay to Portage road – Roads and tracks – Kenepuru Roads Board.

35 A. Chatfield, transport officer, to Sec.-Mgr, Visit to the Marlborough Sounds . . ., 13 September 1967, Transport – General – Marlborough Sounds 1966–72, ABDM W3569 Box 439 ANZ.

36 Dougherty, *The Making of the French Pass Road*, p. 18.

37 F. M. Hanson to Commissioner of Works, 24 February 1958, Marlborough Road District – Torea Bay to Portage road – Roads and tracks – Kenepuru Roads Board.

38 Joy Redwood, interview, 11 March 2014.

39 District Office Wellington – Construction report – Marlborough Sounds & Counties 1905–68, AATE W3399/75, 16/1105, ANZ.

40 Re the date of the road, Tony Redwood, pers. comm., May 2017.

41 Joy Redwood, interview, March 2014; Joy Redwood, pers. comm., May 2017.

42 For an initial account of the Port Gore settlers' situation see Report from interdepartmental committee of enquiry into Onahau channel, 1949, Launch services in the Marlborough Sounds, Pt 1, 1949–50, AAFZ 412 W5704 Box 380, Ag. 84/13/185, ANZ; for the decision see W. J. Broadfoot to T. P. Shand MP, 17 June 1952, Shipping – specific services – Marlborough Sounds steamer & launch services 1949–81, ABPL W4932 7457 Box 175, 49/1/10, ANZ.

43 Paterson, *The Sea was our Boundary*, p. 102 makes the general claim. Report from interdepartmental committee of enquiry (ibid.) lists only three settlers so obliged.

44 Christian, 'Sounds reminiscences', p. 14; AECB 8615 T01/135, 20/21 pt 1, Tourists resorts – Malborough Sounds – General, 1905–57, ANZ (Wellington), Memorandum for Minister of Marine, 7 April 1949.

45 Report from interdepartmental committee of enquiry (ibid.) sets out the general issues. Re the inadequate subsidy see Sec. Marine to Min. Marine, Launch services Havelock to Pelorus Sound, 20 March 1950, Shipping – specific services – Marlborough Sounds steamer & launch services 1949–81.

46 Re the meeting see Paterson, *The Sea was our Boundary*, p. 103. The matters are more extensively set out in Memorandum for Minister of Marine, 7 April 1949, Tourist resorts – Marlborough Sounds – General 1905–57.

47 Paterson, *The Sea was our Boundary*, p. 103.

48 Sec. Marine to Commissioner Transport, Picton Ferry Services, 13 December 1950, Shipping – specific services – Marlborough Sounds steamer & launch services 1949-81.

49 www.nzhistory.net.nz/culture/the-1950s/overview

50 By 1932 cables linked telephones from Waikawa to Torea Bay, Portage to headland to south of Waitaria Bay, Broughton Bay to a point close to St Omer. See Telephone cables, Marlborough Sounds 1932–32, ADOE 16612 M1/639, 6/1/158, ANZ. In Queen Charlotte Sound a wartime submarine cable laid across the sound from West Bay, Curious Cove, to McAlister Cove created a better and direct link with Picton and enabled a growing demand to be met (Furness, *Tahuahua*, p. 110). In the late 1980s underwater cables finally brought improved services to Bay of Many Coves residents (Mason, *Cockle Cove*, p. 105).

51 'Moves to improve Bay of Coves telephone line', *ME*, 2 August 1964.

52 Mason, *Cockle Cove*, p. 106.

53 Jill Clendon, 'Public health nurses in New Zealand: The impact of invisibility', *Nursing Praxis in New Zealand*: www.nursingpraxis.org/172-public-health-nurses-in-new-zealand-the-impact-of-invisibility.html

54 Flora Robb, *St Omer House: Family Life in the Guest House and Some Sounds History* (Nelson: self-published, 2013), pp. 195–96 lists a lot of home remedies, some of which borrowed from Māori medical lore.

55 King-Turner, *Pioneer Nurse*, p. 6.

56 Ibid.

57 Joy Redwood, interview, March 2014.

58 Nola Leov, interview, October 2013.

59 Ibid.

60 Rita Jacobson, pers. comm.; Paterson, *The Sea Was Our Boundary*, pp. 195–96.

61 Tony Redwood, pers. comm., October 2021; Jay Redwood, pers comm. Feruary 2021.

62 Harvey, *Where There's a Will*, pp. 137–39.

63 *AJHR*, 1922, E.–1, Education, p. 3.

64 *AJHR*, 1926, E.–1, Education, p. 11.

65 Noel Moleta, interview, March 2014.

66 Shirley Buckland, *Reflections on a Lifetime* (Nelson: self-published, 2007), pp. 257–59.
67 Joy Redwood, interview, March 2014.
68 Ibid.
69 *AJHR*, 1928, E.–1, Education. p. 16. In 1920, 28 per cent of all adult teachers were uncertified. By 1927 this number had dropped to 8 per cent and would drop to 7 per cent in 1930 – see relevant report, 1930.
70 Loreen A. Brehaut & Mike Turner, *Whekenui School, 1951–62: A Very Remote School* (Picton: Picton Historical Society, 2008), p. 21.
71 Alan Hall, interview, 12 May 2007, Lorreen A. Brehart, Picton Whaling and Heritage Museum.
72 The value of amalgamating in Kenepuru is attested to by transport officer to Sec.-mgr, Department of Education, Proposed amalgamation . . ., 17 May 1966, Transport – General – Marlborough Sounds 1966–72, ABDM W3569 Box 439, ANZ.
73 J. S. Watson, resident teacher, to Sec.-mgr, Education, 14 August 1972, ibid.
74 Nola Leov, interview, October 2013; Hylton Harvey, interview, September 2013. Both were born in the 1920s.
75 Joy Redwood, interview, March 2014.
76 Ibid.
77 Buckland, *Reflections*, p. 81.
78 Robb, *St Omer House*, pp. 130–34, 137; Harvey, *Where There's a Will*, pp. 20, 32–35; Harry Williams, 'Outward-bound from Havelock', undated, Williams private papers; Lorna Orchard, *Time and Tide Waits for No Man* (Blenheim: Yvonne Fell, 2004), p. 15.
79 Nola Leov, interview, October 2013.
80 Joy Redwood, interview, March 2014.
81 Ibid.
82 Debbie Moleta, interview, March 2014.
83 Denise Harvey, interview, August 2016.
84 Joy Redwood, interview, March 2014.
85 Buckland, *Reflections*, p. 49.
86 Denise Harvey, interview, August 2016.
87 Debbie Moleta, interview, March 2014.
88 Harry Williams, 'Life at Kaiuma Bay in the Pelorus Sound, Collingwood', August 1998, Williams private papers, pp. 2, 6, 15–16.
89 Laura Bowdler, Evidence of Laura Bowdler (née Keenan) for Tahuaroa-Watson whānau, Board of Inquiry, New Zealand King Salmon proposal, 2012, para. 30; Mike Taylor, pers. comm., provided the dates and the scope of the orchestra's activity.
90 Heather Heberley, *Riding with Whales: Stories of Great Sounds Women* (Picton: Cape Catley, 1999), 'Ruby Heberley', p. 21.
91 Bowdler, Evidence, paras 31, 32.
92 Orchard, *Time and Tide*, p. 31–33.
93 Re the Terrills' dance see Heberley, 'Ruby Heberley', p. 21; re the Whakatahuri dance see Orchard, *Time and Tide*, pp. 33–33; re the Port Gore men see Buckland, *Reflections*, p. 93.
94 Paterson, *The Sea was our Boundary*, pp. 101–12.
95 Peter Cooke, *Defending New Zealand: Ramparts on the Sea 1840–1950s* (Wellington: Defence of New Zealand Study Group, 2000), pp. 247–48.
96 Ibid., pp. 253–54.
97 'Appreciation of the defence of New Zealand', secret report in ibid., p. 266.
98 For the early discussion around these restrictions see Notes for meeting, 29 April 1942, Prohibited places – Marlborough Sounds 1942–45, AAYT 8490 N1 514, 1724, ANZ; re the prohibitions and residents' evacuation see Naval secretary to Min. Defence, Defence of Marlborough Sounds – traffic restrictions, 21 May 1942, ibid. The restrictions, recognised as inconvenient but inevitable, were as follows: With some (unidentified) exceptions, Tory Channel was to be closed to all inward or outward traffic. Internal traffic to whalers and settlers, and access to the whaling station, was to be by day and under licence. In Queen Charlotte Sound, inward and outward traffic were to

permitted by day, but prohibited at night. At night, only internal licensed traffic was permitted, and net fishing inside the sound was prohibited at all times. Some parts of outer Pelorus Sound were to be closed; within the rest there was to be traffic only by day and under permit. Settlers within restricted areas were to be evacuated; the Bureau of Industry was to consider how farmers would get out sheep and wool.

99 July 1942, Prohibited places – Marlborough Sounds 1942–45, ANZ.

100 Re the Howes guns see Memo, Marlborough Sounds, 20 January 1942, Coast defence – fixed defence – Marlborough Sounds 1941–50, AAYS 8649 AD12/3, ANZ; re the date of the completion of the gun at Whekenui see Kerry Neal & Nola M. Leov, *The Price of Vigilance: The Building of the Gun Emplacements in the Marlborough Sounds, 1942* (Nelson: self-published, 1999).

101 See file from 25 June 1942 to 19 August 1942, Defence works and buildings – Navy Department – Anti submarine fixed defence – Marlborough Sounds – Long Island, AHHL 19111 W1/817, 23/723/2, 1942–43, ANZ.

102 Cooke, *Defending New Zealand*, p. 387 states that the first overture was made in January. However, the secret telegram of which I am aware is dated 4 April 1942 (Naval message, secret, Britman Washington, Defence – Defence of Marlborough Sounds – General – April 1942–March 1943, AAYT 8491 N2/31, 020/5, ANZ). The advantages of the sound were that in the quite possible event that Australian bases were held, developments to house the fleet in New Zealand were to go ahead. Both Auckland and Wellington harbours had their limitations, but QCS could be entered in all weathers, could berth a large fleet and was comparatively easy to defend. There were three good aerodromes at Blenheim (Memo, QCS, 11 August 1942).

103 These were loop indicator equipment that would give the position of enemy ships entering and passing over a field of controlled mines (Construction at Waikawa Bay of naval magazine sites and a mine store and boom defence depot, Defence – Defence of Marlborough Sounds – Boom defence – June 1942–June 1946, AAYT 891N2/31, O20/5/2, ANZ). Authority for the Waikawa Bay magazine sites was given in the last quarter of 1942; the boom defence was approved 27 October 1942 as part of the development of the sound as a fleet anchorage. Neal & Leov, *The Price of Vigilance*, p. 25 describe the workings of the loop indicator equipment. Picton was to have a servicing depot; Cockle Cove was to be used for fuelling and storing ammunition lighters and as a base for the picket boats guarding the boom (Memo, Defence of Marlborough Sounds, Arrangements for fuelling and servicing HDMLs etc', 15 September 1942, Defence – Defence of Marlborough Sounds – General – April 1942–March 1943). Two observation mining stations, in Tory Channel and at Dieffenbach Point, and a boom defence 1.5 km west of Dieffenbach Point were to be built, and four minefields laid: two in Pelorus, one in QCS and one in Tory Channel (Cooke, *Defending New Zealand*, p. 387). A defence officers' post was set up at West Point in East Bay, with a camp at Curious Cove (Neal & Leov, *The Price of Vigilance*, pp. 24–25).

104 Memo, Queen Charlotte Sound – Proposals for future development, undated [early October 1942], Defence – Defence of Marlborough Sounds – General – April 1942–March 1943.

105 Re basic shore facilities see Cooke, *Defending New Zealand*, pp. 388–89; re the minefields see Naval Sec., Defence of Marlborough Sounds – Traffic restrictions, 3 October 1942, Prohibited places – Marlborough Sounds 1942–45; Naval Sec., Prohibited anchorage, Queen Charlotte Sound, 10 November 1942 (ibid.) notes that it was no longer intended to close the area to seaborne traffic; Memo, Minefields in the Sounds, 6 October 1942, Coast defence – Fixed defence – Marlborough Sounds 1941–50, AAYS, 8649 AD12/3, 25/3/3, ANZ.

106 Neal & Leov, *The Price of Vigilance*, pp. 191–94.

107 Nancy M. Taylor, *The New Zealand People at War*, vol. 1: *The Home Front* (Wellington: Historical Publications Branch, Department of Internal Affairs, 1986), pp. 479–90; Notes for meeting, 29 April 1942, Prohibited Places – Marlborough Sounds 1942–45. Correspondence, 18 & 22 August 1942, deals with the decision not to move the residents.

108 Memo, Trawling in Queen Charlotte Sound and Tory Channel, 12 August 1943, Prohibited places – Marlborough Sounds 1942–45. The restrictions were only fully removed (*NZ Gazette*, 14 December 1944, p. 1517) after two requests from the Merchant Service Guild (Merchant Service Guild to Sec.

Navy Dept, 12 August 1943, Prohibited places – Marlborough Sounds 1942–45); Merchant Service Guild, 22 May 1944, ibid.

109 https://nzhistory.govt.nz/war/new-zealand-and-the-second-world-war-overview

110 Nola M. Leov, *The Sounds in Wartime: A celebration of the contribution to the war effort made by an isolated New Zealand community 1939–45* (Te Towaka 50th Anniversary Home Guard Sports Committee, 1996), pp. 57, 59–60. For the names of those killed see lists on pp. 59–60, p. 64.

111 Ibid., pp. 12–13; Robb, *St Omer House*, pp. 177, 180–81.

112 Lorna Mason, *Cockle Cove: Marlborough Sounds Haven for Four Generations* (Picton: Cape Catley, 2000), pp. 73–74.

113 Taylor, *The New Zealand People at War*, pp. 454, 467.

114 Leov, *The Sounds in Wartime*, p. 13. '7.5% of the population [was involved], more than double the proportion of the Home Guard in Great Britain': Ian McGibbon, 'Second World War – Japan enters the war', Te Ara: www.TeAra.govt.nz/en/photograph/34574/home-guard; The *ME* reported meetings of settlers called by the Farmers' Union on 28 December 1940 to look at forming a Home Guard unit. The formation of a further French Pass unit was first mooted at a meeting in February 1941; by July 124 men were in the Pelorus Sound unit, 84 in Picton and Koromiko, and the French Pass unit had been formed, with 30 enrolments – see Leov, *The Sounds in Wartime*, pp. 25–31.

115 Williams, 'Life at Kaiuma Bay', p. 15.

116 Leov, *The Sounds in Wartime*, p. 13. At its greatest strength of 119,000 guardsmen, the Home Guard was 40,000 American rifles and ammunition short (Taylor, *The New Zealand People at War*, p. 478). The national list of basic equipment and rations that each guardsman was to bring on enlisting underlines the extraordinarily makeshift nature of the whole enterprise, as does the call for buckets, kerosene tins, wire, nails, staples, tins with lids, matches, detonators, bottles with corks etc, to be stored at headquarters ('Equipment', *New Zealand Home Guard Manual*, 1942, reproduced in Leov, *The Sounds in Wartime*, p. 35).

117 Leov, *The Sounds in Wartime*, pp. 41–43.

118 Ibid., p. 43.

119 Neal & Leov, *The Price of Vigilance*, pp. 31, 39, 55, 58, 87–90, 93–100, 191–94.

120 Ibid., pp. 203–05.

121 Don Grady, *The Perano Whalers of Cook Strait, 1911–1964* (Wellington: A. H. & A. W. Reed, 1982), p. 87. At Whekenui they acquired accommodation buildings, a recreation hall, butcher's shop, kitchen, store and ablution block; at Fishing Bay they got a number of the prefabricated huts and the army recreation hall.

122 Hylton Harvey, interview, September 2013.

123 Robb, *St Omer House*, pp. 176–78.

124 Rural Women, 'Our history – from small beginnings': www.ruralwomen.org.nz/about_us/history.html

125 Buckland, *Reflections*, pp. 164–65.

126 Debbie Moleta, interview, March 2014.

127 Joy Redwood, interview, March 2014.

128 Deirdre Mackay, *Voices from the Sea: The Stories of Some Nelson and Marlborough Fishing Families* (Motueka: Talley's Group, 2004), p. 195.

129 Ibid, pp. 196–97.

130 Ibid., p. 99.

131 Ibid., p. 121.

132 B. Hippolite, brief of evidence on behalf of Ngāti Toa, pp. 5–6, in Waitangi Tribunal, *Te Tau Ihu o te Waka a Maui: Report on Northern South Island Claims* (Wai 785), vol. 2 (Wellington, 2008), p. 1008; Duff, brief of evidence, pp. 4–7, in ibid., p. 1007.

133 Waitangi Tribunal, *Te Tau Ihu*, vol. 3, pp. 1069–70.

134 Ibid., p. 1053.

135 Ibid., pp. 1094–95.

136 Ibid., p. 1111.

137 Waitangi Tribunal, *Te Tau Ihu*, vol. 2, p. 573.

138 Ibid., pp. 565–66.
139 Ibid., p. 569.
140 Ibid., pp. 569–70.
141 Ibid., pp. 570–71.
142 Ibid., p. 987.
143 Ibid., p. 570.
144 Waitangi Tribunal, *Te Tau Ihu*, vol. 3, pp. 1105–20.
145 Diana Morrow, 'A legacy of loss: Ngāti Awa/Te Ātiawa reserves in Queen Charlotte Sound, 1856–c1970', report commissioned by the Crown Forestry Rental Trust, 2000 (doc D6), p. 108, in Waitangi Tribunal, *Te Tau Ihu*, vol. 3, pp. 1098, 1099.
146 Waitangi Tribunal, *Te Tau Ihu*, vol. 3, p. 1101.
147 Ibid., p. 1131.
148 Ibid., p. 113.
149 Controller and Auditor-General, *Government Planning and Support for Housing on Maori Land*, Appendix: Summary of the legislation about Maori Land (2011): www.oag.govt.nz/2011/housing-on-maori-land/appendix.htm; Hilary Mitchells and John Mitchells, pers. comm., June 2015.
150 Ibid., p. 987.
151 Richard Bradley, pers. comm., August 2017.
152 Ian Pool & Tahu Kukutai, 'Taupori Māori – Māori population change – Population changes, 1769–1840', Te Ara: www.TeAra.govt.nz/en/interactive/31311/Māori-population-1841-2006
153 Cybèle Locke, *'The Poorest Tribe under the Heavens': Ngati Kuia's Socio-economic Circumstances, 1856–1950*, research report commissioned by Crown Forestry Rental Trust, Wellington, 2002, pp. 124–29 indicates the scattered nature of people's holdings. For instance, in 2002, Thomas August Wilson (Wirihana) of Ngāti Kuia and Ngāti Koata descent had land at Kenepuru, Anakoha, Wairau, Te Hora, Bruce Bay and Stewart Island; James Waihaere Mason's family still had land at Anakoha, Ruapaka, Havelock, Māhakipawa and perhaps Kenepuru and Croisilles.
154 Matui Rei, brief of evidence (no. 1), p. 10 in Waitangi Tribunal, *Te Tau Ihu*, vol. 3, p. 1109.
155 Waitangi Tribunal, *Te Tau Ihu*, vol. 2, p. 1120.
156 Ibid., p. 990; Locke, *'The Poorest Tribe'*, p. 90.
157 Locke, *'The Poorest Tribe'*, pp. 113–19, 120–21.
158 Waitangi Tribunal, *Te Tau Ihu*, vol. 2, p. 999.
159 Locke, *'The Poorest Tribe'*, pp. 114–17. For date of closure see Waitangi Tribunal, *Te Tau Ihu*, vol. 2, pp. 1000–01.
160 Waitangi Tribunal, *Te Tau Ihu*, vol. 2, p. 990; Locke, *'The Poorest Tribe'*, p. 90.
161 AANS W5491 6095 Box 325, 4/539, Scenic reserves – Scenic reserves – Sounds County (Marlborough Sounds) 1932–50, ANZ; 'Sounds tracks', *ME*, 6 August 1935.
162 We might note the sporadic work at Okoha in the late 1930s and, in the 190s and 1950s in Queen Charlotte Sound, the work at the freezing works and whaling station and the range of jobs the district's still-existing seasonal agricultural/horticultural ventures offered.
163 Locke, *'The Poorest Tribe'*, p. 114.
164 Ibid., pp. 80–81; Waitangi Tribunal, *Te Tau Ihu*, vol. 2, pp. 1001–02. In 1934 Māori deaths from typhoid were 10 times higher than for Pākehā. Poorly kept statistics show that Māori, at rates far greater than Pākehā, were increasingly dying from respiratory diseases, maternal mortality and typhoid. During 1925–34 Māori infant mortality was about three times that of Pākehā; in 1929 the death rate from respiratory diseases was over eight times higher.
165 J. H. Grace, 'Housing and economic survey', 1938, MS papers 85-173-4/5, ATL 210, pp. 426–27, ATL; Locke, *'The Poorest Tribe'*, pp. 145–46.
166 Waitangi Tribunal, *Te Tau Ihu*, vol. 2, p.1005; Miss Clark to Dr Ellison, 12 February 1930 (H 1 13506 160/52, ANZ), quoted in Locke, *'The Poorest Tribe'*, pp. 81–82; Locke, ibid., p. 95.
167 Ibid., p. 107.
168 Waitangi Tribunal, *Te Tau Ihu*, vol. 2, pp. 990–91.
169 Ibid., p. 1006.

170 B. Wyn Irwin, Medical Officer of Health, to DG Health, 18 October 1937 (H 1 12189 172/21/41, ANZ), in Locke, *'The Poorest Tribe'*, p. 123.
171 Locke, *'The Poorest Tribe'*, pp. 78–79.
172 Ibid., p. 122.
173 Waitangi Tribunal, *Te Tau Ihu*, vol. 2, pp. 990–91.
174 Ibid., pp. 1006–07.
175 Stephen (Bosun) Huntley, Evidence for Tahuaroa-Watson whānau, Board of Inquiry, NZ King Salmon proposal, 2012, para. 72.
176 Richard Bradley, interview, 2014.
177 Waitangi Tribunal, *Te Tau Ihu*, vol. 2, pp. 1010–11. Tony Redwood, pers. comm., October 2021 provided the information on the new school, its attendees, its closure.
178 Morrow, 'A legacy of loss' in Waitangi Tribunal, *Te Tau Ihu*, vol. 3, p. 1099.
179 Huntley, Evidence for Tahuaroa-Watson whānau, paras 61–64.
180 Arthur Huntley, Evidence for Tahuaroa-Watson whānau, Board of Inquiry, NZ King Salmon Proposal, 2012, para. 15.
181 Duff, brief of evidence, pp. 4–7, cited in Waitangi Tribunal, *Te Tau Ihu*, vol. 2, p. 1007.
182 Laura Bowdler, Evidence of Laura Bowdler (née Keenan) for Tahuaroa-Watson whānau, Board of Inquiry, New Zealand King Salmon proposal, 2012, paras 1, 2.
183 Florence Trotter, interview, November 2014.
184 Bowdler, Evidence, para. 22.
185 Ibid., paras. 31, 32.
186 Waitangi Tribunal, *Te Tau Ihu*, vol. 3, p. 1164.
187 *NZ Gazette*, 24 October 1901, p. 2034, Motungarara or Tītī Island, Preservation of Native Fauna and Flora.
188 Consistent with the land's status as scenic reserves, Māori had to agree not to light fires, destroy other than the named birds and fish, take vegetation, or 'interfere' with fences or the stock that might be said to be destroying the habitat (L&S to CCL, 20 September 1918, Permission to take muttonbirds from Chetwode and Tītī Islands, 1918–1966, AANZ W5986 Box 12, 3/356, Pt 1, ANZ).
189 Wiremu Waaka to CCL, 1 March 1937 & 22 March 1937, ibid.
190 Waitangi Tribunal, *Te Tau Ihu*, vol. 3, p. 1156 states that 'From 1960, all further access was denied by the Crown.'

10. New Directions

1 Dataset: Age and sex by ethnic group (grouped total responses), for Census 'usually resident' population counts – 2006, 2013 and 2018 (RC, TA, SA2, DHB), Statistics NZ.
2 Keith Murray, pers. comm., October 2021.
3 Ibid.
4 Joy and Tony Redwood, pers. comm., October 2021.
5 Noel Moleta, interview, February 2014; Noel Moleta, pers. comm., June 2021.
6 Tony Redwood, pers. comm., October 2020.
7 Joy Redwood, interview, March 2014.
8 SCION, Analysis of setback options and harvesting implications for the Marlborough Sounds: www.marlborough.govt.nz/environment/coastal/sedimentation (2017), p. 5.
9 Infometrics, *Picton and the Sounds: 2016 Annual Economic Profile* (2016), pp. 6, 7.
10 Dallas Hemphill, pers. comm., June 2021.
11 John McKenzie, pers. comm., June 2021.
12 Note that the Marlborough Forestry Industry Association argues against historical (before the late 1980s) sedimentation from forestry in the Sounds. See Dallas Hemphill, 'Pine forests in the Pelorus Sound from 1900 to 1970', *NZ Tree Grower*, May 2021, p. 31.
13 Ron Sutherland, Marlborough Forest Industry Association, pers. comm., September 2017.
14 Vern Harris, Executive Officer, Marlborough Forestry Industry Association, pers. comm., June 2021.
15 Dallas Hemphill, pers. comm., June 2021.

16 Forest Owners' Association, 'Commission's ETS change risks forest planting targets', Media release, 21 May 2021.
17 Marlborough District Council, Environment: www.marlborough.govt.nz/environment
18 Andrew Macalister, 'Management strategy the control of wilding conifers', prepared for the Kenepuru & Central Sounds Residents Association Inc (2010): https://static1.squarespace.com/static/51a82c3ce4b080a0192d23d2/t/51b827aee4b0b1ab9202c735/1371023278814/ManagementPlan-Kenepuru+15March11.pdf
19 Marlborough District Council, 'Welcome boost to wilding pine control', media release, 8 September 2020. In September 2020 the government granted $3.7 million for fighting the wilding pines in Marlborough, of which the fund received $335,000 for its 'ongoing and successful programme'.
20 Destination Marlborough, 'Details and data about Marlborough's visitor economy', year ended 2019.
21 Vern Harris, pers. comm., June 2021.
22 Jacqui Lloyd, pers. comm., June 2021.
23 Aquaculture NZ, *Aquaculture for New Zealand: A sector overview With Key Facts and Statistics for 2020.*
24 Information from the Marlborough District Council, based on its Infometrics database for aquaculture, and GDP and employment figures for tourism to March 2016.
25 Bev Doole, 'NZ King Salmon's proposal: What's the catch?' *NZ Listener*, 5 May 2012: www.noted.co.nz/archive/listener-nz-2012/nz-king-salmons-proposal-whats-the-catch/
26 Stephen (Bosun) Huntley, Evidence for Tahuaroa-Watson whānau, Board of Inquiry, King Salmon proposal, 2012; Laura Bowdler, Evidence of Laura Bowdler (née Keenan) for Tahuaroa-Watson whānau, Board of Inquiry, NZ King Salmon proposal, 2012.
27 Wendy McGuinness, 'Think piece 16 – NZ King Salmon: Was it a good decision for New Zealand?' (Wellington: McGuinness Institute, 2013): www.researchgate.net/publication/337208364_Think_Piece_16_-_New_Zealand_King_Salmon_Was_it_a_good_decision_for_New_Zealand
28 Marlborough District Council, *Marlborough District Council Long-term Plan, 2018–28*, p. 173.
29 Schuckard, 'Lip service'.
30 'A jaunt in the *Hinemoa*', *Evening Post*, 24 September 1892, p. 1, Supplement.
31 Miller Consulting, 'Some impacts of roading and flood damage on sounds roads part only – Queen Charlotte Drive and Kenepuru Road, 1985–2010': www.marlborough.govt.nz/environment/coastal/sedimentation
32 'State forests', *Daily Telegraph*, 26 January 1893, p. 2.
33 www.marlborough.govt.nz/environment/coastal/iwi-and-coastal-marlborough
34 Marlborough District Council, *2018–2029 Long-term Plan: Investing in Marlborough* (Blenheim: Marlborough District Council, 2019) p. 328.
35 RNZ, 'Marlborough's new aquaculture rules have a scent of a Treaty breach – iwi', RNZ, 11 May 2021: www.rnz.co.nz/news/ldr/441556/marlborough-s-new-aquaculture-rules-have-scent-of-a-treaty-breach-iwi
36 Waitangi Tribunal, *Te Tau Ihu*, vol. 3, pp. 1190, 1168–75, 1777.
37 Jeffrey Hynes, on behalf of Rangitāne, 22 April 2003 (doc. M12), p. 4 in ibid., pp. 1088–89.
38 Waitangi Tribunal, *Te Tau Ihu* Vol. 3, p. 1109.

Appendices

1 Mike Johnston, *Gold in a Tin Dish: The Search for Gold in Marlborough and Eastern Nelson*, vol. 2: *The History of the Eastern Marlborough Goldfields: The Northbank, Mahakipawa and Queen Charlotte Sound* (Nelson: Nikau Press, 1993), vol. 2, p. 125.
2 'District news', *Nelson Evening Mail*, 21 January 1902, p. 2
3 'Advertisements', *The Nelson Examiner and New Zealand Chronicle*, 21 April 1864, p. 2. Those nominated were applying to vote under the provisions of the Nelson Trust Funds Act 1854 and its amendment in 1863. The act gave one or two votes to both owners and occupiers in relation to the size of holdings; re the Long Island pilot see 'The late wreck', *NZ Spectator and Cook's Strait Guardian*, 14 June 1865, p. 4; re Robert Woodgate: Mike Taylor, pers. comm., in James Wallace,

Timeline, Resolution Bay, Family papers); re James Heberley on Long Island see 'Advertisements', column 2, *Wellington Independent*, 6 November 1869, p. 7. The island seems to have continued to be farmed – see Jas. Norton's application for a new lease – 'Marlborough Land Board', *ME*, 17 December 1903, p. 4. By 1911 the Long Island lease was for some 300 acres – see *ME*, 'Local and general news', 10 July 1911, p. 4.

4 R. J. Paterson, *The Sea Was Our Boundary: The Titirangi/Waitui Story of the Patersons 1929–1977* (self-published, 2011), p. 16.

5 Nola Leov, interview, October 2013; *AJHR*, 1908, F.–1, P&T p. xxiv for when the telegraph office was installed.

6 Re the Stuart brothers see Nola M. Leov & Margaret J. Turner, *Marriages Have Been Arranged: Life in Carluke, Autumn 1893* (Nelson: self-published, 2011). Note that Nola Leov now believes only William, not his brother, settled there then. Re Godsiff see Muriel Washington, 'The Hannah and Henry Godsiff family: Early settlers in the Pelorus Sound', undated, private papers.

7 Nola M. Leov & Margaret J. Turner, *And They Lived Happily Ever After: W. H. Turner's Family 1867–1871* (Nelson: self-published, 2010), p. 38.

8 'The Pelorus Sound', *Nelson Evening Mail*, 23 September 1880, p. 4.

9 'Local and general news: Pelorus Sound', *ME*, 15 June 1898, p. 2.

10 The source of the population figures ('The Census', *ME*, 27 May 1881, p. 2) does not cover the western side of Pelorus Sound, so information on people in, for instance, Gore Bay, Bulwer, Waitaria Bay and down to Tennyson Inlet is not available. Nor is it clear whether these figures include children.

11 Geoffrey Wilson, *Linkwater: A History* (Linkwater: Linkwater Settlers' Association, 1962), p. 67.

12 Nola M. Leov & Margaret J. Turner, *Best Laid Plans: Life in Carluke 1893–1894* (Nelson: self-published, 2011), p. 11; Wilson, *Linkwater*, p. 67 gives the date of the Archers' arrival in Worlds End as 1880. For the detail on Fred Fell see Nola M. Leov & Margaret J. Turner, *The Making of the Bridle Track to French Pass: A Salute to an Early Roadmaker, Jonathan Brough* (Nelson: Copy Press, 2015).

13 Leov & Turner, *Best Laid Plans*, p. 11.

14 Re the early Mills settlements see 'Local and general news: Obituary', *ME*, 30 August 1898, p. 2.

15 Oliver Sutherland, *Arthur Elmslie, Whaler and Gentleman, and Anaru, the Farm at French Pass* (Nelson: self-published 2006), p. 57.

16 This was presumably where Jane Hope's son Orry had leased in 1876. That manuscript spells Creighton as Crichton. At that point he was described as a chemist in Havelock see Hope family letters and Elizabeth's diary, Hope family papers, p. 30.

17 'Personal matters', *Evening Post*, 29 August 1928, p. 11; re the timber merchant stint see 'Obituary', *Evening Post*, 22 November 1941, p. 10.

18 Re the Scarborough Run and its position see 'The Marlborough Sounds: How the Census is taken', *Evening Post*, 9 May 1896, p. 1, which mentions goods being dropped off for Bowden in Endeavour Inlet. Bowden's obituary (*Evening Post*, 22 November 1941) states that he and his brother took up land in Dryden Bay. Were the materials dropped off in Endeavour Inlet, as a sheltered anchorage for the run? This is a possibility if the run was, as Steve Bagley of DOC, suggests, between Dryden Bay and the Inlet.

19 Nola M. Leov & Margaret J. Turner, *Marriages Have Been Arranged: Life in Carluke, Autumn 1893* (Nelson: self-published, 2011); 'The Marlborough Sounds: How the Census is taken'; re Neave see R. J. Paterson, *The Sea Was Our Boundary: The Titirangi/Waitui Story of the Patersons 1929–1977* (self-published, 2011), p. 16. Paterson gives the sale date as 1893 but the *Otago Witness* records the sale in 'Agricultural and pastoral', 11 May 1893, p. 12.

20 Carol Dawber, *The Jacksons of Te Awaiti* (Picton: River Press, 2001), p. 105.

21 For snapshots of small millers in 1903 see *AJHR*, 1903, C.–1 Lands, pp. 38–39. Alongside Brownlees, those millers were bit-players. That year Brownlees milled 3.14 million super feet and employed 58 men. Additionally, the horsepower of the equipment noted for the various small millers should be put alongside Brownlees' 64hp machines ('The timber industry', *ME*, 25 October 1905, p. 3).

22 In 1903 there were eight mills operating in the county, another was about to come onstream and the Harvey mill was soon to be moved to a new site.

23 Frank W. Ponder, *A Labyrinth of Waterways: The Forgotten Story of New Zealand's Marlborough Sounds* (Wellington: Wenlock House, 1986), p. 96.

24 Queen Charlotte Sound is little mentioned in the Sounds' milling history. There were almost no alluvial flats on which the big trees grew, and given milling charges and a lack of significant returns freeholders may have preferred to buy the land without milling rights, and burn the forest to break it in for farming rather than mill it (Brian R. Paton, 'Sawmill pioneers in the Pelorus', unpublished dissertation, Lincoln College, 1892, p. 12). See also *AJHR*, 1903, C.–1. Lands, p. 38 for the miller-specific information.

25 'The timber industry', *ME*, 25 October 1905, p. 3; John Wilson Brownlee, 'A brief history of the sawmilling industry in the Pelorus Sound district' (unpublished, 1939): www.peloruspeople.org.nz/havelockmuseum/index.mvc?ArticleID=2

Select Bibliography

Books

Akerblom, Pat & Barry, *A Finger in So Many Pies: Hon. Charles Houghton Mills, 1844–1923* (Blenheim: self-published, 2009).

Arnold, Rollo, *The Farthest Promised Land: English Villagers, New Zealand Immigrants of the 1870s* (Wellington: Victoria University Press, 1981).

Ault, H. F., *The Nelson Narrative: The Story of the Church of England in the Diocese of Nelson, New Zealand, 1858 to 1958, with an account of the years 1842 to 1857* (Nelson: Standing Committee of the Diocese of Nelson, 1958).

Barnett, Shaun & Chris Maclean, *Tramping: A New Zealand History* (Nelson: Potton & Burton, 2014).

Barrington, J. M. & T. H. Beaglehole, *Māori Schools in a Changing Society: An Historical Review* (Wellington: NZ Council for Educational Research, 1974), 26.

Barrington, John, *Separate But Equal?: Māori Schools and the Crown, 1867–1969* (Wellington: Victoria University Press, 2008).

Barratt, Glynn, *Bellingshausen: A Visit to New Zealand, 1820* (Palmerston North: Dunmore Press, 1979).

Barratt, Glynn (ed.), *Queen Charlotte Sound, New Zealand: The Traditional and European Records, 1820* (Ottawa, Canada: Carleton University Press, 1987).

Beaglehole, Helen, *Lighting the Coast: A History of New Zealand's Coastal Lighthouse System* (Christchurch: Canterbury University Press, 2006).

Beaglehole, Helen, *Always the Sound of the Sea: The Daily Lives of New Zealand's Lighthouse Keepers* (Nelson: Potton & Burton, 2009).

Beaglehole, Helen, *Fire in the Hills: A History of Rural Fire-fighting* (Christchurch: Canterbury University Press, 2012).

Beaglehole, J. C. (ed.) *The Journals of Captain James Cook*, vol. 1: *The Voyage of the* Endeavour, *1768–1771* (Cambridge: Cambridge University Press for the Hakluyt Society, 1955).

Beaglehole, J. C. (ed.), *The Journals of Captain James Cook*, vol. 2: *The Voyage of the* Resolution *and* Adventure, *1772–1775* (Cambridge: Cambridge University Press for the Hakluyt Society, 1961).

Beaglehole, J. C. (ed.), *Banks's* Endeavour *Journal*, vol. 1 (Sydney: Trustees of the Public Library of New South Wales in association with Angus & Robertson, 1963).

Beaglehole, J. C. (ed.), *The Journals of Captain James Cook*, vol. 3: *The Voyage of the* Resolution *and* Discovery, *1779–1780*, parts 1 & 2 (Cambridge: Cambridge University Press for the Hakluyt Society, 1967).

Beaglehole, J. C., *The Life of Captain James Cook* (London: Hakluyt Society, 1974).

Beauchamp, Harold & Ethel Broughton Hazelwood, *Reminiscences and Recollections* (New Plymouth: T. Avery, 1937).

Beck, Russell with Maika Mason, *Pounamu: The Jade of New Zealand* (Auckland: Viking/Te Runanga o Ngāi Tahu, 2010).

Begg, A. Charles & C. Neil, *James Cook and New Zealand: The Voyage of the* Endeavour, *1768–1771; the Voyage of the* Resolution *and* Adventure, *1772–1775; the Voyage of the* Resolution *and* Discovery, *1776–1780* (Wellington: Government Printer, 1969).

Berry, Ken, *Scrutiny on the County* (Blenheim: Marlborough County Council, 1986).

Bester, R. (ed.), *Harvest of Grace: Essays in Celebration of 150 Years of Mission in the Anglican Diocese of Nelson* (Nelson: Standing Committee of the Diocese of Nelson, 2010).

Brailsford, Barry, *The Tattooed Land: The Southern Frontiers of the Pa Maori* (Auckland: Reed, 1981).

Brehaut, Loreen A. & Mike Taylor, *Whekenui School, 1951–62: A Very Remote School* (Picton: Picton Historical Society, 2008).

Brooking, Tom, *Lands for the People? The Highland Clearances and the Colonisation of New Zealand, a biography of John McKenzie* (Dunedin: Otago University Press, 1996).

Brown, Derek, *Stephens Island: Ark of the Light* (Havelock: self-published, 2000).

Buchanan, Rachel, *Ko Taranaki Te Maunga* (Wellington: Bridget Williams Books, 2018).

Buckland, Shirley, *Reflections on a Lifetime* (Nelson: self-published, 2007).

Buick, T. L., *Old Marlborough* (Palmerston North: Hart and Keeling, 1900).

Butchers, A. G., *Education in New Zealand: An Historical Account of Educational Progress Amongst the Europeans and the Maoris since 1878* (Dunedin: Coulls Somerville Wilkie, 1930).

Calder, Alex, Jonathan Lamb & Bridget Orr, *Voyages and Beaches: Pacific Encounters, 1769–1840* (Honolulu: University of Hawaii Press, 1999).

Chapman, G. T., *Chapman's Traveller's Guide through New Zealand: A picture of New*

Zealand, Geographical, Topographical and Statistical (self-published, c.1872).

Condliffe, J. B., *New Zealand in the Making: A Study of Economic and Social Development* (London: Allen & Unwin, 1963).

Cooke, Peter, *Defending New Zealand: Ramparts on the Sea 1840–1950s* (Wellington: Defence of New Zealand Study Group, 2000).

Cowan, James, *The Marlborough and Nelson Districts* (Wellington: Department of Tourist and Health Resorts, 1909).

Cyclopedia of New Zealand (Nelson, Marlborough & Westland Provincial Districts), The (Christchurch: Cyclopedia Company Ltd, 1906): http://nzetc.victoria.ac.nz/tm/scholarly/tei-Cyc05Cycl-t1-body1-d2-d28-d14.html

Daley, Caroline, *Leisure & Pleasure: Reshaping and Revealing the New Zealand Body 1900–1960* (Auckland: Auckland University Press, 2003).

David, Andrew, Rüdiger Joppien & Bernard Smith (eds), *The Charts and Coastal Views of Captain Cook's Voyages: The voyage of the* Endeavour, *1768–1771* (London: Hakluyt Society, 1988).

Dawber, Carol, *Lines in the Water: A History of Greenshell Mussel Farming in New Zealand* (Picton: River Press for NZ Marine Farming Association, 2004)

Dawber, Carol, *The Jacksons of Te Awaiti* (Picton: River Press, 2001).

Dieffenbach, Ernst, *Travels in New Zealand, with contributions to the geography, geology, botany, and natural history of that country* (Capper reprint, 1974: Early New Zealand Books: enzb.auckland.ac.nz).

Dougherty, Ian, *The Making of the French Pass Road in the Marlborough Sounds* (Auckland: No Ordinary Life, 2008).

Elvy, W. J., *Kei Puta te Wairau: A History of Marlborough in Maori Times* (Christchurch: Whitcombe & Tombs, 1997).

Fell, Yvonne M., *Boats for a Lifetime*, 3rd edn (Blenheim: self-published, 2008).

Fitzgerald, Tony, *It's Our Life: An Imperfect History of the Waikawa Boating Club Inc., 1950–2017* (Blenheim: Waikawa Boating Club, 2017).

Forster, Georg, *A Voyage round the World in His Britannic Majesty's Sloop,* Resolution, *during the Years 1772, 3, 4, and 5* (London: Printed for B. White, J. Robson, P. Elmsly, G. Robinson, 1787).

Furey, Louise, *Māori Gardening: An Archaeological Perspective* (Wellington: Department of Conservation, 2006).

Furness, Donald, *Tahuahua: The Story of Blackwood Bay, Queen Charlotte Sound* (Blenheim: self-published, 1974).

Grady, Don, *Still More Grady's People: Still More Unforgettable Characters in the Top of the South Island* (Nelson: Nikau Press, 2004).

Grady, Don, *The Perano Whalers of Cook Strait, 1911–1964* (Wellington: A. H. & A. W. Reed, 1982).

Harvey, G. J. C. (John), *Where There's a Will There's a Way: Memories of My Childhood and Sawmilling Days in the Marlborough Sounds* (Blenheim: self-published, 2008).

Hazelwood, Ethel Beauchamp, *Life at Anakiwa: The First 100 Years 1863–1963* (Anakiwa: self-published, 1974?).

Heberley, Heather, *Riding with Whales: Stories of Great Sounds Women* (Picton: Cape Catley, 1999).

Hoare, Michael (ed.), *The* Resolution *Journal of Johann Reinhold Forster 1772–1775*, in four volumes (London: Hakluyt Society, 1982).

Horton, Tom, *Pelorus District Ambulance, 1967–92* (Havelock, 1991). Held at the Havelock Museum.

Houghton, Philip, *The First New Zealanders* (Auckland: Hodder & Stoughton, 1980).

Howes, Edith, *Marlborough Sounds: The Waters of Restfulness* (Auckland: Whitcombe & Tombs, 1919).

Johnston, Mike, *Gold in a Tin Dish: The Search for Gold in Marlborough and Eastern Nelson*, vol. 2: *The History of the Eastern Marlborough Goldfields: The Northbank, Mahakipawa and Queen Charlotte Sound* (Nelson: Nikau Press, 1993).

Kelly, Henry D., *As High as the Hills: The Centennial History of Picton* (Picton: Cape Catley, 1976).

Kennedy, Julie, *Picton and Queen Charlotte Sound: A Chronology* (Picton: Picton Historical Society, 2013).

King-Turner, Carol, *Pioneer Nurse in the Marlborough Sounds* (Rai Valley: s elf-published, 2004).

Laffan, M. D., B. K. Daly & J. S. Whitton, *Soils of the Marlborough Sounds* (Nelson: Soil Bureau, Department of Scientific and Industrial Research, 1987).

Leach, Foss, *Fishing in Pre-European New Zealand* (jointly published by the *New Zealand Journal of Archaeology* and *Archaeofauna*, 2006).

Leov, Nola M. (compiled by) *The Sounds in Wartime: A celebration of the contribution to the war effort made by an isolated New Zealand community 1939–45* (Te Towaka 50th Anniversary Home Guard Sports Committee, 1996).

Leov, Nola M. & Margaret J. Turner, *And They Lived Happily Ever After: W. H. Turner's Family 1867–1871* (Nelson: self-published, 2010).

Leov, Nola M. & Margaret J. Turner, *Changes: Rai Valley, 1901–1902*, (Nelson: self-published, 2014).

Leov, Nola M. & Margaret J. Turner, *Highs and Lows: Changes in the Lives of the Turners of Carluke, and improving access to the outside world, 1892–1893* (Nelson: self-published, 2011).

Leov, Nola M. & Margaret J. Turner, *Intermezzo: The Fortunes of the Turner Family and the Evolution of Rai Valley, 1885–1892* (Nelson: self-published, 2011)

Leov, Nola M. & Margaret J. Turner, *Best Laid Plans: Life in Carluke 1893–1894* (Nelson: self-published, 2011).

Leov, Nola M. & Margaret J. Turner, *Marriages Have Been Arranged: Life in Carluke, Autumn 1893* (Nelson: self-published, 2011).

Leov, Nola M. & Margaret J. Turner, *Why Carluke? The Turners and their English cousins, 1881–1882*, (Nelson: self-published, 2010).

Leov, Nola M. & Margaret J. Turner, *The Pelorus Guardian and the Park, 1989–1899*, (Nelson: self-published, 2012).

Leov, Nola M. & Margaret J. Turner, *Slough of Despond* (Nelson: self-published, 2013).

Leov, Nola M. & Margaret J. Turner, *The Making of the Bridle Track to French Pass: A Salute to an Early Roadmaker, Jonathan Brough* (Nelson: Copy Press, 2015).

Locke, Cybèle, *'The Poorest Tribe under the Heavens': Ngati Kuia's Socio-economic Circumstances, 1856–1950*, research report commissioned by Crown Forestry Rental Trust, Wellington, 2002.

MacIntosh A. D., *Marlborough: A Provincial History* (Blenheim: Marlborough Provincial Historical Committee, 1940).

Mackay, Deirdre, *Voices from the Sea: The Stories of Some Nelson and Marlborough Fishing Families* (Motueka: Talley's Group, 2004).

Maclean, Chris, *John Pascoe* (Nelson: Craig Potton Publishing/Whitcombe Press, 2003).

Mansfield, Katherine, *Selected Stories* (London: Oxford University Press, 1953).

Marlborough District Council, *2018–2029: Long-term Plan: Investing in Marlborough*, (Blenheim: Marlborough District Council, 2019).

Marlborough Progress League, *Marlborough the Golden, New Zealand* (Blenheim, 1920).

Mason, Lorna, *Cockle Cove: Marlborough Sounds Haven for Four Generations* (Picton: Cape Catley, 2000).

McCaskill, L. W., *Scenic Reserves of Marlborough* (Wellington: Department of Lands and Survey, 1981).

McNab, Robert, *The Old Whaling Days: A History of Southern New Zealand from 1830 to 1840* (Auckland: Golden Press, 1975 [1913]).
Mitchells, Hilary and John, *Te Tau Ihu o Te Waka: A History of the Māori of Nelson and Marlborough*, vol. 1: *Te Tangata me te Whenua / The People and the Land* (Wellington: Huia Publishers, 2004).
Mitchells, Hilary and John, *Te Tau Ihu o Te Waka: A History of Maori of Nelson and Marlborough*, vol. 2: *Te Ara Hou / The New Society* (Wellington: Huia Publishers, 2007).
Mitchells, Hilary and John, *Te Tau Ihu o Te Waka: A History of the Māori of Nelson and Marlborough*, vol. 3: *Nga Tupuna / The Ancestors* (Wellington: Huia Publishers, 2009).
Mitchells, Hilary and John, *Te Tau Ihu o Te Waka: A History of the Māori of Nelson and Marlborough*, vol. 4: *Ngā Whānau Rangatira o Ngāti Tama me Te Ātiawa / The Chiefly Families of Ngāti Tama and Te Ātiawa* (Nelson/Picton: Ngā whānau rangatira o Ngāti Tama me Te Ātiawa, 2014).
Munford, James Kenneth (ed.), *John Ledyard's Journal of Captain Cook's Last Voyage* (Corvallis: Oregon State University Press, 1963).
Neal, Kerry & Nola M. Leov et al., *The Price of Vigilance: The Building of the Gun Emplacements in the Marlborough Sounds, 1942* (Nelson: self-published, 1999).
New Zealand Forestry League, *Rules and Objects of the New Zealand Forestry League (inc)* (Wellington: Watkins, Tyer & Tolan, 1916).
Noonan, Rosslyn J., *By Design: A Brief History of the Public Works Department, Ministry of Works, 1870–1970* (Wellington: Government Printer, 1975).
North, Michael, *The Story of the Friends of Nelson Haven & Tasman Bay* (Nelson: Friends of Nelson Haven & Tasman Bay, 2007).
Orchard, Lorna, *Time and Tide Waits for No Man* (Blenheim: Yvonne Fell, 2004).
Parkes, Elizabeth K., *Better Prospects: The Parkes Family History* (Nelson: self-published, 1986).
Paterson, Lachy & Angela Wanhalla, *He Reo Wahine: Māori Women's Voices from the Nineteenth Century* (Auckland: Auckland University Press, 2017).
Paterson, R. J., *The Sea Was Our Boundary: The Titirangi/Waitui Story of the Patersons 1929–1977* (self-published, 2011).
Pawson, Eric & Tom Brooking (eds), *Making a New Land: Environmental Histories of New Zealand*, 2nd edn (Dunedin: Otago University Press, 2013).
Peart, Raewyn, *The Story of the Hauraki Gulf: Discovery /Transformation /*

Restoration (Auckland: David Bateman/Environmental Society, 2016).
Picton & Sounds Promotion Society, *Picton and the Marlborough Sounds: The finest holiday resort in the Dominion of New Zealand: A descriptive booklet containing views and descriptive matter designed to set forth in a compendius [sic] form the attractions of this picturesque country* (Picton: 1910–11).
Ponder, Frank W., *A Labyrinth of Waterways: The Forgotten Story of New Zealand's Marlborough Sounds* (Wellington: Wenlock House, 1986).
Potton, Craig, *The Story of Marlborough Sounds Maritime Park* (Blenheim: Marlborough Sounds Maritime Park Board, 1986).
Prickett, Nigel, *The Archaeology of New Zealand Shore Whaling* (Wellington: Department of Conservation, 2002).
Ramshaw, Kevin & Bettina Maniatis (eds), *Interislander: A Ferry Tale: Connecting New Zealand for 50 Years, 1962–2012*: https://issuu.com/inflightpublishing/docs/interislander_50th_mag
Reed, A. H., *Marlborough Journey* (Auckland: A. H. & A. W. Reed, 1963).
Robb, Flora, *St Omer House: Family Life in the Guest House and some Sounds History* (Nelson: self-published, 2013).
Rowe, Betty, *Arapawa: Once Upon an Island* (Auckland: Halcyon Press, 1988).
Salmond, Anne, *The Trial of the Cannibal Dog: Captain Cook in the South Seas* (London/Auckland: Allen Lane/Penguin, 2003/2004).
Simpson, Thomas E., *Kauri to Radiata: Origin and Expansion of the Timber Industry of New Zealand* (Auckland: Hodder & Stoughton, 1973).
Soons, J. M. & M. J. Selby (eds), *Landforms of New Zealand* (Auckland: Longman Paul, 1992).
Sutherland, Oliver, *Arthur Elmslie, Whaler and Gentleman, and Anaru, the Farm at French Pass* (Nelson: self-published, 2006).
Taylor, Mike, *The History of Waikawa School, Queen Charlotte Sound* (Christchurch: self-published, 2012).
Taylor, Nancy M., *The New Zealand People at War*, vol. 1: *The Home Front* (Wellington: Historical Publications Branch, Department of Internal Affairs, 1986).
Trotter, Michael M., *Marlborough Sounds Archaeological Survey 1974* (Christchurch: Canterbury Museum, 1974).
Trotter, Michael M., *Titirangi Archaeology: An Interim Report* (Christchurch: Canterbury Museum, 1977).
Trotter, Michael M., *Archaeological Site Survey of East Bay, Arapawa Island* (Christchurch: Canterbury Museum, 1978).

Wakefield, Edward Jerningham, *Adventure in New Zealand from 1839 to 1844 with Some Account of the Beginning of the British Colonization of the Islands* (London: John Murray, 1845), sourced from University of Auckland Library Early New Zealand Books Project.

Willis, Arthur, Gann & Co., *The New Zealand Handbook, or, Guide to the 'Britain of the South': A description of the provinces of . . . together with the latest information on every subject needed by the capitalist-emigrant and the working man* (London: E. Stanford, 1862).

Willmott, Bill (ed.), *New Zealand and the World: Essays in Honour of Wolfgang Rosenberg* (Christchurch: self-published, 1980).

Wilson, Geoffrey, *Linkwater: A History* (Linkwater: Linkwater Settlers' Association, 1962).

Young, David, *Maori Society and the State in Colonial and Post-colonial Te Tau Ihu, 1880–1960: A Survey of Official Archives* (Wellington: Crown Forestry Rental Trust, 1999).

Book chapters & journal/magazine articles

Andrews, J., 'The road', *Journal of the Nelson and Marlborough Historical Societies*, vol. 1, 6 October 1985: http://nzetc.victoria.ac.nz/tm/scholarly/tei-NHSJ04_05-t1-body1-d4-d2.html

Arnold, Rollo, 'The virgin forest harvest and the development of colonial New Zealand', *NZ Geographer* 32 (1976), 105–26.

Barber, Ian, 'Molluscan mulching at the margins: Investigating the development of a South Island Maori variation on Polynesian hard mulch agronomy', *Archaeology in Oceania* 48 (2013).

Barber, Ian, 'Early contact ethnography and understanding: An evaluation of the Cook expeditionary accounts of the Grass Cove Conflict'. In Alex Calder, Jonathan Lamb & Bridget Orr, *Voyages and Beaches: Pacific Encounters, 1769–1840* (Honolulu: University of Hawai'i Press, 1999).

Berthold, Martin, 'Sounds Wrecking Company: Shipwreckers, breakers and recyclers, Wakatahuri [sic], Outer Pelorus Sound', *NZ Marine News*, vol. 56, no. 3 (60th anniversary issue, 2009).

Brooking, Tom, 'Use it or lose it: Unravelling the land debate in late 19th-century New Zealand', *NZ Journal of History*, vol. 30, no. 2 (October 1996), 141–45.

Brough, Jonathan, 'Tracks', *The Colonist*, 31 December 1900, p. 4.

Brownlee, John Wilson, 'A brief history of the sawmilling industry in the Pelorus Sound district' (unpublished, 1939): www.peloruspeople.org.nz/havelockmuseum/index.mvc?ArticleID=2

Burtenshaw, M, G. Harris, J. Davidson & F. Leach, 'Experimental growing of pre-European cultivars of kūmara (sweet potato, *Ipomoea batatas* L. Lam.) at the southern margins of Māori horticulture', *NZ Journal of Archaeology* 23 (2001).

Clendon, Jill, 'Public health nurses in New Zealand: The impact of invisibility', *Nursing Praxis in New Zealand*: www.nursingpraxis.org/172-public-health-nurses-in-new-zealand-the-impact-of-invisibility.html

Cunningham, J. M., 'Obituary, R. H. D. Stidolph: Some reminiscences', *Notornis*, vol. 27 (1980).

Daley, Paul, 'Ataturk's "Johnnies and Memmets": Words about the Anzacs are shrouded in doubt': www.theguardian.com/news/2015/apr/20/ataturks-johnnies-and-mehmets-words-about-the-anzacs-are-shrouded-in-doubt

Doole, Bev, 'NZ King Salmon's proposal: What's the catch?' *NZ Listener*, 5 May 2012: www.noted.co.nz/archive/listener-nz-2012/nz-king-salmons-proposal-whats-the-catch

Egerton, Rachael, 'Unconquerable enemy or bountiful resource? A new perspective on the rabbit in Central Otago', *Australian & New Zealand Environmental History Network*, vol. 9, no. 1 (18 March 2014).

Forest & Bird, 'Manapouri: A Green awakening': www.forestandbird.org.nz/what-we-do/publications/forest-bird-magazine/articles-archive/manapouri-green-awakening

Hemphill, Dallas, 'Pine forests in the Pelorus Sound from 1900 to 1970', *NZ Tree Grower,* May 2021.

Johnston, Judith A., 'New Zealand bush: Early assessments of vegetation', *NZ Geographer* (April 1981).

Keenan, Danny, 'The trouble with the NZ wars', *The Dominion Post*, 4 July 2019.

Laffan, M. D. & B. K. Daly, 'Soil resources of the Marlborough Sounds and the implications for exotic production forestry. 1. Soil resources and limitations to exotic forest growth', *NZ Journal of Forestry* 30 , no. 1 (1985).

McCaskill, L. W., *Scenic Reserves of Marlborough* (Wellington: Department of Lands and Survey, 1981).

McGuinness, Wendy, 'Think piece 16 – NZ King Salmon: Was it a good decision for

New Zealand?' (Wellington: McGuinness Institute, 2013): www.researchgate.net/publication/337208364_Think_Piece_16_-_New_Zealand_King_Salmon_Was_it_a_good_decision_for_New_Zealand

Meihana, Peter N. & Cecil R. Bradley, 'Repatriation, reconciliation and the inversion of patriarchy', *Journal of the Polynesian Society* 127 (2018): 307–24.

Miskelly, Colin, 'Legal protection of New Zealand's indigenous terrestrial fauna: An historical review', *Tuhinga* 25, 25–101.

Orchard, John, 'A short history of sawmilling in the Nydia Bay area', *Journal of the Nelson and Marlborough Historical Societies*, vol. 2, 1 (1987): http://nzetc.victoria.ac.nz/tm/scholarly/tei-NHSJ05_01-t1-body1-d4.html

Perry, Nigel, 'Recollections of the early Waikawa Boating Club' first appeared in *The Seaport News* (November 2007): http://waikawaboatingclub.co.nz/about/history/

O'Regan, Stephen, 'Queen Charlotte Sound: Aspects of Maori traditional history'. In Glynn Barratt (ed.), *Queen Charlotte Sound, New Zealand: The Traditional and European Records, 1820* (Ottawa, Canada: Carleton University Press, 1987).

Robertson, R. T., 'Government responses to unemployment in New Zealand, *1929–35*': www.nzjh.auckland.ac.nz/docs/1982/NZJH_16_1_03.pdf

Schuckard, Rob, 'Lip service: Working group member reflects on the future of aquaculture in Marlborough', 25 February 2021: www.stuff.co.nz/business/farming/300236368/lip-service-working-group-member-reflects-on-the-future-of-aquaculture-in-marlborough

Simpson, Heather, 'Marlborough District Council considers tightening forestry rules': www.stuff.co.nz/environment/74635822/marlborough-district-council-considers-tightening-forestry-rules

Smith, S. P., 'History and traditions of the Taranaki coast: The South Island raids', *Journal of the Polynesian Society*, vol. 18, no. 4 (1909), 186–87.

Trotter, Michael M., 'Marlborough Sounds prehistory', *Map of the Marlborough Sounds*, NZMZ 301, Edition 1 (Department of Lands & Survey).

Trotter, Michael M., 'Settlements, sites and structures around Ship Cove'. In Glynn Barratt (ed.), *Queen Charlotte Sound, New Zealand: The Traditional and European Records, 1820* (Ottawa, Canada: Carleton University Press, 1987).

Wilkinson, Iris (Robin Hyde), 'On the road to anywhere', *NZ Railways Magazine* 10, no. 3 (1 June 1935).

Online resources

Aimer, Peter, 'Aviation: An aviation industry', Te Ara: www.TeAra.govt.nz/en/aviation/page-3

Barnicoat, John Wallis: http://demo.recollect.co.nz/nodes/view/168

Bay of Many Coves website: https://bayofmanycoves.co.nz/about-us

Biotechnology Learning Hub, 'How mussels are farmed in NZ': www.biotechlearn.org.nz

Boast, Richard, 'Te tango whenua – Māori land alienation – Pre-Treaty transactions', Te Ara: www.TeAra.govt.nz/en/te-tango-whenua-maori-land-alienation/page-2

Bowe, Chris, 'The legacy of Picton boat-builder Ernie Lane': www.cleanweb.co.nz/abode/708/documents/Ernest%20Richard%20Lane.pdf and https://waitematawoodys.com/tag/ernie-lane/

Brehaut, Loreen, 'Sounds mailboats': www.theprow.org.nz/enterprise/Sounds-mailboats/#.VTAwcSgVrHg

Burton, David, 'Cooking – Cooking technology', Te Ara: www.TeAra.govt.nz/en/cooking/page-1

Butterworth, Graham, 'Grace, John Te Herekiekie', DNZB, Te Ara: www.TeAra.govt.nz/en/biographies/5g14/grace-john-te-herekiekie

Byrnes, Giselle M., 'Smith, Stephenson Percy', DNZB, Te Ara: www.TeAra.govt.nz/en/biographies/2s33/smith-stephenson-percy

Calman, Ross, 'Māori education – Mātauranga – The native schools system, 1867 to 1969', Te Ara: www.TeAra.govt.nz/en/maori-education-matauranga/page-3

Church, Ian, 'Pezant, Jean Étienne', DNZB, Te Ara: www.TeAra.govt.nz/en/biographies/1p14/pezant-jean-etienne

'Classic wooden boat stories': waitematawoodys.com/tag/chas-bailey-jnr/

Copper Development Assoc. Inc., 'The evolution of the telephone cable': www.copper.org/applications/telecomm/consumer/evolution.html

'Distribution of Electricity by Local Authorities', Te Ara: www.teara.govt.nz/en/1966/power-resources/page-5 (unrevised from A. H. McLintock (ed.), *An Encyclopaedia of New Zealand*, 1966)

Easton, Brian, 'Brexit: How New Zealand might cope': http://pundit.co.nz/content/brentry-how-new-zealand-coped

Envirohistory NZ, 'The end of whaling in New Zealand: The Soviet factor': http://envirohistorynz.com/2011/06/18/the-end-of-whaling-in-new-zealand-the-soviet-factor

Environment Guide: www.environmentguide.org.nz/activities/land-use/a-brief-history-of-town-planning

Evison, Harry C., 'Mackay, James', DNZB, Te Ara: https://teara.govt.nz/en/biographies/1m29/mackay-james

Flude, Anthony G., 'Whaling in early New Zealand': http://homepages.ihug.co.nz/~tonyf/whale/whaling.html, 2001

Forest and Bird, 'Manapouri: A Green awakening': www.forestandbird.org.nz/what-we-do/publications/forest-bird-magazine/articles-archive/manapouri-green-awakening

Grady, Don, 'Guard, Elizabeth', DNZB, Te Ara: www.TeAra.govt.nz/en/biographies/1g23/guard-elizabeth

Grady, Don, 'Jackson, James Hayter', DNZB, Te Ara: https://teara.govt.nz/en/biographies/1j1/jackson-james-hayter

Gregg, Paul, 'Soil erosion and conservation – Legislation and catchment boards, 1940s–1950s', Te Ara: www.TeAra.govt.nz/en/soil-erosion-and-conservation/page-5

Hopa, Ngapare, 'Ngā rōpū – Māori organisations – New Māori organisations, early 20th century', Te Ara: www.TeAra.govt.nz/en/nga-ropu-maori-organisations/page-2

Lange, Raeburn, 'Te hauora Māori i mua – History of Māori health – Health improves, 1900 to 1920', Te Ara: www.TeAra.govt.nz/en/te-hauora-maori-i-mua-history-of-maori-health/page-3

Leov, Nola M., 'The Brownlees enterprise': www.theprow.org.nz/yourstory/the-brownlees-enterprise/#.WUMSTjOB3yt

Leov, L. C., 'Rai Valley sawmills', *Journal of the Nelson Historical Society* 3, 1: www.nzetc.org/tm/scholarly/tei-NHSJ03_01-t1-body1-d8.html

McGibbon, Ian, 'Cobham, Charles John Lyttelton', from DNZB, Te Ara: www.TeAra.govt.nz/en/biographies/5c27/cobham-charles-john-lyttelton

McGibbon, Ian, 'Second World War – Japan enters the war', Te Ara: www.TeAra.govt.nz/en/photograph/34574/home-guard

McKinnon, Malcolm, 'Colonial and provincial government – Julius Vogel and the abolition of provincial government', Te Ara: www.TeAra.govt.nz/en/colonial-and-provincial-government/page-4

McKinnon, Malcolm, 'Marlborough region – Government', Te Ara: www.TeAra.govt.nz/en/marlborough-region/page-10

McKinnon, Malcolm, 'Marlborough region – Transport and communications', Te Ara: www.TeAra.govt.nz/en/marlborough-region/page-9

Ministry for Culture and Heritage, 'Education Act passed into law': https://nzhistory.govt.nz/page/education-act-passed-law
Ministry for Culture and Heritage, 'Homosexual law reform – Setting the scene': https://nzhistory.govt.nz/culture/homosexual-law-reform/setting-the-scene
Ministry for Culture and Heritage, 'Impact of the Korean War': https://nzhistory.govt.nz/war/korean-war/impact
Ministry for Culture and Heritage, 'Scenery preservation in New Zealand': https://nzhistory.govt.nz/culture/scenery-preservation
Ministry for Culture and Heritage, 'The Wairau incident': https://nzhistory.govt.nz/war/wairau-incident
Ministry for Culture and Heritage, 'War work': https://nzhistory.govt.nz/war/second-world-war-at-home/war-work
Mitchells, Hilary & John, 'Wairau Affray': www.theprow.org.nz/maori/wairau-affray
Nathan, Simon, 'Conservation – a history – Changing organisations and ideas, 1985–2010s', Te Ara: www.TeAra.govt.nz/en/conservation-a-history/page-10
New Zealand Maritime Record: www.nzmaritime.co.nz/r301.htm
Nightingale, Tony, 'Government and agriculture – Formation of the Department of Agriculture', Te Ara: www.TeAra.govt.nz/en/government-and-agriculture/page-4
Papers Past: https://paperspast.natlib.govt.nz
Patete, Anthony, 'Patete, Haimona', DNZB, Te Ara: www.TeAra.govt.nz/en/biographies/3p14/patete-haimona
Pawson, Eric, 'Cars and the motor industry – A motorised society', Te Ara: www.TeAra.govt.nz/en/cars-and-the-motor-industry/page-1
Phillips, Jock, 'History and historians – The first half of the 20th century – amateur history', Te Ara: www.TeAra.govt.nz/en/history-and-historians/page-2
Phillips, Jock, 'Whaling – Māori and whaling', Te Ara: www.TeAra.govt.nz/en/whaling/page-4
Phillips, Jock, 'Whaling – Modern whaling and whale watching', Te Ara: www.TeAra.govt.nz/en/whaling/page-5
Pool, Ian & Tahu Kukutai, 'Taupori Māori – Māori population change – Population changes, 1769–1840', Te Ara: www.TeAra.govt.nz/en/interactive/31311/maori-population-1841-2006
Pōmare, Mīria, 'Ngāti Toarangatira – 19th century: Rise and fall', Te Ara: www.TeAra.govt.nz/en/ngati-toarangatira
Popay, Ian, 'Weeds of agriculture – Weeds in pasture, crops and forestry', Te Ara:

www.TeAra.govt.nz/en/weeds-of-agriculture/page-2

Port Ligar history: www.waterfallbay.co.nz/history.html

Rare Breeds Conservation Society of New Zealand: www.rarebreeds.co.nz

Rowe, Betty, profile at International Arapawa Goats Association: www.arapawagoats.com/betty.html

Rural Women, 'Our history – from small beginnings': www.ruralwomen.org.nz/about_us/history.html

Schmidt, Andrew, 'Dental care – Dental nurses to dental therapists', Te Ara: www.TeAra.govt.nz/en/dental-care/page-4

Shoebridge, Tim, 'Mail and couriers – Mail in the 20th century', Te Ara: www.TeAra.govt.nz/en/mail-and-couriers/page-3

Smith, F. W., 'Samuel Ironside and the Cloudy Bay Mission': www.methodist.org.nz/files/docs/wesley%20historical/11(1)%20samuel%20ironside%20.pdf

Stephens, Joy, 'Power to the people': www.theprow.org.nz/enterprise/power-to-the-people/#.WO7nmVKB3MV

Stephens, Joy, 'Havelock': www.theprow.org.nz/places/havelock/#Main_content

Stringleman, Hugh & Scrimgeour, Frank, 'Dairying and dairy products – Cooperatives and centralisation', Te Ara: www.TeAra.govt.nz/en/dairying-and-dairy-products/page-3

Stringleman, Hugh & Peden, Robert, 'Sheep farming – The refrigerated meat trade', Te Ara: www.TeAra.govt.nz/en/sheep-farming/page-5

Swarbrick, Nancy, 'Aerial recreation – Flying powered aircraft', Te Ara: www.TeAra.govt.nz/en/aerial-recreation/page-2

Swarbrick, Nancy, 'Canoeing and rafting – Early canoeing', Te Ara: www.TeAra.govt.nz/en/photograph/13079/rob-roy-canoes

Swarbrick, Nancy, 'Country schooling – Getting an education: 1800s', Te Ara: www.TeAra.govt.nz/en/country-schooling/page-1

Swarbrick, Nancy, 'Country schooling – Wider options: 1900s–1930s', Te Ara: www.TeAra.govt.nz/en/country-schooling/page-2

Swarbrick, Nancy, 'Primary and secondary education – Teachers', Te Ara: www.TeAra.govt.nz/en/primary-and-secondary-education/page-8

Swarbrick, Nancy, 'Rural services – Health', Te Ara: www.TeAra.govt.nz/en/rural-services/page-7

Taonui, Rāwiri, 'Te ture – Māori and legislation – Laws affecting Māori land': Te Ara: www.TeAra.govt.nz/en/te-ture-maori-and-legislation

Tai Awatea Knowledge Net, 'Jacky Guard and his family': http://tpo.tepapa.govt.nz/ViewTopicExhibitDetail.asp?TopicFileID=0x000a4d73

Te Whānau ā Apanui, 'Māori language in the education system': www.apanui.co.nz/aa-home/directory/peter-shields-home-page/the-treaty-of-waitangi/history/tereomaori

Tolerton, Jane, 'Agricultural processing industries – Freezing works, 1880s to the 1970s', Te Ara: www.TeAra.govt.nz/en/agricultural-processing-industries/page-7

Union Steam Ship Company ships list: www.theshipslist.com/ships/lines/unionnz.shtml

Walrond, Carl, 'Roads – Funding road construction', Te Ara: www.TeAra.govt.nz/en/roads/page-5

Watson, James, 'Farm mechanisation – Steam, wind, water and oil', Te Ara: www.TeAra.govt.nz/en/farm-mechanisation/page-3

Wilson, A. C., 'Telecommunications – Early telegraphy and telegrams', Te Ara: www.TeAra.govt.nz/en/interactive/21998/telegraph-spreads

Wilson, John, 'European discovery of New Zealand – Cook's achievement', Te Ara: www.TeAra.govt.nz/en/european-discovery-of-new-zealand/page-6

Official documents

Aquaculture New Zealand, *Aquaculture for New Zealand: A Sector Overview with Key Facts and Statistics for 2020.*

Census and Statistics Office, *Agricultural and Pastoral Production of the Dominion of New Zealand 1922–21, 1932–32, 1940–41*, Census and Statistics Office, Wellington.

Controller and Auditor-General, *Government Planning and Support for Housing on Maori Land*, Appendix: Summary of the legislation about Maori Land (2011): www.oag.govt.nz/2011/housing-on-maori-land/appendix.htm

Department of Conservation, 'A history of wildlife translocations in the Marlborough Sounds' (2008): www.doc.govt.nz/documents/conservation/wildlife-translocations-small.pdf

Department of Conservation, 'Our beautiful environment: 1953 to the present': www.doc.govt.nz/Documents/science-and-technical/OurPicturesqueHeritage.pdf

Department of Conservation, 'Potential effect of mussel farming on New Zealand's marine . . .': www.doc.govt.nz/Documents/science-and-technical/musselfarms03.pdf

Infometrics, *Picton and the Sounds: 2016 Annual Economic Profile* (2016).
Marine Department, *A Preliminary Survey of Mussel Stock in Pelorus Sound*, Fisheries Technical Report 61 (Wellington, 1968–69).
Marine Department, *Pelorus Sound: Mussel Survey December 1969*, Fisheries Technical Report 62 (Wellington, 1971).
Marlborough District Council, *Marlborough District Council Long-term Plan, 2018–28.*
Marlborough District Council, *2018–2029 Long-term Plan: Investing in Marlborough* (Blenheim, 2019).
Ministry of Works and Development, *The Strategy for the Conservation and Development of the Marlborough Sounds* (Wellington, 1977).
Waitangi Tribunal, *Te Tau Ihu o te Waka a Maui: Report on Northern South Island Claims* (Wai 785), vol. 1, 2 & 3 (Wellington, 2008).

Research reports & submissions

Agricultural Bureau of NSW, Module 8: Soil & nutrition: Pastures http://bettersoils.soilwater.com.au/module3/3_08.htm
Bowdler, Laura, Evidence of Laura Bowdler (née Keenan) for Tahuaroa-Watson whānau, Board of Inquiry, New Zealand King Salmon proposal, 2012.
Davies, E. B., 'Molybdenum Research in New Zealand': www.grassland.org.nz/publications/nzgrassland_publication_1959.pdf
Guardians of the Sounds, 'Potential relocation of salmon farms in the Marlborough Sounds', Comments to advisory panel from Marlborough Environment Centre, 2 May 2017: www.guardiansofthesounds.co.nz/topics/aquaculture
Handley, Sean, 'The history of benthic change in Pelorus Sound (Te Hoiere), Marlborough', prepared for the Marlborough District Council (National Institute of Water and Atmospheric Research, February 2015).
Huntley, Arthur, Evidence for Tahuaroa-Watson whānau, Board of Inquiry, NZ King Salmon proposal, 2012.
Huntley, Stephen (Bosun), Evidence for Tahuaroa-Watson whānau, Board of Inquiry, NZ King Salmon proposal, 2012.
Macalister, Andrew, 'Management strategy the control of wilding conifers', prepared for the Kenepuru & Central Sounds Residents Association Inc (2010): https://static1.squarespace.com/static/51a82c3ce4b080a0192d23d2/t/51b827aee4b0b1

ab9202c735/1371023278814/ManagementPlan-Kenepuru+15March11.pdf
Marlborough District Council, 'Sedimentation': www.marlborough.govt.nz/environment/coastal/sedimentation
Marlborough District Council, 'Welcome boost to wilding pine control', press release, 8 September 2020.
Miller Consulting, 'Some impacts of roading and flood damage on sounds roads part only – Queen Charlotte Drive and Kenepuru Road, 1985–2010': www.marlborough.govt.nz/environment/coastal/sedimentation
Whitefield, Geoffrey & Faith Barber, Submission to Historic Places Trust for registration of the Brownlee homestead, 1994–95.

Unpublished papers, reminiscences & theses

Christian, Harry, 'Sounds reminiscences or 40 years in Pelorus Sounds territory', Allan family papers, unpublished, c.1920s.
Godsiff, Ada Elizabeth Grace Hetherington, private papers, undated.
Hope family letters and Elizabeth's diary, Hope family papers.
Leov, Harold Alexander, 'The story of my purchase of Te Towaka and some of the doings that followed', Leov family papers.
Mulcock, Paul, 'The New Zealand branch of the Mulcock family', pt 3: 'The story of Bulwer farm in Pelorus Sound', unpublished.
Paton, Brian R., 'Sawmill pioneers in the Pelorus', unpublished dissertation, Lincoln College, 1982.
Rankin, Keith, 'Unemployment in New Zealand at the peak of the Great Depression', paper for the 1994 Conference of the Economic History Association of Australia and New Zealand, University of New England, Armidale, NSW, Australia, 6–10 July 1994: http://keithrankin.co.nz/NZunem1933
Tortell, Philip, 'Investigation into settlement behaviour of mussels and the hydrology of a selected area with a view to farming the shellfish', PhD thesis, Victoria University of Wellington, 1976.
Wallace, James, Timeline, Resolution Bay, Family papers.
Washington, Muriel, 'The Hannah and Henry Godsiff family: Early settlers in the Pelorus Sound', undated, private papers.
Williams, Harry, 'Outward-bound from Havelock', undated, Williams private papers.

Williams, Harry, Kaiuma Bay, Pelorus Sound, panorama photo, c.1925, Williams private papers.

Williams, Harry, 'Life at Kaiuma Bay in the Pelorus Sound, Collingwood', August 1998, Williams private papers.

Archives New Zealand

AADS, AAFV, AAFZ, AANS, AAQU: Department of Lands and Survey

AANZ: Television One

AAPR: Ministry of Transport

AATE: Ministry of Works and Development

AATJ: Ministry of Economic Development

AAZU: Nature Conservation Council

ABKK: Works Consultancy Service

ABLP: Institute of Geological and Nuclear Sciences

ABMW: Rt. Hon. Wyatt Creech

ABPL: Maritime New Zealand

ACEB: NZ Post Ltd (Norsewood)

ACHL: Public Works Department

ACGO: Department of Internal Affairs

ACHL: Public Works Department

ADOE: Marine Department

ADSQ: Department of Forestry

Films

The Pilchard Fishermen, National Film Unit, 1945, sourced from ANZ: www.youtube.com/watch?v=CBPGSPWFHxE

Outward Bound School, National Film Unit, 1963, sourced from ANZ: www.youtube.com/watch?v=-PiNrVqAXFA

North-East Corner, National Film Unit, 1964, sourced from ANZ: www.youtube.com/watch?v=2Gm7bsRTz9I

Guardians of the Light, DVD, Howard Taylor Productions, Wellington, 2008.

Acknowledgements

BOOKS, I ALWAYS THINK, ARE never the work of just one person. And as I put the finishing touches to the final draft of this, I am struck, once again, by the generosity with which others have given advice, information and support. Christopher Challis, Joe and Heather Heberley, Hylton Harvey, John Harvey and Denise Harvey, Kerry Johnson, Julia Millen, Ian Mitchell, Graeme Moore (who also most valuably gave me a long loan of his extensive collection of published Sounds books), Sally Rhodes, John Shand, Mike Taylor, Joy Tomlinson and Florence Trotter all gave up considerable time to talk to me about their Sounds lives; Joy Redwood and Tony Redwood, Noel and Debbie Moleta and Denise and John Harvey provided fulsome hospitality as well; all generously responded to follow-up questions and a need for elucidation. Pauline McMahon drove me the not inconsiderable distance from Picton to Taradale so I could talk to her brother Colin and sister-in-law Marama.

Others provided further forms of assistance: June Allen generously lent family papers on the settlement at Port Gore; Ron Crosby painstakingly read, commented and provided a useful perspective on an early draft; archaeologist Janet Davidson gave most helpful feedback on a very early draft of the first chapter; Igor Drecki, curator at Cartographic and Geospatial Resources, provided advice on the early mapping of the Sounds; Ray Grose and others within the Department of Conservation tracked down old Sounds place names; Mike Johnson and Mike Laffan responded to questions on mining and soil fertility respectively; Jacqui Lloyd of Destination Malborough commented on tourism in the area; Nigel Prickett made available images and maps from his archaeological history on shore-based whaling; geologist Mike Selby helped me make sense of the Sounds geology; Ron Sutherland of the Marlborough Forest Industries Association, John McKenzie, Vern Harris and Dallas Hemphill, all long involved in Sounds Forestry, gave knowledgeable advice; Philip Tortell carefully explained innovations in mussel farming; Anne Wagenbroot generously loaned her Williams' family papers and elaborated on her family's history; Ian Mitchell advised on the Malborough Sounds Maritime Park; and Keith Murray's long-amassed information on the area proved invaluable.

Institutions and their staff have also played valuable roles in the prodduction of this book. I am indebted to Nicola Legat, Tracey Borgfeldt and Emily Goldthorpe at

Massey University Press for their interest in and production of this publication. Rachel Scott's sympathetic and nuanced editing of a large manuscript was much appreciated. I should also like to thank the Picton Whaling and Heritage Museum and Loreen Brehaut who helped me navigate their collection; the New Zealand Archaeological Society and the Waitangi Tribunal for providing relevant images free of charge — something that an independent researcher always treasures. Particular thanks should go to the Marlborough Archives Heritage Trust and its staff — executive director Steve Austen, archives manager Megan Ross, and Logan Coote, regional collections and archive manager. They have been a source of encouragement and interest from a very early stage and provided generous help as I made choices between the multitude of rich images held in the Marlborough Historical Society Collections at Marlborough Archives.

Four people deserve special thanks. Richard Bradley's rich, multi-dimensional narrative of his boyhood in the Sounds gave the book a depth and reach it would otherwise have lacked. Nola Leov, who sadly died before the book was finished, gave tirelessly of her time, knowledge and perspectives of the world that she knew so well; her enthusiasm and trust in what I was doing were always a great morale boost. Historian Malcolm McKinnon gave unflagging support in the latter stages of this book. Finally, without my husband Tim's sense of adventure, seamanship, unflagging interest and support — and belief that I could write this widely ranging work — it would never have happened.

About the Author

Helen Beaglehole is a Wellington writer. She published a number of well-received books for children and young adults, some of which were published overseas, before turning to non-fiction. This she writes from a strong research base as well as an eye for telling detail. This book is informed by her knowledge and love of the Sounds, where she has tramped and biked, and where she and her husband Tim sailed for over 40 years.

Index

Page numbers in **bold** refer to photographs or illustrations

MASSEY UNIVERSITY PRESS

First published in 2022 by Massey University Press
Private Bag 102904, North Shore Mail Centre
Auckland 0745, New Zealand
www.masseypress.ac.nz

Pages 4–5: Entrance to Pelorus Sound, Robert Percy Moore, Alexander Turnbull Library, Pan-1022-F; page 12: Marlborough Sounds, Whites Aviation, Alexander Turnbull Library, WA-05926-F; pages 18–19: Queen Charlotte Sound, Shellie Evans; pages 40–41: *Tory Channel, Queen Charlotte's Sound*, Charles Heaphy, 1851, Alexander Turnbull Library, A-189-023; pages 76–77: Hay-baling near Crail Bay, Fred Brockett, c. 1908, Museum of New Zealand Te Papa Tongarewa, B.027885; pages 124–25: Te Awaiti, showing James Norton's residence at left behind the boat shed and Riwai Keenan's residence second from right. The Love's schooner, *Charlotte*, is on the beach. Whaleboat *Māori Girl* is nearest the beach, with Riwai Keenan, steersman, and Pumipi Love, headsman. The other whaleboat, *Swiftsure*, carries James Norton, steersman, and James Jackson, owner and headsman. Picton Heritage and Whaling Museum, courtesy Picton Historical Society; pages 160–61: Looking along the shores of Te Mahia, Pelorus Sound, c. 1911, Auckland Libraries Heritage Collections, 35-R1074; pages 194–95: The Hon. William Massey coming ashore to open the Tia Ora post office in the Garfield's home in Northwest Bay, Pelorus Sound, 1914, Marlborough Historical Society, 5097; pages 236–37: Beach at unidentified location, possibly Marlborough Sounds, 1880s, Fredrick James Halse, Alexander Turnbull Library, 1/2-011512-G; pages 286–87: Sheep being unloaded from a boat in the Marlborough Sounds, 1938, Alexander Turnbull Library, PAColl-6304-05; pages 334–35: *Rangatira*, Picton, 1937, Nelson Provincial Museum, 162671; pages 378–79: Tennyson Inlet, Shellie Evans; page 395: Pelorus Sound, Auckland Libraries Heritage Collections, 35-R1086

Design by Megan van Staden
Jacket photograph by Tom Hackett

A catalogue record for this book is available from the National Library of New Zealand

Printed and bound in China by 1010 Printing Asia

ISBN: 978-0-9951431-9-7